DICTIONARY OF SCOTTISH BUSINESS BIOGRAPHY
1860–1960

DICTIONARY OF SCOTTISH BUSINESS BIOGRAPHY

Volume 1: **The Staple Industries**

Extractive Industries
Metals
Civil, Mechanical, Instrument and
  Electrical Engineering
Shipbuilding
Vehicles
Chemicals and Allied Industries
Textiles
Clothing
Leather and Footwear

ISBN 0 08 0303986

DICTIONARY OF SCOTTISH BUSINESS BIOGRAPHY 1860–1960

Volume 2
PROCESSING, DISTRIBUTION, SERVICES

Editors

ANTHONY SLAVEN
SYDNEY CHECKLAND

Associate Editors

Sheila Hamilton, Nicholas J Morgan, Charles W Munn, Brenda M White

ABERDEEN UNIVERSITY PRESS
Member of Maxwell, Macmillan, Pergamon Publishing Corporation

First published 1990
Aberdeen University Press

© Department of Economic History, University of Glasgow 1990

British Library Cataloguing in Publication Data
Dictionary of Scottish business biography.
  Vol. 2, Processing, distribution, services.
  1. Scotland. Business enterprise, 1860–1960—Biographies
  I. Slaven, Anthony
  338.6'092'2

ISBN 0–08–030399–4

Typeset and printed by AUP Glasgow/Aberdeen—A member of BPCC Ltd.

Contents

Contents

SECTOR FOUR: CONSTRUCTION INDUSTRY

SECTOR FIVE: PAPER, PRINTING AND PUBLISHING

SECTOR SIX: OTHER MANUFACTURES

SECTOR SEVEN: GAS, ELECTRICITY AND WATER

Contents

SECTOR EIGHT: TRANSPORT AND COMMUNICATION

SECTOR NINE: DISTRIBUTIVE TRADES

SECTOR TEN: BANKING, INSURANCE AND FINANCE

Contributors to Volume Two

J NEVILLE BARTLETT
University of Aberdeen

THERESA BARTON
University of Glasgow

DORIS BLACK
Glasgow

BRIAN BLENCH
Glasgow Museum & Art Galleries

JOHN BUTT
University of Strathclyde

R A CAGE
University of New England, New South Wales,
Australia

JOHN CALDER
University of Glasgow

LEN CAMPBELL
University of Strathclyde

SYDNEY CHECKLAND
University of Glasgow

MONICA CLOUGH
James Finlay PLC

PATRICIA COLLINS
University of Strathclyde

ANN K COOPER
University of Glasgow

ROBERT D CORRINS
Bell College, Hamilton

MICHAEL S COTTERILL
Scottish Mining Museum, Edinburgh

JOHN M CUBBAGE
Lenzie, Glasgow

P N DAVIES
University of Liverpool

JOHN A H DEMPSTER
Airdrie

KATHLEEN DONALDSON
The Queen's College

IAN DONNACHIE
The Open University in Scotland

GEORGE DIXON
University of Glasgow

MICHAEL J FRENCH
University of Glasgow

ENID GAULDIE
Duncan of Jordanstone College of Art, Dundee

SHEILA HAMILTON
University of Glasgow

THOMAS HART
University of Glasgow

FREDERICK G HAY
University of Glasgow

JOHN KING
London

CHRISTOPHER C LEE
Renfrew District Council

MAUREEN LOCHRIE
Paisley Museum

ALISTER McCRAE
Killearn, Glasgow

DONNY McLEAN
University of Glasgow

JAMES MAIR
Newmilns, Ayrshire

RANALD MICHIE
University of Durham

T E MILNE
University of Glasgow

NICHOLAS J MORGAN
University of Glasgow

MICHAEL MOSS
University of Glasgow Archives

H C MUI
Memorial University of Newfoundland, Canada

L H MUI
Memorial University of Newfoundland, Canada

CHARLES W MUNN
University of Glasgow

J FORBES MUNRO
University of Glasgow

M J ORBELL
Baring Bros Co Ltd, London

SARAH C ORR
University of Glasgow

PETER L PAYNE
University of Aberdeen

RICHARD PERREN
University of Aberdeen

MARIAN QUIGLEY,
University of Glasgow

Contributors

ALEX J ROBERTSON
  University of Manchester

C J A ROBERTSON
  St Salvator's College, St Andrews

RICHARD RODGER
  University of Leicester

IAIN RUSSELL
  University of Glasgow Archives

CHRISTOPHER SCHMITZ
  University of St Andrews

WILMA SEMPLE
  Glasgow

ANTHONY SLAVEN
  University of Glasgow

ROBERT N SMART
  University of St Andrews

BRIAN SPILLER
  Oxford

NORIO TAMAKI
  Keio University, Japan

JAMES H TREBLE
  University of Strathclyde

ALISON TURTON
  House of Fraser PLC, London

WRAY VAMPLEW
  Flinders University of South Australia

LORNA WEATHERILL
  University of St Andrews

RONALD B WEIR
  Derwent College, University of York

OLIVER M WESTALL
  University of Lancaster

BRENDA M WHITE
  University of Glasgow

Abbreviations

Profile Abbreviations (in order of appearance)

b.	born	V Ch	vice chairman
c.	circa	Prop	proprietor
n.d.	no date	d.	died
m.	married	g/v	gross value
s.	son	UK	United Kingdom
d.	daughter	m	million
MD	managing director	s.	shilling
Dir	director	d.	pence
Ch	chairman		

All other abbreviations

AM	Master of Arts, Audio-modulation	DL	Deputy Lieutenant
Anon	Anonymous	Dr	Doctor
BA	Bachelor of Arts	DSM	Distinguished Service Medal
Bart	Baronet	ed(s)	editor(s)
BBC	British Broadcasting Corporation	edn	edition
BBM	Bran, Bone and Muscle	EIC	East India Company
BEA	British European Airways	ESRC	Economic & Social Research Council
BI	British India Steam Navigation Company	FBI	Federation of British Industries
BISNC	British India Steam Navigation Company	FIEE	Fellow of the Institute of Electrical Engineers
BLitt	Bachelor of Letters	ft	feet
BRTMA	British Rubber Tyre Manufacturers' Association	grt	gross registered tonnage
		G & SW	Glasgow & South Western Railway
BSM	British Sugar Manufacturers Ltd	GCC	Glasgow Chamber of Commerce
CA	Chartered Accountant: Chief Accountant	GNSR	Great North of Scotland Railways
		GU	Glasgow University
CEB	Central Electricity Board	GWH	Gigawatt hours
CEng	Chartered Engineer	IBEA	Imperial British East Africa Company
CIE	Commander of the Indian Empire		
CIS	Co-operative Insurance Society	in(s)	inch(es)
Co	Company	IRI	Institution of the Rubber Industry
col	column	Jnr	Junior
cu ft	cubic feet	KBE	Knight Commander of the British Empire
DCL	Distillers Company Limited		

KCSI	Knight Commander of the Star of India	PLUTO	Pipe Line Under the Ocean
KVA	Kilo-volt-amperes	pp	pages
KW	Kilowatt	qv	quod vide (which see; cross reference to another entry)
L & A	Lanarkshire & Ayrshire Railway	RAF	Royal Air Force
lbs	pounds (weight)	RASC	Royal Army Service Corps, now called Royal Corps of Transport
LLD	Doctor of Laws		
LMS	London, Midland & Scottish	RFC	Royal Flying Corps
LMSR	London, Midland & Scottish Railway	RMC	Royal Marine Commandos: Royal Military College (Sandhurst)
LNER	London & North Eastern Railway	RNVR	Royal Naval Volunteer Reserve
Ltd	Limited	s	shilling
m	million	SCIS	Scottish Co-operative Ironworks Society
MA	Master of Arts		
MC	Military Cross	SCWS	Scottish Co-operative Wholesale Society
Messrs	Messieurs		
MechE	Mechanical Engineer	sic	thus used (confirming quoted words)
MI	Military Intelligence: Ministry of Information	SJPE	Scottish Journal of Political Economy
MP	Member of Parliament	SMT	Scottish Motor Traction
Ms	Manuscript	Snr	Senior
NATSOPA	National Society of Operative Printers and Assistants	sq yd	square yard
		SRO	Scottish Record Office
NBR	North British Railway Company	SS Co	Steam Shipping Company
nd	no date	St	Saint
NI	Netherlands India Steam Navigation Company	STUC	Scottish Trades Union Congress
		SUITS	Scottish Universal Investments Limited
No(s)	Number(s)		
NRA(S)	National Register of Archives of Scotland	TIESS	Transactions of the Institution of Engineers and Shipbuilders in Scotland
OBE	Officer of the Order of the British Empire	UK	United Kingdom
		US	United States
obit	obituary	USA	United States of America
p	page	v	versus
P & O	Peninsular & Oriental Steam Navigation Company	VG	Voluntary Group
		Vol	Volume
PhD	Doctor of Philosophy	WC	Water Closet
PKTF	Printing & Kindred Trades Federation	WS	Writer to the Signet
PLC	Public Limited Company	YMCA	Young Men's Christian Association

Acknowledgements

The editors of the Dictionary of Scottish Business Biography owe many debts to the very large number of individuals, companies and institutions whose assistance has made it possible to compile the biographies. First and foremost among these is the Social Science Research Council (now the Economic and Social Research Council) which supported the research programme with funding between 1980 and 1985. We gratefully acknowledge the foresight and faith of the SSRC which has made this publication possible.

The confidence of the SSRC in the value of this work has been echoed in the Scottish business community, which in addition to contributing much information and advice in many of our biographies, has underwritten part of the costs of publication of this large two volume enterprise. The editors express their special thanks to the following for their generous financial support: Burmah Oil Trading Ltd, Malcolm Campbell Ltd, Christian Salvesen Ltd, Coats Patons PLC, The Committee of Scottish Clearing Banks, Low and Bonar PLC, Scottish Development Agency, Scottish & Newcastle Breweries Ltd, Tennent Caledonian Breweries Ltd.

The editors also gratefully acknowledge further financial support from the Carnegie Trust for the Universities of Scotland, the Publications Board, University of Glasgow, and the Macfie Bequest, University of Glasgow.

A work of this scale has drawn upon the experience and knowledge of many individuals, either in personal, family or business connections. The editors acknowledge with pleasure the assistance provided by the following: Messrs A G Barr PLC, James Barrie, Gordon Baxter OBE, Ian Baxter, T Norman Biggart, Harold D Bowtell, Duncan Brand, Mr T Brattin, Mr A F Bryce, Eric McKinnon Buchan, Mr D Buchan, Mr Burnett, Mrs Sheila Calvert, Messrs Malcolm Campbell PLC, Mrs Linda Craig, Graeme Cruickshank, Ms Pat Cunningham, Rev I M P Davidson, George A Dixon, Mr J Edgar, Mrs Greta Edwards, Ms A Escolt, Mr B S Faulkner, Mrs Valerie Ferguson, Andrew Fleming, Albert Gurevitz, Alex Hawson, Hepworth Ceramic Holdings PLC, Dr John Hurll, Mrs E M Kennedy, Elspeth King, James C Letters, Janet McBain, Ian Wilson Macdonald, Mr A MacFarlane, Mr S McGonigle, Charles C McInroy, Mr W McIntosh, A A M Mackay, Dr Alan McKinlay, Mr J M McLean, Charles McMaster, Peter Mathias, Mr D W Mickel, James Miller, Mr J R Pate, Jimmy Reid, Sir William Reid, Mr C J Risk, Mr & Mrs Kenneth W Sanderson, William D Shaw, Carol Smith, Ms Janet Smith, Dr R Smith, Paul Thompson, Gordon Thornton, Mr I S Walker, John Wallace Snr, J G C White, Roy C P Whitson, P J Wordie, Mr F Worsdall, Mr J Harry Young.

In addition we have enjoyed the unstinting support of young research assistants working in Community Projects through the Manpower Services programme. The editors acknowledge heavy debt to: Theresa Barton, Anne K Cooper, William Good, Scott Kerr, Michelle Laycock, Donald J McLean, Patricia McPhee, Liz Meenagh, Marian Quigley, Michael Tough.

A very large debt of gratitude, recorded in full in the Acknowledgements to Volume One, is owed to the librarians, archivists and staff of a very large number of libraries, archives and museums, to the Commissary Office Edinburgh, the Companies Registration Office, the General Register Office (Scotland) and to the Scottish Record Office. We sincerely renew our thanks to all the individual members of staff who unstintingly gave us their support.

Many debts were also incurred in the search for photographic illustrations and our thanks have been recorded appropriately in the text. The editors would however specially thank Mr Andrew Miller, Director of Glasgow District Libraries, for his generous adjustment of charges to enable us to draw so heavily upon the rich photographic resources of the Mitchell Library.

Among the many hundreds of individuals who have helped us in innumerable ways a few require special mention for particular support. Mr Michael Moss, Archivist, the University of Glasgow, has contributed more than generously in the overall research assistance to this project. Professor Peter L Payne of the University of Aberdeen kindly made available his detailed research data on Scottish limited companies. Dr David Jeremy and Professor Leslie Hannah of the Business History Unit, London School of Economics, freely made available information and their assistance in resolving the many problems arising from men who had made part of their business careers in both Scotland and England.

The research funding, and the research staff who began this project in 1980, had disbanded by 1985, and the remaining work has been undertaken on a voluntary basis. The assistant editors have all given generously of their time even though the commitment of new posts and new projects have taken first claim on their time. With protracted authorship and editorship of this second volume the support, friendship and understanding of Mr Colin MacLean, Managing Director, Publishing, of Aberdeen University Press, has been a source of strength and encouragement that has stretched far beyond the bounds imposed by contracts. It has been a special privilege to have been associated with Colin MacLean in this endeavour.

The compilation of this second volume has been both lengthy and arduous: some of the initial typing was skilfully undertaken by Sandra Walker, but nothing would have appeared in print without the commitment, drive, and unfailing contribution made by Mrs Isabel Burnside. She has singlehandedly coped with correspondence, draft papers, proofs, all typing and corrections, and the interface between the editors and the publishers. She knows the text better than the editors, and without her, our best efforts would have been in vain.

Our affection, and our thanks go to her, and all who have helped us.

ANTHONY SLAVEN

Introduction

The publication of this second volume of the *Dictionary of Scottish Business Biography* completes the set of studies that were planned by Sydney Checkland and myself in 1980. A decade of research and authorship has explored a formerly uncharted world, the world of the entrepreneur, the businessman in the setting of his company, and the origins, training, business achievements, and social and political roles of that group of men who created and directed Scotland's greatest companies. For as we observed in the introduction to Volume One, the businessman has been largely omitted from the accounts of the history of our society; and yet the wealth on which the quality of our lives depend is largely generated in the world of business.

The detailed introduction to our first volume in this set of studies set out our objectives, namely to rescue the businessman from obscurity, and to contribute to a wider understanding of business behaviour in the past century or so. We also set out to explore the nature and impact of personality in economic affairs, and to try to discern whether there were characteristics which were common and shared between men of business in different types of activity. The interested reader can refer to Volume One for a full discussion of our aims.

The organising principle on which our work has been based has been to group men together in the sectors in which they conducted their business, and to introduce each group of subjects with a short essay setting out the main features of their industry over the last hundred years. How these men were selected, and why some sectors are smaller or larger than others in the number of biographies included in this study are again set out in detail in the introduction to Volume One.

Since the inception of this study, and since the publication of Volume One, there have been many changes affecting the course of our work. Most difficult to accommodate was the death of my friend and co-editor Sydney Checkland in early 1986. At that stage the content of this volume was barely half complete, and the loss of his advice and enthusiasm was a grievous blow. On a happier note, our colleagues at the Business History Unit in the London School of Economics completed the publication of their five volume set of the *Dictionary of Business Biography*, parallelling our work in England and Wales. This successful outcome gave us some pointers and assistance in completing our Scottish biographies in a better charted British context of business development. That English based work is now to provide the raw material for a new project explaining comparisons with European entrepreneurs, while the completion of the *Dictionary of Scottish Business Biography* will now make it possible to proceed to our ultimate objective. In the future this set of volumes will be complemented by a third volume, *A Biography of Enterprise*, which will explore in some detail the lessons we have begun to learn about the origins, nature and achievements of Scottish Businessmen. A flavour of this is given in the short conclusion at the end of this volume.

ANTHONY SLAVEN

Food, Drink and Tobacco

Food and drink are the basic necessities of life. Without them mankind cannot survive. But, however palatable basic necessities might be, there is a streak in human nature which demands variety, the taste of something new, the indulgence in luxury items. Fortunes have been made, empires have been built on the exploitation of the vagaries of human taste and Scottish entrepreneurs were quick to seize opportunities offered in the period from 1860-1960.

The last half of the nineteenth century saw the rise of the mass market with the significant development of transport, communications and urbanisation. Rising industrial wealth provided opportunities for the luxury market while increased urbanisation of the labouring classes forced the pace of mass production of basic foodstuffs and made possible the purchase of small luxuries. The drink industry flourished on similar lines: although many cities and towns improved their municipal water supplies the opportunities to make money came from the brewing of beer and the distillation of grain based spirits. Drink transcended class barriers and was indulged in from the highest to the lowest ranks of society. Scotch whisky provides one of the few examples of a luxury export commodity which was freely available to all levels of Scottish households. The tobacco trade, once the commercial mainstay of Glasgow and the west of Scotland, declined during the period, with several noted firms such as Mitchell's joining larger tobacco conglomerates by the early 1860s. Thus there is only one entry, William Fraser Dobie for this trade under the generic sector heading of Food, Drink and Tobacco. As in many of the sectors the weight of entries falls in the central belt of Scotland with a distinct bias towards the industrial centres of Glasgow and west of Scotland cotton towns and the Clyde based lines of inter-continental maritime traffic.

The most basic of all foodstuffs is bread. It has seen the greatest intensive change in production from the hand kneaded dough fired on the simple domestic hearth to the fully automated moving multi ovens of the present day. The emphasis on large scale bread production lies in Glasgow with its concentrated working population and the Clyde wharves where American and European grain was landed. In the crowded single rooms occupied by the majority of the Scottish labouring classes, opportunities for home breadmaking were limited. Small single oven bakeries sprang up often serving the street, or the surrounding tenements. Often larger co-operative units founded by workers appeared such as the United Friendly Bakery of the United Co-operative Baking Society founded in Glasgow in the 1860s to ensure purity and hold down prices. These were delivered round the doors by horse and cart. Demand for bread however, ensured the development of wholesale mechanised production of a standard 2 lb white loaf distributed through retail grocery outlets.

Amongst the first to seize the opportunity presented by mechanised production were the four Bilsland brothers, small scale bakers to a man, who amalgamated in 1877 to form Bilsland Bros under the leadership of (Sir) William Bilsland. Bilsland Bros erected a bakery purpose built to accommodate mechanised production. The latest American technology was employed with reel ovens and dough dividers bought from Baker-Perkins of Peterborough. Bilsland's Hydepark Bakery produced around 23,000 loaves per week delivered amongst the 1,600 retail grocery outlets in Glasgow and the suburbs first by horse drawn later by motorised vans.

The new technology meant more than increased production, it increased hygiene by obviating close contact with the operatives. This was especially noticeable in the kneading processes when dough was often trampled by foot. William Beattie designed much of his own machinery in the Dennistoun Bakery with this in mind. Hygienic production was a great selling point in all the food trades in the late Victorian era. Increased sanitary inspection through the various Bakehouse and Factory Acts brought a public awareness quickly identified by bread manufacturers. John Montgomerie went a stage further when he had each individual loaf wrapped, a development

3

previously unknown when enormous trays of unwrapped bread were carried through busy streets littered with horse manure and other health hazards. Montgomerie also grasped the market opportunity for healthy eating by those with delicate stomachs and dispositions. His 'Bermaline' range of flour, bread and invalid rusks were made with a malt extract he developed and patented in 1886. Bermaline was manufactured under licence in 4,000 outlets throughout Britain, 400 of them in London.

Other grain based products were sold with invalids and children in mind such as James Marshall's 'Farola'. A product made from the hard nutritious particles of wheat excluded from commercial flours which were then re-milled to provide an easily assimilated food. The products of Marshall and Montgomerie found favour with leading medical and scientific journals in the 1880s and 90s, though it is debatable whether they approved of Marshall's later successful pasta products with the self advertisement 'the man who put the "Mac" in macaroni'. Household grain products could find their way into the kitchen from the widest possible sources. The thickening agent, cornflour, was a spin-off from the muslin trade when John Polson substituted sago flour with maize flour for starching the muslin goods belonging to the Glasgow merchant, William Brown. Who can forget Brown and Polson's Cornflour?

Grains provide food other than bread. Cakes and biscuits are not necessary adjuncts to life but they can make it sweeter. Scotland has a notoriously sweet tooth and its exploitation provided opportunities in the sugar, sweet, preserves, biscuit and cake trades which carried far beyond the domestic market. Many of the noted names in these trades operated lucrative export markets in the

Glebe Sugar Refinery Co Ltd   COURTESY OF THE MITCHELL LIBRARY

Dominions, America and Europe. Once again the Clyde based west of Scotland economy was the main beneficiary of maritime trade patterns. Sugar found an early base in Greenock. Shipping unloaded raw sugar cane there from the West Indies long before John Golbourne opened up Glasgow as a deep water port in the late eighteenth century when he made the Clyde navigable above Port Glasgow.

The Greenock refineries supplied the brewing, jam, confectionery (sweets), biscuit and cake trades in tradition to the household use of granulated and lump sugars, golden syrup and molasses. Robert Kerr introduced new technology to his Glebe refinery and steered away from the use of beet sugars to cane refining and diversified into the brewing trade. This proved a wise move for in 1900 the Glebe was one of only four of the original 16 sugar refineries left in Greenock.

The Scottish people showed a desire to bite into sweet biscuits and cakes on a variety of occasions both at home and in public. Biscuits and cakes were consumed with fortified wine, with tea, with coffee, in trains, on steamships, on omnibuses, in restaurants, in tearooms, in coffee rooms, at church socials, on picnics, in domestic parlours and kitchens. Market opportunities to satisfy this national obsession were unlimited as shown in this sector and in the Distribution sector. By a strange quirk of fate, or by regional contacts, many of the men who took these opportunities were from the north east of Scotland, though they found their markets either in Glasgow or Edinburgh.

William Gray was an Aberdeenshire Quaker who was educated in England and came to Glasgow in 1854 to take over his deceased brother's partnership in the newly formed firm of Gray Dunn & Co, biscuit manufacturers. The staple produce was ships biscuits. William Gray began to manufacture sweet biscuits and cakes sealed in soldered tins. These were exported by the shipping lines he supplied with ships biscuits. By 1875 he was supplying the domestic market with cakes, bread and 50 varieties of biscuits from a modern factory in the Kinning Park district of Glasgow employing 400 staff. The business drew William Bilsland to its board and eventually Bilsland Bros took over Gray Dunn & Co in 1912. Shortly afterwards William Beattie began to manufacture cakes and biscuits at the Dennistoun Bakery.

(Sir) Alexander Grant apprenticed himself to the one oven bakery of Jocky Stewart in his native Morayshire town of Forres in the late 1870s. In the early 1880s he moved to Edinburgh and found work in the underground bakery of Robert McVitie. McVitie recognised Grant's keen business sense and encouraged him to study chemistry and sent him to Europe to study continental baking. At the same time McVitie took Charles Price, an ex Cadbury salesman, into partnership. Grant became the mainstay of McVitie & Price, rising to general manager when Price entered Parliament as MP in 1901, and chairman in 1910 after McVitie's death. Grant converted McVitie and Price into a private limited company in 1911 with a capital of £150,000. The Scottish firm opened factories in London, 1893, and Manchester, 1914. At Grant's death in 1937, McVitie and Price had worldwide markets for their wide variety of biscuits and cakes.

United Biscuits was formed in 1948 as a holding company by (Sir) Peter MacDonald by merging McVitie and Price with the old established Glasgow firm of MacFarlane and Lang. MacDonald, was also a native of Moray and knew Grant well. He was a lawyer with the Edinburgh legal firm of W & J Burness and was legal adviser to the McVitie & Price board in 1930 and later joined the board as a director. The war years were rigorous and both McVitie & Price and MacFarlane & Lang had to pool their resources and agree cut backs in production. This proved a sound move in the post war years when Weston Foods threatened to monopolise the biscuit and cake market. In 1947 the combined profits of the two companies was £442,554 with assets totalling £2.5m. By 1957 profits had risen to over £2m.

Under Sir Peter MacDonald's chairmanship, United biscuits continued to hold their market position by positive expansionist policies, automated production lines and further acquisitions; William Crawford & Sons in 1962, William MacDonald & Son Ltd in 1965; and Meredith and Drew and KP Nuts in 1966-1968. With the acquisition of William MacDonald's and their 'Penguin' chocolate biscuit bars, United Biscuits had 25% of the UK chocolate biscuit market. Sir Peter

MacDonald's business life reflects the changes he contributed to in the making of the modern biscuit industry. He died in 1983.

The manufacture of sugar based confectionery, or sweets for short, was also a major Scottish concern. Duncan's and Mackintosh both operated from Edinburgh. Keiller's of Dundee who began by making marmalade in 1800 and had a nationwide network of outlets by 1830 began to manufacture sweets in 1887 under John Mitchell Keiller's chairmanship.

The majority of sweet manufacturers were centred around Glasgow where again the imported raw materials of sugar, sorghum, colourings and flavourings were on hand and the export markets for manufactured sweets began their outward journey. The mass production of sweets and chocolate in the mid nineteenth century allowed the Buchanan brothers John, Alexander and Andrew to develop a large complex in the Cowcaddens area of Glasgow by 1870. They used mainly American, Austrian, French and Dutch beet and sorghum based sugars. The Greenock refined West Indian cane sugar found little share in Buchanan's enormous sugar shed which stored up to 8,000 barrels. Citrus fruits came from the Cape Province but Buchanan's had to pay a 2d per pound weight of sweets tax on their exports to the Cape. American imported sugar carried a 30% duty when it was sent back in the form of sugar confectionery. Nevertheless Buchanan's produced around 100 tons of confectionery a week, much of it exported. It was produced by 1,100 staff, many of which were administrative and delivery staff. Buchanan's were amongst the first to employ female office workers and thought their influence as beneficial, but nevertheless they implemented a strict separation of the sexes because of their own religious convictions. Robert Buchanan, affectionately known as 'Sweetie Buchanan' was the salesman and he was well known for leaving small shield shaped religious texts in trains and hotels.

Whilst the majority of entries are concentrated in the confectionery industries there is an outstanding example of entrepreneurial success with current international status. The fame of Baxter's of Speyside is legendary but it highlights a deficiency in Scottish businessmen to exploit the natural advantages of Scottish produce. It is true Scottish food has a wide market, Aberdeen Angus beef and Scotch salmon for instance command a certain degree of gourmet respect. But there is no other Scottish firm of note which shares, or challenges, Baxter's market position as a worldwide provider of quality Scottish foods. What is more most of the ingredients are culled from local Moray sources and produced by local labour. Baxter's independent private limited company status reflects a commitment to the local community seldom encountered in today's business world. William Alexander Baxter's rise was admittedly aided by the seigneurial influence of Ducal custom and introduction to such august establishments as Harrods and Fortnum and Mason's culminating in the ultimate accolade of Buckingham Palace. It was also bolstered by the sound common sense and common sense of purpose of his wife, Ethel Baxter. Nevertheless it is an awe inspiring study of business success founded on natural produce and native Scottish nous. The tartan card has seldom been better played.

Though the Baxter's canned and bottled their products, the east of Scotland provided earlier similar enterprises such as John Moir's of Aberdeen under John Moir Clark and Maconochies. Robert Waddell also bottled his meat products and held respectable UK markets in the early twentieth century. But these efforts were not sufficiently rooted to withstand later market forces.

The early tea trade in Scotland was a cut-throat business with long distance supply lines, indifferent agents and small profits carefully scratched from cash sales. The Edinburgh tea firm of Andrew Melrose and Company rose from origins in the retail grocery trade in the 1820s. The sale of tea grew from retail to wholesale distribution, buying direct from the East India Company tea auctions. When the China tea trade opened in 1834 Melrose was the first to import tea from Canton to Leith. It was not until Andrew Melrose's son, William, took control of tea buying on site in Canton and set up his own agency house that true stability came to the Scottish firm. From Canton, William Melrose supplied brokers in Liverpool, London and Glasgow, wisely watching the rates for bills of exchange, timing the bills arrival to coincide with tea cargoes to reduce interest charges.

William Melrose died in 1863 leaving an estate of only £16,007. A more profitable aspect of the tea trade lay in the plantations themselves.

Tea plantations formed a major support of James Finlay and Company the well established Glasgow firm owned in 1884 solely by (Sir) John Muir. He, too, followed the practice of sending his sons to learn and manage overseas supply lines. The Finlay tea plantations in India and Ceylon were the forcing ground for (Sir) Alexander Kay Muir's business training when he was sent to Calcutta in 1890, returning to Glasgow in 1901 to take control of Finlay's wide range of overseas interests with his younger brother. Sir John Muir died in 1903 but he left behind lucrative profits rising from his earlier plantation investments. In 1902 the Muir brothers diversified into cotton manufacture with Sir Charles Cayzer, opening mills in Bombay. By 1909 they formed a private limited company with an authorised flotation of £1m rising to £2m in 1919 and in 1923 Finlay's went public. Thus the second generation of Muirs brought together the ramshackle collection of private businesses in tea, sugar, cotton, indigo and jute into a major international public company. In 1926 Finlay's bought land in Kenya and estblished the earliest publicly quoted tea plantation there, and broke the Asian monopoly of tea growing.

Robert Paterson & Sons

Coffee drinking was popularised by seventeenth century males in coffee houses. It later became a domestic beverage but large scale consumption was delayed until the last quarter of the nineteenth century when coffee essence was first produced. The drying, roasting and grinding of coffee beans to extract a coffee flavoured essence was pioneered in Scotland by several firms in Edinburgh and Glasgow and captured 80% of the UK market. Two major concerns appeared, Thomas Symington & Co, Edinburgh, and 'Camp' coffee produced by Campbell Paterson. The ease with which coffee could be made using coffee essence virtually guaranteed its success. 'Camp' coffee became the brand leader because of Campbell Paterson's decision to patent the name and to give the product a distinct British logo: the tall bearded Indian Sepoy serving his master the British army officer with 'Camp' coffee. Outside the UK domestic market 'Camp's' major markets lay in the outposts of the British Empire. To boost this jingoistic image Paterson erected castles and bivouacs out of crates of 'Camp' coffee at the major trade fairs. Customers were then invited to sup the product within the make-believe encampments.

Paterson funded the experimental stages of 'Camp' coffee through the proceeds of less exotic products such as pickles, fruit wines and cordials. Amongst them was a raspberry vinegar used in low company to mix with whisky to produce a drink favoured by tavern ladies and went by the popular name of 'Cuddle-me Dearie'. Between this slender connection of the polite world of coffee drinking with that of alcohol related beverages lies the soft drink industry. Andrew Greig Barr was only one of many soft drink manufacturers to spring up in the late nineteenth century borne on the success of the Temperance movement and the Scottish desire to drink something other than water. The Scottish firm of A G Barr has successfully promoted 'Irn-Bru', as Scotland's other national drink. Rather in the nature of the American 'Coke' industry, Barr's have also jealously guarded the secret ingredients of 'Irn-bru'. But Andrew Barr sold numerous varieties of soft drinks before 'Irn-Bru' came on the market. In an age of returnable bottles and syphons he rigorously policed the protection of his own returnable bottle supplies.

The more serious aspect of drinking, that of beer and spirits, is one more readily associated with Scottish products. Scottish beers and Scotch whisky enjoy world renown. Their export markets are enviable and are buttressed by firm domestic consumption patterns. The majority of the major brewing firms originated in the east of Scotland. William McEwan's and William Younger's of Edinburgh and the Alloa firm of George Younger & Co, emerged from a plethora of fairly substantial brewing concerns based in or around Edinburgh and Alloa. The same may be said for Tennent's the Glasgow brewing firm which shook off west of Scotland competition to become a household name.

William McEwan, came from Alloa, but he transferred to Edinburgh for his commercial training in the family connected business of Jeffries in 1851. Family capital backed his own venture into brewing at the Fountain Brewery in 1856. Success came from the large market for quality beers in the industrial central belt of Scotland with its shipbulding, coal, iron and steel industries. all of them 'drouth' giving work. And, like other east coast breweries McEwan found markets further down the coast in the Tyneside area of north east England with a similar industrial base.

The dynamic nature of McEwan's enterprise meant that wherever there was a 'drouth', McEwan's beers slaked the thirst be it in Australia, New Zealand, India, Canada or South America. Exports accounted for £34,000 of business by 1868. When he went into politics 20 years later as a Gladstonian Liberal, McEwan's had a nominal capital of £1m and profits of around £92,000 per annum.

The older established Edinburgh firm of brewers, William Younger was founded in the eighteenth century. By 1852, the fourth generation of Youngers, Henry Johnston Younger, was poised to take advantage of markets similar to those exploited by his contemporary and rival, William McEwan. Younger's fanatical concern for quality control and its wide export market ranked it high on the list of a fiercely competitive industry. Important discoveries in brewing chemistry brought Louis Pasteur to Edinburgh in to inspect the Younger's Abbey and Holyrood breweries, moving H J

Younger to donate £500 to Edinburgh University's building fund in Pasteur's honour. The firm of William Younger's Edinburgh, continued its rise under the chairmanship of his son, Harry George Younger. Harry Younger together with Alexander Bruce his depute chairman, developed the 'tied' house system in Scotland, Tyneside and in London. The way forward in an increasingly competitive market was through amalgamations and in 1931 he was instrumental in the formation of Scottish Brewers by the merging of William McEwan's with William Younger's. He then formed McEwan-Younger Ltd to handle the joint export, naval and military trade of both firms.

The brewing trade had to fight its corner against the powerful Temperance lobby. William McEwan's role as a Scottish brewer-politician was repeated by George Younger of the Alloa brewers, George Younger & Co. He succeeded to the business, originally founded by his father, at the age of 17 in 1868. In addition to building up the firm to become one of the largest Scottish breweries Younger entered politics as a Unionist in 1906 as MP for Ayr Burgh after several previous defeats in 1895, 1899 and 1900. The reasons for the brewers' political involvement are not difficult to find. The enormous capital outlays, development costs, new products, cooperage and bottling plant, extended credit made an assured future imperative in the face of increasing opposition from the Temperance movement. McEwan and George Younger may have served opposing political parties but their major aims for the brewing industry were similar as were those of the English brewer-politicians.

Not all Edinburgh based breweries survived in the cut throat competition for business. William Stewart formed the Edinburgh United Breweries in 1889 from several well established small brewers. The company inherited several 'tied' houses in central Scotland and the north east of England, a reasonable colonial export trade and had the advantage of a popular brew, Disher's Ten Guinea Ale. However, it failed in 1906 in the face of competition from the other major brewing concerns.

More successful was the Glasgow firm of J & R Tennent at the Wellpark Brewery. It had prospered under the management of Hugh Tennent Snr, and his son Charles in the mid 1850s until their deaths in 1864. Tennent's was then run by Trustees for the next 20 years and increased its value to £300,000 by 1870. It had a worldwide reputation for Pale Ales and Stouts. Hugh Tennent came to manage the firm in 1884 when its famous red 'T' for Tennents had been registered for sole use throughout the British Empire by the Trustees. Tennent's already had a considerable export market and Hugh Tennent's contribution was to adopt the production of Lager beer from the Bavarian Lagers he had sampled when on holiday. Lagers from Germany and Austria were already popular imports because of their light sparkling properties. Tennent brought German expertise to Glasgow and rebuilt the plant on German lines of production. Hugh Tennent died in 1890 at the early age of 27. Lager remains Tennent's major product.

The more romantic appeal of the drink industry lies in the cult status of Scotch whisky. In general terms whisky is produced in two ways; malt whisky by using the traditional Pot Still and grain whisky by using the Patent Still method. Malt whisky has a distinctive peaty taste. Blended whisky is a combination of both malt and grain whisky, the varying proportions used in each blend is reputedly the hall-mark of a particular blend of whisky, usually marketed under a 'brand' name.

The whisky industry therefore falls into two groups, the distillers and the blenders. In practical terms many blenders made the backward linkage into distilling to control the distinctive taste associated with their particular brand name. Taste therefore was, and continues to be the ultimate appeal pitched by the producer and the advertiser. The taste of the connoisseur is assiduously cultivated as claims are made that one will instantly recognise a particular brand rather in the manner of those expert in wine tasting.

By the mid nineteenth century whisky was shedding its disreputable image of small scale illicit production by roving highlanders and was tentatively entering into the vocabulary of relatively sophisticated taste and refinement. It is no coincidence that all but one of the biographical entries for the whisky industry were born within the 20 year span from 1850-1870. As such they were reaching the height of their managerial skills in the critical period 1890 to 1930. The whisky industry experienced extreme difficulties in the first decade of the twentieth century. In 1908 a Royal Commission on Whisky, and later Lloyd George's Budget proposals to raise duty by a third to finance his social reforms.

If the marketing of whisky was successful its profitability was astounding as the rise from 'howf' to club location was accomplished by the turn of the century. In the process of gentrification several whisky firms came to prominence such as Walker's, Dewar's and Bells. Brand names emerged with Buchanan's Black and White and Mackie's White Horse taking a major share. In such a rapidly burgeoning market, whisky trade politics and tactics played a recognisable role and led ultimately to the amalgamation of the 'Big Three' whisky blenders with the Distillers Company Limited in 1925.

The Distillers Company (DCL) was formed in 1877 by six Lowland grain whisky producers to reduce competition and achieve economies. The 'Big Three' were the blending firm of Buchanan's who owned the Black and White label, Dewar's, and Walker's who owned the Johnny Walker label. The path to amalgamation was long and tortuous. The Dewar brothers, John and Thomas, were the inheritors of a well ordered whisky concern carefully husbanded by their father since 1846. In 1890 they broke the mould by negotiating a business loan from the DCL in exchange for buying grain whisky from DCL. This allowed the Dewar's to embark on positive business decisions, advertising, and exports. Alexander Walker was the third generation of the Kilmarnock whisky blending firm begun in 1820 by Johnny Walker.

James Buchanan was a self made man. He began with no other capital than supreme self confidence and a reasonable education and built up his business by marketing skills. Buchanan vigorously promoted his blended whisky in a black bottle with a white label by storming the strongholds of popular recognition: The House of Commons and The United Musical Halls Company. He then went on to gain the Royal Warrant for supplying the Prince of Wales, the Duke of York, and finally Queen Victoria. He was a major user of advertising in the press, on railway and on delivery vans. All three concerns had flourishing overseas markets and had entered the lucrative London market by the 1880s.

The ability of the Distillers Company Limited (DCL) to bring the large blenders under its umbrella was mainly due to William Henry Ross, described by some as 'the father of DCL'. His astute mind overcame the whisky salesmen to accomplish his grand plan in the first 30 years of the twentieth century. Ross joined the DCL at the age of 15 in 1878. By 1900 he was appointed as managing director. His rise was due to his personal qualities and by certain inherent management difficulties within the DCL.

Under Ross's guidance the DCL moved surely through the difficult period of the early 1900s when whisky attracted legal scrutiny and became a financial plank in the government's social policy aims. Ross also moved the DCL from being solely a producer of potable spirits and widened its output to encompass the production of industrial alcohol and derivative products. This planned diversification moved the DCL into the chemical industry requiring greater capital outlays. An excellent addition to the DCL combine was the talented (Sir) James Calder when his companies were absorbed by the DCL. Calder brought with him tremendous expertise in brewing and distilling and became a major figure in the DCL's marketing of industrial alcohol.

However, not all blenders or distillers came under the DCL. (Sir) Peter Mackie and Arthur Kinmont Bell of Perth headed notably independent whisky concerns. Peter Mackie's forthright character made him a focus for the political discontent surrounding Lloyd George's increased duty on spirits. His independent business stance was based on the successful overseas and domestic sales of his two major brands of blended whisky; 'Old Smuggler' and 'White Horse'. He owned distilleries to maintain the standard of his blending. So too did Arthur Kinmont Bell whose overseas and domestic markets enabled him to withstand the DCL. Another example is William Alexander Robertson who combined wine broking and sales with distilling and blending whisky. His firm,

Robertson and Baxter, Wine and Spirit Merchants, based in Glasgow, became the training ground of many of those later destined to rise to prominence in the brewing and whisky industries.

The Food, Drink and Tobacco sector provides many examples of men who rose to become Members of Parliament, or took titled rank, or became landed gentry. Their philanthropic contributions to local causes was often quite outstanding. Edinburgh rejoices in the McEwan and the Usher Halls and the chair of Public Health within the university: direct gifts from the profits of the brewing industry. Very few of the biographical entries for this sector can be read without reference to community involvement. Neither can they be read without an appreciation of the extent to which the general public itself had enriched the subjects of these biographies.

BRENDA M WHITE

Andrew Greig BARR,

Soft drink manufacturer; b. 5/5/1872, Falkirk, s. of Robert Barr, cork cutter and aerated water manufacturer and Jane Greig; m. 25/4/1903, Isabel Margaret Gibb, d. of James Gibb, superintendent engineer; no issue; Founder, A G Barr & Co; d. 12/7/1903, Dennistoun, Glasgow; g/v estate: £18,409 7s 7d.

A G Barr & Co, Britain's largest manufacturer of soft drinks, is renowned as the maker of 'Scotland's Other National Drink' otherwise known as *Irn-Bru*. The firm today employs some 1,500 people in eight plants in Scotland and 17 in England and Wales. It takes its name from Andrew Greig Barr who was born in Falkirk in May 1872 and died tragically early in Glasgow in July 1903 at the age of 31. Yet in a few years in the business Andrew Greig Barr had created a locus of operation in Glasgow, and an approach to the business of soft drink manufacture, that was to strongly influence the long term growth and success of the company.

A G Barr was the second son of Robert Barr whose own father had been a cork cutter in Falkirk, mainly supplying stoppers to the bottling trade. This close connection with bottlers led Robert Barr to set up as a manufacturer of aerated water at Burnfoot in Falkirk in 1880. He had seen the demand for cork decline as alternative bottling materials came into the market. When his father set up as a soft drink manufacturer Andrew Barr was then only eight years old and was attending Falkirk High School. He finished his schooling at Stewart's College, Edinburgh, and was then put to banking at the Clydesdale Bank in Falkirk. The family soft drink business was then probably too small to provide immediate employment for Andrew since his elder brother Robert F Barr was already working with his father. Andrew Barr clearly had an aptitude for banking and when the Clydesdale opened a small branch in Larbert he was given the task of operating the business.

While Andrew Barr pursued his early career in banking his father and elder brother were making a success of the soft drink business. The main constraint on growth in the trade was the ability to distribute the bottles. The market was essentially a local one determined by the extent of delivery by horse and cart, out and back from the plant in the course of a single working day. Consequently there was a proliferation of small manufacturers since, in the last decades of the nineteenth century, the soft drink market was growing rapidly. This expansion was partly brought about by the manufacturers themselves who were rapidly extending the choice of soft drinks available to the consumer. Traditionally almost the only non-alcoholic beverage available had been the 'home-brewed ginger beer'. In this expanding consumer market Glasgow was clearly the plum. Consequently in 1887 Robert Barr Snr sent his eldest son Robert F Barr to establish a branch of the business in Glasgow. As the eldest son went to Glasgow, Andrew Barr left the bank, and joined his father to help run the Falkirk business; his younger brother, William S Barr then also came into the business.

Falkirk was the centre of the family business, but Robert F Barr quickly established a successful branch in Glasgow. As a young, but experienced manufacturer, he knew that a good aerated water plant needed space for efficient production. He managed to acquire an extensive site of nearly three acres next to Janefield Cemetery, Parkhead. The new business was established there at 184 Great Eastern Road in 1887. Robert F Barr quickly built up the new establishment on the latest automatic lines. Quality and cleanliness was assured with a process which guaranteed that no worker's hand ever came in contact with the waters throughout the manufacturing. By 1890 Robert Barr was employing over 60 hands in Glasgow and had about 14 delivery vans distributing his products. The new company was one of about 50 such enterprises in the Glasgow district and thrived on producing an ever wider range of drinks. In Glasgow Robert Barr produced lemonade, soda water, seltza, kali or potass water, orangeade, pineapple, cider, sarsaparilla, and also catered for specialist tastes by introducing medicinal beverages. The early Barr range of products included such beverages as ferrugine, hop ale and squash, all of which found a ready sale in the local hospitals.

Andrew G Barr joined his elder brother in the new Glasgow plant in 1892 and for a few years worked jointly between Glasgow and Falkirk. He quickly came to take a leading role in the Glasgow plant. He was aggressive and enterprising and clearly wished to go his own way; so much so that in 1897 he became the sole proprietor of the Glasgow business which thereafter operated quite separately from the family business in Falkirk.

Under A G Barr the Parkhead establishment underwent a major expansion as the young man aimed to capture a large share of the Glasgow soft drinks market. A major new factory, designed by A R Crawford, was built over an 18 month period, and extended quickly in 1901 and again in 1902-03. The most modern plant was purchased and installed from Rileys of London, and the layout was designed to enable each stage of manufacture to be carried out easily. The store-room could cope with 30,000 crates containing a dozen bottles each, this reflecting the new scale of the enterprise. It was in the middle of this phase of expansion that the young A G Barr introduced a new product; in 1901 he created Barr's *Irn-Bru*. At the time of its launch Barr's *Irn-Bru* was only one of a large number of similar products in the market, and no one could have known it would become the foundation of the Barr empire. From the outset the formula was a family secret. The most important part of the Parkhead establishment was the laboratory where syrups and essences were blended and added to the water. A G Barr personally supervised the work of the laboratory and even today the formula for the *Irn-Bru* ingredients is held exclusively by the two senior members of the family. Barr's *Irn-Bru* was immediately popular, but did not become the cleverly phoneticised *Irn-Bru* till 1946.

By the time Andrew G Barr introduced his *Irn-Bru* he had extended the works to employ around 200 persons, and some 150 horses were necessary to cope with deliveries. Advertising was important, and A G Barr had his vans designed with a distinctive white and gold livery carrying the company name in large clear letters.

The young A G Barr also took a close interest in trade affairs and quickly became treasurer of the Glasgow Bottle Exchange Association. He, himself, had pioneered the use of the screw-on replaceable bottle top, making it even more worthwhile to collect and recycle the expensive bottles. The Bottle Exchange Association fulfilled that function since van men would collect empty bottles from the retailers and inevitably find bottles bearing other manufacturers' names in their number. The investment in bottles was indeed so large that Barr frequently went to the law to enforce his ownership of bottles bearing his name and to prevent others from filling them with their own products. In 1903 his firm was pursuing Mathew Bennie, oil and colour merchant in Maryhill, who was using Barr's bottles to sell paraffin; a similar case was pursued against Alexander Smith, a licensed grocer in Old Kilpatrick; yet another case was mounted against a rival manufacturer, Mair and Dougall, who was filling soda syphons in Barr's name with their own product. The company ownership of its bottles was upheld in each of these cases.

By the age of 30 A G Barr had firmly established himself as a major manufacturer of soft drinks in Glasgow; he was also taking a leading role in the trade. As yet, however, he had had little time to involve himself in public affairs. Nevertheless as a young man he was a keen sportsman, enjoying cycling, tennis and cricket. Although he lived and worked in Glasgow he still had firm roots in Falkirk where he was a promoter and member of the Falkirk Amateur Athletic Club.

In 1903, with his new business thriving, Andrew G Barr turned to matrimony; he was married to Isabel Margaret Gibb at Dollar on 25 April. Eleven weeks later he was dead at the early age of 31 after a three week battle with a combination of blood poisoning, and a chill which deteriorated into pneumonia. During his three week illness he made provision in his will that his younger brother, William S Barr, be manager of the new Glasgow factory for a period of 18 months; at the end of this he was to be given first option of purchase at a mutually agreed price with the trustees of A G Barr's estate. This indeed was the outcome, and in 1904 the firm of A G Barr & Co was created as a private limited company with a share capital of £25,000. From then on the two parts of the Barr empire, the Glasgow and Falkirk companies, grew apace, but separately. The two were only brought together in 1959 when A G Barr & Co purchased the Falkirk business to create the core of the present company.

ANTHONY SLAVEN AND DONNY MACLEAN

SOURCES

Unpublished

Certificate of Birth, Falkirk District, No 479, 1872, Entry 153

Certificate of Marriage, Dollar District, No 467, 1903, Entry 5

Certificate of Death, Dennistoun District, No 6443, 1903, Entry 1356
Company Microfiche, No 5653
SRO: SC 36/8/135, Will

Published

The Scots Commercial Record, 10/9/1904
Stratten, *Glasgow and its Environs*, Glasgow, 1891
The Victualling Trades Review, 12/2/1890, 1902

William Alexander BAXTER,

Preserve manufacturer, b. 22/9/1877, Fochabers, s. of George Baxter, master grocer and Margaret Duncan; m. 11/11/14, Ethelreda Adam; 2s.; Pres, W A Baxter & Sons Ltd; d. 20/10/73, Elgin; g/v estate: £13,334.

There can be few happier examples of entrepreneurial success than that of William Alexander Baxter, the Speyside grocer who went to London to sell the Queen some of his wife's strawberry jam and came back with an order. It is difficult to strip such romantic details from William Baxter's business life: it contains most of the elements that dreams are made of. The eldest son of a Fochabers village grocer, he founded 'Baxters', the Speyside food manufacturing firm which grew not on the mass production of essentials for the urban working classes but on the supply of simple foods of great quality to grace the tables of the aristocracy and the royal household.

Baxter's business training began very early. He was six years old when his father wrapped him up in the shop foreman's apron and set him to weighing tea and sugar and other items for the customers. He graduated to errand boy collecting orders on the Friday afternoons after school and delivering them on Saturday. His father always greeted his Friday afternoon return with the words 'Well, did you get any *new* customers?' With such a business dictum guiding him it was no surprise that at 13 he left Milnes High School in Fochabers and joined his father full-time.

But William Baxter's father, George, was more than a local highland village grocer, attending to local needs. George Baxter was also a wholesaler of whisky and of high quality pottery and household items. He bought malt whisky from the local distilleries dotted around Moray and Nairn such as the Minmore Glenlivet, Strathisla, Milton Duff and Glendronach distilleries, blended them and marketed the highly successful results under the trade name of Baxter's

Pure Malt Scotch Whisky which sold at around 42/- per dozen bottles. He went on wholesale buying trips to the English potteries bringing back to the North East of Scotland delicate Minton for the ladies of Elgin and ornate floral patterned ware for the fisherfolks. On his return to Fochabers, George sold them to the local shopkeepers who served this particularly bounteous area of Scotland. On a lighter note he imported German jewellery costing 42/- a gross and sold it at 1/- a piece, and for bedazzled or ageing eyes he had Czechoslovakian spectacles at 6d to 9d a pair.

George Baxter had as his patron the Duke of Richmond and Gordon. He had been one of the Duke's 50 or so gardeners tending the Gordon estate. The Ducal customer was influential, setting the style amongst the local gentry. It was for the Duke, and gentry, that George Baxter went to London and the Continent for fine Dutch cheeses, French patés and wines. Baxter's sent a daily order up to Gordon Castle which included these imported delicacies and Mrs Baxter's home made jellies and jams.

Mrs Margaret Baxter began making preserves as an outlet for her own surplus fruit and because customers who could not pay for their groceries in

COURTESY OF THE MITCHELL LIBRARY

13

cash offered soft fruit in kind. Mrs Baxter's preserves were good and they sold. The 7th Duke of Gordon gave George Baxter the recipe for a thick cut orange marmalade. The recipe had been used in the kitchens of Gordon Castle since 1837. Baxters' named it Castle Marmalade, and this, too, sold very well. Visitors to Gordon castle liked the locally made preserves and gave George Baxter orders to be delivered at their London addresses. So that when young William Alexander Baxter joined his father in the grocery trade he was not actually beginning from scratch. That particularly Scottish egalitarian trait, often portrayed in myth and legend, played some part in the formation of the family business through the already present ties with the Dukes of Gordon and the up-market demand from landed gentry. It was William Baxter's good fortune to have such a background and to live surrounded by the fertile Laich of Moray in which nature appeared to have been especially generous. The Spey valley is renowned for its natural produce: beef, fish, venison, fowl, grain, fruit and vegetables were literally on the Baxter's doorstep.

The promise shown as a six year old did not disappoint. By the time he was 18, William Baxter began to accompany his father on visits to the Potteries, London, and European cities while his younger brother, George, looked after the Fochabers shop. His salesmanship became legendary and was based on a naturally genial disposition allied to native Scottish nous. In 1898 when he was 21, he paid his first visit to Chichester near Goodwood, on the Richmond estates. His companion was the Duke's Steward. They put up in a local hotel which Baxter described as the local farmers club. Liberal tastings of Baxter's whisky brought a 100 case order which was repeated for many years. His sales round was not always so comfortable. His beat in the North East when he sold groceries and preserves to an established clientele began by taking a bicycle up to Wick by train. Once there he cycled all the way back down to Fochabers, in hail, rain and sun, bicycle panniers filled with samples. Much of his business was done after shop hours over a wee dram.

The pattern continued. The Baxters continued to make jams and took on two elderly sisters who were previously employed by another confectionery and jam maker. A small shed at the bottom of the garden behind the Spey Street shop was converted for the purpose. The fruit; strawberry, raspberry, blackcurrant, rhubarb and ginger came from the Baxter's garden supplemented by other local sources and those of the Gordon Estate. And the Baxter family were able to build their own house, Highfield, by Fochabers in 1904. The family then consisted of four sons and a daughter. Only two sons were fated to carry on the family business, William Alexander Baxter and his younger brother, George. The youngest son, John, served as a Corporal in the Seaforth Highlanders and was killed at Arras in 1917. Gordon, another brother, also served in the First World War as Captain in the

RAMC. He survived and became a dental surgeon in Banff.

For William Baxter life continued from 1904 pleasantly. He was part of a tidy growing grocery business with sidelines in preserves and whisky. Change, however, came just prior to the First World War. W A B, as William Alexander Baxter was known, fell ill. He was nursed back to health at Highfield by Ethelreda Adam, a nursing sister from the Watson Fraser Nursing Home, Aberdeen. During his convalescence W A B made the wisest decision of his life; he proposed marriage to Sister Adam and was accepted. They were married in Aberdeen shortly after the outbreak of war, 1914. William Baxter was 37 and Ethel 31. W A B's father, George Baxter, retired about this time. Ethel took over the jam making and William and his younger brother George took over the business.

Much has been written about the Baxter women and each generation of Baxter men has paid tribute to the qualities of the women they took to wife. Ethel was strong enough to suggest that they should begin in business on their own as jam manufacturers and furthermore that they should leave the family grocery business to William's younger brother George. This was a brave decision in wartime for a newly married couple who already had a settled business life in front of them. But Ethel persuaded W A B to approach the Duke of Gordon and Richmond. In the manner of things they met one Sunday morning after church and later that afternoon, by the Spey bridge, Duke and grocer debated the best place to build a jam factory. W A B's original site was deemed inappropriately near the Spey because of flooding and the site suggested by the Duke was adopted near to the railway. They measured out the one quarter acre site together and the conveyancing fees came to 8 guineas. Due to wartime shortages, lack of timber held up the building until late 1915. The first jam made in the Baxter factory was bottled on New Year's morning 1916.

W A B continued his peripatetic journeying as salesman extraordinary around Scotland and England. His customers, important then, have long since faded from view. Names such as Manuel and Webster of Glasgow, Bruce and Glen of Dunfermline, Aikman and Terris of St Andrews, John Marks of St Ann's Square, Manchester, Coopers of Liverpool (qv J G Bishop), and Barrows Stores of Birmingham. All elegant emporiums for fine foods for the upper middle classes and aristocracy.

In 1919 W A B got his first order from Harrods by selling to Mr Jack Stirling, Harrods' buyer and a fellow Scot, a selection of Ethel's best preserves. The whole family were pressed into service to produce the order. W A B's eldest son, Gordon, recalls that he had to 'tissue' the tops of Harrods' jams before he could go out and play football for the local team. Stirling's personal friendship with W A B provided an entré into Fortnum & Mason's of Piccadilly.

W A B approached the buyer, Mr Reilly, whose office was a glass kiosk in the middle of the store, with some trepidation. W A B gave him the sales talk and some of his jam to taste. Reilly gave him an order on the strength of the tasting alone despite the fact that he had not understood a word that W A B had said. With Harrods and Fortnum & Mason as customers it seemed a natural progression that the Duke of Gordon introduced W A B to the Comptroller of Supply at Buckingham Palace. The order was successful and it was for several cases of Little Scarlet Strawberry Jam to be delivered to Balmoral Castle. It confirmed the Baxter's decision to produce only quality goods.

Other successful ventures followed, Royal Game Soup, in its day probably the best known of Baxter's products, came about through the Duke suggesting that W A B should use the game on his Glenlivet and Glenfiddich estates. At that time in the late twenties venison was practically unsaleable, bringing only tuppence a pound free on rail, and caracases were often buried on the hillsides. Ethel took venison, game, partridge and pheasant added port wine and seasoning and canned it as soup and started a fashion for quality canned soups for the elite tables of the artistocracy.

The farming community were introduced to quality control in a novel way when W A B decided on a new product: small whole chickens in natural jelly packed in glass jars. The chickens had to be exactly two and a quarter pounds in weight when killed to fit into the jars. A great incentive was to pay cash on delivery to the Banff and Moray wifies. Baxter's famous beetroot came about when one of W A B's customers, Graham and Co of Banff, Italian warehousemen, received a consignment of understerilised bottled beetroot from a firm in the south. The beetroot fermented and exploded in the shop as W A B was taking an order. The proprietors suggested that W A B should set up in the beetroot business. He did just that, using local produce picked and bottled by local labour.

The major factor in Baxter's success was the ability to seize opportunities for new products which were providentially all around them. They had always been there, William Alexander Baxter capitalised on them. Baxter's became part of the Moray landscape as entrepreneurs and employers. Fochabers became known worldwide from the 1920s when foreign buyers going to London came across Ethel Baxter's excellent preserves, canned soups and bottled foods and ordered them direct from Fochabers.

The wartime years were very difficult. In 1945 when their sons were returning from the services staff was reduced to ten factory workers and one clerkess. In 1945 W A B set up a private limited company with Ethel and their two sons Gordon and Ian, W A Baxter & Sons Ltd with 4,000 £1 shares. By 1956 stock had increased to £26,000. The post-war expansion of 'Baxters of Speyside' came with another generation of Baxter men and women. Ethel Baxter died in 1963

and it fell to Gordon Baxter's wife Ena to carry on the tradition of Baxter wives sharing the credit for expanding the products awaiting an ever increasing market.

Although W A B retired from the role of travelling salesman for his products he remained president of the company until his death in October 1973, aged 96. He oversaw the tremendous expansion of his company: share capital moved from £70,00 in 1967 to £500,000 in 1970, all held in family hands. Not until 1973, the year of his death, did a few Baxter shares fall to a non-family member. Share capital reached £1 million in 1981 and the Baxter family still own 96% of the company's shares.

The small jam factory begun in 1916 is now the core of a vast complex of buildings including the W A B Baxter building opened in 1973, the culmination of five years capital investment by Baxters on Speyside. The original village shop belonging to W A B's father was removed from its site in the Fochabers High Street and rebuilt within the new complex by Gordon Baxter and is now a timely reminder of such small beginnings. Before his death in 1973 W A B was persuaded to recall his personal reminiscences for the in-house magazine. He died just three weeks after dictating his last memoirs. This biography of this fiercely proud Scot who knew that the world was his market place has, naturally, used many of these personal details.

BRENDA M WHITE

SOURCES

Unpublished

Company Registration File, WA Baxter & Sons Ltd, No 23572

Inventory of William Alexander Baxter, SC 26, Elgin Sheriff Court, Reference 1602050DG

Testamentary Disposition and Settlement of William Alexander Baxter, Elgin

The Baxter Story, various other pamphlets and ephemera of W A Baxter & Sons Ltd

Published

The Banffshire Journal, 20/10/73, 22/10/73
The Chamber of Commerce Journal, Summer 1957
The Elgin Courant, 27/10/1923 and 6/12/61
The Elgin Courant & Courier, 10/8/34
The Glasgow Herald, 17/10/73
The Northern Scot, 20/10/73
Scots Magazine, February 1967
The Speyside Courier Series of W A Baxter Memoirs, 1973-74

William BEATTIE,

Master baker; b. 1853, Ballymena, Co. Antrim, s. of Francis Beattie, master baker and Elizabeth Cathcart; m. 31/10/1884, Margaret Barr, d. of Andrew Morton, Inspector of Timber; 2 s., 3d.; Founder, William Beattie & Co Ltd; d. 7/4/1919, Glasgow; g/v UK estate £81,530 5s.

From very humble origins William Beattie rose to be numbered amongst the best known wholesale bread manufacturers in Scotland. He came to Glasgow from Ireland, as a herd laddie, in 1866; he was then 13 years old. Little is known of his life in Ireland, but once in Glasgow he found an apprenticeship with John Roberts, master baker, in Castle Street. His energy must have been prodigious because after serving as a journeyman baker for only a few years he opened in business on his own account in 1876.

Baking was a growth industry in Glasgow during the last half of the nineteenth century. Rapid population growth occurred in crowded areas where people had no facilities to bake their own bread as they had perhaps done in previous generations in rural areas. Beattie therefore seized an open opportunity to expand quickly in his chosen trade of baker. He began business in a very modest fashion, in a small shop and bakery with only two ovens. After two years he moved to larger premises in Bellgrove Street in the East End of Glasgow. A fire in neighbouring premises offered the opportunity to expand and modernise the plant at a cost of £1,700.

Beattie specialised in the making of Vienna bread, which suggests a higher class of clientele than most of his competitors. In 1886 he bought large tracts of land in Paton Street, Dennistoun, from Peter Stewart, paper maker, and built the Vienna Bakery. The bakery, designed by J M Munro and Munro & Co was enlarged several times between 1886 and 1908 at a total cost of £58,000 for buildings and ovens. It consisted of a group of one, two and three storey buildings and as it grew in size it became known throughout Scotland as the Dennistoun Bakery.

In making the move to Paton Street and committing himself to wholesale bread manufacture William Beattie joined the ranks of large wholesale bakers such as J & B Stevenson who had two gigantic bakeries at Cranstonhill and Plantation in Glasgow which produced about 100,000 loaves a day; the United Co-operative Baking Society at McNeill Street; and Bilsland Bros' Hydepark Bakery, built by William Bilsland. The market for wholesale baking was quickened by rapid rail delivery to areas far distant from Glasgow, and the hamper trade to the Western Isles and the Clyde coast resorts.

Until 1913, Beattie concentrated on baking bread and there is evidence that he tried unsuccessfully to emulate John Montgomerie's (qv) malt extract loaf, which the latter had widely patented and retained the sole use of it for his Bermaline products. Nevertheless Beattie was a successful innovator in his own right, designing his own machinery for kneading dough, which replaced the old tradition of trampling the dough by foot, and machinery for sifting flour which obviated over handling by the operatives. The Dennistoun Bakery employed 200 persons around the turn of the century. In 1913 Beattie began to produce confectionery and cakes to counter competition from other bakers such as Bilslands who bought over Gray Dunn & Co, the biscuit manufacturers in 1912. It was also to meet the growing market demand for tea bread, cakes and biscuits stimulated by the increased consumption of tea, coffee, sugar and jam resulting from the considerable price reductions of these commodities during the last quarter of the nineteenth century. This is echoed in the rise of tea and coffee rooms for which Scotland, Glasgow in particular, was famous, reaching its apogee in Charles Rennie McIntosh's Willow Tea Rooms designed for Mrs Cranston.

In 1917 Beattie formed a private limited company, William Beattie Ltd, with a nominal capital of £100,000 in £1 shares, 50,000 preference and 50,000

COURTESY OF THE MITCHELL LIBRARY

16

ordinary. Directors were his eldest son, Francis Beattie, who was on active military service at the time, his brother-in-law, John Morton, the Dennistoun Bakery factory manager, and Thomas Shanks Crosbie, the company cashier. William Beattie held the majority of shares and became chairman and managing director of the new company.

Beattie was a well liked man in the Glasgow business community. He was an extremely active member of the Incorporation of Bakers, becoming Deacon in 1904 and Deacon Convener of the Trades House, Glasgow in 1913 and as such became a member of Glasgow Corporation. After his term of office ended he became a town councillor for the Whitevale ward of Glasgow and during that time was recalled to serve as Deacon Convener of the Trades House when his successor, Mr Hugh Alexander, died whilst holding office. William Beattie was also president of the Scottish Master Bakers Association and the first chairman appointed of the Scottish Bakers Industrial Council, and served on the Whitley Council representing the baking trade of the United Kingdom.

In 1884 he married Margaret Barr Morton. There were five children of the marriage, two sons, Francis and William, and three daughters, Violet, Gladys and Doreen. A few years before his death in 1919, William Beattie bought the mansion Dinieddwigg, by Milngavie where he could display the fine collections of paintings and rare books of which he was a generous patron and an avid collector respectively. His art collection included works by Reynolds, Gainsborough, Raeburn and Sam Bough, in addition to works by the Dutch painter Jacob Maris. It is not surprising therefore to find that William Beattie was for many years a council member of the Royal Glasgow Institute of the Fine Arts.

William Beattie died at a nursing home in Claremont Terrace, Glasgow after a prostate operation. The gross value of his moveable estate was £81,530 3s of which the household furnishings of Dinieddwigg amounted to over £5,000; his collection of paintings was valued at £5,500; his book collection at £5,000 and silver plate at £650. Of the rest of his estate £24,000 lay in life assurance policies, and £39,000 in ordinary and preference shares in William Beattie Ltd. The total estate of William Beattie amounted to £119,653 2s 11 which incurred death duty of £9,143.

BRENDA M WHITE

SOURCES

Unpublished

Companies Registration Office:
SC 9890, Company fiche, Beatties Bakeries Ltd

Stirling Sheriff Court, Vol 167, Inventory Vol 36, Will

Published

The Bailie, 139, 1425, 1589, 1666
Biographical Notices of Glasgow Men, Vol 15
The British Baker, 11/4/1919
Glasgow Herald, 8/4/1919
Hume, J, *The Industrial Archaeology of Glasgow*, Glasgow, 1974
Marks, Richard, *Burrell, Portrait of a Collector*, Glasgow, 1983
Mathias, Peter, *The Retailing Revolution*, London, 1967
Oakley, C A, *Scottish Industry Today*, Edinburgh, 1937
Oakley, C A, *Scottish Industry*, London and Glasgow, 1953
The Scottish Trader
Cunnison and Gilfillan, J B S, *Third Statistical Account of Scotland, Glasgow*, Glasgow 1958

Arthur Kinmond BELL,

Distiller; b. 1870, Perth, s. of Arthur Bell, wholesale wine and spirit merchant and Isabella W Duff; m. Camilla Bruce; no issue; Dir, Arthur Bell & Sons Ltd, Dir, The North British Distillery Co Ltd, Ch, John Shields & Co (Perth) Ltd; d. 26/4/1942, Perth; g/v estate £465,198 5s 6d.

Arthur Kinmond Bell, or 'AK' as he was known in the whisky trade, was the eldest son of Arthur Bell, a wine and spirit merchant in Perth. Arthur Bell had been engaged in the whisky trade since 1851 when he had joined a partnership whose origins dated back to 1825. In 1889 when 'AK' joined the firm its trading activities included the wholesale and retail sale of wine, spirits, malt liquors and tea. Spirits, especially blended whisky, were the most important item accounting for 90% of the modest profits of £1,753. His father had conducted the business according to certain well defined principles: a rigid insistence on quality, a refusal to advertise, a distaste for borrowing from banks, a distrust of agents and, above all, a profound belief that 'slow and sure' was the best approach to business. The adoption of this cautious, plodding style of management can be explained by the father's considerable family responsibilities, certain unfortunate experiences early on in his career and a personality which dictated involvement in every detail of business. This approach made Bells a distinct contrast to larger and more expansive blending firms such as Buchanan, Dewars and Walkers. At the same time, however, Arthur Bell had created a firm with considerable potential for future expansion: his insistence on quality had built up a loyal clientele; his husbanding of the finances had allowed the accumulation of mature whisky stocks, a vital ingredient in any blending firm; and, finally, his use of a network of relations residing in the Empire had laid the foundations for an export trade. His motive in asking his relations to find trustworthy agents was clear:

'My son Arthur has been learning the business with a wholesale firm in Edinburgh for the last three and a half years, and in six months more he will join me here, and I am very anxious to have a good colonial connection, so that he may be independent of the Home Trade which is so much cut up with competition.'

His concern about the home trade proved only partly correct. It was competitive but it was also, during the 1890s, to expand extremely quickly.

'AK' thus entered the firm at a propitious time. By 1895, when he was made a partner, profits had risen to £5,276. In the following year his younger brother, Robert Duff Bell, was also admitted to partnership. Robert's training is not known but he had visited Australia, Tasmania and New Zealand in 1892 and established agencies. With both sons involved in the business, Arthur Bell gradually withdrew leaving management in the hands of his sons. He died in 1900 leaving a personal estate worth an estimated £45,000. By then profits had risen to £11,795, far outpacing the general increase in the demand for whisky.

After his father's death, policy gradually began to alter: more agents were appointed, a modest amount of advertising was undertaken, and, in 1904, the name 'Bell's' first appeared on the firm's labels; Bells thus belatedly joined other blenders in branding their product. These changes, together with a successful attempt to establish Bell's whisky in Canada in 1908, produced an impressive growth in profits which rose to £24,573 in 1913. Given the decline in consumption after 1900 it was a remarkable performance and one reinforced by the very limited drawings which the partners made. An increasing proportion of profits was ploughed back into the business, a feature that was to be of vital importance to the firm in the First World War. Most of the effort behind this expansion came from 'AK' and in 1914, Robert withdrew from active participation in the partnership, his pursuit of leisure proving more compelling than wealth.

The retained profits were mainly invested in mature whisky stocks which by 1915 were valued at £105,000, five times their value in 1900. The firm was thus able to withstand the stock shortages following the Immature Spirits Act of 1915. Indeed, Bells would have been an attractive purchase for any of the larger blenders but 'AK' had a strong streak of independence. With plentiful stocks Bells continued to expand its share of the whisky market and its profits

until 1921 when the firm was converted into a private limited liability company with 'AK' holding the ordinary shares.

Life for an independent blending house in the 1920s proved extremely difficult. Demand continued to fall until 1932, when Bells recorded a trading loss of £10,952. Reserves enabled the firm to survive and, indeed, in 1933 to embark on a policy of expansion with the purchase of the Edinburgh firm of P Mackenzie & Co Ltd. Mackenzie's owned two Highland malt distilleries, Blair Atholl and Dufftown-Glenlivet. A third, Inchgower, was purchased in 1936. Bells thus came later than most blenders to owning its own distilleries. All three were acquired extremely cheaply and put Bells in a good position to benefit from the gradual recovery in demand, most of which came from the export market, the most profitable part of the business by the end of the 1930s. By 1941, with profits of £100,000 Bell's future as an independent blending firm seemed well assured. However, in April 1942, 'AK' died leaving an acute problem of succession. He had no children to follow him in business and his own financial affairs were intricately connected with those of the firm. His younger brother, now aged 70, was recalled from his life as a country gentleman to assume the position of managing-director. He held the post for just over a month until W G Farquharson, a chartered accountant who had joined the firm in 1927, was apppointed chairman and managing-director. Robert Bell died later in 1942, the last member of the family to be represented on the Board. The firm owed £247,000 to 'AK's' estate and family, and in 1949 Bells was converted to a public company in order to raise capital to pay off the loans and to finance a programme of reconstruction.

The whisky trade was by no means A K Bell's sole interest. He was a noted local philanthropist. In 1922, he purchased the Gannochy and Muirhall estates and began the construction of a model housing estate with the intention of providing cheaply rented houses for unemployed railwaymen. The estate, consisting of 150 houses, was completed in 1932. Five years later he founded the Gannochy Trust and in 1941 allocated part of his shareholding in Arthur Bell & Sons Ltd to the Trust. He also purchased Quarrymill Den, a beauty spot on the outskirts of the city of Perth, and presented it to the town. Other activities to benefit from his philanthropy included the allotment garden movement, the Boy Scouts Association, local bands and, above all, his pet enthusiasm, cricket.

Bell was also credited with saving the local linen industry from extinction. In 1936, John Shields & Co Ltd, manufacturers of linen damask, and one of the town's largest employers, went into voluntary liquidation. Loss of export markets and foreign competition were blamed but antiquated equipment and a failure to grasp the significance of artificial fibres also played a part in the firm's demise. Bell acquired the premises, re-equipped them for artificial fibres and re-constructed the firm. For this, and his philanthropy, he was made a Freeman of the City of Perth in 1938.

RONALD B WEIR

SOURCES

Unpublished

SRO: SC 49/31/278, Inventory
   SC 49/32/73, Will
Weir, R B, *Arthur Bell & Sons Ltd, 1825-1900*, Manuscript, 1969
Weir, R B, 'The development of the distilling industry in Scotland in the nineteenth and early twentieth centuries'. (University of Edinburgh, unpublished PhD thesis, 1974)

Published

Anon, 'Bell's O'Perth: An Independent Scottish Whisky House', *The Wine and Spirit Trade Record*, 17/2/1958
House, J, *Pride of Perth: The Story of Arthur Bell & Sons Ltd, Scotch Whisky Distllers*, London, 1976

Sir William BILSLAND,

Master baker; b. 17/3/1847, Ballat, Stirlingshire; s. of James Bilsland, farmer and Annie Blair; m. 16/9/1885 Agnes Anne, d. of Alexander Steven, engineer; 2 s., 2 d.; Partner, Bilsland Brothers, Glasgow; d. 27/8/1921, Garton, Cambusbarron; g/v estate £50,000 5s 0d.

The second half of the nineteenth century witnessed changes both in the patterns of consumption, and the methods of production, of bread. In the developing industrial cities, families which lacked the time, facilities and perhaps knowledge to bake their own bread turned in increasing numbers to the local master baker for the provision of their staple diet. These bakers, themselves, comparatively new phenomenon, with small bakery-cum-shops serving specific residential areas, were gradually being dominated by a few large scale factory bakeries, employing wherever possible new technology in place of physically exhausting labour intensive methods of bread production. In the West of Scotland the first such concern was the United Co-operative Baking Society, founded in 1869. Capitalist enterprise was also active in this field, and in 1881, coinciding with the first International Exhibition of Flour Mill Machinery in London, 'said to mark the beginning of mechanical baking in the United Kingdom', the firm of Bilsland Brothers opened its purpose-built bakery in Hydepark Street, Anderston, Glasgow. The senior partner in this concern was William, later Sir William, Bilsland.

William Bilsland's career had begun some 20 years earlier, when in 1861 at the age of 14 he moved to Glasgow from Bonhill, where he had received his education at Dalmonach School. He was apprenticed to Robert Mitchell, a grocer and provision merchant for nine years before starting his own grocery business in the north of the city with his brother James. In 1872 he leased a small bakery which he operated with his youngest brother, John. Three years later the two bought a second bakery in Greenhill Street, William having given up his grocery business to concentrate on baking. By 1875 William, John, James and Alexander Bilsland had formed a loose partnership operating six bakeries scattered throughout the north of the city. In 1877 William and his three brothers formalised the partnership, which lasted until 1915 when a

COURTESY OF THE MITCHELL LIBRARY

private company was formed, with William as chairman.

The new factory which William Bilsland directed exploited to the full the new technology available to the trade. Much of it was supplied by Baker-Perkins of Peterborough, whose transatlantic activities allowed Bilslands to incorporate the most up-to-date machinery in their plant. William Bilsland was not, however, a baker; the mechanics of the production process, dough-dividers, double ovens and American reel-ovens were supervised by John Bilsland. With a training in the retail trade, William Bilsland's main concern was the actual and potential market for the Hydepark Bakery's standard product, the 2lb white loaf. The company's main customers were found among the 1,600 retail establishments in the city of Glasgow and its suburbs, served by a fleet of motor and horse drawn vans. Sales also extended via the railway to the Western Highlands and Isles and the growing towns to the south and east of Glasgow. Much of the success for the distribution of some 23,000 dozen loaves per week was explained by William Bilsland's particular 'genius' for organisation, and his ability to be identified with the many small grocers of the city was a continual boost for the popularity of Bilsland's bread. He was associated with the North West Grocers and Provision Merchants' Association, and according to one trade journal there was 'no public man in the city of whom Glasgow grocers are prouder'.

The problems of securing a share of an increasingly competitive and complex market were to be faced by the firm after William Bilsland's active career had ended, but he was, as early as 1890, aware that diversification was one method of increasing market share. In that year he became a partner in the baking and biscuit manufacturing company, Gray Dunn and Co at Kinning Park, Glasgow. With his brothers Alexander and John, he revitalised this stagnating concern, rapidly restoring it to the position of one of Scotland's foremost biscuit manufacturers. In 1912 the company was taken over by Bilsland Brothers and its bread production absorbed into the output of the Hydepark plant, while biscuit production remained at Kinning Park.

By 1900 the firm of Bilsland Brothers employed 200 people, with an output of 23,000 dozen loaves per week. The company had acquired a reputation in Glasgow not only for their bread, but also for their methods as employers. William Bilsland particularly was noted for that 'trait which wins and secures the goodwill and loyal service of hundreds of workers'. Employment terms were good in comparison to those of most competitors; the Hydepark factory was light, spacious and clean with good sanitary provisions. Shifts of eight hours were normally worked, and the average wage was, again comparatively, high. In addition, the company made extensive donations to its workers in the form of cash gifts and free bread. However, such paternalism precluded any signs of initative or organisation being shown by employees and William Bilsland, who clearly wished to see his own brand of democracy enforced from the top, strongly discouraged any attempts at unionisation by his workforce.

Bilsland's business activities outside of his baking interests were confined to a small number of directorships concentrated in the financial sector. He was a director of the Scottish Temperance Life Assurance Co Ltd, the Western Insurance Company, and the United Free Church of Scotland Fire Insurance Trust. In 1915 he became an extraordinary director of the Royal Bank of Scotland, a position which he retained until his death. A director of the 'philanthropic' Glasgow Workmen's Dwellings Co, he served as chairman between the years 1913 and 1919. Although not an impressive list, such interests, along with his own baking activities, allowed Bilsland to enter the industrial and commercial elite of the city. His position was further enhanced by membership of a number of trade organisations; he served as treasurer of the Grocers Company of Glasgow, was a member of the Incorporations of Bakers, Hammermen, Gardeners and Coopers, and also the Merchants House and Chamber of Commerce.

Although not directly involved with many charitable organisations, William Bilsland was noted for the generosity with which he gave to a variety of religious and philanthropic groups. He made no specific charitable bequest in his will, but through the company donated at least £1,000 per annum to charities on top of large gifts of free bread. His personal beliefs were such that he began all company meetings with a prayer of thanks to God, a practice which ended only with his death. As a member of the United Free Church he assisted with the practical mission work of his local congregation as well as frequently attending the General Assembly, and serving as a member of the committee to establish a union between Scotland's two major presbyterian denominations. It is probable that his religious views account in part for his strong attachment to the temperance movement and subsequent membership of the Scottish Temperance League; his uncle, with whom he lived whilst attending school at Bonhill was Sir Alexander Leckie, one of the pioneers of the Scottish Temperance Movement. When, in 1886, William Bilsland stood for election as councillor for the Anderston ward (in which his bakery was situated) it is possible that he was in part motivated by his attitude to drink. Temperance was the main issue in most local elections fought in Glasgow between 1881 and 1914, the success of the anti-drink lobby at the polls being reflected in their increasing power over the local licensing courts.

William Bilsland's career as a local politician lasted until 1908, during which time he served as a magistrate for three years (1891-1894); sat on the bench of the licensing courts and acted as convener of the Parks Committee (1892-1905). He continued to serve as a

Deputy Lieutenant for the county and Justice of the Peace until his death. Finally, between 1905 and 1908 he held the office of Lord Provost of the City of Glasgow. It was during this period that he received his baronetcy (1907), an honorary LLD from Glasgow University (1907), the rank of Knight Commander of the Royal Norwegian Order of St Olaf (1906) and the Order of the Sacred Treasure (3rd class). As a member of the council he was elected to the Board of the Clyde Navigation Trust, and he was chairman of the Scottish Departmental Committee on Inebriates, which reported in 1909. Although concerned with public health, most notably sanitation and housing reform, his main impact on the Corporation lay in the provision of leisure facilities for the city. He was prominent in the construction of the municipal galleries at Kelvingrove, even advising the Corporation on the selection and purchase of pictures. Slightly less elevating, but still a suitable diversion from the vices of public houses, was the People's Palace and Winter Gardens, built on Glasgow Green for the working classes of the city's east end. He was a strong advocate of the Free Libraries system, and also, again probably due to his zeal as a temperance reformer, instituted Saturday evening lectures at the city's galleries, and 'musical entertainments' in city parks.

As Lord Provost his activities went beyond extending the boundaries of the city's parks, and he launched an ambitious plan for the extension of the city boundaries, which was finally realised in 1912. He instituted the District Visitors Association, which was in part responsible for preventing the maltreatment of children in the city. During the unemployment crisis of 1908 he was both personally and officially involved with relief schemes for the out of work, but as someone strongly identified with the Liberal cause his activities were not always welcomed by the representatives of organised labour or the ever growing left. Overall, his term in office was typically energetic, with Bilsland taking an active interest in all the sub-committees of the Corporation. Indeed, as contemporaries and obituaries noted, throughout his municipal career he had preferred the bread and butter work of the committee as opposed to the debating chamber, this despite an apparent gift for public speaking.

When William Bilsland died in 1921 he was still playing an active part in the management of his firm. Although retired from all municipal activities he still served as a J P and was a member of the Carnegie Education Trust and a trustee of the National Galleries for Scotland. A change in the pattern of demand for bread and increasing competition from local rivals was forcing the company to alter radically both its production and sales methods. The fact that many of the necessary changes could only be made after

William Bilsland's death indicates both the power that he continued to wield over his fellow directors (even in old age), and also a decline in his innovative drive, probably brought about by many years of living off one successful product. His shares in the company were worth some £21,000 and he ensured by the terms of his will that these would remain firmly in family hands.

William Bilsland's career was marked by an untiring energy, both in his public and business life. Following his death contemporaries agreed that he had broken his health through continual self-neglect in the face of massive commitments. In establishing Bilsland Brothers and overseeing the building of the Hydepark Street bakery he revolutionised bread production in Glasgow. However, although Bilsland's bread was popular it made him no great fortune, his estate totalling only £50,000. In Glasgow he was remembered as much for his public service as for his bread, and it was this which increasingly consumed his time in later years. A 'self-made' man, though with a fairly privileged background, he was perhaps typical of the commercial and industrial elite that was by 1920 slowly losing its grip on the control of the city.

Nicholas J Morgan

SOURCES

Unpublished

Hill Collection, Biographical Notices of Glasgow, The Royal Faculty of Procurators of Glasgow
SRO: SC 36/48/328, Inventory
SC 36/51/193, Will

Published

The British Baker, 2/9/1921
Directory of Directors, 1900, 1905, 19210, 1915, 1920
Glasgow Herald, 29/8/1921, 1/10/1921, 5/10/1921
Glasgow & Lanarkshire Illustrated, Hamilton, 1904
Lanarkshire Leaders, London, n d (c 1911)
Murphy, W S, *Captains of Industry*, Glasgow, 1901
Scottish Trader, 10/2/1900, 11/11/1905, 28/12/1907
Stothers' Glasgow, Lanarkshire & Renfrewshire, Glasgow, 1911
Who Was Who, 1907, 1916
Who's Who in Glasgow, Glasgow, 1909

Alexander BRUCE,

Master brewer; b. 1839, Edinburgh; s. of Robert Bruce, Master bricklayer and Ann Low; m. (1) Catherine Greenlees; m. (2) 27/7/1875, Agnes Livingstone, d. of David Livingstone, African traveller; 3 s., 1 d.; Deputy Ch, William Younger & Co Ltd; d. 27/11/1893, Edinburgh; g/v UK estate: £177,673 8s 10d.

Alexander Low Bruce, in common with William Stewart (qv), was one of a new breed of professional managers who contributed to the success of Scottish brewing enterprise in the late Victorian era. He was born in Edinburgh in 1839, educated at the High School, and joined the firm of William Younger & Company while still in his teens. Within a year he was transferred to the London office, where he was later joined by Henry Johnston Younger. Bruce rapidly assumed increased responsibility for the firm's sales in London and overseas markets. In order to achieve greater penetration in potentially lucrative North American markets Bruce was sent in September 1873 to the United States and Canada with samples, to take orders on the spot, and promote all Younger's products. This sales tour was to take him from New York to San Fransisco and back in four months.

In 1875 Bruce returned to Edinburgh and shortly afterwards became a partner in the firm. It was said that despite the size of incoming correspondence it was usually all opened and read by Bruce before being passed on to the appropriate department. On the inception of William Younger & Co Ltd in 1887 Bruce became deputy chairman and also acquired a substantial shareholding in the firm.

Later in 1891 Bruce undertook another major sales promotion in the Mediterranean, conducting negotiations on the company's behalf with their agents in Gibraltar, Malta and Egypt. During this trip Bruce again proved his sales ability by securing the regimental contract supplying the Black Watch, then stationed in Gibraltar - Scottish beer followed the flag all over the British empire! His hard-headedness as well as his enthusiasm for sales is well illustrated by the fact that he did not budge an inch when faced with the coopers' and maltmens' demand for an increase of 12/- a week and an hour's reduction in the working week, while he proved more generous to salesmen and agents seeking merit payments.

Bruce had other major interests in the drink trade, including the Lion Brewery in London, Guinness & Co Ltd, and in the Edinburgh United Breweries, of which William Stewart was manager. By all accounts Bruce had as good a head for legal as financial affairs and it was he who negotiated the conversion of W B Reid & Co, the Newcastle brewers, into a limited liability company. Part of the agreement was the control of Tyneside tied houses and the transfer of a substantial shareholding to William Younger & Co, plus seats on the board for Bruce and Harry George Younger (qv). Bruce was a director of the Edinburgh & Leith Shipping Co (which carried much of Younger's beer south to London markets), and of the Scottish Widows' Fund. He became a close friend of Andrew Drybrough, another noted Edinburgh brewer.

While native business ability brought obvious financial reward, Bruce also enjoyed considerable social prestige through marriage in 1875 to Agnes Livingstone, daughter of David Livingstone, the African missionary-explorer. According to one contemporary 'he made the interest of the Dark Continent his own' and worked 'to forward the cause of civilisation in Nyasaland and the African Lakes', notably in putting an end to the slave trade. Whether Bruce himself actually visited Africa is not known, though he did have shares in the Africa Lakes Co and the British East Africa Co. He was active politically as a Liberal but like so many others in the Scottish business community at that time was also a Unionist and campaigned against Gladstone's proposals on Home Rule. With Sir John Usher, another successful drink industrialist, he jointly financed the chair of Public Health at Edinburgh University, leaving £5,000 in his will for the purpose. This, he recorded, was in acknowledgement of Pasteur's investigations.

He died in 1893 at the early age of 54 years - of pneumonia preceded by influenza. In its obituary notice *The Scotsman* recorded that 'by this unexpected and dolorous event Edinburgh (had) lost a citizen of rare worth; and the cause of civilisation in Africa, where much of his large heart was centred, one of its warmest friends'. Much later in a history of William Younger, David Keir described Bruce as 'a man wholeheartedly devoted to the Victorian gospel of work' - and he certainly played a distinguished part in the development of one of Scotland's leading enterprises.

IAN DONNACHIE

SOURCES

Unpublished

Records of William Younger
SRO: SC 70/1/327, Inventory
      SC 70/4/273, Will

Published

Donnachie, Ian, *A History of the Brewing Industry in Scotland*, Edinburgh, 1979
Keir, David, *The Younger Centuries*, Edinburgh, 1951

Andrew BUCHANAN,

Wholesale confectioner; b. 1827, Killearn, Stirlingshire, s. of Andrew Buchanan and Jane Forsyth; m. (1) Jean McAdam, (2) Jane Hepburn Boyd; 1 s.; Partner, John Buchanan & Brothers, Glasgow; d. 16/5/1902, Cadder House, Bishopbriggs; g/v estate: £89,601 19s 8d.

Scotland has a notoriously 'sweet tooth'. Not surprisingly this national weakness was recognised quite early and during the nineteenth century thousands of small confectionery firms sprang up to manufacture anything from high class chocolates to jube-jubes and liquorice sticks. The majority of 'sweetie' manufacturers centred around Glasgow, largely because the raw materials of sugar, sorghum, colourings and flavourings were imported via the Clyde from the West Indies and the Americas, and because the increased populations of the Central Belt offered greater marketing opportunities. One of the largest of these firms was that of John Buchanan & Bros, Glasgow, founded in 1858 by three brothers, John, Alexander and Andrew Buchanan. These three were the eldest of ten sons born to Andrew Buchanan Snr in Killearn in the heart of Buchanan territory in Stirlingshire. They had a fairly comfortable home life which was strongly influenced by firm religious principles. All ten sons were educated at the local Venture School whose sturdy, dissenting ethos set it apart from the established Church of Scotland parochial school in the village.

Andrew Buchanan attended the Venture School until he was 15 years old then he left Killearn and moved to Glasgow and entered the provision trade. He worked for 16 years with various firms to gain experience and in 1848 set up business in his own right as a high class provision merchant in the Port Dundas area of Glasgow. His business prospered and ten years later he extended into Parliamentary Road with a retail shop. About 1858 he joined with his brothers, John and Alexander, in forming the partnership of John Buchanan & Bros. His eldest brother John had established a wide connection amongst grocers and sweet sellers and his brother Alexander already had a thriving partnership with a John McIndoe as a general provision merchant. The three brothers set up business in the flat of a mill in Cadogan Street with warehouse premises in Madeira Court. This was a strange venue for a sweet factory but the mechanical gift of Andrew and the business ability of John and Alexander combined to make the venture a success almost from the start. The three brothers kept to their own spheres of interest within the firm. Alexander's talent lay in book-keeping and the counting house, John was an indefatigable traveller and Andrew developed a latent technical talent to rev-

olutionise the machinery used by the firm for producing confectionery.

The Buchanan brothers demanded from their employees certain standards of cleanliness, hard work and artistic appreciation of the art of confectionery. In return they operated a worker incentive scheme paying high piece rates and a bonus based on yearly profits. The Cadogan Street factory employed around 50 women and girls producing about 60 cwts of handmade sweets a week. Business was brisk. The firm moved to larger premises and installed machinery to cope with demand but either quality, price or selection boosted the sales of Buchanan's confectionery to such an extent that the machinery was fully utilised night and day. Because of all this they needed even larger premises. In 1869 they moved into the nucleus of their permanent premises at the junction of Stewart Street and Ann Street in the densely crowded Cowcaddens district of North Glasgow. The premises were previously known as the Phoenix Foundry which produced cannon for the British Army before the Crimean War. The owner, Alexander Gray, an engineer and ironfounder, died and the foundry was abandoned. Such a large block of property in so crowded an area brought few offers and the Buchanans bought the site and buildings at a public roup or auction raising a bond of £3,500 on the property for building purposes.

By a positive policy of buying up adjoining properties in Stewart Street and Ann Street and acquiring further properties in Maitland Street, over the years 1870-1900 the firm of Buchanan Brothers built a large factory complex in the shape of a rough square bounded by Ann, Stewart and Maitland Streets and Dobbie's Loan in Cowcaddens. In 1885 jam making was added to confectionery manufacture and Buchanans now produced 40 tons of sweets a week and 50 tons of jam in the fruit season. The factory complex housed all that was necessary for the manufacture of confectionery ranging from special areas for citrus fruit peeling, areas for flavouring and decoration, to the processing of raw cocoa beans for chocolate. It included enormous sugar sheds where upwards of 8,000 barrels of American, Austrian, French and Dutch produce was stored. These were mainly beet and sorghum based sugars. West Indian cane sugar processed at Greenock found little share in Buchanan's stock reflecting the commercial free trade policy of the time.

Andrew Buchanan and his brothers John and Alexander were operating at the height of the intercontinental Clyde based trade. Citrus fruits were bought mainly from the Cape where one of the younger Buchanan brothers lived and operated a distribution centre there. Essences were bought in from America and special colourings from France and Germany. In addition, Buchanans became major exporters of confectionery with distribution networks in the Cape, America, London and Europe. Market competition was fiercest in the Cape where a tax of tuppence on each pound of sweets was levied and in the United States which operated a 30% import duty on British confectionery. At the turn of the century Buchanans were producing 100 tons of confectionery a week and that in a trade where weight was no criterion of value.

This vast import/export manufacturing business was carried on at the complex at Cowcaddens. A factory of such magnitude situated in the heart of Glasgow could only be extended by building upwards and parts of the complex were six storeys high, housing the counting house, the essence stores, stables, van sheds, engine rooms, warehouses, in addition to the great flats containing the actual manufacture of between 9,000 and 10,000 different varieties of confectionery, much of which was exported.

Andrew Buchanan with his engineering skills and enthusiasm for mechanical production undoubtedly steered the firm of John Buchanan and Brothers Ltd through the first major phase of its expansion from 1880 to 1900. The firm's capacity to meet ever increasing demand was due mainly to his support for mechanised production and to its constant updating and modification. It is estimated that in this period, 1880-1900, confectionery prices as a whole decreased threefold due to lowered costs of raw sugar imports and reduced hand labour costs. The former obviously affected Buchanan's growth but the latter, the decreasing hand labour costs in relation to mechanised production, must be set against the fact that by 1900 Buchanan's total labour force has risen from 50 in the 1880s to 1,100 by 1900, many of which were administrators and delivery staff. The key to Buchanan's success, therefore, lay in its capacity to satisfy increased demand by its production methods. It is useful to note that Buchanans were one of the first large firms to employ female administrative staff in their counting house. They did this from the early 1880s. It was successful, they thought, because of their rigid separation of the sexes within the counting house. However, they also thought that the female influence was beneficial and paid their female clerks from 12s to 18s a week depending on age and experience.

Of the three original partners in John Buchanan Brothers Ltd, Andrew Buchanan was the longest lived. His brother John died in 1881 and Alexander in 1896. Andrew Buchanan was responsible for forming a private limited company in 1894.

Andrew Buchanan's life was devoted to the business of John Buchanan and Brothers Ltd. He held no public offices either in the confectionery trade or in municipal affairs. He did contribute extensively to charitable organisations, following the general Buchanan family ethos of charitable concern for the care of the poor, young orphans, and temperance organisations. It was his youngest brother, Robert Buchanan, who became a director in the new limited liability company, who exemplified the Buchanan's charitable involvement in social and religious rescue work. Robert Buchanan was an intimate friend of William Quarrier who founded the orphan homes of Scotland. He took a leading part in the formation of the Glasgow Foundry Boy's Religious Society and was an ardent worker during the Moodie and Sankey revival. He was known familiarly as 'sweetie Buchanan' and his little shield texts 'be of good cheer' and 'have a faith in God' were to be found in railway signal cabins and waiting rooms throughout the world. He travelled far and never failed to take his well known cards with him.

When he died in 1902 Andrew Buchanan's estate was worth £89,000. With the exception of £25,000 worth of shares held in John Buchanan & Brothers Ltd, his shareholdings show little relation to the confectionery business and its raw material supply lines. He invested mainly in gold mining and oil company shares with varying success. The £1,000 of £1 shares in the Mallina Gold Mine, Glasgow, were valued at only 1s each at his death but, each of the 330 ordinary shares of 10s each in the Orregeun Gold Mining Company of India, London had risen to 41s 6d, and the 200 £1 shares in the Rand Fontein Estates Gold Mining Company, Witwaterstrand, stood at 72s 6d each, and the Consolidated Gold Fields South Africa shares had risen from £1 to £9 11s 3d.

Andrew Buchanan took up residence at Cadder House in Bishopbriggs about seven years before he died. There he enjoyed the life of a country gentleman but still kept his place as head of the firm of John Buchanan and Brothers Ltd. He died at Cadder House on 16 May 1902 after a short illness.

BRENDA M WHITE

SOURCES

Unpublished

Sasines for the Barony Parish of Glasgow, 1869, 1900
SRO: SC 36/48/180, Inventory

Published

Glasgow Herald, 20/5/1902

Glasgow News, 'Typical Industries, Messrs John Buchanan and Brothers', 24/8/1885

Glasgow Post Office Directories

Hume, J, *Industrial Archaeology of Glasgow*, Glasgow, 1974

Murphy, W S, *Captains of Industry*, Glasgow, 1901

Scottish Trader, 26/5/1900, 7/12/1900, 31/3/1939, 20/5/1902

Gilfillan and Cunnison, (eds), *The Third Statistical Account of Scotland - Glasgow*, Glasgow, 1958

James BUCHANAN, Lord Woolavington,

Scotch whisky merchant, distiller and blender; b. 16/8/1849, Brockville, Ontario, s. of Alexander Buchanan and Catherine McLean; m. 5/12/1891, Mrs Annie Bardolph, d. of Thomas Pounder, upholsterer; 1 d.; Founder and Ch, James Buchanan & Co Ltd, London & Glasgow, Dir, The Distillers Co Ltd, Edinburgh; d. 9/8/1935, Lavington, Sussex; g/v estate: £7,150,000.

James Buchanan was the founder of one of the 'Big Three' Scotch whisky companies which made their brand names household words, first in the UK, then in the English-speaking world, between the 1880s and the Great War. His main competitors, John Dewar and Sons Ltd of Perth and John Walker & Sons Ltd of Kilmarnock, were family businesses, each run by the founder's grandsons, that had expanded over many years from their home grounds in Scotland. James Buchanan & Co Ltd was created by one man who brought it from nowhere to the front rank within 20 years. For most of this time it was a marketing company, based in London and with the bulk of its trade in the metropolitan area. After the take-over of its suppliers in Glasgow, Buchanan's became one of Scotland's largest blenders and bottlers. Despite a run of continuous success, Buchanan was mindful of the industry's cycles of boom and depression. In the 1900s he pressed for an amalgamation of the 'Big Three' and their main supplier, The Distillers Co Ltd. In private life, he was a notable philanthropist and a most successful owner and breeder of racehorses.

Buchanan was the third and youngest son of Scottish emigrants to Canada. A year after his birth they returned to Glasgow where his father obtained a post with Charles Tennant & Co, chemicals manufacturers. The boy was educated privately at Larne, Co Antrim, where his father managed a limestone quarry. In his fifteenth year he made a start in business as an office boy with William Sloane & Co, steamship owners and shipping agents, Glasgow, where a cousin was an active partner. Although soon promoted customs house and clearing clerk, he received no increase in pay and after three years decided to move on. He was aged about 19 when he joined his brother William as a partner in W & J Buchanan, hay, grain and seed merchants. After about ten years in this trade, including a period when he worked unsuccessfully on his own account, 'I went', he said, 'to an old distiller whom I knew and told him that if he would pay me, I would represent him in London.'

So in 1879 Buchanan was appointed the London agent of Charles Mackinlay & Co, wine and spirits merchants of Leith. 'In 1884', according to his reminiscences, 'looking to the future, and not satisfied to continue my business career as an agent, I made up my mind to start business on my own account.' and, he mused, 'sometimes I marvel at the supreme self-confidence that upheld me - a young man without capital and practically no knowledge of the business I was embarking in: a stranger too among strangers in this great City of London. The extraordinary thing is that the possibility of failure never once occurred to me. I had it always before me in my mind that sooner or later I was bound to make a success.'

He was already convinced that the English public was 'certainly inclining towards the use of Scotch whisky.' (So were the Walker and Dewar brothers; they set up London Offices in 1880 and 1884 respectively). To unlock the potential of the London market, it was necessary to offer a branded product that was more attractive to the English taste than the whiskies commonly sold in public houses. Buchanan set out 'to find a blend sufficiently light and old to please the palate of the user.' For help in devising it, he enlisted the skills of W P Lowrie, a Glasgow wine and spirit broker, one of the largest stockholders in the Scotch whisky industry. Having found it, he agreed to draw all his supplies from Lowrie in return for extended credit and a loan to start up his business. Interest-free loans and low overheads (cheap premises, few employees and no advertising) were significant factors in the early years when Lowrie 'largely contributed to my prosperity.'

Lowrie undertook production of the brand, in cask and in a plain bottle of black glass with a white label designating 'The Buchanan Blend of Fine Scotch Whiskies'. Buchanan was able to devote himself entirely to marketing: 'I was on the quest for business night and day, getting introductions and getting to know people wherever I could.' He made rapid headway. 'When I look back on the strenuous years I went through in building up my business,' he recalled, 'continuous and unremitting hard work, I think, was the principal factor in my success, with the abiding faculty of taking pains and giving attention to small matters. Tact and a natural facility for making friends of my customers was another great help to me in those joyous days when the building process was going on, for I loved my work and I saw and felt it growing in my hands.'

Buchanan intended that his brand should be preferred, and seen to be preferred, by those whose custom was taken to imply a seal of approval. The first battle in this campaign was won in 1885 when he secured the contract to supply the refreshment department of the House of Commons, held until then by his former employers, Mackinlays. The value of the contract lay in its presentation as a mark of confidence in the product. The words 'As specially selected for the House of Commons' were printed under the brand name on the front label of the bottle, and a reproduction of the letter of appointment on the back label.

The United Music Halls Company, owner of most

of the leading variety theatres in London, was another target. Repeated attempts to gain some of its bar business were rebuffed. The company was controlled by the head of a large firm of accountants. Buchanan invited Mr Newsom Smith to audit his accounts and courtesies were exchanged. Subsequent approaches, carefully timed and delicately executed, achieved their object, 'I need hardly say that I brought off the business I desired and very soon my whisky was the dominant brand in all these London music halls.'

By 1889 Buchanan's brand was on display in the most important bars and public houses in Central London. This core business was the base for the company's rapid expansion in the 1890s. Success in winning orders from the railway companies helped to make the brand known outside the capital. Overseas sales were conducted through a firm of export merchants in the city until Buchanan recruited one of its employees in 1895 to set up an export department. With capable assistants to mind the shop, he undertook voyages to the main overseas markets for Scotch whisky (Australia, South Africa, New Zealand and Argentina) to obtain first-hand information on market conditions and to appoint distributors.

After building eye-catching new offices in Holborn, Buchanan was able to accommodate 200 employees, as against seven in 1889. The company opened its first Highland distillery, also in 1898, and became entitled to describe itself as 'Scotch whisky distillers' - a significant advantage at a time when some distillers, alarmed by the growth of blended whisky, had mounted a campaign to disparage it. At the end of the year, James Buchanan & Co obtained the ultimate accolade for its product on being granted Royal Warrants of Appointment to supply the Prince of Wales, the Duke of York, and finally Queen Victoria.

A campaign to expand sales outside London began in 1899 with the appointment of a sales agent in Scotland and of a regional office and distribution depot in Bristol. Branches at Birmingham, Manchester and Leeds followed within a few years. From 1898 onwards, the main illustrated weeklies carried a notable series of advertisements based on paintings commissioned by Buchanan himself. The subjects included sporting scenes, pedigree dogs and members of the upper classes taking appropriate refreshment. All were intended to reinforce the brand image of top quality. From the turn of the century the brand name was changed to 'Black & White', derived from the black bottle and white label of its distinctive pack. Advertisements were first placed in provincial newspapers in 1904 but not in the national press until the following year. The company was a major user of advertisements on the sides of tramcars and buses. Buchanan regarded his elegant delivery vans, their well-trained drivers and horses, as a most effective form of advertising. Their loading-up parade outside his premises was one of the sights of London for a quarter of a century.

'Once fairly started in my new office and store',

Buchanan recollected, 'my business increased phenomenally, no doubt due in large measure to the publicity and the unrivalled position of my new premises.' In 1903 James Buchanan & Co Ltd was registered as a private limited liability company with an authorised capital of £1 million. The issued capital was £700,000, of which the founder held 98%. The value of the Company's sales in its first year of trading exceeded £1 million, compared with £180,000 in 1896-97, the last year before the move to Holborn. Its main supplier, W P Lowrie & Co, was unable to put up the capital to provide greater bonding, blending and bottling capacity for the growing volume of the Buchanan trade. Buchanan took over Lowrie in 1906, reformed it with a capital of £500,000 and rebuilt and re-equipped its warehouse. The new building was the largest bonded store of its kind in the world. The press noted that 'the employees number 658 and the total staff of this great firm is about 1000.' The company took vertical integration a stage further by becoming the first Scotch whisky firm to make its own bottles, and by undertaking the manufacture of packing cases.

'Whisky alone could not absorb his untiring energy', the magazine *Vanity Fair* noted in a profile of James Buchanan. His career as a successful owner of race-horses had begun in 1899. Four years later, he bought Lavington Park, an estate of 3,000 acres (1,214 hectares) on the Sussex Downs. Here he created one of the finest stud farms in the world. A contributor to a society magazine, *The World*, interviewing him there in 1909, saw him as:

'One of those strong characters that go steadfastly on their way, regardless of obstructions. His vigorous powers of organisation and mastery of detail have built the world-famous business that bears his name - but he holds the theory that life to be happy must be compounded in due degree of activity and pleasure, and he has many hobbies. He shoots ... he breeds pedigree cattle, sheep and thoroughbred horses, but it is not hard to guess that he derives more satisfaction and enjoyment from his racing establishment than from all the rest combined.'

The country round Lavington was ideal for riding, a favourite recreation since boyhood. At Torridon, his estate in the North West Highlands, he enjoyed salmon fishing and stalking. With Lord Aberdeen, he bought 20,000 acres in British Columbia, with the aim of developing fruit-farming and assisted immigration. He served, with characteristic energy, on the committee of the Tariff Reform League.

Unlike the Dewars and Walkers, James Buchanan had no son to provide for the succession. To undertake the responsibilities of day-to-day management, he appointed William Harrison as managing director in 1911. Two years earlier, the principals of the 'Big Three' had begun to discuss the feasibility of amalgamation. The original object was to contain the costs of aggressive competition, both in advertising expenditure and in discounts to customers. The main argument revolved round the valuation of the three companies. Buchanan, the keenest to amalgamate, told the others that he would sell his company for £20,000 or £30,000 less than it was worth to achieve the benefits of a merger. Walker's, having been narrowly overtaken as the market leader by Buchanan's, were adamant that the issue should not be prejudiced by 'one or two of their bad years'. In 1915 Buchanan's and Dewar's went ahead without Walker's by forming a holding company, later known as Buchanan-Dewar Ltd. It had an authorised capital of £5 million, issued in exchange for the ordinary capital of the two companies, valued after investigation of their accounts over the past ten years. A statement informed the public that

> 'We shall be able to co-operate in many different ways to reduce expenses and lessen competition, and we shall have the largest stocks in existence of fine old whiskies. It is a financial amalgamation only, to enable us better to meet the high taxes and the high prices of raw materials. There will be no interference with the policy of the firms and with the conditions under which they work.'

Wartime restrictions on distilling caused a prolonged shortage of mature whisky. The great blenders, with orders far in excess of their capacity to meet them, snapped up any stocks of mature whisky, and malt whisky distilleries, that came on the market. Some of Buchanan-Dewar's acquisitions were made in conjunction with Walker's, or with their main suppliers of grain whisky, The Distillers Co Ltd. Such negotiations led in 1925 to a merger of all three companies under the style of the last name. The grand design envisaged by James Buchanan had finally been realised. As Lord Woolavington, he joined the board of the enlarged Distillers Company, but in his 76th year, he was no longer concerned with management. He was an elder statesmen.

As a county magnate, he had served as High Sheriff of Sussex in 1910. He was created a baronet in 1920 and a baron in 1922. The last honours were his appointment as GCVO and an honorary doctorate in law from the University of Edinburgh. Thus a record of philanthropy dating from the 1890s received recognition. Although he otherwise ensured that his benefactions were made anonymously, some of his gifts for public objects necessarily became known. His interest in animal husbandry prompted a donation of £10,000 to endow Animal Breeding Research at Edinburgh University, and one of £5,000 to the West of Scotland Agricultural College. He put £50,000 at the King's disposal for the restoration of St George's Chapel, Windsor Castle, and gave £125,000 to the Middlesex Hospital, London, to endow the Woolavington Wing, and £10,000 to the London Hospital,

both for the benefit of paying patients of moderate means.

Woolavington's achievements in the racing field made him a nationally-known figure. In 1922 he gained the prize that had eluded him in over 20 seasons: he won the Derby with *Captain Cuttle*. Four years later he repeated this feat with *Coronach*, which went on to win the St Leger and the Eclipse Stakes. His pleasure was all the greater because he had bred both horses from his own stallion, *Hurry On*, the St Leger winner of 1916, at Lavington Park. The 1926 season, when he headed the list of winning owners for the second time, was the peak of his racing career. His horses carried his colours to the end.

BRIAN SPILLER

SOURCES

Unpublished

James Buchanan, Select Letter Book, 1888-1902

James Buchanan & Co Ltd, Minute Books of Directors' meetings, 1903-1936

John Dewar & Sons Ltd, A J Cameron papers (correspondence with Sir John Dewar and Sir Thomas Dewar)

Dr R B Weir, 'The Distilling Industry in Scotland in the Nineteenth and Early Twentieth Century', unpublished PhD thesis, University of Edinburgh, 1974

Published

Atherton, F W, *History of the House of Buchanan, with an introduction by Lord Woolavington*, James Buchanan & Co Ltd, 1931

The Field, 17/8/1935

Ross, W H, 'History of the Company', *The DCL Gazette*, January 1923 to January 1929

Spiller, Brian, *The Chameleon's Eye: James Buchanan & Co Ltd, 1884-1984*, James Buchanan & Co Ltd, 1984

The Times, 10/8/1935, 12/8/1935, 19/8/1935

Vanity Fair, 20/11/1907

Wine & Spirit Gazette, 24/8/1907

Woolavington, Lord, 'Autobiographical sketch', *DCL Gazette*, 8/1928

The World, 3/6/1908

Sir James Charles CALDER,

Brewer; b. 28/12/1869, Alloa, s. of James Calder, brewer and timber merchant and Cecilia Mackenzie; m. 1904, Mildred Louisa, d. of Col Richard Manners; no issue; Partner & Dir, James Calder & Co; Ch, MacDonald, Greenlees and Williams (Distillers) Ltd; Dir, Distillers Company Ltd; d. 22/8/1962, Ledlanet, Milnathort.

James Calder had financial interests in the brewing, distilling and forestry industries but his main entrepreneurial activity was in distilling. His career, from 1886 when he joined the family firm of James Calder & Co until 1941 when he retired from the Board of the Distillers Company, spanned the transformation of the Scotch whisky trade from an industry owned by independent capitalists to one dominated by a single large firm.

As the younger son of James Calder, a prosperous timber merchant and brewer in Alloa, his future was already planned for him. After formal education at Perth Academy and St Benedict's College, Fort Augustus, he joined the family business and was apprenticed to the firm's agents in Glasgow. Three years later, in 1889, he was placed in charge of Bo'ness Distillery which his father had purchased in 1873 and subsequently (in 1876) converted from a pot still (malt whisky) to a patent still (grain whisky) distillery. His main achievement at Bo'ness was to further extend the production of yeast, a source of revenue of considerable importance to patent still distillers in the highly competitive environment following the collapse of the grain distillers' cartel (the United Kingdom Distillers' Association) in 1888. Calder remained at Bo'ness until 1903, having been made a partner in James Calder & Co in 1890 and a director when the firm adopted limited liability status in 1892. With the earlier acquisition in 1880 of Glenfoyle distillery, a pot still distillery, the firm was well placed to participate in the blending trade (the mixing of malt and grain whiskies) then undergoing a very rapid expansion. Through the sale of malt and grain whisky, James Calder came into contact with the Leith blending firm of Alexander & MacDonald and was made a partner in 1895. Such links between distillers and blenders were becoming increasingly commonplace as distillers sought access to the fastest growing section of the whisky market and blenders sought security of supply. Alexander & MacDonald participated in the whisky boom of the 1890s and built a new pot still distillery, Stronachie distillery at Forgandenny, Perthshire. With the reduction in the demand for whisky after 1900, the firm's affairs were re-arranged and control of Stronachie distillery was acquired by James Calder & Co Ltd. James Calder was involved in the controversy over blending and appeared as a witness before the Royal Commission on Whisky in 1908, arguing for a definition of whisky which would embrace both pot and patent still products, a view confirmed by the Commission.

The crisis in the whisky trade, exacerbated by the increase in spirit duty in Lloyd George's 'People's Budget' of 1909, produced a great deal of talk about amalgamation. The name of James Calder & Co Ltd was frequently mentioned as a possible partner, both by 'The Big Three' blenders (Buchanans, Dewars and Walkers) for whom the firm would have given an alternative source of supply of grain whisky to the Distillers Company Ltd (DCL), and by the DCL which saw Calder's as an important competitor in the yeast and spirit trade. Calders preferred to remain independent, though from time to time they co-operated in fixing prices and restricting output. The continuing decline in spirit consumption and the wartime restrictions on the trade, especially the Immature Spirits Act of 1915 which heightened the existing shortage of mature whisky stocks, hastened the merger movement. In 1919 Alexander & MacDonald combined with two other blending firms, William Williams & Son Ltd of Aberdeen and Greenlees Brothers of London, to form MacDonald, Greenlees and Williams (Distillers) Ltd with James Calder as chairman. James Calder's extensive knowledge of the trade was also sought by other distillers for reconstruction schemes. In 1922, for example, he advised the owners of Balmenach distillery, at Cromdale, Moray, and was appointed chairman of the reconstructed company.

Following the death of his father in 1917, he assumed the chairmanship of the family timber business and during the First World War held the posts of deputy timber controller (1917-19) and timber controller (1920) at the Board of Trade. For this public service he was made CBE in 1920 and received a knighthood in 1921.

Amalgamation talks between the DCL and James Calder were resumed almost immediately after the war. Calder's had acquired a controlling interest in a second patent still distillery, Gartloch, in 1907 and the possibility of the firm entering the DCL offered the DCL control over all Scottish patent still distilling capacity save only for the North British distillery whose unique 'co-operative' constitution placed it beyond threat of takeover. In August 1921 provisional agreement was reached between DCL and James Calder, the agreement being finalised eight months later. It provided for the transfer of properties, plant and working stock to the DCL in exchange for 20,000 DCL ordinary shares, some 6% of DCL's ordinary share capital, and a seat on the DCL Board. James Calder, a tough negotiator, kept the ownership of the unsold whisky stocks, the most valuable part of the firm given the post-war shortage.

If the merger marked the end of James Calder's career as an independent distiller, it did not terminate his interest in the Scotch whisky trade. He kept his seat on the DCL Board following 'The Big Amalgamation' of 1925 between the DCL, Buchanan-Dewar and Walkers, and played an active part in the management of the greatly enlarged company. In December, 1925 he brought MacDonald, Greenlees & Williams into the DCL, continuing as chairman of the new subsidiary firm. In 1926 he formed part of the deputation from the DCL Board which led to the firm investing in the production of potable spirit in Australia, a response to the introduction of import tariffs on Scotch whisky. He was appointed to the new management committee of the DCL in 1936 with responsibility for industrial alcohol, yeast, malt extract, methylated spirit, the works department and the gin trade in the USA. The last was probably his most signficiant contribution for it gave the DCL a firm foothold in the American liquor trade following the repeal of prohibition. It also brought Calder into contact with Joseph Kennedy, reformed bootlegger and head of Somerset Importers, one of DCL's main brand agents. His relationship with the Kennedy family was maintained when he acted as host to Joseph Kennedy and the young John F Kennedy when they toured Scotland during Joseph Kennedy's period of office as US ambassador to the Court of St James. Calder retired from the management committee in December 1940 and from the Board in July 1941.

Despite his substantial involvement in the Scotch whisky trade, Calder had extensive interests in brewing and forestry. He held directorships in several brewing firms including the family brewing firm, though his younger brother, John, played the more active part. Calder owned saw mills in the north of Scotland and plantations in Germany and the United States. His plantation in the Black Forest was used by an associated company of the DCL for experiments in the production of wood sugar from timber which were technically, though not commercially, successful. During the Second World War he was appointed director of home timber production (1940-41).

Sir James was a leading lay member of the Roman Catholic Church in Scotland. He also held a number of public offices being a Justice of Peace for Kinrossshire and a Deputy Lieutenant of the county from 1930. He owned estates at Ledlanet, Milnathort and Lingford Hall, Norfolk. His leisure activities included golf, shooting and fishing, and he was chairman of the syndicate which owned the Grimersta river in Lewis. He married Mildred Louisa, the daughter of Col Manners, the Royal Scots, in 1904. They had no children. Lady Calder died in 1936, Sir James in 1962, aged 92.

RONALD B WEIR

SOURCES

Unpublished

Board & Management Committee Minute Books of the DCL

McMaster, Charles, 'James Calder & Co (Brewers) Ltd, The Shore Brewery Alloa'

Weir, R B, 'The Development of the Distilling Industry in Scotland in the nineteenth and early twentieth centuries', (University of Edinburgh unpublished PhD thesis, 1974)

Published

The DCL Gazette, January 1925
Perthshire Advertiser, 25/8/1962
Scottish Biographies, Glasgow, 1938
Who Was Who, Vol VI

John Moir CLARK,

Provision manufacturer; b. 1835; adopted son of Benjamin Moir, provisions manufacturer; bachelor; MD, John Moir & Son Ltd, Aberdeen; d. 3/9/1896, London.

John Moir Clark was a second generation manager of the firm of John Moir and Son, preserved provision manufacturers, 54 Virginia Street, Aberdeen. He developed the company established in 1822 by his grandfather, John Moir whose family originally came from Leith. In its early years this firm specialised in meat preserving, in the first instance preserving salmon for export and then adding meat, game, soups and other fish to their range of tinned and bottled products. It was claimed that they were pioneers in the canning business and were the first company in Scotland to use this method of packaging their products. Their business was gradually extended within Scotland and they moved further afield. In the Crimean War they were important suppliers of canned meats and other preserved foods for both the British and French governments. A substantial export trade with India, China, and Australia already existed when John Moir Clark entered the firm and it also supplied a large proportion of the provisions used on vessels sailing from London, Liverpool, and Glasgow.

With the death of John Moir control of the firm had passed to his son Benjamin who managed it with his nephew and adopted son, John Moir Clark. John Moir Clark appeared to have gradually assumed the management of the business and made the decision to diversify its activities. In 1869 he bought an estate at Garthdee on the western outskirts of Aberdeen which he turned over to the production of fruit and vegetables. In this way some 135 acres were adapted to supply raw materials for the preserving works in Aberdeen with the cultivation of strawberries, raspberries, gooseberries, black and red currants, carrots, turnips, peas and beetroot. The vegetable refuse from the market gardens was put to use as feed in an adjacent pig-rearing establishment, also owned by John Moir Clark. This experiment does not seem to have been entirely successful, possibly because the gardens so near the city were a temptation to marauding townspeople. In any event they were sold towards the end of the 1870s.

On his uncle's death in 1872 John Moir Clark assumed sole responsibility for the company, and after the sale of the market garden property he severed his personal connection with Aberdeen and moved to London. He was then 37 years old. At the same time the decision was made to form what had hitherto been a family partnership into a limited liability company. In 1880 the firm was floated as John Moir and Son, Ltd with a capital of £50,000 and John Moir Clark was its first managing director. The head office of the company was established in London although the premises were still retained in Virginia Street. He was anxious to continue with the preserved fruit and vegetables so this side of the firm's operations were transferred to premises at Deptford leaving Aberdeen to specialise in the preparation of preserved meats. Under Clark's management branches were set up at Seville in Spain and at Wilmington, Delaware in the United States. Some years before his death in 1896 he ceased to take an active part in the business and the chairmanship of the board of directors was undertaken by Robert Milburn.

RICHARD PERREN

SOURCES

Published

Bremner, David, *The Industries of Scotland; their Rise, Progress and Present Condition,* Glasgow, 1869; reprinted Newton Abbot, 1969

Fraser, G M, *The Old Deeside Road,* Aberdeen, 1921

In Memoriam, Aberdeen, 1896, Obituary

MacKinnon, L, *Recollections of an Old Lawyer,* Aberdeen, 1935

John Alexander DEWAR,
(Lord Forteviot of Dupplin),

Wine and spirit merchant; b. 6/6/1856, Perth, s. of John Dewar, wholesale wine and spirit merchant and Jane Gow; m. (1) 24/6/1884, Johann Hume, d. of William Tod, farmer; 1 s., 5 d.; (2) 22/3/1905, Margaret E, d. of Henry Holland, merchant; 1 s., 1 d.; Partner, Dir, Ch, John Dewar & Sons Ltd; Dir, Distillers Company Ltd; d. 23/11/1929, Dupplin Castle, Perthshire; g/v estate: £4,405,977 12s 10d.

The last quarter of the nineteenth century saw the development of a number of highly successful firms in the Scotch whisky industry amongst which one of the most successful was John Dewar & Sons Ltd of Perth. The firm had been founded in 1846 by John Dewar, the son of a crofter. Born in Aberfeldy in 1806 and educated at the parish school, he was trained as a joiner but in 1828 moved to Perth to take up an offer of employment with a wine merchant. He was made a partner in 1837 and nine years later decided to begin his own business. When he died in 1880 the business was still very much a local one though it made sufficient profit to sustain a sizeable family and to leave an estate worth £34,796.

Two of his seven children, John Alexander, his second surviving son, and Thomas Robert (1864-1930), his fifth, joined the firm in 1879 and 1881 respectively. Both had been educated at Perth Academy and had undergone the customary apprenticeship in another wine and spirit firm, John with Condamine & Co of Leith, Tommy with Forrest & Turnbull of Leith and later, Robertson & Baxter of Glasgow. Together the brothers were to create a firm whose product became a household name. Profit figures offer some indication of their achievement. When their father died profits were a mere £1,321. By 1900 they were £59,000 and by 1925, when the firm merged with the Distillers Company, they were £1,198,154.

The way the firm expanded is difficult to understand without an appreciation of the quite different characters of the two brothers. John was a cautious, dour individual very much absorbed by finance and administration. Tommy, by contrast, was a flambuoyant extrovert, extremely effective at marketing whisky. John spent his entire career in Perth whilst Tommy pioneered new markets in England and overseas. Their business attributes thus complemented one another, much more so than did their political loyalties for John was a Liberal, Tommy a Conservative and Unionist.

John was made a partner in 1879, Tommy in 1885. The firm's progress was very modest until, in June 1890, John approached the Distillers Company and was granted a credit of £12,000 provided Dewars confined their purchases of grain whisky to the DCL. The credit, soon increased to over £75,000, freed resources for investment in whisky stocks, branch offices and a sales tour by Tommy Dewar between 1891 and 1893 when he visited 26 countries, appointed 32 agents and arranged for opening consignments to each country he had visited. The tour cost the firm £14,000, a hefty increase in costs when current profits were less than £7,000 a year, but it established Dewars on a world wide basis. These sales trips became a hallmark of the firm's approach to exporting. Tommy undertook another in 1898 and by 1914 the firm's representatives had made five such campaigns.

Although Dewars continued to enjoy expanding home sales despite the declining demand for spirits in Britain after 1900, exports were critically important for they were almost three times as profitable as home sales. With the largest volume of export sales amongst 'The Big Three' blending firms (Buchanans, Dewars and Walkers), Dewars were well placed in the amalgamation discussions which began in 1909. An amalgamation of 'The Big Three' proved unattainable in the pre-war years but Buchanan and Dewars merged in a holding company, Scotch Whisky Brands Ltd in 1915. This was subsequently renamed Buchanan-Dewar Ltd in 1919, and merged along with John Walker & Sons Ltd in the DCL in 1925.

John Dewar played a more important part than his brother in the merger discussions, partly through his mastery of financial detail and partly because through the credit arrangement with the DCL he had established a close and friendly relationship with W H Ross (qv), the managing director of the DCL. After 1900, both gradually developed a common set of beliefs about the problems facing the Scotch whisky industry. Both wished to see greater stability in the trade, a reduction in the influence of speculators, and an end to certain 'unbusiness like methods', especially 'the very extravagant distribution of advertising material'.

Persuading the various interests, particularly those of the Walker family, that an amalgamation between 'The Big Three' and the DCL was desirable proved extremely difficult. John Dewar's contribution was to urge that 'we must take a wide view and not be too trifling': it was the future earning power of the combine that was vital, not the precise valuation put on the family interests. He was also instrumental in persuading the other participants that Ross should be the chairman of the combine. His only major disagreement with Ross was over the location of the head office. Dewar, following the advice of his financial adviser, Sir Gilbert Garnsey, argued that London was essential if the company was to have the confidence of the city. Ross thought it inconceivable that the leading firm in the Scotch whisky industry should be based outside Scotland, a view that ultimately prevailed.

John Dewar and Tommy Dewar were appointed to the board of the DCL in 1925 but were too far advanced in their careers to play a significant part in shaping future developments as the company became increasingly drawn into the non-potable spirit and chemical trades in response to the decline in whisky consumption.

John Dewar had many interests beyond the whisky trade as a politician, town and county councillor, landowner and agriculturalist. He became a member of Perth Town Council in 1883, aged 27, was elected treasurer in 1888, and served as Lord Provost from 1893 to 1899 pushing through locally important housing and sanitary reforms. In 1900 he became Member of Parliament for Inverness-shire, the only Liberal candidate in Scotland to supplant a Unionist at that election. He retained the seat until 1916. In 1907 he was created a baronet and in 1916 elevated to the peerage as Baron Forteviot of Dupplin, the first of 'The Whisky Barons'. His title derived from the estate of Dupplin which he purchased from the Earl of Kinnoull in 1910, the sale being sanctioned by the Court of Session as the estate was burdened with debt. It cost £249,000. As a landowner, Lord Forteviot set about the task of rural regeneration, building the model village of Forteviot in the style of a small Dutch township.

Part of his fortune was used for philanthropic purposes. An estimated £50,000 was devoted to projects such as the restoration of St John's Church as a war memorial, the building and equipping of a maternity ward at Perth Royal Infirmary, and the building of a new model lodging house in Skinnergate. He also founded the Forteviot Charitable Trust with an endowment of £60,000 for the benefit of the City of Perth and its inhabitants. Other public service included chairing two commissions of enquiry into medical conditions in the Highlands and Islands of Scotland, membership of Perth County Council and Education Authority, and chairmanship of the Territorial Force Association.

Lord Forteviot died in November 1929 leaving an estate worth £4,405,977. His brother, Lord Dewar, died on 11 April 1930 with property valued at over £5m. Lord Forteviot's investment portfolio was valued at £3.996m, 81% of which was invested in the Scotch whisky trade, mainly in the DCL. Of the remaining 19%, 8% was in government stock, 5% in insurance companies, 3% in investment trusts and 2% in banking. His heir, Col, the Hon John Dewar, MC, had been appointed to the board of DCL in 1925 and was appointed chairman in September 1937.

RONALD B WEIR

31

SOURCES

Unpublished

Dewar, J & Sons Ltd, Cameron Papers

Weir, R B, 'The development of the distilling industry in Scotland in the nineteenth and early twentieth centuries', PhD thesis, Univesity of Edinburgh, 1974

Published

Anderson, J L, 'History of the House of Dewar', *DCL Gazette*, April 1929-January 1930

Glasgow Herald, 25/11/1929

William Fraser DOBIE,

Tobacco manufacturer; b. 16/9/1862, Paisley, s. of George Dobie, tobacco manufacturer, and Annabella Fraser; m. 1901, Annie R Hislop; Ch, George Dobie and Son; d. 1/3/1930, Paisley; g/v estate: £39,269.

William Fraser Dobie was born in Love Street, Paisley in 1862. His father was George Dobie, a leading public figure in the town, who had inherited a tobacconist's business from his uncle in the 1840s. The business had been founded in 1809 in High Street but moved to Orchard Street in mid-century before moving to a brand new factory in the Greenhill area of the town in the 1880s. The firm then traded as George Dobie and Son. It did not register under the Companies Acts until 1927 at the time when William Dobie, without an heir, had begun to contemplate his retirement.

William Dobie gained the Barrie medal for Classics at Paisley Grammar School in 1878 but nothing else is known about his education although it is likely to have been the conventional one for the sons of middle ranking businessmen, that is, local schools followed by an early entry into the family business where experience would be gained over a number of years in all departments. Dobie is, therefore, likely to have been active in the family business by 1880. He became a partner in 1888 and this left his father, George, more time to devote to public affairs. George Dobie retained his connection with the firm until his death in 1910 although it seems likely that effective control lay with his son William.

For many years the company's speciality product was known as 'Dobie's Thick Black and Bogie Roll'.

This was a relatively unsophisticated product although the demand for it sustained the firm for many years. By the late nineteenth century, however, the market was beginning to demand more sophisticated products, especially as more women were taking up the smoking habit. At that time William Dobie assumed effective control of the company and responded to these changes by diversifying the product. A range of speciality tobaccos, including cigarettes, was introduced. The cigarettes were marketed as 'Gold Standard' and the pipe tobaccos were marketed under the trade mark 'Four Square' with a design in red squares for the matured Virginia tobacco and blue squares for the mixture. The trade marks were registered in more than 100 countries. Dobie apparently saw the need for attractive packaging for his products. Quality alone would not sell them. These met with great success although Dobie resisted the temptation to market Empire tobaccos, perhaps believing that these were inferior tobaccos, which some of them undoubtedly were. The firm did not begin to sell these tobaccos until 1931, the year after Dobie's death. These were such a success that the company had to double its productive capacity and it is difficult therefore to escape the conclusion that Dobie had carried his resistance to these types of tobacco for too long.

Dobie was greatly interested in new technology and in 1908 he purchased the long established Glasgow firm of J & T Hodge who had been the first Scottish company to use cigarette making machines. The purchase of this firm also brought with it a useful trading connection, for the American cousins of the Hodge family had done much to establish the tobacco industry in Kentucky and were still a very active organisation. Dobie built on this connection. George Dobie and Son conducted all the processes from treating the raw tobacco leaf to selling the finished product. It was a very small company compared to the giants of the industry but its continued success proved that scale was not essential to a continued and healthy existence.

Dobie also had a subsidiary business which manufactured tallows of various kinds. These were speciality products and included edible sweet fat and superior qualities of tallow for lubrication, manufacturing purposes and dip candles.

In his private life William Dobie was an enthusiastic volunteer. He joined the Renfrewshire movement in 1882 and in a long period of association he held every rank from private to lieutenant-colonel. His regiment was originally known as the 2nd Renfrew Volunteers before becoming the 2nd (Princess Louise) Argyll and Sutherland Highlanders. It subsequently became the 6th Argyll and Sutherland Highlanders in the Territorial Force. He retired from the volunteers at the time of his father's death in 1910. Dobie was associated with many local organisations including the Paisley Savings Bank, which he served for a time as chairman. He was a Justice of the Peace for the

County of Renfrew. In 1926 he became a Fellow of the Scottish Antiquarian Society.

Dobie made his home at Edgemont, Castlehead in Paisley and at Stonihill, Portencross at West Kilbride where he lived in some style with his wife Annie, daughter of George R Hislop, gas engineer for the burgh of Paisley. When Dobie died of pneumonia in 1930 various bequests were made to his sister and cousin and to several workmen. The bulk of his estate of £39,000 was left to his wife.

CHARLES W MUNN

SOURCES

Unpublished

SRO: SC 58/45/33, Calendar of confirmations
     SC 58/42/112, Inventory
     BT 2/14590, Companies Registration

Published

Anon, Typescript history of George Dobie and Son, Paisley Museum, n d
Anon, *The House of Dobie*, Paisley Museum, n d
Glasgow Chamber of Commerce Journal, Vol 19, No 2, 1936
Glasgow Herald, 3/3/1930
Paisley and Renfrew Gazette, 8/1/55, 24/12/55, 7/4/56
Paisley Daily Express, 12/1/55, 12/8/55, 21/12/55, 2/8/56
Transactions of the International Engineering Conference, Glasgow, 1938
Scottish Trader, 21/1/1899

Sir Alexander GRANT,

Biscuit manufacturer; b. 1/10/1864, Forres, Morayshire, s. of Peter Grant, railway guard and Elizabeth Norrie; m. 29/7/1887, Elizabeth Simpson Norris; 1 s., 2 d.; Ch and MD, McVitie and Price Ltd; d. 21/5/1937, Edinburgh; g/v UK estate: £1,039,976 5s 9d.

Alexander Grant was long associated with the great Edinburgh bakery and biscuit manufacturing business of McVitie and Price. His obituaries described him as a striking example of a Scottish self-made man, a man of great force and character, which seems an apt description for a man who rose from being a baker's boy to a successful and esteemed businessman and millionaire.

Grant was born in 1864 in Forres, Morayshire. His early years were not easy. His father, Peter Grant, a railway guard for the Highland Railway died while Grant was still at school. He was educated at Forres Academy and when he left school he entered a writer's office. However, he found this kind of work not to his taste and instead apprenticed himself to a baker known locally as 'Jocky' Stuart. For the next few years Grant was trained in this one-oven establishment.

After this initial training Grant moved to Edinburgh where he obtained employment in the underground bakery of Mr Robert McVitie in Queensferry Road. Despite the prevailing conditions in the baking industry - long, uncertain hours and low wages, Grant was not deterred. No work came amiss, and he gained useful experience in the manufacture of articles other than bread and rolls. Robert McVitie took a keen interest in Grant, and it was under his guidance and encouragement that Grant's ambitious character flourished and the foundations for his business career were laid. McVitie encouraged him to attend classes and to study chemistry. Moreover, McVitie provided Grant with facilities that allowed him to travel on the continent, allowing him to learn about the different branches of the baking industry. About this time McVitie entered into partnership with Charles Price, an ex-salesman for Cadbury's under the style of McVitie and Price, for the manufacture of biscuits. This new departure led the firm to phenomenal success, of which Grant played an increasingly large role.

The increased knowledge Grant had gained under McVitie's encouragement was soon put to use when, before he was 30 years old, Grant was appointed foreman of the cake department in the biscuit factory in Merchant Street. This was a new departure that McVitie had decided on in the St Andrew's biscuit factory. It was an immediate success, and from this point Grant's career went from strength to strength. When the St Andrew factory burned down Grant was sent to Malten, near York, to organise and carry on a temporary factory while new premises were being built at Gorgie Road, Edinburgh. On his return to Edinburgh he became inside manager of the new factory. He was also associated with Robert McVitie in establishing biscuit works at Willesden, London. When Mr Price retired from the business in 1901 to become an MP Grant became general manager, and on the death of Robert McVitie in 1910 Grant acquired a controlling interest in the concern. The firm was converted into a private limited company in June 1911, with a share capital of £150,000, divided into 100,000 cumulative preference shares at £1 each and 50,000 ordinary shares at £1 each, and Grant became chairman and managing director of McVitie and Price Ltd.

McVitie and Grant both found success in the baking industry; it was a growing industry - rapidly increasing populations developing in cities had no facilities to do their own baking and needed an alternative source; and there was also a growing demand for items other than bread and rolls, such as cakes, biscuits and teabread. The firm of McVitie and Price was only too willing to take advantage of these demands and provide bread, cakes and biscuits and it was in this atmosphere that the firm continued to expand and develop markets both at home and abroad. Quality of material was of first consideration to the firm and it established a wide reputation for quality biscuits and specialities. Goods of a fancy and attractive nature made for ready sale; packaging and display were important for appearance and tins were adapted for window dressing purposes. The firm was well known for its *Vailima* biscuits, oval *Rich Tea* biscuits, *Butter creams* and *Ginger cake*. New varieties were frequently introduced, usually with great success. In 1905 *Little Mary Wafers* and *Little Veribest Wafers* were introduced, and both lines were unqualified successes. The firm also added to its list that year *Continental Mixed*, *Miladi Cakes*, *Sandringham Shortcakes* and *Bermuda Biscuits*. Most traders found these lines very saleable and as new lines were introduced the firm continued to retain its high reputation for excellence.

To accommodate the expansion of the firm's business another branch was opened in England. It was called the Edinburgh Biscuit Works and was opened in Willesden, London, in the 1890s, and it became well-known for the range of biscuits it produced. The firm was innovative in the goods it produced. For example, in 1891, George Andrew Brown, one of the firm's London salesmen and directors introduced the sandwich biscuit. The volume of trade continued to increase and there was recognition for the firm in 1903 when McVitie and Price were appointed biscuit manufacturers to His Royal Highness the Prince of Wales. Around 1914 the erection of a third factory in Manchester was begun and was partially completed to enable the firm to manufacture supplies for the troops. This was not the first time McVitie and Price had supplied the troops. In December 1899 they had sent out $1,000 \times 2$ lb tins of oatcakes to the First Battalion Gordon Highlanders who were engaged in the Boer War. The firm continued its phenomenal success and developed a position of importance in biscuit production in the whole of Britain under Grant. Some time before his death in 1937 an important extension was made to the Edinburgh factory and it was opened by the Duchess of York. The floorspace of this extension was 35,000 sq ft and it was decided that no pillars should be erected to interfere with the layout of the plant. By Grant's death the firm had, under his management, developed far beyond the sanguine anticipations of its founder, McVitie, it had expanded far beyond the limits of Scotland and Britain and had markets worldwide for its superior quality products.

Apart from his successful business career Alexander Grant was also well known for his philanthropic and benevolent activities; he was a generous benefactor to many Scottish institutions and organisations. In 1923 he gave £100,000 to establish an adequate endowment fund for the National Library of Scotland, which allowed the valuable books and manuscripts of the Advocate's Library to be taken over and housed. A further £100,000 was given by him towards the cost of erecting the new library buildings. These donations reflected how necessary Grant thought that Scotland should have a national library. He also enabled the publishing of Sir Walter Scott's letters to be completed. Grant was a generous benefactor to Edinburgh University. He gave £50,000 to help ease the burden of the University's building debt and in 1929 he gave sums amounting to £50,000 for the building of a new Department of Geology which became known as the 'Grant Institute of Geology'. He donated a further £50,000 to the University in 1930. Grant was one of the chief contributors to the financing of the Scottish National War Memorial at Edinburgh Castle. In 1924 he made a gift of £5,000 to the Scottish Federation of Grocers and Provision Merchants Association which was to be used in a benevolent fund for aged grocers and for those who had fallen on difficult times. In 1920 he cancelled for five years the interest on £100,000 which his firm had invested in war stock, this being the equivalent of a total grant of £25,000 to the Treasury.

One of his last, and perhaps best known, examples of generosity before his death was the presentation of a magnificent service of silver, linen and cutlery and glassware for the Palace of Holyrood House. This gift marked the completion of efforts to make the palace worthy once more for royalty. It was the finishing of the palace; from now on the King would not have to bring his own furnishing. This gift was made anonymously but Grant's anonymity was not preserved and it became well known that he had made the handsome donation of £10,000 to provide the service. The banqueting silver, which comprised 4,000 pieces, weighed 18,000 ounces, and the complete service was placed on exhibition in the national galleries, an opportunity for demonstrating Scottish skill and craftsmanship, as everything connected with the gift was of Scottish manufacture.

Alexander Grant took considerable interest in the development of his native town of Forres. He presented a public park to the town and frequently gifted large sums of money on behalf of the Lossiemouth golf course; he gave financial assistance in the formation and development of the golf course. He was also a generous benefactor to the town of Nairn, where he gave generously to many of its institutions and charities. He gave important support to the reconstruction of Nairn Harbour which allowed the town's fishing community to carry on its trade. He donated £100 a year to the Town and County Hospital, £5,000 for the renovation of the local swimming baths, and sums varying from £50 to £100 to the local cricket, football and other clubs. It is estimated that Grant gave away circa £750,000 and his thoughts on the donations for the Advocates Library clearly reflect his opinion about all of his benefactions: 'I have always felt it was the duty of everyone, who wanted to build up a big business, to have larger ideas in the giving away, as well as in the taking. I am a great believer in the "passing on" habit.'

His generosity did not go unrecognised. In 1923 he received the freedom of the City of Edinburgh, when tribute was paid to his philanthropic and benevolent activities. In 1924 he received the freedom of Forres and he also received the freedom of Nairn. Grant was created a baronet in 1924 and in 1925 the honorary degree of LLD was conferred on him by the University of Edinburgh.

The conferring of the baronetcy excited a large amount of interest when it was associated with an act of kindness by Grant to his close personal friend Mr Ramsay MacDonald, PM. The matter was even raised in parliament. Both Macdonald and Grant were Morayshire men, and Grant's father worked with MacDonald's uncle on the Highland railway. Soon after MacDonald had entered office Grant lent him a Daimler car and £40,000 in securities. In the next honours list, he duly became Sir Alexander Grant in recognition of his many philanthropic activities, and in particular of his donation of the Advocates Library to Scotland. Neither Grant nor MacDonald saw any connection between the baronetcy and the £40,000, but only a short time before there had been the honours scandals under Lloyd George. Many of the daily papers carried lead stories about it. Grant wrote to MacDonald, 'Cheer up, it is only the opinion of good people that matter and that guides public opinion however loud the others may be.' At the end of 1924 MacDonald returned the shares and the car to Grant, but by then the damage had been done. The whole issue was seen by some as an attempt to make political capital out of an act of kindness on Grant's part and was wholly unwarranted. However, in the McVitie and Price affair MacDonald was seen to have behaved with extraordinary imprudence.

The demands of his business life left Grant little time for other interests. When business did not require him to stay in Edinburgh he preferred to relax in the beauty of his native area of Morayshire. He never sought the social life that his wealth could command, and had a few intimate friendships. He married Elizabeth Simpson Norris in July 1887 in Inverness, and they had one son and two daughters. His recreational interests were motoring and golf - his great interest in golf being reflected in all his gifts to the Lossiemouth and Nairn golf courses. Grant described himself as a life-long Conservative, although he did support the Liberal candidate for West Edinburgh in 1924. He was also a Justice of the Peace, though he took little other active interest in public office. He was also described as a good and practical Christian which was reflected in his philanthropic activities. In 1937 while attending the Coronation celebrations in London, Grant caught a chill, and on his return to Edinburgh pneumonia developed. Lord Harder, a royal physician, was in attendance toward the end of Grant's illness. Grant died on 21 May 1937 at the age of 72. He left an estate of £1,039,976 5s 9d. His son, Robert McVitie Grant and his son-in-law, Hector Laing, carried on the business which Grant had developed into one of the most important biscuit making concerns in the country, and one of worldwide repute. Grant will be best remembered for his business skill and his great force of character and his many philanthropic activities, particularly the creation of a national library for Scotland.

THERESA BARTON

SOURCES

Unpublished

SRO: SC 70/1/982, Inventory
SC 70/4/733, Will

Published

Adam, James A, *A Fell Fine Baker. The Story of United Biscuits*, London, 1974
Glasgow Herald, 22/5/1937
Marquand, David, *Ramsay MacDonald*, London, 1977
Oakley, C A, *Scottish Industry Today*, Glasgow, 1937
The Scotsman, 21/5/1937
Scottish Commercial Record, October 1899, December 1899, March 1903
Scottish Trader, 15/3/1902, 19/9/1903, 25/2/1905, 7/1/1911, 17/6/1911, 28/5/1937
The Times, 22/5/1937
Who Was Who, Vol III

William GRAY,

Biscuit manufacturer and baker; b. 16/7/1812, Kinmuck, Aberdeenshire, s. of James Gray, farmer, and Mary Cruickshank; m. (1) Hannah Ostle; (2) 17/6/1851, Margaret Sarah Pace; 4 s., 2 d.; Snr Partner, Gray Dunn & Co, Biscuit Manufacturers and Bakers, Kinning Park, Glasgow; d. 31/1/1880, Pollokshields, Glasgow; g/v UK estate £21,865 1s 9d.

William Gray was born at Kinmuck in Aberdeenshire in July 1812, the son of James Gray, a farmer there. In 1818 James emigrated with his family to America where they stayed for five years until returning to Kinmuck in 1823. Little is known of William Gray's subsequent education, but as his father became a convinced member of the Society of Friends in early manhood it is likely that he was educated at one of the small number of Quaker schools in England. By mid-century William's elder brother John had moved to Glasgow to work as a representative for the English Quaker biscuit manufacturers Huntley and Palmers. John Gray saw the potential that existed in the west of Scotland for biscuit manufacture at a time when the industry was in its infancy and mechanical manufacturing processes only recently perfected. Although Glasgow boasted a large number of bakers the majority were still small and localised enterprises of a traditional kind - none were specialised biscuit producers. He explored this idea with two friends, Peter Dunn and Archibald Campbell, partners in Campbell & Dunn, a Glasgow firm of millers and grain merchants, both of whom responded positively. As a result in 1853 John Gray established the firm of Gray Dunn & Co in partnership with both Peter Gray and Archibald Campbell, although Campbell acted as a sleeping partner, retaining a working interest in the grain milling business. The firm's factory was at Kingston in the south of the city, where they initially produced mainly hand-made biscuits.

During this period William Gray had moved to London where he was employed as an agent for Moorlands, the Quaker sheepskin firm. However in August 1854 his brother John died in Glasgow as cholera swept through the city. William was summoned urgently to Glasgow to take his brother's place in the business, which he did despite lack of experience and capital. Despite the death of its founder the firm was nicely placed to take advantage of the growing demand for biscuits, either as a luxurious accompaniment to fortified wines or tea on middle-class tables, as a convenience food for travellers of all classes, or as a staple food for seafarers. Such was the growth of the firm that by 1860 the partners were exploring new sites for possible expansion, settling on ground close by at Kinning Park which they feued in 1860 and subsequently used as a security for a loan of £2,000.

In 1862 Archibald Campbell withdrew from the partnership to be replaced by James Dunn, Peter Dunn's son by his first marriage. In the following year the firm moved to purpose built premises at Stanley Street, Kinning Park, where in addition to widening their range of biscuit production they began to bake bread on a massive scale. Under William Gray's supervision the firm established a network of retail outlets for bread production, with over 22 shops in all the main thoroughfares of the city.

In 1865 Peter Dunn died, leaving William Gray as the senior partner in the business. James Dunn withdrew from the partnership at the same time, taking with him the £9,700 of capital that his father had invested in the firm. In order to make up this loss a network of Quaker buiness contacts was scoured by Gray until he found a suitable backer in James Thompson, a card-manufacturer from Kendal, who sent his younger brother John Thompson to Glasgow to act for him in the partnership where he supplied a degree of mechanical expertise. The firm continued to add to its product range and market, not only through direct retailing in Glasgow, but also through the development of a substantial export trade: products were 'sent everywhere within the domains of civilisation, and for all classes of consumers' claimed a newspaper account of the early 1870s. From ship's biscuits, (3 tons of which were produced every ten hours), to gingerbread ('manufactured here upon a liberal scale'), to expensive Sultana cakes, soldered in tins to prolong freshness; all these products were despatched from Glasgow bearing the increasingly well-known name of Gray Dunn. For the local housewife 14 ovens served to provide 'an honest and excellent article', white bread, mainly in 2 lb loaves.

At 63 years of age William Gray could have been forgiven for a degree of self-congratulation - having assumed control of a business with which he had little familiarity he had guided it with intense energy to a place of international prominence by 1875. No doubt however his religious beliefs would have prevented any such complacency - he was a prominent member and elder of the local Quaker meeting, serving as clerk to the meeting, and as clerk to the General Meeting for Scotland. He was remembered in the *Annual Monitor* as a man of humility, 'a liberal giver, and a kind and judicious helper of the poor and needy'. He was prominent in the Quaker peace movement in the city, and also travelled regularly to attend the Quaker Yearly Meeting in London. However any hope of relaxation in these latter years was shattered for William Gray in January 1875, when the Stanley Street factory was totally destroyed by fire. The reconstruction of the factory and the reorganisation of the firm was to be William Gray's last contribution to the business. In order to meet the added demands made on the firm John Thompson was formally added to the partnership, as was William's eldest son James Henry Gray. The new partners borrowed heavily (some £10,000 from the cotton spinner George Grant) on the security of the still only partially developed site in Kinning Park in order to finance the rebuilding of the works. However by the end of the year production was fully under way, supporting a workforce of around 400 hands. The firm boasted over 50 varieties of biscuits, a wide range of 'toothsome' cakes, and both machine and hand-made bread. The new factory, whose internal appearance was like 'that of a considerable printing office machine department', offered all the possible savings of automation in every area of production, whilst retaining a high-quality end-product.

William Gray died in January 1880 after an illness that had lasted about a year. He left £21,865, of which £19,756 represented capital in Gray Dunn & Co. In his will he instructed that this sum should remain with the company, and that his son James Henry should manage the business for his trust estate, asking that his second son William Jnr be assumed as partner on attaining majority. The conditions these sons faced were far less favourable than those experienced by their father. The closure of export markets through the imposition of tariffs, particularly in Norway and Sweden, led to a concentration on the home market where competitors were increasingly effective at undercutting prices (and often quality). Already by the 1890s Gray Dunn were an old company in a new world, and the decision taken in 1890 to merge with Bilsland Brothers, the Anderston bakers who eventually took the business over in 1912, was seen as one way of coming to terms with radically altered trading conditions.

NICHOLAS J MORGAN

SOURCES

Unpublished

Companies Registration Office, SC 13345, Gray Dunn & Co Ltd

Library of the Society of Friends, Dictionary of Quaker Biography

SRO: Register of Sasines, Renfrewshire, 1855-1890
    SC 58/42/32, Settlement and Inventory of Peter Dunn
    SC 58/42/47, Inventory, William Gray
    SC 58/45/1, Trust Disposition and Settlement, William Gray

Published

Annual Monitor, London, 1880
Bootham School Register, York, 1971
British Baker, Confectioner and Purveyor, December 1891
The Friend, 20/11/1901
Glasgow Herald, 1/2/1880, 1/5/1940
Marwick, William, 'Some Quaker firms of the nineteenth century', Part I, *Journal of the French Historical Society*, Vol 48, 1958
Marwick, William, 'Some Quaker firms of the nineteenth century', Part II, *Journal of the French Historical Society*, Vol 50, 1962
Scottish Trader, 6/12/1902, 13/2/1904, 27/1/1906, 8/1/1910, 2/8/1913
Slater's Directory for Scotland, 1860, 1867, 187

John Mitchell KEILLER,

Confectionery manufacturer; b. 1/1/1851, Dundee; m. 1883, Mary Greig; 1 s.; Partner & Ch, James Keiller & Son Ltd., Dundee; d. 2.1/1899, Morven, Aberdeenshire, on board yacht *Earl King*, en route to the West Indies; g/v estate: £435,367 12s 5d.

John Mitchell Keiller was the head of the third generation of the great confectionery and preserve manufacturing family of Dundee. He was fortunate, therefore, to inherit a company, James Keiller & Son, which already enjoyed an established nationwide reputation. However, John Keiller was only 26 when he gained control of the family business on the death of his father, and it was a measure of his maturity and entrepreneurial skills that the company continued to expand until his own untimely death at the age of 48.

The family concern had been founded in 1797 by his grandfather, James Keiller (1775-1839), producing confectionery for the local market in Dundee. Keiller was to become famous for a product which sprang from a business blunder of James Keiller - marmalade. Marmalade was first produced by his wife Janet after James had mistakenly purchased bitter Seville oranges. From 1800 the firm began the first commercial production of marmalade, again concentrating on the local market. Preserves proved so popular that by 1830 Keiller's orange marmalade had gained a nationwide market and production of preserves overshadowed the confectionery side of the business.

John Mitchell Keiller was groomed from an early age for his place in the family business. After attending the High School of Dundee, he spent some years at Edinburgh University before rounding off his education with two years on the Continent perfecting his French and German. Keiller then entered the family firm aged about 20 years as assistant to his father, then chairman of the concern. The young

Keiller proved to be an excellent businessman and was soon promoted to partner. In the early 1870s, he persuaded his father to establish a factory in the Channel Island of Guernsey to circumvent the high import duties on sugar on mainland Britain. It was John who ensured that 'Keiller's Dundee Orange Marmalade' was one of the first trade marks registered when the British trade mark registry was established in 1876. The following year, aged 26, John Keiller assumed control of the company on the death of his father.

Keiller's flair for business became apparent in the rapid expansion of the company from 1877. He completely re-modelled the Dundee factory utilising the latest technology and expanded the confectionery business once more with a range of sweets including traditional lozenges, gums and rock. In 1880 when the sugar duties were relaxed, Keiller switched production from Guernsey to a new factory at Silvertown in London. This not only met demand for Keiller's products in England, but it was hoped to provide a base for expansion into the export market. To this end, John Keiller travelled widely throughout Europe, the United States and to the British Colonies of Australia and New Zealand promoting the family products. He proved a most energetic entrepreneur and was certainly not content to live on the past reputation of the firm he had inherited.

From 1877 until 1893 John Keiller controlled the company directly. Then in August of that year, the firm was converted into a limited liability company with capital of £300,000. Under the articles of agreement, Keiller was to remain chairman of the company as long as he retained a seat on the board of directors. However, in practice, although he was nominally chairman, ill-health forced Keiller to leave most of the administration to his managing director, Mr William Boyd.

As well as a substantial interest in the family business which on his death amounted to £140,708 6s 8d in preference shares and £92,481 10s in ordinary shares, Keiller had a wide range of investments. His inventory was reputed to have been 'the largest ever recorded at Aberdeen'. Keiller had substantial interests in several investment companies such as the Third Scottish American Trust Co Ltd (£5,643 10s 3d). He also invested in railway companies thoughout the world. He had shares worth £8,108 17s 1d in the North British Railway Co, some £4,000 invested in three Indian railways and over £19,000 invested in American railroads. He also invested in telegraphic communications and electrical construction companies.

Although Keiller was one of the most prominent businessmen of his day, he did not enjoy the high public profile of many of his contemporaries. He was only rarely connected with local boards. He served as Justice of the Peace for Dundee and Dundee District, president of the Dundee Chamber of Commerce and sat for one year on the Harbour Trust. A conservative,

he never became involved in local politics. He was, though, an active philanthropist. He made several large donations to local hospitals including a gift of £2,000 in 1896 to the Dundee Royal Infirmary of which he had been a director. It was in the fields of education and the arts that Keiller received most recognition in his native city. He believed that education was the key to improvement of the working class. Therefore, in 1887 he donated £10,500 to the Albert Institute to pay off its debts. His motive was to preserve the Free Library which he believed was vital for the spread of education in Dundee. When it was discovered that the debt was less than originally anticipated, Keiller insisted on paying the agreed amount so that the Library could purchase a further 572 books. Meanwhile, Keiller's love of gymnastics prompted him to donate a challenge cup for Dundee schools. He cared deeply for his workers instituting holidays and social events and in his will left £20,000 to establish a benevolent fund for employees.

Keiller became a patron of the fine arts in Dundee. He both promoted the work of local artists and allowed works from his own collection to be exhibited in the city. On his death, his private collection was valued at £15,500 and contained works by Constable, Turner, Raeburn and Millais. He donated several paintings to the Dundee Public Galleries and was a promoter of the Dundee Exhibition. In all his philanthropic activities, Keiller remained in the background preferring his actions to speak for him.

In his last years Keiller suffered severely from ill-health. He retired from Dundee to London or his estate at Morven in Aberdeenshire. His love of yachting provided some compensation and he spent some six months of every year on trips combining business and pleasure. It was on board his yacht, The *Earl King*, that John Keiller died on 2 January 1899 bound for a cruise in the West Indies. His ill-health and early death robbed Scotland of one of its most notable entrepreneurs, a truly internationally-minded businessman. Within a year of his death, both of his great factories in London and Dundee were destroyed by fire. Yet such was the reputation built up by John Keiller, the board of directors were able to raise easily the £100,000 loans needed for rebuilding.

PATRICIA COLLINS

SOURCES

Unpublished

SRO: SC 1/36/136, Inventory
   SC 1/37/120, Will

Published

Bremner, D., *The Industries of Scotland*, Edinburgh, 1869

Dundee Year Book, 1899

Glasgow Herald, 6/2/1899

Millar, A H, *Glimpses of Old and New Dundee*, Dundee, 1925

Scottish Trader, 27/3/1897, 7/1/1899

The Times, 7/1/1899

Robert KERR,

Sugar refiner and manufacturer; b. 1850, Greenock, s. of John Kerr, shipowner and sugar refiner, and Isabella Dougall; m. (1) Margaret Sharp Galbraith; (2) Mary Broadfoot; 3 s., 1 d.; MD, Glebe sugar Refining Co, Ltd; d. 1/6/1922, Greenock; g/v estate: £150,160 14s 1d.

At the turn of the twentieth century, Robert Kerr was one of the most notable figures in the Greenock sugar industry. Beginning his career as a clerk in his father's company, the Glebe Sugar Refining Co, Kerr rose to become its managing director. As well as his business interests, Kerr was also prominent in Greenock civic life and local politics.

Robert Kerr belonged to one of the great sugar dynasties of Greenock. In the mid-1840s his father John (1823-1872), partnered by Abram Lyle, had owned the Diamond Shipping Line, trading coal to and sugar from the West Indies. In March 1865, they moved into the manufacture of sugar, founding the Glebe Sugar Refining Co in partnership with James and Walter Grieve and C P Hunter. At its launch, Robert joined the company as an articled clerk determined to learn about the business at all levels of production. By 1882 he had worked his way up to become joint managing director when the Lyle family sold their share of the business to concentrate their interests in England.

Under Kerr's skilful management, the Glebe refinery expanded greatly. He was quick to incorporate new technology such as steam powered vacuum pans which reduced the wastage during cyrstallisation that had marred the earlier open-pan system. In 1891 the company received nationwide recognition when it concentrated only on the refining of sugar cane, thereby reversing the growing trend towards utilisation of sugar beet. While the Ker Street Refinery was closed for refurbishment for cane refining, Kerr purchased another Greenock refinery to maintain production. Kerr also diversified the range of products through the establishment of two new companies. In 1885 he founded the Brewers Sugar Co Ltd, to supply sugar to the brewing trade and later in 1896 established the Western Sugar Refineries Ltd for the manufacture of sugar products for the grocery trade and confectionery products. In particular Kerr's companies became famous for the production of golden syrup and loaf sugar (sugar cubes).

As well as an openness to technical innovation and product diversification, Robert Kerr emphasised the importance of effective modern marketing methods. He advertised widely in both trade journals and national press stressing the purity of products bearing the Glebe trade mark 'free from beetroot and all acids'. The firm won awards for successful marketing at trade exhibitions such as the London Grocery Exhibition of 1899.

The success of Kerr's companies, with production trebling between 1882 and 1899, was all the more remarkable in being accomplished at a time of great crisis in the Greenock sugar industry. In 1900, the Glebe was one of only four of the original 16 sugar houses in Greenock still in production. Kerr too, however, had his share of setbacks. In 1899, in particular, the company received much unwelcome publicity with the collapse of a tenement in the town's Argyll Street which was being used to store sugar. Kerr attempted to sue the owner of the property, Mr A Patterson, a local ham curer, arguing that the building was unstable at the time of rental. However, a counter-suit was accepted that Glebe had overloaded the property and damages of £1,834 19s 11d were awarded to Patterson.

While managing the Glebe, Kerr became active in the Greenock Harbour Trust, intent on improving the port facilities. He acted as convenor of the Harbour Committee until 1886 during which time the James Watt Dock was built.

In later life, Kerr diversified his business interests, with directorships in the Greenock and Port Glasgow Tramway Co (1900-1909), the London and Lancashire Fire Insurance Co (1900-22) and William McLean Ltd (1920-22). He also served as president of the Greenock Provident Bank. His prominence in the Greenock business community was reflected in his two terms of office as president of the local Chamber of Commerce.

Robert Kerr was a member of the United Free Church, acting as office bearer for the Greenock Parish. He was well-known for his charitable work sitting on the committees of several local charities including the Blind Society Infirmary and the Seaman's Friends Society. He also served as Justice of the Peace for Renfrewshire and Honourary Sheriff-Substitute. Politically, Kerr's sympathies had lain with the Conservatives until the Home Rule Bill whereupon he had joined the Unionists. He was president of the Greenock Unionist Association until 1911. Robert Kerr advocated stronger links within the British Empire and presided over Joseph Chamberlain's visit to Greenock. He had risen to prominence through his championship of the anti-bounty campaign in Greenock. As a result he was asked to stand as a candidate in the 1900 election on the retiral of Sir Thomas Sutherland. Kerr, however, declined the invitation as he did a similar request to stand for the constituency of South Ayrshire. Instead he preferred to supervise the electoral campaigns of others, such as James Reid who won the Greenock seat in 1900. Robert's love of politics was continued by his eldest son, John, who became a Bailie on Greenock Town Council. Robert was also well-known for his sporting aptitude. He enjoyed rugby but his first love was cricket and he was associated for 50 years with the Greenock Cricket Club, from his playing days in the first eleven until his years as club president. Again this interest was shared with the next generation in his younger son James.

Through his entrepreneurial skills, Robert Kerr had built up the premier sugar company in Greenock until it occupied six sites throughout the town. He had presided over the growth of the Glebe and Brewers Cos at a time of great difficulty in the Scottish sugar indusry. That the concerns had depended largely on Robert Kerr's management skills is seen by the later years of his life. In 1921, the Brewers Co, then under the management of his son James, ceased production and the refinery was purchased by Caird and Co and demolished. In the crisis of the 1920s, there was no Robert Kerr to come to the rescue of the Greenock sugar industry.

PATRICIA COLLINS

SOURCES

Unpublished

SRO: SC 53/41/30, Inventory
      SC 53/47/19, Will

Published

Fairrie, G, *The Sugar Refining Families of Great Britain*, London, 1951
The Greenock Telegraph and Clyde Shipping Gazette, 1/6/1922
Hutcheson, J M, *Notes on the Sugar Industry*, Greenock, 1901
Murray Smith, R, *The History of Greenock*, Greenock, 1921
Scots Commercial Record, September 1899, 24/2/1900
Scottish Trader, 10/6/1899 and 18/4/1903

Sir Peter MacDONALD,

Company chairman; b. 20/2/1898, Edinkillie, Darnaway, Moray, s. of William Macdonald, gamekeeper and Annie Cameron; m. 18/2/1929, Rachel Irene Forgan; 1 s., 2 d.; Ch, United Biscuits Ltd.; d. 21/7/1983.

Sir Peter Macdonald was the main architect in the foundation and fortunes of United Biscuits Ltd, one of the largest biscuit manufacturing groups in Scotland in the post-1945 era. As chairman of the company from its formation in 1948 he was largely responsible for the company's direction and expansion. However, Sir Peter's management role in United Biscuits was a later development in his career and indeed a departure from his profession as a solicitor in Edinburgh in the inter-war period. However his contribution to the business world does merit some consideration.

Born on 20 February 1898, Peter Macdonald grew up in a family which had crofting origins. His father held the prestigious post of head gamekeeper to the Earl of Moray. Peter Macdonald attended Forres Academy but the First World War interrupted any further continuation of his education and he in fact volunteered for military service. He first served with the Scottish Horse unit, then the 9th Battalion of the Black Watch and finally the Lovat Scouts which was a contingent largely composed of soldiers whose background was in hill-farming or gamekeeping.

His return to civilian life saw him join the Moray Estate office, moving to Edinburgh to work for Gillespie and Paterson, the laird's Edinburgh lawyers, where he gained considerable experience including work in the factoring department. Under the peacetime provisions to ex-service men, Macdonald attended law classes at Edinburgh University and it became apparent that law was more appealing to him than estate business. He was apprenticed to the then small firm of W & J Burness. He also became a Writer to the Signet on 28 March 1927.

The first connection with the biscuit trade came in the 1930s when Peter Macdonald renewed his acquaintance with Sir Alexander Grant whom he had known as a youth in Moray. Both were members of the Edinburgh Morayshire Club and served as secretary and president respectively. Sir Alexander Grant had been the driving force behind the successful development of McVitie & Price Ltd from 1887 when he had joined the firm as foreman and through the years as chairman and managing director it was his expertise and drive which jointly contributed to the progress of the firm. Peter Macdonald became legal adviser to the McVitie & Price Board in the 1930s. He was very close to Sir Alexander and zealous in carrying out his wishes. When Sir Alexander Grant died in 1937 it was he who naturally became closely

Register of defunct and other companies
Scots Commercial Record, June 1901, November, 1902,
    November, 1903, 18/7/1903
The Scotsman, 4/2/1926
Scottish Trader, 3/5/1902, 2/7/1904
The Times, 19/10/1900, 6/8/1901, 4/2/1926

James MARSHALL,

Food manufacturer; b. c 1838, Rothesay, s. of James Marshall, cotton spinner, and Elizabeth Carswell; m. (1) Elizabeth Patterson, (2) Mary Carswell Gow; 4 s., 2 d.; Founder & MD, James Marshall (Glasgow) Ltd; d. 28/5/1928, Glasgow; g/v UK estate: £74,481 3s 6d.

The second half of the nineteenth century witnessed radical changes in the ways in which foodstuffs were prepared, processed, packaged and marketed. The revolution which transformed food retailing and gave multiple-retailers a predominant place in the market had profound implications for those concerned in food preparation. Increasingly retailers demanded pre-packed goods in convenient sizes for sale - consumers expected such goods to be attractive in the appearance and pure in their content. Firms such as Liptons (qv) were increasingly responsible for packaging many of the goods they sold, as a gradual process of vertical integration took place in this and other retailing companies. However there lay within the increasing market for packaged and convenient foods enormous opportunities for specialist producers with the necessary entrepreneurial flair to establish a profitable niche. One such man was James Marshall, who pioneered the production of a range of pre-packaged wheat-based foodstuffs, gaining his company a lasting nationwide reputation.

James Marshall had been born in Rothesay in 1838, where his father was a cotton-spinner. Little is known of his early years, although evidence from later life suggests a scholarly education and a youth with a passion for the acquisition of knowledge. Marshall moved to Glasgow in his early twenties to work in the flour mill of W & W Glen (later A & W Glen), flour merchants and millers at Cheapside Street in the city's Anderston district. At this time there were around 25 millers in the city, some producing agricultural feeds, but the majority producing flour for the city's ever-increasing number of commercial bakeries. The increase in the consumption of bread, partly due to its comparative cheapness as a result of the importation of European and American grain into the Clyde, alarmed nutritionists. Generally brought as a 2 lb loaf baked from highly refined white flour, it formed an increasingly significant part of the working-class diet. Proprietary flours and breads, such as Montgomeries' Bermaline (qv), were one response to this problem. Marshall's, however, was to look at new ways of preparing and marketing nutritious wheat-based foodstuffs for mass consumption.

Although created a partner of Glens in 1865 Marshall chose to forsake this position and establish his own businnss in 1878, when he set up the Ibrox Flour Mills in the city's south-side. Here he set about producing a variety of 'farinaceous substances widely known as Marshall's Preparations of Wheat'. Principle among these was to be semolina, consisting of the fine, hard and nutritious particles of wheat normally excluded from commercial flours. Cheaper than bread, and with a higher protein and carbohydrate content, Marshall's Semolina was, in the words of *The Lancet* 'a highly valuable form of food'. Other millers produced semolina - what distinguished Marshall's variety was that it was pre-packaged in attractive cartons, the first such product to become available on the market. Marshall's Semolina was launched in 1885; in the same year James Marshall entered into partnership with his brother, Thomas, a trained engineer who was an active food reformer. The capital of the new firm was £12,000, with James Marshall providing £7,000 and Thomas Marshall £5,000. In addition Thomas brought both mechanical skills to the business and an enthusiasm for the production of a range of wheat-based health foods. Together the brothers launched farola, a very fine grained semolina, 'pleasing to the most fastidious, and easily digested by the most delicate'. Farola was marketed as a product with an infinite variety of uses - as a health food, an invalid food, as a base for blancmanges and other 'ornamental table dishes', and as an infant food. Its purity was recognised by *The Lancet* and a variety of regional medical journals, whose endorsements formed the basis of much of the firm's advertising. In 1886 the excellence of farola and Marshall's Semolina was recognised with an award of two gold medals at the Edinburgh and Liverpool exhibitions.

The apparent success of the new firm masked considerable difficulties, both financial and personal. An over-ambitious level of production combined with high marketing costs forced the partnership into liquidation in 1887. Between June 1885, the start of the partnership, and December 1886, the firm recorded sales of semolina and farola worth some £11,000. During the same period the cost of raw materials accounted for £4,300, operating expenses £3,700 and advertising £4,700. With insufficient resources to sustain a loss of somewhere between £1,500 and £2,000 and creditors (mainly advertisers) pressing for payment, sequestration was the course adopted by James Marshall. There followed a bitter dispute between the two brothers which saw the reconstruction of the business into two firms, James Marshall continuing at the Ibrox Flour Mills, and

Thomas A Marshall setting up at Morrison Street, Kingston. As the two brothers battled for market supremacy Glasgow was plunged into an unprecedented semolina war. Thomas Marshall claimed to have retained the old firm's trade-mark, 'The Heart of the Wheat', warning customers that 'without it none are genuine' - under this mark he sold semolina and oat flour. James Marshall, on the other hand, retained the old firm's particular brand-names, pronouncing himself sole proprietor of Marshall's Semolina and Farola. Both sought to expand through the preparation of new wheat-based products. Thomas Marshall introduced Kassama Food, 'a delicate nourishing preparation got wholly from wheat', which, it was claimed, 'obtained almost a world-wide celebrity'. James Marshall expanded his products to include Tritola, a large grained semolina, Granola, a whole-meal semolina, and Ptyaloid, a pure vegetable digestive of starch, particularly recommended for cases of 'weak digestion or debility'.

These years of reconstruction were difficult for James Marshall - starting from a much reduced base the new firm struggled to make a profit, recording losses in 1887, 1888, 1890 and 1893. Staffing levels were pruned to a bare minimum, and Marshall cut his own salary by over two-thirds of its 1885 level. In 1888 a new packing plant and office was opened in the east end of Glasgow; in the same year a small warehouse was opened in Pimlico. In 1889 Marshall obtained official patents for Marshall's Semolina and Farola, and the trade-mark 'The Finest of the Wheat'. Although the problem of direct competition was lessened after the closure of Thomas A Marshall's firm in 1894, following Thomas Marshall's death in July of the previous year, extensive advertising remained an expensive imperative. Between 1887 and 1900 the firm had an average annual advertising bill of £1,863, compared to annual profits of £1,662. Newspapers, magazines, billboards and 'advertising bags', all carried slogans praising the virtues of the various Marshall products. Other avenues were also pursued in order to keep product names before the eye of the market; for example, Marshall reached an agreement with the bakers McFarlane Lang (for whom his son, James P Marshall worked as a bakery manager) allowing them to use the trade-marks Farola and Granola for biscuits based on these products.

In 1900 James Marshall converted his firm into a limited liability company with a paid-up capital of £10,000 in £10 shares, which were distributed by Marshall among his family. James Marshall remained managing director of the business, his only fellow director being James P Marshall, still an employee of McFarlane Lang. In 1904 James P Marshall established his own bakery at Copeland Road in Govan; in the same year the earlier arrangement over use of trade marks with McFarlane Lang was formalised - Marshall sold them the sole right to the title Granola, and also an unused trade-mark Farella - in exchange McFarlane Lang reconveyed to Marshall their right to use farola for biscuits. This latter product was increasingly, in the words of the company minute-book, 'of first rate importance to us'. As generations of mothers will attest (and a file of unsolicited testimonials in the company's archives confirm), farola possessed legendary properties for transforming the most sickly infant into a healthy (not to say fat) and contented child. This fact became one of the main elements in the promotion of the product which accounted for around 35% of the company's sales.

In 1906 James Marshall further increased the family membership of the business by bringing his sons Thomas and Allan (already serving as company secretary) onto the board; three years later his fourth son, Edward Nixon Marshall, became a director at the age of 18. Delegating authority did not come easily to James Marshall, and despite giving his sons specific departmental responsibilities he retained throughout 'the ultimate decisions on matters of policy'. There was little change to the product range in the pre-war years, but a continued emphasis on increasing the market; advertising ran at around £2,500 per annum, and slowly a small but significant export trade was established, largely with British colonies, particularly Kenya. The 1914-18 war saw the majority of the firm's production diverted to provisioning the British Army and although home markets were quickly re-established after the war exports sank to a tiny fraction of all business. Nonetheless the impact of the war was felt sharply; two members of the family, Allan and Edward, joined the forces and in February 1918 Captain Allan Gow was killed on active service. 'We had hoped', wrote James Marshall in the Company's minute-book, 'that he and Tom would be the mainstays in the future'. Thomas Marshall, continuing his own job at home, also undertook the secretarial duties of his elder brother, and in addition spent evenings engaged in volunteer work. It is not unlikely that his 'painstaking devotion to the practical department of our work' described by his father, and his additional duties, contributed in part to his death from pneumonia in 1926. When Allan Marshall died his father was 80 and the blow was considerable; he was for a short period absent from business, and suffered from increasing blindness from 1919 onwards. Nonetheless, despite the further tragedy of Thomas's death he returned to play an active role in the company, which he was to maintain until the day before he died.

Working closely with his son Edward, James Marshall still sought to increase sales through ever-more ingenious forms of advertising. In 1922 the firm undertook extensive market-research in Manchester, Newcastle and Sunderland, when 93,000 housewives were quizzed on the properties of farola. Few trade fairs and exhibitions were not graced by a Marshall's display and sales-point, although after each a meticulous analysis was made of costs against increased sales. In addition recipe books were available from Glasgow by post, as were a variety of free-offers - principally calendars and tea-trays. During the inter-war years the average advertising annual budget was well in excess of £6,000 whilst annual profits averaged around £7,500. The firm produced an average of 980 tons of semolina and farola a year. Sales, however, were still dominated by the Scottish market, particularly Glasgow; other important concentrations were in the north-east of England and in Belfast and Dublin. Exports increased slightly in the mid-twenties but fell again as the depression set in in the 1930s. It was during the 1920s that an idea pursued in the pre-war years was revived; the production of pasta products had failed due to difficulties in perfecting the drying process. These were overcome in the late twenties, leading to the production of a variety of pasta products, then largely unknown to the British table. In the following yeas Marshalls were to become famous as much for being 'the firm that put the Mac in Macaroni' as they were for the production semolina or farola.

On 28 May 1928 James Marshall died from heart-failure; he left a widow, Mary Carswell Gow, his second wife, and two surviving sons. His estate, valued at £74,000 (£29,000 of which were shares in James Marshall Ltd) was divided between his children and their offspring, with complex provision being made for keeping shares of the company in family hands. Almost half of the value of his household possessions were taken up by books in his extensive library at his home at Eglinton Drive, Glasgow, an indication both of his inquiring mind and of the blow that blindness must have been to him. Although active in the United Free (later United Presbyterian) Church, Marshall had given his lifelong attention to his family and his business, 'his whole life', as they were described in a moving testimony to him in the company's minute book. 'Although conservative by nature ... his strong conviction was through to success'; this was a route he pursued through 'attention to details, scrupulous economy in unessentials' and by being willing to 'take great risks' when required. Although the scale of his business was modest he achieved a unique and profitable place in the increasing market for prepackaged quality foodstuffs in the Victorian and Edwardian era, nourishing at the same time future generations of Scottish entrepreneurs, many of whom would have profited from following his example.

NICHOLAS J MORGAN

SOURCES

Unpublished

Companies Registration Office, 4747, James Marshall (Glasgow) Ltd

Glasgow University Archives, UGD 233, James Marshall (Glasgow) Ltd
SRO: SC 36/48/398, Inventory
SC 36/51/219, Will

Published

Glasgow Chamber of Commerce Journal, 5/5/1936
Glasgow Herald, 30/5/1928
Glasgow Post Office Directories, 1855-1930
Industries of Glasgow, Glasgow, 1888
Victualling Trades Review, 1/9/1893, 8/9/1893

William MELROSE,

Tea merchant; b. Edinburgh, 17 March 1817; s. of Andrew Melrose, tea merchant; m. 1856, Eliza Laura Bella, d. of Rev. Henry Stedding; no issue; Agent, Andrew Melrose & Co, tea merchants; d. 1/3/1863, London; g/v estate: c £16,000.

William Melrose climaxed his business career by managing with considerable success a one-man agency in Canton during the mid-nineteenth century. Unlike most merchants trading with China, he and his co-venturers dealt exclusively in tea, a difficult trade. The profits yielded by their transactions were largely achieved by a close attention to the markets in China and Britain and a careful co-ordination of operations on both sides of the trading link. To do so required a thorough knowledge of the prices and qualities of tea by agent and principal and close co-operation between the two. William and his father Andrew, the major organiser of the ventures, were eminently qualified for the roles they played. In addition to the possession of ample expertise, the father had acquired sufficient capital and credit and had established effective commercial connections to prosecute the trade. Indeed, he was the driving force behind the ventures.

Andrew Melrose, 1789-1855, was born in Penicuik, son of a tenant farmer. He was apprenticed with Robert Sheppard, a prominent Edinburgh grocer with a chain of four shops, one as far away as Aberdeen. One of Andrew's fellow apprentices was James Richardson (1789-1860), with whom he maintained strong personal and business relations throughout his life. At Sheppard's retirement in 1812, Andrew opened his first shop at the head of Canongate and from the beginning gave special prominence to the sale of tea. He very quickly became the leading tea dealer and grocer in Edinburgh: a second shop was acquired in 1815, a warehouse in 1816, a third shop in 1820 and in 1825, a second warehouse. There was a corresponding rise in his cash and credit transactions. Bank deposits jumped from £22,000 for the year 1815 to £45,000 in 1816 with a monthly credit balance of about £1,000. Within two years his account with major suppliers increased from £10,700 to over £58,000 in 1817. From then on, expansion continued at a slower pace. By 1847 the annual balance sheet of Andrew Melrose and Company showed assets of £74,487.

In his drive to extend business, Andrew adopted various commercial techniques to reduce costs and increase sales. Two major policies dominated his purchasing of stock: shortening the line of supply by buying at the first and cheapest source and eliminating extended credit. Most of his tea, for example, he bought at the quarterly auctions of the East India Company (hereafter EIC) and not from London wholesalers. Sugar came directly from merchants and refiners, much of it from his friend James Richardson, the Glasgow sugar merchant. Even items such as salt, soap and cocoa were bought from manufacturers. Gouda cheese was imported from Rotterdam and wine directly from the continent. By 1830, his search for supplies had been extended to Bordeaux, Cognac, Hamburg, Malaga, Naples, Oporto, Port St Margo and Smyrna. When the China trade was opened in 1834, he was among the first to import tea from Canton to Leith and continued to explore that source by trying various Canton agency houses: Jardine Matheson and Company, Russell and Company, Y L Murrow and Jamieson How and Company. The governing consideration was the capital and credit resources at his disposal.

To extend the latter, Andrew took advantage of the joint venture, an informal organisation among friends and business acquaintances that increased capital resources and used the skills and experience of each for the benefit of all. Among Andrew's co-venturers, the most frequent was James Richardson. From the beginning of their careers, the two were involved in sugar ventures. But there were many others, for example, James Duncan and Robert Schaw of Leith and John and Thomas Black, Andrew's former commission agents. Andrew also engaged in ventures with overseas correspondents such as the Russells of Canton and the Hardmans of Calcutta. For the medium-sized businessman, it was a very useful and flexible form of enterprise. Andrew made extensive use of it; in 1845 he was involved in 12 ventures of various kinds.

Andrew was equally aggressive in his search for custom. Shops and warehouses were sited in strategic spots to attract wholesale and retail customers from all ranks and places. One shop, for example, was close to the carriers quarters; another was on elegant George Street. Carriers were also used, almost as hawkers, to extend his trading area; and for a short period commission agents were employed to reach a wider range of customers. Andrew, like his master Sheppard, was an avid and effective advertiser. The 'cheapest teas in Scotland ... for ready money' were featured on all billheads and in large block letters on circulars and newspaper advertisements. It was not

an idle boast. A quick turn-over, small per unit profit and cash transactions characterised his sales policy.

By the 1820s Andrew Melrose and Company was firmly established. Annual profits were modest but regular. During the decade, 1820-30, they ranged from £1,250 to £2,400. Following comtemporary practices, most of Andrew's share was ploughed back and by 1834 his capital account in the Company amounted to £16,500 and his credit unimpeached.

In one area Andrew did not achieve his usual success; the early ventures into the China market were not encouraging and after a few years his annual investment dropped to about £1,500. Between 1834 and 1845 Andrew's principal buying agent was Jardine Matheson and Company but the handling of his orders was far from satisfactory. The company was itself heavily involved in the tea trade as a means of remitting the enormous funds accumulated from opium dealings. As a result, its transactions in tea frequently conflicted with the interests of its principals. Nor did Andrew obtain much satisfaction from other agency houses he tried. He soon realised that in order to prosecute the trade successfully a far more responsive agent was necessary, one eager and able to serve the interests of his principals. On William, his second son, Andrew rested his hopes and ambitions. The choice was a wise one.

William received his initial introduction to business at Andrew Melrose and Company. After serving a seven year apprenticeship, he completed his training as tea taster and buyer with Ewart Maccaughey and Company of London, a firm of prominent tea brokers dating back to the early eighteenth century. Tea brokers occupied a pivotal position in the trade, particularly after the China market was opened. Under the EIC's monopoly, they examined the quality and character of all tea offered for sale at each quarterly auction and published their judgment in a catalogue which served as a guide to the buyers. In addition to being the recognised masters of the qualities of tea, the brokers had acquired a familiarity with the different demands of various markets in the country. Tea was a product with an infinite variety of sorts and qualities and tastes varied both geographically and socially. After the trade was opened, the China agency houses, few of which had experience in the tea trade, required the services of well-trained tea tasters who possessed commercial knowledge and the brokers supplied such needs. Indeed, when the EIC decided in 1790 to install a tea inspector in the factory at Canton, it sent a member of a brokerage firm. During a period of over 40 years, five appointments were made: four brokers and one from the EIC's tea warehouse department. Of the four, two were from Ewart Maccaughey and Company. The firm had, therefore, considerable knowledge of the China market well before free trade. For a career in the China tea trade, no better house could have served William's purpose. Andrew Melrose had had a long and satisfactory association with Ewart Maccaughey and Company and was personally acquainted with several members of the firm. William remained with the firm for two years cultivating the art of tea tasting and acquiring a general knowledge of the trade. They were, William thought, arduous but fruitful years.

In 1842 William obtained a post in Canton as tea taster for Jamieson How and Company, a substantial house originating in Glasgow with branches in Liverpool, Calcutta and Canton. The firm exported cotton and other goods from Britain, opium from India to China and returned the proceeds largely in tea. The circuitous transactions were typical of the activities of many merchants trading with Asia but opium remained the major source of profit. In that trade smaller merchants had to compete not only among themselves but also against such well established giants as Jardine Matheson and Company and Dent and Company whose duopoly dominated the China trade of the mid-century, a period that witnessed the failure of many medium sized concerns. Before William left for Canton Andrew stipulated that during the term of contract William was not to trade on his own account. It was a mutually advantageous arrangement that assured the employer of William's undivided attention and effort and at the same time protected William from the hazards of the trade before he could acquire sufficient experience in it. As he later testified, a thorough mastery of the quality of teas and commercial experience were equally necessary for success. During the four years that William remained with Jamiesons, he worked hard and diligently, never leaving Canton for the healthier climate of Macao. And it took its toll. At the expiration of his three year contract, William began trading on his own but all his activities were cut short in the spring of 1846 by a very serious illness. Early in 1847, sufficiently recovered to travel, he made his way back to Scotland to recuperate at Pittendreich, near Lasswade, Midlothian, the family estate.

In June 1848, with his health restored, William returned to China as buying agent for Andrew Melrose and Company and some of Andrew's business associates including, among others, James Richardson of Glasgow and Robert Schaw of Leith. William's commission as agent was fixed at 5% for tea purchased and shipped. Nothing was to be paid for negotiating bills of exchange but he was permitted to share in some joint ventures, his father providing the capital to a maximum of £10,000 per trading season. He was also allowed to trade on his own account and to act as agent to other importers. Andrew was responsible for organising the ventures and recruiting the capital. And William was well financed. During the first year, Andrew himself paid out over £71,000 for bills negotiated by William. But Andrew had achieved his aims. William was a well-trained tea taster and experienced in the China trade. His warm, friendly relations with his father and regard for his own future assured the personal concern with the business that was essential for success.

In the ensuing five years William managed his small agency single-handed, purchasing tea by selling bills of exchange drawn on his principals. His knowledge of the trade was skillfully employed and he worked tirelessly to achieve the end of all concerned, 'to make a little money', as Richardson put it. Commercial documents, often in triplicate, were clearly and accurately drawn and mailed in time to reach Scotland well before the tea arrived. And he wrote long detailed letters, frequently 9 to 11 closely written pages, on the state of the tea market in China, the activities of his competitors and the fluctuations in the exchange and shipping rates. His principals were fully informed on his actions and the reasons for them, particularly if he had departed from instructions. They in turn reported in detail the results of his shipments and advised on future purchases in terms of the British market. There was, in short, a continuous exchange of views which guided the action on each side, a frank and thorough correspondence which Andrew had been unable to obtain from his earlier agents. It contributed not a little to the success of the ventures.

William's clerical work was time-consuming, often requiring him to work late at night in order to catch the mail with the latest news. But his major attention was given to buying and shipping the tea and selling his bills of exchange. The absence of comprehensive banking services in Canton rendered the selling of bills a tricky matter. The place of origin of the bills, the destination to which they were sent, their denomination and usance together with the current demand influenced the rate of exchange. All these were carefully explained to his principals so that they would supply bills most easily sold. But equally crucial was the energy, skill and persistence of the seller and on this score William's performance was second to none as his rates testify. And in so far as the movements of the exchange allowed, he timed the sale of the bills so that they would not reach Scotland too far in advance of the tea, thus saving his principals heavy interest charges. Few agency houses would have acted similarly.

In purchasing tea, William watched market fluctuations closely and bought when prices seemed favourable. At the same time, he noted carefully the quantity and sorts shipped to Britain by his competitors and avoided buying those sorts which in his judgment were being overdone. As he repeatedly explained, for a medium sized venture, attention should be focussed on teas neglected by other shippers and for which the demand at home was restricted but steady. He favoured the better quality sorts needed for blending and chose wisely. In organising a shipment for a full cargo, he was faced with the fact that in the Chinese market the first and second quality were rarely simultaneously available; hence, the worry of failing to secure the second after having bought the first, both necessary for a large shipment. William also paid particular attention to the demands of the local market to which the tea was despatched. What suited London might be unsaleable at Liverpool. And through his contacts in Britain particularly Ewart Maccaughey and Andrew Melrose and Company, he was well informed on the prices realised in the different British markets and directed shipments accordingly.

To despatch the tea home, William considered the rates of freight, the safety and speed of the ship, the timing of the voyage and the ship's destination. For a full cargo, freight rates were negotiated but for small shipments William often obtained much reduced rates by breaking bulk for which he had to attend to the loading to ensure a safe stowage of all his goods. For technical knowledge on ships, William consulted with his friend, Y L Murrow, a shipbuilder. The duration of a voyage was sometimes a matter of chance. In 1851 William chartered the *Auguste and Bertha*, reputedly a fast ship; its passage was, however, much delayed, fortunately, as it turned out. The ship arrived in time to catch a favourable turn in a market that had been very depressed. Luck too, as William fully realised, played a part in the success of a venture.

When the tea reached the shores of Britain, it was Andrew who directed the sales. To effect a profitable sale, the first essential was the faithful and reliable service of a tea broker. Andrew's long experience in the trade enabled him to select the most reputable brokers: in London, Ewart Maccaughey; in Liverpool, Littledale and Company; in Glasgow, William Connal and his London associate, W J Thompson. The broker, in addition to unloading and storing the tea and arranging its sale, advised on the upset prices. The final decision lay of course with the importer. Here, Andrew's knowledge of local markets was a valuable asset.

In the revealing example of the sale in Glasgow of the cargo by the *Naomi*, his evaluation, higher than either of the two brokers consulted, determined the upset prices. The results of the auction vindicated his judgment. Clearly, a knowledgeable tea dealer had an advantage over importers who dealt in a multifarious collection of goods. A difference in the sale price of as little as a half-penny per pound could put the seller on either side of the ledger. Moreover, parcels not favourably received could be withdrawn from the sale to be disposed gradually at one or another of Andrew's shops. As a further precaution, William was frequently instructed to send a cargo from Canton to Cork for orders. As mail reached Britain usually two months ahead of the cargo, the arrangement allowed the importers to land the goods at the most favourable market and to save on transportation and warehouse charges.

In all, five years strenuous effort enabled William and his principals to make a respectable profit. The total investment of Andrew Melrose and Company in joint ventures with Richardson and sometimes William amounted to over £194,000 and the average net profit was 13%. The figures for individual ventures ranged from 5% to 35%, with no year registering

a loss. It was an incredible achievement. William's share amounted to £5,835, a major portion of his total credit balance of nearly £11,000, the remainder being derived from his own trade.

William left Canton towards the end of April 1853 with intentions to return. The market for tea had turned unfavourable and he thought a brief absence desirable. But after his departure, trading conditions in Canton continued to deteriorate. The reports from his Canton friends together with the reorganisation of Andrew Melrose and Company after Andrew's retirement, convinced William that little was to be gained by returning. From 1854 William's assets were invested mainly in railway stocks, yielding an annual income of over £500. A year after Andrew's death in March 1855, William married Eliza Laura Bella, the daughter of Rev and Mrs Henry Stedding and settled in Manchester. In the summer of 1862, William and his wife moved to London where he died in March 1863, leaving an estate valued at £16,000.

The years William resided in Canton are often represented as a period of thorough-going revision in Sino-European relations during which life for foreigners was hazardous and trade at best precarious. It is a description little supported by William's records. Possibly, personal detachment from those events which stir later historians and a consuming concern with trade diverted William's attention. And yet, his monthly letters reveal regular full working days without disturbance or interruption and he had nothing but praise for his Chinese suppliers. One wonders if the well-hashed political and diplomatic accounts have not over-emphasised the obstacles to peaceful commerce.

H C MUI & L H MUI

SOURCES

Unpublished

Andrew Melrose Archives:
    Bills Payable Book from 1826
    Historical Documents, Andrew Melrose & Co
    Miscellaneous letters to Andrew Melrose, 1845-51
    Miscellaneous material relating to China Trade
    Papers connected with direct shipments from China
    Personal Ledger from 1815
    Private Ledger, 1818-96
    Sales Ledger 'O' Wholesale, 1841-54
    Town Ledger No 1, 1841-56
    Wages Book, 1815-51
Jardine Matheson Archives:
    B1/134, B1/136 & B1/137, Correspondence in
      Great Britain
    B6/iii, B6/iv, B6/v, B6,vi, Europe Letter Book

Principal Probate Registry, London: viii (1863), The Will of William Melrose

SRO: Inventory & Will of Andrew Melrose, 1855

Published

Checkland, S G, 'An English Merchant House in China after 1841', *Bulletin of the Business History Society*, XXVII, September 1953

The Chinese Repository, 1830-51

Costin, W C, *Great Britain and China, 1833-60*, Oxford, 1937

Directory of Edinburgh

Directory of Glasgow

Directory of Liverpool

Directory of London

Directory of Manchester

Fairbank, J K, *Trade and Diplomacy on the China Coast, 1842-54*, Stanford, California, 1969

Macgregor, D R, *The Tea Clippers, 1849-69*, London, 1952

Marriner, Sheila, *Rathbones of Liverpool, 1845-73*, Liverpool, 1961

Marriner, Sheila & Hyde, F C, *The Senior: John Samuel Swire, 1825-98*, Liverpool, 1967

Morse, H B, *International Relations of the Chinese Empire*, New York, 1910

Mui, H C & Mui, L H, 'Andrew Melrose, Tea Dealer and Grocer of Edinburgh 1812-33', *Business History*, IX, January 1967

Mui, H C & Mui L H (eds), *William Melrose in China, 1845-1855: The Letters of a Scottish Tea Merchant*, Edinburgh, 1973

John MONTGOMERIE,

Maltster, miller and baker; b. 1850, Torblarhan Farm, Lochgilphead, Argyll; s. of Alexander Montgomerie, farmer and Agnes Ferguson; m. Elizabeth McNichol; 2 s., 3 d.; MD, Montgomerie & Co Ltd, Glasgow and Haddington; d. 28/6/1928, Glasgow; g/v estate £41,808 0s 5d.

Throughout the nineteenth century the pattern of baking bread altered, especially that in urban centres, due mainly to social changes. For many city dwellers the facilities to bake bread were not available. To cater for this, small grocers and dairies began to bake bread and rolls in their back premises. They supplied streets, sometimes districts. Towards the middle of the century more sophisticated organisations began to appear amongst bakers and by the last decades of the nineteenth century there was a discernable movement towards wholesale bread baking for sale to retail outlets. This was especially noticeable in the Glasgow area where the large and growing populations of the late nineteenth century offered valuable markets to wholesale bakers. By the middle of the 1880s Glasgow already had at least three major concerns supplying bread wholesale; they were the United Co-operative Baking Society, the Bilsland brothers, Hydepark premises and William Beattie's Dennistoun bakery.

This narrowing of opportunities in wholesale bread manufacture in Glasgow was recognised by John Montgomerie when he came from Rothesay as a master baker to set up business in Partick in the early 1880s. He quickly realised that though the opportunity for producing a quantity of bread was limited, the opportunity for producing a quality product existed. In 1886 he launched his new product onto the market, the 'Bermaline' loaf; rusks and infant biscuits, taking care to patent the name and the production process. Bermaline products contained the added ingredient of a malt extract which, it was claimed, made it especially suited for those with weak digestions. Claims were also made for its nutritional value. With its selling points based firmly on the appeal to gastatory valetudanarianism, Bermaline became a highly successful commodity. By the end of the century, within 14 years of its launch, Montgomerie had over 4,000 agents baking Bermaline bread through the UK, 400 of these in London.

Bermaline became a household word and it is possible that John Montgomerie's ability to gauge demand for such a loaf and allied products was based on his early training and experiences. He served his apprenticeship in Rothesay, a well known Clyde holiday resort and, as a journeyman baker at the age of 19, spent the next five or six years travelling the world by working his passage on sail and steam vessels either as steward or chief baker. He spent several years working for the Anchor Line as chief baker on vessels trading between Glasgow and New York. In his mid-twenties he left the sea and returned to Rothesay where he set up a baking business of his own which he operated with considerable success for eight years.

In the early 1880s, restricted by an island's limitations, he sold his flourishing business and erected his own bakery in Partick, a thriving burgh on the banks of the Clyde by Glasgow. The Glasgow International Exhibition of 1885 gave him the opportunity to supply pastry to various exhibitors, such as the Tea Planters Association of Ceylon which began to make him known in the trade. It was after this that he launched his product, Bermaline, on to the market in 1886.

At the outset the malt extract for Bermaline was provided by another firm but the difficulty experienced in obtaining the genuine article persuaded John Montgomerie to look for factory premises to manufacture malt extract himself. This carried the dual purpose of securing supplies and safeguarding his patent. He also needed secure supplies of barley and wheat grain of a certain standard and this was not possible under his old system of organisation. In order to finance his ambitions John Montgomerie set up a limited company, Montgomerie & Co Ltd in 1892, becoming managing director and chairman. He took as his co-directors two reputable chartered accountants, W F Trotter, Edinburgh, and J Martin Newton, Glasgow. But, by 1897, only £10,000 of the £40,000 nominal capital had been subscribed. In 1897 he issued an increase of capital, advertising the fact that current shares had reached a tax free return of 15% per annum. To publicise the increased capital issue John Montgomerie forecast that it took up to 40,000 sacks of flour to utilise all the Bermaline extract he produced to make Bermaline bread. With sales of the extract increasing at 100% annually the prospects for Montgomerie milled flour were limitless.

Montgomerie's publicity brought in enough capital to purchase flour mills and 15 acres of land at Haddington. The Haddington mills were established prior to the Reformation being rebuilt several times before the last owner, Mr Hogarth, had re-equipped them with the first steam-powered roller milling process to be installed in Scotland. It was there that Montgomerie & Co Ltd began to mill Scots-grown wheat for Bermaline bread. The mills also included a small water-powered oatmeal mill. Almost immediately the company erected a substantial maltings factory, five storeys high, built at a cost of £11,000. The barley for the malt was purchased locally at the Haddington market from farmers. It was then steeped for a certain time, after which it was spread on the floors and allowed to germinate for 11 days. The germination process being completed, the barley was removed to the top floor of the kiln where it underwent partial drying and then subsequently removed to the under-floors where it was thoroughly dried. It was then forwarded to the Bermaline works at Partick and converted into Bermaline extract. At Partick it was mashed in large tuns where the starch in the barley was converted into maltose and dextrine. It was then afterwards run off into vacuum pans and evaporated to the proper consistency and finally filled in large drums and forwarded to the agents over all parts of the world. It was Montgomerie's proud boast that only home-grown Scotch barley was employed in the manufacture of Bermaline.

An indication of the value to the local economy of siting the Bermaline mills and maltings at Haddington, in terms of local labour employment in the factory and utilisation of local farm produce, can be gained from the following example: The mills were situated on the banks of the River Tyne and the bridge which led from the mills to Haddington was extremely derelict. John Montgomerie wanted the Council to build a new bridge, the expenditure for which totalled about £9,000. His appeal met stiff opposition within the local council. However, John Montgomerie was loyally supported by the provost, the magistrates and the majority of the council. Together with the help of the county proprietors, including the Rt Hon A J Balfour who subscribed £100, and Miss Balfour and Lord Harrington who subscribed £200 and £100 respectively, and a bazaar organised by the ladies of the county which brought in £5,000, the bridge, a handsome structure, was eventually built and named the Victoria Bridge being dedicated to the recently deceased Queen Victoria.

The value to Glasgow of John Montgomerie's enterprise came in 1901 when the organisers of the Glasgow International Exhibition chose John Montgomerie's Bermaline bakery to represent Glasgow's baking industry. The exhibit, a working model of a bakery, formed an annexe to the Machine Hall, 85 ft wide and 25 ft deep. It included three areas, the working bakery, a malted confectioners department, and a sales shop. The bakery was fitted out by T Melvin & Sons, Glasgow, with three large ovens illustrating the Scotch, Irish, and English systems of baking. The confectionery plant for the manufacture of the malted confections was supplied by Morton & Sons, Wishaw. As a token of appreciation to the City for this recognition, Montgomerie's built a sugar model of the Exhibition, 8 ft long and 4 ft wide. It contained nearly 600 pieces of mica used for glazing miniature windows. It was lit with electricity and occupied a prominent position at the Exhibition. When the Exhibition closed, Montgomerie's presented the model to the City of Glasgow.

The increased supply from the Haddington mills and maltings placed enormous strains on the Bermaline bakery at Partick and in 1910 John Montgomerie opened extensive new bakery premises at Govan. The Govan Bermaline factory, named the 'Great White Bakery', laid great stress on the hygienic production methods fully in keeping with the firm's already established dietary image. When the Bermaline loaf appeared in 1886 it had won three medals relating to health and excellence in its first year, bringing it to the notice of leading medical journals such as the *British Medical Journal*, the *Hospital Gazette,* the *Chemist and Druggist* and the *Sanitary Review*. The opening of the Great White Bakery was attended by some 2,000 invited guests. This carefully fostered medical image was furthered by emphasising hygienic production. The plant was powered by electricity, a clean power source; the fully mechanised process eliminated hand labour as much as possible; The use of nickel in surfaces exposed during bread manufacture, the use of white tiling and mirrors and specially monitored temperature gauges in all departments, were all used to create a germ-free environment. Staff health monitoring, which included a pre-employment tuberculosis check, also extended to dressing rooms, clean uniforms and baths.

By far the greatest innovation at the Great White Bakery, which contained both hygienic principles and salesmanship, was that each Bermaline loaf produced at the bakery left it ready wrapped and sealed in fine quality grease-proof paper. This ensured that Bermaline bread reached the customer's table without being exposed to the contamination present on the dusty, germ laden streets, which had been a feature of bread delivery in the past. By 1903 the health risk of dust was a recognised factor in tuberculosis prevention. Loaves of bread were constantly at risk during the delivery processes from the hygienic surroundings in bakeries when they were carried by horse drawn vehicles through busy streets to their point of destination. Once there, the loaves were often dropped onto the filthy streets during delivery, picked up, dusted down, and sold to unsuspecting customers. However, the wrappers were in themselves a form of advertising. Each one bore the firm's name, and loaves were delivered to retailers throughout the city by smart vans and uniformed vanmen all prominently displaying the name of Bermaline Bread. John Montgomerie was perhaps one of the first bakers to wrap his bread as a matter of course. Bilslands did not begin to wrap their bread until the 1920s.

It was through such emphases on nutrition and hygiene that John Montgomerie built up the name and fame of Bermaline, backed by sound commercial judgment and innovatory techniques. In the early period the Bermaline patent undoubtedly secured Montgomerie's success. Overt attempts to break the patent were frequent and unsuccessful, and there was constant industrial espionage to re-create the exact constituents of the Bermaline extract. In addition to patenting Bermaline bread, John Montgomerie also patented draw plate ovens. The Great White Bakery operated 24 such ovens each capable of firing 40 dozen loaves at a time.

During the 1914-18 war Montgomerie's entire output was commandeered by the War Ministry of 1917, Flour Mills Control Committee. Initial postwar difficulties reduced share dividends to 5% but by the mid 1920s these were overcome and profits reached £27,000 in 1925 with profits averaging around 15% in the mid/late 1920s. By 1928 John Montgomerie saw his Bermaline products selling under licence in South Africa, India and Denmark.

John Montgomerie's early foray into local politics at Haddington was short-lived. After two years the demands of business recalled him and his public service ceased. He was associated with the Incorporation of Wrights and Tailors, Glasgow and the Glasgow Chamber of Commerce. He died at his home, Ettrick Bank, Partick, Glasgow, on 28 June 1928. The gross value of his moveable estate was £41,808, most of which was taken up by oil and rubber shareholdings, investment and insurance holdings with about £16,000 relating to John Montgomerie & Co Ltd. He left no charitable bequests and his entire estate was divided between his five children, two sons and three daughters.

BRENDA M WHITE

SOURCES

Unpublished

Companies Registration Office: SC 4229, Company fiche
SRO: SC 36/48/400, Inventory
　　　SC 36/51/220, Will

Published

The Bailie, No 1715, 30/8/1905
Cunnison, J and Gilfillan, J B S, (eds), *The Third Statistical Account of Scotland - Glasgow*, Glasgow, 1958
Glasgow Herald, 29/6/1928, also company reports 1912-1928
Glasgow Post Office Directories
Hume, R, *Industrial Archaeology of Glasgow*, Glasgow, 1974
Scots Commercial Record & Scottish Trader
Stratten, *Glasgow and Its Environs*, London, 1891

Sir Alexander Kay MUIR,

Landed proprietor; b. 20/4/1868, Glasgow, s. of Sir John Muir, merchant, and Margaret Morrison Kay; m. (1) 1910, Grace, d. of J A R Newman; (2) 1924, Nadejda Constanza Iranea Garrilla Euphorosyne Stancioff, d. of Dmitri Stancioff, Bulgarian Ambassador to Great Britain; no issue; Ch, James Finlay & Co Ltd, Glasgow; d. 4/6/1951, Blair Drummond House, Kincardine; g/v estate: £909,056 7s 4d.

Alexander Kay Muir was born in Glasgow on 20 May 1868, eldest son of John Muir (qv) 1st Baronet, to whom he succeeded in 1903, and Margaret Kay, his wife. He was educated like his father at Glasgow High School and briefly at Glasgow University, not taking a degree but joining his father's Glasgow counting house, James Finlay & Co, of which John Muir became sole proprietor in 1884. He was sent to Calcutta in 1890, aged 22, and was soon joined by his next brother James Finlay Muir; each took charge in turn after the retirement of a trusted Senior, R Williamson, at the end of 1890. Both had inherited their father's business acumen, but like many sons managing overseas concerns they were kept on very tight leads, receiving long visits from both parents and constant letters of instruction. In one surviving one dated 18 October 1898 (when A K Muir was 29) John Muir wrote him 14 pages of detailed instruction.

The regrouping of the Finlay tea interests into four limited companies, the Consolidated Tea and Lands Co Ltd, the Amalgamated Tea Estates Co Ltd, the Kanan Devan Hills Produce Co Ltd and the Anglo-American Direct Tea Trading Co Ltd (geographically scattered through India and Ceylon but grouped according to elevation, and thus quality of teas) had only just been completed. These, unlike the jute mills, were the first sterling public companies in the Finlay group registered and controlled from Glasgow. The Boards were made up almost entirely of the eminent sons-in-law who had married John Muir's eight daughters. His advice on the tea companies was that 'I wish you and James eagerly to watch that in every respect they are managed ably and with the utmost economy. We are likely to have hard times and great difficulty in making dividends satisfactory to our ordinary shareholders.'

Both A K and J F Muir returned to Glasgow when their father had his first stroke in 1901, A K Muir taking control of the Glasgow office. In 1902 a minute of co-partnership, the first since 1884, was drawn up between the two Muir brothers under their own names, and as Trustees for Sir John's estate, with R Sinclair (Sir John's private secretary) on the one part and A M Brown, Cotton Works' manager, Gryffe Castle, on the other. Sir John died in 1903. Profits

continued to swell as Muir's early capital investments in plantations began to give returns. Sir Kay Muir became senior partner of James Finlay and Finlay Muir & Co, and chairman of the four Glasgow registered tea companies, and the Trustees' proprietor of the private company of Webster Steel & Co.

During this period Finlays continued to be Owner's Agents for the Clan Line in six ports. In 1902 Sir Charles Cayzer (qv) sponsored the move into cotton manufacture in India, making Finlay Muir's Bombay office his managing agent, through his acquisition of an existing low-grade mill, renamed Swan Mill and re-equipped with modern spindles and 600 looms. Swan became a public company owned by Finlay Muir & Co in 1908 and Finlay, Muir & Co also then floated Finlay Mills in Bombay with a capital of 1,800,000 Rupees. The purpose built mill contained 30,000 Northropp Ring-spindles and a further 600 looms. Competition with imported low grades of cotton cloth from Japan later forced further heavy investment in high-count machinery and into advanced equipment for bleaching, dyeing and finishing, based on experience gained in their Scottish mills. The switch to high counts and good finish, producing fine muslins, paid handsomely. After 1934, when these changes were completed Finlay Mills captured a large slice of the top end of the market in Asia. A third mill, Gold Mohur, was added in 1912.

A M Brown died in 1906 and the Muir brothers turned James Finlay & Co from a partnership into a private company with authorised capital on flotation of £1m, on 27 May 1909. All the shares were held by members of the now extensive Muir family. The average profit of the years 1912/1913 was £103,813. During the war years of 1914-1918 the company modestly prospered on production of the wartime staples of jute (sand-bags), tea and cotton khaki-dyed cloth, though a high proportion of British employees were absent on war service. In 1919 capital was increased to £2m, Sir Kay Muir held 6,454 shares, each of his three brothers 3,227, the Trustees of his father's estate 32,265 out of a total of 50,000 issued. In spite of heavy losses 'due to the exceptional fall in value in 1920' rapid recovery in 1922 produced a profit of £173,417 and a further issue of 50,000 ordinary shares at £10 each was made. However it was in response to these pressures that the decision was made in 1923 to convert the business to a public limited liability company. The £10 shares were divided up into £1 shares and put on the market at £2.10 each. Assets included buildings in West Nile Street, Glasgow and the two Scottish cotton mills at Deanston and Catrine. Not modernised since mid-nineteenth century, the mills had been much written-down in book figures, although they were increasingly profitable in output. The value of the Indian properties had also grown 'in excess of book figures' in the cautious words of the Accountants. Cash derived from the tea companies was at this point used to acquire for the new company the Muirs' old private firm of Webster Steel & Co, (with South African interests) for £257,300.

Sir Kay Muir retired from the chair in 1926 leaving his equally able second brother James Muir to take over. A third brother, John, took little part in the firm and was at one period cattle-ranching in Wyoming. Matthew, the youngest, had managed the business in Calcutta for two years, where he had emulated Kay's prowess on the polo fields. He served in the 1914-18 war, returning to act on the boards of various Finlay companies. He died in 1922 following an accident in the hunting field.

Sir Kay Muir continued as a director of Finlay companies, and a majority shareholder, but devoted the rest of his life to country pursuits. He had purchased Blair Drummond, near Doune and his mother's home at Deanston House. The large mansion had been built in 1868 and the estate, formed and improved originally by Lord Kames in the eighteenth century, was a fertile and extensive one. Muir's first marriage was in 1910 to Grace Newman of Co Cork, widow of Major H Villiers Stuart of Co Wexford, Ireland. She died in 1920. In 1924 Sir Kay Muir caused a sensation by his second marriage to Nadejda Stancioff, then aged a little over 20, eldest daughter of Dimitri Stancioff, late Premier of Bulgaria and Bulgarian Minister in London. She had attended the Versailles and Lausanne Conferences with her father from the age of 14 and figures in memoirs as 'The Conference Kid'. The marriage was a very happy one and Lady Nadejda Muir's cosmopolitan background, united with Sir Kay's hospitality and his sporting interests made Blair Drummond the scene of notable house parties. One obituary in *The Times* (8 June 1951) was almost entirely devoted to this aspect of Sir Kay's career and to 'hospitable Blair Drummond [and] those sparkling gatherings where sport and international politics blended so harmoniously'. Blair Drummond was transformed in both World Wars into a convalescent Hospital, run in 1939-45 by Lady Muir with a characteristic mix of ruthless charm and efficiency. Sir Kay died on 4 June 1951 aged 83 and Lady Muir did not long survive him. There were no children.

Sir Kay succeeded to his father's political interests, following him as vice-chairman of the West of Scotland Liberal Unionist Association and as chairman of his local constituency association of West Perthshire. In 1909 he was adopted by the Unionists as prospective parliamentary candidate for the Partick Division of Lanarkshire, then the largest single constituency in Scotland. However, despite growing popular enthusiasm for his candidature Sir Kay Muir was forced to withdraw from the field, apparently on the advice of his doctor. He was replaced by Archibald Maconochie (qv), the food processor and former Unionist MP for East Aberdeenshire. At the two elections of 1910 he lost the seat on each occasion to the Liberal, R Balfour, by a margin of some 500 votes.

Sir Kay epitomised the second-generation Glasgow merchant of his period, shrewdly converting his autocratic father's large but ramshackle collection of privately owned businesses into a major international public company with important subsidiaries in the East. During his tenure of the chair the two remaining Indigo companies were converted into Sugar Mills under Finlay's managing agency and much more general agency business was taken up in India and Ceylon. The Clan Line and other shipping and insurance agencies were satisfactorily maintained and in 1926, at the end of his tenure, the important decision was made to take up land in Kenya and establish the earliest publically quoted tea plantation company there, the African Highlands Product Co Limited. This was established by his brother James on the model of successful Finlay experience in South Indian tea estates and broke the Asian monopoly of tea growing.

Sir Kay had made many shrewd private investments during his lifetime. He held shares worth £58,000 in Shell Transport, £51,000 in Dunlop Rubber, £32,000 in Imperial Tobacco and £31,000 in British Aluminium. This compared with shares worth only £14,438 in the various Finlay companies. However, whilst his personal estate was entered in his inventory as £909,056 the bulk of his wealth, some £1,341,090 was entered in the separate inventory Account No 4. This sum comprised his share in the residue of his father's trust estate and possibly also gifts he had made within five years of his death. In all his estate was proved at £2,343,491 gross, but death duties levied at 80% on his personal estate reduced this total to £1,636,642. He made generous bequests to members of his own and his two wives' families. The largest portions of his estate (25% each) were left to his wife and to his heir John Harling Muir, the elder son of his brother and constant business associate J F Muir of Braco Castle, Perthshire. J H Muir also inherited the estate and mansion of Blair Drummond.

MONICA CLOUGH

SOURCES

Unpublished

James Finlay PLC, with acknowledgement to the Board of Directors and Secretary; family papers, with acknowledgement to Sir John Muir 3rd Bart.
SRO: SC 44/48/28, Inventory
    SC 44/48/28, Will

Published

Anon, (C Brogan), *James Finlay & Co Ltd, Manufacturers and East India Merchants 1750-1950, n d*

The Bailie, 'Men You Know Series', No 1848, March 1908, No 1942, 5/1/1910
Directory of Directors, 1951
Glasgow Herald, 6/6/1951, 7/9/1982
The Times, 8/6/1951, 13/6/1951, 14/6/1951
Who Was Who, Vol 5, London, 1961
Who's Who in Glasgow, Glasgow, 1909

Campbell PATERSON,

Essence manufacturer; b. 1852, East Kilbride, s. of Robert Paterson, vinegar merchant and Agnes Campbell; m. 1872, Mary Anne Davidson; 3 s.; Senior Partner, Robert Paterson & Co; Founder, Camp Coffee. d. 1920, Channel Islands.

Campbell Paterson was the second of seven children born to Robert Paterson, an enterprising vinegar and pickle manufacturer, and his wife Agnes Campbell. The family originated in East Kilbride and the father, Robert Paterson opened a small vinegar and pickle business in Hutcheson Street, Glasgow in 1851, a year before Campbell's birth in 1852. The family must have been reasonably affluent for Robert Paterson kept his house in East Kilbride and also had a house on the outskirts of Glasgow at Shawhill, Pollok. The eldest son, also named Robert, did not enter the family business but was apprenticed to a brushmaker and eventually opened his own business in that trade. Campbell Paterson was taken as partner by his father when he was only 16 years of age in 1868. Ten years later when his father retired and went to live in Skelmorlie on the Clyde coast, Campbell was joined by his younger brother, Walter (b 1861) who became junior partner in the firm which then became known as Robert Paterson and Son.

When Campbell Paterson joined his father as partner he began to market their traditional product under the name of 'Paterson's Golden Grain Vinegar', and introduced cordials and fruit wines to their range. Raspberry vinegar was a speciality of Paterson's and was manufactured to meet the demand for 'Raspberry' in the spirit shops where it was mixed with whisky to produce a drink favourable to the female palate and was popularly called 'Cuddle-me-Dearie'. Campbell Paterson's main business contribution was that he recognised another market opening for a beverage, only slightly related to whisky, in the form of coffee which he manufactured in essence form under the trade name of 'Camp Coffee'.

The vogue for mass consumption of coffee came with the lowering of raw material prices and duty on coffee beans and sugar in the latter quarter of the nineteenth century. The drinking of coffee was not new. Coffee houses were recognised meeting places for males from the seventeenth century, and domestic coffee drinking was not unknown amongst the more affluent classes. The market for a commercial product came in the mid-1870s when the drying, roasting, grinding, and subsequent extraction of a coffee flavoured essence was pioneered by several firms in Edinburgh, and in Glasgow by Robert Paterson and Son. Scotland did in fact become the major centre for the manufacture of coffee essence, capturing about 80% of the market. 'Camp Coffee' became the market leader through Campbell Paterson's far sighted precaution of taking out a patent and trade mark to protect his product and the aggressive sales marketing and advertising policy he pursued.

It is not certain when Campbell Paterson began to experiment with coffee essence, but the transition from one form of popular beverage to the more sedate image of coffee essence manufacture was clearly evident in 1888 when he bought the initial nucleus of his famous works at Charlotte Street and Greendyke Street overlooking the Glasgow Green. The experimental stages were funded mainly through the continued sales of 'Golden Grain' vinegar, pickles, sauces and ketchups which, together with his fruit wines, made up the bulk of Paterson's output. A decade later, in 1898, Robert Paterson & Son were termed 'manufacturing chemists' and their 'Camp Coffee' had a Colonial and Dependencies distribution network founded mainly on expatriate custom. Canadian, Australian and New Zealand markets were especially strong, but stringent ad valorem tariffs on both essence and bottles kept Paterson's from expanding into the lucrative American market.

The colonial outpost image of 'Camp Coffee' with its familiar logo of a kilted British officer attended by an Indian Sepoy was fully exploited by Paterson at trade fairs and exhibitions where the 'Camp Coffee' stand grew more adventurous with each passing year. Full scale castellated fortresses made from 'Camp Coffee' cases and Bivouacs shaped as caves inside which people were lured to taste the coffee were common place exhibits which earned Paterson's product international acclaim and recognition. But, underlying the aggressive marketing policy lay the actual constant warfare to keep the monopoly of coffee essence firmly within Campbell Paterson's own camp.

In 1904 the partnership between Campbell and Walter Paterson was terminated and Campbell took his own sons, Robert and James Davison Paterson as his new partners, continuing to trade under the style of Robert Paterson & Sons. Walter Paterson then began to manufacture a rival coffee essence under the registered trade name of 'Kit Coffee' and formed the Kit Coffee Company Limited. Campbell Paterson successfully sued his brother, Walter, for canvassing 'Camp Coffee' customers and selling them 'Kit Coffee'. Walter was bankrupted and his company together with the registered trade mark of 'Kit Coffee' was sold to Messrs John and Robert Jarvie. Once again Campbell Paterson went to war in defence of his product with a successful but protracted law suit against the Jarvie's and had the trade mark, 'Kit Coffee' expunged from the trade register.

An early indication of Campbell Paterson's determination to direct the course of 'Camp Coffee' came in the 1890s when his partnership with Walter was still extant. Much of Paterson's domestic trade was carried on with small private retailers. In the closing decades of the nineteenth century a trade war developed between the independent retailers and the Co-operative stores which with their dividend and cut price groceries distributed through the wholesale co-operative societies threatened the livelihood of the small retail grocers. A Traders Defence Association was formed against the Co-operatives and Paterson's, together with R & W Scott, the jam makers from Carluke and James Marshall, Semolina manufacturers strongly supported the independent traders. Paterson's refused to employ co-operators and in a tit-for-tat retaliation the Scottish Wholesale Co-operative Society, (SCWS), boycotted Paterson's 'Camp Coffee'. However, with the massive export trade achieved by his product, Paterson could withstand the SCWS ban quite well.

The sales of 'Camp Coffee' continued to increase at a prodigious rate with 30 dray loads of cases leaving the Charlotte Street works daily. In 1909 Campbell Paterson and his sons formed a private limited company and made coffee essence their sole product. The shift from 'cuddle-me-dearie' to the polite world of coffee essence manufacture was complete.

Campbell Paterson died on the Channel Islands in 1920.

BRENDA M WHITE

SOURCES

Unpublished

Census Returns for Glasgow, 1871
Companies Registration Office: SC 28, 145, Company Fiche, R Paterson and Sons Ltd
SRO: SC 58/42/49, Inventory
    SC 58/45/3, Will

Published

Cunnison, J, and Gilfillan, J B S, *Third Statistical Account of Scotland: Glasgow*, Glasgow, 1958
Edinburgh Chamber of Commerce Journal, Vol XXX, No 2, November 1948
Glasgow Chamber of Commerce Journal, Vol 20, No 12, December 1937
Glasgow Post Office Directories
Hume, J, *Industrial Archaeology of Glasgow*, Glasgow, 1974

John POLSON, Jnr,

Starch and cornflour manufacturer; b. 5/2/1825, Paisley, s. of John Polson, Snr, starch manufacturer and Jean Malcolm; m. 13/7/1859, Mary B Shanks, d. of Thomas Shanks, engineer; 1 d.; Snr Partner, Messrs Brown & Polson, Paisley; d. 10/8/1900, Castle Levan, Gourock; g/v estate: £307,405 15s 0d.

John Polson was born on 5 February 1825 the son of John Polson Snr and Jean Malcolm. The family was already well established in the Paisley business community. Polson was educated at the local grammar school and at the Andersonian College in Glasgow where he was said to have distinguished himself. On 13 July 1869 at a Baptist ceremony in Johnstone he married Mary B Shanks (1832-1911), the daughter of engineer Thomas Shanks, the first Provost of Johnstone. They had one daughter, Alice Mary, who married A Cameron Corbett, MP for Tradeston who later became Baron Rowallan.

The background of John Polson like so many Victorian businessmen in the West of Scotland lay in tenant farming stock. Polson's great grandfather migrated from Caithness in the mid-eighteenth century and settled in Paisley. Polson's grandfather became a tenant of the lands of Millarston and supplemented his income by hand-loom weaving. His father John was brought up in the weaving trade but its decline led him to open a small shop selling haberdashery with his brother William. At some point they became muslin manufacturers. The Polson's co-operated with a firm of Glasgow muslin manufacturers called William Brown & Son who had recently moved to Paisley. The two businesses were ultimately amalgamated.

John Polson Snr and William Brown expanded into the business of bleaching, starching and scouring at Thrushcraig, mainly for their own product. In the process of research for the most suitable starch for their finished muslin goods they used a preparation of sago flour. Polson began to wonder if sago starch might have wider domestic uses.

In 1843 John Polson Snr died aged 43 and the firms of Messrs William Brown & Son and Messrs John Polson & Co were amalgamated as Brown and Polson.

In addition to the powder starch which they prepared from sago flour the firm began to manufacture starch from wheat and later from maize. The result of these experiments was the branding of maize starch as 'cornflour'. The product was highly successful and was sold throughout the world. Premises at Thrush-craig were supplemented by the acquisition of works at Barterholm and Colinslee. Manufacture was eventually concentrated at Carriagehill on a three and a half acre site. In 1893 the firm celebrated its jubilee.

John Brown Jnr inherited a partnership in an established family business and was certainly no first generation entrepreneur. It does seem, however, to have been John Polson who worked on the production of cornflour from maize, having realized that objections to maize largely concerned its fatty content. He developed a process for producing pure starch which was patented in 1854.

Clearly the business and John Polson prospered, and gradually he began to direct his energies towards more public affairs and private interests. Polson's material culture was very affluent; in Paisley he lived at 'Westmount' and at Gourock resided at Castle Levan. In 1871 he acquired the manors of Tranent and Cockenzie near Edinburgh.

In matters of religion Polson was a member of the United Presbyterian Church which tended to attract so many of the West of Scotland's most aspiring entrepreneurs. Polson was an elder at Thread Street Church. At the factory he always kept in view the biblical motto to the effect that 'unless the Lord do build the house they who build it labour in vain'. Polson was a subscriber to the Scottish Temperance League although not a strict teetotaller. In common with other second generation businessmen he was able to devote a great deal of time to philanthropy. He subscribed regularly to the infirmary in Paisley as well as providing a public hall in Tranent and 50 houses for fishermen at Cockenzie which were sold at cost price.

Like most United Presbyterians Polson was a Liberal and a supporter of Gladstone until the Irish Home Rule issue. He was vice president of the local Liberal club. With the Home Rule split Polson joined the Unionists, indeed it appears to have been Polson who promoted the meeting of the Glasgow Chamber of Commerce which condemned Gladstone's measure by a large majority.

In local affairs John Polson was very active, becoming a Justice of the Peace and Commissioner for both Renfrewshire and Haddington. He was chairman of the first School Board of Tranent, and chairman of the Parochial Board of Tranent. In addition Polson was active in the Paisley Philosophical Institution, the Paisley Art Institute, the Royal Society of Arts, the Royal Scottish Agricultural Society, the Royal Statistical Society, and the Choral Society.

Membership of these societies reflected his recreational pursuits. Polson was very interested in art and literature and he had a valuable collection of paintings which were regularly exhibited in Paisley Museum. The garden at Westmount was evidence of Polson's keen interest in botany and his particular love of trees. He gave botany prizes to the pupils of the John Neilson Academy and was involved in the restoration of Paisley Abbey, donating £1,000 to the project.

As well as a frequent newspaper correspondence Polson wrote about *Monaco and its Gaming Tables* and other papers denouncing gambling and in 1882 a series of articles on *Affluence, Poverty and Pauperism*. Polson's views on poverty reflect those of many of the middle class business community influenced by Thomas Chalmers and the Charity Organisation Society. He wrote in opposition to the 'selfishness of indiscriminate charity' and looked back to the results of such folly in ancient Greece and Rome. The solution he saw was a bold attack on pauperism in its stronghold that is to say he wanted the abolition of outdoor parochial relief. With only the poor houses left in view he felt that people would 'strain every nerve to keep away from them'. Within the poor houses he advocated the division of deserving cases, that was to say those suffering from chronic disability, and the undeserving, who were to be kept in a state of degradation. Churches would take charge of their own poor and all cases would be investigated. Anyone not fit for the poor house Polson 'would leave to the Church of Scotland'.

Polson's attitude towards the deserving and undeserving was further demonstrated by his introduction of 'profit-sharing'. A yearly bonus was paid to workers based on the firm's profits provided they were not 'guilty of misdemeanour'. This was paid directly to the savings bank which Polson believed everyone should be helped to find their way to.

In common with other contemporary biographical material on West of Scotland businessmen, the character and personality of Polson is described in glowing terms. It is, however, possible to read into the terms 'striking personality', 'strong individuality' and 'not the sort of man to appeal to the multitude, neither was he the sort of man to care that he did not, a belief that, like other Victorian manufacturers, he was a hard-headed, self-satisfied, shrewd man of business.

John Polson died at Castle Levan, Gourock on 10 August 1900. He had been in indifferent health for some years and died following a short illness.

The value of Polson's gross personal estate was £307,405 15s 0d. His major investment was his partnership share in Brown & Polson valued at £90,326 2s 9d, and goodwill estimated at £33,000. Other investments included substantial sums in the popular Irrawaddy Flotilla Co Ltd as well as Shaw Saville and Albion Co Ltd and the British India Steam Navigation Co Ltd. Like most businessmen of the period in western Scotland his investments outwith the family business were relatively conservative in nature and limited in extent. Polson's true wealth position was of course greater than that indicated by the confirmation figures which did not include valuations for dwelling houses or agricultural lands. Estate duty was set at £21,422 19s 2d.

CHRISTOPHER C LEE

SOURCES

Unpublished

SRO: SC 58/45/11, Will

Published

Murphy, W S, *Captains of Industry*, Glasgow, 1901
Paisley & Renfrewshire Gazette, 5/1/1878, 15/7/1878, 16/11/1878, 30/11/1878, 21/10/1882, 28/10/1882, 4/11/1882, 11/11/1882, 16/11/1882, 24/3/1883, 19/4/1890, 7/1/1893, 11/8/1900, 18/8/1900, 25/8/1900, 1/9/1900, 8/9/1900
Scots' Commercial Record, August 1900, November 1900
Scottish Trader, 18/8/1900

John ROBERTSON,

Preserve manufacturer; b. 1859, Paisley, s. of James Robertson, preserve manufacturer, and Marion McFadyen; m. Jane Neilson; 3 children; Principal Partner, James Robertson & Sons, Preserve Manufacturers; d. 18/4/1937, Paisley; g/v estate: £258,148.

The firm of James Robertson and Company was founded in Paisley in 1864 by James Robertson. The business expanded quickly and grew to have factories in London, Manchester and Bristol, as well as Paisley. There was also a plant in Boston, USA. It is not clear exactly when John entered the business but there is no doubt that his main talents lay in marketing. A strong brand image was established with the 'Golden Shred' label for marmalade and the famous golly motif was introduced by John following a visit to the USA in 1912.

John Robertson followed the example of his father in many things, not least in his public services. He entered the Town Council in 1904 as one of the representatives of the Eighth Ward and after serving two terms as a magistrate and a further period as treasurer of the burgh he was appointed Provost in 1913, a post which he held until 1918. In his public role he took an interest in industrial developments far beyond his own industry. In particular he made strong endeavours to improve shipbuilding facilities on the lower reaches of the River Cart. He was also the originator of a scheme to construct a new bridge over the Cart at Inchinnan, an undertaking which was completed in 1923. By that time he had retired from the Town Council but had accepted the task of chairing the committee which was charged with the responsibility of erecting a war memorial in the town. That task was completed in 1924. During the war he took a great interest in the Sailors and Soldiers Families Association and in the provision of comforts for the men of the Paisley Territorial Units.

After the war Robertson's charitable interests centred on the Royal Alexandra Infirmary. He became a director of the Infirmary in 1914 and later served for eight years as its vice president. In 1927 he was elected as its president and served for a further four years. He made a number of gifts, not least the £500 he donated in 1925 to pay for the installation of radio throughout the hospital.

John Robertson was awarded the CBE in 1918. He was also a Justice of the Peace and served as Sheriff-Substitute for Renfrewshire. He died in April 1937.

CHARLES W MUNN

SOURCES

Unpublished

SRO: SC 58/42/126, Inventory
      SC 58/45/39, Will

Published

Evening Citizen, 19/4/1937
Glasgow Herald, 19/4/1937
Paisley and Renfrewshire Gazette, 10/10/1914
Scottish Trader, 23/4/1937

William Alexander ROBERTSON,

Wine and spirit merchant, and whisky and blends; b. 1833, Fife; Founder, Robertson & Baxter, Wine & Spirit Merchants, Glasgow; d. 30/08/1897, Troon; g/v estate: £186,000.

William Alexander Robertson was born in Fife in 1833 and moved to Glasgow in his late teens to find his fortune. He secured a position working for D Lade & Co who were wine and spirit merchants with a shop in the centre of the town. By 1854 William Robertson, just 21 years old, had progressed sufficiently far in the firm to be mentioned as an employee in the Glasgow Post Office Directory. Two years later Daniel Lade amalgamated with Bulloch & Co, owners of the large Camlachie distillery in the east end of Glasow, to form the firm of Bulloch Lade & Co. W A Robertson rather than join this new concern decided to go into business on his own. In partnership with another wine and spirit merchant, Robert Thomson, he set up as a commission merchant at 162 Hope Street, Glasgow in 1857. Imitating their larger competitors, the partners chose to act as wholesalers rather than open their own shop. There is no record of how their infant business fared in the commercial crisis that rocked the city towards the end of their first year's trading when the Western Bank collapsed in November. They did not lose their confidence accepting the agency for the Greenock Distillery Co in the midst of these difficulties. Convinced that trade would improve the partners moved during 1858 from Hope Street to Virginia Street in the heart of the Merchant City. Towards the close of the year they judged that the time was right to bring their first cargo from Bordeaux. On 10 January 1859 the *Auguste Louise* docked at Greenock with 55 quarter casks consigned to the firm. Altogether eight shipments were received by the partners during the year, containing ports, sherries, brandies and clarets. During the year Robertson & Thomas became agents for the Fettercairn distillery in Angus and the Dutch Geneva distillers J H Henkes of Delftshaven. In the first six months of 1860 the partners' import trade grew more than four-fold. This achievement no doubt reflected the massive reductions in duty on French wines and spirits, a consequence of the commercial treaty signed on 23 January.

At the end of June 1860 Robert Thomson left the firm to open his own business in Howard Street, Glasgow. W A Robertson took his clerk John W Baxter into partnership to form the firm Robertson & Baxter. Although the first full year of trade in 1861 for the new firm was complicated by downturn in the economy resulting from the outbreak of the America Civil War, W A Robertson continued to search for further agencies. Early in 1862 he was rewarded with the appointment of Robertson & Baxter as Glasgow representative of the celebrated port house of Cockburn Smithes & Co, the great claret house of Widow D Johnston & Co, and for the popular *Ponce de Leon,* a blend of sweet sherry, brandy, sugar, syrup, oranges, and other flavourings. By promoting these additions to their list, Robertson and Baxter pushed their imports to over 27,000 gallons by 1864. Other prestigious agencies quickly followed. The sherry house of Partick Garvey in 1865 and the following year the rum producer De Verage & Co and the newly revived Talisker distillery on Skye. Although W A Robertson had traded in whisky since he started in his business, he had not purchased any on his own account. In the autumn of 1866 the firm began investing in large stocks of whisky, suggesting that they had entered the recently established blending business. This possibility is borne out by a change in the firm's advertised business from 'merchants and commission agents' to 'wine and spirit brokers', confirming their intention to remain as wholesalers. Shortly after notifying their customers of this alteration, they were also able to tell them they were now agents for one of the greatest Champagne shippers, J Bollinger & Co.

Robertson & Baxter's trade fell away in the last two years of the 1860s as a consequence of a downturn in the economy as a whole. In addressing these difficult times the partners explored possible diversifications, half heartedly taking delivery of the three chests of tea in April 1869. Unconvinced W A Robertson chose instead to enlarge their existing business through the acquisition of further agencies. In the course of the year he was invited to represent the famous Bordeaux wine merchants, Cruse et fils, who had recently acquired the legendary Chateau Pntet-Canet which produced one of the most popular clarets in Scotland. As a result of receiving two other agencies the firm's trade leapt the following year to over 70,000 gallons.

By 1872 when J W Baxter retired, Robertson & Baxter was one of the principal wine and spirit concerns in Glasgow. Engaging Thomas W Wightman from Alnwick in Northumberland to help him manage the firm, W A Robertson moved his business house to a more fashionable address at 48 West Nile Street, Glasgow, to the west of the city centre. Trade fell away over the next three years, dwindling to 18,000 gallons in 1875, the lowest level for 14 years. Sensing that urgent action was required to restore the fortunes of the business, W A Robertson despatched Thomas Wightman to Edinburgh to open a branch in Leith, chiefly to sell 'new make' and 'matured' whiskies on the broking market. His position in Glasgow was taken by John Marshall, a fellow Northumbrian. This action had the desired effect and matters improved. However, the economy began to sag in 1877 and by the spring of 1878 Britain was sliding into recession. Prudently W A Robertson took immediate precautions drastically reducing his stocks. This may have been more a matter of luck than good judgment. The whisky market was confused and perplexed during

1877 by the formation of Distillers Company Ltd which immediately embarked on a price war with the larger pot distillers. Seizing this opportunity to acquire stocks of malt whisky cheaply, unscrupulous merchants formed the Whisky Ring. W A Robertson, with his commitment to quality products, refused to be associated with such tactics and began tentatively to explore the possibility of building his own distillery on the island of Islay.

The setback of the crisis year 1878 was quickly eclipsed for the whole wine and spirit trade by a catastrophe of even greater proportions caused by tiny phylloxera aphis which laid waste the vineyards of France, Spain and Portugal in the next decade. Between 1879 and 1881 Robertson & Baxter traded at a very low level while W A Robertson considered the future. Cautious by nature, he did not revive his plans to build a distillery until 1881 and then only with the support of William Ford & Sons, wholesale and retail, tea, wine, spirit and produce merchants of Leith. Built over the next three years at a cost of £30,000, Bunnahbhain distillery, as it was christened, was to be operated by a new limited liability company the Islay Distillery & Co. Robertson & Baxter's trade recovered dramatically in 1883 ro reach over 92,000 gallons. The lion's share was made up not of whisky but of rum which was enjoying a renewed fashion with the increased difficulty in obtaining brandy. To satisfy his customers for fine wine W A Robertson turned to Germany where growers for almost ten years had taken concerted and effective action to control phylloxera. He secured agencies from four Hock and Moselle houses. These additions to Robertson & Baxter's list helped to keep business buoyant throughout 1884. By the winter, however, it was becoming clear that the wine and spirit trade was becoming seriously over-stocked and the more wary merchants like W A Robertson slashed their orders for the coming year. This action was most timely as during 1885 the economy turned down sharply and demand for wines and spirits slumped.

In meeting further adversity W A Robertson yet again looked for ways of enlarging his custom. He began shipping large cargoes of American rye whisky, started dealing in the fashionable liquers, dabbled in German brandies, and took on the agency for dessert wines from Tarragona. Resenting the action of DCL in maintaining grain whisky at artificially high prices during a time of recession, he joined with the Edinburgh pioneer blender Andrew Usher in establishing North British Distillery Co in 1885. This concern over the next two years constructed a new grain distillery near Haymarket in Edinburgh. Similarly W A Robertson was receptive to overtures from William Grant, one of the promoters of the Glen Rothes distillery at Rothes on Speyside commissioned in 1879, that his business should be amalgamated with the Islay Distillery Co to counter the activities of the 'Whisky Ring'. W A Robertson had no difficulty in persuading his directors and a new company, the

Highland Distilleries Co, was floated on 6 July 1887. It shared an office with Robertson & Baxter at 48 West Nile Street, Glasgow, and at the first meeting of the directors W A Robertson was elected chairman. During the first year of trading Robertson & Baxter marketed 86,000 bulk gallons of whisky from Bunnahabhain and 88,000 bulk gallons from Glen Rothes, numbering nearly all the best known brokers and blenders amongst their clients.

The continental wine and spirit trade began to recover in 1888 with the worst of the phylloxera over in Bordeaux, Charente and the Jura. Sensing that trade was set fair to regain lost ground, W A Robertson secured two important agencies for Maire et Fils, the Burgundy negotiations, and Welsh Bros, the well-known Madeira shippers. Business boomed and by 1890 stocks taken into Robertson & Baxter's Glasgow bonds exceeded 110,000 gallons. Trade continued to be buoyant in the opening years of the decade with a surge in growth of sales of blended whiskies. In marketing their blends W A Robertson concentrated on breweries and public houses in Scotland and the North of England. Although competition was fierce he was determined to market well-balanced blends, as keenly priced as possible. He incorporated inexpensive Irish whiskies into his recipes and in 1891 secured the agency for Highland Park distillery on Orkney. At the same time he purchased, on behalf of Robertson & Baxter, Glenglassaugh distillery at Portsoy in Banffshire, transferring it immediately at a handsome profit to Highland Distilleries. Despite the drop in turnover in 1894, he was now sufficiently confident in the future to help James Scott, the manager of the Clydesdale distillery at Wishaw in Lanarkshire, to float a company to acquire the business from the existing proprietor.

In December 1894 Robertson & Baxter was converted into a limited liability company. The assets of the firm were valued at the colossal sum of £318,516, testimony to W A Robertson's phenomenal success in the 40 years since his name first appeared in the Glasgow Directory. Shares in the new enterprise were distributed to his sons, to his two junior partners, and to clients and customers. During the first year of trading, business was slack; but in the next two years sales, particularly of whisky, burgeoned. To keep pace with demand, W A Robertson joined in a syndicate to build the Tamdhu-Glenlivet distillery at Knockandhu on Speyside. At the height of his powers, W A Robertson died suddenly on 30 August 1897 at the age of just 64. His obituary in the *National Guardian*, a weekly newspaper that was the principal voice of the Scottish wine and spirit trade, was unequivocal in its praise:

'He was a personality of outstanding importance in the wholesale trade in Scotland and his demise creates a vacancy which will be extremely hard to fill. As a shrewd businessman Mr Robertson had few equals, and, though cut off at a comparatively early age he lived sufficiently long to see his business become the most important of its kind in the country.'

He left £186,000 mostly made up of his stake in Robertson & Baxter; but including a wide spread of other investments. He had a small parcel of shares in the Bruichladdich Distillery Co of Islay, the Gulf Line Associates, Lanarkshire Steel Co, the North British Distillery Co, St Andrews School for Girls, the Glasgow blending firm of Wright & Greig, a stake in Dr Robert Bell's patent for heating and ventilating railway carriages, and shares in the Brighton & Hove, Sussex Auxiliary Supply Association Ltd. Outside the world of business W A Robertson was a keen golfer, helping to found the club at Troon, where he had his country home. He was, also, noted for his generous and unostentatious support of philanthropic works.

MICHAEL M MOSS

SOURCES

Unpublished

Moss, Michael, *History of Highland Distilleries PLC, 1888-1988*

Records of Highland Distilleries, deposited in Business Record Centre, University of Glasgow, (UGD 217)

Records of Robertson and Baxter, deposited in Business Record Centre, University of Glasgow, (UGD 231)

Published

Moss, Michael, *History of Robertson and Baxter, 1858-1990*, forthcoming, 1990

William Henry ROSS,

Distiller; b. 19/6/1862, Gowanside, Carluke, Lanarkshire, s. of John Ross, farmer and Euphemia Forrest; m. (1) 21/8/1888, Annie Gilmore Pollock, d. of David Dalglish, cotton mill manager; 2 s., 1 d.; m. (2) Florence Ridley; m. (3) Gladys Murdoch; M D and Ch, The Distillers Co Ltd; d. 22/8/1944, Edinburgh; g/v estate: £246,071 12s 6d.

Ross has been variously described as 'the father of the DCL', 'the genius of the Distillers Company',

'the Abraham Lincoln of the Trade', and simply as 'one of the most outstanding figures in the Scotch whisky industry'. Ross, an austere, reserved, almost withdrawn individual offers a sharp contrast to the great whisky salesmen but he came to assume a dominance over the affairs of the Distillers Company and the Scotch whisky industry during the first 30 years of the twentieth century.

He was born on 19 June 1862 at Carluke, Lanarkshire, the youngest son of John Ross, a tenant farmer. In 1863, the family moved to a new tenancy on the Dundas estate near South Queensferry. Ross was educated at the local school and from the age of ten at George Watson's College, Edinburgh. His first job, aged 15, was in the Grassmarket branch of the ill-fated City of Glasgow Bank. Twelve days after the Bank collapsed, on 14 October 1878, Ross joined the Distillers Company Limited (DCL) as a junior clerk. DCL had been formed in April 1877 by six Lowland grain whisky (or patent still distilling) firms who saw the Company as a means of reducing competition and achieving internal economies.

Between 1878 and 1900 Ross made rapid progress through the ranks of salaried employees. In 1884, aged 22, he was appointed accountant and cashier. Five years later he became the company secretary and in 1897 he took the dual post of general manager and secretary. In 1900, at the early age of 38, he was appointed to the Board as managing director, the first salaried employee to reach Board level. These rapid promotions owed much to three factors. The first was his willingness to make good a prematurely curtailed formal education through private study of accountancy. In this he was encouraged by two of DCL's more active directors. The second was an acute managerial problem in the DCL arising from an agreement amongst the vendors of the old family firms that they would continue to act as managers of *their* distilleries. This created an intense conflict of interest between the managers' traditional loyalties to their family distilleries and their new allegiance to the DCL, nearly bringing about a dissolution of the firm in 1881. Such conflict was resolved, particularly after the appointment of a fixed (rather than rotating) chairmanship in 1888, by centralising decision taking and by recruiting salaried managers. Centralisation offered opportunities for functionaries wih no previous connections with the old firms and whose loyalty was therefore undivided. Ross, both as accountant and later as secretary, became a key figure in the permanent chairman's implementation of centralised control and thus in the belated realisation of the promised economies of the amalgamation. Lastly, there was plenty of scope at the top level of the Company for the promotion of a hard working and diligent employee. The DCL inherited a Board with an exceptionally top heavy age structure. Of the nine members of the original Board, seven had either died or resigned by 1888, and replacements from the founding families tended to display increasingly less interest in management. The few active directors were thus keen to bring on new talent from within the company.

Until 1900, Ross remained a figure little known to the Scotch whisky industry in general. The events which made him a leading figure were related to the downturn in spirit consumption after 1900. In December, 1898 the Leith blending firm of W & G Pattison ended its meteoric rise in a scandalous financial failure. Ross, anticipating the likely damage to the stability of the trade, mounted a collective rescue bid. This failed but Ross gained valuable goodwill from the effort and from the financial assistance offered by the DCL to the numerous wholesalers caught up in the Pattison debacle. Next, in 1905, came the famous 'what is whisky' case, the prosecution of a retailer for selling blended whisky, the very product on which the expansion of the industry had been built. Ross marshalled the combined forces of the patent still distillers and a majority of the blenders to fight the case. The DCL acted as paymaster. When the Government was finally persuaded to appoint the Royal Commission on Whisky of 1907-09, Ross was cast in the dual role of leader of the patent still distillers and close ally of the blenders; the resulting definition of whisky momentarily satisfied both parties. These events received wide publicity but it was to the pressing problem of excess productive capacity that Ross was devoting most of his time.

Free market forces offered a possible solution but not one favoured by Ross who instead saw consolidation as the only way 'to preserve what trade there is left and to enable such trade to be conducted on the most economic basis'. Consolidation commenced in 1902 and until 1914 was mainly confined to the production side of the industry. Wartime measures, especially the Immature Spirits Act of 1915, radically altered the situation. The Act created an enormous shortage of mature whisky stocks, prices rose and some 50 wholesale firms took advantage of high stock values to liquidate and leave the trade.

DCL thus became increasingly reliant for its grain whisky fillings on a limited number of large blenders; conversely, the blenders viewed with increasing concern DCL's growing control over grain whisky supplies through consolidation and wartime restrictions on production. In this inherently unstable situation Ross persuaded 'The Big Three' (James Buchanan & Co Ltd, John Dewar & Sons Ltd and John Walker & Sons Ltd) that it made more sense for them to join DCL in making joint purchases of mature stocks rather than pushing prices up against each other. The first of many such deals, the purchase of Dailuaine-Talisker Distilleries Ltd in 1916, had the great virtue in Ross's eyes that: 'It may be the beginning of bigger things! At any rate it will draw us closer together.' Such indeed proved to be the case and by 1923 serious discussion of an amalgamation between the DCL and 'The Big Three' were underway. By then DCL had acquired 15 patent still distilleries, leaving only four outside its control.

Amalgamation had been a favoured but largely unfruitful topic of conversation amongst the blenders since 1909 when Price Waterhouse, the accountants, had prepared a scheme to merge 'The Big Three'. Although Buchanan and Dewars formed a loose alliance under a holding company, Scotch Whisky Brands in 1915, the larger merger with Walkers and some of the other big blenders proved singularly elusive. There were many reasons: the lack of a mutually agreeable financial basis, family interests, personal antagonisms and, not perhaps least, the fact that 'the principals are all too well off to sit down for days and months if need be, to work all this out ...'.

Ross's participation in the talks with his previous experience of amalgamations and his lack of any personal financial interest in the outcome proved decisive. Although intensely loyal to the DCL his loyalty was not interpreted in the same way as that of self-made men like Buchanan or the Dewar brothers. He was seen more as a civil servant than a businessman, a man who could stand aside from the factions and bring hitherto irreconcilable competitors together. As an accountant the financial intricacies of mergers were an ever stimulating source of intellectual challenge rather than an unfathomable mystery. With some £3m of undisclosed reserves in the DCL he met the challenge supremely well! Two features of 'The Big Amalgamation' of 1925, the second largest in British industry during the inter-war period, owed everything to Ross. One was that DCL rather than Scotch Whisky Brands became the holding company; the other was that the holding company remained registered in Scotland despite considerble opposition from the blenders and their financial advisers. The idea that the largest company in the Scotch whisky trade should be domiciled in London was anathema to Ross. The final accolade for Ross, described by one of the blenders as 'correct and straight in all his dealings', was their insistence that he should chair the Board.

Although Ross regarded the amalgamation as his crowning achievement, he was also responsible for two other notable developments in the DCL. In the 1920s he took the company into making direct investments in Australia and Canada, mainly to circumvent tariffs but which he also justified, in line with currently fashionable thinking, as evidence of the Company's 'Imperial Spirit'. In the short run the world depression of 1929-32 made these ventures unprofitable but with recovery and the repeal of prohibition in the United States they proved beneficial. More challenging, but for different reasons, was the policy of diversification which, like consolidation, was a response to the slump in potable spirits consumption.

In 1929, Ross compared the way American distillers had overcome the effects of prohibition by moving into industrial alcohol with his own Company's attempts to move from 'the Whisky Age' to 'the Alcohol Age'. Demand for industrial alcohol rose from five million proof gallons in 1900 to 52 in 1938. A successful consolidation policy was vital to diversification for other patent still distillers also turned to industrial alcohol production. Ross was one of the guiding lights behind the formation of the Industrial Spirit Supply Company in 1907 and later, in 1920, the Methylating Company, both cartels complementing DCL's efforts to amalgamate this side of the business. As industrial alcohol became an increasingly important feedstock for the chemical industry between the wars, it spawned a wide range of derivative products. In 1900, DCL's product range consisted of grain whisky, malt whisky, gin, yeast, malt extract and carbon dioxide. To these by 1939 had been added industrial spirit, acetone, acetic acid, acetaldehyde, acetates, esters, resins, plastics, plaster board and power alcohol. Diversification took the DCL into the chemical industry and posed a new range of problems quite unlike the Scotch whisky industry: capital requirements were greater, fundamental research was needed, there were other large scale competitors (home grown and foreign) and a different type of management expertise was needed. Although Ross set the DCL on the road to diversification, his achievements were less long lasting. During and immediately after the First World War, Ross recruited new directors to develop the industrial side but 'The Big Amalgamation' of 1925 created a Board in which the blenders formed a majority. Some of the blenders, even as potable spirit consumption continued to fall, were always inclined to view the industrial side as a short term insurance policy and during the early 1930s sucessfuly prevented the adoption of a divisional structure. They also prevented the rationalisation of distribution, an idea dear to Ross's heart though one which given brand loyalty amongst consumers was probably misconceived. Ross's chairmanship was thus marked to some degree by personal disappointment over the lack of acceptance of his ideas. It was also marred by personal tragedy when, on a business trip to DCL's Australian subsidiaries in 1929, an accident on board ship severely damaged his sight. His other faculties remained unimpaired and his speeches to the annual shareholders' meetings continued to reveal a mind ever ready to analyse the problems of the industry. His chairmanship remained an active one until his retirement in November, 1935.

Although Ross was very much the personification of the DCL and, in a sense, came close to making the DCL the Scotch whisky industry (such was its control of distilling and blending), a notable feature of his career was the amount of time devoted to the wider problems of the industry. This side of his career made its heaviest demands during the First World War in negotiations with Lloyd George over his anti-drink policies and with the Ministry of Munitions in its ever increasing demands for extra spirit for munitions purposes. Ross was fully alive to the threat to the trade posed by the anti-drink campaign whether at home, in the shape of the Scottish Temperance Act of 1913, or abroad, in the form of prohibition in the USA. The Anti-Prohibition Campaign Council of which he was chairman produced a unified response by brewers, distillers and retailers, something which had been conspicuously lacking before the War.

Ross left the DCL a wealthy man by the standards of his day but a poor man by the standards of the blenders. His salary at its peak in 1931 was £12,000 a year. He received an annual pension - from the Employee Superannuation Fund he had been instrumental in creating - of £2,000 a year plus another £2,000 voted by the Board in recognition of his distinguished service. During his retirement he married as his second wife, Florence Ridley, the first nurse who had tended him and, when she died, he married her successor, Gladys Murdoch. Ross died on 26 August 1944 leaving an estate of £246,072. His investments, valued at £225,126 were mainly in the DCL (54% of the portfolio), government stock (19%), tobacco companies (6%), investment trusts (5%) and insurance companies (3%). He left £5,000 to Edinburgh City Corporation for a bandstand in Princes Street Gardens (the Ross Bandstand), £8,000 to the Royal Edinburgh Infirmary extension fund and £40,000 to the W H Ross Foundation for the Study and Prevention of Blindness, a research institute he had established in 1935. His eldest son H J Ross, later became the chairman of DCL in 1948.

RONALD B WEIR

WRITINGS

'History of the Company', *DCL Gazette*, January 1923-January 1929

SOURCES

Unpublished

The Distillers Company Ltd, Board and Management Committee Minute Books
SRO: SC 70/1/1115, Inventory
  SC 70/4/798, Will
Weir, R B, 'The Development of the Distilling Industry in Scotland in the Nineteenth and early Twentieth Centuries', University of Edinburgh unpublished PhD thesis, 1974

Published

Glasgow Herald, 23/8/1944
Scottish Biographies, Glasgow and London, 1938
The Times, 24/8/1944
The Victualling Trades Review, August 1900
Who Was Who
Wilson, R, *Scotch: the formative years*, London, 1970

William STEWART,

Brewer; b. 1847, Grandtully, Perthshire; m.; 3 s., 4 d.; MD, Edinburgh United Breweries; d. 17/6/1930, Droitwich; g/v estate: £32,446 1s 0d.

William Stewart, like Alexander Bruce (qv), is an interesting example of the career-manager who rose through the ranks in late Victorian brewing enterprise, and for a time was associated with the important but ill-fated Edinburgh United Breweries. Stewart, son of a Perthshire farmer, was born in 1847 and educated at Perth. Coming to Edinburgh in 1862 he entered the service of the Edinburgh & Glasgow Railway Company as a clerk under his uncle - also William Stewart - who was the goods manager. By 1865 he had moved to the brewing trade and gradually worked his way through various clerical and managerial posts to become manager of the Edinburgh & Leith Brewery, otherwise known as Robert Disher & Company.

The Edinburgh & Leith Brewery dated back to 1820 and occupied much older premises belonging to Robert Stein & Company, a firm with eighteenth century origins. The company, though small, had a high reputation, its speciality being 'Disher's Ten-Guinea Ale', one of the strongest ales brewed, and sometimes called the 'Burgundy of Scotland'. According to one contemporary it was so matured that it tasted like barley wine and was highly recommended by medical men for invalids' use, some even claiming 'that it is superior in effect to port wine'.

Despite the popularity of its ales and perhaps as much due to the ferocity of local competition from brewing giants like William Younger and William McEwan, the Edinburgh & Leith brewery was at a low ebb. It says much for Stewart's managerial skills that after five years - if one estimate is to be taken at face value - its return on capital was 25% per annum. Certainly it was the most important firm in the merger that created the Edinburgh United Breweries in 1889.

Next to William Younger and William McEwan the Edinburgh United Breweries was the third largest Scottish company before George Younger of Alloa sought limited liability in 1897. The new company united the Edinburgh & Leith Brewery with George Ritchie & Son of Bell's Brewery, Robin Macmillan & Company of Summerhall Brewery, and David Nicholson & Son of Palace Brewery. The authorised capital was £450,000, £125,000 of which was in ordinary shares of £10, and a further £125,000 in 6% cumulative £10 preference shares. Additionally there was £200,000 worth of 5% debentures. Sir W Hamilton Dalrymple became chairman and Stewart, managing director. The company inherited tied properties in central Scotland and north-east England and also had a fairly extensive free trade, notably in Disher's Ten Guinea Ale. A modest export trade focussed on India and New Zealand, where the company had agents. A depot was established in Newcastle with other agencies in Glasgow, Dundee, London and Cardiff.

Stewart immediately instituted a rationalisation programme, with the Edinburgh & Leith concentrating on strong ale, the Palace Brewery on 54/- pale ale, and Ritchies on pale ale, mild ales and porter (a dark, highly hopped brew popular before the development of lighter beers). But despite his efforts the firm was over-capitalised from the outset and at an early stage ran into financial difficulties. The annual report of 1890 indicated that the capital was fully paid up 'despite rumours to the contrary' and, moreover, the firm's situation was hardly helped by a Court of Session case the following year that revealed fraudulent accounts at the Palace Brewery. While it was maintained that the company's beer had a bad reputation among its agents, it seems more likely that its problems arose from its financial structure. Undoubtedly the interest on debentures - the largest of any Scottish brewery company before 1898 - caused difficulties. But by accident rather than design and thanks to the general brewery boom of the period, Stewart managed to keep the company afloat until his ultimate retiral in 1906.

On his death in 1930 aged 83 he left an estate valued at £32,000, mostly stocks and shares in leading investment and industrial enterprises, including the North British & Mercantile Insurance Co, Commercial Bank of Scotland, North British Distillery Co, William McEwan & Co Ltd, the Distillers Co, and Scottish Oils Ltd. Four years later in 1934 the Edinburgh United Breweries - a somewhat less than successful merger - were finally wound up.

IAN DONNACHIE

SOURCES

Unpublished

Scottish Brewing Archives
SRO: SC 70/1/835, Inventory
      SC 70/4/651, Will

Published

Directory of Directors, 1903, 1904, 1905
Donnachie, Ian, *A History of the Brewing Industry in Scotland*, Edinburgh, 1979
Journal of the Institute of Brewing, 1930
Men of the Period, London, n d, c 1900
The Scotsman, 18/6/1930

Hugh T TENNENT,

Brewer; b. 1863, s. of Charles Stewart Parker Tennent, Brewer and Maltman; Bachelor; Manager, Wellpark Brewery, Glasgow; d. January 1890; g/v estate: £230,226 13s 6d.

Although Hugh Tennent had a tragically short life and was in active management of the famous Wellpark Brewery in Glasgow for just six years, he was clearly a dynamic and enterprising businessman who greatly influenced the future development and prosperity of the firm long after his untimely demise.

The 1880s was a time of considerable expansion in the brewing industry, and this was reflected not only in the scale of new enterprises, but also in the competition for new markets and the striving after new products.

J & R Tennent, probably always the largest brewing firm in the West of Scotland, had expanded its business rapidly from the mid-nineteenth century. The Wellpark Brewery built up a large general business and a specialist trade in pale ales and stouts. In 1855 the value of the business was put at £220,000 and was said in the 1850s and 1860s to have made

'large and increasing profits', mainly under the management of Hugh Tennent Snr and his son, Charles.

Both father and son died in the same year, 1864, and with Charles' offspring all being minors, including two sons, Archibald and Hugh, the business was thereafter run by trustees on behalf of the family for upwards of 20 years, 1864-1884. Obviously they were very successful, for by 1870 the Company was worth £300,000, making it a multi-million pound enterprise by modern standards. The firm already had a world wide reputation, both for the excellence of its pale ales and its other products.

Under the Tennent Trust the Wellpark Brewery was itself greatly expanded; the malt barns were extended; a new cooperage built; and sawmills and a printing works added. Everything could be done at the Brewery, from the malting of barley to the printing of labels for bottles and cases. In 1876, as it happened, the famous Tennents' red 'T' trademark was registered for sole use throughout the British Empire (the firm having large colonial sales as well as in the home market).

Hugh Tennent assumed a management role in his late teens, for his older brother, Archibald, was apparently in poor health and took no active interest in the business. Hugh bought over his brother's share and took sole control of the company at the age of 21 in 1884.

A few years earlier, in 1881, Hugh Tennent had visited Bavaria with a physician friend Dr Wyllie Clarke, and there realised the attractive qualities of lager beer. With the firm's export trade in mind, this lighter brew seemed a logical new product. It travelled well and like all lighter ales would be consumed avidly by customers in hot climates. Even at home he recognised a growing demand for imported lagers, mostly German and Austrian, whose light, sparkling appearance and taste had considerable appeal at a time when there was a swing away from traditional dark, heavy, beer.

So Tennent, in 1885, began lager brewing at Wellpark, with two continental brewers, Dr Emil Westergaard, a Dane, and Jacob Klinger, a German, as consultants, and Wyllie Clarke in charge of operations. Lager brewing for export proved so successful that Tennent decided to build a completely new lager brewery at Wellpark. He brought in the German firm, Reldinger of Augsburg, and work began in 1889. The plant was built entirely on the German model - even German coopers being imported to manufacture the cellar casks needed for maturation. Tennent had clearly realised that lager brewing, with lower temperature fermentation followed by extensive periods of cold storage, differed very little from traditional Scottish techniques of brewing 'keeping beers' for overseas shipment.

The lager brewery was completed in 1891, but sadly Hugh Tennent did not live to see it, for he had died the previous year, aged only 27. He was unmarried and had no family. Earlier in 1883 he had purchased the property of Dunalastair in Perthshire for a reputed £200,000, and this with the rest of his estate was divided among his relatives. A second Tennent Trust was set up to run the business, but as it transpired Hugh Tennent was the last member of the family to be in direct control of this important and dynamic enterprise.

IAN DONNACHIE

SOURCES

Unpublished

Scottish Brewing Archive, Records of J & R Tennent
SRO: SC 36/48/128, Inventory
SC 36/5/100, Will

Published

Donnachie, I, *A History of the Brewing Industry in Scotland*, Edinburgh, 1979
McMaster, C and Rutherford, T, *The Tennent Caledonian Breweries*, Edinburgh, 1985
Scottish Wine, Spirit and Beer Trades Review, 26/4/1887

Robert Davidson WADDELL,

Provision Manufacturer; b. 1855, s. of John Waddell, carting contractor and Catherine Davidson; m. 6/8/1879, Mary Jane Tait; 1 s., 2 d.; MD & Ch, R D Waddell Ltd; d. 2/3/1929, Glasgow; g/v UK estate £5,555 11s 4d.

Robert Davidson Waddell was born near Airdrie in 1855 to John Waddell and his wife Catharine Davidson. He attended Kirkcaldy Academy and after leaving school served his apprenticeship as a sausage maker with Messrs Annackers Ltd, a well known Glasgow firm of meat processors. In 1878 he began trading in his own right as a pork butcher in the Gallowgate, Glasgow but soon opened a number of branches throughout Glasgow specialising in pork and other meat sausages. By 1885 Waddell had built a large factory at Mount Street (West), where he manufactured sausages, puddings, pies, potted heid, haggis and saveloys; products which made him a household name in Scotland and England. Further expansions to his business in the late 1880s culminated in the building of the largest sausage factory in Scotland, at Napiershall Street, Glasgow. This was a large ornate renaissance style block of six storeys high plus attics and the total cost of the buildings amounted to £47,000.

Waddell's sausages and allied meat products were claimed to be manufactured under extremely hygienic conditions. This was a pre-requisite for publicity in the late Victorian period when the public consciousness of health risks associated with contaminated foodstuffs was heightened by the Public Health Acts relating to Foodstuffs and the increased vigilance of informed sanitary inspection of food manufacture, retailing premises and abbatoirs. Waddell's publicity stressed the hygienic preparation of his food products and Waddell himself patented most of the steam powered machines for mincing, filling and packing sausages. This obviated the need for personal handling by the operators. Customers were invited to inspect the works at Napiershall Street to see for themselves the standards of cleanliness.

Sausages, once the nearest contact the poorer classes had with meat, were rising in popularity with the middle classes. By 1910 Waddell advertised his wares as being made from the best, Sandringham reared young pigs and sold a 'regal' sausage at ten pence per pound in one pound and half pound bunches. Waddell always exhibited a well stocked stand at the London grocers' exhibition at Islington and the Glasgow and Edinburgh International exhibitions. His stands were colourful and cleverly advertised. Gold medals and complete sell-outs of the entire stand were commonplace happenings in the Edwardian era. He was a pioneer of glass containers for meat products and sold to many high class grocery concerns such as Coopers Stores (qv J G Bishop).

With increased sales Waddell had warehouses in Belfast, Edinburgh, and in 1909 bought out the London meat concern of Cunninghames and de Fourier Ltd to give him London warehousing facilities. In 1914 Waddell formed a private limited company with an authorised capital of £40,000 of £1 shares, of which Waddell held 36,781 shares. At the time Waddell owned 19 shops in Glasgow, 14 elsewhere in Scotland and two in Belfast, in addition to the three warehouses. In 1921 share capital was increased by £20,000, the majority of which was held by Waddell and his only son, Robert Bulloch Waddell.

Robert Waddell actively promoted the training of those entering the grocery trade by presenting a competition silver cup to classes at the Technical College. He was also a passable violin player and kept a collection of violins including a Stradivarius. He was a Deacon of the Incorporation of Coopers and an ex-president of the Palette Club.

Robert Waddell died at his home, Rednock, Eglinton Drive, Glasgow on 2 March 1929. The gross value of his moveable estate was suspiciously small, £5,555 11s 4d, much of which was accounted for by his holdings in R D Waddell Ltd and his personal effects. Despite the fact that Waddell left 18,686 shares in R

71

D Waddell Ltd which were originally floated at £1 each, they were now only worth 2/6 d and accounted for £2,335 of his personal estate. The 1,503 shares of £1 each in Cunninghame and de Fourier Co Ltd had no value at all. This may have some connection with the fact that the year prior to his death Waddell acquired William Annakers Ltd. Annakers was, of course, the place where Waddell had served his apprenticeship. Annakers had vastly increased their business since then and had built a large renaissance style sausage factory at William Street, Anderston, in 1889 at a cost of £8,000. A far cry from Annakers earlier establishments which provided generations of Glasgwegians with the eponymous yardstick for filthy disorder: *Annaker's midden*. The cost of buying Annakers, therefore, may in fact have effected the end value of Waddell's own personal estate. The generous spirit present in the bequests made in his will to family and dependents actually outran the amount of realisable estate available.

The business was carried on by his son Robert Bulloch Waddell who, at the time of his father's death, held a majority of the shares. In 1946 the Zwanenburg family became directors and took over the firm. The firm of R D Waddell Ltd was wound up in 1957.

BRENDA M WHITE

SOURCES

Unpublished

Companies Registration Office: B72/9620, Company Fiche
SRO: SC 36/48/418, Inventory
SC 36/51/226, Will

Published

Glasgow Herald, 4/3/1929
Glasgow of Today, 1888
Post Office Directories, Glasgow
Hume, J, *Industrial Archaeology of Glasgow*, London & Glasgow, 1974
Industries of Glasgow, Glasgow, 1888
Municipal Glasgow - Its Evolution and Enterprise, Glasgow, 1914
Scottish Trader, 1886-1929

Sir Alexander WALKER,

Distiller; b. 22/3/1869, Kilmarnock, s. of Alexander Walker, wine merchant and Isabella McKemmie; m. 1895, Rosaline, d. of Arthur S Josling; 2 s., 2 d.; Ch, John Walker & Sons Ltd, Distillers & Blenders; Dir, The Distillers Co Ltd; d. 13/5/1950, Troon; g/v estate: £558,299 1s 11d.

Alexander Walker was the third son of Alex Walker, chairman of John Walker & Sons of Kilmarnock, a firm founded in 1820 and which by the 1880s was one of the largest whisky blending firms in Scotland. He was educated at Ayr Academy and subsequently had legal training as well as a trade apprenticeship with Robertson & Baxter Ltd, wine and spirit merchants, of Glasgow. He joined the family firm in 1888 and two years later became a director. In 1913 he was appointed a joint managing director. During the First World War he undertook work for the Ministry of Munitions on the control of raw materials and was a member of the Munitions Disposal Board, being knighted in 1920 for his service. In 1923 John Walker & Sons Ltd became a public company with Sir Alexander as chairman. Two years later the firm merged with the Distillers Company and Buchanan-Dewar Ltd, and Walker joined the Board of the DCL.

Walker had earned a reputation for his independent views on trade matters before 1925, especially in his evidence to the Royal Commission on Whiskey where he argued unsuccessfully for a 50% malt whisky component in blends. His maverick manner was also evident, much to the frustration of the other parties, in the long series of talks leading to the amalgamation. Much of the delay in securing the amalgamation may be attributed to him. Greater interest attaches to his role on the DCL Board between 1925 and 1939. Few of the proprietors of the blending firms were active contributors to the development of the DCL but Walker, as one of the youngest directors (56 in 1925), became exceedingly influential.

The amalgamation confirmed the DCL's premier position in the whisky trade as a vertically integrated combine. Faced, however, with a sharply falling demand for potable spirits the company turned its attention to the production of industrial alcohol and via this into solvents and other chemicals including, by 1939, plastics. Diversification, initially relying on imported technology and subsequently on the firm's own research and development, generated a series of complex problems. These included relationships between the DCL and other much larger chemical firms such as ICI and I G Farben who were already established in fields DCL sought to enter; the sheer scale of the necessary capital investment, quite different from previous experience of potable production; a highly unsettled technology in which the choice of the cheapest raw material lay between molasses, where DCL had invested heavily, gases from oil, and coal using only partially perfected processes; and, the most appropriate organisation for the firm. The last of these was a particularly sensitive issue as the capital for diversification had to come from DCL's potable activities and the dominant representation on the Board was the blenders, not all of whom took a charitable view of the long-run potential of the industrial side of the business regarding it as a short-term insurance policy in case the potable market took longer to recover than expected. On the industrial side, some of the directors responsible for building up the business wished to see the company adopt a divisional structure in which the company would be split into two divisions, whisky and industrial.

In 1931 during the absence of the chairman, W H Ross (qv), from illness, a small Finance and Executive Committee was formed as a temporary contingency measure. Walker was a member and argued successfully for a greater degree of centralised control over the firm's activities. Four years later this resulted in a new management structure which rejected the divisional approach and established a management committee in which each member controlled a number of subsidiary companies and departments. Walker was placed in charge of research and development, and much of the chemical interests. His chairmanship of the management committee from 1937 to 1939 saw the DCL adopt a definite policy in relation to chemicals which moved it into the marketing of finished products in addition to the production of raw materials. The ICI/DCL 'spheres of interest' agreement was negotiated, and joint research initiated with Shell and Anglo-Iranian on alcohol production by synthetic processes. Joint ventures between the DCL and the British Government on the production of strategically important chemicals were also commenced prior to 1939.

Walker's contribution to the development of DCL lay in his perception of the problems which accompanied the firm's late entry into the chemical industry. His interest in technical matters and his presence on the research committee reassured the blenders whose profits funded diversification that 'the tail would not wag the dog'. In the context of the 1930s he bridged the gulf between potable and non-potable activities. In the longer run, many of Walker's technical personnel were to provide the next generation of top management.

Walker had several other directorships, most notably in Glenfield & Kennedy Ltd, McDougall's Timber Co Ltd and British Home Stores Ltd. His other activities included membership of the Ayrshire Electricity Board, chairmanship of the Ayrshire Gas Supply Committee and chairmanship of a Board of Trade Committee set up to investigate the feasibility of a gas grid for the West of Scotland. He was a Trustee of C K Marr's bequest for the erection of a college at Troon to provide special facilities for further education, and became chairman of the governors when Marr College opened in 1934. He made gifts of building land to the Burgh of Troon and promoted the Troon Bathing Pool. In 1944 he donated £10,000 to the Town Council for the establishment of a health centre for the treatment of rheumatism. In 1946 Sir Alexander was presented with the Freedom of Troon, the first person to receive the honour, in recognition of his services to the town. By then he was the only survivor of the nine commissioners appointed to govern the burgh when it was formed in 1896.

Walker married Rosaline Josling in 1895. They had two sons and two daughters. He left an estate worth £521,204, some 23% of which was represented by his shareholding in the Distillers Company.

RONALD B WEIR

SOURCES

Unpublished

The Distillers Company Ltd, Board and Management Committee Minute Books
SRO: SC 6/44/157, Inventory
 SC 6/46/89, Will
Walker J & Sons Ltd, Board Minute Books and other company papers
Weir R B, The development of the distilling industry in Scotland in the nineteenth and early twentieth centuries, University of Edinburgh, unpublished PhD thesis, 1974

Published

Boyd, T, 'History of the House of Walker', *DCL Gazette*, April 1930-October 1930
Wilson, R, *Scotch: the formative years*, London, 1970

George YOUNGER,
Viscount Younger of Leckie,

Brewer; b. 13/10/1851, Alloa, s. of James Younger, brewer and Janet McEwan; m. 1879, Lucy, d. of Edward Smith, Physician; 3 s.; Ch, George Younger & Co, Alloa; Pres, Scottish Licensed Trade Association; Dir, National Bank of Scotland, Lloyds Bank Ltd; d. 29/4/1929, London; g/v UK estate: £327,642 16s 9d.

George Younger, Viscount Younger of Leckie, was both chairman of one of the largest breweries in Scotland and perhaps the most prominent of the brewer-politicians of the period. Younger, the eldest son of James Younger and his wife Janet, eldest daughter of John McEwan of Alloa, was born in 1851. He was educated at Edinburgh Academy and had only just gone to Edinburgh University in 1868 when his father died and he left to take charge of the business, though only 17 at the time. Dating back, like its Edinburgh namesake, to the mid-eighteenth century, the original business in the Meadow Brewery had already expanded considerably in his father's time - for James Younger in the 1850s first leased then purchased the Candleriggs Brewery from another old Alloa firm, Robert Meiklejohn, and pursued a policy which gradually extended the enterprise in both home and colonial markets.

After his father's death the firm was nominally run by trustees until 1875, but Younger was apparently in effective control virtually from the outset. Under his management - which coincided with the general boom in the industry - the Younger enterprise grew dramatically. The growth of the firm can be readily appreciated from the extension of plant during the late Victorian and early Edwardian period. The Craigward Maltings were begun in 1868 (later reconstructed and extended in 1904), and new pneumatic maltings built at the Candleriggs Brewery in 1895. A second large maltings was completed in 1899. Bottling - particularly for export - was increased rapidly after 1885, the plant being extended in 1889 and moved to new premises four years later. This was subsequently extended in 1895 and 1900, and in 1903 chilling and carbonating plant was installed for home beers.

When the business became a limited liability company in 1897 the properties included the Candelriggs and Meadow Breweries, the Craigward and Station Maltings, Kelliebank export bottling stores, Eglinton home bottling stores and the Craigward cooperage. The purchase price was £500,000, payable by the issue to the vendors of the whole of the ordinary and deferred share capital, with the balance in cash. Younger became chairman, and other members of the family joined the board. In 1898 the ordinary capital was increased by 12,500 shares of £10 each and the

deferred by 12,500 shares of £10 each to enable the company to acquire two breweries in County Durham, the Sunderland brewery of R Fenwick & Co and the Chester Brewery, Chester-le-Street.

With Younger at the helm the firm expanded and rationalised its home market, much as McEwan did by concentrating sales in the industrial lowlands of Scotland and the north of England. He also greatly expanded sales in colonial outlets, notably in India, Singapore, the Far East and South Africa, with such success that the export and home bottling plant were separated and a new home bottling plant opened in 1912. A glass bottle works opened in 1908 and was floated as a separate company some years later in 1919 with George Younger & Sons Ltd holding a quarter of the capital.

Younger first entered politics by way of Clackmannan County Council (the smallest county authority in Scotland) to which he was elected in 1890 and of which he was convenor, 1895-1906. But he had greater political ambitions, and having contested the parliamentary seat of Clackmannan and Kinross unsuccessfully in 1895, 1899 and 1900, and that of Ayr Burghs in 1904, was ultimately returned there in 1906 and remained as Unionist MP until 1922. Younger joined the Conservative opposition to the reforming Liberal government of the period and took an active part in the Commons, making a notable attack on Lloyd George's 'People's Budget' of 1909, which advocated super-tax and land value duties. Ultimately this was rejected by the Lords, thus beginning the quarrel that led to the Parliament Act of 1911. Younger himself was created a baronet that year - perhaps a measure of respect on the part of his political opponents. On one occasion he fainted in the Commons and after recovering remarked 'tell Lloyd George I'm not dead yet'.

As in business however it seems his major contribution lay in party management, for in 1917 at the invitation of Bonar Law he became chairman of the Conservative Party organisation - then dormant because of the war and Conservative participation in the Coalition government. He was partly responsible for the success of the Coalition in the 'Coupon' election of 1918 - an endorsement device adopted by the Conservatives and Liberals to avoid sacrificing seats to Labour and Independent Liberals. He was extensively involved in discussions on the Reform Bill of 1918 for he made himself something of an authority on franchise and registration questions.

Another of Younger's objectives was the reform of the House of Lords and the establishment of a more effective upper chamber, a policy supported in general by the Coalition. On this and other grounds he opposed several early attempts to break up the coalition, but later in 1922 changed his mind and supported Bonar Law at the meeting in the Carlton Club which effectively spelled the end of the Coalition. He was much criticised by those Conservatives who had wanted to stay in the Coalition, and Lord Bir-

sufficiently established to participate as sole Scottish exhibitor in the China, Porcelain and Earthenware class of the Great Exhibition in London, alongside prestigious English manufacturers such as Worcester and Derby. The company displayed not only highly artistic and decorated products in classical patterns but also blue transfer-printed wares appropriate for the fast-growing mass-market. Several of these patterns were registered designs affording some protection from imitation. It also displayed terra-cotta vases in the Manufacturers from Mineral Substances class.

The firm became highly successful, eventually employing some 800 persons, the most extensive single pottery establishment in Scotland. Astute attention was paid to the frequent introduction of new designs, maintenance of a broad range of types of wares, the differing requirements of both the cheap mass-produced and expensive highly decorative markets, the distinctive needs of the export trade and the overall dependence of the firm on technical development of appropriate porcelain and earthenware bodies. Accordingly its reputation was considerable: 'no other factory', says Fleming 'did more to establish the good name of Scottish pottery than Bell's Pottery'. In particular hand-painted china tea services, often with Scottish landscapes, rivalled the better quality products of Staffordshire. Large quantities of wares were shipped to export markets particularly in North and South America and the East Indies.

However, like other once-large Scottish pottery companies, Bell's did not survive the increasingly competitive and turbulent trading environment of the late nineteenth and early twentieth centuries. Matthew Bell died in 1870 and John in 1880, his death precipitated, it is said, by the financial stresses encountered by his companies consequent upon the collapse of the City of Glasgow Bank in 1878. Within six months of his death, and despite the considerable capital assets of his estate, sequestration proceedings were begun by his creditors. The difficulties were compounded by the fact that he died intestate and without issue; he had married, unlike his brother Matthew, but his wife, Ann Milner, died, it is said, within six months of their marriage and he did not remarry. The pottery was purchased as a going concern by a joint stock company formed by James Murdoch, Bell's works manager, and a number of Glasgow merchants, some nine months after John Bell's death. Although the established export markets particularly in the East Indies were cultivated efficiently with the creation of designs based on indigenous motifs, generally the quality of the wares declined while dependence on re-issued old designs increased. Employment by the late 1880s was down to 500 or 600. Competition from Staffordshire potteries, establishing retail outlets in Glasgow, and from continental manufacturers under suspicion of dumping their wares, took its toll. According to the Glasgow News of 1885:

'Glasgow at the moment is flooded with pottery productions similar to those of these works ostensibly from Staffordshire, but for the most part, probably, from foreign ports. The articles come as consignments for realisation at whatever they may bring, and if from Staffordshire, then Staffordshire is in a bad way; while if from foreign ports, the question arises whether such consignments will pay the shippers and be continued.'

The rising price of fuel at the turn of the century also had its effects. The loss of land to the enlargement of the Buchanan Street Station by the Caledonian Railway in 1902 accelerated the decline, and the firm was voluntarily wound up in 1910 on the death of Murdoch. Another previous manager, Joseph Turner, acquired what remained of the company as a wholesaling concern, eventually in partnership with former cashier, John Weir. But by then J & M P Bell & Co Ltd was a shadow of its former glory. It effectively ceased in 1928, though Weir struggled on with the title, printing dairy names on milk bottles, at two successive locations in Glagow up to his death in 1941.

According to Weyers a key factor in the decline was the loss of 'artistic direction to anticipate and lead public taste', a direction presumably provided personally by John and Matthew Bell and not replaced on their death. Their artistic interests certainly were well known and extended beyond the pottery company; they amassed a large collection of paintings, tapestries, statues and classical antiquities. It was possibly to house their growing collection that John moved from the family residence at 245 St Vincent Street to Bardowie House, Milngavie. Certainly it was their objective to provide suitable galleries for their collection in having designed and built the Italianate Mansion of North Park House, Glasgow. Begun in 1869 and completed in 1871, after Matthew's death, it became John's home address from 1873 until his death there, some seven years later. The collection, possibly intended to become a bequest to the City, was sold in Glasgow and London; the paintings inexplicably realised much less than he was reputed to have paid for them. North Park House was sold in 1884, having been empty since his death, to house the Queen Margaret College, incorporated the previous year, and shortly to become part of the University of Glasgow in 1892. In 1935 it was sold to the British Broadcasting Corporation.

Little is known of John Bell's other activities, either commercial or private. The Govan Tube Works provided malleable iron pipes for the shipbuilding industry. It may have been acquired around 1870; at the time of the sequestration of his estate it still employed 100 workers, but apparently it had been a loss-making concern for some time and that only John Bell's philanthropy and his financial successes elsewhere allowed it to continue. J Bell & Co, East India merchants, and Bell & Co, commission brokers,

Rangoon, appear to represent the ends of an important trading link for the pottery company, though possibly other goods were handled as well. All three businesses were disposed of along with the pottery in the course of the sequestration. The total assets realised amounted to over £357,000, of which the pottery accounted for £136,000 and his private assets, personal and heritable, £68,000. With total liabilities of £194,000, creditors were eventually paid in full. His businesses fell victim to a liquidity crisis partly arising from general circumstances of the time but partly due to his failure to make a will, a surprising omission for one who had a close familiarity with the law. He appears to have had no involvement in public affairs, though he evidently had the wealth which would have accorded him influence. Only in the specialist field of ceramic collecting is his artistic entrepreneurship still appreciated.

FREDERICK G HAY

SOURCES

Unpublished

Quail, G, *The Sequestration of John Bell*, unpublished paper to the Scottish Pottery Society, 1983
SRO: SC 36/48/104, Inventory

Published

Fleming, J A, *Scottish Pottery*, Glasgow, 1923
Glasgow News, 6/4/1885
Weyers, J, 'The Rise and Fall of Bell's Pottery', *Scottish Field*, October 1969
Weyers, J, 'The Treasure Glasgow Lost', *Glasgow Herald*, 27/6/1981

Robert BROWN,

Fireclay goods manufacturer; b. East Kilbride, 15/7/1810, s. of John Brown, tenant farmer and Jean Aikenhead; m. 29/12/1838, Isabella Henderson; 3 s., 8 d.; major firms: Robert Brown and Son, Ferguslie Fireclay Works, Paisley; d. 6/5/1895, Paisley; g/v estate: £2,163 10s 6d.

Robert Brown was born on 15 July 1810, the eighth of nine children of John Brown and Jean Aikenhead, at Ranger House, a small tenanted farm near East Kilbride. The family moved to a larger farm on the outskirts of the village of Neilston in 1815. During his childhood Brown's fingers were injured in a domestic accident and because this made him unfit for more typical manual trades, his parents sought to provide him with a classical education at the Neilston Parish School, with a view to his proceeding to university. Despite the market opportunities in nearby Paisley, the family fell victim to economic circumstances. Unable to meet the rent on account of the collapse in agricultural prices, they were obliged to move to a small-holding on the southern outskirts of Paisley in 1824 and Robert Brown's formal education came to an abrupt and regretted end. After various menial employments, and an apprenticeship in the ironmongery trade, which still failed to provide him with a steady occupation, he eventually joined the staff of the *Glasgow Chronicle* newspaper. From there he moved to occupy the responsible post of town chamberlain of Paisley in 1834. Evidently he had begun to show the qualities of character which were to stand him in good stead in later years, and, with his family now resident in Paisley, to forge the personal links which were so important an element in his business and civic success. The treasurer of the then newly-reformed town council was influential in his obtaining the post, and he was able to find acceptable guarantors of his fidelity to the extent of £1,000.

Robert Brown quickly established a reputation for efficiency and ability, and capitalised on such formal education as he had received. As well as looking after the day-to-day expenditures and receipts of the town council, he performed the duties of master of works; he assisted in the presentation of the Cart Navigation Act and was appointed treasurer of the Trustees of the Cart Navigation in 1835. Deposit-taking facilities were opened both by the town and the Cart trustees and for these funds he was treasurer also. Amidst the rigours of the depression of 1842 the town council and the Cart trustees were found to have over-reached themselves financially, and in view of this insolvency the financial affairs of both town and navigation were placed under control of parliamentary trustees in 1843; Robert Brown was appointed treasurer to the trustees. In addition, from 1840 he acted as agent for the Atlas Insurance Company. He thus acquired a considerable ability in financial accounting on the basis of learning by doing.

In the meantime a foundation was being laid for independent enterprises. As town chamberlain he handled applications for exploitation of mineral deposits in town land, and thus witnessed the expansion of brick-making in the locality, partly encouraged by the railway links being forged with Renfrew, Glasgow and Ayr in the mid-1830s. The lease for one particular brickfield in the north of Paisley was unwanted by railway contractors who had exploited it, and Robert Brown entered into a partnership to purchase it in 1840, to manufacture bricks, field drainage pipes and tiles. His partner was James Craig, an elderly experienced brick manufacturer who, perhaps significantly, had previously served as town chamberlain of Paisley.

In addition Robert Brown must have been aware of the involvement of prominent Paisley businessmen of the time in the rapidly expanding activity of share dealing, and have absorbed from his contacts with them the rudiments of trading in shares, complementing his growing capabilities in financial accounting. When, in 1845, he failed in his attempt to become treasurer of the Trustees of the Clyde Navigation, he nevertheless gave up his secure and highly appreciated tenure of the town chamberlainship in favour of the risky role of sharebroker in the hope of improving his financial position. Although it was not an auspicious time for an initiative in this direction - within two months of becoming the 59th member of the recently formed Glasgow Stock Exchange Association the 'mania' in railway shares collapsed and with it the volume of trading in shares - he clearly demonstrated an ability which attracted responsibility. In 1847 he was elected to the association's committee. Perhaps significantly, the chairman of the association was at that time James Watson, Paisley-born and schooled, broker to an influential Paisley draper, Peter Brough, whose successes in share dealing allowed him to become subsequently a significant benefactor to the town.

So between 1845 and 1852 Robert Brown pursued the unlikely combination of brick-making and stockbroking - arguably he was the first Paisley-based stockbroker. But with the balance moving in the direction of manufacturing due to the thinness of share broking, another opportunity arose which proved to be a decisive factor: he purchased a three-acre property in the west of Paisley containing a thick and high-quality deposit of fireclay, which had been discovered incidentally in a search for blackband ironstone deposits. Exploitation began under the name of the original partnership, even though Craig had died five years previously. In 1852 he resigned from the Stock Exchange and by 1853 Robert Brown was trading under his own name, and placing greater emphasis on the development of the Ferguslie Fireclay Works. In addition, he integrated brick-making with brick-building, both residential and industrial, in Greenock and Port Glasgow as well as Paisley.

The fireclay business flourished with the growing adoption in the town of coal as a domestic fuel, aided by its improved availability thanks to the railway; a demand was generated for firebricks and chimney cans. The housing boom of the late 1850s and 60s added to the impetus. A wider market was sought: depots were opened in Glasgow (1856), Belfast (1858), Greenock (1859), Dublin (1861) and export markets in USA were tapped; industrial applications were found, particularly retorts for use in the gas industry, also rapidly expanding; firebricks for use in foundries, and later plumbago crucibles for metal manufacture. Improved sewerage systems generated a demand for

pipes, and a new works was established by Robert Brown at Shortroods in Paisley in 1861. This was associated with a second mine to exploit the same fireclay seam, but there it was of lesser quality. Leases were entered into for the exploitation of clays in adjoining properties, linked by private railway from 1872. Sanitary earthenware was added to the range of products.

The capital for this expansion appears to have been raised by taking advantage of rising land prices and ploughing back trading profits in the earlier years of operations, placing the firm in a sufficiently strong position to weather the difficult conditions of later years. The land on which the Ferguslie Fireclay Works was established originally cost £450; by 1860 the £240 debt to Paisley Abbey (from which it seems the land had originally been purchased) had been repaid and the National Bank of Scotland was willing to lend £3,000 on the land as security for the purchase of Shortroods; by 1875 this had been repaid and the following year the same bank was prepared to advance £10,000 on the same security. Other property in Smithhills purchased by Robert Brown was good for £2,500 (also from the National Bank) in 1859 and £5,000 in 1878, by which time depressed trade necessitated borrowing to meet working capital requirements. By 1874 Robert Brown owned 34 acres of property in Paisley. By the collapse of the property boom it would appear that the fixed capital of the firm had been established. No substantial capital indebtedness remained by 1890.

Towards the end of the 1860s Robert Brown had been joined in business by his eldest son, John Brown, but he died in 1886. By 1885 his grandson, also Robert Brown, had become involved, eventually assuming a managerial role in the firm; he had effective charge of the firm from 1892/3, particularly during his grandfather's final illness. Robert Brown died on 6 May 1895, aged 84. His grandson, though one of the trustees of the estate, was appointed by the trustees to manage the business. Some trustees, however, had doubts as to the legality of this arrangement, and litigation was eventually initiated by one of Robert Brown's sons-in-law in 1899, culminating in the appointment of a Judicial Factor. This had an extremely detrimental effect on the profitability of the enterprise. In 1902 a company was formed to acquire the business from the trustees, with Robert Brown (grandson) as managing director, incorporating the old title as Robert Brown and Son Ltd. However, the momentum had been lost. After ups and downs of trade in the 1920s the company went into liquidation in 1934, nine years after the death of Robert Brown. Purchased by Associated Clay Industries and substantially expanded to cope with the post-war demand for sanitary ware for housing schemes, it eventually became part of a local competitor, Armitage Shanks, in 1976.

In addition to establishing a highly successful manufacturing business, Robert Brown became active in civic affairs. In 1854 he was elected unopposed to the town council, representing the Fourth Ward, succeeding Peter Brough. He was immediately appointed a junior magistrate, in the following year senior magistrate, and in 1856 he became Provost of Paisley. However he retired from the council at the end of his first term of office in 1859, becoming a Justice of the Peace. His efforts for the local community became focussed on education. The long-established Grammar School was at the time fragmented into separate English, Classical and Commercial Schools. Through Robert Brown's influence these were eventually united in new premises as the Paisley Academy in 1864. He subsequently became involved in the Paisley School Board after the Education (Scotland) Act of 1872. He also made significant contributions to the High Church, Paisley. He became an elder in 1839 whilst town chamberlain, a member of its Ecclesiastical Trustees from 1873 (chairman from 1875 to 1877), superintended its extensive renovation completed in 1880, and was a benefactor on more than one occasion. He also served on the restoration committee for Paisley Abbey in 1862.

His active involvement in party politics appears to have flourished in 1868, when he gave his enthusiastic support to the subsequently unsuccessful Conservative candidate Colonel Campbell, in the Parliamentary election. Thereafter he appears to have been instrumental in the foundation of the Paisley Conservative Association in 1878; he was elected president of it in that year, and continued as honorary vice president throughout the early 1880s. Despite his efforts, however, Paisley did not return a Conservative candidate during that period.

His schooling at Neilston, as well as having a material bearing on the course of his career, also left him with a lifelong interest in literature and the arts generally. During an ill-fated excursion into the grocery trade in Glasgow at the age of 16 he became a subscriber to the Bridgeton Library, the following year joining the New Street Library in Paisley. He attended theatrical performances and informal musical evenings in Paisley, and by 1844 had begun seriously to build up a library, which eventually included two Burns' manuscripts and a unique collection of books and pamphlets relating to Paisley and district. Between 1885 and 1886 he compiled extensive autobiographical notes. In the latter part of his life his literary interests blossomed into a series of publications: *History of the Paisley Grammar School* (1874); several memoirs of local poets - *Charles Fleming* (1878), *Ebenezer and Andrew Picken* (1879), *William Alexander* (1881) - and eventually a two-volume collection, *Paisley Poets* (1890); *History of the High Church, Paisley* (1880); a two-volume *History of Paisley* (1886); finally, a history of the *Paisley Burns Clubs* (1893). Burns appears to have been a special interest, and he became a member of the Paisley Burns Club in 1875, soon after its reconstitution, and president in 1877. He had broad historical interests as

well: he was a member of the Glasgow Archaeological Society, the Ayrshire and Galloway Archaeological Society, was made a Fellow of the Society of Antiquarians of Scotland in 1882 and was a member of the Scottish History Society from its inception in 1887. He also served on the management of the Paisley Free Library and Museum, the Philosophical Institution, and the Government School of Science and Art (subsequently the Paisley College of Technology).

Robert Brown married Isabella Henderson in 1838, the daughter of the sub-collector of assessed taxes in Paisley and niece of Andrew Henderson, painter and proverbialist. Although his wife gave birth to some 11 children several died in childhood, and he was survived by only one son and four daughters. His wife, who was five years his junior, died in 1898. His surviving son had gone to Australia and took no part in the continuation of the business. The bulk of Robert Brown's estate consisted of the assets of his business and his remaining properties in Paisley and Dublin.

Evidently a man of great personal ability, Robert Brown was able to take effective advantage of the circumstances in which he found himself, given considerable impetus by the education which he had received in such an accidental fashion. No doubt also the exigencies of economic circumstances during his early manhood exerted their own discipline. Whatever their origin his achievements spanned a wide range of practical and intellectual interests and involvements, and his contribution to the community of Paisley was substantial, even if overshadowed by those of such contemporary families as the Coats and the Clarks.

FREDERICK G HAY

SOURCES

Unpublished

Brown, R, Autobiographical notes and diaries

Published

Brown, R, *History of Paisley*, Vol II, Paisley, 1886
Glasgow Stock Exchange Association Records, 1844-1898, Glasgow, 1898
Paisley and Renfrewshire Gazette, 11 May 1895 and 5 June 1954
Paisley Daily Express, 7 May 1895

Alexander Willison BUCHAN,

Stoneware manufacturer; b. 20/6/1833, Portobello, s. of William Buchan, grocer and wine merchant, and Mary Willison; m. 2/8/1856, Hester Strover Hardy; 7 s., 4 d.; Founder, A W Buchan & Co, Portobello; d. 1/6/1914; g/v estate: £11,795 14s 11d.

Alexander Willison Buchan was born on 20 June 1833, one of five sons of William Buchan, grocer and wine merchant, in Portobello, near Edinburgh, and Mary Willison whom he had married in 1828. Nothing appears to be known about Alexander's education. In his early life he was employed in the Leith firm of Matthew Buchan & Co, spirit rectifiers and wine and spirit merchants. After they ceased business around 1858 he became a commercial traveller. Around 1867 he leased a long-established pottery in Portobello.

At that time the pottery was operated by the Tough family, in addition to their Musselburgh Pottery, manufacturing salt-glazed stoneware pottery. They in turn had purchased it from Milne and Smith in the 1850s, successors in 1848 to Milne Cornwall & Co. The pottery had originally been established towards the end of the eighteenth century by Antony Hilcote (or Hillcoat) according to Baird, by W & C Smith according to Fleming, or William Jameson according to McVeigh. Around the turn of the century or soon thereafter, it became the soapworks of George Morrison & Son, until their liquidation; in 1826 it was acquired by Creelman's Abercorn Brickworks, before being occupied by Hugh and Arthur Cornwall in 1830, when the manufacture of quality salt-glazed stoneware was resumed, continued in 1840 by Milne, Cornwall & Co.

Alexander Buchan took up the lease in partnership with Thomas F Murray, but not until four years later did he style himself 'stoneware manufacturer', continuing during these years as a commercial traveller, possibly in connection with the wine and spirit business. Murray may have been associated with the Caledonian Pottery, Glasgow. They traded as Murray and Buchan until Murray's retiral in 1877, whereupon the Portobello site was purchased and the title of A W Buchan & Co assumed. According to Baird the company initially produced decorative ware known as Portobello faience, before specialising in commercial dip-glazed stoneware, a proportion transfer-printed with customers' trade marks. The principal products became stoneware whisky jars (for the trade in Scotland and north of England) and cream and butter jars. Trade was built up in other utilitarian and commercial products: beer and ginger beer bottles, jam jars, varnish and rennet bottles. There is some evidence that a small amount of art pottery was also produced. A significant export trade was developed with South Africa and Canada. During part of this period Buchan designated the pottery the Waverley Potteries.

Alexander Buchan was joined in his business by one of his sons, Samuel Milne Buchan, who became a partner in 1890. Another son, Carlyle Buchan, also became a partner ten years later by which time the Waverley Potteries employed some 100 persons. Other sons did not enter the business. Of the other five, Matthew Buchan became an electrical engineer, for a time at the neighbouring Waverley Electric Works, while Robert Buchan became a concert violinist; both predeceased their father. There were also four daughters by Alexander's marriage to Hester Strover Hardy, grand-daughter of Admiral Hardy; she also predeceased her husband. Alexander Buchan died on 1 June, 1914.

With the introduction of casting plant in 1920 the firm developed new lines, chiefly hot-water bottles, while continuing established products, though the substitution of glass for many of these significantly reduced the market. During the Second World War principal items were rum jars for the Admiralty and, according to E McKinnon Buchan, Samuel Buchan's son, who joined the firm in 1921,

'at the request of the Board of Trade ... as many hot-water bottles as possible for the Home Market.'

The post-war situation entailed the introduction of more domestic lines and hand-painted artwares for both domestic and export markets in Canada, USA, South Africa, New Zealand and elsewhere. Following the death of Samuel in 1941 and Carlyle in 1949, the firm was continued by other members of the Buchan family at its original location, until 1972 when it was moved to new premises at Crieff, called the Thistle Potteries. Employment by 1948 was down to about 70, less than a third female, and currently is around 30.

At the time of his death in 1914 the bulk of Alexander Buchan's personal estate was a portfolio of stocks and shares covering a wide range of activities, many abroad including a number of mining companies. Two mortgage bonds on farms in the Orange Free State possibly testify to his travels in pursuit of markets for the products of his firm. Given the commercial nature of most of the wares produced by the Waverley Potteries the name of Buchan is not particularly well-known. He is significant perhaps more for keeping alive and bringing into the twentieth century the activity of stoneware pottery production, which once flourished so widely in Scotland.

FREDERICK G HAY

SOURCES

Published

Baird, W, *Annals of Duddingston and Portobello*, Edinburgh, 1898

Buchan, E McK, 'History of Stoneware Pottery in Edinburgh', *Journal of the Edinburgh Chamber of Commerce*, Vol XXX, 2, 1948

Cruickshank, G, 'Waverley Potteries, Portobello' in *Scottish Pottery Historical Review*, No 7, 1982

Fleming, J A, *Scottish Pottery*, Glasgow, 1923

McVeigh, P, *Scottish East Coast Potteries*, Edinburgh, 1979

Robert COCHRAN,

Earthenware manufacturer; b. 1811, Dumbarton, s. of Alexander Cochran, ship's master and Christian McFarlane; m. c 1838, Mary; 2 s., 1 d.; (2) c 1855, Agnes Gibb; 1 s., 1 d.; Partner, Robert Cochran & Co, Glasgow; d. 7/8/1869, Milngavie, Dunbartonshire; g/v UK estate: £50,339 11s 11d.

Robert Cochran was born in Dumbarton in 1811, one of at least three children of Alexander Cochran, ship's master, and Christian McFarlane. Nothing seems to be known of his childhood or education.

His earliest recorded business venture appears to have been in 1834, when he entered into partnership with James Couper (qv), then on the way to becoming an influential figure in the glass and ceramic industries in Glasgow. This partnership operated a glass and china warehouse at 36 Buchanan Street, formerly run by Archibald Geddes and Robert Alexander Kidston, pottery and glass manufacturers, trading as Geddes, Kidston & Co. The partnership continued and developed Couper's earlier involvement in the marketing of these products; it acted as agent for Kidston's Verreville Pottery, the Anderston Bottle Works of William Geddes and the Glasgow Flint Glass Company. Both partners appear to have become involved in manufacturing firstly in 1835 when in conjunction with John McCall they acquired the Port Dundas Pottery for a brief period. In 1838 the warehouse was disposed of, and the partnership took over the Albion Flint Glass Works, St Rollox, which had been established by James Rennie Geddes and others in 1836. The following year Alexander Cochran, Robert's brother, joined the partnership, and in 1842, when Couper left to become involved

successively in the Caledonian Pottery, the City Pottery and the City Flint Glass Works, the brothers' enterprise became known as A & R Cochran.

Around this time Robert's interests seem to have moved in the direction of pottery manufacture, possibly encouraged by his earlier role as agent for the Verreville Pottery. Certainly, by 1846 he had become the managing partner of the Verreville Pottery, along with Robert Alexander Kidston, who had purchased it some 12 years earlier from John Geddes; he in turn had been responsible for the introduction of pottery manufacture into what had been since 1777 an enterprise specialising in the production of fine crystal for the home and American export markets. After trading for a year as Kidston, Cochran & Co, Robert Cochran became sole partner, the firm's name changing to Robert Cochran & Co. Kidston, with earlier experience of china manufacture in Glasgow, had put considerable efforts into the development of the quality of the Verreville wares, bringing potters and decorators from renowned English potteries as well as from France and Flanders. However such elaborate and expensive china wares failed to find adequate markets. Robert Cochran reorientated the enterprise in the direction of mass production of domestic earthenware, and was responsible not only for the introduction of various labour-saving measures, but also for a number of patented innovations in pottery technology which subsequently became widely used. Fine china was replaced by more durable bodies such as 'Ironstone China' and 'White Granite', which were successful in both home and export markets in North America and Ireland. Handpainting gave way to transfer-printing, a much cheaper repetitive form of decoration suited to the mass market. J Arnold Fleming says of him:

'Robert Cochran ... had a better trained business mind than any of his predecessors. He gave Scottish pottery a tremendous impetus, and did not dissipate his energies on variety. Besides, he formed an extremely shrewd opinion of the limited capacities of his workers, and also the conditions of "potting" in Scotland. He, therefore, set himself to build up a large output of good, sound white domestic earthenware, nicely finished, and attractively but inexpensively decorated.'

Opportunites for opening new markets in Canada were favourable in the mid-nineteenth century and Robert Cochran endeavoured to take advantage of these. However, the four-acre site at the Verreville Pottery had by this time reached its capacity, and any further expansion of the business entailed the construction of an entirely new pottery. Adjacent to the St Rollox Flint Glass Works was vacant ground on which Robert Cochran was able to establish the new Britannia Pottery. Building commenced in 1857, and despite set-backs to the North American export trade due to the American Civil War it was eventually to provide employment for some 600 workers due to the success with which the firm exploited the mass production market, particularly for blue and white transfer ware. According to Fleming much of the finance for the construction and equipping of the pottery came from successful speculation in American dollars, an incidental benefit arising from Robert Cochran's efforts to establish pottery warehouses in Canada and America in those unsettled times. Certainly the pottery once completed was large and fully mechanised: the three-acre site was occupied by '... one of the largest potteries in the country at that time. Money was not spared in installing the best appliances available. ... Between Verreville and Britannia one of the first private telegraph connections were (sic) made in Scotland ... The whole layout of this factory was a great advance on any then existing, even the potteries in England had no finer plant. More machinery was placed in this factory than any previous one.'

The particular form of earthenware which represented such a significant component of the output of the Verreville and Britannia potteries required large quantities of calcined flint and Cornish stone. This had to be ground down before being used. Robert Cochran integrated the grinding of these and other materials into his business by the acquisition of the North Woodside and Garrioch Mills, Glasgow, both powered by water from the River Kelvin and originally employed for the milling of grain.

Partially paralysed for a few months before his death, Robert Cochran died on 7 August 1869, leaving a widow (his second wife), three sons and a daughter. The bulk of his personal estate of some £50,000 was his interest in his business. In his will he made arrangements for the Verreville and Britannia potteries to be purchased by Robert Cochran Jnr (his eldest son), Alexander Cochran (his second son) and James Fleming, (qv) who had operated the North American end of the business between 1858 and 1863, returning in that year to take over the management of the Britannia pottery. In the event, Robert Cochran Jnr became proprietor of the Verreville, while the Britannia continued under a partnership of Alexander Cochran and James Fleming, the latter continuing to manage the operation. Both establishments continued to trade under the name of Robert Cochran & Co, the Verreville until it ceased operations in 1918, and the Britannia until 1896, when J Arnold Fleming joined the partnership, the firm then becoming known as Cochran & Fleming; notwithstanding Alexander Cochran's retiral in 1902 the title was retained until Fleming sold the pottery to the Britannia Pottery Co Ltd, a partnership of the Wolfson family in Glasgow, in 1920. The firm ceased to trade in 1935 and was removed from the Register of Companies in 1954.

Despite apparently having no formal training either as a potter or as an engineer Robert Cochran, Snr, made a very considerable contribution to the development of the pottery industry in Glasgow. Evidently an astute businessman he had a clear appreciation of the type of product required by the emerging North American market and an ability to identify the technological developments which were necessary to ensure that such markets could be supplied at competitive prices. In 1861 he employed 550 workers (250 of them women and children), and by the 1880s the two potteries together possibly provided employment for over 1,000 workers, constituting probably the largest enterprise in the Glasgow pottery industry of the day.

FREDERICK G HAY

SOURCES

Unpublished

Quail, G, 'The Britannia Pottery', unpublished paper to the Scottish Pottery Society, 1982
SRO: SC 36/48/62, Inventory
    SC 36/51/56, Will

Published

Blench, B, 'The Elusive James Couper, Snr', *Scottish Pottery Historical Review*, No 8, 1984
Fleming, J A, *Scottish Pottery*, Glasgow, 1923
Industries of Glasgow, Glasgow, 1888

James COUPER,

Ceramic or glass retailer and manufacturer; b. 3/6/1797, s. of James Couper, Officer 3rd Battn, Royal Artillery; m. 1816, Mary Nicol; 4 s., 1 d.; Founder, James Couper & Sons, City Glassworks, City Pottery; d. 25/11/1884, Glasgow.

James Couper was one of the most influential figures in the ceramic and glass trade in Glasgow during much of the nineteenth century. Of his early life little is known apart from his marriage in 1816 and his reputedly having taken part in the attack on Harvey's dyke in 1823.

His first business venture was as owner of a 'china and stoneware' shop at 24 Candleriggs in 1826, to which was added glassware three years later. He sold the business to William Barr in 1834, at the same time entering into partnership with Robert Cochran (qv) in a 'glass and china showroom' at 36 Buchanan Street. The following year the two entered a partnership with John McCall to run the Port Dundas Pottery. This venture was shortlived and dissolved in 1835. Three years later the lease on the Buchanan Street warehouse ran out and the contents auctioned. Cochran and Couper then took over the running of the St Rollox Glass Works, carrying on dealing in china and earthenware, as well as glass, from the works till 1840, when Couper entered another partnership, with James Murray, running the Caledonian Pottery & Townhead Grinding Works, which continued till 1850.

In October 1850, Couper tried to lease a factory for his eldest son James (1821-1912) without success but in December of the following year he purchased

the land opposite Bell's Pottery in Dobbies Loan from the Edinburgh and Glasgow Railway Company: glass kilns were speedily established and the following year pottery kilns. The 'City Pottery' was heavily subsidised by profits from the 'City Glassworks' and in 1855 was leased to David Neil for 11 years but was sold in 1858, and incorporated into the glassworks. Two of his sons, James Jnr and Roderick Alison bore the burden of management along with William Haden Richardson of Stourbridge. The major development of the glassworks had little to do with James Snr who in 1852 was elected to the Town Council for the Provan ward.

Till the end of his life he lived on a fixed annual payment from the company and spent much of his time on civic duties. He was a radical and 'a Reformer in pre-Reform bill days', an advocate of Free Trade. He was associated with John McAdam in the radical movements of the latter part of the century, chaired the fund raising meeting for the defence of Watt and Park after the 'Cagliari' incident of 1857, received John Bright on his visit to Glasgow in 1858, and, as a supporter of Italian unification helped establish the Garibaldi Fund in 1864.

At a more local level, Couper served in various positions in many charities and institutions - as a preceptor of Hutcheson's Hospital, trustee of Glen's School, Anderson's College and Atkinson's bequest. He was on the council of the Philosophical Society of Glasgow, chairman of the Mechanics Institute, laying the foundation stone of its James Salmon Snr designed building in Bath Street in 1861. In 1870 he retired from the council but in 1877 he was appointed bailie of Provan for life.

In 1884 he established a trust to administer his interests. The trustees - his two sons James Jnr and William, with William Haden Richardson, were to administer all his properties and interests and to pay the income to him during his lifetime. With regard to the Glassworks of which he and James Jnr were joint proprietors he expressed the wish that his copartner should have the option of acquiring his interest on his death. When James Jnr took up this option in 1885 he paid £4,750.

James Couper Snr died on 25 November 1884 at the home of his son James Jnr, having established the most important of Glasgow's glassworks. *The Bailie* summarised his character as 'pleasant and chatty ... an agreeable and interesting companion ... above all things a Glasgow worthy'.

BRIAN BLENCH

SOURCES

Unpublished

Sederunt book of Trust of James Couper Snr, Strathclyde Regional Archive T- MS58
Quail, G, MS, The City Pottery, Glasgow

Published

The Bailie, 10 March 1880
Blench, B, *Scottish Pottery Historical Review 8*, 1983/4
Glasgow Post Office Directories
Quail, G, *Scottish Pottery Society Archive News 2,* Spring 1988

William DOUGLAS,

Firebrick manufacturer; b. 4/5/1855, Corshill, Dreghorn, Ayrshire, s. of John Douglas, tile manufacturer, and Jean Steel; m. Margaret Littlejohn; 4s. 1 d.; MD, Douglas Firebrick Co Ltd; d. 2/6/1937, Kilwinning, Ayrshire; g/v estate: £2,112.

William Douglas was the eldest of a family of two sons and one daughter. His father, John Douglas, was a tile maker and William was born at the tile works at Corshill near Dreghorn in 1855 where his father worked. Four years later the family moved to Stevenson where his father set up his own tile making business. There was then a substantial demand for the new cylindrical tiles to drain the water out of the stiff clays of much of the farmland in the west of Scotland. John Douglas was well placed to meet the local demands and it is clear that his business prospered.

William Douglas joined his father's business which developed from tile making into firebrick making. He quickly developed an interest in the geology of clays and an expertise which was very valuable in his father's line of business. By the 1880s William Douglas had become a member of the Glasgow Geological Society, and he quickly became known for his knowledge of fireclays in particular.

In the course of his work with his father William Douglas travelled extensively in the Ayrshire countryside seeking out fireclay deposits. This and his interest in geology convinced him that the Dalry district possessed commercially workable deposits of highly refractory fireclays. By 1910 he had located samples which he sent to London for testing and analyis by Mr J F Norman. The results confirmed Douglas' belief, and in 1911 he obtained an option on the lands of Monkcastle, and the following year he negotiated a lease with the landowner, Colonel Blair. The horizons of clay he then exploited were named 'Douglas Fireclays' by the Geological Survey of Great Britain, in recognition of his exploratory work. At the same time he collaborated with E M Anderson of the Geological Survey in investigating samples of clay revealed at low tide at Saltcoats on the Ayrshire coast. This proved to be a high quality bauxite clay, the Ayrshire bauxite clay, which Douglas then exploited in developing the production of high alumina firebricks.

William Douglas' leases of the lands of Monkcastle with its extensive Douglas fireclays, together with his commercial recognition of the potential of the Ayrshire bauxite clays, led him in his mid fifties to establish his own company, the Douglas Firebrick Co Ltd, near Dalry. After working with his father he had also become associated with the Lylestone Brickworks, but now he established his own company in three stages. His mine to work the Douglas Fireclays on the Monkcastle estate was opened early in 1912 adjacent to the Glasgow and South Western Railway Line. Within 18 months he added a quarry working the Ayrshire bauxite clays on the lands of High Smithstone. The following year, in May 1915, his firebrick works came into operation. He was by then confident of the quality of his clays, having used the Lylestone Brickworks as a pilot plant to test them in manufacture between 1912 and 1915.

The Scottish fireclay industry comprised a large number of relatively small producers together with a few large manufacturers like the Glenboig Union Fireclay Co and John G Stein & Co Ltd. The industry had begun in the 1830s in the Garnkirk and Glenboig districts of north Lanarkshire around the developing iron industry, and then extended into the Bonnybridge and Armadale areas. The Ayrshire district had never rivalled these centres of fireclay and firebrick production, and coming late into the industry, William Douglas built his success on the special qualities of his raw materials and of his products. He concentrated in producing high alumina bricks, with an alumina content in the range of 35/37% to 42/44%. His company made products in the highest quality end of the market; in addition to high alumina bricks he also manufactured bricks and products of special design and shape and insulating bricks, to meet the needs of almost every type of industrial furnace.

In the early days the entire output of his work was of hand moulded shapes, and the best craftsmen at the works could produce up to 3,000 squares a day, each brick measuring 9 ins × 4.5 ins × 3 ins. In the 1920s the arrival of a public electricity supply at the works enabled Douglas to introduce the semi-plastic brickmaking process for standard shapes and sizes; in the 1930s the dry-press process was undertaken to produce bricks of special shape and size. At the same time Douglas introduced the then new tunnel kilns fired with gas generated from anthracite in a fully mechanised production process.

Throughout these developments almost the entire output of the brickwork came from the Douglas Fireclays and Ayrshire bauxitic clays. Materials were only imported for the manufacture of a very few special products such as very high alumina content firebricks with alumina of 65% or more.

The market for the products of the Douglas Firebrick Co was dominantly local and Scottish, but from the outset of the company, Douglas had established a special relationship with the Morgan Crucible Co, based at Battersea. In 1915, impressed with a demonstration test of the Douglas Firebrick, Leonard Harvey of Morgan's furnace department had ordered a load of Douglas fireclay. Later that year Morgan ordered its first consignment of bricks and linings for their tilting furnaces. In the following year the Morgan Crucible Co gave Douglas a contract for 3,000 tons of refractory bricks, these to be produced in kilns similar to those in operation at their Battersea plant. Indeed the Morgan Co sent bricklayers from Battersea to Dalry to build the kilns. Such a specialised relationship quickly produced a financial and sales agreement between the two companies in November 1917. This link ultimately led to the Douglas Firebrick Co becoming a wholly owned subsidiary of the Morgan Crucible Co in February 1970.

William Douglas came relatively late to independent proprietorship and manufacture in the firebrick business. Even so, he never gave up his geological interests. His advice was widely sought on all matters relating to fireclays. Indeed he acted specifically as an adviser to the government Geological Survey Department, and was also for a time president of the Scottish Employers Council for Clay Industries. He remained very much a man of local interests. Married with four children, he lived in Kilwinning close by his works, and was involved in the Dalry Parish Council, and in recreation was a member of the Kilwinning curling club. He continued actively to manage his business and died in harness in his eighty-third year, having previously taken steps to secure the future of the company by transferring shares to his sons. His successful transfer of his interests in his own company meant that he largely escaped the attention of the tax man; his personal estate at death was valued at only £2,112, an improbable indicator of his achievement in a long and successful business and geological career.

ANTHONY SLAVEN

SOURCES

Unpublished
SRO: SC 6/44/120, Inventory
      SC 6/46/64

Published
The British Clayworker, June 1937

Douglas, Richmond, 'The Evolution of the Refractories Industry in Scotland and some outstanding personalities associated with it', Presidential Address, The British Ceramic Society, *Transactions of the British Ceramic Society*, Vol 55, No 12, December 1956

Douglas, Richmond, 'The Douglas Firebrick Co Ltd, Its Origin and Development 1910-1970', *Kilmarnock Weekly Standard*, 7/9/1970

Glasgow Herald, 4/6/1937

Kilmarnock Herald and Ayrshire Gazette, 5/6/1937

James DUNNACHIE,

Firebrick manufacturer; b. 1835, Pollokshaws, Renfrewshire, s. of William Dunnachie, bleacher, and Martha Ramsay; m. (1) Jane Henry, 20/8/1860; m. (2) Elizabeth Levack; 3 s., 2 d.; MD, Glenboig Union Fireclay Co Ltd, Glenboig; d. 8/1/1921, Glenboig, Lanarkshire; g/v estate: £10,297 16s 2d.

James Dunnachie was one of the most important entrepreneurs of the Scottish fireclay industry and his rise to prominence was linked closely with the development of the brick industry in the West of Scotland and in particular with the Glenboig Union Fireclay Co Ltd. The Glenboig fireclay brick became famous world-wide in the late nineteenth century and early twentieth century due to two factors. The first was the excellent quality of the natural mineral resources of the Glenboig clayfields and the second was the entrepreneurial expertise and innovative skill of James Dunnachie.

The importance of refractory materials to many branches of industry, not least those of iron and steel, cannot be underestimated and with the growth of the iron and steel trades in the West of Scotland in the nineteenth century there came the development of the firebrick industry. As the new steel production methods of Bessemer and Siemens-Martin open-hearth developed, a demand arose for a suitable type of brick which would withstand very high temperatures without expanding or contracting. The Glenboig product was one of the main ones to meet that need with properties largely alkali free and with a high degree of infusibility.

There had been a brickworks on a small scale at Glenboig since 1836 under the managements of John Hillcoat, John Thomson and Messrs Thomson MacLean & Co respectively. In 1860 James Dunnachie, then aged 25 years, took up the post of manager to Thomson MacLean & Co. Five years later when one of the partners died and another retired, Dunnachie took over the business. He formed the Glenboig Fireclay Co with two partners, John Hurll and John Young, firebrick manufacturers in the neighbouring areas of Garnkirk and Heathfield.

This partnership was dissolved in 1872 with Hurll and his two sons Peter and Mark (qv) continuing to trade at the old works and Dunnachie leasing the six-sevenths unlet portion of the Glenboig clayfield to build the Star works under the name of James Dunnachie & Co. His partners now were James Craig, a coal and brick master in his own right in Kilmarnock,

COURTESY OF THE MITCHELL LIBRARY

and John Wilson, a Glasgow tube manufacturer and later Liberal MP for Govan.

James Dunnachie and Co made a bright start to its business. Dunnachie had already begun to develop his inventive skill with a patent in 1870 for a brick drying stove, and in 1876 at the British Association's Glasgow meeting he exhibited a Glenboig Fireclay Bessemer Tuyere. Major awards were received between 1875 and 1882 from many international exhibitions including Melbourne, Sydney, Paris and London, reflecting the high quality product which the Glenboig clay produced. In addition to this, further fame came to Dunnachie and Glenboig when he took out a patent for a continuous regenerative gas kiln in 1881. This was applauded by metallurgists and scientific experts and was reckoned to be the earliest development of the application of gas to firebrick burning. Many people, including Sir William Siemens, had tried to develop such a regenerative kiln without much success. Previous kilns had wasted fuel in the manufacturing process and there was much heat wastage as the bricks cooled down. The basic principle was to regenerate the heat contained within the actual manufacturing process. Dunnachie's kiln consisted of ten chambers with two 4 cwt gas producers and was sufficiently different in method from the Siemens' system to merit the patent being taken out.

The Dunnachie kiln was a simple construction which enabled temperatures within the kiln to be regulated and the mixture of air and gas to be controlled; it also permitted the use of cheap slag as fuel with considerable savings in fuel costs. It also upgraded working conditions by improving the atmosphere in which the men had to work; increased output and reduced labour costs were also achieved. It was estimated by Dr Thomas Egelston, an American scientist who had visited the works and later presented a paper on the Dunnachie kiln, that savings in the cost of manufacture amounted to almost 75% over previous systems. The new process enabled 300,000 bricks to be manufactured per month. The older method using the Newcastle kiln was reckoned to produce a costing of 8s 2d per thousand bricks. The Dunnachie hopper kiln, another invention in 1865 which was the forerunner of the regenerative kiln, reduced this to 6s 6d per thousand but the gas regenerative kiln reduced this even further to 2s 9d per thousand. In 1885 Frederick Siemens purchased an interest in the patent which was licensed to various producers in several of the American states.

Dunnachie and his Star works developed successfully in Glenboig for ten years side by side with the Glenboig Fireclay Co of John Hurll. But by 1882, despite Dunnachie's inventive success, sharpening competition for markets in a period of recession in iron and steel making forced the two Glenboig operations to amalgamate to form the Glenboig Union Fireclay Co Ltd. The authorised capital was £150,000 in £10 shares. John Hurll was chairman, his son

Peter, secretary, and James Dunnachie was appointed managing director. Restrictions were placed on the Hurlls to prevent them from trading separately in the same business for a period of 15 years. Competition may have been one spur to the amalgamation, but the Hurlls were obviously attracted also by Dunnachie's patent for his new gas kiln and by his 31 year lease over the Glenboig clayfields.

Following the merger, works were opened in Cumbernauld in 1882, Gartcosh in 1890 and the Gartsherrie clayfields in 1896. Much of this resulted from a fear of competition and a jealous guarding of the Glenboig position. Innovations were made regularly and earned the works the descriptive labels of 'modern' and 'model': these included a laboratory for the chemical analysis of the various products and for the control of production quality. Dunnachie's son, Archibald, was employed as chemist. A telephone was installed in 1887 and electric lighting in 1894. Throughout the period from 1882 - 1914 a new plant was installed, old machines and kilns updated. In the mid 1880s contemporaries touring the works spoke of a water reservoir and filtration process which supplied pure water to workmen's dwellings. They also noted large numbers of workers' houses in Glenboig which were company built and the presence of a school and chapel.

In a very short space of time markets were extended throughout the globe. Dunnachie travelled extensively seeking new markets, and indeed, any new methods. This vigorous sales policy was reinforced with the appointment of agents in Russia, America, Canada and elsewhere. A trade catalogue of 1893 listed over 400 products ranging from ordinary firebricks to pipes, chimney cans and ornamental garden ware. In the UK important contracts were held with the Royal Arsenal and the Admiralty. The company was also sole makers for Scotland of basic bricks for the Gilchrist-Thomas dephosphorising process. By 1920 fifty awards or medals had been received for the company's products at international exhibitions.

Yet, despite these obviously successful indicators, as managing director, Dunnachie's business life was not without problems and crises. Litigation was brought in 1883 against John Young, the former partner, who had been using the Glenboig trade name on his own bricks. An ex-employee, John G Stein (qv), set up a rival company after a disagreement in 1886 and quickly became one of the Glenboig company's toughest rivals. Indeed, there were several such episodes for Dunnachie and his directors over the use of the name Glenboig on bricks which had not been produced by their company. The Dunnachie kiln was not available to the Scottish firebrick industry, the company reserving the patent rights over the use of the kiln.

In general, the apparent prosperity and international reputation of the Glenboig Union Fireclay Co concealed a less happy picture. Dunnachie had to enforce a series of wage reductions in 1884, 1885 and

1892 in trade recession: the company also had to raise bank finance to meet its immediate needs in 1884 and 1893. The restrictive trade agreement with the Hurlls, preventing them from trading independently in the business, also provoked disagreement, and in 1888 they left the new company in a dispute when Hurll's sons were discovered carrying out test borings in the area.

The years from 1882 to 1893 were therefore marked by fluctuating fortunes, but from 1895 to 1914 the company enjoyed a resurgence of activity with increased sales and improved dividends. In 1883 sales figures totalled £74,156 giving profits of £9,030 and a dividend of 9%: after fluctuation in the 1890s, sales reached £136,574 in 1906: profits were recorded as £28,725 and dividends were paid at 12.5%. The company had for a decade thus been the largest of its kind in the world employing over 600 persons including 50 moulders. Glenboig was then a village of over 1,300 people. This compared with 120 people in 1861 when only one moulder had been at work. Dunnachie's enterprise had transformed not only the brick industry and his company, but the village and district of Glenboig itself.

Even then all was not plain sailing: labour relations at Glenboig were reputedly always smooth and cordial, but a ten month strike for higher wages in 1901 by clay miners severely disrupted production and Dunnachie carried out his threat to employ a professional strike-breaker who put Lithuanian workers in to replace the miners. Litigation also continued to pursue the company, and from 1908-1911 Dunnachie was involved in a law suit against the Caledonian Railway Co over the right to extract minerals under the Garnkirk junction: a legal wrangle with the income tax authorities further detracted from the straight run of success.

Dunnachie had effectively managed the business since its inception, and he ultimately became chairman in 1900 on the death of John Wilson. Shortly after, in 1910, with some 50 years in the business, Dunnachie withdrew to semi-retirement. His son, James Jnr, who had been general manager of the brickworks department then joined the Board. In 1920, after 60 years association with the company, the workers honoured him with a special celebration in Glenboig, presenting him with a testimonial gift.

Unlike some of his business associates, Dunnachie confined his business sphere of activity to the Glenboig company. He held only one other directorship, in the New Zealand Crown Mines Co Ltd for a short period. As an employer, he took part in early attempts to form a Fireclay Manufacturers Association in the late 1880s, the main purpose being to regulate prices. This Association did not last long, and it was only in 1917 that a British Association was formed with a separate Scottish Council. Dunnachie, however, was president of a British Clay Workers Association in the 1890s.

Little is known of Dunnachie's earlier life, prior to

Sir James Fleming

his arrival in Glenboig in 1860. This was the year in which he married for the first time and information from the marriage certificate suggests that his occupation was a commission agent. His father was a bleacher and a strict teetotaller. Dunnachie's brother, Thomas who became works manager in 1874, had previously been a school teacher and was well known as a lay preacher and lecturer to the Scottish Temperance League. Dunnachie followed the family tradition in his support of the temperance movement in which both he and John Wilson, chairman and former partner, were active. He served on the District Licensing Court in Airdrie as well as being a Justice of the Peace for the County of Lanark in 1898. In politics he was a Liberal Unionist but he declined to stand for office in any municipal or parliamentary election. His other interests included active membership of the Clan Donnachie Society. He studied fine art, and possessed a valuable collection of modern art. His will reflected this interest, with its main preoccupation being the disposal of items to his family.

In his lifetime he was responsible for the setting up of the Workmen's Institute in Glenboig. During the First World War, Dunnachie's initiative on behalf of the Red Cross Society transformed the Institute into a war hospital with 60 beds. Despite Dunnachie's contribution to the development of Glenboig it has been noted by Harold, a historian of the Glenboig company, that there is no lasting memorial to Dunnachie in Glenboig, not even a street named after him.

When Dunnachie died on 8 January, 1921, just a few weeks after his sixtieth anniversary celebrations, he left a very modest estate of £10,297 16s 2d, some few thousand short of the £20,000 plus 2d per ton royalties which he received in 1882 when the company bought over his patent rights. He left a widow, his son James and two married daughters, his sons, Archibald and William having died in 1904 and 1917.

SHEILA HAMILTON

SOURCES

Unpublished

Companies Registration Office: SC 1150, Glenboig Union Fireclay Co Ltd, Company file
Harold, J, 'The Glenboig Union Fireclay Co Ltd, 1882-1921', unpublished undergraduate dissertation, Department of History, University of Strathclyde, 1972
Information from Hepworth Ceramics Ltd, Sheffield
Register of Sasines, 1879
SRO: SC 35/31/19, Inventory
SC 35/33/7, Will

Published

Airdrie and Coatbridge Advertiser, 1/1/1921, 15/1/1921
The Bailie, 'Men You Know Series', No 1525, 1902
British Clayworker, November 1920, February 1921
Directory of Directors, 1891, 1901, 1911
Gaskell, E, *Lanarkshire Leaders*, London, 1908
Glasgow Contemporaries at the Dawn of the Twentieth Century, Glasgow, 1901
Glasgow Herald, 10/1/1921
Glasgow Today, 1901
Patents Records, Mitchell Library
Rhodes, Daniel, *Kilns, Construction and Operation*, London, 1968
Singer, F and Singer, S S, *Industrial Ceramics*, London, 1963
Stock Exchange Official Year Books
Stratten & Stratten, *Glasgow and Its Environs*, London, 1891
Transactions of American Institute of Mining Engineer, Vol XV, 1886-7

Sir James FLEMING,

Pottery manufacturer; b. 1831, Rutherglen, s. of John Fleming, millwright and Ann Pinkerton; m. 7/2/1871, Mary, d. of James Smellie, grocer; 2 s., 1 d.; Partner, Cochran & Fleming; Ch, West of Scotland Insurance Office Ltd; Dir, Scottish Reinsurance Co Ltd; d. 24/5/1914, Rutherglen; g/v UK estate: £70,242 4s 1d.

James Fleming was born in Rutherglen in 1831, one of at least four children (two sons and two daughters) of John Fleming, a millwright, and Ann Pinkerton. His school education was obtained initially at Rutherglen Parish School, and subsequently in Glasgow at the School of Art. He received military training in the Rutherglen Company of the Blythswood Highland Light Infantry.

Intending to enter the legal profession, he worked in a Glasgow law office for a short period before taking the decisive step around 1850 of becoming a clerk in the firm of Robert Cochran & Co, earthenware manufacturers, proprietors of the long-established Verreville Pottery in Glasgow. His progress there was such as to merit his being appointed at the age of 27 to take over the firm's warehouse in Montreal, opened two years earlier to provide a base for exploitation of the rapidly growing North America market; this initiative was complemented by the firm starting construction of much-enlarged capacity in the form of the entirely new Britannia Pottery in Glasgow. After the Canadian operation had been moved to Toronto, the bottom fell out of the trade with the outbreak of the American Civil War in 1861. His earlier military training equipped him for service in the Northern Army; in turn this left him with first-hand experience of the disruption of the war-riven American economy and led to his encouraging the proprietor of his firm, Robert Cochran (qv), to speculate in the considerably depreciated American currency. The success of this venture provided sufficient capital to allow the enlargement of the Britannia Pottery so that the company was well positioned to benefit from the rapid expansion of trading opportunities when hostilities ended.

James Fleming returned to Scotland in 1863, and was appointed manager of the Britannia Pottery - one of the largest potteries in the country at that time - at the age of 32. Six years later, on the death of Robert Cochran, Alexander Cochran, his younger son, entered into a partnership with James Fleming to operate the Britannia Pottery, the latter continuing as managing partner. They were joined in partnership by J Arnold Fleming, James' eldest son, in 1896, the title of the firm changing to Cochran and Fleming.

James Fleming retired in 1911, his son carrying on the business until its sale in 1920. His involvement in pottery manufacture was not limited to Glasgow: according to Arnold Fleming he was for many years a partner with W H Grindley in the Woodland Pottery, Turnstall, and his younger son J Hamilton Fleming became a director of that company. Nor was pottery his only business involvement. James Fleming was also vice chairman and subsequently chairman of the West of Scotland Insurance Office Ltd, a position he occupied until his death; he was a trustee of the City and County House Purchase Company, and a director of the Scottish Reinsurance Company Ltd, John Gray & Company Ltd and the Heritable Investment Bank Ltd.

From 1863 James Fleming found himself managing a large, modern and highly mechanised pottery with already-established overseas and domestic trade connections (including a London showroom in Holborn), operating at least initially in a buoyant market. What was required of him was to ensure the smooth operation of the business and a steady succession of product design changes - new shapes of wares and new patterns - to maintain the firm's market position. The former appears to have been attained at least in part due to his sympathetic personality, his concern for the well-being of his workers and their conditions, and his own energetic involvement in the firm. In 1871 he moved his residence from Rutherglen to Glasgow to be nearer the works. (Alexander Cochran, his partner from 1869 to 1902 appears to have preferred a subsidiary role in the firm and he moved from the family home in Glasgow to Crawfurdland near Kilmarnock, and later Kilwinning in the mid-1870s). The succession of new shapes and patterns, some specific to particular American, Colonial and Eastern markets, is well documented and was achieved by the employment of a number of able designers, decorators and engravers. His own early education at the Government School of Design in Ingram Street, precursor from 1840 of the Glasgow School of Art, together with the requirements of his business, left him convinced of the necessity of sound training in art and design as a means of preserving Britain's position in an increasingly competitive trading world. Accordingly he devoted a growing proportion of his energies to furthering the provision of education in general, and art education in particular, and it is in respect of the latter that his contributions were given public recognition. His first public responsibility was to commence six years' service on the Glasgow School Board, created by the Scottish Education Act of 1872; he was elected to it by a substantial majority in 1879 as the Free Education candidate, a testimony to the Liberal sentiments which he apparently upheld in his youth. During his period of service he became chairman of the Teachers and Teaching Committee, and, significantly, chairman of the Science and Art Classes Committee.

In 1882 he was appointed a governor of the Glasgow

School of Art and a Trustee of its associated Haldane Academy, in 1887 becoming chairman in succession to Sir James Watson (qv). *The Bailie* said of him: 'Mr Fleming's assumption of office marked the beginning of a new era for the School; he imparted energy to all its operations, and devoted himself heart and soul to the furtherance of its best interests ... the citizens of Glasgow should never forget the obligations they are under to him for the judicious and well-directed manner in which he has started and fostered schemes that had in view the promotion in our midst of sound and progressive practical art knowledge'. Under his chairmanship the young and dynamic headmaster of the school, Francis H Newbery, was given support for a number of innovations which assisted the school to attain national and international standing. Newbery shared James Fleming's conviction of the importance of links between design and industry and commerce, and a major step forward was the establishment of the Technical Art Studios in 1892, to offer 'a complete cycle of Technical Artistic Education applicable to the Industrial Arts of the City of Glasgow.'

By 1892 the Governing Board had been reconstituted to give representation to the principal public bodies in the city. Haldane Academy had disappeared from its title, and concerted efforts had been begun to provide a custom-built Glasgow School of Art to replace the dark and cramped Corporation Buildings in Sauchiehall Street to which the School had moved from Ingram Street in 1869. James Fleming played a leading part, in conjunction with Francis Newbery, in raising funds from various sources; The Bellahouston Trustees £10,000, the Corporation of Glasgow £5,000, the Government £15,000, two public subscriptions, approximately £30,000. Cautiously planned and executed in two stages the first was begun in 1896 and completed the following year, and the second in 1907, completed in 1909. Inevitably more memorable than the conception, administration and funding of this major development in art education in Glasgow was the inspired choice of architect in Charles Rennie Mackintosh.

James Fleming had other educational commitments: on his retirement from the Glasgow School Board he was appointed a member of the City Educational Endowments Board, which he remained for several years; he was a governor of the Royal Technical College; he was a member of the Rutherglen School Board. He had a special interest in the welfare of Rutherglen, his birthplace, and returned around 1888 to reside in Woodburn for the remainder of his life. On the artistic side of his life he was a member of the Royal Glasgow Institute of Fine Arts and the Glasgow Art Club, and at the interface between art and industry he was convener of the section of the Glasgow International Exhibition of 1901, devoted to Applied and Industrial Art. His own business had exhibited under the name of Robert Cochran & Company Ltd at the 1888 exhibition, and as Cochran and Fleming at the 1901, 1905 and 1911 exhibitions.

A Liberal from the start, his involvement in party politics was limited to the local stage, though his activity there was considerable, as was his influence. He became member and president of the Glasgow Liberal Council, and was a founder-member and one-time chairman of the Glasgow Liberal Club. He resolutely resisted overtures to become a parliamentary candidate or even a town councillor, however, a stance attributed by his obituarist to his 'retiring disposition, and modest ambition' which perhaps unusually accompanied such energy and determination. W S Murphy saw irony in the fact that 'so fervent a believer in popular franchise should find his chief channels to public service on non-elective boards' (p 241). He was also involved actively in the temperance movement, and was a member of the United Free Church; he was a Justice of the Peace for Glasgow and for Lanarkshire; he was a generous contributor to Rutherglen charities and towards the end of his life he donated a bandstand for Overtoun Park, Rutherglen.

James Fleming died on 24 May 1914, at the age of 82. He had been predeceased by his wife Mary Smellie or Smillie, and was survived by two sons, John Arnold Fleming and James Hamilton Fleming, and one daughter Alice Mary Fleming. As none was yet 21 years old in 1892, the date of a codicil to his will, it seems that he may have married relatively late in life - possibly in the late 1870's. At his death he left a personal estate of over £70,000, of which nearly £56,000 was in commercial stocks and shares covering a range of interests but with a preponderance of railways, shipping and mines, both in Britain and abroad, largely North and South America. In addition he had a heritable estate of over £20,000. In recognition of his varied public services he was knighted by King Edward VII in November 1906.

Very evidently a man of considerable energy and foresight, he combined the management of a highly successful pottery company, employing upwards of 400 workers (in 1888), with a productive involvement in public affairs of an essentially local scope. Even although he was not responsible for the foundation of either the commercial or the educational institution with which he is primarily associated, he had the vision and determination to initiate appropriate developments of them, and the temperament to convince others of their desirability - an inspired manager rather than an entrepreneur in the classical sense.

FREDERICK G HAY

SOURCES

Unpublished

Quail, G, *The Britannia Pottery*, unpublished paper

to the Scottish Pottery Society, Glasgow Branch, 1982
SRO: SC 36/48/254, Inventory
SC 36/51/166, Will

Published

The Bailie, No 1418, 20/12/1899
British Clayworker, June 1914
Fleming, J A, *Scottish Pottery*, Glasgow, 1923
Glasgow Herald, 9/11/1906, 25/5/1914, 28/5/1914
The Glasgow Style, 1890-1920, Glasgow Museum and Art Galleries, Glasgow, 1984
Industries of Glasgow, Glasgow, 1888
Murphy, W S, *Captains of Industry*, Glasgow, 1901

John HOWIE,

Fireclay manufacturer and coalmaster; b. 1833, Newhouse, Hurlford, Ayrshire, s. of William Howie, coalmaster and Margaret Paterson; m. Mary Paterson; 3 s., 2 d.; Founder and Partner of J & R Howie, Fireclay Manufacturers, Hurlford; Dir. Hurlford and Skerrington Collieries and Plann Brickwork, Crosshouse; d. 22/9/1895, Newhouse, Hurlford; g/v estate: £43,874 14s 11d.

The history of the Howie family of Newhouse, Hurlford, mirrored the social and economic changes of central Ayrshire during the nineteenth century. They took full advantage of the opportunities which came their way, firstly on the agricultural and then on the industrial scene, and the career of John Howie, coalmaster and fireclay manufacturer, marked the culmination of the family fortunes. Many of those who were to become leaders in the industrial field benefited from initiatives during the eighteenth century agricultural improvements in which Ayrshire played a large part. On the break-up of the Earl of Marchmont's estates in the county in the 1770s, Howie's paternal grandfather bought the farm of Parkhouse at Hurlford, inclusive of mineral rights. By the end of the Napoleonic Wars, coal extraction had begun on the adjacent lands of Skerrington and Barleith and within a few years William Howie, father of John, had joined those who were first to reach the main coal by opening up pits on his small estate, attached to the newly built residence at Newhouse.

At this period coal was mined for a limited local market for use in lime burning, tile-drain production and for domestic consumption. Primitive communications prevented rapid exploitation, but as early as 1819 coal depots had been established in Kilmarnock and long lines of carts, travelling from Hurlford, were supplying a growing demand for the excellent household coal of the district. William Howie promptly became associated with this trade. As the century progressed Kilmarnock was transformed from the busy market town, familiar to Robert Burns in the 1780s, to a rapidly expanding manufacturing centre. The combined parishes of Kilmarnock and Riccarton had grown from 12,000 in 1811 to 26,000 by 1851, engaged chiefly in the production of carpets and textiles, and boots and shoes, based on the raw materials of the surrounding farming area. Economic activity quickened pace with the spread of the railway into Ayrshire, with a connection to Kilmarnock in 1843 and, on the construction of the Portland Iron Works in 1846, an extension to Hurlford.

William Howie died in 1852, leaving to his son John a number of productive coalmines. Very early he was aware of the value of a by-product of his pits and within a year had built a brickworks. The coal seams lying between Dalry and Hurlford rested on rich beds of fireclay. The clay was extracted with the coal, and as a necessary process in production, by weathering, could be stored in bings for future use in the manufacture of high-grade building bricks. Demand was already high with the railway acting both as customer and distributor and, with a boom in the construction industry, in the provision of factories and houses in the Kilmarnock district and throughout the west of Scotland. The market for coal might occasionally falter during the second half of the century, but with successive new developments the appetite for fireclay goods continued unabated.

The courage and enterprise of a youth of 20 to start off in a new direction, albeit on the strength of inherited collieries, were matched by the skill with which he mastered the techniques of production, and recruited a workforce which would make the firm one of the leading manufacturers of fireclay wares in volume, appearance and quality. All his life Howie was alert to new opportunities for his products. The first divergence from brick-making was to meet the needs of farmers with large herds of cattle in a district which specialised in dairy farming. He started to exhibit at cattle shows run by the numerous agricultural societies, first locally and then nationally, and within a few years had won over 100 major prizes. To the general run of domestic fireclay goods, chimney cans, sinks and washing tubs, butter crocks and pickling dishes, vases, garden edging and finials, a wide range of agricultural products was added, including cattle and pig troughs, horse mangers, stable bricks and milk coolers. These encouraged the development of the high quality glazes, essential for hygienic handling in the home and farm, which became known in the trade as Hurlford yellow-glazed ware. The firm was also renowned for its patent water filter which was a market leader for a number of years.

The fireclay of the district excelled in the pottery field for strength and durability, and its capacity to withstand physical and thermal shock. It was used as a refractory in all the industries where heat-resistant materials were an integral feature of production, but primarily in the coal-gas industry which burgeoned during the second half of the nineteenth century. John Howie's business quickly expanded into this sphere, and he followed up with the production of drain and sewerage pipes on a large scale for the water supply industry and public and private sewerage systems, after the passing of the Public Health Act of 1875. His firm's fireclay pipes were made impermeable by the application of an internal glass lining and an external salt glaze and were supplied in vast quantities throughout Great Britain and Ireland. Foreign orders were never of major importance in the history of the firm, although a good, steady trade was maintained last century in Europe and in colonial territories, and latterly through agents in South America, principally to Argentina and Uruguay.

In 1867 John Howie's younger brother, Robert, had become a partner. Educated at the Andersonian University and the University of Edinburgh, he made little impact on the firm before he died in 1871, leaving John once again sole partner in the enterprise. By 1875 the works covered more than three acres and contained five steam engines, brick-making machinery, two sanitary pipe-making machines, five pan mills and a pug mill, as well as brick and paving-tile presses and the numerous moulds necessary for an ever-widening variety of products. In 1886 Plann Brickwork situated near Crosshouse railway station was acquired and thereafter the manufacture of sewerage pipes and fittings, chimney cans, vent linings and ridge tiles was mainly concentrated there, while vitreous enamelled fireclay products were developed at Hurlford. Plann proved a valuable asset in times ahead, not only for its established brickwork, but also for the opencast clay and deep-mined coal and clay pits in the vicinity. They replaced the collieries in Hurlford, nearing exhaustion, the last of which were lost through flooding in the 1920s. Seven collieries were in turn opened up around Crosshouse, securing supplies of coal and fireclay for the future. Even before the acquisition of the Plann works the industry originally based on a by-product had pushed Howie's mining operations into a subsidiary position. It is doubtful, however, if the numbers employed at both plants ever exceeded 500 and, with increased mechanisation, that figure was further depressed in later years until it settled at approximately 200 at Hurlford and 150 at Plann.

In the last 20 years of his life John Howie continued to be the driving force of his firm. During that period emphasis was placed on the manufacture of the sanitary ware which characterised the lasting reputation of the company. Described as vitreous enamelled fireclay, it was in essence fireclay with a white glaze finish, produced by an engobe of china clay imported from Cornwall. Giving a hard lustrous surface it was resistant to abrasions, stains and heat and the sanitary wares produced from it were most suitable for use in schools, hospitals, laboratories and factories. White and coloured facing-bricks were also copiously manufactured for slaughter houses, underground stations, common entries, public lavatories and wash-houses, adding a distinctive feature to late Victorian and Edwardian architecture.

With the multiplication of water supply schemes at the end of the nineteenth century, and a limitless demand for sanitary ware operating, John Howie died in 1895, leaving the business in a strong competitive position in this and in the more traditional products of the firm. The value of his estate was £43,874 of which a quarter came from lucrative investments in five continents, notably in mining companies in Southern Africa, North and South America and Australia. His penchant for speculation involved him in ownership of shares in more than 70 companies, the great majority in gold mining in South Africa, including a highly desirable stake in the Consolidated Gold Fields. He had widespread interests in transport companies, service industries and in property at home and abroad, one-fifth share in the Saline Valley Coal Co, Dunfermline and a £3,000 investment in J Gebbie & Co, Lace Manufacturers, Kilmarnock. Much of his leisure time must have been devoted to studying the market.

A lifelong Conservative in politics Howie took little part in public affairs, but was for a time an elder in the established church at Hurlford and chairman of Riccarton School Board. His charitable activities included the distribution of coal each winter to the poor of the district, and the houses he provided for his miners were generally of a higher standard than elsewhere in the Ayrshire coalfield. The paternalist attitude of many of last century's employers was also present in John Howie, but he appeared to go further in his responsibility towards the firm, its employees and their dependents. From the terms of his will he seemed to believe that even his natural heirs might not be worthy enough to inherit. He requested that the 15 acres of land at Hurlford, used for the brickwork and fireclay manufacture, along with the workmen's houses, be offered to his three young sons 'if they are fit to run the business, if not, to sell as a going concern.'

As it transpired his eldest son, Fred C Howie, continued the style and practice of management established during his father's lifetime, and set the standard for another half century. There was strict supervision in all the company's arrangements with careful selection of sales and technical staff, quality control, good business methods in attention to correspondence and liaison with customers, and a highly efficient troop of salesmen soliciting orders and specifications throughout the country. In 1903 Howie's was registered as a limited company with a nominal capital of 80,000 £1 shares the bulk of which was divided equally among the three sons and two daughters. The eldest son became managing director, while the younger sons, Robert and Henry, entered the firm as managers of the company's pits and of the Plann Fireclay Works at Crosshouse. J & R Howie & Co entered a period of expansion with the erection of new kilns and the introduction of modern production methods. With continually updated designs and wider ranges of sanitary ware it kept abreast of its chief competitors, leading to a further allocation in 1931 of £60,000 in 10% cumulative preference shares. An obituary of John Howie mentions his indomitable perseverence and assiduous attention to duty. No doubt he was totally immersed in the affairs of his business and took pleasure in them, but after he died at the age of 62 others enjoyed the fruits of his creation.

JAMES MAIR

SOURCES

Unpublished

Catalogue of Vitreous Enamelled Fireclay Sanitary Ware, J & R Howie, n d.
SRO: SC 6/44/58, Inventory
        SC 6/46/25, Will

Published

Kilmarnock Herald, 28/9/1895
Kilmarnock Standard, 28/9/1895
The Weekly Supplement, 15/11/1888 and 14/3/1890
Wilson, Matthew, *The Ayrshire Hermit and Hurlford Sixty Years Ago,* Kilmarnock, 1875

Mark HURLL,

Coalmaster and fireclay manufacturer; b. 1849, Lanarkshire, s. of John Hurll, firebrick manufacturer and Isabella McGlastion; m. n.d., Jessie Cowie; 3s., 1d.; Founder and Ch, P & M Hurll Ltd; Dir, Mount Vernon Colliery Company; d. 21/6/1928, Hillswick, Shetland; g/v estate: £54,307 12s 6d.

Well into the early part of the nineteenth century deposits of fireclay situated in the Lanarkshire area had been worked to a small extent in the making of small quantities of firebricks. Then extensive deposits of fireclay were discovered in the neighbouring areas of Garnkirk and Glenboig. The presence of these valuable beds of clay led to the founding of several important producers of refactory materials, such as G & R Stein, P & M Hurll and the Glenboig Union Fireclay Company, and to the development of a flourishing firebrick industry in the west of Scotland.

One of the significant figures during the early years of fire manufacturing in Scotland was John Hurll, the father of Mark Hurll. Little is known about his early life. He left Ireland in the early 1820s and came to work for the Garnkirk Coal Company about 1835. By 1851 he was brickyard operations manager at the Garnkirk Works. Soon afterwards he joined in partnership with another Garnkirk employee, John Young. They established a fireclay works at Cardowan, about half a mile west of Garnkirk, which came to be known as Hurll, Young and Company and which produced glazed sewage pipes and firebricks. Their business expanded, and this led to the acquisition in 1862 of the Heathfield works from Ferguson, Miller and Company. In 1865, along with James Dunnachie (qv) Hurll and Young formed the Glenboig Fireclay Company to operate the Old Works at Glenboig, of which Dunnachie was manager. However, this partnership did not last.

When the partnership was dissolved in 1872, John Hurll and his sons, Peter and Mark, continued to trade at the Old Works, John Young purchased the Heathfield and Cardowan Works, and James Dunnachie leased the 6/7th unlet portion of the Glenboig clayfield, where he built the Star works under the name of James Dunnachie and Company. For the next decade the Hurlls and Dunnachie continued to trade side by side. Competition was keen between the two works. The refactory industry depended heavily on the iron and steel producers for its custom and when, around 1882, a decline in the growth of the iron and steel industries led to diminishing markets it was decided that in the best interests of both works to cease competing against each other and to form one establishment. The new company was called the Glenboig Union Fireclay Company Ltd. The company had an authorised capital of £150,000 in £10 shares. John Hurll was chairman, Peter Hurll was secretary, and James Dunnachie was managing director. The vendors who sold to the union company works, leases and goodwill, bound themselves not to start in the same line of business for 15 years from the date of sale.

In the same year as its establishment the company purchased the Cumbernauld Works as suitable for the production of blast furnace blocks. By 1883 the first blocks were being exported to Bilbao in Spain. Production rapidly expanded and as markets continued to expand so new works were acquired. However, the partnership did not last. The Hurlls left the Company in 1888 after a disagreement over their rights to conduct fireclay business in the Glenboig area contrary to the vendors agreement of 1882 when Peter and Mark were found to have been carrying out test borings in the area.

Their father having retired from the fireclay business, Peter and Mark entered into partnership. Using their knowledge and experience gained in the organisation and management of the older works they set up a rival business, Peter and Mark Hurll, at Gartliston, less than a mile to the south of Glenboig. Business expanded rapidly, built up, according to a company catalogue, on the merit of the products of the works, because the raw fireclay was of excellent quality, and the methods of manufacture and business outlook of the partnership were thoroughly up to date. The firebricks produced at the Gartliston works were stamped *Hurll,* and as demand increased for *Hurll* products a second pit had to be sunk at Glenboig in 1895, and works were also built at Garnqueen. The bricks were popular for their long life and strength when subjected to high or rapidly varying temperatures. The bricks did not 'spoil' or break in furnaces, thus there was no weakening of the brickwork or damage to the contents of a furnace from falling pieces. The *Hurll* bricks, blocks and retorts manufactured at the Gartliston and Garnqueen works were sold in Britain and the colonies in Europe and in many countries abroad.

Business continued to expand, and two more partners were assumed, John Henry Hurll, Peter's son, and Emile Francois Duvoisin, a fireclay manufacturer. In 1908, one firm was registered as a private limited company with an authorised capital of £50,000 in £1 shares. All were made permanent directors, and Peter Hurll was made chairman and Duvoisin was made secretary. 1908 also marked another important development for the company with the discovery of a valuable seam. A seam of fireclay was investigated near Manuel, Linlithgowshire. This seam had been worked previously in the mid nineteenth century, but only to a small extent. Further investigation found clay that proved to be highly aluminous and of a very constant composition peculiar to this district. A mine was driven. Firebricks from this clay were marketed under the brand *Klint,* and were bricks of a high standard for use in high melting point natural aluminous refractories. *Klint* bricks were used where conditions were exceptionally severe, and there was an increasing demand for such bricks, especially from firms where pulverised coal or oil fuel was used, or where it was important that a furnace should be kept under heat continuously.

Peter Hurll died in 1911, and Mark took over the chairmanship. Under his guidance the firm continued its high standard of produce. The advertised products included firebricks of several kinds, gas retorts, tiles and other products which were used by firms for steel and iron furnaces and ladles, chemical and glass furnaces, locomotives, fire-tube and water-tube boilers, and pottery kilns. To maintain the quality of their products at a uniformly high standard only the true first-quality seam was worked and the best raw material extracted. To meet increasing demand it was necessary to open new works. As well as the works in Glenboig the company started new works at Garscube and Knightswood which produced firebricks and sewer pipes. In the Drumchapel area of Glasgow the Hurlls worked the blaze bings: the waste materials of brick-making. These waste materials could be utilised by crushing and then moulding the material into bricks under high pressure.

Despite his heavy involvement in fireclay manufacture, Mark Hurll had been trained in his earlier years as a mining engineer, and he spent some time in Germany to further his training and to expand his knowledge of new processes. On his return to Scotland in the early 1870s he was associated with several collieries, as well as the Hurlls brick manufacturing business, and in the Post Office Directory for 1890 he is described as a coalmaster at Letterick Colliery, Blantyre. By this date he was also involved in the fireclay industry with his brother Peter, and his knowledge and experiences as a mining engineer were put to good use in the investigation of seams and the sinking of pits for the company's works.

The company faced tough competition from the other fireclay manufacturers in the Lanarkshire area, especially from James Dunnachie's Glenboig Union Fireclay Company Limited. Indeed various complaints had been made against the Hurlls by Dunnachie over a number of years. For example, in 1905, the Glenboig company claimed that *Hurll* bricks were being used in an Irish contract which had specified *Glenboig* brand. In another case, May 1909, a Hurll advertisement in a Belfast paper claimed *Glenboig manufacture*, but by February 1910 the Hurll agent in Ireland had agreed to drop this nomenclature. Such complaints were bound to arise with the two companies using Glenboig addresses. Competition continued to be keen between the two companies. There is no available information about how Peter and Mark Hurll Ltd was affected by the outbreak of war in 1914, but it is probably that they faced similar difficulties to those of its rivals; the loss of overseas trade and labour shortages. Increased orders from the home market went some way to cover the loss of foreign markets and mechanisation was an answer to labour shortages, but to what extent the company was involved in these changes or in the post war is not known.

The year 1920 saw some changes in the company. The authorised capital of the company was increased to £75,000 when a further 25,000 £1 shares were issued. In that year, also, Mark Hurll was made managing director of the company. Mark was still dividing his time between his fireclay interests and his coal interests. He was a director of the Mount Vernon Colliery Company as well as managing director of Peter and Mark Hurll Ltd. Despite his heavy business involvements Mark still had time to enjoy a few outside interests. He was a keen angler and made several trips to Shetland in pursuit of this sport. He married Jessie Cowie and had four children; John McGlashan, a captain, who died in 1915, Mark and Thomas Rennie, who followed their father into the business, and Margaret.

On 21st June 1928, Mark Hurll died suddenly on holiday at Hillswick, Shetland from heart failure, he was 79. He left an estate of £54,307 12s 6d. His two sons carried on the brick making industry which Mark and Peter had built up. From one establishment in Glenboig the brothers extended their business to Gartliston, Garnqueen, Linlithgow, Knightswood, Garscube and Garscadden. The company of Peter and Mark Hurll also outlived its nearest rival, the Glenboig Union Fireclay Company Ltd, and only went into liquidation in 1980.

THERESA BARTON

SOURCES

Unpublished

SRO: SC 36/48/400, Inventory
   SC 36/1/220, Will
Harold, J, 'The Glenboig Union Fireclay Co Ltd, 1882-1921'. Unpublished undergraduate dissertation, Department of History, University of Strathclyde, 1972

Published

Catalogue of Peter and Mark Hurll Ltd, nd
Fleming, J A , *Scottish Pottery,* Glasgow, 1923
Glasgow Herald, 23/3/1928
Glasgow Post Office Directories 1885-1890
McLean, A (ed), *Local industries of Glasgow and the West of Scotland*, British Association for the Advancement of Science, 1901
Quail, G, *Garnkirk Fireclay,* Bishopbriggs, Glasgow, 1985

Alexander Dixson JENKINSON,

Glass manufacturer; b. 14/10/1853, Edinburgh, s. of Alexander Jenkinson, ceramic and glass manufacturer; m. Edith Telford; 1 s.; Sole Partner, Alexander Jenkinson, China Pottery and Glass Merchant, and Edinburgh and Leith Flint Glass Company; d. 27/3/1909, Edinburgh; g/v estate: £31,193 9s 4d.

Alexander Jenkinson's business career is associated with the two companies established by his father Alexander Jenkinson (1821-1880) who had started his retail business, selling ceramics and glass at 10 Princes Street, Edinburgh in 1872. The following year he had become associated with the Edinburgh and Leith Flint Glass Company at 33 Leith Walk. This was an auspicious moment for other Edinburgh glass manufacturers had attracted favourable attention at the Paris Exhibition of 1867 and demand for their products was rising. In 1874, 34 Leith Walk was acquired and the next year Professor Archer, director of the Edinburgh Museum of Science and Art (now the Royal Museums of Scotland, Chambers Street) noted the quality of the company's products, particularly those in the Venetian style. The new combined works were still too small and Alexander Jenkinson Snr concerned for the future of his two small sons William and Alexander decided that even more extensive premises were required in order to develop the production side of the family interests.

The new works were less than a mile away from Leith Walk but allowed space for better planning of the factory. They were built by the side of the Edinburgh, Leith and Granton loop of the North British Railway and incorporated a 12 pot furnace as well as improved warehouse, packing and office facilities. The eldest son William worked in the Prince's Street shop while Alexander was responsible for the warehouse. Only two years after the establishment of the new works the company exhibited at the Paris Exhibition of 1878 where the products were described as 'placed by all critics amongst the best works of the class that have been sent by Great Britain in competition with the hitherto unrivalled fabrications of Germany and France. They are a credit to Scotland.'

William Jenkinson died aged 28 on 5 December 1878 and Alexander Snr only 13 months later on 11 January 1880. The latter left personal estate valued at £9,961 1s 3d which included stock at Prince's Street to the value of £6,340 16s 2d, at Norton Park to the value of £1,320 6s 8d while the plant was valued at only £100 and fittings at £10! The younger son therefore took over both family businesses. Jenkinson expanded the family manufacturing business;

in the 1880s wares, gas and electric light shades, were produced to meet the vastly increased public demand for such fittings, while at the same time the company began to move away from the coloured 'Venetian style' wares towards the manufacture of high quality crystal suitable for cutting and engraving. In addition a new technique was introduced with engraved portions of glass polished, previously they had been left matt, combined with polished backgrounds and cutting. This development met with equal popular success.

Not only did Jenkinson extend the range of the company's products but he expanded its marketing operations. In 1895/6 a second shop was opened at 20 Morningside Road, Edinburgh, while customers abroad included both Pitcairn's and Tiffany's in New York and Parsons of Canada: Government contracts included the Admiralty, and numerous wholesalers and retailers throughout the UK.

He died at the age of 55 at 4 Carlton Terrace, Edinburgh, as a result of heart disease. His estate totalled £31,193 9s 4d (duty paid £1,770 15s 10d). The assets of the Edinburgh and Leith Glass Company of which he was the sole partner were valued at £1,754 18s 8d, not including the premises. The retail outlet with Princes Street having been sold to J A Nesbit, George Street, Edinburgh, contributed £1,527 8s 4d to the total. Stocks held by the deceased were valued at £6,958 6s 10 in Scotland, £10,685 in England, £2,714 17s 6d in Ireland and £1,376 5s abroad, making two-thirds of the estate. The glassworks was inherited by his son, Stanley Noel Jenkinson (1886-1982).

BRIAN BLENCH

SOURCES

Unpublished

SRO: SC70/1/493, Inventory
      SC70 /4/408, Will
MS Edinburgh Central Library: Alexander Jenkinson founder of Edinburgh Crystal (1821-1880) by H A Basterfield

Published

Woodward, H W, *The Story of Edinburgh Crystal*, Dema Glass Ltd, Edinburgh, 1984

John MONCRIEFF,

Ink and glass manufacturer; b. 1834, Cherrybank, Perth, s. of Alexander Moncrieff, handloom weaver and Jane Skene; m. Christina Robb; 2 s., 2 d.; Founder, North British Glassworks; d. 30/9/1899, Perth; g/v estate: £71,717 14s 11d.

Moncrieff was born, the son of a handloom weaver, at Cherrybank, Perth, where he received his early education at the village school, to the age of 13. In 1847 he was apprenticed at the ink and glass works of John Todd, continuing to study at night classes. By the age of 21 he had been appointed manager of the works, building furnaces and experimenting on the nature of glass. He started work on his own account about 1865 in small premises at South Street. Perth, moving in 1881/2 to St Catherine's Road.

Gauge glasses were the staple product of the business. Based on his own studies and advice from outside specialists the firm developed a boro-silicate glass able to withstand chemical attack from boiler steam and also liable to fracture due to variations of temperature. Widely exhibited, Moncrieff's gauge glasses won awards all over the world and by the end of the century production had expanded from 100 lbs per day to over 1 ton. Waste glass was used to make ink bottles and in the 1890s the manufacture of ink was added to the company's activities. Moncrieff used tank furnaces and made several improvements to them.

Apart from being an astute and innovative manufacturer, Moncrieff had a deep concern for the city of his birth. A pronounced radical he espoused the Liberal cause in parliamentary and local affairs serving as vice-president of both the Perth Liberal Club and Perth Liberal Association. He was a town councillor for five years and a member of the school board for 12. An evangelical in religion he served as manager and president of the Evangelical Union contributing substantially to the building of an elegant church for the sect; not surprisingly he was a director of the Perth Bible Society and the Perth Gospel Temperance Society. Moncrieff was also a sportsman witnessed by his presidency of the Perth Bowling Club and membership of the Tay Fishing Syndicate. An obituarist described him as 'an excellent type of self-made man and a citizen who was greatly respected'.

At his death he left an estate in excess of £70,000 of which the glassworks accounted only for some £3,000. His wife inherited Elmside, Balhousie and its contents with an annuity of £1,000 per annum, annuities to his daughter, and his wife's sisters and the business equally between his two sons Thomas Robb and John Jnr. In 1905 the sons incorporated the firm as a limited liability company under the name John Moncrieff Ltd.

BRIAN BLENCH

SOURCES

Unpublished

SRO: SC 49/31/178, Testamentary settlement and Inventory
SC 49/31/182, Corrected Inventory

Published

Fleming, J A, *Scottish & Jacobite Glass,* Glasgow, 1938
Perthshire Courier, 3/10/1899
Perthshire Advertiser, 2/10/1899

John SHANKS,

Sanitary engineer; b. 1825, Paisley, s. of William Shanks, handloom weaver, and Helen Gowens; m. (1) Isabella Mills; (2) Jessie Turnbull Smith; Founder, Shanks & Co Ltd, Barrhead; d. 18/12/1895, Barrhead; g/v estate: £18,872 17s 6d.

John Shanks was a prime example of the Victorian 'self-made man'. Beginning his working life as a plumber, he pioneered what was to become the premier sanitary engineering firm in Britain. He was an astute businessman, a skilled inventor of many sanitary appliances and remained active until the last year of his life when ill-health finally forced him to retire.

Little is known about the early life of John Shanks. His father, William, was a Paisley handloom weaver and John was apprenticed as a plumber to Wallace and Connell of Glasgow. He worked as a journeyman plumber in the Paisley area until he was 30 years old when he transferred his business to the neighbouring town of Barrhead. While maintaining his plumbing business here, John Shanks began to devise and patent improvements to sanitary ware. He began with cheap portable bath tubs, finally devising fixed domestic appliances. He prided himself on his products being good quality, hard-wearing and of reasonable price.

In 1875 he founded Shanks and Co, Sanitary Engineers, with his brother Andrew who had also been a plumber. The firm began on a small site in Main Street, Barrhead, employing eight people. With John as senior partner, the business expanded rapidly. Two decades later, the firm occupied a seven-acre site and employed 600 men, Barrhead's single largest employer. It was John who was the innovator of the company, taking out some 100 patents by 1894.

All stages of the production of sanitary ware were completed on the Main Street site from iron-moulding to enamelling so that employees were engaged in 20 different trades. Shanks established his own pottery to ensure both uniformity of quality and economy in production. John Shanks always remembered his employees, providing in his will an extra day's pay to employees who had been with the company for six months on the day of his death.

Shanks and Co quickly established itself as Britain's leader in sanitary engineering. The company gained a reputation for reliable and durable goods. This reputation was confirmed when the Prince of Wales succumbed to fever and investigations in Buckingham Palace discovered that every sanitary applicance was defective except the Shanks Patent Number 4 water closet in the servant's quarters. Shanks products were soon to be found in hospitals and public buildings throughout Britain and became the first choice as fitments on the passenger liners of the late nineteenth century. John Shanks had recognised the market potential of sanitary ware in a period when individuals and local authorites were growing aware of the needs of public health. He took particular pride in designing equipment for hospitals such as the Western Infirmary, Glasgow and Paisley Infirmary. Nor was the

COURTESY OF STRATHCLYDE REGIONAL ARCHIVES

company's reputation confined to Britain. It was Shanks who supplied the Melbourne Metropolitan Board of Works. At his death, John Shanks' share of the company was valued at £18,000. His drive and business skills were maintained by his son John and nephew William who began as apprentices with the firm, working their way to managerial level as their fathers had done.

The Shanks family also played a prominent role in the civic life of Barrhead as befitting the town's largest employers. John Shanks was an active supporter of the Conservative cause until the Home Rule Bill whereupon he became a Liberal Unionist. He was well-known in Barrhead as a moral man. For ten years he was president of the Barrhead Evangelical Union and manager of the United Presbyterian Church. He was very active in the temperance movement led by Rev William Clark and in later life was elected to the first Neilston Parish Council although he was forced to retire because of ill-health. Members of the Shanks family filled several of the seats on local boards and it was John's nephew William who became the first Provost of Barrhead in 1893 when the town was declared a burgh.

John Shanks was a pioneer of sanitary engineering in Scotland. He was a well-known and prolific inventor, and respected businessman who had been quick to appreciate the market potential of the growing awareness of public health in the late nineteenth century. He dominated the market for sanitary appliances, creating the foremost sanitary engineering firm of his day whose reputation was to remain long after his death.

PATRICIA COLLINS

SOURCES

Unpublished
SRO: SC 58/42/59, Inventory
      SC 58/45/9, Will

Published
Glasgow Herald, 23/12/1985
Murphy, W S, *Captains of Industry*, Glasgow, 1901
Murray, R, *The Annals of Barrhead*, Glasgow, 1942
Paisley Daily Express, 19/12/1985
Pride, D, *The Parish of Neilston*, Neilston, 1910

John Gilchrist STEIN,

Brick manufacturer; b. 1/8/1862, Clackmannan, s. of John Stein, brickmaker and Janet Hunter; m. 23/11/1883, Annie Henderson; 4 s., 7 d.; Ch and MD, J G Stein and Co Ltd, Brick Manufacturers, Bonnybridge; d. 16/10/1927; g/v estate: £99,714 11s 4d.

John Gilchrist Stein was one of the leading figures in the Scottish brick-making trade in the late nineteenth and early twentieth centuries. This was a time which saw the rise and peak of brick manufacture in Scotland and in particular the production of fire-bricks using the abundant fireclay seams of the mid-central Scotland belt between Glenboig and Bonnybridge.

Stein's early life fostered his interest in the brick-making trade. His father, John, (1835-1882) had emigrated to Philadelphia, USA, with other members of his family in the 1850s. He was a skilled brickmaker to trade. He sent for and married a Scots girl in 1859. The tensions and unrest of the Civil War prompted their return to Scotland where John Gilchrist Stein

was born in 1862. His father returned to the brick-making trade as manager of the Winchburgh Brick-works and it was here that John Gilchrist began to learn the trade as an apprentice to his father after attending the local parish school. It is believed that from the age of 14 John Gilchrist Stein may have attended Gillespie's School in Edinburgh.

In 1882 when his father died, aged 47, John Gilchrist Stein sought to take over his father's place as manager but this was declined. He then moved west to the Cumbernauld Pipe Works, owned by the Glenboig Union Fireclay Company Ltd, which was to become one of the largest brick-making concerns in Scotland headed by another 'doyen' of the trade, James Dunnachie (qv). During his time at Cumbernauld, Stein worked closely with an Austrian who developed a secret formula for glazing pipes. When the Austrian left and received royalties for his formula, Stein suggested that he should get his share because as foreman he had worked closely with the formula. This was refused and Stein was sacked. This seemed to fire Stein's ambition and determination to do one better than Dunnachie. The brick trade was certainly one of rivalry with many firms setting up in competition at the same time.

Stein's next job was as a salesman with the Bonnybridge Silica Company at 27/6d per week. His real aim was to set up on his own and after two years as salesman and careful saving and financial help from his wife's family he took up a lease on the clayfields over two acres in an area called Milnquarter, near Bonnybridge. He commenced mining operations on the 17 November 1887 with six employees. The early business was concerned with selling tap hole clay to the steel industry after mining it on an open cast basis. This brought in some business while work began on a brick stove. However the costs of the mining operations and foundations had used up most of the original capital of £300 and so an injection of capital was needed. One of the local ironfounders, Malcolm Cockburn who was a customer of Stein joined the business putting in £600. The total capital was £1,200 with Stein's share attributed to the lease, the mine and the plant. This extra capital pushed Stein on his way and in the autumn of 1888 he built and fired his first kiln with a capacity of 5,000 bricks, all hand-made.

By 1894 the works had expanded to five conical kilns, numerous other buildings and plant and the works were valued as a going concern at £2,800. Two years later disagreement arose in March 1896 between Cockburn and Stein over the level of Stein's salary. Stein bought out Cockburn's share after sealed bids were lodged for the company. Stein now pushed ahead with new plans and developments, not least was the introduction of machinery to manufacture bricks rather than by hand. He extended his operations to Denny where he leased a bing of fireclay and ganister waste from William Baird & Company to produce common building bricks. These Anchor works at

Denny had a capacity of 150,000 bricks per week and continued until the shale was exhausted in 1931.

Meanwhile at Bonnybridge the first steps were being taken to make the first firebricks by machine. Two problems had to be overcome. The first was the need to overcome the prejudice against machine made bricks after so many years of hand-making. The second was the problem of Stein's bricks being recognised as quality bricks in their own right against the reputation of the famous Glenboig brick. Certainly these problems seem to have been overcome fairly quickly as Stein's reputation grew but the competition from Glenboig was always there.

The Milnquarter works were improved in 1900 with the building of new kilns, a 13 chamber continuous kiln, which was developed on the same lines as Hoffman kilns used at the Denny works but modified by Stein. The company history noted that Stein 'thought out alternative ideas to cut down work and improve quality, then took the risk and made it work'. Other improvements around this time included electric lighting and workmen's houses.

Expansion was still on Stein's mind and the Glenboig rivalry ever present. In 1902 he took out a mineral lease at Castlecary at the branch of the London and North-Eastern Railway on the south and the Midland and Scottish Railway on the north, a vital location for the transportation of goods. The costs of sinking mines and laying foundations were such that further capital was required and at this stage the decision was taken to become incorporated as a limited company.

On the 20 April 1905 J G Stein & Company Ltd came into being. The authorised share capital was £100,000. This was divided into 5,000 £10 Preference shares and 5,000 £10 Ordinary shares of which 2,500 Preference and 4,000 Ordinary were issued. This raised £25,000. The major shareholders included the Henderson shipowning family, Robert and George Dobbie, ironmasters, and three of the company's employees. The directors were Stein, Harry Henderson, Peter Forfar, a banker, and later in 1907 Stein's son Alan was company secretary, having joined the company in 1904. When Forfar and Henderson retired in 1911 two of Stein's sons, Alan and Norman, replaced them.

With Stein's drive and enthusiasm expansion at Castlecary and Milnquarter continued apace. Further developments included the extension of the continuous chamber system to 52 chambers and the continual search for higher quality bricks and new combinations of refractory materials including the silica brick. By 1927 Castlecary alone was producing 1,000,000 bricks per week. Further developments in the 1920s included the significant exploration of clayfields at Manuel near Linlithgow and the opening of the new brickworks there in 1927.

The story of J G Stein and Company Ltd was therefore one of success and continual expansion. At the heart of the company development was the forceful and dominant John Gilchrist Stein. His personality can be revealed by his involvement in three court cases. In 1899 the first episode arose over the delay in delivery of new plant to the Milnquarter works in 1899 and the subsequent failure of the machinery to meet its specifications led to Stein's refusal to settle his account and the plant manufacturers, Rowleys of Lincoln sued for settlements of their bill. The court case and subsequent appeal went against Stein. This was in 1900. Then in 1903 an order for a pump to clear water in one of the shafts failed to appear and Stein sent two letters and a telegram to the supplier, Joseph Evans of Wolverhampton, expressing his disquiet at the delay. Another court case ensued, this time for slander and Stein won this case on appeal. During the 1914-18 war government intervention decided brick prices and customers, which Stein found hard to accept; when the Glenboig brick was priced higher than his, he again went to court to have the matter decided but failed. These incidents seem to reflect Stein's passionate concern and involvement with the running of his business which he placed above all else.

Indeed he devoted his life to his business. He was a teetotaller and non-smoker, a stern disciplinarian, had little interest in the church or politics and only latterly took up the sport of fishing. He was concerned for the welfare of his employees and erected workers' houses, a football field and bowling green and built a hall used as both a canteen and recreation room.

His main activity outside the business was in fact directly related to the industry itself. After the experience of the First World War Scottish brickmakers realised the need to strengthen their position by combining. After the setting up of the Employers' National Council for the Clay Industries, Scotland saw the setting up of the Scottish Employers' Council for the Clay Industries in 1917. This came about through the initiative of Stein and William Douglas (qv) of the Douglas Firebrick Company. Stein was its first president. One of the council's jobs was to fix prices and Stein this time made sure that the Glenboig bricks were the same price as his own.

Stein had become the foremost brick manufacturer in Scotland and it was at this point in his life that ironic tragedy struck. In 1927 while inspecting the Castlecary works he tripped over a brick and grazed his shin which turned septic. His leg had to be amputated but it was not enough to save his life and he died on 16 October.

The brick industry had lost an eminent figure and his family a much loved father and husband signalling the end of an era. However in his two sons Alan and Norman he passed on all the expertise of the brick manufacturing tradition. They proceeded with the development of the Manuel works using new techniques and modern power plant. By 1971 the Manuel works were one of the largest in the world under the name GR-Stein Refractories. The achievement and success of John Gilchrist Stein cannot be underestimated not only in terms of his development of a successful business but for his entrepreneurial skills which he devoted completely to the manufacture of bricks.

SHEILA HAMILTON

SOURCES

Unpublished

Calendar of Confirmations, 1927

Published

British Clayworker, Vol XXXIV, 1925 and Vol XXXVI, 1927
Falkirk Herald, 19/2/1939
Falkirk Mail, 22/10/1927
Glasgow Herald, 18/10/1927, 11b
Sanderson, K W, *Stein of Bonnybridge*, Privately Printed, Edinburgh, 1985
The Refractories Journal, November, 1927

Grateful thanks to Mr Kenneth Sanderson for his invaluable help

SOURCES

Unpublished

Companies Registration Office:
  File No 2614, H & A G Alexander & Co Ltd
Register of Sasines, Glasgow, 1865-1900
Register of Sasines, Lanark, 1865-1900
SRO: BT2/6011, Buchanan & French Ltd
SC 36/48/279, Inventory
SC 36/51/176, Will

Published

The Bailie, Nos 1360, 1379, 1875, 2248
Butt, J, *Industrial Archaeology of Scotland,* Newton
  Abbot, 1967
The Cabinet Maker & Art Furnisher, May 1893,
  February 1894, June 1894, October 1899, January
  1900, March 1901, April 1907, July 1917
Edinburgh Post Office Directory, 1878-1885
Evening News, 10/7/1917

Charles Stuart BROWN,

Tea chest and aluminium foil manufacturer; b. 6/6/1873, Bathgate, s. of Peter Stuart Brown, tea chest manufacturer and Elizabeth Chapman; m. 17/9/1915, Elizabeth Wilson Blyth; 1 s.; Ch, Acme Tea Chest Co Ltd; d. 26/8/1960, Water Yett, Lochwinnoch.

Charles Stuart Brown was born at Bathgate on 6 June 1873 the son of Peter Stuart Brown and Elizabeth Chapman who had married in Edinburgh on 8 September 1864. Charles was the second of seven children. He was educated in Inverness and at Allan Glen's School in Glasgow.

The family were originally from Aberdeenshire. Peter Stuart Brown was by training an industrial chemist and spent some time in Inverness. From 1908 he resided in Lochwinnoch, Renfrewshire. By his grandson's admission Peter was the 'bright spark' of the family, both innovator and entrepreneur he had many interests. At one stage he owned a chemical plant near Irvine on the Ayrshire coast where he produced sulphate of ammonia. He also had an interest in agricultural fencing. For the Acme Tea Chest Company he patented and produced a plywood tea chest. This was an important innovation for the tea trade as a whole, which had previously relied on hand sawn planks which tended to split. The chests were previously lined with lead which made them very heavy. From Germany, Peter Stuart Brown brought the original method for making aluminium foil which was a much more suitable lining for the plywood chests. Peter died in 1915.

Charles Stuart Brown joined the family business having served in the 18th Imperial Yeomanry Glasgow Regiment during the Boer War. Under Charles Stuart Brown the business expanded. The aluminium linings were produced through a subsidiary company, Empire Aluminium Ltd. Charles Stuart Brown travelled extensively, establishing a foil plant in Colombo, a tea chest business at Cooch Behar in North India and a plywood plant at Nyasaland. In Britain there was, in addition to the Acme plant at Polmadie in Glasgow, a factory at Enfield. Before and during the First World War Charles Stuart Brown worked at Wilmington, North Carolina, making plywood and exporting timber to Britain.

Among the firm's major customers in Africa, in the years after the Second World War, were Joe Lyons, Dixon Anderson and the Scottish Co-operative Society. In the Far East they worked closely with James Finlay, who acted as their agents and secretaries in Colombo, and Harrison Crossfield.

The aluminium foil had other outlets of course, and the Glasgow based company produced foil for milk bottle tops, butter wrappers, chocolate, pharmaceutical foil for pills, powdered milk satchets, condensor foil for radios, radar and television. One of the largest markets was for cigarette packaging. These were world wide outlets and before the Second World War included America.

Acme's biggest competitor was Venesta Limited, which ultimately took it over before being swallowed up itself by Tube Investments and subsequently by Alcan. Charles Stuart Brown retired with Venesta's successful takeover in 1957. Since 1900 he had been having problems with his sight and by 1936 was totally blind. Despite this disability he continued as chairman and travelled abroad to visit subsidiary companies.

Charles Stuart Brown had married Elizabeth Wilson Blyth the daughter of a lawyer on 17 September 1915. Elizabeth was trained as a nurse at the Glasgow Royal Infirmary but left to work in a private nursing home in Glasgow. It was in the nursing home that she met her husband who was recovering from an operation. The family home was at Auchengrange, overlooking Castle Semple Loch and the village of Lochwinnoch. They had one son, Wilson Stuart Brown.

Charles Stuart Brown seems to have taken little part in public affairs. He was, according to his son, distinctly 'unpolitical'. In religion he was a presbyterian and a member of Lochwinnoch Parish Church, although not an elder. He was an enthusiastic painter before he lost his sight and had been a member of the Glasgow Art Club. In recreational terms his real passion was for horses which he bred and raced, not always successfully. He kept a good stable at Auchengrange and was an enthusiastic member of the Lochwinnoch Agricultural Show Committee and the Lanark and Renfrew Hunt. Charles Stuart Brown died, aged 86, on 26 August 1960.

CHRISTOPHER C LEE

SOURCES

Unpublished

Information supplied by Mr Wilson Stuart Brown

Published

Glasgow Herald, 27 August 1960

Matthew Henry FORREST,

Timber merchant and sawmiller, b. 27/11/1876, Glasgow, s. of James Forrest, sawmiller, and Mary Frew; m. Isabella Mary Edmiston, d. of John Edmiston, auctioneer; 1 s., 1 d.; Dir & Ch, Brownlee & Co Ltd, City Sawmills; d. 4/3/1941; g/v estate: £122,595.

Matthew Henry Forrest, Harry, was one of the second generation of Forrests in control of Brownlee & Co, of the City Sawmills, Port Dundas. His father James Forrest, was the elder brother of William Forrest (qv), both sons of Janet Brownlee, the elder sister of James Brownlee founder of the business. His father married Mary Frew in 1859, but Harry Forrest was not born until 1876, two years after his father had become a director of the company.

Harry Forrest was schooled at Allen Glen's in Glasgow. On completing his schooling around 1891, he was placed with the firm of White & Hogart, timber measurers, to learn something of that skill. He became a supervisor of the labourers moving timber in the public yards, mostly at Yorkhill. After a few years there he joined James Brownlee & Co in 1895 shortly before his twentieth birthday; he was principally employed as a traveller, visiting carpenters

and joiners' shops to gain orders for the City Sawmills. In this capacity Harry Forrest was only one of some ten members of the Forrest and Brownlee families then in managerial and director positions in the business. In 1910 his uncle William Forrest retired as chairman, and Harry's elder brother John succeeded to the chairmanship. Harry himself then succeeded to his uncle William's place on the board; he was 33 years of age and had about 20 years experience in the timber trade.

Brownlee & Co was organised in a number of specialised departments, and Harry Forrest was responsible for the soft wood and joinery department. There was a particularly great demand for the products of this department during the First World War, and this kept Harry Forrest extremely busy. Nevertheless, during the war, Harry was active in the Volunteer Movement. He had long been an active member in the Mounted Section of the First Lanarkshire Rifle Volunteers, and during the war he held the rank of captain. He was also much involved in the organisation of the 'citizens army'.

By the end of the First World War Harry Forrest was working closely with his chairman brother John, and was gradually beoming an effective and efficient

COURTESY OF MRS FORREST

second in command. Brownlee & Co was by then the largest sawmill enterprise in Scotland. At this stage Harry Forrest also represented the family and the company in the public affairs of the industry, becoming president of the Scottish Timber Merchants and Sawmillers' Association between 1923 and 1925. In the 1930s he became a member of the executive council of the Timber Trades Federation, and served on many local and national committees, spending increasing amounts of time in London and elsewhere as a public figure in his industry.

In 1932, in the depth of the depression, his brother John died and Harry Forrest succeeded him to the chairmanship of Brownlee & Co at the age of 55. Even in this new position he continued to represent the company and the industry in its various committees, and his expertise was much in demand. In 1939 he agreed to become assistant area officer of the timber control in Glasgow; but when it became apparent that this would be a full-time post he withdrew, since he could not run Brownlee & Co at the same time as being a full-time civil servant.

Throughout these years Harry Forrest lived close to his place of work, moving to the nearby community of Bishopbriggs. His early interest in playing rugby changed to a passion for playing golf; he was indeed a joint founder of the Bishopbriggs Golf Club. In addition he was successively president and vice-president of Bishopbriggs District Horticultural Society. His public service also involved him as a Justice of the Peace for the City of Glasgow, and he was also for many years vice-president of the North Lanarkshire Unionist Association.

His death in 1941 was sudden; he had indeed been at business that day. He left a personal moveable estate of £122,595, of which £59,473 represented shares in Brownlee & Co. Harry Forrest had been a member of Brownlee & Co for 50 years; indeed he was the sole survivor of those who had been in the company at the time of its taking public company form in 1896. Thereafter control of the business passed to a third generation of Forrests and a fourth generation of Brownlees.

ANTHONY SLAVEN

SOURCES

Unpublished

SRO: 36/48/570, Inventory
      SC 36/51/277, Will

Published

Carvel, J L, *100 Years in Timber: Brownlee & Co, City Saw Mills 1849-1949*, Glasgow, 1950

Directory of Directors
Glasgow Herald, 6/3/1941
The Timber Trades Journal, 15/3/1941

William FORREST,

Timber merchant, b. 1838, s. of John Forrest and Janet Brownlee; m. Margaret Risk; 2 s.; Dir & Ch, Brownlee Co Ltd; d. 9/2/1913; g/v estate: £81,846.

William Forrest's route into business lay through his family connections. His mother Janet, was elder sister to James Brownlee, the founder of the City Sawmills. William and his elder brother James both entered the family business.

William Forrest was the fifth of seven children of George Forrest and Janet Brownlee. His father farmed Kilcadzow Farm at Carluke. William was born in 1838 and had completed his elementary education at the parish school before his uncle James set up in business as a sawmiller in 1849 on the banks of the Forth & Clyde Canal at Port Dundas. This was an ideal location, since timber could be brought in from the Baltic by way of Grangemouth and the canal, while timber from the Americas and elsewhere could be brought in from the Clyde through the canal from Bowling.

Both William Forrest and his brother James joined the Brownlee's business for training rather than following their father into farming. Practical experience and knowledge of timber was gained by William Forrest under the direction of his uncle James; more especially he acquired knowledge of the financial side of the business from Henry Stewart, who joined the firm in 1852 as cashier, but quickly became manager and ultimately a director in the company.

James Brownlee's firm developed rapidly, till by 1870 it had outgrown its original site. A new location was required and one comprising some 14 acres was purchased at Craighall Road close to the original City Sawmills. The new site fronted the Forth & Clyde Canal on one side while connecting directly with a branch of the North British Railway Co on the other. Consequently it was ideally located for the receipt, processing and distribution, of large volumes of timber. This extension of the business was quickly followed by a reconstruction of the management. In 1874 Robert Brownlee, the founder's brother, Henry Stewart, William Forrest and his brother James, together with George Christie Young, another nephew of James Brownlee, all became directors. Soon afterward, James Brownlee, the founder of the business, retired in 1878, and his place at the head of the firm was taken by his brother Robert.

In spite of these changes, Henry Stewart remained as the managing director and he in turn was closely assisted by William Forrest, who was by then specialising in the purchase of timber for the mills. When Stewart died in 1887, William Forrest then 49, became responsible for the overall direction of the business. When Robert Brownlee died the following year William Forrest was effectively in command of the enterprise. It was by then a considerable business, not only with a large modern mill at Port Dundas employing over 400 men, but had large sawmills also at Grangemouth and Kilmarnock. The company was then among the largest sawmill enterprises in the United Kingdom and a major supplier to the timber trade. Sales of timber were held every six to eight weeks, and special premises to hold 200 agents were constructed at Port Dundas.

Under William Forrest's management the City Sawmills was a major supplier to the expanding housebuilding trades in Glasgow and district, and also to the very wide range of local industries. House-

building, public works, the coal industry and shipyards, were all major customers for the City Sawmills products. The annual throughput of the company in the last decade of the nineteenth century was around 100,000 tons of timber. The firm was clearly operated as a close knit family consortium. Members of the Brownlee and Forrest families held the directors' positions and functioned as specialists at the head of the various branches of the business. Below them were skilled foremen in day to day charge of each section and responsible for the plant, its employees and its management. On this basis William Forrest converted the partnership to a public limited company, registering it in Edinburgh on 29 March 1896 as Brownlee & Co Ltd, of which he was first chairman.

It is clear that William Forrest had little time for, or interest in, affairs outside his own company. His first entry into broader public affairs was in 1896, when at the age of 64 he became a ratepayer's representative on the Clyde Trust. He served on the Trust till his death in 1913, becoming convener of the committee on rates in 1910. He was a skilled and shrewd manager rather than an innovating entrepreneur.

Outside the business he was devoted to his large family of eight, and to his church, the Cambridge Street United Free Church. His stewardship and long involvement in the City Sawmills, made him a wealthy man. His personal estate at death in 1913 was £81,846, of which £15,676 was held in shares and debentures in Brownlee & Co Ltd. The remainder of his wealth was in a very wide portfolio of shares in local mining and iron companies, railways, and overseas mining concerns, especially in Africa. His death at the age of 75 came after a number of years of poor health which had seen him devote less and less of his time to the business. Even so he did not retire from the chairmanship until 1910; even then, like so many other Scottish men of business in family firms, only death finally separated him from a daily interest in his company's affairs.

ANTHONY SLAVEN

COURTESY OF BROWNLEE & CO

SOURCES

Unpublished

SRO: SC 36/48/244, Inventory
SC 36/48/255, Will

Published

Carvel, J L, *100 Years in Timber: Brownlee & Co, City Saw Mills 1849-1949*, Glasgow, 1950

Glasgow Herald, 10/2/1913
Glasgow Today, 'Brownlee & Co, The City Saw Mills', 1888

Joseph JOHNSTONE,

Master cabinet-maker; b. 1860, Salford, s. of Robert Johnstone, cabinet-maker and Catherine Conchar; m. 13/7/1882, Jane Clark, d. of Alexander Muir, lime quarrier; 2 s., 3 d.; Founder, Joseph Johnstone Ltd; d. 13/1/1931, Lochwinnoch, Renfrewshire; g/v estate: £2,047 8s 6d.

Joseph Johnstone was born in Salford in 1860, the son of Robert Johnstone, a cabinet-maker, and Catherine Conchar. Robert Johnstone set up business in Beith, Ayrshire, where his son, Joseph, joined him after an education at a local school. Later, Joseph settled in nearby Lochwinnoch, where he set up business on his own. Lochwinnoch was just three miles from Beith, a town noted for the production of high quality furniture, and which no doubt supplied Joseph Johnstone with a reserve of skilled labour. Markets, too, were easily accessible, with Glasgow just 15 miles away. From beginnings in a small mill in 1884, new plant was gradually built up over the years, until, by the time of his death in 1931, Johnstone's Viewfield Works were the largest furniture manufacturers in Scotland.

The success of Joseph Johnstone was due to the coupling of craftsmanship with the techniques of mass production. Parts were standardized and employees skilled in one operation, the various articles of furniture passing along the production line towards completion, and being polished and finished according to the type and grade of wood; there were different polishing departments for mahogany, lime, oak etc. The emphasis on standardization and production-line skills was reflected in the ease with which production could be switched quickly to meet demand: initially every type of furniture was made at the Viewfield Works, but eventually Johnstone decided to specialise in chairs and dining room chairs, and finally to concentrate specifically on dining room furniture, particularly tables and sideboards.

Standardization and mass production techniques did not, however, detract from the quality of product: craftmanship remained a priority - modernity was employed alongside quality and good taste, and the more expensive lines of furniture were left in the hands of skilled craftsmen who carried out hand carving on these articles of furniture.

The company was made into a private limited company in 1922, with a capital of £20,000 in shares of £1. It remained very much a family concern; Joseph Johnstone was chairman, owning 6,499 shares; his sons, Joseph H Johnstone and William Johnstone, as directors, held 1,000 and 999 shares respectively; while his daughters, Janet W Johnstone, Catherine Johnstone and Mary E Johnstone held 499, 500 and 500 shares respectively. Janet W Johnstone was also a director until her death in 1937, while Catherine Johnstone took up a directorship in 1931.

Modern techniques continued to be the firm's watchword, as could be seen in its production of laminated and ply woods, which the firm made at the Viewfield Works. Yet, here again quality was kept to the fore; instead of a veneer surface, Johnstone's plywood consisted of fixing solid oak boards on to the front and back of the plywood. On the technical side, machinery was designed at the Viewfield Works for specific use in the plant, and was constructed in the nearby town of Johnstone, which was an important centre of machine tool making and light engineering. The Viewfield Works also had its own power-plant and generated its own electric light.

Joseph Johnstone was extremely active in local affairs, and engaged in numerous areas of public life - the chief of which were politics, local government, education and health. He was a leading member of Renfrew County Council until his death, and in which capacity he served on a great many committees. He was vice-convener of the county in 1919. In 1930 he was appointed convener of the Public Health Committee, a post for which he was well suited, having been long associated with the King Edward Memorial Fund, set up before World War One by Thomas Glen-Coats Bt, to combat tuberculosis. He was also for a time on the executive of the National Insurance Committees Association of Scotland, and for 26 years on Lochwinnoch School Board.

During the Great War, Johnstone acted as chairman of the Renfrewshire Advisory Committee and Military Service Act, and was a member of the Naval and Military Pensions Committee, of the Scottish Joint Parliamentary Recruiting Committee and of the Scottish Joint Parliamentary War Aims Committee. In the commercial sphere he was chairman of the National Services Furnishing Trades, Central Joint Committee for Great Britain, and of the Joint Advisory Committee of the Furnishing Trade of Great Britain, in connection with the training of disabled servicemen. For these services he received an OBE in 1918, the year in which he was elected to Parliament as a Liberal, for the coalition government as member for East Renfrewshire, a seat which he held for four years.

Joseph Johnstone died on 13 January 1931 at his residence, Calder House, Lochwinnoch. His estate amounted to £2,047 8s 6d of which his interest in

Joseph Johnstone Ltd was £437 10s. He was survived by his two sons and three daughters.

JOHN CALDER

SOURCES

Unpublished

BT/12040, Joseph Johnstone Ltd
SRO: SC 58/42/114, Inventory
    SC 58/45/33, Will

Published

The Cabinet Maker, January 1931
Glasgow Chamber of Commerce Journal, Vol 18, 4/4/1935
Glasgow Herald, 14/1/1931
Hansard, 1919, 1920, 1921, 1922, Vol 124, 137, 148, 158
Paisley & Renfrewshire Gazette, 17/1/1931
Who Was Who, Vol 3

George PATERSON,

Timber merchant; b. c.1849, Stirlingshire, s. of George Paterson, timber merchant, and Mary Stark; m. Jessie Ann Gordon, 2 s., 2 d.; MD, A G Paterson & Co Ltd, Timber Merchants; d. 10/11/1928, Glasgow; g/v estate: £21,028.

George Paterson never ran a large business corporation and never took any active role in public affairs. Rather he ran a medium sized business showing steady rather than spectacular growth. His contribution therefore was not that of a major business figure but that of a middle ranking businessman whose company enjoyed a comfortable existence. It was, however, an increasingly competitive market. In the Glasgow business directory of 1836-7 there were 24 wood merchants while in the directory for 1923-4 there were 136 names in that section. A & G Paterson was the only name which appeared in both lists.

The company was founded in Lanark in March 1824 by two brothers, Alexander & George Paterson; the latter was the father of George Paterson. George was his father's third son. He received a good education, spending time at Glasgow University and at universities in Berlin and Leipzig. Apparently he was intended for a career in chemistry but in 1871 he entered his father's business and three years later became a partner.

The company moved its headquarters to Glasgow in the 1830s, largely because its major customer was the Tennant's chemical works. It maintained sawmills at Bonnybridge and at Kincardine on Forth from where the wood was taken along the Forth and Clyde Canal to Port Dundas. At first most of the wood was purchased in Fife. Alexander Paterson, one of the founders, sought supplies further afield principally in the north of Scotland, eventually making his home in Invergordon. The Invergordon and Glasgow sides of the business were divided in 1856, with Alexander's family taking the Invergordon side and George's the Glasgow side. The Glasgow Paterson's continued to buy timber from their cousins but supplies were insufficient and they soon began to buy wood for themselves in the north of Scotland. It was this aspect of the business which was developed by the young George Paterson.

A large part of George's business career was spent in Aberdeenshire where he managed the company's affairs. In particular he attended to the saw mills on Deeside. The company also invested considerable sums of money in purchasing young woodlands which would ensure future supplies of timber. After about 20 years there his elder brother died and he moved to Glasgow to become managing director of the firm which was still based in the St Rollox district of the city. In 1904 George registered the firm as a limited company.

An extremely busy business career, which included the eventual oversight of 20 sawmills, prevented George Paterson from taking an active part in public affairs but he was a man of wide culture who enjoyed the company of his many friends.

CHARLES W MUNN

SOURCES

Unpublished

SRO: SC 36/48/403, Inventory
    SC 36/51/220, Will

Published

The Bailie, 27/8/1924
Glasgow Herald, 12/11/1928
Timber Trades Journal, 17/11/1928

Hugh S ROWAN,

Ship furnisher, b. 20/3/1891, Greenock, s. of John Rowan, ship furnisher and Isabella Gordon Shearer; m. (1) Dorothy Heath; (2) Sheila Evelyn Pasmore (Blair); 1 d.; Ch, Rowan & Boden Ltd; d. 15/2/1956; g/v estate: £179,581.

The world leadership in shipbuilding established by the River Clyde in the last quarter of the nineteenth century created a huge demand for supplies of materials for the ships, since shipbuilding is largely an assembly trade. Not only were plates, angles and pumps in demand, but the vessels required furnishing all the way from basic deck covering to cabinet work, upholstery, and the most elaborate furniture. It was this opportunity that lay behind the establishment of the partnership of John Rowan and John Boden in 1909. John Rowan had previously been in business from about 1890 as J G Rowan & Co, Cabinetmakers and Ships' Furnishers. The office was in Bothwell Street, Glasgow, and the workshop in Greenock. By 1900 this small firm was also advertising itself as 'office furnishers'. In 1909 Rowan & Boden appeared in the Glasgow directory as ships' furnishers and in 1913 the partnership converted itself into a private limited company.

Hugh S Rowan was born in March 1891 in Greenock and went to school there at Greenock Academy. His subsequent training is obscure, but it seems most likely that he went directly to join his father in the family business. His progress in the business was to be interrupted by the First World War. He served first in 1914 in France with the Cameron Highlanders, and was then commissioned in the Royal Garrison Artillery; he was awarded the MC and gained the rank of major. At the end of the war he rejoined Rowan & Boden.

The 1920s were not particularly good years for ships' furnishers. Shipbuilding was in a long depression and the Clyde yards were building vessels at barely half the pre-war level of output. Nevertheless the reputation of Rowan & Boden was good and they gained several important contracts with European and British lines. In the 1930s conditions were even more difficult but again Rowan & Boden's reputation stood them in good stead. Among the contracts they won were for furnishing part of the *Queen Mary* and *Queen Elizabeth*.

Hugh S Rowan became chairman of Rowan & Boden in 1934. Under his direction his company opened new premises on the new Hillington industrial estate. In the Second World War he was again in service and his involvement with the armed forces gave him an interest in the employment of disabled men. After the war he became chairman of Haven Products Ltd a company set up on Hillington estate and geared to the employment solely of disabled men.

In the decade after the war the Clyde and other British shipyards were busy, and Rowan & Boden prospered. The company converted to a public limited company in 1949 with a capital of £380,000. Hugh S Rowan was chairman and two members of the Boden family, E J Boden and Sydney Boden were joint managing directors. The only non-family director was R C Blackie as company secretary. During this period the company opened a second factory at Hillington and also acquired all the shares of Roanoid Plastics Ltd. In the 1950s the company carried on its business as both manufacturers and contractors for floor, deck and industrial protective compositions, and also through its acquisition of Roanoid Plastics, became suppliers and manufacturers of plastic moulded hardware, and industrial plastic mouldings. The original business of ship and general furnishing continued, but diversification protected the company moving it out of its formerly very specialised market dependency. In the mid 1950s the company was recording annual net profits of around £150,000.

Although the products, activities and markets of Rowan & Boden grew, the firm remained located in Hillington with its head office in Paisley. Hugh Rowan remained a Renfrewshire man living at various times in Kilmacolm and Bridge of Weir. He was a staunch churchman being a member of St James Church, Kilmacolm, leaving it £1,000 in his will. In local politics he was a member of Kilmacolm Parish Council from 1924 to 1932; he was also a Justice of the Peace. Rowan was twice married, first in 1917 to Dorothy Heath and later to Sheila Evelyn Pasmore or Blair with whom he had one daughter and a step-daughter. His personal estate at death was £179,581 of which £148,867 represented his shares in his own company. It appears that Rowan had taken no steps to transfer his shares to avoid death duties. His sudden death in 1956 at the early age of 64 consequently meant that £98,871 was paid out in estate duty. A rapid reorganisation then followed in the company. E J Boden became chairman while Sydney Boden remained as managing director. Younger managers then joined the board including J R Organ, a nephew of Rowan. Rowan himself had had no sons and with his death the Rowan name passed from the membership of he firm.

ANTHONY SLAVEN

SOURCES

Unpublished

SRO: SC 58/42/193, Inventory
      SC 58/45/93, Will

Published

Glasgow Herald, 16/2/1956
Post Office Directories
Rowan, Hugh S, *Scottish Biographies*, 1938
The Times, 17/2/1956

Peter SIME,

Timber merchant; b. 9/1/1847, Dundee, s. of John Sime; m. Jane Ann Gordon; 2 s., 3 d.; Partner, Bell & Sime Ltd, Timber Merchants, Dundee; d. 3/11/1918, Dundee; g/v UK estate: £34,492 4s 0d.

Peter Sime was a leading member of the timber trade in Scotland during the late nineteenth and early twentieth centuries. In 1871 at the age of 24 he went into partnership with James Bell who was his junior by a year. Both men were at that time master joiners and their first business was as joiners and jobbing builders. As custom grew they progressed to supplying joinery materials to the trade and also the heavier types of timber used in house building. This development provided a bridge whereby the firm were eventually able to enter the trade as timber merchants proper and direct importers. In 1877 an opening in the timber trade of Dundee appeared with the withdrawal from business of Wm Kirkland and Sons, one of the larger firms within the city. Bell and Sime were sufficiently well established at this time to survive the shock of the failure of the City of Glasgow Bank in 1878, which had severe repercussions on all industries and trades in Scotland. In Dundee the imports of timber were 59,643 loads in 1876, but this had declined by 44% to 33,381 loads two years later. The firm's trade in heavy timbers required them to erect the Balgay Sawmills at Lochee and to rent a yard near the harbour to store their timber. The disappearance of yet another of the older Dundee timber firms in 1878 provided a further reduction of competition and an opening which the vigorous partnership of Bell and Sime were able to exploit. A year or two later they abandoned the joinery and building business entirely to specialise solely as timber merchants and soon after transferred the whole of their business to the harbour site which came to house Dundee's largest sawmill. By the 1880s the firm had grown to become the largest timber business in the city and in 1893 it was necessary to convert from a partnership into a private limited liability company.

The company had a capital of £100,000, and the two partners were managing directors.

Bell and Sime reinforced their leading position within the Dundee timber trade by organising meetings between the three largest firms in the city from January 1885 onwards to regulate competition. Besides themselves the two other participants in these arrangements were Fleming and Barry Ltd and James Donaldson and Sons of Tayport. At first the agreement took the form of a common price list for all three firms as well as a joint undertaking to limit the number of public sales which each held each year. In April 1898, James Bell and Peter Sime initiated an arrangement whereby the three firms pooled their profits which were then redistributed according to a pre-arranged formula. This formula was probably based on the relative size of the participants' sales and stock for a few years prior to the start of the agreement. This agreement lasted until Peter Sime's death.

The firm was the first to introduce the import of American log timber into Dundee by steamer and by the First World War they had a large number of steamers trading between Dundee and the timber ports of the Baltic coast. Peter Sime took a leading part in these arrangements and he travelled widely on the continent visiting sources of supply and acquainting himself with the products on offer from the various sawmills of Norway and Sweden. He was also in the habit of attending the London and Liverpool mahogany and hardwood markets where he became well known. A genial and kindly personality, combined with a comprehensive knowledge of the qualities of timber, made his services as a surveyor and arbiter in disagreements between traders in great demand, not only in Dundee but over the East coast of Scotland generally.

He played a part both in church activities and also in civic offices, including the Dundee Harbour Board, although he does not appear to have been as active on the civic side as his partner James Bell. With Bell, Peter Sime was one of the promoters of Logie Parish Church and was a keen supporter of that institution for the years when he was connected with the congregation. A change of residence meant that for a number of years he was a member of St Mary's Parish Church. He was also a member of the Dundee Guildry.

RICHARD PERREN

SOURCES

Unpublished

SRO: SC 45/31/84, Inventory
SC 45/34/37, Will

bungalows became the desired forms of housing. As if this were not enough builders found themselves facing a total dislocation in the supply of building materials exacerbated by massive shortage in specialised areas of labour, particularly bricklayers whose services were now at a premium.

And yet those builders who chose to remain in the business in the inter-war years faced unprecedented opportunities for growth. On the one hand there lay local authority building contracts. Even councils such as Glasow's, with only minimal experience in housing projects (but more than other local authorities in Scotland), could not contemplate significant direct-labour projects until the 1930s. Central authorities, with a firm grip on the purse-strings of subsidies, ensured that contracts were widely tendered for, and actively discouraged favouritism being shown either to direct-labour or building guilds. So firms such as John A Mactaggart & Co were able to profit by providing building services to local authorities under contract for specific schemes, including the largest single development in Scotland at Mosspark, worth some £1.8 million. Mactaggart was also quick to take advantage of government subsidies to private builders for the construction of houses for rent, building extensively in Glasgow through the Western Heritable Investment Company. Mactaggart & Mickel, run by Mactaggart's son and Andrew Mickel built subsidised properties for rent, but also turned to the slowly developing market for owner-occupied housing. Here they provided both flatted and cottage accommodation, and also distinctive bungalows. Building was not restricted to Glasgow, but slowly expanded in the west of Scotland and also in Edinburgh. In the Capital private building was dominated largely by one building type, the bungalow, and increasingly by one builder, James Miller.

Miller, like Mactaggart & Mickel, was increasingly aware of the importance of design, both for its own sake, but also as a marketing tool. Both these firms advertised heavily and mimicked the marketing ploys developed by the large English house-builders such as Costains or Laings. They provided a variety of payment-plans and mortgages for would-be owners, and at the top of the market offered the facility for individual architect-designed houses. Nor did these builders only innovate in house types and marketing techniques. Increasingly they came to experiment in new types of materials, both for private developments and local authority schemes. Local authorities encouraged experimentation with concrete and artificial stone, and with flat-roofed designs, such as those pioneered by the Glasgow builder John MacDonald. The majority of Miller's 'traditional' bungalows were built using an artificial stone facing, whilst Mactaggart made extensive use of both concrete and artificial stone, in the manufacture of which he and Mactaggart & Mickel had invested. John Lawrence was committed to new building techniques, and owed the success of his business partly to his exploitation of gypsum based 'Bellrock' bricks. Few builders however went as far as Lord Weir, who advocated the construction of a utility house, made from a wooden-frame with steel walls, as a means of solving both the post-war housing crisis and relieving unemployment among engineers and steel-workers.

Despite public enthusiasm and government encouragement Weir's ideas had been met with hostility from the building trades and local authorities. However, after the second war private builders universally looked to new building techniques to meet the demands for public housing. Millers, Mactaggart & Mickel and John Lawrence were among a number of firms who formed the Scottish Housing Group, formed to erect selected types of non-traditional houses on a standardised tendering and contractual basis. The group was formed by Ralph Whitson of Melville, Dundas and Whitson, who designed with Dr W A Fairhurst a house built around a reinforced concrete frame. James Miller and John Lawrence also developed non-traditional house types of which large numbers were built in the years 1945-1955. No builder contributed as much in this field as Harry Cruden whose firm specialised in the construction of non-traditional house types of which over 25,000 were built between 1945 and 1960. Crudens also crossed the barrier between low-rise non-traditional housing and the development of massive mixed housing developments for local authorities in the 1960s. As high-rise techniques came to dominate public building so specialised contractors, many from south of the border, were called in to build. At the same time the vitality of private sector building was assured through the continued success of firms such as Mactaggart & Mickel and John Lawrence, and also James Miller and Partners, whose success in the post second world war era lay partly in diversification into contracting and open-cast coal mining.

Few productive industries can have left such an enduring and visible record of its output as has building; on the other hand few are shrouded in as much anonymity and surrounded by as much misunderstanding. A handful of biographies can resolve neither of these difficulties, but they can serve to remind us of the vitality of the construction industry, of its complexities and innovations, of its personalities and problems, and most of all of its essential contribution to modern life in Scotland.

NICHOLAS J MORGAN

Peter ANDERSON,

Mason and contractor; b. 1848, Auchterarder, Perthshire, s. of John Anderson and Alexis Martin; m. Margaret McIntosh; 1 s.; Founder and Ch, P & W Anderson Ltd, Glasgow; d. 21/3/1922, Auchterarder, Perthshire; g/v UK estate £34,313 4s 10d.

Peter Anderson was born at Auchterarder in 1848; he was trained there as a mason, but anxious to exploit the opportunities for employment offered by Scotland's fastest growing city he moved to Glasgow in the early 1870s. There he worked as a tradesman, setting up in business with his younger brother William at Elphinstone Street, Govan in 1877. Together the two brothers created a small thriving business which was to expand rapidly during the 1890s, the period that witnessed much of the redevelopment of Glasgow's city-centre, becoming for a short time one of Scotland's largest building firms.

The basis of the firm's steady growth had been masonry contracts for tenements, villas and mansion houses, and small public buildings. However their rise to prominence was to be through their association with prestigious city-centre contracts, working on difficult restricted sites, employing advanced construction methods. On many of these contracts they worked with some of the kingdom's most eminent architects. If relationships with architects were important then so also were the relationships that Peter Anderson had forged with a number of key institutions in the city who were to provide the firm with a series of essential large contracts. Most significant was the redevelopment of the City's Royal Infirmary - between 1910 and 1912 the firm was awarded three contracts worth £187,210 for mason work on the new hospital complex which replaced the late eighteenth century building designed by R and J Adam. In the city-centre the Caledonian Railway Company provided contracts worth £174,000 between 1901 and 1909 for the construction of a 16 bay extension to the Central Station Hotel, and for offices for the company in Glasgow's Union Street. Contracts worth £160,000 were won for the original construction work on David Barclay's Royal College of Science and technology in 1903, and for additions and extensions in 1909 and 1910. The firm also undertook a number of important civic projects; building schools, halls and fire stations for the School Board and Corporation, and in 1906 undertaking the mason work on the Mitchell Library.

The majority of these contracts had been distinguished not only by their sheer scale and technical complexity, but also by the degree of craftsmanship that they demanded. It was in their ability to meet all three of these demands, and thus service both the designs of architects inspired by Italianate and Renaissance traditions, and also meet the ambitions of sponsoring companies, that Anderson's astonishing growth was achieved. Contracts included John Keppie's and Charles Rennie Mackintosh's striking Glasgow Herald Building (1893-95), James Salmon's elaborate Mercantile Chambers in Bothwell Street (1897-98), and James Thomson's Liverpool London and Globe Insurance Company's office in Hope Street, a contract worth £40,000 between 1898 and 1900, described by the authors of *The architecture of Glasgow* as 'a vast pile ... a building to make one wonder rather than admire'. Perhaps their greatest technical achievement was the steel-framed Northern Assurance Building in St Vincent Street whose construction exemplified the problems of building in confined sites; the architect J A Campbell's solution to this was to reduce 'wall space to a minimum producing an almost entirely glass facade' at the rear, made up of 'towering bays of steel framed windows'. In all, between 1896 and the outbreak of the war the company carried out contracts in and around Glasgow worth at least £2,250,000.

In response to the increasing demands on the business Peter Anderson and his brother converted their firm to a limited liability company in 1907 with a registered capital of £100,100 divided between 6,000 ordinary shares and 4,000 preference shares of £10 each. Peter Anderson was appointed chairman, and with 2,700 ordinary shares was the largest shareholder in the business; the company's two other directors were his son John and his brother William, both of whom held 1,350 shares. By 1912 two of William Anderson's sons, Robert T and John T Anderson, had become members and shareholders of the firm, each receiving 200 of their father's shares.

The outbreak of war in 1914 brought a halt to the flow of projects that had prompted the company's expansion. However, with Peter Anderson's encouragement, and under the active management of his son John in London, the firm wholeheartedly threw themselves into the war effort, where they were in particular associated with a number of projects at Gretna, with the result that the scale of their operations and their workforce grew enormously. In 1917 Peter Anderson offered the company to the War Office as a working unit, and as a result of the acceptance of this offer a large part of the workforce, by then numbered at around 15,000 men, were recruited to the Royal Engineers. Among these was John Anderson, by then managing director of the firm, who became a Major.

By the end of the war Peter Anderson had effectively retired from the active management of his business, although he retained the position of chairman. He increasingly divided his time between his south-side Glasgow home and Auchterarder, where he died from heart disease in March 1922. He left personal estate valued at slightly over £34,000, which included his 1,300 shares in P & W Anderson (valued generously at par) and over £13,000 invested on the Savings Bank and Thrift scheme which he and his son had set up to encourage savings among their employees. The majority of his estate was left to his son, Sir John, who had been knighted in 1920 for his war time services. Sir John Anderson, managing the business from London from where he also indulged in agricultural pursuits on estates in Bedfordshire, thus became the largest shareholder in the company, the capital of which had been increased in 1921 to £290,000, with 40,000 shares. The attempt to increase the capital of the business in 1921 was the first warning sign of the difficulties Andersons were to face in the post-war depression. Having expanded massively before and during the war they found themselves starved of the contracts they needed to sustain themselves. The result was that by 1925 the company faced insuperable financial problems, going into liquidation with assets valued at only £70,000, compared to liabilities of £500,000. Not all was lost; the business that Peter Anderson had worked so hard to build was at least partially rescued by his brother William, who along with his two sons bought the Glasgow side of the business from the liquidators, establishing a leaner, and fitter, P & W Anderson (Glasgow) Ltd. Sir John Anderson retired from active business, taking up writing and lecturing on the philosophy of thought.

NICHOLAS J MORGAN

SOURCES

Unpublished

BT 2/6928
SRO: SC 36/48/332, Inventory

Published

The Builders Journal, 28/11/1906
The Glasgow Building Trades Exchange Yearbook, 1896-1913
The Glasgow Herald, 5/6/1920, 31/3/1922, 10/2/1925, 15/4/1963
Gomme, A and Walker, D, *The Architecture of Glasgow*, revised edn, London, 1987
Hume, John R, *Industrial Archaeology of Glasgow*, Glasgow, 1974

John BEST,

Public works contractor; b. 1839, Kilmarnock, Ayrshire; m. Mary Finlay; 3 s., 1 d.; Founder and Ch, John Best & Sons Ltd, Edinburgh; d. 30/6/1908, Warriston House, Edinburgh; g/v UK estate: £348,168 13s 7d.

By the time of his death in June 1908 John Best was managing director of probably the largest public works contractors in the east of Scotland. The list of contracts to his credit stretched northwards from Bradford and Bolton in England through the east of Scotland, west to Ballachulish and across the Irish channel to Donegal and Cork. Specialising in reservoir and harbour works Best undertook a range of work which challenged both his technical and managerial skills. His success in overcoming these difficulties was reflected both by the healthy state of the limited company which he left behind him to be managed by his three sons, and by his substantial personal fortune of in excess of £348,000.

Best was born in Kilmarnock in 1839 where, following an elementary education, he served an apprenticeship as a joiner to his uncle William Scott. It was with Scott that, following his apprenticeship, he learnt the basic skills of estimating for and managing contracts; following his uncle's death, Best completed the outstanding work of the firm before seeking contracts on his own account. His first major work may well have been as principal in the partnership of Lawson & Best (with the contractor George Lawson of Rutherglen), building in 1880 the Roseberry reservoir as part of Edinburgh's Moorfoot water scheme, a contract worth £33,000. He undertook a number of minor railway contracts around the same period, including work for the Monkland Railway and the Broughton and Peebles Branch Railway. These were followed by a number of harbour extension contracts, including the Govan Graving Dock, the Albert and Edinburgh Docks, and the Imperial Dock at Leith, worth £14,500 in 1885.

The gradual accumulation of capital and expertise allowed Best, with the assistance of his three sons and an established managerial staff, to expand his business considerably in the early 1890s. Unlike many other Scottish firms Best also looked to England for work, obtaining the first of an important series of contracts in the north of England in 1893 for the construction of the Gouthwaite reservoir for Bradford Corporation. Completed between 1893 and 1903, during which time the contract suffered a major setback due to storm damage at the site, the work was worth, at final measurement, £144,000. In 1902 Bradford Corporation again employed Best, this time to build the Angram Reservoir as part of the Nidd Valley water scheme. Five years later the firm won the contract for Bolton Corporation's Delph reservoir, worth £218,400. Best also undertook work in Ireland, including three major contracts in 1898; the Cork, Blackrock Package Railway Company's line to Crosshaven, the Loch Erne drainage scheme, and the Admiralty contract for the construction of a new jetty at the Admiralty Dockyard at Halbowline. The spread of contracts underway naturally led to a delegation of responsibilities on particular contracts to his sons John, William and Alexander, and also to contractors agents such as William Sloan and William Main. Labour was generally acquired at the site, some of it being local and some itinerant navvies following either the firm or contracts around the country. Plant - locomotives, cranes and excavators - were frequently moved from site to site, with the company maintaining depots at Craigleith Quarry in Edinburgh, over which they held a lease, and Warriston in Penicuik, the home of John Best.

In addition to the work in England and Ireland Best, who throughout this period remained in sole control as the only partner in the business, continued to work throughout Scotland on a variety of projects. Between 1892 and 1900 the firm undertook the construction of a wet dock, a graving dock and other extensions at Newhaven Harbour west of Leith on the Firth of Forth. This contract for the Leith Harbour & Dock Commissioners was followed by another for the construction of new gates and locks for the Old Dock at Leith. In 1898 a contract was obtained for the Ballachulish extension to the Callander and Oban railway, the same year in which Best began his fateful association with the Edinburgh City water works at Talla. The main contracts for the construction of the service railway to the Talla site and the reservoir had been won admist some controversy by James Young & Son, the Edinburgh contractors, Best obtaining a single contract for the construction of an aqueduct between the Tweed and Broughton syphons, worth some £87,728. In the late summer of 1899 Youngs, and the remaining family member of the firm Robert Young (qv), went into liquidation, leaving over three-quarters of the reservoir unbuilt. The contract was readvertised, with Best this time getting the work, with a value of £150,000.

The Talla contract was not easy to complete; labour was short owing both to the dispersal of Young's workforce, and to the mobilisation of many for the South African war. A tunnel collapse in 1901 and persistent conflicts with the city engineers further delayed progress. Drunkenness, which had bedevilled Young's workforce was less problematic; Best sought both to control and profit from the prodigious drinking propensities of his workforce who were housed in a number of wooden huts around the site, by taking the lease on the Crook Hotel at nearby Broughton, ensuring that a siding was built on the reservoir's service railway at Crook to allow navvies easy access. John Best was prominent in the management of the Talla contract, although it was important enough to also involve his son John Jnr and William Sloan; at 66 Best was in his prime actively promoting the rapid growth of his company. It was in the course of one visit to the Talla site in 1905 that Best was involved in a serious accident as his car was in collision with a cart at Broughton - he never fully recovered from his severe injuries, which led to his untimely death three years later in June 1908.

John Best's refusal to bring either his sons or managers into partnership led to a crisis following the accident in 1905. Action was quickly taken to convert the firm into a limited liability company, with John Best Jnr, William and Alexander Best as directors, and John Best as director and chairman. The share capital of £50,000 was fully paid up, with John Best holding 18,000 shares and his sons 10,000 each. The company's permanent staff, Main, Sloan and the cashier Robert Brydon, along with two civil engineers Thomas Philips and John James, all held 200 shares. The new company took over all the old firm's existing work, which included in 1906, in addition to the Angram Reservoir, contracts for a graving dock at West Hartlepool for the North Eastern Railway Company and the associated Seaton Snook railway to a nearby steelworks. The Talla contract had been successfully completed, as had a contract for Drumbowie reservoir for the Falkirk and Larbert Water Trustees.

After providing for his wife during her lifetime, and setting aside a small sum to produce an income for his daughter, John Best left the residue of his estate, around £300,000, to his three sons. Best had invested shrewdly and carefully - nearly a third of the sum was held in bonds and mortgages; £47,000 was invested in British railway companies, and a similar sum in overseas railways and tramways. The remainder was held in generally small investments in Scottish companies and overseas mining concerns. His substantial personal fortune probably offers a fair representation of his lifetime's accumulation of wealth, as events overtook any plans he may have had to divide money among his sons through partnerships in his firm. As such it reflects a highly successful business career, at the height of which John Best, very much in the tradition of the self-taught Scottish contractor, personally controlled a sophisticated and complex business carrying on major projects in various parts of Britain with a combined workforce of around 1,200 men to be managed, housed and fed. Best's name was associated with important public undertakings throughout the North and Scotland, where his business ranked with firms such as McAlpines, Brand, Young and Morrison & Mason. There is every reason to think that Best's career would have been even more notable had it not been for his accident on the road to Talla.

NICHOLAS J MORGAN

SOURCES

Unpublished

SRO: BT 2/6376, John Best & Sons Ltd
    BT 2/13194, John Best (Edinburgh) Ltd
    SC 70/1/482, Inventory
    SC 70/4/399, Will
    GD 310, Records presented by John Best (Contractors) Ltd

Published

Building News, 1/5/1885, 1/7/1908
Engineering, 9/9/1898
The Scotsman, 1/7/1908
Tait, W A, *Edinburgh and District Water*, Edinburgh, 1905

James BRAND,

Public works contractor; b. 20/9/1831, Montrose, s. of Charles Brand, mason and contractor and Margaret Falconer; m. 1863, Jane Gordon, d. of William Gordon, Procurator Fiscal, Banffshire; 5 s., 3 d.; Snr Partner, Charles Brand & Sons; d. 15/1/1904, Bournemouth; g/v UK estate: £113,593 18s 9d.

James Brand was born in Montrose in 1831, the son of a mason and contractor, Charles Brand, who carried on business in the vicinity of Montrose. James was educated first at a dame school in Montrose and then at the town's academy where he was taught arithmetic and rudimentary Latin - by his own confession he was a lazy student, leaving school to go 'into the workshop, determined to qualify for making my living as a workman'. His practical education began in the employment of his father, but shortly afterwards he was sent to work for his uncle, William Brand, who was supervising the construction of Ardross Castle for the China merchant William Matheson. Brand spent three years at Ardross learning the principles of man management and the rudiments of the building trade from those employed at the site; 'my familiar

COURTESY OF THE MITCHELL LIBRARY

135

association with workmen gave me a knowledge of their point of view which has been of great use to me since; besides, the training in mechanics which has also been of great advantage'.

During Brand's apprenticeship his father was gradually expanding his business, with contracts for viaduct construction on the Aberdeen Railway between Forfar and Arbroath, and a share in a combine of contractors (known as Mitchell Dean & Co) who tendered for the extension of the Aberdeen railway to Inverness. Charles Brand also built a number of mansions in the north east, many to the design of the architect James Ross. In 1851 James Brand returned from Ardross and was sent by his father to work as clerk of works on the Episcopal Church at Arbroath. The first stage of the contract for the Inverness line began in 1852, Brand moving to Huntly with his father to work on their share of the contract there. The second stage of the contract saw Brands working on the final section of the line running into Aberdeen - James Brand was agent for the contract and timekeeper - 'I had also all the levels to give and setting out as we had no engineer'. The demands for completion ahead of the tourist season meant six months almost continuous labour, although following the opening of the line in 1854 James Brand remained in Aberdeen for a year attending to line maintenance. Brand's father joined a second consortium (Mitchell Brebner & Co) to contract for sections of the Great North of Scotland Railway (GNSR), being given the line from Elgin to Keith across the Spey valley and through the valley of Mulben, including the construction of the viaduct at Boat O'Brig, where James Brand worked as agent between 1856 and 1858. Poor surveying of what was a naturally treacherous environment left Brand with severe difficulties calling for improvisation on site - as was often the case the ingenuity of the contractor was required to make up for the shortcomings of the professionals. He later recalled that he owed a good deal of his training to this contract.

With James Brand taking an increasingly important role in the family business (he had been sole manager since 1853, and became partner with his father in 1859) the firm acquired a number of large contracts in the late 1850s and early 1860s, a time of general slackness in railway works. Although they tendered for work in the south their successful bids were for contracts in the north and north-east, often because few others either had the skill or desire to work in the difficult geological conditions and hostile climate. Even then Brand regretted that they frequently under-tendered in an attempt to secure work. During this period they built the line from Keith to Dufftown (on which they lost £10,000 following a viaduct collapse) for the GNSR and a section of the Strathspey Railway (1861-63), the latter involving part payment in shares in the company to the value of £4,000, which sub-sequently realised only £1,000. The firm's next major contract was not until 1865 when Brand began a 30

mile line from Bonar Bridge to Golspie in Sutherland, a contract worth in total £100,000 on which the firm made a 10% profit largely due to Brand's shrewd management. During the completion of this contract James Brand was employed by the directors of the Highland Railway to survey their proposed Dingwall & Skye line with a view to his being offered the contract. Brand's estimate for the work, which reduced the projected costs considerably by avoiding heavy excavation work and the extension of the line to Loch Akin, was accepted by the directors on the condition that he take shares in the company. With his experience of the difference that shares could make to the profit on a contract from the firm's work on the Strathspey Railway still fresh in his mind, Brand refused to accept the contract, leaving him little prospect of work.

It was at this point that James Brand made the decision to move the focus of the firm's operations to the central lowlands, although his enthusiasm for the move was limited. It was his father who prompted the move, arguing, according to Brand, that 'if I did not go then, as I was approaching 40, I might never go into a wider field'. The decision proved, in the short term, a disaster. Brands tendered for two contracts on the Ayrshire line of the Glasgow and South Western Railway (G & SW), working from the Lugar iron-works through Cumnock to Ayr. Brand's recollection of the work was stark, and reflected on the importance of accumulated experience to the successful con-tractor: 'it was a mistake, and I was sorry, as the work was heavy and we were not trained to work in that country, and we lost all the money we had made'. There followed in 1868-70 a contract for the Balerno branch of the Caledonian Railway Company, which also made a loss for the firm, and then the first of an important series of contracts on the Glasgow tramways, acquired largely through the rec-ommendation of G & SW's chief engineer. Although required to work with sub-contractors (A & J Faill) on the first ten-mile line in 1871, a subsequent extension for the Corporation and a line for the Govan and Greenock tramways saw the company back in profit, bringing in around £4-5,000. The tramway work overlapped with a contract for the Hamilton section of the Bothwell railway, including a viaduct over the Clyde, worth around £80,000. The firm made a profit of £5,000 on this, despite substantial rises in craftsmen's wages during the building boom of the mid 1870s and indifferent management by the contract agent, James' youngest brother David.

Between 1875 and 1882 Brand acquired a number of varied contracts which saw the firm consolidate its position in the lowlands, expand into Ireland, and broaden its field of technical expertise. Among these was one in 1875, a small diversion of the Caledonian Railway line on the south-side of Glasgow, that paid a profit of 40% (£9,500), largely due to the method of excavating adopted by Brand which allowed work to continue regardless of through traffic, thus reducing the time taken on the contract to only nine months. Between 1876 and 1877 the firm built tramways at Dundee and Bridge of Allan. In 1878 the firm began work on the Grangemouth docks, a contract valued at £260,000, which took over 12 months longer than planned to complete largely due to difficulties in securing foundations in difficult ground. The consultant engineer for the Railway Company on the project was Sir John Wolfe Barry. Brand, displaying the contempt of the practical man for the theoretical, complained later that 'it paid fairly well on the whole, but scarcely what it should have done if properly designed at first' - the profit on the contract amounted to in the region of £26,000. Brand also obtained a number of small contracts for harbour works on the east coast, and for building docks for Denny's of Dumbarton (1880-84), and Donegal Quay at Belfast (1882-85); the latter too was the victim of poor design work, although in this case extravagance in the original plans allowed Brand to increase his profit to some £11,000 through careful revision of specifications and materials.

In 1882 Charles Brand formally retired from the firm, leaving James Brand as sole partner in the business; he died three years later in January 1885. Although James Brand was responsible for the management of the firm, a number of full time employees supported his efforts, notably Andrew Smith, who had joined as an apprentice on the Keith-Dufftown line later coming to specialise in book-keeping and estimating; Thoams Mason (qv) who had supervised the early tramway works before moving to work on Stobcross Docks, and David Brand, who had acted as agent on the Bothwell line and at Grangemouth. Although maintaining a fairly stable management the firm was always dogged by a shortage of labour; 'our greatest difficulty in carrying on engineering works has been that we have never been able to man the work sufficiently' complained Brand in 1904. This was despite the fact that Brand was acclaimed for his 'consideration for the large bodies of men he employed', a result possibly of his early experiences at Ardross - 'labour disputes', wrote the *Glasgow Herald*, 'rarely occurred among his workmen'.

The year of Charles Brand's retirement saw the firm undertake one of its most ambitious contracts, the eastern section of the City and District Railway, the first underground line to be built in Glasgow. The work was extremely difficult and slow - underpinning of buildings at Buchanan Street, for example, reduced progress on that section to seven yards of tunnel per month, whilst at Queen Street Brands built the low-level station without interruption to the main line station above by supporting the existing station during excavations by a complex arrangement of columns and girders. The line was completed in 1886, with the contract yielding a 15 per cent profit on £130,000. The expertise gained during this contract, and the skill with which it had been executed, led to Brand's involvement in Glasgow's two other major underground railways, the Glasgow District Subway and the Caledonian Railway's Glasgow Central line. The former contract, worth in total £180,000 involved both sections running under the Clyde. The latter, involving two contacts from Bridgeton in the east of the City to Trongate in the centre and involving a workforce of over 1,000, was priced at £600,000 (Brand put the final cost at £900,000) and was 'thought so risky that almost no one would take it'. In both, Brands successfully deployed a sophisticated system of shielded compressed air chambers to allow tunnelling to progress safely and rapidly. The outcome of the Central contract was however disappointing. At arbitration the Caledonian Railway disputed his claim, despite the fact that Brand's work had been described by Sir Benjamin Baker, the civil engineer who had overseen the first three of London's underground lines, as 'one of the most difficult pieces of work under streets so full of traffic that had been undertaken in his time'. Brand was bitter that the much lauded Sir John Wolfe Barry, of whom he did not hold a high opinion, made an award as arbitrator which greatly favoured the railway company.

There were other disappointments during this period - Brand's acquired expertise for railway building in the crowded urban environment was not matched by an ability to work with water in the countryside. He was unsuccessful in tenders for both Craigmaddie Reservoir outside Glasgow and the Thirlemere aqueduct. Both of these contracts went to Scottish competitors. In 1898 Brand took a contract with the Caledonian for a second project at Grangemouth Docks worth in excess of £600,000 - the contract was offered partly in settlement of the disputed claim over the Central Railway. Sir John Wolfe Barry was also consulting engineer at Grangemouth - 'like most of the works from the same engineer', recollected Brand, 'it had to be much altered'. Barry delayed and hindered the project with suggestions that ranged from the 'absurd' to the 'impracticable' - further delays arose due to disputes with the resident engineer, the weather, and conflicts with the local authority over diversions of sewers. Nonetheless the contract did pay - this was largely due to two experiments conducted by James Brand - the first was the deployment of a German excavator that shifted almost 100,000 yards of soil in a month, and the second the use of a suction dredger which was also brought from Germany. It was during the Grangemouth contract that James Brand was joined by his son, Harry F Brand, a graduate of Glasgow University who had been trained as a consulting engineer in both Glasgow and London (where he had worked as an assistant engineer to Barry). Harry F Brand began work on the contract in 1899, and took over its management in 1901.

The Grangemouth contract saw the construction of a new partnership to manage the business. In 1903 Harry F Brand, Donald Stewart Arbuthnot (Brand's son-in-law) and the cashier Andrew Smith were all assumed as partners. Business was fairly healthy; in addition to Grangemouth, which was not completed until 1908, the firm had contracts at Rosslare for harbour works (1906) and for the Inverness to Aviemore line of the Highland Railway. In 1909 they received the contract for raising the level of Loch Arklet in Stirlingshire, a contract notable for the use of hydro-electric power generated on the site by the contractors for driving drills, cranes, and in the admiring words of the *Glasgow Herald*, 'greatest of all Highland miracles, an ariel railway stretching miles onwards to Loch Lomondside'. This innovative use of natural resources marked the impact of the energetic Harry Brand (later Sir Harry) on the business. In 1918 he was responsible for moving the base of the company from Glasgow to London where, using the expertise they had gained under the streets of Glasgow, they carried out numerous contracts on the London Underground in the inter-war years. Sir Harry Brand was eminent on a national scale - he was a founder member and chairman of the Federation of Civil Engineering Contractors, chairman in 1927-28, and president from 1936-1940.

James Brand effected a gradual retirement from the family business following the formation of the new partnership in 1903. He did not however forsake the public work upon which he had spent so much time during his life. In 1904 he sat on the Glasgow Municipal Commission on the Housing of the Poor in his capacity as former chairman of Glasgow Parish Council. Brand had first joined the Barony Parochial Board in 1875 - he served continuously (with the exception of one year) until the reforms following the Local Government Act of 1894 which saw the creation of the merged Glasgow Parish in 1898, of whose council he served as chairman until 1901. The merger was the result of a long standing campaign to bring the two parochial boards together which had begun in 1881, largely with a view to providing a single hospital for the city's sick poor. Brand was chairman of the new council's hospitals committee, where he continued to agitate for reforms in the accommodation provided for the poor. In particular he argued that 'many lives could be saved if those who apply for relief from sickness ... could be induced to accept hospital treatment' - this he continued, could only be done if the stigma of the poorhouse was removed from medical treatment by the provision of parochial hospitals. As a result of his efforts the council undertook to build one 1,200 bed hospital to house the chronic sick, the aged and infirm, and children, and two smaller hospitals for the acutely ill. The subsequent construction of the imposing general hospital at Stobhill marked the end of Brand's career as a parochial officer, although he did give detailed verbal and written evidence to the Royal Commission on the Poor Laws in 1909.

Brand was also notable in Glasgow for his service to the City's Catholic community, for which he received the Knighthood of St Gregory. He had been born an Episcopalian but had been received into the Catholic church shortly after his marriage in 1863 to Jane Gordon, the daughter of William Gordon, Procurator Fiscal in the county of Banffshire. Brand served for many years on the Scottish Catholic Schools Committee, and was also chairman of the Caledonian Catholic Association. He was remembered by the *Catholic Observer* as a generous benefactor to many Catholic causes, and only shortly before his death he had purchased ground in Glasgow for the construction of church halls. Of his family two of his five sons were Jesuit priests, whilst two of his three daughters were Good Shepherd nuns.

James Brand died in Bournemouth in January 1909 whilst trying to escape from the harshness of the climate in which he spent so much of his working life. He was 77 years old, and during his career had accumulated a modest fortune of some £130,000, distributed between a bewildering variety of investments. He divided his estate between his children, giving, in the case of those in religious orders, half their share to the order to which they belonged. During his career Brand had successfully taken his firm from a provincial to the national stage. They had undertaken profitably contracts which other firms would have not contemplated, involving the marshalling of vast resources of men and materials, and the exercise of considerable ingenuity and expertise. Frequently one of the main obstacles to success was, in Brand's opinion, the interference of professionals. Brand, 'with a Napoleonic grasp, both of ideas and detail', managed the firm, its contracts and its men, on the basis of skills he had acquired throughout his working life, many of them stemming from his apprenticeship with the craftsmen at Ardross. It was a life he recalled shortly before his death in his memoirs, which he wrote as 'some of my children have been urging me, as I am too old to do any more work, to amuse myself and prevent time from hanging heavy on my hands'. It is from this that much of the detail of his remarkable life has been drawn.

NICHOLAS J MORGAN

SOURCES

Unpublished

Glasgow University Archives, UGD/8
Information supplied by Duncan Brand
Memoirs of Mr James Brand (lent by his family)
SRO: SC 36/48/215, Inventory
       SC 36/51/149, Trust disposition and settlement

Published

The Bailie, No 928, 30/7/1890, January 1909
Building Industries, 10/6/1890, 15/2/1909
Building News, 16/1/1885, 2/5/1890
Engineer, 22/1/1909
Engineering, 15/1/1875, 21/9/1882, 1/2/1882, 22/1/1909
The Glasgow Herald, 18/1/1909, 5/4/1910, 2/7/1910, 23/8/1910
Glasgow Municipal Commission on the Housing of the Poor, *Minutes of Evidence,* Glasgow, 1904
The Glasgow Observer, 23/1/1909
North British Daily Mail, 6/2/1893
The Times, 7/7/1951, 18/7/1951

Harry H CRUDEN,

Housebuilder and contractor; b. 14/8/1895, Fraserburgh, s. of Lewis Cruden, fishcurer and Margaret Smith; Clara Madelaine Buck; Founder and Ch, Crudens Ltd, Musselburgh; d. 1/3/1967, Longniddry, East Lothian.

Harry H Cruden was born in Fraserburgh in August 1895, the son of Lewis Cruden, a fishcurer. He was educated locally and trained as an engineering draughtsman, serving a three year apprenticeship with a Fraserburgh firm. Like many young men of the period his training and career was interrupted by the 1914-18 war. At the age 19 he volunteered for service with the Gordon Highlanders, and following his commission was seconded to the East African Rifles in Kenya. After the war he remained in Kenya, working as a coffee planter, and then travelled to China before returning to Scotland in the late 1930s. There he worked as a timber merchant and manufacturer in a business owned by his wife, Clara Madelaine Cruden, in Musselburgh slightly to the east of Edinburgh. The firm dealt in all aspects of the timber trade and during the second war specialised in the production of ammunition boxes and other munitions-related products.

What catapulted Cruden's career from the mundane to the memorable was the single minded pursuit of an idea - that essential to the recovery of Scotland at the end of the second war was the production of houses, and that a satisfactory rate of house production could only be achieved through innovation in the method of house building, and particularly in the use of non-traditional building techniques. Such techniques were not new - builders and local authorities throughout Scotland had sought to reduce building costs in the inter-war years by gradually adopting 'non-traditional' methods and materials. The government had commissioned the Scottish Special Housing Association with the task of developing non-traditional solutions to the housing problem. Moreover in Kenya Cruden would have been more than familiar with the principles of prefabrication which informed the construction of many residential and public buildings, a good number of which were exported in kit-form from the United Kingdom. What Harry Cruden attempted was a single solution - the Cruden House, designed partly by himself and partly by a team of draughtsmen and engineers. The result was a steel framed house with external walls of concrete slabs, with roofs covered with concrete tiles. The interior walls comprised prefabricated timber frames, lined originally with plasterboard, although tests to the suitability of this material to withstand fire (following numerous outbreaks in completed houses) led to its replacement by plasterboard. Other internal components were all prefabricated. The house was approved by the Department of Health for Scotland in 1946, being costed at between £1,240 to £1,340 each. There followed five house types of various designs, each intended for production.

The government made it clear in 1945 that the emphasis of post-war housebuilding would be on non-traditional methods. In Scotland, where need was greater and resources more scarce a special subsidy was provided to local authorities until December 1947 to meet any extra cost that might be incurred in building by new methods - in addition firms such as Crudens were given a guarantee by the Department of Health for Scotland that a fixed number of houses would be contracted for by local authorities. Initial orders for the house were made by the Secretary of State for Scotland, although contracts were made between Crudens and the local authority for whom

the houses were being erected. Schemes were built either directly, by contractors, or by the SSHA throughout Scotland. However the total number of houses erected in the post war period must have surpassed even the ambitions of Harry Cruden. In Scotland as a whole 116,601 permanent non-traditional houses were erected between the end of the war and December 1954; slightly less than 13,000 of these (or 11 per cent) were Cruden houses. Only one firm, Weirs of Cathcart, provided more houses during the same period. In all, in excess of 25,000 Cruden Houses were built by 1960.

In order to accumulate the expertise and organisation necessary for this widespread housebuilding Harry Cruden formed a combine, Cruden Houses Ltd, with a number of prominent Scottish building firms. These were chosen to give a strong regional flavour to the enterprise, Alexander Hall from Aberdeen, Alliance Construction from Dundee, J Wright & Co from Edinburgh, and Laidlaws from Glasgow. Each firm contracted to undertake the erection of the various Cruden houses in their own locality, with Halls, for example, building from Aberdeen to Shetland.

By the mid-1950s the demand for non-traditional houses of the Cruden type was diminishing as conventional materials became readily available. The Cruden House itself lost its concrete walls as bricks became easier and cheaper to use. It was Harry Cruden's task to steer his company into new directions from the substantial base they had achieved in such a short time. The company looked towards the construction of prefabricated steel-framed factory and garage units, hospital, school and church building as a way of deploying their expertise. In their workshops they built pre-cut or pre-formed timber components for themselves and other contractors - by 1959 2,800 flush doors were being produced weekly. Harry Cruden retired as managing director of Crudens Ltd in 1957, taking up the post as chairman. He was succeeded by M R A Mathews, aged only 25, a trained quantity surveyor. Crudens continued to expand their field of enterprise, particularly in the area of contracting for large public and commercial projects. In 1965, for example, they won the contract for the North British Rubber Company for two factories at Newburgh, Midlothian. They were also involved with local authorities in the design and construction of massive housing developments in Edinburgh and Glasgow. Later projects included shopping developments (Sauchiehall Street in Glasgow, the Wellgate Centre in Dundee, the Eastgate Shopping Development), hopsitals (Queen Mother's Hospital in Glasgow, Ninewells Hospital in Dundee) and other public buildings (the David Hume Tower at the University of Edinburgh and the Meadowbank Stadium).

In 1943 Harry Cruden and his wife had converted their small business into a limited company, with a capital of £1,000, which was not fully paid up until 1946, the year that the Cruden House went into full production. In addition, as production grew, a number of other companies were established, including Cruden Houses Ltd, Cruden Concrete Ltd and Cruden International Design Ltd. Harry Cruden remained in overall control of all of these firms. The share capital of Crudens Ltd was increased from £1,000 to £60,000 by 1957, the increase in value accruing from the capitalisation of reserves of profits. In 1967 a further £150,000 was added to the capital of the company by the same procedure. These new shares had all been allotted to the Cruden Foundation (originally known as the Cruden Trust), a charitable body established by Harry Cruden and his wife. By 1967, the year of Harry H Cruden's death the Foundation held 249,985 of the company's 250,000 shares.

Clara Cruden died in 1965, and two years later Harry Cruden died of cancer. He had created one of Scotland's largest building and civil engineering firms on the basis of a single idea which he had pursued with resourcefulness and imagination. Cruden was well known, not only for the successes of his firm, but also for its benevolent attitude to his employees. He had acquired no great wealth, preferring to divert profits to the Cruden Foundation, a charitable body with a wide remit for supporting public and educational undertakings. His career provides an admirable example of the success that can accrue from the pursuit of innovation.

NICHOLAS J. MORGAN

SOURCES

Unpublished

Companies Registration Office
SRO: SC 22525, Crudens Ltd
SC 33862, Crudens Building and Civil Engineering Ltd
Information supplied by Crudens Ltd

Published

Builder, 21/6/1946, 1/1/1965
Building Industries, December 1947, February 1948, February 1949, March, June, July, October and November 1950, January 1957, April 1963
Mackie, W, *A century of craftmanship, Alexander Hall & Son (Builders) Ltd*, Aberdeen, 1980
Scottish Office Building Directorate, *A Guide to non-traditional housing*, Edinburgh, 1987
The Scotsman, 3/3/1967

Hugh KENNEDY,

Builder, contractor and property investor; b. 1824, Netherton, Glasgow; s. of William Kennedy, forester and Mary Hunter; m. 11/10/1854, Agnes, d. of Moses Hunter, timber merchant; 3 s.; Founder, Hugh Kennedy and Sons, railway and public works contractors, Glasgow; d. 31/10/1895, Glasgow; g/v estate: £21,620 13s 10d.

Hugh Kennedy, the son of a forester, was born at Netherton, Glasgow in 1824. He began his career as an apprentice joiner and cartwright with Thomas Baird, a small builder in Govan. By 1847 he was working on his own account as a joiner, and by 1853 was firmly established in Partick, having as his base a large yard in Merkland Street, feued at some £70 per annum. His business increased steadily; he was described as a builder in 1860, a builder and contractor in 1865, then a railway contractor and finally by the time of his death in 1895 the firm of Hugh Kennedy & Sons bore the title of Railway and Public Works Contractors. Through his involvement in these different aspects of the construction industry, Hugh Kennedy established himself as one of the leading railway contractors in Scotland, and one of the largest owners of rented accommodation in the City of Glasgow and Burgh of Partick.

The growth of Kennedy's business as a contractor should be set firmly in the context of the economic development of Glasgow and the various Clyde ports and resorts with their increasing demands for housing and more sophisticated means of urban transport. Many of his earliest contracts were provided by the Clyde Navigation Trustees; Kennedy took on a variety of large and small jobs such as the construction of a timber wharf at South Quay, Govan, worth £6,000. Kennedy's association with the improvement of the river and its wharfage did not end with the Trustees. He completed contracts for the shipbuilders A & J Inglis and had a close personal link with David Tod of the firm Tod and McGregor. He carried out considerable private contract work for this company and was possibly responsible for the construction sheds built at their yard in 1854 which were destroyed, at a cost of some £20,000, by the gales of 1856. David Tod acted as a financial guarantee on much of Kennedy's work for the Clyde Navigation, and in 1872 Kennedy was purchasing land in Partickhill from his Trustees for housing development.

It was probably the expertise which Kennedy gained in the construction of piers which won him his first railway contract. The firm built the Craigendoran railway and pier, piers at Garelochhead and in 1888 the pier and station at Gourock. All these transport developments were required to meet the growing industrial and leisure demands of Glasgow's popu-lation. In this last respect, Kennedy's most publicly acknowledged work was the Wemyss Bay Railway Station and Pier, built in 1865. The growth of this resort, highly popular with Glasgow's bourgeoisie, was directly dependent on the construction of its railway connection. Other railway works were the No 2 contract of the Greenock and Ayrshire Railway (1865), worth some £128,000, the Whiteinch Railway and Tramway (1872-76) worth £17,000, the Strath-endrick and Aberfoyle railway in the Western Highlands and the Temple Contract on the Glasgow City and District Railway (1885). Kennedy also took on contracts with the major railway companies for the construction of engine and goods sheds. Bridge build-ing and tunnelling were common features of much of this work, and the firm tendered for individual bridge contracts, notably the construction of the new Partick Bridge over the Kelvin in 1877, worth £19,000. Expertise in tunnelling was exploited by Kennedy's eldest son William, when he took over his father's firm and later when controlling his own company, William Kennedy Ltd (qv).

The nature of Kennedy's work reveals an increasing level of sophistication, both in the projects themselves and in the plant required to complete them - Kennedy

COURTESY OF THE MITCHELL LIBRARY

was employing steam piling machines and dredgers as early as 1855 on the Erskine Ferry contract, one which was complicated both by the winter weather and the stipulation that the ferry service should not be interrupted. His 1861 South Quay contract stipulated that only steam piling engines were to be used, no fewer than four being kept constantly at work. The main materials employed on such jobs was timber and masonry, any extensive iron-work requirements being let by sub-contract. Railway contracts would require the use of contractors' locomotives, steam navvies, cranes and mobile sawmills and stone-crushers. Even on the comparatively small Partick Bridge contract, Kennedy was obliged to employ a Goliath Travelling crane, two static cranes of two and three tons each, a centrifugal pump and a mortar mixing plant both driven by separate eight horsepower mobile engines: furthermore, as with any contract, a mobile smithy and engineering shed would have to be supplied. Site organisation demanded a well managed workforce - Kennedy employed several long-serving supervisory workers, notably Daniel and David Anderson, and John Barclay who worked as a manager for 30 years, supervising many of the firm's bridge-building projects.

Hugh Kennedy's career as a public works and railway contractor was complemented by his activity in the sphere of property development and private building. He purchased land for building in Partick, Partickhill and Kelvinbank. Whilst some feu contracts obliged him to commence development, others allowed speculation: in 1853 he feued 6,848 sq yds in Partick at 4s 6d per sq yd, which by 1867, he claimed, owing to the 'rapid progress which of late years Partick has made in population, trade and building' was worth 9s per sq yd, and suitable for 'speedy disposal' as 'good advantage' was certain. With a few exceptions, notably involving land in the parish of Kilbarchan, Renfrewshire, Kennedy's property dealings were all confined to Glasgow. He acted mainly by himself, although on one occasion he did feu 4,946 sq yds of ground in fashionable Hillhead jointly with Henry Cowan and Joseph Taylor, Writer. By 1892 this particular piece of land and the building on it was in the possession of Kennedy's sons, as trustees for the firm. Kennedy built mainly three or four storey tenements, most of them containing houses of three rooms and a kitchen. Tenants would have ranged from highly skilled artisans and white collar workers to the professional classes. His building activities were not confined to Partick or Kelvinbank; at the time of his death he also owned homes in the growing middle-class suburb of Crossmyloof in the south of the city.

Although Kennedy retained only a small proportion of the homes he built, these were enough to make him one of Glasgow's largest owners of residential property. He had absolute faith in the soundness of property as an investment. When he died he owned property with a yearly rental of nearly £8,000 (a total value of somewhere in the region of £108,000). He instructed his trustees to 'hold and retain' his heritable properties as he considered that 'from their situation (they) will probably increase in value with time'. After paying off any debts on his property they were to use any outstanding balance in the estate for 'the purchase of heritable property'. In the event there were debts of nearly £70,000 over Kennedy's property, representing some 65% of the total purchase price.

The raising of loans on heritable property, land and buildings, was Kennedy's main source of capital for his building activities. Between 1850 and 1886 Kennedy raised loans to the value of £119,517 on the security of property in Glasgow. Of some 45 separate loans only two came from institutional sources. One in 1873 from the City of Glasgow Life Assurance Company for £2,000, which was repaid within five months of being granted, and a second from the Union Bank of Scotland, granted to Hugh Kennedy & Sons in 1886 for £20,000. Of the remainder, 20 came from family trust funds, and 23 came from a variety of industrialists, widows and acquaintances. John White, grain merchant and local councillor in Partick lent Kennedy £5,500 in 1883. In 1855 Kennedy received two loans totalling £5,400 from James and David Paton, textile manufacturers at Tillicoultry, whilst between 1860 and 1861 he received four loans worth £8,050 over newly completed tenements in Radnor Terrace from the trustees of Charles Tennant Dunlop.

Following the collapse of the City of Glasgow Bank, two of these loans were assigned by trustees to Robert McLaren, iron founder of the Eglinton Foundry, who had lent Kennedy some £2,500 in 1874. Unlike other large-scale builders, most notably Robert McAlpine (qv), and despite an apparent lack of accounting skills which led to a complaint in 1866 that 'The Kennedy's books are imperfectly kept - they have not been balanced for about five years and result of his business could not be ascertained', Kennedy ably survived the financial crisis of the late 1870s. Such was his standing that in 1880, when the building industry in Glasgow was generally regarded with suspicion following revelations of mal-practice in the bankruptcy courts, he raised £14,500 on heritable property, more than he had done in any previous year.

Kennedy would clearly have diverted some of these loans towards financing his railway and other contracting work, though there was a notable slump in his loan raising during periods of extensive contract work. Cash-flow shortages, caused by long and slow paying contracts, would have been eased by the half-yearly injection of sums representing rentals on property he owned. Typical of the problems a contractor could face was Kennedy's dispute with the Whiteinch Railway Company. Having been obliged to purchase £2,000 worth of stock as a condition of gaining the contract, he later became involved in litigation over payment for work completed and interest due on such sums, complaining that 'it is very hard lines for me having so much stock and no prospect of dividend'. At such times rentals, or short term loans (it was during the Whiteinch contract that the City of Glasgow Life Assurance loan for £2,000 was made) would be vital to maintain liquidity. If there may have been a financial link between house-building and contracting, there was certainly a physical one. Many of Kennedy's red-sandstone tenements were built of stone taken from quarries leased whilst constructing railways on the west-coast, notably at Wemyss Bay.

Hugh Kennedy married Agnes Hunter, daughter of Moses Hunter, a Partick timber-merchant, in 1854. By 1892 all three of his sons had joined his business, with the eldest, William (qv) taking the leading role. Kennedy was an active member of the Partick High Free Church, serving as deacon of the congregation. He was a member of the Incorporation of Wrights, being elected Deacon in 1872, and to the Master Court in 1883. He followed in the footsteps of his business associate, David Tod, by becoming a Magistrate for the Burgh of Partick in 1860, and Lord Provost in 1878, retiring after two terms in office in favour of Andrew MacLean of Barclay Curle and Co in 1883. Among other magistrates were his father-in-law and his step-brother. One of his many duties as magistrate was to preside over the proceedings of the Dean of Guild Court, responsible for approving all planned building in the Burgh. As Provost he was responsible for the attempts by the burgh to not only maintain its independence from Glasgow, but also to expand its boundaries into Kelvinside. He was involved in the improvement of Partick's recreational facilities and took a keen, if not self-interested, concern in housing in the Burgh; he also actively supported the new Partick Academy, built in 1877. Among his leisure interests was gardening, and he was a regular prize-winner at local horticultural shows.

Hugh Kennedy suffered a stroke in 1890 and died some five years later on 31st October, 1895, aged 71. He left a personal estate of £21,620, but the nett value of his estate after the payment of debts and duties was £52,000 which was held in trust for his children. He was a joiner by trade, a house builder, a shrewd investor in housing and land, a skilled valuator, a contractor managing men, machinery and materials under frequently hostile conditions, and an active public figure. The number and variation in the contracts he undertook reveal a sophistication both in appraising work and in carrying it out, whilst the balance between the financing of these operations suggests a forerunner to the larger property developing and building companies of the twentieth century. His involvement in all spheres of the construction industry, and his consequent ability to vary his product according to demand, enabled him to prosper in a period when so many other Scottish builders and contractors perished.

NICHOLAS J MORGAN

SOURCES

Unpublished

GU Business Archives: UGD 8/51, 194 Railway Collection

Morgan, N J, 'Report on House Ownership and House Management in Glasgow, 1900', 1982

Register of Sasines, Ayrshire, 1866

Register of Sasines, Glasgow, 1850-1895

Register of Sasines, Renfrewshire, 1850-1895

SRO: SC 36/48/154, Inventory
    SC 36/48/117, Additional Inventory
    SC 36/51/115, Will

Strathclyde Regional Archives: TCN 12/484, 500, 507, 574, 676, 705, 741, 814, Clyde Navigation Papers
    T-TH 1/29/7, Trades House of Glasgow
    T-TH 1/29/23, Trades House of Glasgow

Published

The Bailie, 29/6/1881

Clydebank and Renfrew Press, 8/12/1907

Deas, James, The River Clyde, Glasgow, 1888

Glasgow Herald, 9/11/1895

Glasgow Post Office Directories, 1847-1895

Greenhorne, William, History of Partick, Glasgow, 1928

Hume, J R, Industrial Archaeology of Glasgow, 1974

Illustrated Railway Guides, 1859

Industries of Glasgow, Glasgow, 1888

Industry in Glasgow Scrapbook, Mitchell Library, Article 24

Lindsay, Charles C, 'The Design and Construction of Partick Bridge', Proceedings of the Institution of Engineers & Shipbuilders in Scotland, XXI, 1877-78

McIlwraith, The Glasgow & South Western Railway, Glasgow, 1880

Partick and Maryhill Press, 9/11/1895

Partick Observer, 30/6/1877, 7/7/1877, 8/9/1877, 27/10/1877, 30/11/1877

Partick Star, 6/11/1895

John LAWRENCE,

Builder; b. 17/10/1893, Glasgow s. of John Lawrence, joiner and Deborah Johnston; m. Annie McKirdy 1926; 2s., 2d.; MD, John Lawrence (Glasgow) Ltd; d. 26/1/1977, Blanefield.

John Lawrence was born in Govanhill Street, Glasgow in 1893. His first home was modest, a room and kitchen. His father, John Lawrence, was a joiner from Inverness-shire and his mother Deborah Johnston came from Ireland. John's relationship with his father was never very good, but his mother was one of the great influences in his life. Lawrence was educated at Calder Street school, where his best subject was mental arithmetic. He left school at 14, as the family needed another income, and became an office boy with a grain broker. He wanted to become a joiner but his father had aspirations for his son to have a white collar job. After three years Lawrence gave up his office job against the wishes of his family and the advice of his employer to start his apprenticeship as a joiner.

During his apprenticeship John Lawrence went four nights a week to night school and then to the Royal Technical College. While he was in his early twenties he became a foreman for Mactaggart and Mickel (afterwards a rival builder). In 1926 he married a local girl, Anne McKirdy, and by his own admission 'made every stick of furniture for our first home'. The Lawrences had two sons and two daughters.

In 1924 John Lawrence borrowed money from his aunt to start his own business. The first contract was to build council houses at Shotts and he did everything, including laying the foundations. Business cannot have been all that good for he shortly emigrated to the United States. This was not a successful move, the family were unhappy there and a year later they returned to Glasgow. In 1930 Lawrence built his first house for sale at Busby. Right from the start he was interested in modern building techniques and the business prospered.

With the outbreak of war in 1939 the construction industry was hit with a depleted labour force. John Lawrence turned to building air-raid shelters and hospitals. After the war he was involved in rebuilding large parts of Clydebank which had been badly bombed.

After the war much of John Lawrence's success was based on his interest in standardisation and pre-fabrication techniques, which drew whenever possible on Scottish resources. Perhaps his major contribution to the Scottish building industry was his discovery of gypsum, a plastic made of white rock powder. He made the discovery while visiting a friend who built sets for Alexander Korda's film studios. Bricks were in short supply after the war and John Lawrence saw the possibilities, and developed the powder into bricks which had considerable properties of warmth and strength. He was to sell these bricks in 19 different countries. He called his new houses 'Bellrock' and building time was substantially reduced. The properties of 'Bellrock' were demonstrated by Lawrence at the Pentagon and the Kremlin. The new building material and techniques helped to make him a very wealthy man and the controller of the largest private building organisation in Scotland. Lawrence kept his wealth a closely guarded secret and would never admit to being a millionaire. His successes continued and by 1963 he was chairman of eight companies. He was also president of the Atlantic Gypsum Co; he was on the committee of the Scottish Building Research Station and chairman of the Scottish Housing Group. Lawrence was also involved in the Scottish Contractors' Consortium which had a joint capital of £35 million in 1965. The consortium aimed to stop contracts going to English companies. In the post war years Lawrence gave Scotland a new phrase 'A Home of Your Own'.

With his new wealth Lawrence was able to indulge himself in little extravagances, such as having an office which was an exact replica of the headmaster's study at Eton. From here he personally paid his foremen each week. In 1965 he employed 1,800 men. Not all Lawrence touched turned to gold, for example the 1970 proposal for a £9 million tourist centre at Strathblane collapsed when Sir Hugh Fraser withdrew in 1973.

John Lawrence's doctor advised him to develop a hobby as a diversion from the business world. His reaction was to become a shareholder in Rangers Football Club and in 1963 he became the club's chairman. The club's identification with the protestant cause in the West of Scotland brought John Lawrence into a great deal of controversy. A member of Lawrence's family has said that he himself was not anti-catholic but that he was rather an 'unbiased protestant'. He was a church-going man and picked his church according to the ability of the preacher. Lawrence's decade at Ibrox witnessed the club's success at Barcelona in 1972 when it won the European Cup Winners' Cup; it also saw the Ibrox disaster of January 1971 when 66 persons died. John Lawrence, who was now 80, was called to give evidence as a witness. In 1973 he resigned as chairman following a power struggle and his doctor's advice.

For the home of his own, John Lawrence built a mansion house in the Blane valley. Apart from the house and his Rolls-Royce, his tastes were simple, he was somewhat fastidious about his health, he did not smoke and only drank moderately in later years. His favourite holiday resort was Rothesay, but he occasionally visited his daughter at her home in Tangier.

In politics John Lawrence was a Conservative. His charitable interests and activities were considerable, but in an anonymous fashion. He gave more than many people realised, for example in 1972, £5,000 to the Chest and Heart Association.

John Lawrence died at his home, Levern Towers of a coronary thrombosis on 26 January 1977, aged 83. His wife had pre-deceased him in 1969. His funeral was held in Killearn Kirk.

CHRISTOPHER C LEE

SOURCES

Published

Daily Express, 27/2/1963
Glasgow Herald, 3/5/1951, 10/4/1959, 10/2/1963, 17/3/1965, 21/9/1970, 24/9/1970, 12/9/1972, 8/1/1973, 20/6/1973, 10/9/1973, 7/12/1973, 7/5/1974, 28/1/1977
Glasgow Herald, Reserve Biography, 1967
Glasgow Illustrated, Vol 9, No 66, September 1967
Scotland, Scottish Council for Development and Industry, August 1955
Sunday Mail, 23/4/1972
Sunday Post, April 1965
Who Owns Who, UK and Republic of Ireland, 1980, Vol 1

William Hepburn McALPINE,

Building contractor; b. 31/10/1871, Hamilton, Lanarkshire; s. of Robert McAlpine, master bricklayer and Agnes Hepburn; m. 6/4/1898, Margaret Donnison, d. of Thomas George Bishop, grocer; 3 s., 2 d.; Partner & Ch , Robert McAlpine & Sons; d. 20/2/1951, Henley-on-Thames; g/v estate: £141,351 2s 2d.

William Hepburn McAlpine was the second son of Robert (qv) and Agnes. He spent his childhood in Hamilton, but in 1882 he moved with his family to Clydebank, where his father's construction company built a factory for the Singer Manufacturing Company. In 1884, the McAlpines moved again, to Kerelaw House, near Stevenston in Ayrshire, when Robert McAlpine and Co won the contract to build the first section of the Lanarkshire and Ayrshire Railway. William was sent to continue his education at Ayr Academy.

William had ambitions to become a lawyer, but his father required the assistance of his sons to run his prospering business. In 1887, William left school and joined his elder brother, Robert Jnr, working on the Lanarkshire and Ayrshire Railway (L & A) contract.

Robert McAlpine lacked the formal education which both his sons received, and he hoped that they could help him supervise the firm's office work. But Robert Jnr and William were given experience of working in various aspects of the construction business, as clerks and timekeepers, and assisting the site managers and engineers. In 1889, William was sent to Longford in Ireland with his young cousin, Archie Johnstone, to manage a contract for the construction of a small reservoir and water pipeline there. He returned the following year and helped manage several jobs in the Glasgow area. On one of these contracts, for the construction of a section of the Glasgow Distict Subway, William spent long hours underground. While working there, he became seriously ill, suffering from exhaustion and the effects of working in the damp, fetid atmosphere of the tunnels. He was sent to Switzerland for several months to recuperate.

It had become obvious during the L & A contract that while Robert Jnr was emerging as an enthusiastic and promising engineer, his brother possessed a talent for business organisation and administration. After Robert took his two sons into partnership in May, 1893, William gradually took charge of Robert McAlpine & Sons' head office in Glasgow.

Between 1890 and 1900 McAlpine's annual turnover rose from about £40,000 to over £280,000, and by 1914 the figure exceeded £500,000. The firm undertook larger and more difficult contracts. By 1906 it employed up to 7,000 men, and owned plant with an estimated value of about £200,000. As the firm continued to grow, and as his father grew older and began to withdraw from the day-to-day business of running the firm, William had to spend more of his time at head office. There, he and the office manager, J D Ferguson, maintained a tight control over expenditure. Every effort was made to eliminate waste, and contract managers were required to submit weekly reports on site costs to enable the office staff to maintain an accurate picture of the firm's financial situation. William, who personally supervised the construction of the L & A Extension lines, 1898-1904, the construction of the Prince's Dock Branch Joint Railway and the widening of a section of the Wemyss Bay Railway during the same period, was able to take charge of individual contracts only occasionally after this. However, despite the vast amount of work to be done at head office, he continued to find time to pay regular visits to each McAlpine site, to see for himself what problems had to be tackled there, and to suggest ways in which savings might be made on site costs.

On 6 April, 1898, William married Margaret D Bishop, the daughter of Thomas G Bishop (qv), founder of Cooper and Co, provision and tea merchants in Glasgow. Robert Jnr and his sister Mary had also married children of the grocery tycoon, and the close ties between the two families led to a strong business connection between the two firms. Coopers were often invited to open provisions stores on McAlpine's sites in remote areas, to keep the navvies supplied with food and other goods. When Cooper's jelly works in Glasgow was destroyed by fire in 1907, McAlpine rebuilt it.

The period 1899-1902 was one of financial crisis for McAlpine. A combination of factors, which included a dramatic rise in the price of labour and materials, long spells of bad weather, and the development on some sites of unforeseen engineering problems, resulted in a serious drain on the firm's reserves of capital. As it became more difficult to find the money to pay for men and materials required to continue the work, less work could be done, and less income was received from monthly payment instalments from clients. Claims by the contractor for extra expenditure incurred on a contract were not usually settled until the work was finished, when the client also released the sums held as security for the satisfactory completion of the contract. Yet McAlpine failed to complete a single major contract between 1897 and 1901, and completed only three out of eleven before 1903. It began to look as if the firm might be forced to withdraw from two of the most troublesome contracts, those for the construction of a section of the Talla water pipeline and of a graving dock at Hebburn-on-Tyne: the penalties which could be incurred for doing so might well have driven the firm out of business. In November 1900, at the height of the crisis, Robert Snr contracted pleurisy while visiting the Hebburn site. He was sent off on a cruise to recuperate, leaving William to deal with the financial problems without the benefit of his father's experience and advice.

William succeeded in placating several angry clients, who were demanding that more plant and labour be sent to the worksites and were threatening to take contracts out of McAlpine's hands unless the firm made better progress with the works. On three contracts greater progress was made after cash advances were received from the clients. To enable work to continue on the other contracts, William sought a loan from the firm's bank.

James Young & Sons (Ltd) (qv), a firm of Scottish contractors which encountered similar problems to McAlpine during this period, and which was wound up in 1899, had an overdraft of nearly £30,000 with the Bank of Scotland. At the Clydesdale Bank, McAlpine had credit facilities of just £3,000, and when Robert Snr asked for an extension of this overdraft, after his return to Scotland in the spring of 1901, he was informed that the firm would have to provide security for any additional loan. McAlpine's assets at this time consisted mostly of plant and materials on sites, and were unsuitable as security for a loan. However, in June 1901 William and his father-in-law visited the bank, and Thomas Bishop agreed to act as guarantor for a loan to McAlpine of £5,000.

Bishop subsequently put up a further £10,000 in guarantees, enabling McAlpine to extend the overdraft at the Clydesdale up to £25,000. With the money raised in this way, McAlpines were able to complete all the work on their books, and most of the contracts showed profits after claims had been settled. The overdrafts were discharged by 1904.

In 1906, William's brother Malcolm opened the firm's London office. At first he found it difficult to gain acceptance in civil engineering circles there, but by 1914 McAlpine had established a good reputation as reservoir builders in England and Wales, and the firm was gaining recognition as a major British, and not just Scottish, concern. During the First World War McAlpine undertook large numbers of war contracts and were involved in other projects south of the border. Head Office moved to London from Clydebank in 1916, and those members of the McAlpine family not already living in England moved there shortly afterwards.

William was the last to leave Scotland. In 1910 he took charge of the Methil Dock contract in Fife, when the enormous expense involved in building a sea wall there in rough weather, and of replacing plant and repairing works damaged by frequent storms, threatened to break the firm. His sound management was a major factor in McAlpine's success in completing the contract in 1913 but the long hours which he worked at Methil, and the stress involved, undermined his health. During the period 1914-18, he was in overall charge of McAlpine's major war contracts in Scotland. His offer to William Weir (qv), Director of Munitions in Scotland, to build the huge £1.3 million National Filling Factory at Georgetown, near Paisley, at cost price plus a commission of just 1% to cover administration charges, was eagerly accepted. McAlpine also undertook smaller contracts for the Ministry of Munitions in Scotland, and completed work valued at £450,000 on the ill-fated Loch Doon School of Aerial Gunnery project, before the Air Ministry abandoned it in 1918.

William's health, which had been poor before 1914, was made worse by his exertions during the war. The death of Ebenezer Hepburn, his uncle and a close friend, came as a sad blow, and by 1918 William was on the verge of a breakdown. He recovered, however, and in 1920 moved from his beloved Ravenscourt home, near Glasgow, to Micklem. He later purchased a house near Redhill, before finally settling at Badgemore House, in Henley-on-Thames.

By the end of the First World War, William's father was over 70 years of age, and while he was still consulted on important business matters he was quite content to leave the affairs of the firm in the capable hands of his sons. Robert Jnr, too, had gone into semi-retirement after the war leaving William as the senior active partner in the firm.

It was due to William's initiative that McAlpine became involved in Britain's young sugar beet industry during the 1920s. The firm built a factory at

Wissington in Norfolk, for British Sugar Manufacturers Ltd (BSM), in 1925. Like other sugar beet companies, BSM encountered great difficulties in establishing their business, and William persuaded his partners to offer the company financial assistance. The firm accepted shares in BSM as part of the payment for building the factory, and McAlpine's Secretary, J R Milne, sat on the BSM board during the first months of its existence. William and Malcolm both held debentures in the company, William's alone being for £60,000.

McAlpine also became informal partners with the Dyer Company of Cleveland, Ohio, which specialised in designing and building sugar beet factories. In partnership, the two firms built factories at Peterborough, Bardney, Brigg and Selby for sugar beet companies. Dyer designed the factories and machinery and took charge of construction, while McAlpine provided finance and put their organisation and equipment at Dyer's disposal. The profits from each contract were divided equally between the two firms. When the Second Lincolnshire Beet Sugar Company Ltd issued debentures worth £51,500, to raise money to extend the factory at Brigg in 1929, William took up the complete issue. He ignored criticism made in the press by established sugar importers that the beet sugar industry was over-subsidised by the government, relied too heavily on foreign expertise and machinery, and could never be viable, and he permitted the companies to pay a large proportion of the cost of building their factories by issuing McAlpine with ordinary and preference shares. Most of McAlpine's shares in beet sugar companies were disposed of by 1936, when the companies merged to form the British Sugar Corporation Ltd.

William also found time during the twenties to involve himself directly with two of McAlpine's largest construction projects. He supervised the extension of Tilbury Docks and, at the end of the decade, took charge of a similar contract at Southampton. Both contracts were completed successfully, and William remembered them with great satisfaction in later years.

In November 1934, Robert McAlpine Jnr died, just 13 days after the death of his father. William became chairman of Sir Robert McAlpine & Sons, which had remained very much a family concern since it was founded in 1868. About 40 of the McAlpines and their relatives were working for the firm in the early 1930s, and several of Sir Robert Snr's grandsons became partners during the decade. William's sons, Thomas, Robert Edwin and Malcolm, Sir Malcolm's son, Robin, and Sir Alfred's son, Alfred James, were all given the same practical experience of the business of construction which their fathers had received, before they too became partners in the firm.

During the Second World War, McAlpine undertook large numbers of important war contracts. When peace 'broke out' once more in 1945, the firm had undergone further changes. In 1940, four years before his death, Sir Alfred, with his son, established a new construction company in Cheshire. William and Sir Malcolm were the only surviving sons of Sir Robert Snr at the end of the war, but were content to relinquish the reins of control of McAlpine to the new generation of partners, while continuing to offer advice and involve themselves in important business matters. On 20 February, 1951, William died at Badgemore House after a bout of pneumonia.

The gross value of his estate amounted to £141,351 2s 2d in 1951, although he put much of his personal fortune into trust funds for his children and grandchildren. During his lifetime William also endowed the Physiotherapy Department of East Surrey Hospital and, with his brothers, the Neurological Department of Middlesex Hospital, where his youngest brother, Douglas, became a consultant in 1924.

William was a deeply religious man, his Presbyterian beliefs having been moulded by his mother and her brother Ebenezer. His disapproval of excessive drinking was well known. While his retiring nature and religious outlook sometimes gave him a reputation for being dour, this image was a false one. He shared his father's and brothers' great love for sport, and especially for golf, shooting and tennis. He also took great pride in the achievements of his wife and his daughter, Marjorie, as horseriders, and set up a riding school at Badgemore House.

William was a quiet man, who attracted little public attention but who played a crucial role in the history of Sir Robert McAlpine & Sons. Civil engineering contracting is a notoriously risky business, and William's strict control over the firm's expenditure and his sound financial management laid the foundation on which McAlpine's success was built.

IAIN RUSSELL

SOURCES

Unpublished

Hadie, Alec M, 'The Story of Sir Robert McAlpine and His Family', (with the company, c 1960)

McAlpine Archives: various documents

Twiname, Eric, 'Fragments of McAlpine History' (with the company, c 1970)

Published

Childers, J Saxton, *Robert McAlpine: A Biography*, Oxford, 1925

Sir Robert McALPINE,

Building contractor; b. 13/2/1847, Newarthill, Lanarkshire, s. of Robert McAlpine, underground manager in coal mine and Ann Paterson; m. (1) 12/6/1868, Agnes d. of William Hepburn, master shoemaker; 6 s., 4 d.; (2) 21/8/1889, Florence Christina, d. of William Palmer, doctor; 1 s., 2 d.; Founder, Robert McAlpine & Sons, dock, railway and public works contractors; d. 3/11/1934, Oxshott, Surrey; g/v estate: £205,794 9s 7d.

Robert McAlpine was the son of an underground manager who worked in a colliery near the village of Newarthill, Lanarkshire. His father died in 1853 and at the age of ten years Robert left the local school and worked to augment his family's income as a trapper in the pits. When he was 15 he graduated to working with the men at the coal face, but two years later left to become a bricklayer's apprentice in Coltness, returning to work in the mines there during the winter months when building work was scarce. In 1868, after completing his apprenticeship, Robert went into business on his own account as a jobbing builder. He married shortly afterwards and settled first in Motherwell and later in Hamilton.

To begin with Robert worked on small building and repair jobs, until in 1872 he won his first major contract to build 100 miners' cottages in the Hamilton district for the iron and coal magnate William Smith Dixon (qv). To pay for the labour and materials required to start this big job, Robert successfully applied for a loan from the City of Glasgow Bank, whose Hamilton agent was his friend, and a future Provost of Hamilton, John Clark Forrest. The successful completion of the cottages provided Robert with the capital to undertake other large building contracts on the railways and at pit-heads and ironworks in Lanarkshire. By 1877 he was regularly employing several hundred men, and he leased three brickworks at which he made bricks for use on his own sites and for sale to other builders. The annual turnover of his business had grown to over £100,000 and Robert had become one of the leading building contractors in the Hamilton area.

During the late 1870s Robert won building contracts elsewhere in Scotland, ranging from minor railway stations in Edinburgh to quarrymen's houses in Argyll. He also became a speculative builder. In 1875 he began to invest his profits from building and brickmaking in plots of land in Hamilton, Blantyre and Motherwell. The local iron and coal industries had prospered during the 1870s, and large numbers of people had flocked to Hamilton and the surrounding towns in search of employment there. Other builders were making huge profits by building houses to meet the increasing demand for accommodation in the area,

and Robert decided to follow their example. He used his land as security for loans which he negotiated with various individuals and investment companies. The money raised in this way was used to purchase still more ground and to pay for the labour and materials needed to build houses. Robert built over 500 houses and about 50 shops in tenement blocks during the following three years, and he intended to build a little garden suburb near Hamilton. Unfortunately for the young builder, however, a nation-wide depression began to bite in the West of Scotland in 1877. As the market for coal and iron shrank, unemployment in the Hamilton area grew, and demand for working class housing slumped. Robert had expected that the income from the selling and renting out of his properties would enable him to meet the interest payments on his heritable bonds and to pay off his ordinary creditors. Instead, with his houses either empty or let at low rents, and with the recession in the building trade affecting his other sources of income, Robert was forced to abandon his housebuilding venture. As the recession deepened, so his financial position became more perilous. Theoretically his heritable and ordinary debts of around £90,000 and £3,000 respectively were covered by assets worth over £110,000. But as these assets were almost entirely in the form of unwanted land and houses, Robert was unable to realise them. In May 1880 he was forced into bankruptcy.

The sequestration of his estate must have come as a great blow to Robert's confidence and pride. He had built up a valuable business from almost nothing, moved into a mansion, Udston House, and become a well-known figure in Hamiltonian society. In 1878 he had been elected to Hamilton Town Council, representing the Burnbank Ward in which he had built most of his houses. Udston House was eventually sold, and Robert did not seek re-election to the Town Council in November 1881, but by then he had already begun to rebuild his business. In January 1880 he had entered into a partnership of convenience with his cashier, William Richmond, knowing that if he became a bankrupt he would be unable to raise credit and salvage his ailing contracting business by himself. Although this partnership came to an end with the bankruptcy, Robert continued to direct the affairs of Robert McAlpine & Co while Richmond, now the sole partner, remained in the background. The firm soon began to win contracts to build signal boxes, station buildings, houses and even a small pier for railway companies in central Scotland and the West Highlands. They completed most of a £10,500 contract to build the Oban Hydro before the company financing that project got into financial difficulties in June 1882 and subsequently went into liquidation. Robert's personal fortunes were boosted when he was discharged from bankruptcy on 28 August 1881 and he could again become a partner in his firm. And he was given a golden opportunity to re-establish his business when in the summer of the following year

McAlpine & Richmond, as the firm had become known, won a contract worth £300,000 to build a new sewing machine factory at Kilbowie, Clydebank for the Singer Manufacturing Company.

Winning the Singer contract was one of the most important events in Robert's business career. He had never before worked on a contract worth over £30,000 and exactly how he managed to persuade Singer that his small firm was capable of building what was then the largest factory in Europe is uncertain. But when the factory was completed in 1885 the contractor was widely praised for the speed and quality of the work done there. The profits from the Singer contract put Robert's business back on a sound financial footing, enabling him to dissolve the partnership with Richmond in January 1883 and to invest in plant required to enable him to enter the lucrative world of civil engineering contracting.

In May 1884 Robert won the first of four contracts to build the original 21 mile section of the Lanarkshire and Ayrshire (L & A) Railway. Robert had worked under the consulting engineer employed by the L & A, John Strain (qv), while engaged on minor building jobs on the Callander and Oban line, and this may have helped him to win these first major railway-building contracts. It took six years to complete the new lines, but although the L & A contracts were not a success financially, they gave Robert McAlpine & Co the opportunity to acquire a team of engineers, the necessary plant, and most important of all the experience and a reputation in this line of work, which were all essential if Robert was to compete successfully for other large railway contracts. And Robert did establish a name for himself as a railway contractor. Between 1884 and 1904 his firm built nearly 150 miles of railway lines in Scotland and Ireland, attracting world-wide attention to the work involved in building the spectacular Mallaig Extension to the West Highland line between 1897 and 1901. Robert McAlpine & Sons, so called after Robert's eldest sons, Robert Jnr and William (qv) became partners in May 1893, also began to build reservoirs, docks, and pipelines while continuing with the traditional side of the business by building gasworks, warehouses and railway stations. By 1904 the firm's annual turnover had grown to about £450,000, its workforce to around 7,000 men, and the McAlpines had established themselves among the ranks of Scotland's leading railway, dock and public works contractors.

Robert McAlpine's success in rebuilding his firm was due to several factors. One was his adventurous use of new construction techniques. During the 1870s he had been given the nickname 'Concrete Bob' because of his wide use in the construction of his houses, of what was a fairly novel building material in Scotland. Concrete was cheap to use, doing away with the need to employ large numbers of relatively highly paid bricklayers and stonemasons on a site, and Robert found that when it was mixed with granite chips or slag from the iron works it could be used to make durable building blocks, doorsteps and lintels. He was later to use mass concrete extensively in the construction of railway bridges, viaducts, retaining walls and tunnels, often colouring the concrete with iron oxide to give it the appearance of red sandstone. The McAlpines first began to use reinforced concrete on a large scale in 1904, when the prefabricated floors installed at Singer's cabinet works and at a Glasgow warehouse were constructed of 'Ferrolithic' - concrete made with slag from steel furnaces. They later took out licenses to use reinforcing techniques developed by the Frenchmen Hennebique and Coignet, and developed their own system of building tunnels using prefabricated, reinforced concrete segments which were keyed together on site.

Other factors included Robert's willingness to invest large sums in buying labour-saving machinery, such as steam excavators and steam cranes, to speed up the work involved in earth-moving, and in newly developed plant such as the electric rock drill and the steam lorry, which first appeared on McAlpine's sites in 1893 and 1902 respectively. To save on material costs, Robert often leased a quarry near a site where a large amount of concrete or masonry was required, or built a brickworks to which clay or sand excavated there or on other sites was carried. The extensions to the Singer factory in Clydebank were built of bricks made at nearby Dalmuir from clay excavated at the site of College Goods Station in Glasgow.

By 1905 three more of Robert's sons, (Thomas) Malcolm, Alfred and Granville, had become partners in the firm. Each of his sons was given a sound practical training in all aspects of site and office management, and along with a team of loyal and experienced engineers and managers which Robert had built up over the years they ensured that Robert McAlpine & Sons continued to prosper. After an illness in 1900, Robert had begun to leave an increasing amount of the day-to-day administration work of his firm to his sons, and his departure on a world cruise in 1906 was only the first of many long holidays he was to take in his later years. But Robert remained an active partner. He continued to make up tenders himself for the most important contracts during the first decade of this century, and he was always consulted on important business matters. Indeed it was Robert's decision in 1904 to begin to build the Radnor Park housing scheme on the hill to the north of Singer's Clydebank factory.

The 'Holy City' acquired its nickname because of the similarity which McAlpine's flat concrete roofed tenements bore, when viewed from the south, to pictures of Jerusalem. The estate was built primarily to provide the firm with an alternative source of income to that derived from contracting. As in Lanarkshire during the 1870s, the land was mortgaged to provide the capital to build houses. By 1914 McAlpine owned nearly 1,300 houses and shops in Radnor Park, about 1,200 of them in traditional three and four storey tenements in the 'Holy City' and another 100 in a little garden city of cottage tenements and villas to the west. During the 1870s Robert had entrusted the factoring of his houses to his foreman, Thomas Brock. For the Radnor Park estate, however, and for about 350 tenement houses which were built in the Ladyburn and Bogston areas of Greenock 1907 - 10, established local firms were employed as factors. In 1908 McAlpine's head office was moved from Glasgow to Radnor Park, where the firm had already built a brickworks and a fitting, a joiners' and an engineering repair shops.

In 1904 Robert McAlpine & Sons completed their first contract in England, the construction of a graving dock at Hebburn-on-Tyne, and in 1906 Malcolm McAlpine travelled south to open an office in London. It took several years for Malcolm to establish McAlpine's name in the capital, but by 1914 he had won four large reservoir contracts for the firm in England and Wales. During the First World War the number and value of McAlpine's contracts in the south increased dramatically, and in 1916 head office was moved once again, from Clydebank to London. Between 1914 and 1918 McAlpine completed over £5 million of war contracts alone, building aerodromes, army camps and munitions factories all over Britain and in France. On 2nd July 1918 Robert McAlpine was created a baronet in recognition of his firm's contribution to the war effort and 'for public and patriotic service for many years in the provision of workmen's dwellings and the creation of garden cities'. Sir Robert celebrated by donating £15,000 to help set up the Institute of Agricultural Botany at Cambridge.

Sir Robert McAlpine & Sons continued to prosper in the post-war years. They were employed by several local authorities in Scotland and England to build housing estates and new roads, while they continued to win factory, railway, dock, and other public works contracts. In 1922 they won the prestigious contracts to build Wembley Stadium and the British Empire Exhibition buildings. In 1929 they were members of the consortium which purchased Dorchester House in Park Lane and demolished it, opening the luxury Dorchester Hotel on the site in 1931. Sir Robert played little part in all this, however. After the war he virtually retired from an active role in the firm's affairs, leaving the business in the capable hands of William, Malcolm and Alfred. He continued to entertain important clients, to pay visits to sites and to offer advice whenever it was sought, but Sir Robert's latter years were mostly spent away from the world of construction. He continued to travel widely, taking at least one long holiday abroad each year. At home he was a keen race-goer, enjoyed playing golf and tennis until nearly 80 years old, and was an enthusiastic poker and bridge player. Despite his poor early education he became a great reader, and was particularly fond of the works of Robert Louis Stevenson, Robert Burns and Anatole France, and of books on philosophy and natural science. Sir Robert

was abstemious all his life. He used to boast that he did not taste whisky until he was 30, and he drank only an occasional glass of wine or whisky in later life.

Sir Robert moved to England from Greenock in 1910, and in 1916 he settled at Knott Park, Oxshott in Surrey. He died there on 3 November 1934 at the age of 87, after contracting cancer of the prostate gland. The gross value of his estate at his death was given at £205,794 9s 7d, although much of his personal fortune had been placed in trust for the benefit of his daughters, his youngest son, Douglas, and the family of his deceased son Granville.

IAIN RUSSELL & GEORGE DIXON

SOURCES

Unpublished

Hardie, Alec M, 'The Story of Sir Robert McAlpine and His Family', c 1960
McAlpine Archives: various documents
Twiname, Eric, 'Fragments of McAlpine History', c 1970

Published

Childers, J Saxton, *Robert McAlpine: A Biography*, Oxford, 1925
Russell, Iain, *Sir Robert McAlpine & Sons: The Early Years*, Carnforth, 1988 (published privately)

John Campbell McKELLAR,

Architect and builder; b. 1/11/1859, Glasgow, s. of Robert McKellar, bleacher, dyer and sometime property developer; m. Jessie Nisbet Hood, d. of Rev Robert Hood; 1 s.; Founder, MD and Ch, John C McKellar Ltd., Glasgow; d. 27/3/1941, Glasgow.

John Campbell McKellar was born in Glasgow in November 1859, the son of the bleacher and dyer Robert McKellar of Newlandsfield, Pollokshaws. He was educated at Queens Park Collegiate School, and in 1875 began an apprenticeship to the Glasgow architect James M Munro. Having become a member of the Institute of Architects McKellar was employed as Munro's chief assistant until 1883, when he left to establish his own practice at West George Street. In 1884, in order to increase his business, he added house-factoring and property management to the services he offered. McKellar took on a variety of architectural contracts during this period, ranging from alterations to tenements, tenement designs proper, shops, engine sheds and kilns. From 1888 McKellar began to build speculatively, designing his own tenements and employing contractors to build them. Many of these were initially retained by McKellar as an investment, providing crucial cash-flow to finance other projects, and additional heritable security to raise loans. Between June 1881 and the start of 1896 he had undertaken 17 such projects, building in all 89 tenements throughout the city. His efforts concentrated on two distinct areas: the first was at Crossmyloof on the south side of the city, a favoured area for lower-middle class tenemental development by other prominent builders such as James Ferguson, Hugh Kennedy (qv) and John McTaggart (qv). Here considerable attention was paid to the style of both the internal and external design and layout of the buildings, which commanded annual rents of between £20 and £23 for two and three apartment houses. The second area was in the north-west of the city at Kelvindale and Maryhill. Here he

was following in the footsteps of his father, who although originally trained as a bleacher, had speculated heavily in property in the north-west of the city in the 1870s and 1880s, laying out roads (notably Bilsland Drive), feuing land to builders, and building himself. During this period McKellar also continued his general architectural work - in 1891 he was commissioned to design the Hood Memorial Church in Muslin Street (where his wife's father had served as minister) in the east end of Glasgow, and there followed a number of other important contracts for the Congregational Church.

In 1894 McKellar entered into a short-lived partnership with the house factor John McKellar, formerly a partner in Robert Stobo & Co, one of the largest firms of property managers in the city. The new business, McKellar and McKellar, combined John C McKellar's architectural expertise with considerable experience of John McKellar, who brought to the partnership a substantial portfolio of properties throughout the city. However the arrangement proved less than satisfactory to a man of John C McKellar's undoubted ambition, and in 1896 he formed what was possibly Glasgow's first limited liability building and property owning company. The prospectus for the new company claimed that by 1896 the 33 tenements that McKellar had retained ownership of, containing 320 dwelling houses and 16 shops, were worth £70,000, yielding a return of £1,867 after payment of interest on bonds. In addition between 1891 and 1896 McKellar had made a profit of £2,000 a year on the feuing of land and the creation of feu-duties and ground annuals. This latter device was widely employed by builders in Glasgow, who, it was claimed, could safely build at a loss providing they had first created ground burdens, the purchase of which commanded a high price from conservatively minded investors. The capital of the company was set at £40,000 - McKellar was the main shareholder although his reputation in the City and its environs attracted a flood of would-be subscribers. McKellar was appointed managing director of the company: its other directors were as prestigious a group of business leaders as could be wished for: the confectioner William Pettigrew, the butcher William Hood, the merchant Robert Crawford, and Alexander Frew, a civil engineer easily identified with many of Glasgow's most ambitious construction projects. A later addition to the board was Lord Provost Sir John Ure Primrose. In 1899 the capital of the company ws increased to £100,000, to 'place the company in a stronger position for taking advantage of property and ground'.

The new company continued to build along the lines pursued by McKellar, although the minute books reveal a sometimes uneasy relationship between a man cast in the mould of a thrusting Victorian entrepreneurial builder and a conservative board of directors careful of their responsibilities to shareholders. McKellar himself chose sites for development, often buying land on his own account which

COURTESY OF THE MITCHELL LIBRARY

151

he subsequently sold to the company at cost; he continued to design the buildings although this was done on contract through his architectural practice, John C McKellar (later McKellar & Gunn). The company acted only as a main contractor, employing a master of works on its staff but no craftsmen. Gradually older properties were disposed of (by 1901 all the property south of the river had gone) whilst many of the new ones were retained for rent and others sold. At the same time the company began to concentrate building and ownership in Kelvindale and particularly in Partick. In addition they diversified into the ownership of tenement property in the seaside resort of Troon, and office-buildings in Glasgow, purchasing Gresham House in West Nile Street for £24,000 in 1903. The company also acquired a 25% stake in the newly formed Langside Estate company, formed in 1901 to develop lands on the city's south side.

The company's minute-books, a rare if sometimes sparse insight into the thinking of Edwardian builders, show clearly the strategies which were being pursued. It was the company's intention to 'acquire sites in very populous localities which were not utilised to their best value ... as with increases in population shop and house rents are always on the increase'. They followed the expansion of industry, and were delighted to note in 1906 that 'a splendid block of 12 tenements was just being completed on the very spot where the immense activity was being set up by Messrs Yarrow ...' Design and amenity remained a priority; the tenements erected in shipbuilding areas (many in the heart of the district that spawned the infamous rent-strikes of 1915), although often less ornate than those built elsewhere, were nonetheless 'of a highly improving kind'. Between 1900 and 1906 the company built (or were in the process of building) between 80 and 100 tenements, containing in the region of 1,200 houses. In addition some of the land acquired from McKellar at its formation (at Bilsland Drive and Eastpark in Maryhill) had been successfully feued to other builders for development. Annual profits stood at around £6,000, and the confidence of the directors was high.

In 1906, at the same time as continuing with these tenement projects, McKellar launched the company on an adventurous scheme to build 'modern self-contained houses' of three and five rooms on the Hillington Park estate south west of the city centre. The houses, apart from their use of the ubiquitous red sandstone, were built to a style more reminiscent of the home counties in the 1920s or 1930s than Glasgow in 1906, and were clearly influenced in design (both internally and externally) by the Glasgow school of architects and designers. 'This scheme', said the directors, 'was along the lines of modern progress ...' McKellar, who had originated the novel design devised a similarly imaginative style of marketing. The houses were advertised promiscuously under the slogan 'Become your own landlord', not only in the staid property pages of the *Glasgow Herald*, but as far afield as the *Sunday School Magazine*, the *British Congregationalist*, the *Scottish Temperance League Magazine*, the *Scottish Reformer* and the *Scottish Pictorial*. In addition adverts were carried on the Glasgow District Subway and the Paisley tramcars, whilst an illustrated booklet was prepared for the information of would-be purchasers. To lure aspiring owner-occupiers McKellar devised a variety of schemes for payment on the basis of a single deposit with the balance of the purchase price being repaid over ten years by quarterly or half-yearly instalments. Hardly surprising now, the whole scheme was revolutionary in the context of Edwardian Scotland.

Thirty houses were built in the first phase of the Hillington development, but a combination of circumstances prevented any further progress, the property being first feued to other builders to develop and ultimately sold to Glasgow Corporation for a housing scheme. Sales had been disappointing - as late as 1915 the company still had four houses which were let and could not apparently be sold. Secondly the firm found building increasingly unprofitable as the trade depression of the mid-1900s set in. And thirdly, as the company's minutes and accounts show so graphically, the passing of the 'People's Budget' in 1909, with the introduction of Increment Duty on both builder's profits and the creation of new feu-duties, both, as we have seen, means favoured by McKellar for financing schemes on ground owned by the company, brought building operations to a complete and final standstill. The company dismissed its master of works following the passing of the Budget, and with the exception of one or two minor operations they never built again. 'For over twenty years prior to the passing of the Finance Act', McKellar told the Royal Commission on Housing in Scotland in 1913, 'I built continuously either on my own behalf or on behalf of my Company, but during the last five years I have not been able to lay one stone upon another'. Profits fell steadily after 1909 (from £2,449 in 1909 to £266 in 1910), and the mistaken optimism shown by McKellar in the spring of 1914 on the revival of the property market were dashed by the war. Much of the tenement property owned at the outbreak of war was retained by the company, despite the effect on income from property of increased rates and the Rent and Mortgage Restriction Act. But as the balance sheets and ledgers show, the company increasingly took on the role of an investment trust. In 1909 non-heritable investments had accounted for 10% of the company's assets, but by 1929 nearly half of its capital assets were held in this form. In the same year revenue from investment dividends and sales matched the company's income from property.

McKellar's views on the subject of national and local government intervention in the property market were not confined to the increasingly gloomy pages of the company minute book. He was a leading member of the property-owning lobby in Scotland and a prominent Conservative. Consequently, like a number of other builders, he expressed his views to enquiries, trade periodicals and newspapers. More often than not his invective was directed against the Finance Act of 1909, and the sinister growth of municipal involvement in the housing market (which he had spoken against strongly to the Royal Commission in 1913). 'Private enterprise cannot operate successfully ... against a Government scheme to build and let houses at uneconomic rents', he argued, alleging that by subsidising local authority building the government was 'still at war with economic law against which it cannot win'. In 1934, addressing the company's annual general meeting in that year, having deplored (as he did every year) the effect of the 1909 Finance Act on the company's building activities, he went on to explain that the company felt obliged to invest in stocks and shares in companies which operated outwith the City boundaries; boundaries which, he hoped, would 'not be extended until we are freed from the Hitlerite rule of unreasonable and unfair Socialists and Communists, who aim at the confiscation and theft of property that cannot be removed out of their reach ...' Although innovative in his approach to building and marketing McKellar's political views led him to adopt a position that was increasingly anachronistic at a time when builders in both Glasgow and Edinburgh were proving that successful and highly profitable businesses could be run by effecting a mixture of local authority contracting and subsidised and unsubsidised private building. In his rejection of this pragmatic approach to his business he condemned his company, if not to penury, then at least to stagnation.

McKellar continued to act as managing director and latterly chairman of the company until shortly before his death in 1941. He was predeceased by his wife, Jessie Hood, who had died in 1925. His son, Robert H McKellar, had been a director of the company for some years, in addition to being a partner in a local firm of house-factors and valuators. John C McKellar took on a number of other business commitments such as directorships of the Yorkshire Insurance Trust and of the Scottish Heritable Trust. In his leisure, when not lambasting the evils of local and central government intervention in the property-market, he could be found either yachting on the Clyde or golfing at Troon. As one of the largest developers in the city in the late nineteenth century his contribution to its growth had been prodigious; his innovative development at Hillington Park was an ambitious attempt to bring owner-occupation to a city where even the most wealthy were loath to invest in dwellings. However in his negative reaction to post-war developments in the construction industry he showed that he was at heart an entrepreneur of the nineteenth century school, and not of the twentieth.

NICHOLAS J MORGAN

SOURCES

Unpublished

Glasgow University Archives, GUA UGD/208, John C McKellar Ltd
Glasgow Valuation Rolls database
Information supplied by Mr Frank Worsdall
SRO: SC3172, John C McKellar Ltd, Companies Registration Office
Strathclyde Regional Archives, Dean of Guild Court application books

Published

Building Industries, 16/11/1922, 19/1/1925
Glasgow Post Office Directories
Glasgow Contemporaries at the Dawn of the Twentieth Century
Glasgow Herald, 21/1/1909
Partick and Maryhill Gazette, 29/3/1907
Royal Commission on Housing in Scotland, Minutes of Evidence, Vol 2

Sir John MACTAGGART,

Builder; b. 30/9/1867, Anderston, Glasgow, s. of Neil Mactaggart, coppersmith and Anne Auld; m. (1) Margaret Lockhart Curtis, d. of Robert Curtis, master blacksmith; (2) Elizabeth Anne Orr, d. of Rev David Orr; 1 s., 1 d.; Founder and MD, J A Mactaggart & Co Ltd; MD, Western Heritable Investment Co Ltd; d. 24/11/1956; g/v UK estate: £32,339 17s 3d.

Although the Scottish construction industry produced a number of men of enterprise and vision few can match the achievements of Sir John Mactaggart. His building work was of immense importance to the development of Glasgow and the West of Scotland between 1890 and 1940, and he also made major contributions to housing policy in Scotland, the United Kingdom more generally, and the United States. In the course of these activities he did much to challenge the traditional structure of the Scottish building industry, which, dominated as it was by craft skills, tended to deter innovation. In addition he was a generous benefactor to his native city, gifting parkland in 1930, and giving generously to the Empire Exhibition of 1938. He was a promoter of the Scottish film industry, and on a wider stage promoted international understanding through the American and British Commonwealth Association, which he founded in 1941.

John Mactaggart was born in September 1867 in Glasgow, the son of a coppersmith there, Neil Mactaggart, whose family had moved to Glasgow from Campbeltown in the early 1830s. John Mactaggart received a formal education in the city, destined, according to one source, for the civil service. However he instead joined the firm of Robert Mickel & Co, timber merchants and sawmillers at Broomloan Saw Mills, in Govan. Here Mactaggart, described as a 'wizard with figures', was trained in the office as a mercantile clerk. In 1887 Mickel moved his sawmilling business to Bo'ness, where he established a large and well equipped 'steam joinery works' - Mactaggart remained in Glasgow at the firm's office in Waterloo Street where, as chief accountant, he dealt increasingly with the property and building side of Mickel's business. This was an extensive operation: between 1889 and 1898 Mickel built 'something like 1,500 houses' in and around Glasgow. In 1898, at the age of 31, Mactaggart left the security of Mickel's firm to join in a partnership with the builder Robert Pollock. The two set up a workshop in Kelvin Street, when in addition to storing plant and materials they manufactured concrete steps; an office was opened at 65 Bath Street. Building projects were undertaken in the vicinity of Springburn, where the firm built 12 tenements between 1898 and 1900.

The partnership between Mactaggart and Pollock was shortlived: in 1901 Mactaggart again left the comparative security offered by partnership with an older and more experienced builder in order to set up his own firm, J A Mactaggart & Co, specialising not only in building but also plastering and the manufacture of concrete pipes, steps and lintels. In addition to contract work Mactaggart began a series of large tenement building projects in the city, concentrating largely on sites in the west end and the south-side Pollokshaws district - in all he built 2,330 houses between 1901 and 1914. The majority of the houses were designed for middle class tenants, who like the majority of urban Scots chose to live in apartments with a small number of large rooms; less than 3% of the houses were of one apartment, 46% of the houses had two apartments, the remainder ranging from three to five apartments. Annual rents for these houses averaged (in 1911) £19, well above the city's average of £13 14s. The houses had a high standard of internal amenity, with internal WCs, and in nearly 80% bathrooms (many years later Mactaggart was to announce himself to a Scottish Office enquiry as 'the man who had made Glasgow bathroom conscious').

The success of his firm during these years, when the building trade fluctuated from a peak at the turn of the century to a trough in the years leading up to the first world war (exacerbated by the impact of Increment Duty in 1909) was due to a combination of personal involvement and delegation:

> By attending personally to the buying of all ground and materials, by having a regular monthly cash-day, and by allowing my foreman an interest in the turnout of their work and giving them the usual employers control over the workmen, a good standard of economy has been maintained.

Cash flow was maintained through the retention of a number of the properties for letting; by 1911 Mactaggart had a portfolio of 83 tenements in the city worth around £200,000, providing an annual rental of nearly £14,000. In addition these properties formed a secure basis for raising loans to finance building operations and land purchases. Mactaggart did not confine his operations to tenement building on his own account: he was contracted to build 44 cottages for J W Gordon Oswald on the Scotstoun estate, to provide houses largely for the English workers being brought to Glasgow to work in Yarrow's new shipyard there, which had been opened in 1908. Unlike his tenements these houses were brick built, with an unusual flat roof formed of concrete and asphalt; the cost of construction to him as a contractor, he later estimated, was the equivalent to that of a two roomed tenement flat.

Although the 1914-18 war offered many opportunities to those involved in the construction industry the production of houses came largely to a standstill. Government had already recognised the deficiencies of housing in Scotland with the setting up of the Royal Commission on Housing in 1913; Mactaggart increasingly a self-styled expert on housing questions, was an outspoken critic of the composition of the Commission, arguing that the failure to include an informed representative of the building or property-owning interest compromised the integrity of its proceedings. The root of the housing problem, he argued in a lecture at Glasgow University, lay in the imposition of penal local-taxes on property, burdening house-owner and householder alike. Expanding this argument in his evidence to the Commission, he suggested that few Scots would opt for larger houses until rates were reduced, making them a more economical proposition. In addition he pesented the Commissioners with an eloquent and impartial summary of the benefits of the tenement system of housing, which was largely ignored in the recommendations. Mactaggart was also involved in the debates over housing that arose from the Clydeside rent-strikes in 1915, resulting in rent restriction and a fundamental destabilisation of the housing market. He later claimed that the suggestion for rent restriction had come from him (although he had included rate restriction in his proposals); 'as the one who suggested the Rent Restriction Acts I feel my responsibility for others and the large number of people in Scotland who are overcrowded because no one will finance the production of better houses'.

The cessation of hostilities saw Mactaggart completing a number of wartime contracts, including work in Glasgow for Fairfields, and for the Admiralty at Gourock. The pressure to improve housing standards had gained momentum during the war, leading first to the pledge to provide 'Homes Fit for Heroes', and then in 1919 to the Addison Act, providing a virtually unlimited subsidy to local authorities, who for the first time were obliged to embark on housing schemes. Mactaggart was successful in gaining large contracts on some of the earliest schemes in Glasgow, such as Riddrie No 2 (brickwork worth £87,000), Riddrie No 4 (joiner work worth £27,000), and Greenhead (joiner work worth £70,000). However the contract that propelled his firm into the forefront of housebuilding in Scotland was for the Mosspark housing scheme. Glasgow Corporation had determined that this scheme for 1,502 houses, then the largest in its plans (and the largest in Scotland), should be let to a single contractor in order to gain the benefits of economy and efficiency that this would offer. This decision provoked the wrath of the various trade associations in the West of Scotland, who argued that it should be let in the traditional fashion by craft. Notwithstanding these objections the single contract was put to tender in the summer of 1920 (the committee having earlier rejected an unsolicited bid from Robert McAlpine (qv) to build it). Mactaggart was finally confirmed as the successful contractor in September, amidst considerable opposition from the supporters of the building interest on the Corporation.

The scheme was worth £1.8 million, and involved the construction of houses in a development designed to meet all the criteria laid down for post-war cottage housing by the Tudor Walters report. In order to provide the necessary financial and managerial back-up to carry out these contracts Mactaggart had converted his firm into a limited company in October 1919, with a capital of £30,000. John Mactaggart was managing director of the new company; his son Jack Auld Mactaggart and Andrew Mickel were the other directors. Both were veterans of the war; Mickel had worked previously for Robert Mickel (his uncle), he had designed some of the tenements erected by Mactaggart and had also been in business as a builder and contractor since 1909. Jack Mactaggart and his mother Margaret were the two largest shareholders in the business, with 5,000 shares each; John Mactaggart held 4,000 shares, whilst his daughter Isa Mickel held 1,000 shares.

The Mosspark contract provided the opportunity for Mactaggart to challenge many of the constraints which the traditional organisation of building contracts imposed on the would-be general contractor. These included the payment of piece-rates, direct negotiation of overtime (which was normally agreed through local craft associations), and the erosion of restrictive practices. As a result disputes with trade-associations (both employers and employees) were legion. In addition the desperate shortage of building materials held up progress and increased costs. At one time it was estimated by the Scottish Office that the Mosspark contract could easily consume all the bricks available for domestic construction in Scotland. In order to overcome the shortage of bricks Mactaggart turned to concrete blocks as an alternative building material, speeding up production and reducing cost on houses by around £17. Further efforts to speed up production included the use of a bricklaying machine ('the difficulty was finding a method of stopping and restarting it when it came to window and door openings'), and cement and plaster guns. Criticisms of the quality of the houses built at Mosspark were not long in emerging from the local press; Mactaggart's response was to offer to undertake the factorage of the scheme and effect all repairs at a fixed price less than that being paid by the Corporation on its existing houses.

Although the opportunities for speculative building were slight in the early 1920s Mactaggart did not lose sight of the private market. In 1919, with rents still controlled as a consequence of the wartime legislation Mactaggart had helped to establish, he sought to overcome the problems of falling income from rented property through the introduction of '25 year terminable annuity bonds'. Offered initially to tenants in houses at Broomhill, Glasgow, rented at over £30 per year, the bonds cost £225 for a four bedroom house; in return the tenant got possession of the property for 25 years at pre-war rent levels, but assumed all responsibility for repairs and rates. Capital was paid back annually without interest, and loans of up to £150 were available to help prospective purchasers. The ingenious scheme faced the implacable opposition of the tenants involved, who like most urban Scots were not prepared to make any capital outlay on their homes. They resisted alleged threats of eviction if they refused to buy bonds and forced Mactaggart to withdraw the scheme, which he argued, had been inspired by the Labour Party's housing policy based on money without interest. Mactaggart however was still concerned to provide houses on the private market, and he used the depressed conditions of the 1920s as an opportunity to build up a substantial land-bank for future developments. Initially he concentrated on areas on the outskirts of Glasgow; purchases were made not by Mactaggart but by a consortium comprising his wife, Margaret Mactaggart, his daughter Isa and sister Jeanie, and the wives of Jack Auld Mactaggart and Andrew Mickel. The most significant acquisitions for the estate of King's Park to the south of the city, and the 114 acres of the Kelvinside estate in the city's west-end, purchased in 1923 for £33,000, supported partly by a loan provided by J A Mactaggart & Co Ltd.

Late in 1924 plans were submitted for the first development at King's Park, but these were overtaken by a reorganisation of Mactaggart's business affairs. These stemmed from the 1924 Housing Bill, then being piloted through parliament by Labour Minister of Health and Shettleston MP John Wheatley. One of the most important features of the Bill was its encouragement to builders to build houses for rent aided by direct subsidy. This 'partnership with private enterprise', as it was later described, had arisen largely from the discussions which Wheatley had had with Mactaggart during his extensive lobbying of the housing interest in Glasgow during the framing of the Bill. The two had a firm relationship, stemming partly from the leading role Wheatley had played for Glasgow Corporation in negotiating the Mosspark contract with Mactaggart. However Wheatley and Mactaggart had a long association through the latter's involvement in politics in Glasgow: Mactaggart, a Liberal in his youth, had joined the Scottish Labour Party in 1889, remaining a member until 1902 when he resigned to rejoin the Liberals. He was active in local politics serving as secretary of the Glasgow Liberals; the veteran Red Clydesider Harry McShane recalled that a Saturday afternoon entertainment for Glasgow socialists was to heckle Mactaggart as he chaired the regular Liberal meetings at the Palace Theatre. However Mactaggart refused invitations to stand for election to the Corporation, and later three requests to stand for election to parliament. Based on this common interest in politics and particularly housing economics, there developed a clear respect and understanding between Mactaggart and Wheatley, and Mactaggart was determined to make good his encouragement of the clauses in the Bill promoting subsidy-aided private building. However

the immediate future for his son Jack Mactaggart and Andrew Mickel lay in private building for owner-occupation, and following the voluntary liquidation of J A Mactaggart Ltd in 1924 they reconstructed the company as Mactaggart & Mickel Ltd, a business in which John Mactaggart had no direct financial interest.

Mactaggart's vehicle for a continued involvement in housebuilding was the Western Heritable Investment Company Ltd. Originally established in 1896 to purchase heritable property in and around Glasgow, the business had languished since the war, its only asset a single tenement on the south side of the city. Mactaggart moved to take over the company in September 1925, increasing its capital from £5,000 to £30,000, divided between himself, his wife, his daughter and grandson. The capital of the company was increased in 1927, 1929 and 1931, by which time it stood at £150,000; the Mactaggart family shareholding had increased during this time to reflect the new capitalisation, while Mactaggart & Mickel Ltd had become substantial shareholders in the business themselves. John Mactaggart was managing director, Lena Orr Mactaggart (his second wife) and his son and daughter were directors. Early in 1926 the Western Heritable Investment Company made the first of a series of applications to the Dean of Guild court for permission to build houses at King's Park on a site adjoining a Mactaggart & Mickel development. The land was purchased (or withdrawn) by Mactaggart from the land bank established earlier by J A Mactaggart & Co. The houses were all four apartment, four in a block, cottage flats, similar in design to those built earlier by Mactaggart for the Corporation. They were designed with hollow walls, to be built of a variety material including brick and concrete blocks. Initially these houses attracted a subsidy of £13 10s. under the 1924 Act, conditional on their being let at 'pre-war' rent levels. In addition the company was financed by the local authority through loans of 75 per cent of the estimated value of the completed houses. By 1930 they had completed 1,356 houses, with another 1,512 under construction. Loans over these properties were estimated at £950,000.

Mactaggart's attempt to complete his share of the King's Park development under the same subsidy level was obstructed by an increasing reluctance on the part of both the Scottish Office and the Corporation to finance his operations, and by the gradual withdrawal by Central government of the Wheatley subsidy. Notwithstanding the clear tension that existed between the various parties Mactaggart made a generous gift to the Corporation in May 1930 of the mansionhouse and grounds of the Aitkenhead estate adjoining the King's Park development, on the condition that the land be preserved as a public park for the city. By 1931 agreement had been reached for an additional 1,364 houses to be built at King's Park with a £9 subsidy and 75% loans. This and similar schemes involved massive building operations - Mactaggart estimated the labour requirement at around 900 men - but the rewards were self-evident as demand for the houses continued to be buoyant. With the King's Park land largely exhausted Mactaggart built subsidised brick and concrete tenements at Kelvinside, adjoining the Mactaggart & Mickel land bank there, and in 1932 was building a mixture of cottage-flat house types on land at Cardonald, Glasgow, owned by the Corporation. In all the Western Heritable Company built 6,038 houses for rent under subsidies offered by the 1924 Act, largely within Glasgow. This was the equivalent of, often more than, the entire publicly owned housing stock of many a Scottish burgh, and the company was required to develop and maintain letting, managerial and maintenance procedures similar to those required of local authorities. Property management became a second occupation for Mactaggart, and the procedures adopted by his company were held up as models for local authorities to copy in a report of 1938.

John Mactaggart was 65 in 1932, and yet there was little indication of his taking an early retirement, despite the impending withdrawal of the subsidies to private builders. In addition to his recently acquired but long-term commitment to the management of his housing developments in Glagow he had begun to take an interest in the London property market. One of his first major projects there was the development of luxury flats on the Park Lane site adjoining the Dorchester Hotel, built between 1935 and 1938 to the designs of the Glasgow architect Joseph Wilson, who had designed the majority of the Western Heritable cottage flats. These speculations continued before and after the war through two new companies, the London Heritable Investment Company Limited and Grove End Gardens Ltd, formed to build and manage luxury flats in St John's Wood. He also spread his wings to include New York in his expanding property empire - as in Scotland, so in America he was regarded as a leading authority on housing. In 1936 he was asked to prepare a memorandum for President Roosevelt's advisers, much of which was later incorporated in the New Deal. Nor did he spare Glasgow from his ever fertile thoughts on the housing question. In March 1938, at a dinner hosted by the Corporation to celebrate his knighthood (awarded that year for his contribution to housing), he hit the headlines with a new scheme to relieve overcrowding through widespread grant-aided renovation of tenement properties. New building could never proceed rapidly enough to meet the growing pressure for accommodation, he argued; £100 would be sufficient to convert one and two roomed houses to three roomed houses, making the most of the existing structure. These ideas met with a cool response from local authorities who saw new-build as the answer to their problems; nonetheless Mactaggart revived the idea after the war, and was ultimately to be vindicated by the swing to the restoration and renovation of tenement properties that marked Scottish housing policy in the 1980s.

Mactaggart possessed a breadth of vision that took him beyond the parochial concerns both of his business and native city. His interest in things American prompted him to establish the American and British Commonwealth Association in 1941, which was merged with the English Speaking Union in 1947. Earlier, in 1938, he had been the principal financier of the Peace Pavilion at the 1938 Empire Exhibition designed to illustrate the work of the League of Nations. His interest in the social sciences (one of his listed recreations in *Who's Who* was 'health research') led to an invitation (duly accepted) to serve as president of the Economic Research Council; whilst his expertise in matters relating to property saw him elected to the office of president of the National Federation of Property Owners from 1950 to 1952. He gave both his time and money: his gift to Glasgow of Aitkenhead Park was only one of a number of generous donations to the city and its institutions. His enthusiasm for documentary film and the Scottish Film industry was marked by a gift of £5,000 towards the construction of the cinema at the Empire Exhibition. In his will he explained that the 'nature of my estate prevents me from making any other public bequests'. His total estate at confirmation stood at £32,339; he owned heritable property valued at £129,975, over which loans had been raised to the value of £135,475. Ultimately his final estate for the purpose of duty payment was calculated at only £23,233, although this failed to reflect the 'full and adequate provision' Mactaggart had made for all his family in earlier years. He was mourned widely, and had clearly earned in his lifetime the place attributed to him in death by the obituary writer of the *Glasgow Herald*, 'in the front rank of Scottish industrialists'.

NICHOLAS J MORGAN

Writings

'Housing and planning', *Proceedings of the Royal Philosophical Society of Glasgow*, Vol lxviii, Glasgow, 1943

SOURCES

Unpublished

Companies Registration Office: SC 3247, Western Heritable Investment Company Ltd
SC 13539, Mactaggart & Mickel Ltd
SRO: BT 2/10648, J A Mactaggart Co Ltd
SC 36/48/855, Inventory
SC 36/51/416, Will
Register of Sasines, Glasgow

Strathclyde Regional Archives:
DTC 8/20/38/1-2
Dean of Guild Court Application Books 1895-1939
Dean of Guild Court (sample plans at various years)
University of Glasgow, Glasgow Valuation Rolls database, 1911
Information kindly supplied by Mactaggart & Mickel Ltd

Published

Builder, 30/11/1856
Building Industries, March 1938
Glasgow Corporation, Minutes of the Housing Committee
Glasgow Herald, 15/11/1913, 19/2/1919, 20/2/1919, 21/2/1919, 24/2/1919, 22/9/1920, 22/5/1956, 24/8/1922, 7/4/1923, 2/5/1930, 1/1/1938, 9/2/1938, 3/12/1947, 26/11/1956
Glasgow Post Office Directory, 1885-1945
McShane, Harry, *No mean fighter*, London, 1978
Royal Commission on the Housing of the Industrial Population of Scotland, *Minutes of Evidence*, Edinburgh, 1921, Vol ii
Survey of London, Vol xi
The Times, 26/11/1956
Who Was Who

Sir Thomas MASON,

Public works contractor; b. 1844, Airdrie, Lanarkshire, s. of John Mason, builder, and Marion Hamilton; m. (1) Jeanie Paton; (2) Charlotte Wyllie; 2 s., 3 d.; Dir, Morrison & Mason Ltd, contractors, Glasgow; d. 26/4/1924, Glasgow; g/v estate: £138,129 10s 3d.

When Sir Thomas Mason died in 1921 few others could have claimed to match his intimate and distinguished association with the development of Glasgow, in both his business and civic activities. Born in Airdrie in 1844, the son of a builder, Mason had come to Glasgow to be educated at Anderson's College 'the best private school on the South Side' of the city in the middle class suburb of Laurieston. On leaving school he was apprenticed to be a mason, starting work as a journeyman in Edinburgh at the age of 17. There followed a period of six years during which he worked both as a sub-contractor on railway works and as a mason for other contractors. In 1867 Mason

approached the contractor James Brand (qv) seeking employment on a contract for a line for the Glasgow & South Western railway through Cumnock. Impressed by the young man's apparent skill and obvious ambition Brand appointed him as foreman mason, leaving him largely responsible for the construction of the Ayr viaduct. On completion of the contract Mason spent five years in charge of Brand's tramway contracts, which included the first to be let by Glasgow Corporation in 1870, and one for the Govan and Greenock Tramway Company. In 1875 Mason left Brand to manage (on a commission basis) his first major contract, the No 1 contract of the Stobcross (later Queen's) Docks in Glasgow. This undertaking, which involved blasting through some of the hardest boulder clay in the city and the sinking of sophisticated concrete-cylinders as foundation for the more orthodox rubble quay-walls, was a turning point in Mason's career. Having acquired considerable experience of the problems involved at Queen's Dock, and a degree of capital, he joined the builder John Morrison as junior partner in the firm of John Morrison & Co, to assist in tendering for, and managing future contracts on the Queen's Dock complex.

Mason's partner was a native of Dunoon, the son of a master builder, and a trained mason, who had moved to Glasgow to start a business of his own in

the mid-1850s. In Glasgow Mason worked as a foreman to other contractors and also as a builder in his own right. Probably his most extensive speculation involved the clearing and redevelopment of the Main Street area of the Gorbals, undertaken under the auspices of the Glasgow City Improvement Trust. Morrison purchased land from the Trustees in 1866 on the newly formed Main Street on which he subsequently built, in addition to 11 tenements and public halls, the Royal Princess (now Citizen's) Theatre to the designs of the architect James Sellars, incorporating in its facade the original portico for the city centre Union Bank building. In 1881 Morrison's residential property, including tenements elsewhere in the city, was worth some £16,000. By 1911 much of this had been disposed of (including the Main Street site, sold in 1896 to the theatre lessee for £32,500), although Morrison continued to engage in minor speculations in villa building on the city's south side, where he had lived in increasing splendour since his arrival in Glasgow.

When Mason joined the business Morrison was in the course of completing a series of prestigious contracts for public buildings in the city centre. These included the Merchants House (1874-77) and the city's Stock Exchange (1875-77), both designed by John Burnet Snr (the latter in a highly ornate Italian Gothic style, demanding stonework of the highest quality), and the General Post Office in George Square (1875-76). Mason's expertise allowed the firm to branch out into public works contracting; the first contract in this field being the second stage of the Queen's Dock, worth some £61,000. There followed a number of important railway contracts; the construction of new lines into St Enoch station and an extension to the College station in Glasgow, and the Paisley canal line of the Glasgow and South Western railway. Between 1884 and 1886 the firm built the first section of the Cathcart Circle, Glasgow's south side commuter railway, a contract worth in excess of £77,000 that had been taken over following the failure of the original firm, Alex Coghill & Co. Significantly it was Mason's drive that took the firm south of the border for the first time to build the massive Citadel station on the main line at Carlisle. Mason was also responsible for the firm's first adventure into water related works: in 1886 the firm won the contract for the Mugdock tunnel, part of Glasgow's Loch Katrine water works, worth £40,000, and in the following year they won the first of three contracts for the Thirlmere reservoir project for Manchester water works committee. The Thirlmere aqueduct contract was undertaken jointly with William Arrol (qv) and was the first of a number of important collaborations with Scotland's greatest structural engineer. In addition to these extensive activities the firm also undertook the construction of increasingly larger public buildings in and around Glasgow: the offices of the Clyde Navigation Trust in Glasgow (1883-86), the George A Clark halls in Paisley (subscribed for by the Clark cotton thread manufacturing family), and perhaps most significantly the municipal buildings in Glasgow (1883-88), a 'swaggeringly opulent building' for the main offices of the Corporation built at a total cost of over £500,000.

In 1879 the name of the firm had been changed to Morrison & Mason, ten years later the company was floated publicly as Morrison & Mason Ltd, with a capital of £100,000, divided into shares of £100. The two partners in the old firm held the majority of shares, 290 each (although by 1890 Mason was the largest shareholder with 325); they were the only directors of the company, with John Morrison acting as chairman. Small holdings of ten shares were allocated to James and John Morrison Jnr, sons of John Morrison, John Mason, the eldest son of Thomas Mason, and a number of senior employees. William Arrol purchased 65 shares in the company in 1890. The floatation had possibly been effected in order to raise capital during the Thirlmere contract which was slow paying and subject to tortuous arbitration proceedings - in addition Mason had loaned the new company £10,000 and substantial credits were obtained from the Union Bank.

Between 1890 and the start of the war Morrison & Mason continued to expand the scope of their operations. Waterworks continued to be a speciality; in addition to the continuing work at Thirlmere the firm won contracts for the Black Rigg diversion (part of the Loch Katrine works, worth some £88,000), the Craigmaddie service reservoir (1893-94), the Nidd Valley aqueduct (1894-99), the Birmingham Corporation water scheme (1900-04), and in 1904 the Ystoradfellte reservoir for Neath Rural District Council and the Chew Valley reservoir, the latter for Ashton and District water works committee, worth in excess of £103,000. In 1914 they were awarded the contract for the Lower Laithe reservoir for Keighly waterworks committee, a project that was interrupted both by the war and by persistent labour troubles, not being completed until 1924. The company were also employed on a number of major dock-building projects for Clydeside shipbuilders, including an extension to Fairfield dock in 1890, the construction of J & G Thomson's new dock at Clydebank following the acquisition of the firm by John Brown's of Sheffield, and a sub-contract for excavation work on Arrol's construction of Yarrow's new dockyard at Scotstoun in 1907. The move towards rearmament was significant in providing the company with some of its most lucrative work. In the following year they won their largest contract, worth £1,000,000, for the construction of lock-gates at the entrance to Portsmouth naval dockyard; this was followed in 1907 by a second admiralty contract at Portsmouth worth £500,000 for a graving dock for Dreadnoughts. This work, which was continued during the war, was followed by a number of contracts for harbour defences and fortifications throughout the country.

Although their public works contracts were taking

159

them further afield from Glasgow, Morrison & Mason did not lose their intimate connection with the development of the city or its services. Bridge building was one new area - they had worked as sub-contractors to Arrol on the construction of the Caledonian railway bridge over the Clyde in 1876 but now undertook a series of important contracts in and around Glasgow, including in 1890 the Great Western Bridge (with Arrol as sub contractor for the steel work), the Glasgow Bridge (1895) and the Rutherglen Bridge, completed in 1896. Between 1898 and 1899 they built the tidal weir on the Clyde at Glasgow Green. In 1896 the company began the construction of the City's Ruchill fever hospital which was completed in 1900; between 1905 and 1908 they were responsible for the reconstruction of the Rottenrow Maternity Hospital. They built a number of offices during the massive redevelopment of the city centre that took place between 1890 and 1914, including the offices of the newly formed Central Agency in 1897 (one of several contracts undertaken for J & P Coats), and in 1909-10 new offices for the *Glasgow Herald*.

Between the formation of the limited company in 1889 and the end of the war the company returned consistent annual profits. In the decade 1889-98 they averaged £11,500; in 1899-1908 they averaged £14,000, and in 1909-1918 £13,000. The company followed a policy of paying high dividends, only below 10% on four occasions, and frequently (with bonuses) up to 15%. Morrison & Mason never quite achieved the peak reached by firms such as McAlpines, but they were nonetheless a successful and profitable business, capable of securing and executing contracts throughout Britain. In 1919 John Morrison died of heart failure; Mason, the only remaining director, arranged for the sale of the company to Sir William Arrol & Co at a price of £120,500, following which Arrols put the separate business into liquidation. Mason, a substantial shareholder in Arrols, was also a director and chairman of that company, (he also served as chairman of the Scottish Tube Co Ltd). Thomas Mason was active in the management of Morrison & Mason throughout the business's lifetime; he was, as we have seen, particularly responsible for attending to the side of the business which dealt with public works, where tendering was adventurous and profits high. Mason was a foil to Morrison's more conservative business instinct, and it was undoubtedly his energy that saw the company expand not only its field of expertise, but also its sphere of operations. However, despite his commitment to the business Mason also undertook an impressive public life, which led to his knighthood in 1909.

His involvement in the government of the city began through his philanthropic service in the Incorporation of Masons and the Trades House - as deacon convener of the latter body he was an ex-officio member of the town council. He was subsequently elected to serve as councillor for the city's eighth ward in 1891 (he was a Liberal and had chaired the city's Liberal club); during his term of office he was chosen to represent the city on the board of the Clyde trustees, a position which he resumed in 1893 as a representative of the Merchant's House until 1919. During this period he was convener of the Trust's works committee (1896-1907), deputy chairman (1907-08) and chairman (1908-19), and as such was associated with major developments relating to the city's shipping trade. In addition to the continued deepening and widening of the river this included the installation of hydraulic power at Princes dock, the construction of the Clyde ore terminal, the building of Meadowside Quay and the Trust's contiguous granaries, and the construction of the Rothesay dock at Clydebank. During the years in which Mason was involved with the trust, and largely as a result of the works he had initiated and overseen, the tonnage of shipping coming in and out of the Clyde almost doubled, from slightly over 7 million to just under 14 million registered tons. The revenue of the trust increased from some £354,000 to £633,000. Mason was also concerned about cross-river communications, and was a propagandist for the construction of a new bridge in the west of the city to relieve traffic congestion on central routes. His advocacy of this scheme was the subject of some derision in both the local and engineering press; it is however worth observing that the site for Mason's bridge was almost identical to that chosen for the city's Kingston bridge built in the 1970s. In typical Glasgow style Mason was a jealous guardian of the trust's independence against proposals for a merged authority taking in all the major Clyde ports.

Sir Thomas Mason was typical of those Victorian and Edwardian businessmen who seemed able to cram at least eight days into the working week. And yet he was not a slave to his business, public or charitable commitments - he travelled widely, and lived in splendour at Craigie Hall on the south side of the city. He indulged himself in the ownership of race horses, owning at one time a small stable, and latterly a small number of horses trained at Newmarket. As such all business ceased in the autumn for the Western Meeting at the Ayr race-course. Nor did Mason possess the fiery temperament that one sometimes associates with successful men-of-affairs; *The Bailie* magazine, although not the most objective of sources on such matters, exceeded even its own standards of obsequiousness when it described Mason as 'one of the most lovable of men'. When he died of heart failure in 1924 Mason left an estate of £138,129 to his widow (his second wife, Charlotte Wyllie) and his children. Mason was certainly remembered as one who had given his all for his adopted city, but for business historians and historians of the construction industry he is more notable as the genius behind one of Scotland's most successful contracting businesses.

NICHOLAS J MORGAN

WRITINGS

The improvement of the River Clyde and harbour of Glasgow, 1873-1914, London, 1916

SOURCES

Unpublished

SRO: BT 2/1937, Morrison & Mason Ltd
SRO: SC36/48/301, Inventory
  SC 36/51/184, Trust disposition and settlement of John Morrison
  SC 36/48/354, Inventory of Sir Thomas Mason
  SC 36/51/203, Trust disposition and settlement of Sir Thomas Mason
Strathclyde Regional Archives, T-MAs 323, Morrison & Mason Ltd
Information supplied by R A Smith

Published

The Bailie, No 573, 10/10/1883, No 938, 8/10/1890, No 1388, 24/5/1899
Bowrell, H D, *Reservoir Railways of Manchester and the Peak*, Newton Abbot, 1982
Building Industries, 15/5/1890, 15/7/1890
Building News, 20/3/1885, 5/4/1890
Engineering, 2/5/1924
Glasgow Contemporaries at the Dawn of the Twentieth Century
Glasgow Herald, 8/8/1896, 25/1/1899, 16/1/1908, 2/5/1910, 20/9/1910, 26/3/919, 28/4/1924, 30/4/1924, 2/5/1924
Glasgow Post Office Directories 1850-1920
Kernachar, J, *The Cathcart Circle*, Falkirk, 1980
Riddell, F, *Clyde Navigation*, Edinburgh, 1979
Scottish Trader, 22/5/1897
Shipping World 11/7/1897

Andrew MICKEL,

Builder; b. 1878, Glasgow, s. of Andrew Mickel, hosiery manufacturer and wholesale draper and Helen Weir; m. 26/9/1907, Frances McWhirter, d. of William McWhirter, electrical engineer, Glasgow; 2 s., 1 d.; Ch, Mactaggart & Mickel Ltd, housebuilders, Glasgow; d. 21/7/1962, Largs, Ayrshire.

Andrew Mickel was born in 1878 in Glasgow, the son of a hosiery manufacturer. Following schooling at Bellahouston Academy and the Glasgow High School he joined the extensive joinery and building business owned by his uncle Robert Mickel, at Bo'ness, where he had established a large and well equipped 'steam joinery works'. Mickel was formerly apprenticed as a joiner, going on to act as manager to his uncle on his many building projects in and around Glasgow. This was an extensive operation: between 1889 and 1898 Mickel built 'something like 1,500 houses', ranging from single-ends to seven apartment flats. In addition he worked on house and office-building projects in the west-end of London undertaken by his uncle.

In about 1909 Andrew Mickel established his own firm, first at Byres Road, then at Bath Street, Glasgow, building 'tenements, villas and cottages'. He was, as he later explained to the Royal Commission on Housing in Scotland in 1913, an advocate of cottage building, following the general lines of design set out by the Garden City Movement. He studied not only planning and design, but also the land question, travelling to Canada before the war to examine the system there. His advocacy of cottage building was supported by a thorough commitment to private enterprise and owner-occupation; he was not sympathetic to the prospect of extensive local authority building and advocated instead a Government sponsored Housing Loan Fund to support widespread cottage building. A keen supporter of the volunteer movement he enlisted at the start of the first war and served in the Royal Scots and Royal Enginers before returning to Glasgow in 1919.

On his return to the city he joined in business with John Mactaggart (qv), whom he had first met when the latter worked as an accountant for his uncle. Mactaggart had ambitious plans to capture the promised flood of house-building contracts that were to be issued under the terms of the Addison Act of 1919, which laid the responsibility to build general needs working class housing on local authorities. In order to provide the necessary financial and managerial back-up to carry out these contracts Mactaggart had converted his firm into a limited company in October 1919, with a capital of £30,000. John Mactaggart was managing director of the new company; his son Jack Auld Mactaggart and Andrew Mickel were the other directors. Jack Mactaggart and his mother Margaret were the two largest shareholders in the buiness, with 5,000 shares each; John Mactaggart held 4,000 shares, whilst his daughter Isa and Mickel held 1,000 shares each. The pressure laid on the three directors of the company was immense, particularly following the acquisition of the contract for the Mosspark housing scheme worth some £1.8 million. However in 1924 the business was voluntarily wound up, as John Mactaggart chose to devote his energies to the Western Heritable Investment Trusts, a company he had acquired to take advantage of the opportunities for subsidised building offered by the Housing (Wheatley) Act of that year. The contracts of the old company were acquired by Mactaggart & Mickel, set up by Andrew Mickel and Jack Mactaggart in 1925, with a capital of £20,000. Jack Mactaggart was the largest shareholder (10,000), with Mickel owning 8,000 shares; in 1933 the capital of the firm was increased to £30,000 and two of Andrew Mickel's sons, Francis (who had joined the company in 1927) and Douglas acquired shareholdings of 2,000 and 1,200. Two directors, Walter Grieve and the banker James Ledingham (a director of Western Heritable) joined the board in 1934 and 1939.

The company built initially in two prime locations on the outskirts of the city, one at Kelvinside in the west end, the other on the more extensive site at King's Park on the south side. Developments were sited on parcels of land drawn from a land-bank which John and Jack Mactaggart and Andrew Mickel had built up in the early twenties, transferring the titles of the land to their respective wives and daughters for security. Mickel's concern with the primacy of design informed the lay-out and style of houses; a Mactaggart and Mickel house was to be both 'thoroughly modern in every respect' and at the same time 'so attractive and artistic that those living in it may be justly proud of it'. Built with brick walls ('for dryness, warmth and durability this method of construction is the equal of stone'), the houses were fitted out to a high standard, with oak mantles in living rooms and Dutch tile fireplaces in bedrooms. Power points were supplied in all the main rooms, and electricity also provided an additional hot-water supply. Particular attention was paid to sanitary fittings ('we venture to claim that no houses offered anywhere are so far advanced in these respects'), which included pedestal lavatory basins. Five apartment houses built to this standard (the ones described were at Kelvinside) sold for between £775 and £875, bringing domestic luxury to a small but growing group of would-be home owners. Houses at King's Park, available from 1925, were sold at prices ranging from £500; 'here are houses ...' proclaimed a later advert, 'obtainable on a scheme that makes purchase easier than paying rent'.

Advertising and publicity were one of the key's to the company's success; a two storey house was built in Central Station in 1928 to promote interest, leading to the sale of 100 houses in a week. The same device was used in 1934 to promote sales on a scheme in Clarkston. In 1931 an exhibition bungalow (illuminated by fairy-lights) was built at Eglinton Toll, a busy thoroughfare for the city's south bound travellers. The firm's motto, 'Builders of Fine Homes', had been coined as early as 1927, and was used to build an image of reliability, which rested partly on the emphasis laid on traditional workmanship. The image of the house and the home was projected as a selling point to attract those who wished to move from cramped flatted accommodation with all the disadvantages of multi-occupied buildings. One of the products that Andrew Mickel introduced to Glasgow was the bungalow, which had not been built on any extensive scale before the 1920s. Mactaggart & Mickel were building them at King's Park by 1929, using designs based on the colonial model. Selling at prices from around £575 these houses, which offered all the convenience of a tenement flat and the prestige and privacy of homeownership, were enormously popular. They were also cheap and easy to build; the company managing to get construction down to ten days on one site. In 1931 the company claimed they had sold 130 bungalows in a development at Newlands in Glasgow in 24 hours, claiming a 'world's record in house purchase'.

In 1933 Andrew Mickel expanded the range of the firm's activities to include building in Edinburgh, where 500 houses were built between January and November for renting. Douglas Mickel supervised the company's first developments there, which included further estates at East Pilton (260 houses) and Colinton Mains (352 houses). At this time the company also plunged into modernism at their prestigious Broom estate where, claimed an advert in the *Glasgow Herald*, 'striking modern architecture is well expressed without losing anything of the dignity of house design', providing the 'ideal home' in a 'perfect setting'. Eventually included in the Broom estate were two blocks of luxury two-bedroomed flats, 'designed primarily for those who wish to live in the country with easy access to the town, and without the responsibility of house ownership', rented at £250 per year. Although the houses that were built did not incorporate all the features originally advertised, notably the flat roofs, the estate was an enormous success, cementing the name of Mactaggart and Mickel in the minds of the public as Scotland's leading quality home builder.

The war saw a virtual cessation of housebuilding, although Mactaggart & Mickel were involved in an experiment with Paisley District Council in 1940 to develop a prototype woodless house at Gallowhill, in order to allow the completion of a housing scheme for which timber could not be released. Andrew Mickel was deeply involved in the war effort through his service in the Home Guard in which he served as colonel; the company were involved in various wartime projects, including air-raid shelter construction, and defensive installations at Clydeside oil stores. In addition the company had begun to take contracts for hospital building (at Killearn and Buchanan Castle) and school construction (at Pollok) which were continued after the war when building was subject to severe government control.

By the end of the war Andrew Mickel was past the normal age for retirement, and his active work with the company began to reduce. However in 1953 he was appointed a Deputy Lieutenant for Lanarkshire, having served variously as a County Councillor for Dumbarton and a Justice of the Peace for Glasgow. He had been involved in a number of trade and charitable organisations, such as the Incorporation of Gardeners, the Clydesdale Merchants Society and the Glasgow Discharged Prisoners Society, and with his sons had gifted a public hall for the use of the elderly in Clarkston. By the time of his death in 1962 the company was firmly in the hands of his family; Jack Mactaggart had played a diminishing part in the firm's affairs and had retired in 1942. Conversely Andrew Mickel had played an important role in the management of the Western Heritable Company in which Jack MacTaggart had become involved with his father; Mactaggart & Mickel becoming substantial shareholders in the company. Although Frank Mickel had died suddenly in 1961 his place on the board had been taken by his son Derek, with Douglas Mickel acting as chairman following his father's death. Although less flamboyant than the Mactaggart's Andrew Mickel was nonetheless equally responsible for the revolution in housing that the firm which bore both their names helped to bring about throughout the Central belt, his insistence on design and style setting out a formula from which the firm were never to depart.

NICHOLAS J MORGAN

SOURCES

Unpublished

Companies Registration Office: SC 13539, Mactaggart & Mickel Ltd
Strathclyde Regional Archives:
  AGN 826, '50 Years of Kings Park'
  TD 554/66, Sales Brochure
Dean of Guild Court Application Books 1895-1939
Dean of Guild Court (Sample plans)
Information kindly supplied by Mr D W Mickel of Mactaggart & Mickel Ltd

Published

Building Industries, 16/10/1922, 16/11/1975, 16/1/1932, April 1934, January 1939, October 1940, December 1945, June 1946, October 1949, March 1950
Glasgow Herald, 27/11/1951, 31/7/1961, 4/8/1961, 23/7/1962
Glasgow Post Office Directories, 1890-1945
McKean, C, *The Scottish Thirties: an architectural introduction*, Edinburgh, 1987
Royal Commission on the Housing of the Industrial Population of Scotland, *Minutes of Evidence*, Edinburgh, 1921, Vol II
The Scotsman, 31/7/1961, 23/7/1962

Sir James MILLER,

Builder and architect; b. 16/3/1905, Edinburgh, s. of James Miller, architect; m. 9/9/1933, Ella Stewart, d. of John Stewart, butcher, Edinburgh; 3 s., 1 d.; Founder & Ch, James Miller & Partners Ltd, housebuilders and contractors, Edinburgh; d. 22/3/1977, Edinburgh.

James Miller was born in 1905, the second son of an Edinburgh architect. He was educated at George Heriot's school in the city and subsequently studied architecture in night-classes at Edinburgh College of Art whilst serving as an apprentice to his father, a position he had occupied since 1919. Three years later his father died, leaving James to continue as principal of the business (known as James Miller - Architect) at the age of only 17. It is not clear what nature of work was being pursued by the practice at this time, but under the direction of James Jnr the firm was pushed towards the field of house-building.

Local authority house-building dominated production at the time, leaving both a residual need for owner-occupied accommodation, and in Edinburgh an increasing demand for fashionable, but cheap, private housing from new sections of would-be house purchasers. It was to this market that Miller directed his attention, embarking on his first large venture in 1927 with a development of semi-detached bungalows at Queensferry Road, Blackhill. With two public rooms, three bedrooms and a kitchenette boasting the 'latest labour saving devices' the bungalows sold at £840 each, with a down-payment scheme (financed by building societies) available to those who could afford an initial balance of £170. The 12 houses were easily sold after imaginative illustrated advertising in the *Scotsman* attracted sufficient purchasers in a single day. Nonetheless, although they offered comfort and a convenient location for city-centre work their price was high at a time when English firms such as Taylor & Woodrow could provide their markets with semi-detached houses at around £450 each. Miller's response was to be a cheaper design, the Type A bungalow, that dominated, and formed the basis of the success of, his firm's business in the inter-war years.

The Type A comprised two public rooms, two bedrooms, bathroom and kitchenette. Reconstituted stone was used for the facing material and concrete was used wherever possible to keep down the cost of construction. The unit price was £475, with purchase guaranteed by a deposit of £25 and weekly payments of 17 shillings. Developments mushroomed throughout Edinburgh, at Craigleith, Corstorphine and Craigentinny. In 1932, a year in which economic conditions might have threatened expansion, output peaked, with nearly 600 applications for building permits being lodged by the firm. With demand still buoyant Miller had realised, as had his counterparts in the south, that growth could only be sustained by a rapid throughput of product aided wherever by standardisation. Even in this period the firm only built from a standard range of six bungalows and houses, although the emphasis on appearance and quality was always retained - to provide 'a home of their very own with town convenience and a real country atmosphere' for purchasers who were attracted through advertisement and the Miller company booklet, *Home*. Behind this progress there lay a shrewd policy for the acquisition of land on the fringes of the city for future building use, often acquired at prices which initially seemed to far outweigh their value but which ultimately confirmed the astuteness of the purchaser.

The rapid growth of the business persuaded James Miller and his brother John Manson Miller, who had joined him from a background in motor retailing to assist managing the firm, to convert what had been a limited partnership into a private limited liability company. In 1934 James Miller and Partners was registered with a capital of £50,000; shares were owned by three family members, James Miller (17,500) and John Miller (5,000), who were the two directors of the company, and their elder brother the lawyer Lawrence Steadman Miller (5,000). Lawrence had overseen the company's formation, and was later to be appointed a director. James Miller took a typically modest view of the contributions of the three brothers to the business, 'Lawrie supplied the brain,

Jack the brawn. I just came in between'. The central role of the family in the firm's ownership and management was not to change during James Miller's lifetime: although the capital of the business was increased massively after the war to £500,000 the newly created shares went either to the existing shareholders (James Miller's personal share in the firm was increased to 60,000 shares in 1955), their relatives, or to trusts representing the children of the three brothers.

In the period leading up to the start of the second war James Miller consolidated his firm's position as the leading housebuilding concern in the capital. Miller was personally responsible for this side of the business, and for experiments that were pursued in house design. Borrowing heavily from the modern movement the company built a number of houses that not only incorporated some of the nautical motifs that were common to the 1930s, but also dabbled with flat-roofed houses and bungalows. By 1936 the firm were also involved in the construction of modern private flats in the city. The company also diversified its interests in a number of ways. A garage was built at Liberton and others were acquired for management; the company was involved in the management of a number of cinemas, including the *State* in Leith which James Miller had designed, and dance-halls. James and John Miller were also directors of the builders merchants and joinery firm John and James Lawrence, one of the leading suppliers of pre-cast stone in Scotland.

The outbreak of war saw the company plunged into a hectic period of work in the national interest, with a workforce that was limited through the loss of staff to the services. In addition it witnessed the growth of the contracting side of the company's work, which had previously been limited to a small number of Admiralty contracts for the construction of beach defences on the east coast. Contracts included airfield and factory construction. In addition to opening London and Birmingham offices Millers formed a relationship with the London contracting firm L J Speight & Partners, who were taken over in 1942. In 1941 the company had been requested to undertake open-cast mining contracts for the Government in Yorkshire, an activity which was to become of increasing importance to the business in the post war years.

Housing became a prominent part of the firm's business after the cessation of hostilities. However in the first instance, with private building strictly regulated by government, Miller's acted as contractors to local authorities throughout the United Kingdom erecting thousands of a variety of non-traditional house types. By 1950 the company had also designed their own non-traditional house, the Miller 'No Fines' house, with factories at both Craigleith and Granton producing standardised joinery work and pre-cast concrete, employing around a thousand workers. It was in the standardisation of components that the novelty of Miller's house lay - built of either brick or cellular concrete it was described as a 'non-traditional house with a traditional background'. By 1955 a little under 7,000 of these homes had been built. With the gradual relaxation of building controls by the Macmillan government the company were able to resume private housebuilding, working with an expanded range of house-types. As before James Miller played a leading role in the process of developing these new houses; design and planning remained a lifetime's passion for him even though the pressures of running a large business and public commitments determined that family holidays often presented the only opportunity for creative work.

The housing side of the business - still in the 1950s the most important part of the company's work - remained under James Miller's personal control; mining (which continued after the war in Yorkshire and Northumberland, and would eventually account for around 30% of turnover) and contracting was handled by his brother John. Increasingly the work of the company was managed by specialist office-staff, with two sons of James Miller, James and Roger, assuming managerial responsibilities in the 1950s. The increasing range of activities undertaken witnessed the gradual evolution of a group structure reflecting various specialities - in 1961 contracting became the responsibility of Miller Brothers and Buckley, which in turn became Miller Construction in 1970 with the formal creation of the Miller Group, which included Miller Homes Northern. The new structure witnesses the departure of James Miller from active management of the Miller Group; however his retiral was only nominal, and with a number of long-serving members of staff he established Heritable Development Consultants, a private company that undertook a number of successful speculative developments in addition to consultancies before being integrated with the Miller Group.

Since 1936, in addition to his considerable business achievements, James Miller began a distinguished career in public service when he was elected a town councillor in Edinburgh. He became a magistrate in 1942, and served as city treasurer in 1946. Between 1951 and 1954 he served as Lord Provost of the city during which period he was knighted. Showing a remarkable thirst for such work he then turned his attention to London, becoming a sheriff in 1956, an Alderman for Bishopsgate in 1957, and Lord Mayor in 1964. Despite the burdens of public service in Edinburgh James Miller had not noticeably reduced his contribution to the company; the London appointment was more challenging and saw him hand over the reigns of the business for a year to his brother and two sons. As both a builder and an effective civic leader James Miller was familiar with the complications of laws, bye-laws and regulations. His distaste for the unnecessary trouble and distress these could cause led him to form the Simplification Society, an unsuccessful attempt to lobby for the introduction of straightforward laws and government forms.

Sir James Miller was a man of vast energy and imagination whose primary objective, of creating a successful family based building firm, was surpassed by the eventual business he left, the Miller Group, that largest private construction company in Scotland. He led by example, being seen to work at all levels of the company. But work was not an obsession - he enjoyed sailing and indulged in this leisure pursuit when time was available. Nor was he a man without compassion or kindness; he was noted for his generosity towards Edinburgh institutions, and gifted two boats for training and educational purposes, one in memory of his son Malcolm Miller, who died in 1961. James Miller retired from his Miller Group directorships in 1973; he died four years later, leaving his wife, Ella, two sons and a daughter.

NICHOLAS J MORGAN

SOURCES

Unpublished

Companies Registration Office: SC 18135, James Miller & Partners Ltd
Information supplied by the Directors of James Miller & Partners Ltd

Published

Builder, 12/2/1932, 11/3/1932, 2/9/1932, 28/10/1932, 12/1/1934, 25/1/1935, 11/3/1938, 29/7/1938, 6/7/1951, 4/7/1952, 9/1/1953
Glasgow Herald, 21/3/1977
McKean, C, *The Scottish Thirties: an architectural guide*, Edinburgh 1982
The Scotsman, 21/3/1977
The Scottish Daily Express, 30/9/1964

Gavin SHANKS,

Public works contractor; b. 16/5/1865, East Shawhead Farm, Old Monklands, s. of Alexander Shanks, farmer, and Marion Flemming; Bachelor; Partner, Shanks & McEwan, Joint Founder and MD, Shanks & McEwan Ltd; d. 3/4/1943, Hamilton; g/v estate: £145,817 12s 10d.

Shanks and McEwan Ltd had been formed into a public company in 1924 when it had become clear that one of the firms two partners, Sandy McEwan, was becoming seriously ill. McEwan died at the end of November 1924 aged 68, leaving the company under the control of Gavin Shanks, then nine years younger than his late partner. Shanks came from a farming family in Monklands, where his father was tenant on Shawhead Farm at Whifflet; he had joined in partnership with McEwan running a small contracting business that specialised in modest contract work on water and sewage projects. They undertook local authority schemes at East Kilbride, Stirlingshire, Galashiels and Peterhead, and also built a gas-works at Inverkeithing. They had in addition conducted minor works on the Glasgow District Subway. 'Sandy McEwan was a Master Builder', wrote a company brochure, 'while Guy Shanks was more interested in muck shifting': 'the big man', as he was known in the firm, was to make moving muck his business.

The First World War brought considerable opportunities for work for all contractors. These were not only to meet the obvious needs of war such as shore defences and army camps but also to sustain the production of essential raw materials that fed the munitions industry. Scottish steel making firms were urged to expand their productive capacity by the government and later the Ministry of Munitions with a resultant massive investment in new and replacement plant. McEwan in particular was responsibe for gaining the firm a series of furnace building contracts with five steel companies, including Beardmores, Colvilles, and Stewart and Lloyds, at ten different sites. Perhaps the largest single project was at Beardmore's Mossend Steelworks, where the partners built a melting shop comprising six furnaces. The steel works contracts occupied the firm not only during the war, but also for a few years afterwards, as the momentum gained during the war pushed expansion forward. However at the same time, as depression set in and industrial opportunities receded, Shanks was seeking out road and water works for the company, successfully tendering for heavy work at Loch Coulter for raising banking and cutting pipe tracks, in all worth around £80,000. In addition they purchased the Airdrie Hill Quarry as a source of aggregate and (building on their contacts in the steel industry) began to exploit waste furnace slags in road building; they also began to tender for contracts to tarmacadam road surfaces.

The major road contract that Shanks had been seeking came in 1924, on the Glasgow to Edinburgh Road project. At the same time he engineered a coup by taking the contract let by the Clyde Navigation Trustees for the first Shieldhall Dock from under the nose of Robert McAlpine (qv). McAlpine had tendered around £800,000 for the main part of the project, to sink the foundations and build the concrete basin walls, but he was undercut by Shanks and McEwan, who bid £721,716. The Trustees were reluctant to let the work to a relatively untried contractor rather than employ one they had used successfully (at Yorkhill) in the past, but with government funds helping to finance the contract it went to Shanks and McEwan. The contract was not to run smoothly; the General Strike disrupted progress, and fluctuating prices for building materials forced the cost of the work upwards. However the contract was completed by October 1928, albeit at a cost of £200,000 in excess of the original tender. Worse than these operational difficulties however was the kidney disease that afflicted Sandy McEwan. To secure the business, which had contracts on hand worth well over a million, the decision was taken in early November to convert the partnership to a limited liability company. The capital was set at £150,000, 80,000 £1 shares were allocated equally between Shanks and McEwan, although the latter was too ill to serve as a director, his place being taken by the solicitor John McMurdo. Later in the same month McEwan died leaving Shanks in effective control of the new company.

The Shieldhall contract, the first in a projected series of four, had promised a continued flow of work for the company, but depressed trade led to the shelving of such ambitious plans. In 1928, with little work available in Scotland Shanks began to seek contracts south of the border, winning substantial railway contracts in which the company had little experience, at March (near Peterborough), Nottingham, Bromsgrove and Bristol (for the rebuilding of Temple Meads station), and also (between 1930 and 1933) the East India Dock Bridge at Barking in Essex. In 1932 Shanks also revived a wartime contact with Stewarts and Lloyd who had, under the guidance of Sir Allan MacDiarmid (qv), begun to develop their installation at Corby in Northamptonshire. Shanks gained work there both for the construction of the new plant and for maintenance, a lifeline to liquidity during the depression, which saw an end to the rush of southern contracts. Work did come in Scotland; 1932 had seen work commence for the Galloway Power Company on Clatteringshaws Dam, near New Galloway, whilst in 1935 the firm won the contract for the Stirling and Falkirk Water Board's reservoir in the Denny Hills for road diversions and embankment construction, worth £118,650.

By the outbreak of war the firm's business had largely receded to repair and maintenance contracts on the road they had built in the inter-war years, and service contracts at Corby, and also at Ardeer for Nobel's Explosives. The war brought no contract bonanza to the business as the mainstay of the company, Gavin Shanks, fell ill in late 1942, dying in April 1943. He left £145,000; with neither wife nor family to benefit this was left to nephews and nieces. A man of strong character and strong physical presence he had always been directly involved with his company and its work. That Shanks and McEwan re-emerged after the war as one of Scotland's largest civil engineering contractors, covering a wide range of contracting and maintenance activities, owed much to the solid foundation and reputation established for the business by Shanks in the 1920s and 1930s.

NICHOLAS J MORGAN

SOURCES

Unpublished

Companies Registration Office, SC 13388, Shanks & McEwan Ltd
Information supplied by Shanks & McEwan Ltd.
SRO: SC 37/42/90, Inventory
         SC 37/43/37, Trust disposition and settlement

Published

Building Industries, 16/9/1922
Evening Times, 22/8/1935
Glasgow Herald, 5/4/1943
Riddell, John F, *Clyde Navigation*, Edinburgh, 1979

Robert Barclay SHAW,

Wright and builder; b. 1852, Glasgow, s. of William Shaw, wright and contractor, and Janet Barclay; m. Margaret Dykes Cook; no issue; Ch and MD, William Shaw & Sons Ltd, Glasgow; d. 13/6/1905, Annick Lodge, near Irvine; g/v UK estate: £37,566 14s 1d.

Robert Barclay Shaw was only 19 when he succeeded to the business of wrights and builders which his father William had established in 1848. A prominent member of the Incorporation of Wrights (serving as Deacon in 1864), William Shaw had built up a firm that drew its main business from commercial, industrial and public contracts in and around Glasgow. Under the management of his son Robert the business continued to operate in these spheres, but in addition it extended into speculative house-building in Glasgow and also into the field of specialist exhibition construction.

The contract that brought Shaw to the attention of Glasgow's wider public was for the construction of the Moorish buildings for Glasgow's 1888 Exhibition in Kelvingrove Park, designed by the architect James Sellars. The main building for the Exhibition covered nearly ten acres, and was built at a cost of some £80,000. Shaw employed some 1,000 men on the contract during which, as *The Bailie* magazine enumerated, 'there were used about 5,000,000 bricks, 750 tons of iron, 700,000 cubic feet of wood, 70 tons of nails, 40 tons of bolts, 250,000 square feet of glass and 50,000 square yards of corrugated iron'. The contract, which also included most of the exhibition's out-buildings, and wright-work on many of the exhibitor's stalls, was virtually completed within five months. The competence with which Shaw dealt with this remarkable piece of construction work placed him at the fore of the contractors for the city's next great exhibition in 1901, held on a site adjoining the Kelvingrove Museum and Art Gallery, which had been built partly from the proceeds arising from 1888.

The contract for the 1901 Exhibition was worth some £80,000. As in 1881 one of the hallmarks of the work was the degree of speed and efficiency with which the work was conducted under the direct supervision of Shaw and his manager William Smith. The main hall, the Eastern Palace, and other buildings, were designed in a Spanish Renaissance style by James Miller, whose later work was to make such an impact on Glasgow's city centre. Construction took around a year, during which time Shaw also built the exhibition concert hall (£20,000) and a £15,000 bridge across the Kelvin. It was shortly after the completion of the Exhibition that Shaw converted his business into a limited liability company with a nominal capital of £250,000. Shaw held 5,760 £1 preference shares and 3,200 £1 ordinary shares and was chairman and director, along with Smith and secretary John Craig.

By this time the company could boast a wide portfolio of building work, that ranged from the erection of extensive temporary structures through to conventional tenement building. Shaw had purchased land at Pollokshields on Glasgow's south side where he had begun to build tenements in 1890, largely to the design of the architect George Bell. These blocks contained extensive apartments, some having upper floor flats with attics designed as billiard rooms. The company had carried out library contracts for the Corporation, had built the Langside tram depot (£20,000) and had shared contracts for additions to the Victoria Infirmary. They had also used the skills gained on exhibition work to move into arena construction, building stands at Hampden Park for Queens Park Football Club in 1904. Contracts were also taken outside the city, and in 1905 they won the entire contract for the new Kilmarnock Post Office. The exhibition work had clearly made Shaw appreciate the extent to which new techniques of prefabrication and standardisation could be applied to building; he became one of the first directors of the short-lived Paristagan Company, formed to realise the plans of the engineer John Dougan for the mass production of timber-framed concrete houses.

Robert Barclay Shaw died suddenly in June 1905 at the age of 52 of a malignant disease of the liver. At the time he was living at Annick Lodge near Irvine on the small estate he had purchased there in 1895; nine years later he bought a second rural estate at Knockgerran near Girvan. With no children to support he divided his estate up between his wife, senior employees, and two substantial benefactions. One to the Royal National Lifeboat Institution to fund the purchase of a lifeboat (the 'Barclay Shaw Lifeboat'), and the other to the Trades House of Glasgow to establish the 'Barclay Shaw Bequest' to provide pensions for wrights and others in the city. Some surprise was expressed in the city that Shaw was not given a military funeral; he had been an enthusiatic member of the Third Volunteer Battalion of the Highland Light Infantry, becoming a colonel and commander of the battalion in 1904. His interest in things military fitted nicely with the talents that had made his business so notable, and also relatively successful. For if Shaw was skilled in anything it was in managing complex logistical problems, whether on a real building site or a mock battlefield, involving the deployment and supervision of large numbers of men and supplies. It was to this skill that Glasgow's International Exhibitions of 1881 and 1901 owed their success.

NICHOLAS J MORGAN

SOURCES

Unpublished

BT 2/5201, William Shaw & Sons Ltd
SRO: SC 7/28/2, Inventory
      SC 7/30/2, Trust disposition and settlement

Published

The Bailie, 6/6/1888
Building Industries, 15/8/1890; 10/12/1907
Dougan, John, 'On the Paristagan system of building with concrete', *The Proceedings of the Philosophical Society of Glasgow*, 25, 1893-94
Glasgow Building Trades Exchange Annual Review
Glasgow Herald, 14/6/1905
Glasgow of Today, Glasgow, 1888

Hume, John, *Industrial archaeology of Glasgow*, London, 1974
Worsdall, Frank, *The city that disappeared*, Glasgow, 1981

Sir James STEEL,

Builder; b. 13/3/1829, Cambusnethan, s. of James Steel, farmer and Marion Reed; m. 8/8/1883, Barbara Joanna, d. of Alex Paterson, United Presbyterian minister; no issue; Founder, James Steel, builder, Edinburgh; d. 4/9/1904, Edinburgh; g/v estate £114,197 5s 4d.

James Steel was apprenticed as a mason in Wishaw in the 1840s. Within the space of 20 years he had developed his own successful building firm in Wishaw, and achieved sufficient local prominence to serve on the Wishaw Police Commission and on the Parochial Board. The basis of Steel's early success remains unclear, as do the reasons for transferring his building interests to Edinburgh in 1866. What is certain is that this decision, Steel's accumulated expertise in the building industry, and the continued growth of Edinburgh combined to make him the largest builder in the city by the 1890s, and its largest ratepayer.

Steel's Edinburgh building operations were of such proportions as to justify the development of both a quarry (at Gunnerton, Northumberland) and specialised and mechanised woodworking shops away from the building sites (at Maxwell Street and Comely Bank). This integrated operation was a highly unusual feature of the Victorian building industry and Steel further extended his organisation to include the functions of land developer, feuar and landlord, coordinated from offices at 2 Torphichen Street. Only a few non-residential properties were built by the firm, but between 1880 and 1904 James Steel built 148 houses and 129 tenements in Edinburgh, a building programme equivalent to at least £15,000 annually throughout the period.

The firm built houses for all sections of the market. Three major concentrations of building activity reflected this. The earliest consolidated development was on the Wester Dalry estate, commenced in 1869 and largely composed of working class tenements. Steel was active in each stage of development - as estate developer sub-feuing portions of the land and controlling lay-out, road widths and building quality, as a builder, and as landlord for some of the properties from which he and his trustees continued to derive a rental income until the 1930s. This pattern of buying land in anticipation of future building demand was a central tactic in Steel's business strategy. However, while many builders did likewise, what distinguished Steel was his vertically integrated building interests from estate development, to building and to landlordism which allowed him a greater degree of flexibility and control over his operations than other builders. Although Steel continued to build on the Dalry estates sporadically until the 1890s, the initial phase was completed by the mid-1870s when attention was then directed towards a second concentration of building activity. This was upper middle class housing built to a high design standard on extensive lands feued from the Heriot Trust by 1877. The exclusivity of the social tone of this development was reflected in its location on the western periphery of the New Town and the classical Georgian elegance was mirrored, albeit more modestly, in Steel's development of Douglas, Eglinton and Glencairn Crescents, Palmerston Place, Belgrave Terrace and Place, and Buckingham Terrace. These and a number of adjacent streets were built in the later 1870s and 1880s by Steel as self-contained, stonefronted residences with the latest sanitary, gas and other amenities, and finished with quality hardwood. Unlike the Dalry estate where rental and feuing income accrued to Steel's trustees until 1938, these superior properties were promptly sold outright.

The third type of development was the Learmonth-Comely Bank area. Principally lower middle and middle class housing on the remnants of the Dean estate in the late 1880s and early 1890s, this represented a return to tenement building for in the years 1878-1885 when the Heriot feus were being developed this had dwindled to less than 10% of building operations. This third phase was strengthened when in 1894 Steel bought from Colonel Learmonth 78 acres adjacent to the Dean properties. Already active nearby, Steel's building interests were easily and rapidly switched to the Learmonth estate. Between 1895 and 1904, 59 houses and 70 tenements were built in the Comely Bank and Learmonth area in response to lower middle and middle class demand.

Steel's annual rental income in 1904 was £17,428; his feuing income £4,734. The scale of such property income is demonstrative of his continued heavy commitment to land and property management and development. His retention of feudal superiority and strict monitoring of feuing conditions gave Steel control over large tracts of northern and western Edinburgh; his activities never strayed into eastern or the southern suburbs of the city. Capitalised at a modest 25 years purchase, Steel's feus and rental properties alone were worth £554,000 and judged against a building

investment of approximately £500,000 Steel's contribution to the physical development of Victorian Edinburgh was not simply as a builder, for which he is best known. The proceeds of the building operations, and those of land transactions and property rental, all of which interests were solely owned by Steel, were largely redeployed within the firm, for future expansion, though Steel still managed to accumulate a moveable estate in shares, debentures and loans valued on his death at £112,000. Except for a few properties already proposed at the time of his death, new building activities ceased in 1905 and the trustees - James Steel builder - Cambusnethan (son of brother Thomas), Hugh Percival, mason, Edinburgh (son of sister Mary), Alexander Allan, architect, Edinburgh (son of sister Agnes), and William Babington WS - managed the firm's property interests, principally its rental and feuing income an the sale of lands and properties as conditions dictated until 1938.

Within a few years of moving to Edinburgh, James Steel was active in local politics. He had had previous experience of public service in Wishaw, but first came to notice in Edinburgh in his opposition to the proposed St. Mary's reservoir project in 1871, and though defeated in that year, was elected in 1872 for the George Square ward which he uninterruptedly represented as Liberal councillor, bailie (from 1888) and Lord Provost (from 1900) until his retiral from local politics in 1903. Steel was not an initiator of municipal projects. His main contributions were informed, specialist comments on committees such as Cleaning and Lighting, Plans and Works, and Streets and Buildings where his business experience proved invaluable. He also served on the boards of utility undertakings, the Infirmary Board and Heriot's Hospital (school). Civic honours followed this extended public service when he represented the City of Edinburgh at the funeral of Queen Victoria and the coronation of King Edward VII, and in 1903 the King knighted Steel on the occasion of a royal visit to Edinburgh. Steel possessed many influential personal friends and contacts, partly through his council interests, partly through his directorships in several local companies, notably the Niddrie and Benhar Coal Co. and the Broxburn Oil Co. which he helped to found, but mainly because his business undertakings brought him into contact with landowners, solicitors and other professional groups, and individual wealthy house purchasers. Sir James Steel, Bart. took the title of 'Murieston, Mid-Calder', with the motto, *Firmiter et Durabile,* wholly appropriate not only to the man, but to his business interests, and no less to the houses he built.

RICHARD RODGER

SOURCES

Unpublished

Edinburgh District Record Office:
    Dean of Guild Registers and Plans, 1860-1904
    Feu Chartularies, Wester Dalry Estate
SRO: SC 70/1/455
       SC 70/1/456
       SC 70/4/366
Register of Sasines, City of Edinburgh

Published

Anon, *Scotland of Today: Edinburgh, Its Capital,* Edinburgh, 1890
Anon, *Lord Provosts of Edinburgh 1296-1932,* Edinburgh, 1932
Building News, 9/9/1904
Edinburgh and the Lothians at the Opening of the Twentieth Century, with Contemporary Biographies, ed by W T Pike, Edinburgh 1904
Glasgow Herald, 5/9/1904
The Scotsman, 5/9/1904
The Times, 5/9/1904

William TAWSE,

Public works contractor; b. 1880, Yorkshire, s. of Peter Tawse, book-keeper to Easton Gibb , contractor; m. Louise Gordon; 1 s., 1 d.; Ch, William Tawse Ltd, contractors, Aberdeen; d. 6/4/1940, Banchory, Kincardineshire; g/v UK estate: £60,783 11s 8d.

William Tawse was trained as a public works contractor on the streets of Aberdeen, where he worked for his father, Peter Tawse, after leaving school at the age of 16. Peter had set up a contracting business in 1896, having been dismissed as manager of John Fyfe's (qv) Kenmay Quarry in order to make room in the business for Fyfe's sons. A year's salary by way of compensation provided the initial capital for the venture, the skill came from six years working with Fyfe, and ten years working as a cashier with the contractor Easton Gibb, which had involved travelling extensively to work on railway and waterworks contracts in the north of England and the Midlands. It was during one such contract in Yorkshire that William Tawse was born in 1880. William had attended Robert Gordon's School in Aberdeen before joining his father's business, where his first job was shifting stone on a contract for the Aberdeen docks railway.

Work was plentiful for the new company, at a time when much of the centre of Aberdeen was being redeveloped, and when much of its infrastructure was being renewed or extended. In addition to road, paving and harbour work the firm were responsible for the construction of the Girdleness outfall sewer, part of the Aberdeen waterworks, which involved the tunnelling under the Dee and St Fittick's Hill. Contracts were also undertaken in Dundee and in the northern highlands. Peter Tawse died in March 1907; his son William took over the management of the business in partnership with Howard Anderson. The two were well matched with: 'Howard Anderson preferred the practical side; William Tawse attended to public relations and developed his flair for imaginative constructive thinking'. It was this flair, his 'remarkable commercial imagination and great aesthetic resources', that was responsible for the success of the company. He approached business according to his mood - 'he uttered the thought that was uppermost in his mind at the moment, did what happened to be before him to do, and if he found himself in difficulties he usually though sometimes only eventually contrived to get out of them, although it was seldom that he did not show repentance for an indiscretion ...' In addition the horizons of the company were widened by the demands of war, which saw them execute under great pressure of time and resources, a variety of contracts ranging from the Invergordon naval station to the Lenabo aerodrome and light railway.

In the inter-war years the firm found its niche in road construction and bridge building, although railway work, swimming pool construction, docks and waterworks were also undertaken. Tawse was responsible for remaking the Braemar to Ballater road, and later for two massive undertakings; the roads through the Great Glen and Glencoe. Although neither engineer nor architect Tawse exerted tremendous influence on the outcome of the projects his firm undertook to realise, both in appearance and method of construction, and was credited as having a 'great deal to do with the beauty, as well as the efficiency' of the Glencoe route. Concrete bridge building was a particular speciality of the firm, who were responsible for all the modern bridges over the Don, in addition to the viaduct at Dornie, Ross-shire, and bridges throughout the highlands and islands. The firm also continued the reconstruction of Aberdeen's roads and main drainage, and undertook various contracts in Dundee, Perth and throughout Angus.

William Tawse died in 1940, leaving the company in the hands of his son and Howard Anderson. Bertram Tawse, a Cambridge graduate and former trainee with Sir Alexander Gibb and Partners, built a business on the platform created by his father that in 1966 became part of the Aberdeen Construction

as Young, both as an individual and on behalf of his company, stood in the Court of Session in Edinburgh facing sequestration proceedings and liabilities in excess of £240,000. Unlike many of his contemporaries, Young earned no glowing portraits in the national or trade press - his death following a second bankruptcy in 1905 went unrecorded, and he left insufficient estate to appear in the printed Calendar of Confirmations. Nonetheless, for all this ignominy his career, both at its height and depths, is one worthy of the business historian's attention.

James Young & Sons was founded in 1866 when James Young Snr, who had worked as a contractor since 1846, retired from active business due to ill-health, leaving his firm and its goodwill to his sons, James and Robert. Little is known of the education of these two, although it can be assumed that in common with many they would have mixed a formal schooling with a technical and practical education conducted on-site. Certainly the early success of the firm under the two brothers suggests they possessed both the skills required to make competitive and realistic tenders for works, and also the technical and managerial skills to carry them through. The two brothers made an early specialisation of waterworks which was to account for much of the firms' business. In 1873 they won the first of a series of contracts in connection with the Moorfoot works, the second phase of the Edinburgh waterworks, worth in all £150,000. These various contracts included the construction of the Gladhouse Aqueduct, the laying of the main pipe from Gladhouse reservoir. The works were conducted between 1873 and 1880 and marked the start of a long-standing relationship between the firm and the Edinburgh District Water Trust which was to be essential to the firm's prosperity. In 1887 they won a contract from the Trustees for the construction of new filters at Alnwickhill in connection with the Moorfoot scheme worth £47,000. A further contract in 1894 for the construction of a storage tank at Craiglockhart was worth £10,000 whilst the contract for the Talla Railway, the first stage in the third phase of the City's waterworks, was worth £60,000.

Through their work for the Edinburgh city fathers, the company developed a growing reputation throughout the east of Scotland and the borders which brought them more local water contracts. It also enabled them to enter the field of railway contracting at a time when railway building in Scotland, both the redevelopment of central terminii and the construction of suburban and country lines, was accelerating rapidly. They completed the Galashiels Water scheme in 1879 and from that year onwards proceeded to undertake a number of large and lucrative railway works. The first was the contract for building the Queen Street tunnel in Glasgow for the North British Railway Company (NBR), worth some £110,000. Further NBR contracts followed for the Stirling Bridge, 1880, the Marshall Meadows deviation

railway, 1884, Portobello and Corstorphine stations (1887), Cowlairs bridge, 1890, the four and a half mile Alloa and Kincardine Railway, 1891, and the rebuilding of Alloa dock, 1893. Whilst conducting these NBR contracts the company undertook a variety of other work such as the construction of Ayr docks and esplanade, 1881, the Paisley New Rye water shceme, 1883 and the Water of Leith purification scheme, 1890.

By the mid 1890s the company had become one of the largest of all of Scotland's public works firms, with contracts stretching across the central belt and south to the borders. The workforce comprised some 2,000 men. The business was recording an average annual profit (according to a prospectus issued in 1899) of £10,271. Although subsequent events were to show this figure was more probably between £3,000 and £4,000 there was little reason to challenge Robert Young's later assertion that 'our business was always prosperous'. The position that the company had reached was reflected in an accumulation of prestigious contracts in the second half of the 1890s, including a section of the Loch Katrine water scheme, 1869, worth £57,000, alterations to Waverley Station, 1898, worth £110,000 and the construction of the Talla Railway. Youngs also diversified into building works in Edinburgh, undertaking both small projects such as North Canongate School and tenements at Pleasance for the NBR, and, more famous, excavation and masonry work for the building of Jenner's Princes Street warehouse.

The apparent success of the firm under the management of the two brothers, assisted by a third, John A Young, hid a reality of severe under-capitalisation. As the firm extended the range and size of its undertakings so its need for plant, materials and funds for wages increased. Payment for contract work, normally in Scotland arranged on a monthly or quarterly basis according to a precise measurement of the work completed, was at best of times slow, and was always subject to dispute and arbitration between the contracting parties. Alleged extra work not envisaged at the time of tender, or alleged deficiencies in the work completed, could all delay staged payments for many months. Substantial capital reserves to overcome these cash-flow problems were thus essential, as was a ready fund of credit from trade suppliers. But Youngs, as was to become apparent, were drastically short of capital, a shortage which was compounded by an apparent paucity of financial skills on behalf of the two brothers, particularly Robert. They failed to make precise valuations of the plant in the company's possession, worth upwards of £80,000, and whilst the brothers employed auditors to make up annual balance sheets they rarely saw them themselves, and saw none after 1896. Thus although their knowledge of the firm's financial position was slight, they continued to tender and win contracts on the basis of the reputation they had established over 30 years during which time they had outlasted many a bankrupt competitor.

The inevitable crisis for the company came in 1898. On the surface business had never been better. The company had five contracts in progress worth over half a million pounds, the largest of which were the Talla reservoir main contract worth £153,000, and the contract with the Caledonian Railway company for the Lanarkshire and Ayrshire Railway, worth £311,000. But Youngs' bankers were pressing for a reduction in the firm's overdraft of nearly £27,000, and it became apparent to the two brothers, that with only 'about £35,000 to £40,000' of capital in the firm they were going to have difficulty in satisfying the Bank of Scotland and financing the prodigious programme of work they had undertaken. Their resolution to float the firm as a public company was followed almost immediately by the death of the elder brother James, leaving Robert to manage affairs which were clearly beyond his capacity.

These financial difficulties were compounded by a growing controversy in Edinburgh over the Talla water scheme, where a large and vocal body favoured an alternative site for the new reservoir at St Mary's Loch near Cappercleuch. The Water Trust Commissioners were accused of 'unaccountable extravagance' in their execution of the work, not least because the tender from Youngs for the main contract was some £15,000 more than the lowest tender received. Youngs apparently won the contract because of their long-standing relationship with the water commissioners, but a sub-committee of the Edinburgh Citizen's and Ratepayers Union concluded that 'the Trust had taken a fatherly interest in the contractors and shown them consideration which they had not shown to the citizens of Edinburgh'. Further public concern was aroused by allegations of poor management at the works, and particularly that work was being delayed owing to drunkenness among the contractor's navvies. In 1897 James Young had proposed to the Commissioners that a club be set up at the site to serve food and liquor to workers; this, it was argued, would lessen the nuisance caused by itinerant spirit dealers who sold liquor from hand carts at all hours, and also benefit the workers as profits would be allocated to a sick and accident fund. The club was established in early 1898, but the allegations of drunkenness continued, and following alleged scenes of debauchery at the site on Christmas day 1898, the Commissioners were forced to hold an inconclusive inquiry into events. David Lewis, the noted temperance reformer, who was a vocal critic of the Talla scheme from its outset, concluded that 'the execution of few such public undertakings in this country has been attended by so melancholy a record of drinking, drunkenness and mortality among its workers as was the case at Talla.' What was not clear to many was that Youngs were to be one of the main victims of the Talla scheme.

It was against this background that Robert Young carried out the proposal to form a limited company. The floatation was managed by John Kerr, managing director of the contracting firm John L Kerr Ltd at Manchester and Leith (who had assisted Robert Young in managing the business since the death of his brother), and Arthur Drummond of the accountancy firm Arthur Drummond & Co, Edinburgh (appointed at Kerr's suggestion). The new company was to have a share capital of £10,000 divided into 5,000 preference shares of £10 and 5,000 ordinary shares of £10. In all 4,390 preference shares were issued to 213 shareholders. Robert Young was to receive £50,000 in ordinary shares in the new company and a further £50,000 in cash to be relieved of the old firm's contracts. James Young's estate was to receive £25,000 in cash and shares. However, the arrangement went severely awry - there was no formal adjustment of accounts between the old and the new firms and Young was not formally relieved of his responsibility for the contracts underway; the majority of the contracting parties refused to recognise the new company and held Young liable for the completion of the contracts. In additions he received no payment of ordinary shares. Of the new company's directors (who included Robert and John A Young, Kerr, James Scott a London wine merchant and the civil engineer Douglas Westland) only one, Westland, was formerly qualified to hold office as a holder of 25 or more shares. Robert Young, appointed managing director for ten years 'in order to continue good management' seems to have little contact with the business of the company and formally resigned in June when his personal affairs had brought him to the verge of bankruptcy. There were no minuted meetings and no accounts kept from the date of the completion of the floatation in early 1899 to its liquidation in August. The affairs of the business as revealed to shareholders were shambolic - work on all the major contracts was behind schedule, but finances were even worse - the assets of the company stood at under £9,000 whilst liabilities were calculated at £245,987. Young himself was liable to claims of in excess of £70,000 with assets belonging to himself and the old firm of little over £16,000.

Robert Young's bankruptcy, his personal sequestration and that of the firm, was followed by the sequestration of J L Kerr in 1900, and in 1901 his brother John A Young. Only the accountant Arthur Drummond appears to have escaped unscathed from the disastrously botched floatation. But Young, despite his disgrace, the loss of all his possessions and of the family home in Polwarth Terrace, was not deterred from the attractions of the construction industry. By November 1899 he was working for the Edinburgh quarrymaster and contractor David Scott, with whom he continued until early 1902 when Scott retired. At this point Young moved to Glasgow where he set up as a house-builder under the style R Young & Co. With loans of £80 from his wife and £180 from the contractor John Waddell he planned to erect two tenements in Craighall, supported by advances of £1,600 from the Standard Building Society and

£1,100 from his lawyer A A Stewart. The buildings, completed at the end of 1903, failed to reach the asking price of £3,000 leaving Young heavily out of pocket. Worse was to follow when he entered into a contract with George Stuart for the masonry and brick work on five tenements. While this work was underway, Young was discharged from the 1899 bankruptcy; unfortunately Stuart himself was sequestrated in August 1904, turning an expected profit on the contract of around £600 to a loss of around £1,200. With assets of only £129, and creditors arising from the Stuart contract claiming £1,280, Young found himself in the Court of Session for the second time in the space of six years.

Even to the most hard-headed business historian there must be something rather appealing about Robert Young, a man who as far as it can be deduced was good, if not very good, at his job, but who at the same time was bad, if not very bad, at his business, and possibly even worse in his judge of character. His dilemma was a lack of capital to continue doing what he was good at, combined with a lack of skills to manage the increasing scale and complexity of the business (itself a product of success). Although this was exacerbated by some of the peculiarities of the construction industry, it was not a situation unique to contractors or builders. Nor was Robert Young's response, a reliance on less than trustworthy advisors and builders prone to the same problems as himself, particularly original. But his career deserves to be remembered - he was, with his brother, one of the most successful public works contractors of the day, and many of his completed contracts still form the infrastructure which serves modern central Scotland.

NICHOLAS J MORGAN

SOURCES

Unpublished

SRO: BT2/4/65, James Young & Sons Ltd
CS 318/49/335, Report on Sequestrated estate of James Young & Son, etc
CS 318/50/358, Sequestration of Robert Young, builder

Published

Bowtell, H D, 'Rails to Talla', *Stevenson Journal*, October 1966

Building Industries, 16/6/1890, 15/10/1890, 15/11/1890

Engineering, 21/6/1895, 20/9/1895, 10/4/1896, 23/4/1897, 30/4/1897, 8/10/1897, 18/2/1898, 22/12/1899

Glasgow Herald, 4/3/1899

Leslie, N, 'The Edinburgh Water Works', *Minutes of the Proceedings of the Institute of Civil Engineers*, Vol LXXIV, 1882-83

Lewis, D, *Edinburgh Water Supply, a sketch of its history past and present*, Edinburgh 1908

The Priestman Dredger, Excavator and Elevator, London 1882

The Scotsman, 20/10/1893, 16/9/1899, 20/9/1899, 27/10/1899, 24/11/1899

Tait, W A, *Edinburgh District Water, notes relating to the old and new works*, Edinburgh, 1905

Tait, W A, 'The Talla Water Supply of the Edinburgh and District Water Works', *Minutes of the Proceedings of the Institution of Civil Engineers*, Vol CLXVII, 1906-07

Paper, Printing and Publishing

In the litany of credits conferred on Scottish manufacturing industry in the nineteenth and twentieth centuries the role of the paper, printing and publishing sector has received little praise. Yet it was a sizeable sector of the economy containing several large organisations and a number of smaller businesses. Its direct contribution to the economy was substantial but its indirect contribution was probably even greter for it provided a direct input into literacy and numeracy which are the foundations of all developed economies, as well as making an impact on the wider world of education. Its major value, therefore, is akin to the service sector industries where what is provided is valued, not so much for what it is, but for what it does. For the most part the output of this sector is required for the information, or pleasure, or instruction imparted by the printed word.

In the eighteenth century Scotland already had a printing, paper and publishing industry which, by the standards of the time, was quite well developed. Indeed this was a hallmark of Scotland's place in the Enlightenment and of its role as a well educated nation. In the mid-nineteenth century, however, this sector of the economy began to make substantial progress. From being not much more than a cottage industry in 1800 the newspaper industry had more than 200 titles by 1900. There was a similar quantum change in the book printing part of the industry and the emergence, for the first time, of a market for printed ephemera such as greetings cards. In the twentieth century the trend in the newspaper industry was towards larger scale operations and this often meant loss of control from Scotland. It also resulted in a move towards trivialisation. The trend towards metropolitanisation was less noticeable, but still marked, amongst the book publishers. The market, however, continued to expand.

There are many factors which contribute towards an explanation of why this sector should experience such growth in the nineteenth and twentieth centuries. Demand and supply factors seem equally important but there are also exogenous variables such as the repeal of the Stamp Act in 1855 which laid the foundations for the modern popular press. Foremost amongst the supply factors was the technologial progress which was made, especially with the introduction of rotary presses which did so much to speed up production and, therefore, to lower costs. The inclusion of photographic material in books and magazines was slow to take place but when it began to happen the result was to produce a further increase in the demand for books, magazines, newspapers and postcards. Indeed in this last respect a new part of this sector was created by the advent of technology which enabled printers to reproduce photographs. The railway age also assisted in the creation of a mass market by improving the facilities for distributing newspapers and other printed works. Indeed John Menzies saw the opportunity to create a new retailing system for reading material within railway stations.

Demand factors were also important. Foremost amongst these was the increased literacy and numeracy which developed out of improved educational provision dating from the 1870s. Further improvements in education in the 1920s, 1940s and 1960s ensured that the demand for textbooks would always be buoyant. But this also resulted in an increase in the demand for lighter reading materials as the reading habit spread to all sections of the community. Improved living standards and higher real incomes in most sections of the community also contributed greatly to the demand for reading material. Reading became an important leisure time activity for a large number of people and this was especially so for children. Perhaps the reason that Victorian children could be seen and not heard was that they were too busy reading to make any noise. The catalogue of books published for children was quite simply enormous.

The paper, printing an publishing sector of the economy attracted a diverse group of businessmen. If they had anything in common it was their interest in the printed word. Most were highly education but by no means all received a university education. Several of them, such as William and Robert Chambers and W G Blackie were authors in their own right whose publications included their own material. Most were involved in printing and publishing but the Chambers brothers were rather unusual in being involved in paper making, writing, printing and publishing.

Many of the businessmen who became involved in this sector, whether by inheritance or by their own initatives, had diverse interests outside their main businesses. For example, Sir William Collins had interests in education, temperance, yachting and the Free Church. At least three of these interests brought business to the company and Collins became one of the leading printers of the Bible and many other religious works. Similarly his interests in educational matters led his company into the printing and publication of school textbooks following the expansion of compulsory schooling in the 1870s. Others such as Walter Blackie had farming interests, while Thomas Nelson was closely involved with the Edinburgh investment trust movement. Indeed so close was Nelson to the investment community that his biography could have been included in the Banking, Insurance and Finance sector.

The very nature of publishing as a profession demanded that its practitioners had a high public profile. The high-mindedness of much of what was published and the self-perception of readers

Collins Display Board at Empire Exhibition of 1938   COURTESY OF WILLIAM COLLINS PLC

Collins: A Thomson Letterpress machine in Cathedral Street, Glasgow, c1958

usually combined to create an opportunity for publishers to strike a chord with readers if their own life styles were reflected in what they published. Many of these men sought, and found, office as Lord Provosts of their cities and this often meant that they were involved in the public development programmes of their day. William Chambers, for example, had a great interest in public health matters and was involved in the setting up of the Pilrig Model Dwelling Company. He was also closely involved in the reintegration of St Giles Cathedral and bore a large part of the costs himself. Walter W Blackie's interest was in educational matters. He was chairman of Glasgow Academy, governor of the Glasgow and West of Scotland Technical College and Clerk of the General Council of Glasgow University. Some men in this sector found time to have a range of interests, both public and private, which reflected their energy and enquiring minds in a dramatic way. John Maurice Clark ran T & T Clark but he also had interests in church affairs, the volunteer movement, the Edinburgh Merchants' Company, many charities, he held several directorships, was Deputy Lieutenant of Midlothian, a governor of Donaldson's Hospital and father of four children. Many of the men in this sector also took a great interest in foreign travel, a fact which was often reflected in the books which they published. Walter W Blackie even became a Fellow of the Royal Geographical Society.

Several of the men selected for inclusion in this sector were closely involved in the development and use of new technologies. This was clearly essential for the paper makers such as A G Pirie who transformed a relatively modest local firm into a company with an international reputation. There was, however, something of the dilettante about Pirie for he largely ignored his company for more than a decade and only falling profits brought him back to build it up again. Those who were engaged in both printing an publishing tended to become closely involved in the technology of their industries, Walter W Blackie, William Hope Collins, Robert Gourlay, Thomas Nelson and Harben J Valentine all had skills which enabled them to install and run machinery and some of them made a contribution to the development of new technologies.

Valentine & Sons Ltd: Despatching Room, Westfield Works
<small>COURTESY OF ST. ANDREWS UNIVERSITY PHOTOGRAPH COLLECTION</small>

New technologies often lead to the creation of new products or even new businesses. Paper, printing and publishing was no exception. Harben J Valentine mastered the collotype and photochrome printing processes and the result was that a modest photography business expanded into a major company with worldwide interests.

Other businessmen in this sector used a modest base to expand into related, and more extensive areas. D C Thomson inherited a small newspaper publishing business and used it to create national markets for newspapers, magazines and children's comics.

Although many of the businessmen in this sector often faced severe competition, either locally or internationally all of them were blessed with an almost continually expanding market for their products. Their problem was how to satisfy demand which is an easier management problem than that faced in other sectors of the economy.

CHARLES W MUNN

Walter Graham BLACKIE,

Printer and publisher; b. 21/3/1816, Glasgow, s. of John Blackie, bookseller and Catherine Duncan; m. Marion Brodie (date unknown); 2 s., 6 d.; Partner, William Blackie & Son; d. 5/6/1906, Glasgow; g/v estate: £128,882 12s 7d.

In the nineteenth century books were the major leisure industry in Britain. There was, therefore, a great demand for the printed word and a number of companies were established which met that need. One such company was Blackie & Son which was founded in Glasgow in 1809 by John Blackie Snr and John Blackie Jnr as printers and publishers.

Walter Graham Blackie was the brother of John Blackie Jnr, Lord Provost of Glasgow. He was educated at Buchanan and Connal's Latin School and James Rennie's writing and arithmetic school after which he studied under Rev Andrew Gray at Kincardine Manse near Doune. All this prepared him for studying classics at Glasgow University and he also spent a year in Germany at the Universities of Leipzig and Jena. It was at Jena that he took the degree of Doctor of Philosophy in 1840. On his return to Glasgow he entered the family firm in which his two brothers were already engaged. This was not his first entrée to the business however, for while he was a student he had worked in the printing department and, on his return to Glasgow, it was this department which occupied his time. He soon assumed control of printing and remained in charge for many years.

It is not surprising however, that, in view of his education, it was the literary side of the business which gradually attracted and held his attention. He took a great interest in geography and was the initiator and editor of the *Imperial Gazetteer*. To help him in this work he learned to read many European languages. Besides Latin and Greek he read German, French, Italian, Spanish, Danish, Norse and Dutch. In recognition of this work he became a Fellow of the Royal Geographical Society. This interest of Blackie's was highly significant for the development of the firm, for it began their involvement with educational texts which, supplemented by children's books, underpinned the profitability of the firm for many years, especially after the coming of compulsory education in the 1870s. Blackie's books sold extensively throughout the Empire.

Walter Blackie's interests in education were personal as well as professional. He was Lord Dean of Guild in 1885-7 and chairman of the Merchant Company. As such he was, ex officio, a manager of the Royal Infirmary and when his term finished he continued at the Infirmary - this time as an elected member. In this capacity he played a large part in the movement for having the Royal Infirmary's medical school incorporated as a college with the intention of affiliating to the University under the Universities Act of 1889. The fact that he was one of the Commissioners under this Act doubtless helped in the formulation of St Mungo's College, of which he became principal - an office which he held until 1898. Other educational offices included the chairmanship of Glasgow Academy, the governorship of Hutcheson's Hospital and of the Glasgow and West of Scotland Technical College. He was also Clerk of the General Council of Glasgow University from the time of its inception in 1860 until 1871. He was awarded an honorary LLD in 1886.

Blackie's other great interest was the church. He and his family came out with Dr Chalmers in the Disruption in 1843 and for many years he was an office bearer in Free St John's Church until 1859 when he was one of the founders of Kelvinside Free Church. He was session clerk of that church from its opening until his death although he was emeritus session clerk for the last few years of his life. He was active in the higher courts and committees of the church and did not shrink from the controversies which pre-occupied his fellow churchmen in the second half of the century.

His other major business interest was as a director of the Clydesdale Bank which he joined in 1880 in the aftermath of the City of Glasgow Bank failure. He became deputy chairman in 1887 and served as chairman from 1888 to 1890. He retired from the board in 1898 at the age of 82. His period of tenure at he bank witnessed a number of national and international financial crises including the theatened failure of Baring Brothers but the Clydesdale Bank enjoyed a period of almost uninterrupted growth in deposits and numbers of branches.

Politically Blackie was a Liberal but despite his apparent love of controversy and debate he never sought political office. When he died in 1906, at the age of 90, the value of his moveable estate was £128,882 almost half of which was his shareholdings in Blackie & Son Ltd (the firm had become a limited company in 1890). Most of the rest of his wealth was held in the shares of other Scottish companies including Clydesdale Bank Ltd, North British Locomotive Co Ltd and J & P Coats Ltd.

CHARLES W MUNN

SOURCES

Unpublished

SRO: SC 36/68/201, Inventory
SC 36/51/141, Will

Published

The Bookseller, 10/6/1906
Glasgow Herald, 6/10/1906, 8/6/1906, 12/6/1906
Glasgow News, 6/6/1906
The Times, 7/6/1906, 14/6/1906.

Walter Wilfred BLACKIE,

Printer and publisher; b. 31/7/1860, Glasgow, s. of Walter Graham Blackie, publisher and Marion Brodie; m. 2/10/1889, Anna Christina Younger; 1 s., 4 d.; Ch, William Blackie & Son; d. 14/2/1953, Helensburgh; g/v estate: £142,998 8s 7d.

Walter Wilfred Blackie was the third generation of the family to run the Glasgow based printing and publishing house of Blackie & Sons Ltd. He was the third son of Walter G Blackie (qv) who chose an education for his son very similar to that which he had, himself, received. Several years at the Glasgow Academy were followed by a period at a Gymnasium in Elberfeld in Germany from where he returned to take up a place at Glasgow University. He graduated with a BSc. This was followed by a brief spell in the family business but he had the wanderlust and in 1880 he left for Canada where he worked in farming and the timber trades before moving to New York where he took an appointment in the publishing house of Appleton. The Appletons were friends of his father. He returned home in 1884 to resume work in Blackie & Sons.

His major interest, throughout his working life, was in the educational side of the business and helped by educational reforms which greatly expanded the demand for books, he increased the range of textbooks and, concomitantly, the number of books for children.

In 1918 his elder brother Alexander Blackie died and Walter succeeded him as chairman - a post which he held until his retirement in 1937. Although his own major interest was in publishing he nevertheless ensured that the company was equipped with the best printing technology. From the late nineteenth century the publishing activities of the firm had outrun its printing and binding capacity with the result that a great deal of work had to be sent elsewhere for printing. This was rectified in 1929 when the firm opened the new Villafield Press - a new purpose built, and well designed factory at Bishopbriggs, on the outskirts of Glasgow. The lay-out capacity and quality of work at the new factory, together with the new machinery capable of colour printing, gave rise to widespread comment and admiration. The factory was chosen for a visit by the International Engineering Congress in 1938. By that time Walter Blackie had retired but his major contribution to the growth of his company was widely recognised. There was, however, one sense in which his chairmanship was not successful for some other printers and publishers had begun to produce paperbacks, but Blackies made no move in this direction and this was to have serious implications for the company after the Second World War.

Throughout his life Walter Blackie never lost his early interest in farming and he became a member of the Board of Governors of the West of Scotland Agricultural College at its formation in 1899. Later he became convener of the finance committee and vice-chairman of the board.

Blackie's other great interest was in art and he was early to recognise and patronise the talents of Charles Rennie Mackintosh whom he commissioned to build his new home in Helensburgh which he called Hill House. This house, which was built within budget, is now acknowledged, together with its furnishings, to be one of Mackintosh's best commissions.

Blackie's interests were walking and reading and he was a member of the Caledonian Club, Western Club and Royal Northern Yacht Club.

At his death in 1953 his moveable estate was valued at £144,405. More than £60,000 of this was his shares in Blackie & Son Ltd. The bulk of the rest of the estate was made up of a myriad of small holdings in government securities, tea companies, distillers, brewers, chemical companies and investment trusts.

CHARLES W MUNN

SOURCES

Unpublished

SRO: SC 65/35/90, Inventory
      SC 65/36/55, Will

Published

Directory of Directors, 1951
Glasgow Herald, 16/2/1953
Who Was Who, Vol V, 1951-60.

William CHAMBERS,

Proprietor and Manager; b. 16/4/1800, Peebles, s. of James Chambers, cotton agent, and Jean Gibson; Proprietor and Manager, W & R Chambers, Edinburgh; d. 20/5/1883, Edinburgh.

Robert CHAMBERS,

Proprietor and Manager; b. 10/7/1802, Peebles, s. of James Chambers, cotton agent, and Jean Gibson; m. (1) 1829, Anne Kirkwood, (2) 1867, Mrs Robert Forth; Proprietor and Manager, W & R Chambers, Edinburgh; d. 17/3/1971, St Andrews.

Chambers Edinburgh Journal, published between 1832 and 1956, was the vehicle which brought the brothers William and Robert Chambers into a working partnership which was to create the firm of Chambers Publishers. It also brought to the English speaking world among the first 'respectable and cheap periodicals', which aimed to 'entertain and instruct, altogether apart from political or sectarian prepossessions, and so, as far as possible, gain universal confidence'.

The Chambers brothers launched the Edinburgh Journal on 4 February 1832; William was then 32 and Robert 30, but they were already well experienced in the book and publishing trade. William was the eldest in a family of six, of four sons and two daughters. Robert was only two years his junior and they closely followed each other in schooling. Born in Peebles where the family had lived for many generations, both went to local schools. William began schooling at the age of five in Kirstie Cranston's Dame School, moving from there to James Gray's Parish School where he and his younger brother Robert undertook most of their elementary education. They next transferred to James Sloane's Grammar School. While the Bible had been the basic text in James Gray's School, Sloane's Grammar School introduced the brothers to the classics; even at this early age Robert was the more studious and intellectual, taking strongly to Latin which William disliked. The brothers' education was rounded out at home where their mother improved their penmanship, and their father brought to them all the classics of English literature through his subscription to Sandy Elder's Circulating Library. This also brought the brothers into contact with the Encyclopedia Britannica which Robert in particular devoured.

William and Robert began their life in a prosperous merchant family, their father James being in business in Peebles as a cotton agent for several Glasgow firms.

He also undertook putting out to handloom weavers of whom about 100 were on his books. This comfortable existence crumbled in 1812 when James Chambers became insolvent through injudicious credit given to French prisoners of war. Hoping to recoup the family fortunes the Chambers left Peebles for Edinburgh in 1813 just as William completed his formal education. The family still had sufficient resources to apprentice William to an Edinburgh bookseller in 1813, and set his feet on the first step in his printing and publishing career. Robert however, had still to complete schooling, and stayed behind in Peebles to finish his year at the Grammar School. In 1814 he transferred to Benjamin Mackay's Academy in Edinburgh. Unfortunately his father failed to make a success of his employment in Edinburgh and his mother opened a small shop to supplement the meagre family resources. The family had intended that Robert should train for the ministry, and in 1815 they had hoped to see him complete his studies at Mackay's Academy and also enter the humanities class at Edinburgh University. There were no funds to permit this, and Robert completed his schooling at Mackay's Academy finally leaving in the spring of 1816 with no clear career open to him.

Robert first had a number of short lived jobs as a clerk and a copyist in merchant houses. He also undertook some tutoring. In view of his uncertain progression William suggested to the family that Robert should open a secondhand bookstall in Leith Walk. Old school books and family tomes formed Robert's first stock and he set up his bookstall for the first time in 1818. The following year, William also opened a secondhand bookstall, having completed his apprenticeship.

Although the brothers both had secondhand bookstalls on Leith Walk it is clear that they worked closely together and indeed lived together at that time. By 1822 both William and Robert had made enough in the secondhand book trade in Leith Walk to leave it behind and move upmarket in the book trade to the new town of Edinburgh. During the next ten years both brothers worked independently in the book trade, and developed distinct interests. William learned more about the technical aspects of printing and bookbinding, while Robert began his first serious attempts at authorship. In 1822 he published his first volume Illustrations of the Author of Waverley, following it with a more successful and popular volume in 1822 Traditions of Edinburgh. In the next few years he published prolifically both in volumes and in contributions to a variety of papers and periodicals. William also tried his hand at authorship, contributing with Robert to the Gazetteer of Scotland and produced his Book of Scotland to complement Robert's successful publication Pictures of Scotland.

During this period Robert was establishing himself as a young man of letters, and in 1830 he became editor of the Edinburgh Advertiser. At this stage both brothers were deeply interested and involved in issues of local and national political interest, like the Reform

Movement. Robert was more conservative than William and wrote pungently in the *Edinburgh Chronicle* on virtually every aspect of local controversy.

This climate of popular intellectual ferment affected every level of society, and two developments occurred in the 1820s which were to have a lasting influence on the direction taken by the Chambers brothers. In Edinburgh the well known publisher Archibald Constable planned to introduce 'Constable's Miscellany', a series designed to produce two books in weekly parts at prices which would make them available to the expanding working class readership. One volume was to emphasise 'entertainment' while the other was to focus on matters 'historical and useful'. At the same time in London, Henry Brougham established in 1826 the 'Society for the Diffusion of Useful Knowledge' which introduced two libraries, the 'Library of Useful Knowledge' and the 'Library of Entertaining Knowledge'. Constable died in 1826 before bringing his ideas forward commercially, but the way had been signposted to produce 'respectable, cheap books'.

The message was not lost on William Chambers who was a very able businessman with an eye for market opportunities. In 1831 he proposed to Robert that he should help him to produce a weekly periodical to be called 'Chambers' Edinburgh Journal'. Unlike previous journals which mainly reproduced work which had appeared elsewhere Chambers planned to fill the new journal with new material specifically written for the publication. Robert reluctantly agreed to write some contributions for his brother and James, another brother who was also a bookseller, was to be the publisher. Robert's involvement was critical; he had already written some 23 volumes and was to write the larger part of the contributions for the journal in its early years.

William was right in arguing that the market was ripe for a cheaply priced mass circulation weekly magazine. The first issue of 4 February 1832 sold 25,000 copies priced at a penny ha'penny. Three issues later the *Edinburgh Journal* was on sale in London, and by the summer of 1832 Robert had joined William to work full-time on the new publication. The brothers' editorial policy in selecting and including material in the journal was to emphasise 'dignity and merit' and to exclude anything that would offend good taste. The contents were at first exclusively for a Scottish readership, ranging over thrift, Scottish biographical sketches, folklore, the formation of Scottish society, and so on. When the London market opened up, Scottishness *per se* was diluted in favour of contents of more general interest, including articles on natural history, science, literature, history, and travel. Fiction was also included the articles ranging widely and set in all corners of the globe. This very wide range of content emphasising the provision of information for readers, was in response to the appearance of the competitor *Penny Magazine* established by William Knight for the Society for the

Diffusion of Useful Knowledge, hard on the heels of the appearance of Chambers' *Edinburgh Journal*. The *Penny Magazine* was Chambers' main rival, outselling the Journal in England till it ceased publication in 1846.

When the Journal first appeared William acted as editor, but in 1833 Robert took over that responsibility while William concentrated on managing the busines of W & R Chambers. The problem was not simply how to produce the editorial material for the Journal, but how to overcome the problems of rapid and large scale production at low cost. William's technical knowledge of the trade allowed the brothers to exploit new trends in printing and publishing. At the end of 1833 they installed their first steam printing press; it came into operation in January 1834 and answered the problem of speed and large volume production. The next problem to be tackled was that of the simultaneous distribution of the new magazine in the main cities of Britain. This was overcome by the Chambers brothers adopting the relatively new technique of stereotyping; this was the production of copies of the plates for printing the Journal and despatching these copies to other locations so that the content could be printed in more than one place simultaneously. By the end of 1833 the *Edinburgh Journal* became the first periodical in Britain to be published simultaneously in the three main capital cities of Edinburgh, Dublin and London. The Chambers brothers also quickly installed the best papermaking machines, which permitted them to produce large quantities of the required sized paper at need.

These editorial and publishing policies were pursued systematically; between 1832 and 1841 the journal achieved an average weekly sale of 59,000 copies, the peak sale in the period having reached 80,000. Until 1835 sales were roughly equal in the Scottish and English markets, but by the early 1840s nearly 70% of total sales was made through the London agency. Moreover sales of monthly compendiums had overtaken weekly issue sales by that time. By 1845 the Chambers were utilising ten steam printing presses and employed 150 of a staff in Edinburgh to produce 50,000 sheets of paper a day for their publishing activities.

The innovation of the Journal brought success to the Chambers brothers and in 1841 they both received the Freedom of Peebles, their native town. While the Journal was the flagship of their educational enterprise in these years it had not been alone in bringing education and entertainment to the masses. William and Robert also introduced a series of volumes in their Chambers' Educational Course which was inaugurated in 1835. The series was designed to embrace all aspects of education and Robert was a prolific author in its cause. He contributed many volumes including the *History of the English Language and Literature*; *The Introduction to the Sciences*; *General Knowledge*; *History and Present State of the British Empire*, and *Exemplary and Instructive Biography*. Not surprisingly this enormous output drained Robert's energies and in 1841 he indicated to his brother that he wished to withdraw from the business, or at least to reduce his activities, in order to give himself time to pursue his scientific interests. Consequently by 1843 Robert had substantially withdrawn from the business while William had taken over editorial responsibilities in addition to the management of the firm. A new series of the Journal was introduced relying less on Robert's contributions.

During the 1840s Robert Chambers researched and wrote widely on scientific matters. He had acquired an interest in fossils around 1837, and pursued his writing on the subject in the seclusion of his St Andrews home from 1841. In 1844 he published anonymously *Vestiges of the Natural History of Creation*. This preceded by some 15 years Darwin's *Origins of the Species*. It aroused huge controversy, since it hinted at scientific laws as the basis of development of all forms of life, rather than a divine creative process. There was some suspicion that Robert was the author of this 'aetheistic text' and he had to withdraw his nomination for election as Lord Provost of Edinburgh in 1848. During the 1840s he published widely on geological matters including his text on *Tracings of the North of Europe* and *Ancient Sea Margins*. This effort earned him the Fellowship of the Geological Society of London and the Fellowship of the Royal Society of Edinburgh. Even so he had not abandoned his interest in literature; his other great work of the period was his four volume study *The Life of Burns* which was published in 1851.

Even though Robert was pursuing his scientific and literary interests it is clear that he still had some involvement in the business. In 1848 the two brothers drew up their first formal partnership, and it is clear that William was by then anxious that Robert should resume a more active role in the firm. In the following year William bought the estate of Glenmoriston near Peebles for £25,000, and began to indulge in country pursuits. Robert was drawn more into the business and in 1853 a new copartnery was drawn up in which Robert held 18 shares and William 6 shares, this indicating his desire to play a lesser role in the business.

Where William had carried the burden of the business in the 1840s, this was to be Robert's role in the 1850s. The great project which was on both the brothers' minds, was to extend their earlier series, *Chambers' Information for the People* to develop *Chambers' Encyclopaedia*. The first of ten volumes of their encyclopaedia was produced in 1859, and the first edition of the set was completed in 1868. Robert and William regarded this as their crowning achievement in bringing cheap and instructive literature to the people.

By the 1850s Robert and William Chambers, and their establishment in the High Street in Edinburgh, were held in high repute. At their premises the brothers had established a library for their employees, and a savings bank to encourage thrift. They had also established a school for the younger boys, and a Sunday Evening School for both the boys and girls. It is clear that William and Robert did not regard themselves simply as publishers; they were also authors and editors working through their ownership of a printing and publishing concern to bring education to all the people. Indeed in 1860, Sir James K Shuttleworth declared that he regarded the Chambers brothers, 'as among the foremost educators and therefore civilisers and Christian teachers of the time'.

The brothers had reached this pinnacle of approval by knowing each other's mind intimately, and by pursuing common goals even when one or other gave little time directly to the publishing enterprise. They had jointly shared the burden of launching the Journal in the 1830s, but in the 1840s William had effectively run the firm while Robert pursued his scientific interests. Conversely Robert had taken over the reins in the 1850s while William partially retired to follow his country interests. In the 1860s there was yet another change over as Robert once more withdrew from the firm to live for a time in London to work on his *Book of Days*. This was a vast compilation of legends, folk customs, historical incidents and scientific data, all arranged under days of the year. This work so taxed Robert that his health deteriorated and after its publication in 1864 he wrote little of substance before his death in 1871.

Robert had been able to go to London to work on his *Book of Days* because William was by then bored with country life and was keen once more to take on the management of the business. His return to Edinburgh also drew him into public affairs through his long standing interest in social reform. In the 1840s William had been involved in the Sanitary Reform Movement, and had contributed a study of Edinburgh to Edwin Chadwick's collection of information on urban public health following the cholera outbreaks of 1848. In 1849 he had helped establish the 'Pilrig Model Dwelling Co', and he resumed this interest in city improvement. In 1865 William was elected as Lord Provost of Edinburgh, and piloted through the council and then put through parliament, the 1867 City Improvement Act. The plans to remove old houses and open up new streets and dwellings were only partially completed in his term of office; he was indeed re-elected to see the work through. One of the new streets established at that time, Chambers Street, bears his name. His contribution to the public health movement was recognised by the conferring of the LLD by Edinburgh University in 1872.

William Chambers' interest in the redevelopment of Edinburgh also led him to propose the restoration and reintegration of St Giles' Church, which since the Reformation had been broken up into four separate places of worship. The lengthy restoration proceeded in three phases between 1873 and 1883, and was largely underwritten by Chambers personally. William Chambers lived to see the completion of this great enterprise but died only two days before he was due to preside over the dedication service of the restored St Giles. Indeed the first religious service to be held in the reintegrated and restored St Giles was William Chambers' funeral service on 23 May 1883.

William Chambers' death in 1883 brought to an end a period of more than 50 years of educational endeavour in publishing in which William and his brother Robert had taken a leading role in bringing education to a mass readership. However, in spite of their hopes of educating the working man, it is clear that the main market for their Journal, and their educational and moral publications, lay in the expanding middle class market. It is doubtful if their works ever penetrated beyond the top layer of craftsmen among the aristocracy of labour. Nevertheless they were, as Shuttleworth maintained, great popular educators, and their drive and perseverance brought them both honour and wealth. Both had a driving ambition partly fuelled by their earlier adversity. In William's case this induced a powerful egocentricity and arrogance, as he universally proclaimed himself to be a self-made man. Robert was more modest but neither he nor William were easy personalities. They were above all men of conviction and purpose whose achievements in printing and publishing made them truly 'publishers for the people'.

ANTHONY SLAVEN

SOURCES

Unpublished

Cooney, Sandra Miles, *Publishers for the People: W & R Chambers,* unpublished Mss

Published

Chambers, William, *Memoir of William and Robert Chambers,* Edinburgh, 1872

John Maurice CLARK,

Publisher; b. 7/3/1859, Edinburgh, s. of Thomas Clark, publisher and Eliza Davidson; m. Helen Marder Douglas, d. of the Rev H M Douglas; 3 s., 1 d.; Senior Partner, T & T Clark, Edinburgh; d. 24/5/1924, Edinburgh; g/v estate: £139,270 9s 11d.

Sir John Maurice Clark, for 43 years the senior partner in the theological and legal publishing firm of T & T Clark of 38 George Street, Edinburgh, was born on 7 March 1859 at 12 Forth Street, Edinburgh, the elder son in a family of two sons and three daughters born to Thomas Clark (1823-1900), and Eliza Maule Clark, nee Davidson. After attending Mr Hunter's school for four years, the young John Clark went to Edinburgh Academy in 1870, joining the class supervised by an outstanding master, Dr James Clyde. Clyde was a stimulating teacher, and several of Clark's class-mates went on to illustrious careers. While at the Academy, Clark took prizes in writing, French, German and book-keeping before leaving earlier than might have been expected in 1874; the following year he matriculated in the Arts Faculty at Edinburgh University where he appears to have attended classes only on a casual basis, for there is no record of his having graduated. The late 1870s found him studying publishing in Leipzig. The heir apparent was being groomed for his life's work in the family firm. At the age of 21, in 1880, he was taken into partnership.

T & T Clark had been founded in 1821 by John Maurice's great uncle, Thomas Clark. In 1846 his father became a partner and, after the founder's retiral some years later was sole partner until 1880. Under his guidance, the firm continued to thrive in a quiet way serving the very specialised legal and theological markets. In an era of rapidly-changing theological views, the works he published represented the moderately progressive position. Initially, a major emphasis was on the issue of translations of continental theological works (such as those which appeared in the *Foreign Theological Library*), but as English language writers in the UK and America began to seize the initiative, so he was quick to cultivate relationships with the US, especially with Scribner and Welford, later Charles Scribners' sons.

John Maurice inherited his father's skill, intuition, decisiveness and integrity, and also, more importantly, came to share the particular ethos that pervaded the firm. Writing to his son in Leipzig in 1877, Thomas Clark urged him in all his business dealings to 'have the fear of God before his eyes', and to remember that 'a publisher [had] a great responsibility, such as even few men in very responsible positions [had], and that in his selection of publications he [might] do much for the advancement of God's cause in the world.' John Maurice seems to have shared this outlook: his own attitude to the tension in which motives spiritual and motives commercial had in consequence to be held is illustrated by his comment to Arthur J Gossip regarding one of the major projects edited by James Hastings: 'I can't speak for Christ, and I would like to do something for Him. Well, I can take this risk, seeking to help a little. But, with Hastings editing it, there is no great risk at all!' This may seem rather ambiguous, but in fact throughout his career, John Maurice, as his father had done before him, consistently published some highly speculative, or occasionally manifestly uneconomic works primarily because he felt that they made valuable contributions to theological enquiry and only secondly because of the lustre which such titles would impart to the Clark list.

Thomas Clark retired in 1886, the year in which he was knighted by Queen Victoria at the Edinburgh International Exhibition with which, as Lord Provost of Edinburgh, he was closely involved. Thereafter, John Maurice was sole partner until, in 1894, he received his brother Thomas George Clark into partnership, but he remained the dominant force behind the firm's development.

Guided by John Maurice's energy and dynamism (albeit that, until his death in 1900, Sir Thomas' advice was sought on all important decisions) T & T Clark entered what was undoubtedly its most influential phase. In three areas his contribution was particularly significant.

Firstly, while not neglecting the firm's links with the continent of Europe, he worked hard to develop the transatlantic connection in which he considered the future lay, working closely with Scribners and other houses to sell Clark works into the North American market. Even more significantly, two major co-operative ventures, the *International Theological Library* and the *International Critical Commentary* were launched in collaboration with Scribners. If these moves were a response to the increasing esteem in which English language theologians, so long perceived to be lagging behind their continental counterparts, were now held, the *International* series and other Clark ventures contributed significantly to the standing of British and North American theological scholarship.

Secondly, John Maurice was committed to the development of major theological works involving large investment and considerable risk. For example, the first printing of 750 copies of Moulton and Geden's *Concordance to the Greek Testament* (1897) cost £1,031 16s 1d, while the first two impressions of the first volume of the *Dictionary of the Bible* (1898) cost a total of £3,349 0s 10d. These were significant sums for a firm whose average annual turnover was only £11,500. But because John Maurice's judgments were mature, and because for the most part he was fortunate in his editors and contributors, these were sound investments.

Thirdly, and of major importance, he was successful in building a lasting relationship with James Hastings (1852-1922) whose editorial genius was to shape the firm's future. Hastings first came to John Maurice's attention in 1889, as founder-editor of the *Expository Times*, which T & T Clark took over from January 1890. Soon, under his editorship, a stream of reference works beginning with the *Dictionary of the Bible* poured from the presses of Morrison and Gibb bearing the Clark imprint. It is difficult to imagine how the firm would have developed had it not been for the link with Hastings, for he not only brought major titles into its list, but also introduced to the Clarks a wide spectrum of theological writers, and thereby greatly increased the prestige of the imprint. The crowning achievement of the John Maurice/Hastings partnership was the *Encyclopaedia of Religion and Ethics* which appeared in 12 volumes between 1908 and 1921. A survey of world religion, the *Encyclopaedia* contained work by 886 leading international authorities. An index volume was later issued. Where proposals from Hastings had a reasonable chance of being commercially viable, John Maurice backed them unwaveringly.

As a result of all these developments, the firm was highly regarded in the theological community. Its influence certainly grew while John Maurice was at the helm. (Few legal works were being published by the end of the nineteenth century). But there does not seem to have been any significant financial growth. Detailed figures are available for the three financial years beginning 1896-97. Turnover reached £10,036 8s 4d in 1896-97, £12,152 4s 0d in 1897-98, and £13,104 16s 9d in 1898-99. The return on investment after all overheads had been taken into account was extremely modest: 4.94% in 1896-97, 2.83% in 1897-98, and 4.98% in 1898-99. The business was therefore only a qualified success in financial terms. Over 1896-97, the firm had 685 titles in print; by 1897-98 the figure had risen to 706, while the following financial year saw a further rise to 720 titles.

For all his innovative qualities, John Maurice was no radical. He had, it was said, 'a distinct liking for the old courtly ways associated with the publishing houses which have played an important part in the industrial life of Edinburgh'. And like the members of other nineteenth century Scottish publishing dynasties, and like his father before him, John Maurice was energetically involved in public affairs. On an ecclesiastical front he was active in Lady Glenorchy's Church in Edinburgh with which his grandfather had been associated since 1822. From 1843 this congregation was part of the Free Church of Scotland until in 1900 it joined in the union of Free and United Presbyterian Churches. On a military front, he was associated for 29 years with the 7th Battalion (the Leith Battalion) of the Royal Scots, which he commanded for five years, retiring as Colonel in 1910. He was vice-chairman of the Midlothian Branch of the Territorial Force Association and undertook arduous duties as National Service Representative for the county during the Great War. On a commercial front, he was an extraordinary director of the British Linen

Bank, a director of the Scottish Life Assurance Company, and, perhaps more esoterically, of the Labugama (Kelani Valley, Ceylon) Rubber and Tea Co Ltd. In 1884, he joined the Edinburgh Merchant Company, and, following in his father's footsteps, was elected an assistant in 1900, was treasurer in 1910, and master the following year. On a civic front, he was Deputy Lieutenant of Midlothian, a director of the Philosophical Institution, a governor of Donaldson's Hospital, and was associated with many charitable bodies. He received the Volunteer Officers' Decoration, and, upon his father's death succeeded to his Baronetcy. His leisure activities included riding, fishing, and latterly, motoring; and he was an enthusiastic spectator at rugby matches.

John Maurice married Helen Marder Douglas, the daughter of Free Church minister Henry M Douglas of Kirkcaldy, apparently around 1885. They had four children, Thomas, Henry James Douglas, Isabella Douglas, and John Maurice Jnr.

He retired from the business in 1923. His brother Thomas George, unable to contemplate settling down in the firm after the upheaval of military service in the Great War, had retired earlier, in 1919. John Maurice was therefore succeeded by his son Thomas, who was sole partner until being joined by a cousin in 1930.

On 27 May 1924, Sir John Maurice Clark died at his home at 17 Rothesay Terrace, Edinburgh. It was felt by some that the excessive demands which he had made on himself, both in his business and in his extra-mural commitments, had led to his death at a comparatively early age. The death certificate gives the cause of death as 'carcinoma of stomach and liver'.

John Maurice's moveable estate in the UK and overseas which totalled £139,270 9s 11d, was widely invested. Only a small proportion of this total could have accrued from the profits of the firm.

JOHN A H DEMPSTER

SOURCES

Unpublished

Birth certificate
Death certificate
Dempster, John A H, 'The profitability of progressive theology publishing in late nineteenth century Scotland as illustrated by the experience of T & T Clark in the 1880s and 1890s', Ph D dissertation, University of Strathclyde, 1987
Information from the Archivists of Edinburgh Academy and Edinburgh University
SRO: SC 70/1/716, fol 313, Inventory
        ODV/4956-36, Will
T & T Clark Deposit in the National Library of Scotland (Dep 247)

Published

Edinburgh Academy Chronicle, 71, 152
Expository Times, 35, (1923-24), 477-78
Glasgow Herald, 28 May 1924
Gossip, A J, 'Reverend James Hastings, D D', *Expository Times*, 51, (1939-40), 7-9
Harvey, James, *In Memoriam Sir Thomas Clark*, Edinburgh, n d
Harvey, James, 'The Publishing House of Messrs T & T Clark, Edinburgh', *Expository Times*, 51, (1939-40), 10-13
Scotsman, 28 May 1924

Edward COLLINS,

Papermaker; b. 1848, s. of Joshua Heywood Collins, papermaker and Jane Johnstone; m. Clara Harriet Millington; Partner, Edward Collins & Sons, Glasgow; d. 24/7/1900, Glasgow; g/v estate: £199,011 5s 11d.

Edward Collins was the only son of papermaker Joshua Heywood Collins whose mill at Kelvindale was a well established family business and one of the largest paper-manufacturers in the country. J Heywood Collins was also a director of Drake Walls Mining Company Limited, the Lanarkshire and Dumbarton Railway Company, Northern Assurance Company and Young's Paraffin Light and Mineral Oil Company Limited.

Edward was thus no rags to riches businessman but a member of a business family which was operating in Glasgow in the second half of the eighteenth century. Edward's great grandfather had begun papermaking at Kelvindale, and later the shortage of water on this site necessitated a move to Dalmuir where a site was leased. The Kelvindale property was retained and with improvements to the river in the 1840s Edward's grandfather was able to move back to Kelvindale. On the site of the Balgray Snuff and Paper Mill the family business underwent a considerable expansion and a lot of new building was undertaken.

The family origins were not in Scotland. Edward's great grandfather moved to Edinburgh then Glasgow from Cumberland. The family was not native to this part of the world either and it seems not unlikely that the Collins family was of European origin. It is interesting to note that papermaking was first introduced into Glasgow by Nicholas Deschamps, a Huguenot refugee. The Collins family were unusual among the Glasgow business community in that many of the children were educated abroad in France and Germany, another reason perhaps for suspecting links with the continent. Whether or not the papermaking Collins' were connected with the publishing Collins' is impossible to say.

Edward's father, Joshua, was a difficult man, shrewd and hard headed but lacking in imagination and enterprise. At 18 he was in charge of the firm's 'counting house' and had to cope with what appears to be his father's unstable mental condition. When his father died in 1866 Joshua and his elder brother Edward ran the business together - it flourished and the assets had nearly doubled by 1871, from £79,424 to £123,309. The two brothers never got on well. Joshua had the responsibility of the business from an early age and had little interest outside it. Edward was a more outgoing character who was involved in everything from hunting and mountaineering to the church and the Justice of the Peace Courts. The brothers eventually split when Joshua wanted his daughter's prospective husband, the 20 year old Henry Ball, admitted as a partner. Edward felt he was too young and inexperienced. In 1871 Edward sold his share to Joshua and left him as the sole partner. The business moved into the hands of a junior branch of the family where it remained until 1920 when it was merged into a larger public company.

Joshua could not manage the firm on his own and in due course assumed his son Edward and his grandson, Charles, to partnership. The business clearly continued to prosper. Joshua died in 1894 and Edward and Charles ran the business. Edward and his wife Clara lived at Highfield House, Kelvindale. They spent part of the year at Calderwood Cooke near Blantyre and they also had a farm at Balgray. Most of Edward's wealth was tied up with the family business but, he also had money invested in joint-stock companies such as 1,000 shares in the Lanarkshire and Dunbartonshire Railway Company which at his death were worth £24,742. Edward Collins also invested in the Allan Steamship Line and the City Line. Several thousands of pounds were also invested in overseas concerns such as Rio Tinto, the Canadian Pacific Railway Company, and the Mysore Gold Mining Company.

During the winter of 1900 Edward Collins suffered from a number of attacks of influenza which brought on long periods of depression. On Tuesday, 24 July Edward and his family returned to Glasgow from Calderwood for a brief visit. While Clara Collins and her son were in the garden Edward shot himself in the head. Death was instantaneous. There were few glowing tributes in the press to Edward, the Partick and Maryhill Press simply reported the facts. Edward's estate of £199,011 5s 11d was left to his family.

CHRISTOPHER C LEE

SOURCES

Unpublished

SRO: SC 36/48/172, Inventory
     SC 36/51/126, Will

Published

Partick & Maryhill Press, 27/7/1900.

Sir William COLLINS,

Printer and publisher; b. 12/10/1817, Glasgow, s. of William Collins, printer and publisher, and Jane Barclay; m. (1) Annabella Proudfoot Glen, 9 children; (2) Helen Jamieson, 2 children; Ch & Man Dir, William Collins Sons & Co Ltd; d. 20/2/1895, Edinburgh; g/v estate: £163,985.

Sir William Collins was one of that select band of late nineteenth century Glasgow businessmen who built an important company of world stature yet who found sufficient time to have a very high public profile and to devote himself to public service and to several worthy causes. His contribution therefore was not just to the business sector but to the city and the wider community.

William Collins was born in Glasgow and received his education at Glasgow Grammar School which he left at the age of 12 to begin an apprenticeship in his father's printing and stationery business. He was admitted as a partner in 1848 at a time when the firm was diversifying into publishing. This expansion was well judged for the market for all kinds of literature was growing at a prodigious rate, not just for popular reading material but for school books and religious texts.

When his father died in 1853 William Collins continued the business on his own until 1865 when he took into partnership two of his assistants, followed three years later by his two elder sons William Collins Jnr and Alexander G Collins. The firm was converted into a limited liability company in 1880 with most of the shares being held by various members of the Collins family. By the time of Sir William's death in 1895 the company was one of the largest of its type in the country and employed nearly 2,000 workers. It had offices in London and several cities throughout the world.

William Collins was greatly interested in the welfare of his workers and in 1887, to mark the jubilee of the firm, he presented the employees with the Collins Institute, a handsome building, close by the works, which was fully equipped for educational, social and cultural purposes.

In particular the business expanded because the market for books was growing and Collins did not let his opportunities slip by. The growth in the number of churches was especially important in creating a great demand for Bibles and devotional works. The coming of compulsory education also produced a new generation of readers and with it a demand for textbooks of all kinds. These together with the greater literacy of the population as a whole ensured that publishers who were well organised and who could print books as well as publish them were well placed to develop their businesses in a buoyant market.

As with so many of his contemporaries, however, business was not enough to consume all of William Collins' energies. He inherited his father's zeal for the temperance movement - an enthusiasm which earned him the sobriquet of 'Water Willie'. More seriously his interest in the temperance movement enabled him to use his position on the Glasgow School Board to ensure that temperance teaching figured on the curriculum of Glasgow schools. He was, for many years, president of the Scottish Temperance League. He gave of his time, talents and money to almost any project associated with temperance and in 1881 his friends in the movement erected a drinking fountain in his honour at the gates of Glasgow Green.

In 1868 William Collins was nominated for a seat on the Town Council respresenting the Fifth Ward, the area of the city where the Collins factory was located. He was returned without opposition and was re-elected four times. He was soon involved in the work of a number of committees but took a particular interest in the city's financial affairs. He became a magistrate in 1873 and, despite his views on temperance, it was always said that he acted with strict impartiality in the granting of drinks licences. As a member of the Improvement Trust he supported the scheme for acquiring open spaces throughout the city.

William Collins was appointed Lord Provost of the city in 1877 and held the office until 1880. It was Collins therefore who had the task of being Lord Provost at the time of the collapse of the City of Glasgow Bank in 1878. He convened a public meeting and ensured that subscriptions were opened for the relief of distress arising out of the failure. More widely Collins instituted a series of social meetings, or conversaziones, for leading citizens, for Christian workers and temperance reformers and other groups in the city. All were tee-total gatherings. He was knighted for his services to the city in 1881. Following his retirement from the council in 1881 he took very little active part in civic affairs although he did join the School Board in 1888.

Throughout his life Collins main leisure activity was yachting and he was one of the oldest members of the Royal Northern Yacht Club. He owned successive steam yachts and spent time every year in sailing round the west coast of Scotland.

In politics Collins was an advanced Liberal but he resisted all entreaties to stand for Parliament. Despite this he was an ethusiastic supporter of dis-establishment, local veto, crofter legislation and home rule. He was Justice of the Peace and a Deputy Lieutenant of the county of the city of Glasgow and of the county of Lanark. His religious adherence was to the Free Church and he was originally a member of Free St John's, which his father helped to found. In later life he was an office bearer in the Free College Church. He was also a director of the United Evangelistic Association.

CHARLES W MUNN

SOURCES

Unpublished

SRO: SC 36/51/112, Will
    SC 36/48/151, Inventory

Published

Directory of Directors, 1893
Glasgow Herald, 21/2/1895
Keir, D, *The House of Collins*, London, 1952
North British Daily Mail, 21/2/1895
Paper and Printing Trades Journal, May 1895
The Times, 21/2/1895.

William Hope COLLINS,

Printer and publisher; b. 5/9/1903, Kilmacolm, Renfrewshire, s. of Sir Godfrey P Collins, sometime Secretary of State for Scotland, and Margaret J F Henderson; twice married, second to Lilian Wallace; 1 s., 1 d.; d. 21/8/1967, Glasgow.

William Hope Collins was educated at Wellington College and at Woolwich Military Academy from where he entered the army, serving in the Royal Artillery. He resigned from the army in 1928 to enter the family business, William Collins Sons & Co Ltd. He was aged 25. The company was already more than 100 years old having been established in 1819. Based at Townhead in Glasgow Collins was involved in the printing and publishing of Bibles and educational books, children's books, fiction and non-fiction, reference books of all kinds, diaries and commercial stationery. These were sold all over the world and there were offices in London, Australia, New Zealand, South Africa, Canada, USA and the West Indies.

The company which Hope Collins entered in 1928 was therefore a large, well established and active organisation. From the outset Collins particular talents were on the mechanical side of the business. It was in the printing works that he began to make his contribution under the then printing manager, Mr James Paterson. Hope Collins was a fast learner and soon acquired a wide knowledge of the printing trade. Often, and quite unofficially, he would handle the machines himself either during the lunch-breaks or after hours in the evening shifts. He rapidly acquired a similar practical knowledge of stationery and bindery work. In 1932 he visited the United States and toured the United Kingdom to examine equipment and works design. As a result of his visits he placed orders for over £100,000 worth of printing and binding equipment. Not content with that he diversified his interests into the publishing side of the business where he took over the children's book department to which he later added the educational books department.

Hope Collins' years with the firm were marked by almost unbroken progress. In 1928 10 million books were produced and by the time of his death in 1967 this had risen to 30 million. In the same period diary production rose from 1.5 million to 7 million. Output on the stationery side of the business made similar progress. Needless to say considerable extensions to the company's printing and warehouse capacity were added. The Montgomery Building in Cathedral Street (now the library for Strathclyde University) was opened in 1953. A new printing works was opened at Bishopbriggs to the north of the city - a foretaste of things to come when the whole head office, printing and warehousing operation moved there in 1978.

Hope Collins, as managing director, worked closely with his cousins Sir William A R Collins, chairman and managing director, and Ian G Collins, vice chairman and managing director. All three were responsible for the general management of the company's affairs at home and overseas, with each having particular departmental responsibilities.

Hope Collins main responsibilities lay on the 'works' side of the business where he was involved in the maintenance of the high standards of quality for which the company was renowned. He was also involved in the welfare schemes which the company ran for its workers. For many years William Collins and Sons had a reputation for taking good care of its employees and, as the man in charge of the 'works',

Hope Collins had the task of ensuring that this reputation was maintained. He was fully aware that reputations are not maintained by standing still so he led the company in the 1950s in the development of pension and profit sharing schemes and in the creation of a health and welfare department with a full-time doctor and nursing staff. There was also a visiting dentist, optician and chiropodist. The dining and recreation facilities in the Collins Institute in Collins Street were maintained and further developed.

Throughout his working life Hope Collins took a keen interest in the affairs of the associations and trade unions connected with the printing industry. In 1938 he was asked to assume the presidency of the Company of Stationers of Glasgow. Ten years later he was appointed president of the British Federation of Master Printers and quickly became a valued member of the negotiating committee of that body for the printing industry in Great Britain. He also served as president of the Scottish Alliance of Master Printers. In 1966 he was appointed president of the International Bureau of Master Printers in Europe.

He was a man who made a favourable impact on all who had dealings with him. Even the trade unionists, and printing and publishing was a highly unionised business, felt that he brought fair-mindedness and goodwill to his meetings with them. For his part he believed that honesty and understanding were essential ingredients in all his inter-personal relationships. He was awarded the CBE in the New Year Honours list in 1961 for his work on behalf of the printing industry.

Outwith his work Hope Collins had many other interests. During the Second World War he commanded the Ayrshire Battalion of the Home Guard and was an intelligence officer with the Ministry of Home Security. In 1956 he was appointed zone controller for Western Civil Defence (Scotland) and he retained this appointment until his death in 1967.

In 1953 he served on the Scottish Committee of the Council of Industrial Design and three years later he became a member of the Board of Scottish Industrial Estates. In 1960 he was elected president of the Glasgow Chamber of Commerce having served for two years as vice president and since 1947 as a director. He was also a member of the State Hospitals Board and was for some years honorary treasurer of the British Sailors Society in Scotland.

His hobbies were flat racing and shooting. He kept one or two horses in training in Yorkshire and he shared a Lanarkshire grouse moor with a friend.

On 11 August 1967 Hope Collins became ill while driving his car near Argyle Street in Glasgow. He crashed into a wall and died in hospital 11 days later. The memorial service for him, which was held in Glasgow Cathedral, was attended by almost 1,000 people.

WILMA SEMPLE

SOURCES

Unpublished

Recollections of Collins employees

Published

Glasgow Chamber of Commerce Journal, 1967
Glasgow Herald, 23/8/1967
Keir, D, *The House of Collins*, London, 1952

John GALLOWAY,

Paper manufacturer; b. 1841, s. of John Galloway, farmer and Elizabeth Luice; m. Jessie Black Sloan; 1 s., 1 d.; MD, The Guard Bridge Paper Company Ltd; d. 29/7/1914, Seggie House, Guardbridge; g/v estate: £85,299 1s 8d.

John Galloway spent most of his career as manager and managing director of The Guard Bridge Paper Company Ltd. Although he had no part in founding the company, he was crucial to its growth in the 30 years before the first world war. He was not involved in other businesses although he held a number of local offices (Justice of the Peace, chairman of the Leuchars School Board and president of the Fifeshire Agricultural Society) and was interested in farming. A third of his estate at death (£30,847 out of £85,299) was in shares in The Guard Bridge Paper Company Ltd; another third was invested in the Bank of Scotland and the rest was in a portfolio of shares in (mainly) Scottish companies and enterprises. He stands as a good example of a paternalistic, professional manager.

The history of the company and Galloway's career there, after October 1873, were closely associated, although these were also favourable years for the manufacture of high quality paper. The company, whose Articles of Association were signed in April 1873, had a slow beginning and was not in profitable production for two years. This was partly because none of the directors had previous experience of papermaking. The mill used the site of the Seggie distillery, owned by the Haigs; by the late 1860s Seggie was not required for distilling and they sought to convert the buildings to papermaking but there were problems in finding a suitable manager in the first year. Galloway had come to Guard Bridge as the

mill clerk and the month after he arrived he took over as temporary manager. By the beginning of 1875 he was firmly established and after this the board minutes record most decisions, from the purchase of machinery to the annual trip for the workforce, as being 'left to Mr Galloway'. Under his management the mill became established as a producer of high quality paper, with expanding output and profits.

In the first 25 years the mill grew from having a single machine with an annual capacity of about 1,500 tons to four machines producing 8,000 tons a year by 1900. One reason for the steady growth was that both Galloway and the other directors were willing to expand the business in the expectation of increased profits, some of which were invested in the mill. Growth took place by the addition of a new plant and there were no dramatic innovations at this time, although there were gradual increases in productivity and quality improved considerably. The company was recognised as an enterprising one and 'among the most perfectly organised ... in Great Britain'. It was also able to exploit the buoyant market for fine printing and specialised papers with trade through wholesale merchants and an agency in London from the 1870s. Galloway's experience in a wholesale stationer's in Glasgow (Lumsden & Sons) may have helped here in identifying the potential for the highest quality papers, but the Haigs also had London connections, so it was not Galloway's experience alone that counted.

In the decade before he died he continued as manager, although he was joined by James Hodge in 1909 as joint manager. (He became manager on Galloway's death, until his own death in 1923). There was no expansion at this time, so that, although a new machine was planned in 1912, production was much the same in 1913 as it had been in 1899, at about 8,200 tons a year. A number of problems faced the mill, although it is hard to see how far these were due to faltering management on Galloway's part and how far due to external pressures. The formal records of the company show that there were some managerial and labour problems that could have been the result of stress at the end of a long period of control by one powerful individual. There was some conflict about who was to replace him although the details are not well documented. Galloway certainly wanted his son to succeed him but the board and the other managers there disagreed. (John Galloway Jnr left the company in 1916 and founded his own works at Balerno Bank). But there were other problems; the mill had grown to need more formal supervision of the complex buildings; there was a lack of scientific and technical skill, so that Galloway even found it impossible to retire in 1911 because no-one else was available to plan the fifth paper machine; there was no research and development or quality control tests on paper. There were also new pressures from the workforce for union recognition and for increases in wages. All this meant that production tailed off immediately before the war, and Guard Bridge itself suffered more during the conflict than other mills.

The company also housed much of the workforce by the end of the century, largely because there had been difficulties in recruiting labour as the mill expanded. It is not clear whether Galloway was responsible for the housing policy of the company, but houses were built and the company took some part in the life of the village of Guardbridge that grew up around it. By the early twentieth century about 350 people were employed in the mill, most of them from the village of Guardbridge, although some came from the surrounding areas and Leuchars; about two thirds of the workforce lived in company houses by 1914. In dealing with the village, the company maintained the attitude that its purpose was to make paper, not to run a housing trust; there is no indication that Galloway took an interest in creating a 'model' village, although the housing was built to a higher standard than that of private landlords.

Galloway was a paternalistic manager, relying on the authority of his personality and on personal contact with the work people. His obituary refers to 'kindly control' over staff and employees, but this should not be taken too literally, for paternalism has its frightening side. There certainly were paternalistic gestures, such as the annual day trip every year for the whole workforce, and the building of the Jubilee Hall in 1897. Stories about him tend to draw attention to his rude manners towards work people and he was recalled as a frightening person, with the power to dismiss people at will. His success seems to have lain in a capacity to involve himself in all commercial and technical aspects of the company's activities, and to command hard work and loyalty from other people. All these are personal characteristics that are hard to pinpoint, but they came together at a new mill in favourable circumstances, enabling Galloway to be a successful businessman in a local context.

LORNA WEATHERILL

SOURCES

Unpublished

Cupar Sheriff Court, Register of Inventories, 1914
Letters, minute books and reports, Guard Bridge Paper Mill Company archives

Published

Glasgow Herald, 30/7/1914
Paper Maker and British Paper Trade Journal, 1/8/1914

Renfrewshire and Ayrshire Leaders, c 1911
Weatherill, Lorna, *A Century of Paper Making*, Guardbridge, 1974.

Robert GOURLAY,

Banker and newspaper publisher; 1840, Glasgow, s. of James Gourlay, bank manager and Jeanie Cleland; m. (1) 12/3/1868, Mary Brown Hastings, d. of James Moffat, farmer; (2) 6/6/1899, Jane, d. of Duncan McPhail, cotton spinner; 3 s., 2 d.; Manager, Bank of Scotland, Glasgow, Ch, George Outram & Co Ltd; d. 27/12/1916, Glasgow; g/v estate: £61,295 2s 1d.

In 1855, James Gourlay, ex-draper, retired accountant, town councillor and magistrate, and founder of the Commercial Travellers' Society of Scotland, accepted the agency for the newly established Laurieston branch of the Bank of Scotland in Glasgow. In the following year his son, Robert, having completed his education at the Glasgow High School and Glasgow University, eschewed a favoured career at the bar and joined him as an apprentice. When he retired from the position of manager of the Bank of Scotland in Glasgow some 50 years later Robert Gourlay was 'said to be the most popular man in Glasgow'. His philanthropic connections were such that he was described as being 'the universal treasurer of all the Glasgow charities'. He had served, or was serving, as a director of the prestigious Burmah Oil Company, the African Lakes Company, the Scottish Provident Institution and the 'philanthropic' Glasgow Workmen's Dwellings Company. In addition to this he was, and continued to be until his death, chairman of the highly profitable publishing company, George Outram & Co Ltd, proprietors of, among others, the *Glasgow Herald*.

Gourlay's banking career was, if not spectacular, then at least successful. He gained experience of everyday banking procedure throughout Scotland whilst serving in the Inspector's Department in Edinburgh Head Office. At the age of 29 he was back in Glasgow as sub-manager of the city branch, and ten years later in 1879 was appointed manager. Contemporaries agreed that 'popularity', rather than any intellectual capability, was responsible for Gourlay's success. He admitted himself that personal relationships contributed towards his progress; of David Davidson, treasurer of the Bank of Scotland between 1863 and 1879, he remarked, 'He was my best friend, and gave me early and rapid promotion'. This popularity was also seen as the main reason for the great increase in business that came to the Bank of Scotland during Gourlay's period as manager, which coincided with a rapid extension of branches into the growing middle class suburbs of the city. Critics were less sanguine, for whilst acknowledging the importance of growth (by 1900 the bank was the second largest in Glasgow) many felt that a popular agent led to bad debts, and that the expansion of custom was achieved without due regard to its quality. Even the kindest appraisals of Gourlay's banking career concluded that 'he is apt, like Candide the optimist, to take too favourable a view of borrowing human nature, and to think that all mankind are as well disposed as himself'.

If Gourlay's personality was one reason for his popularity, then no doubt another was his extensive association with Glasgow charities. Hospitals, soldiers and sailors' families, deserted mothers, friendly societies and educational institutes all benefited from his presence. Although he left only £100 to charity in his will he was known during his lifetime to be very generous with his time and money. In 1901-02 he served as Dean of Guild, and was thus an ex-officio member of Glasgow Council; this was his only intrusion into local politics. As a 'zealous' member of the United Presbyterian Church he was a strong supporter of the movement to unite this and the Free Church. He was a founder member of Belhaven United Free Church and spent some time in the Highlands assisting the dispossessed ministers and congregations following the union of the two churches. His religious interest involved him in the Glasgow United Evangelistic Association, the Glasgow Medical Missionary Society and the Religious Trust and Book Society of Scotland. All of these associations were essential for the success of a particular type of businessman in Glasgow, and through them Gourlay entered the orbit of some of the city's most exclusive and influential sons.

Robert Gourlay's connection with George Outram & Co began with him acting as representative for the trustees of James Pagan, editor of the *Glasgow Herald* between 1853 and 1870, and a partner in the company. Pagan had held only one of 28 shares, which he had purchased for £2,750 in 1854, partly financed by a loan of £1,000 from Gourlay's father, James. As a trustee Gourlay inherited a position of considerable power: Pagan had played a major role in the day-to-day management of a company where nearly half of the shares were held by inactive trustees. Only two partners regularly attended meetings, and thus Gourlay, along with the company's counting house manager, Alexander Sinclair (who was also a trustee), was able to exert much influence on company policy. By 1880 these two were sufficiently established to be offered shares in the partnership, along with J H Stoddart, the then editor of the *Glasgow Herald*. Gourlay's one-twenty-fourth was priced at £8,900. By the time Outrams became a limited liability company in 1903 with a capital of £300,000, Gourlay was

in effect the second largest shareholder. He owned himself five shares of £2,500 each: James Pagan's trust, which he continued to represent, was also allocated five shares out of a total of 120. In 1899 Gourlay had taken a second wife, Jane McPhail, daughter of a Glasgow cotton spinner, who brought with her ten shares in the company. This block of 20 shares was second only to the 25 owned by James Cameron Dun Waters, who although a director, was not active in running the new company.

The financial experience and expertise gained in the world of banking came to Gourlay's assistance as a member of Outrams. In the face of declining growth, falling profits and increased expenditure, he pressed for the employment of an independent accountant to act as auditor and advisor to the company. When this was introduced in 1876, following a change of editorship in 1875, an immediate improvement was brought about in the firm's fortunes. In order to formalise the arrangement that had developed by which a few partners controlled most of the company's decisions, a business committee of three was established in 1883 to act on all urgent matters. Robert Gourlay was a founder member, and remained on the committee until the limited company was formed. The three partners acted on financial matters, and were responsible for the policy by which only a moderate dividend was paid to the shareholders in order to strengthen company resources. This policy was vindicated when the outbreak of war in 1914 brought with it a massive increase in the cost of newsprint, which could only be met out of company reserves. Issues relating to the mechanical and production side of newspaper work were also dealt with here.

Whilst the partners seem to have been aware of the measures necessary to ensure company efficiency, they were apparently unable to appreciate the demand for printed matter that was emanating from an increasingly literate and news-conscious population. The *Glasgow Weekly Herald,* established in 1864, and the *Evening Times,* founded in 1876, were both published as a response to the innovations of competitors. The prime motivation of the efficient, but conservative, partners was to preserve the profits accruing to the company from the *Glasgow Herald.* Any new paper, they felt, would threaten these funds. One startling exception to this policy was the introduction of a *Sunday Times* by the company on August 2, 1914. Faced with the need to publish news relating to the outbreak of war in Europe, and in the absence of senior editorial staff, the decision and responsibility for producing Scotland's first Sunday newspaper lay safely with Robert Gourlay. The newspaper, published in the format of the *Evening Times,* carried no advertising and, at Gourlay's request, it contained no sports news but instead a weekly sermon. Despite the boost which this gave to the sales of the *Evening Times,* the directors ruled that Sunday publication should cease at the end of the war. It was paradoxical that Gourlay himself was a member of the church lobby which the company was trying so hard to appease.

When Robert Gourlay died in 1916 the ten shares he owned in the company (on her death Janet McPhail had left five shares to her husband and five to a nephew), along with one-fifth of two jointly owned shares, were given the conservative valuation of £26,000 (this was based on the 1903 purchase price of £2,500). Under the terms of his will these shares were to remain in the hands of either trustees or his family. His eldest son, James, succeeded him as chairman. Robert Gourlay's personal estate totalled £61,295; apart from his interest in Outram's the main components of this were insurance policies totalling £17,648 and shares in New Zealand and Australian Land and the Bank of Scotland worth jointly £7,542. Obituaries agreed that the death of this popular man marked the passing of an era 'where business concerns were never allowed to overwhelm the social graces of life'. Certainly 'social grace' appears to have been a major determining factor in Gourlay's career, but how far it can be applied to his contemporaries is a matter of some doubt.

NICHOLAS J MORGAN

SOURCES

Unpublished

SRO: SC 36/48/274, Inventory
SC 36/51/174, Will

Published

Bassett, H H, *Men of Note in Finance & Commerce*, London, 1900
The Bailie, 10/5/1905
Evening Times, 2/8/1914, 27/12/1916
Glasgow Herald, 11/5/1908, 28/12/1916, 30/12/1916
Scottish Bankers' Magazine, April 1917
Scottish Banks & Bankers, Ch XI
The Times, 28/12/1916
Who's Who in Glasgow, Glasgow, 1909.

John Ross MENZIES,

Wholesale publisher and distributor; b. 16/9/1852, Edinburgh, s. of John Menzies, wholesale publisher, and Rossie Marr; bachelor; Ch and MD, John Menzies & Co Ltd; d. 5/3/1935, North Berwick; g/v estate: £137,949.

John Menzies is a great Scottish institution. Its railway bookstalls in the past, and its high street stores today, purvey the retail side of a business strongly based in the wholesale book, periodical, and newspaper trades. John Ross Menzies was the elder of two brothers, John and Charles Menzies, sons of John Menzies who founded the business in Edinburgh in 1833.

John Menzies Snr was born in Edinburgh in 1808, and after schooling went to London to learn the bookselling trade, where he was apprenticed to a publisher, Charles Tilt. John Menzies returned to Edinburgh in 1833 and set up as a bookseller and publisher in a small way in premises in Princes Street. His London contacts proved valuable and set him into the agency and wholesale side of the trade. In 1837 he was appointed as Scottish agent to Chapman & Hall, the publishers of the *Pickwick Papers*; in 1841 he secured the agency for the magazine *Punch*, this establishing his involvement in the wholesale distribution of periodicals. The retail and wholesale book trade occupied John Menzies till about 1855 when he extended his interests into wholesale newspaper distribution to newsagents. Two years later he began what was to become the real fortune maker for the company; the railway bookstalls. The first John Menzies railway bookstalls were opened in 1857 at Perth, Stirling and Bridge of Allan.

This phase of expansion coincided with the birth of John Menzies' first son John Ross Menzies in 1852. John R Menzies and his brother Charles T Menzies were both to enter their father's business after school. The business was changed to a partnership, John Menzies & Co in 1867, at about the time the elder brother entered the business. As the young brothers began to play a part in the company it took on new directions, moving out of its Edinburgh and the east of Scotland markets to establish a presence in the west. The first Glasgow wholesale branch was opened in 1868, and company bookstalls were opened in Greenock, Ayr, Dumfries and Kilmarnock, between 1872 and 1873. By this time John Menzies was reducing his active involvement in the company, and the two brothers took on a more managerial responsibility. When their father died in 1879 the business passed to the sons.

With the two young partners in control, John Menzies & Co rapidly extended its wholesale warehouse network, and for the first time penetrated into England, establishing a railway bookstall in Carlisle in 1888, following this with a wholesale branch there in 1898. In expanding the business the brothers worked long hours and under John R Menzies leadership, the company developed a policy of career development for its employees. J R Menzies argued that the employees through their own efforts 'promoted themselves'. The company promoted the establishment of a rambling club in 1886, and in both Edinburgh and Glasgow they established social and sports clubs, each supporting hockey and football teams.

Under the guidance of John R Menzies and his brother Charles the profits of the company climbed steadily to average some £8,000 per year in the 1880s, rising to about £15,000 by the turn of the century. This vigorous expansion of profit came more from the railway bookstalls than from the other activities of the company. When John Menzies took the form of a limited company in 1906 it then operated about 357 station bookstalls. This made John Menzies one of the top five bookstall network companies in Britain, being second in size only to W H Smith & Co Ltd which controlled over 500 bookstall sites in England. The prospect of destructive competition across the border between Menzies and Smith led to a gentleman's undertaking between John R Menzies and Sir William Acland of W H Smith & Co, to the effect that Menzies would not use their Carlise base to further penetrate the English market. This unwritten agreement lasted until 1959 when John Menzies acquired Wymans.

With the formation of John Menzies & Co Ltd in 1906 John R Menzies became chairman and he and his brother Charles were also joint managing directors. The two managers of their Glasgow and Edinburgh houses, William Dawson and Robert Dickie, were elected directors. These arrangements did not change the policies of the firm. The management continued to open new wholesale buildings in the main Scottish towns. Advertising, an innovation which was to prove a great stimulus to growth in wholesaling, was introduced in Edinburgh in 1913 and in Glasgow eventually in 1926. By this later date John Menzies & Co had swept aside all Scottish competition, and in 1927 John Ross Menzies retired at the age of 75, though retaining his position as chairman.

During his years at the head of the company John Ross Menzies had lived for some time at Darn Hall, Peeblesshire, where he enjoyed the sports of shooting and fishing. He also kept a residence in London and had a wide circle of literary and artistic friends. In his younger days he had also been an active yachtsman on the Clyde, and was a considerable golfer well known at both St Andrews and North Berwick. When he retired from the firm he went to live in North Berwick, to continue to enjoy his golf. When he died there in March 1935 he was in his eighty-third year, and had piloted his father's partnership and company into Scotland's leading wholesale and retail organisation in the book, periodical and newspaper trade. The railway bookstalls had been the vanguard of the

company during his stewardship, but by the time of his death they were entering upon a decline, preparing the way for the diversification that was to follow when younger members of the family took control.

ANTHONY SLAVEN

SOURCES

Unpublished

Birth Certificate, Midlothian District, 1852, Entry 395
Death Certification, North Berwick District, 1933, Entry 10
SRO: SC 40/40/47, Inventory
    SC 40/43/18

Published

Graham, (ed), H M, *The Menzies Group*, John Menzies & Co, Edinburgh, 1965
Menzies & Co, J, *The House of Menzies*, Edinburgh, 1958
The Scotsman, 6 March 1935.

Thomas NELSON Jnr,

Printer and publisher; b. 25/12/1822, Edinburgh, s. of Thomas Nelson, bookseller, and Margaret Black; m. Jessie Kemp; 2 s., 2 d.; Ch, Thomas Nelson & Sons; d. 20/10/1892, Edinburgh; g/v estate: £630,867.

Thomas Nelson Jnr was one of the best known businessmen in late nineteenth century Edinburgh. His father had started a book-selling business earlier in the century but his health was precarious and this factor alone forced Thomas's elder brother William to abandon a professional education to help in the family business. Thomas never seems to have had the opportunity of higher education and left Edinburgh High School at the age of 17 to assist his brother.

Thomas and his brother William were a good team although later events were to show that Thomas had the better head for business. At first Thomas's interests were mechanical and he ran that side of the business which consisted of not much more than a book-binding workshop. Very soon, however, his interests were to widen and in 1844 he set up the London branch of the business and the firm of Thomas Nelson and Sons, printers, publishers and booksellers was effectively established two years later. New departments were gradually added and the works at Hope Park in Edinburgh became a substantial book production factory where all types of work associated with book production were carried out save for paper and type making.

The Nelson's timing was perfect as they caught the rising demand for all forms of popular literature but their greatest strength was in reading material for children. Thomas Nelson himself edited a monthly magazine called *The Children's Paper* which had an enormous circulation. His own particular favourite subject was geography and in his treatment of it, in various publications, he was highly innovative. For example it was Nelson who, in addition to measures of latitude and longitude, introduced scale miles into his maps and atlases. Thomas Nelson wrote and edited a number of books himself but his great love was always for atlases.

His talents on the scholastic side of the business did not mean that his early interest in the mechanical side were forgotten for in 1849 he invented a rotary printing press which was shown at the Great Exhibition at Crystal Palace in 1851.

When the Education Acts were passed in the early 1870s Nelson moved quickly to supply the textbooks which he knew would be in demand. Beginning with a series known as the *Royal Readers* he followed that with books on history, geography, English language and literature. From that time forward the school book department became the backbone of the business.

In 1878, by which time there were about 600 employees, the firm suffered a disastrous fire which completely destroyed the Hope Park premises. While the fire was still burning Nelson sat down in a nearby office and began the process of re-building the company. He ordered new machinery from London, Paris and New York and he arranged with other local printers to produce copies of Nelson books. Within days he had arranged to build new stock rooms and, on his own property at St Leonards, new machine rooms were erected. These formed the nucleus of the new establishment at Parkside. Despite the fire the firm was able to carry on its business with scarcely a break. This was due, almost entirely to Thomas Nelson's energy and imagination.

This great energy which he possessed was undoubtedly an asset to him but it was often stretched to its utmost for Nelson was not good at delegating and he carried the burdens of business on his shoulders. This was even more the case after the death of his brother in 1887.

In his later years Thomas Nelson became a director of John Bartholomew and Company who were renowned for their maps. In addition to his printing and publishing interests Thomas Nelson took a lively and very active interest in the Edinburgh financial community and particularly in those organisations concerned with investment in North America. At the time of his death he was a director of the Scottish Provident Institution, the Scottish American Investment Company Ltd, and Western Ranches Ltd. His investment portfolio reflects even wider interest and includes shares in the Arizona Copper Company Ltd, the Edinburgh and San Fransisco Redwood Company Ltd, the Alliance Trust, the Edinburgh American Land Mortgage Company Ltd and many more. He also held several mortgages over properties in the southern states valued at over £20,000. These investment activities met with very mixed fortunes and the timber companies were especially unsuccessful but there is no denying that Nelson got a great deal of enjoyment out of these pioneering investment activities. John Clay, one of his associates in the Scottish American Investment Company Ltd, described Nelson as 'small in stature, physically rather weak but mentally a giant'.

Thomas Nelson did not have much of a public life but he was an active Free Churchman and took a special pride in Free St George's. Indeed the Nelson company was effectively the official publishing house for the Free Church. Its *Monthly Record, Children's Record*, and other official documents were all printed by Thomas Nelson and Sons.

Nelson was also interested in politics and during the American Civil War he, unlike many British businessmen, sided with the North. Having visited the United States several times and set up a branch of the business there he was naturally a great admirer of American political institutions and business enterprise. In British politics Nelson was a Liberal and ultimately a strong supporter of Gladstone.

Nelson did not marry until he was 40 years of age and, about that time, he purchased a valuable property adjoining the Queen's Park in Edinburgh where he built the mansion house of St Leonards. A few months before his death he purchased a beautiful residential estate on the shores of Loch Etive. In his will, in addition to provisions for his family he made substantial bequests to the Free Church and to a wide range of local charities most of which were involved in the relief of sickness and destitution.

CHARLES W MUNN

SOURCES

Unpublished

SRO: SC 70/1/316, Inventory
SC 70/4/265, Will

Published

Clay, J, *My Life on the Range*, Oklahoma, 1962

Glasgow Herald, 21/10/1892

Grieves Scrapbooks, Vol 5

Jackson, W Turrentine, *The Enterprising Scot. Investors in the American West after 1873*, Edinburgh, 1968

Kerr, W G, *Scottish Capital on the American Credit Frontier*, Austin, Texas, 1976

The Paper and Printing Trades Journal, December 1892

The Scotsman, 21/10/1892

The Times, 21/10/1892

Alexander George PIRIE,

Paper manufacturer; b. c 1836, Newhills, Aberdeenshire, s. of Francis Pirie, paper manufacturer and Euphemia Hogarth; m. (1) 30/10/1861, Jane Mary, d. of Thomas Hogarth, cotton manufacturer; 1 d.; (2) 10/1/1867, Barbara Hill, d. of David Watson; 2 s., 2 d.; Ch & MD, Alexander Pirie & Sons, paper manufacturer, Aberdeen; d. 13/1/1904, Stoneywood, Newhills; g/v UK estate: £140,719 2s 11d.

Alexander George Pirie, elder son of Francis Pirie, paper manufacturer, was born at Waterton House, Newhills, near Aberdeen in 1836. He was educated at Rugby and Cambridge University but left without graduating owing to the poor state of his father's health and in 1856 entered the family paper manufacturing business, Alexander Pirie & Sons, at Stoneywood, situated by the River Don five miles north west of Aberdeen.

His father and his uncle, Alexander Pirie II, sons of the firm's founder, had begun a programme of expansion in 1848 when the Stoneywood factory was still a relatively modest concern with only two papermaking machines and a labour force of 180 persons. Two additional papermaking machines were installed at Stoneywood and an old cotton mill nearer Aberdeen, the Woodside works, was acquired in 1856 and used for preliminary operations such as sorting and cutting rags. In 1862 another old cotton mill, the Union Works, near the centre of Aberdeen was converted into an envelope making factory. By 1869 output of paper of all kinds exceeded 3,000 tons a year, including one million envelopes per day produced at the Union Works. The total number of employees exceeded 2,000. Meanwhile in keeping with the larger size of the firm it had been decided in 1868 to constitute the firm into an unincorporated joint stock company with a nominal capital of £360,000 in £50 shares.

The papermaking operations of the Piries were also extended in another direction, along the Dee valley. In 1856 a paper mill was purchased at Peterculter by the River Dee, seven miles west of Aberdeen, and although the mill was launched as an independent concern, the Culter Mills Paper Co Ltd, in 1865, the Pirie family retained a substantial financial interest in the firm for a number of years and until 1883 Alexander Pirie & Sons acted as sole selling agent for the Culter Mills papers.

A G Pirie played an important part in these developments. He was made a partner in Alexander Pirie & Sons soon after joining the firm and when Alexander Pirie II decided to play a less active part in management and take up residence on the Continent at the end of the 1850s, A G Pirie became the leading managerial figure. He also became the first chairman of Culter Mills Paper Co Ltd.

The death of his father in August 1870 left him the largest shareholder in Alexander Pirie & Sons, owning one third of the capital, and this dominant position was basically unchanged until the company, which had been officially registered as a limited company in 1881, was reconstituted in 1898. Throughout the period, with one brief interlude, he remained a director of the firm. Yet soon after his father's death he ceased to play a very active part in management and for nearly 20 years he devoted himself mainly to other pursuits, generally residing on his sporting estate at Lechmelm, Ross-shire or at his house in London. A dispute with other directors shortly before his father's death and a subsequent unsuccessful lawsuit against his fellow director and step brother, F L Pirie, may have influenced his decision but it is significant that he also resigned as chairman of Culter Mills Paper Co Ltd, where there was no similar friction, on the grounds that in the future he intended being absent from Aberdeen for some time.

During the 1870s and early 1880s Alexander Pirie & Sons continued to expand though at a more modest rate. Two additional, wider, papermaking machines were installed and by 1887 output had increased to 5,600 tons a year. The most striking improvement perhaps was in envelope production which reached 12 million envelopes a week by 1879 and a few years later it was claimed that the firm was accounting for a third of total UK production. Profits too were buoyant. They exceeded £50,000 a year for nine years in succession from 1874 to 1882 and the dividend declared on the share capital of £360,000 averaged just under 11.5% a year from 1874 to 1888.

However in the face of increasingly fierce competition from other British producers and from abroad the profitability of the company deteriorated rapidly towards the end of the 1880s. Profits fell to £30,439 in 1889, barely exceeded £2,000 the following year, and in 1891 there was a loss of nearly £7,000 on the year's operations.

In this changed atmosphere A G Pirie resumed active management of the firm and from 1891 until his death in 1904 he served as chairman of the company. He embarked immediately upon a major improvement programme extending over some ten years. By 1898 nearly £60,000 had been spent on new plant and buildings quite apart from normal repairs. The bulk of this had been found from reviving profits but the need for further capital to complete the programme was a major reason for the decision to reconstruct the company in 1898 and raise its nominal capital to £1,000,000 of which £200,000 was to be obtained by issuing preference shares to the general public. The shares were heavily oversubscribed and after the debenture holders in the old company, mainly members of the Pirie family, had received substantial cash payments there remained an appreciable sum available to permit a further investment of £65,000 over the next five years.

As a result of the modernisation programme output was increased - initially to some 7,000 tons a year - the office was enlarged, modern facilities such as electric light and a telephone exchange were installed, and costs were reduced by various means including the use of fuel economisers and higher pressure boilers. However one of the principal objectives of the investment was to improve the quality of the firm's products. The various types of paper made - principally fine writing paper, drawing paper, good quality ivory boards for visiting cards and menus, and paper for cheques, charts, envelopes, and books - were designed to sell in the middle and upper spectrum of the industry's price range. Yet A G Pirie consciously decided to move 'up market' and concentrate production still further on high quality products where profit margins were more generous.

Special attention was paid to the finishing processes, especially those which gave the paper a very fine surface, and the firm's paper finishing facilities were completely reorganised. A calender house 100 feet wide and 200 feet long was constructed which housed among other equipment a new Eck Calender from Germany with ten rollers capable of imparting a fine smooth surface to paper 100 inches wide. Even more impressive was the new four storey Finishing House 300 feet long and 240 feet wide costing more than £32,000. As part of this policy the output of tub-sized paper was deliberately increased by some 25% at the expense of the cheaper engine-sized paper and it was estimated in 1902 that this measure alone increased profit margins by £10 per ton of paper sold.

The expansion of exports was an important part of the strategy for increasing sales of high quality papers. Pirie's papers already possessed an international reputation. A G Pirie strengthened and extended this overseas network and in 1902 he was able to boast to shareholders that no other paper manufacturer was represented 'either by a resident or travelling representative to the extent your company is in every civilized country on the globe - Cuba and the Philippines for the moment excepted'. As a result of this policy exports nearly doubled between 1879, the first year for which statistics have survived, and 1903, whilst their share of total sales increased from 14% to 24%.

The fruits of A G Pirie's efforts were apparent in the annual balance sheets. Profits recovered rapidly once the investment programme had begun. In 1895 they exceeded £35,000 for the first time since 1888 and over the next five years averaged nearly £39,000 a year. Even in the years immediately after 1900 when the economy was less buoyant profits exceeded £31,000 each year from 1901 to 1904.

At his death in 1904 Alexander Pirie & Sons was one of the leading paper manufacturers in Great Britain and probably the most important producer in Scotland. A G Pirie had made a powerful contribution towards establishing this position. In the late 1850s and in the 1860s he was one of the main architects in transforming a relatively modest local business into a large prosperous firm with a national reputation, and from the beginning of the 1890s, when financial disaster was looming, he took control once again and spent his remaining years restoring and reconstructing the ailing giant to a condition near to its former vigour.

Pirie took little part in public affairs and held no public offices, but was keenly interested in political events. He was a staunch Tory and strongly supported the campaign for Tariff Reform.

He had artistic tastes and was a collector of precious stones and paintings. In 1901 he presented 11 drawings and etchings by Queen Victoria and Prince Albert to the city of Aberdeen, some of which are currently housed in the City Art Gallery.

He was a keen sportsman, devoting his leisure hours to yachting, hunting, and cricket. He had a sporting estate at Lechmelm, Ross-shire and played cricket for Aberdeenshire, excelling as a batsman.

A G Pirie died on 13 January 1904 at his residence in Stoneywood, Aberdeenshire. He was survived by his second wife Barbara Hill Pirie, daughter of a Glasgow merchant, and two sons and two married daughters - Helen Mary Russell, the wife of a London stockbroker, and Ada Isobel Gully who married the son of the Speaker of the House of Commons. The two sons, Francis David Pirie and George Laurence Pirie, were both directors of the family firm when he died. His first wife was Jane Mary Hogarth, daughter of a former Aberdeenshire cotton manufacturer. Their only child, Jenny Euphemia, married the Rev James Philby.

In addition to his estate at Lechmelm, Ross-shire, Pirie held a long lease on a house in Queen's Gate, London, visiting both properties on frequent occasions. His principal residence in later years was Stoneywood House, Aberdeenshire. He left an estate valued at £141,000.

J Neville Bartlett

SOURCES

Unpublished

Sheriff's Court, Aberdeen:
   1/37/125, Inventory
   1/36/149, Will

Published

Aberdeen Journal, 14/1/1901, 18/2/1901

Bartlett, J Neville, 'Alexander Pirie & Sons of Aberdeen and the Expansion of the British Paper Industry, c 1860-1914', *Business History*, Vol XXII, No 1, 1980

Bartlett, J Neville, 'Investment for Survival: Culter Mills Paper Co Ltd, 1865-1914', *Northern Scotland*, Vol V, No 1, 1982

Bremner, D, *The Industries of Scotland*, Edinburgh, 1869

British and Colonial Printer and Stationer, 1/12/1879

Court of Session Cases, Third Series, Vol XI, Edinburgh, 1873, Alexander George Pirie v Frances L Pirie, 19/7/1873

Cruickshank, J, *Alexander Pirie and Sons Ltd, Paper Manufacturers, Stoneywood and Waterton Works, 1770-1945*, Aberdeen, 1945

Papermaker and British Paper Trade Journal, 16 Sept. 1901

Scotsman, 15 Jan. 1904

World's Paper Trade Review, 6 July 1913

David Couper THOMSON,

Newspaper proprietor; b. 5/8/1861, Dundee, s. of William Thomson, merchant and shipowner, and Margaret Couper; m. Margaret, d. of John McCulloch, Ballantrae; 3 d., Ch and MD, D C Thomson & Co Ltd, Dundee; d. 12/10/1954; g/v estate: £225,433 10s 10d.

David Couper Thomson devoted 70 years of his long life to the development of his newspaper empire. When he died in 1954 at the advanced age of 93, the name D C Thomson was indistinguisable in the minds of a large readership from 'Oor Wullie', 'The Broons', 'Black Bob', 'Desperate Dan', and many other characters. In his lifetime Thomson demonstrated an extra-ordinary ability to provide the public with what it wanted and achieved a virtually saturation readership for his many publications.

When David Thomson was born in Dundee in 1861 no-one could have guessed that he would spend the larger part of his adult life in the newspaper business. His father William Thomson was then a successful merchant clothier who also extended his interests into shipping. His father established the Thomson Line of steamships which traded extensively to North America and the Mediterranean. It was to be expected that the son of a successful businessman would follow in his father's footsteps. Indeed that is what happened for after basic schooling at Newport Primary School and then Dundee High School, David Couper Thomson entered the family shipping business in 1877 at the age of 16. Since his father's business was in steamships young David was despatched to Glasgow to undertake some engineering training. He did not indeed return full-time to the business in Dundee until 1884 when at the age of 23 he was taken into partnership with his father in the shipping business.

David Thomson's direct involvement in his father's shipping business was not to last for long. During the 1870s his father had acquired three Dundee newspapers as part of his expanding business. He owned the *Dundee Courier*, the *Argus*, and the *Weekly News*. Consequently in 1886 William Thomson established a new firm that of W & D C Thomson to operate his newspaper interests. Then aged 25 the young D C Thomson was given the responsibility of operating the new concern. Two years later David was joined by his younger brother Frederick to share that responsibility.

The first phase of the development of the D C Thomson newspaper empire began with the active promotion of the two local papers, the *Courier* and the *Argus*, as outspoken and opinionated publications on local affairs. But the more innovative aspect of their involvement was in the acquisition of a tired and ineffective Tariff Reform publication called *My Weekly*. This was quickly regenerated and converted into a working girl's weekly magazine. With the unerring eye for a market niche that was to become the hallmark of the Thomson empire the two brothers quickly saw that the local market among the mill girls was ripe for that kind of publication. In their first 20 years the Thomson brothers developed a successful recipe for their publications focussing on popular culture, homily, morality and romanticism, always stressing respectability and responsibility. This formula carried their publications to a wide readership and by the end of the century the Thomson newspaper empire was outgrowing its initial premises at 34 Lindsay Road.

The second, and bold, step in developing the Thomson business in newspapers, came in 1905. In that year a new company D C Thomson & Co Ltd was formed with a capital of £60,000. This was a private limited company with the capital divided in

£10 shares. The father William Thomson and his two sons David and Frederick held all but four of the shares divided equally among them. The other four shares were held by each of the wives of the three Thomsons together with Francis Thomas Mudie. It is clear that by 1906 with David Thomson at the age of 45 and his brother two years younger, that their father had largely withdrawn from any active interest in the newspaper side of the family enterprises and that the brothers were in complete command.

The decade before the First World War was one of active expansion for the Thomsons. In 1906 the firm moved to new and larger premises in Dundee in Meadowside. By 1913 offices had been opened in Manchester to serve the North of England; and in 1915 the Thomsons opened premises in Glasgow at the same time as introducing the *Sunday Post*. No one could have known at that point in time how important the *Post* was to become in the development of the Thomson business. This very vigorous expansion of the publishing and newspaper business clearly placed strains upon the two brothers. Tragically the younger brother Frederick died in 1917 and in the midst of the war David found himself in sole control.

Left to himself David Thomson increasingly pursued a line of development in his publications in which his own notably conservative views were given some prominence. While it is rare for a newspaper proprietor's own views to have momentous influence on public affairs D C Thomson did achieve this distinction in 1922. At the end of the war Thomson came to regard Winston Churchill's views with considerable suspicion, and between 1920 and 1922 he mounted a steady campaign of criticism against him. Churchill was indeed unseated in 1922 and it has generally been believed that the anti-Churchill campaign pursued by Thomson in his papers had a significant effect on that outcome. Churchill himself, according to his biographers, certainly believed that to be the case.

Thomson was a man of deeply conservative views and it is also clear that he had considerable local political influence. He was a Deputy Lieutenant of Dundee for more than 50 years and held the position as governor of the University College for more than 60 years. He was also a director of the Dundee Chamber of Commerce and of the Dundee Eye Institution. Even so his personal political views and his deep conservatism had not significantly affected the way in which his business was conducted in terms of employment. The firm was clearly a family firm run on strongly paternalistic and autocratic lines, but the workforces had never been forbidden or prevented from taking part in union affairs. That freedom of membership of unions was to be brought to a dangerous head in the 1926 General Strike. During the Strike many of Thomson's operatives who were members of NATSOPA withdrew their labour in sympathy with the strikers in the heavy industries. Thomson predictably was outraged.

The General Strike had in fact coincided with another major development for D C Thomson. Earlier in 1926 Thomson took over the Dundee business of John Leng & Co who were owners of the rival *Dundee Advertiser*. This brought to an end a protracted period of stiff local competition. As a consquence of the strike Thomson merged the *Advertiser* and the *Courier* into one publication thereafter. Moreover while he had been able to keep his own papers in publication throughout the strike, at least in skeleton form, he now took steps to ensure that his publication would never be upset again.

The cessation of the General Strike was the occasion for D C Thomson to introduce what became known as the 'document'. Thomson agreed to re-employ his NATSOPA printers provided they sign the document which committed them to do a number of things. Anyone wishing re-employment, and signing the document, was obliged to give up his union membership. Moreover he was obliged to tender an apology for having disrupted the work of the paper, and in addition had to promise never to undertake such disruptive activity again. In effect D C Thomson & Co had introduced a non-union shop. Anyone wishing to be employed by Thomson had to be aware that they were only able to be taken on under non-union conditions. It was further made plain that if anyone in Thomson's employment wished to become a member of a trade union then they would have to leave Thomson's in order to do so.

This was the beginning of Thomson's vigorous anti-union posture in operating his newspapers. Not surprisingly a good number of his former employees found the new terms of employment unpalatable and decided not to accept them. A number indeed succeeded in establishing a rival publication called *The Dundee Free Press*. This publicaton was hostile to Thomson and had a lifespan of seven years during which it conducted an active campaign against the position taken by Thomson. An anti-Thomson platform could not however sustain the paper and it closed in the depths of the depression in 1933.

In the aftermath of the General Strike D C Thomson clearly entered a third phase in development as a non-union shop. By 1933 the local union based newspaper opposition had been seen off and David Couper Thomson now in his seventies was making way for the managerial experience of his nephew Harold Thomson. The 1930s in fact inaugurated a phase of remarkable initiative and expansion in the Thomson organisation. In 1932 a new woman's magazine *Secrets* was introduced. There followed in rapid succession in 1933 the *Hotspur*, in 1934 *Family Star*, in 1937 the *Dandy*, and in 1938 the *Beano*. This was a mixture of children's comic strips together with yet more women's magazines. Harold Thomson's influence was notable here and he built the future success of these operations around the managerial and editorial experience of Albert Barnes and the remarkable graphic artist talents of Dudley D

Watkins. It was in this phase too that the *Sunday Post* began to be shaped as a mass readership Sunday publication under the expert guidance of Harold Thomson and Albert Barnes.

As the Second World War commenced the Thomson organisation had laid the foundations for remarkable success with its new generation of children's comics, women's magazines, and its flagship the *Sunday Post*. D C Thomson's influence was to be seen in all these publications. He retained a high degree of anonymity in that no copy ever bore an editor's or journalist's by-line. The organisation itself was reclusive and no one found it easy to meet with or to discuss business with the Thomson management. Characteristically the management was conducted by the small group of family owners together with a small team of loyal specialist managers and designers. This management style developed a remarkably successful formula which by the 1940s was producing over 30 papers and magazines covering all levels of readership from the under fives to the adult population. All the publications whether for children, women, or the more general public, focussed on the popular end of the respectable working class and lower middle class readership. This had been the market area sketched out by David Thomson in the 1880s and was still the mainstay of his vast empire at the end of his life in the early 1950s.

In the end indeed, D C Thomson died as he had lived; fighting the unions for the right to run his empire as he chose with total disregard for the consequences. Although D C Thomson himself no longer ran the day to day business of the publications his views were still adhered to. In March 1952 it was discovered that an operative in the Glasgow office, who had been in their employment since 1921, had been a secret member of NATSOPA since 1939 in complete defiance of the document. The man was dismissed and a major strike action ensued. The STUC blacked the Thomson organisation and soon had the support of more than 47 unions. Widespread disruption of publication, distribution and sale of Thomson papers and magazines followed. So serious was the affair that the government of Winston Churchill ordered an enquiry into the matter. The report heavily criticised D C Thomson's anti-union stance but to no avail. Although the strike was eventually called off there was no reinstatement of the union men in the D C Thomson organisation. Shortly thereafter David Thomson died in 1954 at the advanced age of 93. His non-union citadel was intact and his empire through its newspapers, its women's magazines, and its comics, together with its unique *Sunday Post*, had a saturation circulation in the mass popular market. Few newspaper proprietors had had such a successful career nor one which had made a more profound impact upon the general public.

ANTHONY SLAVEN AND MARIAN QUIGLEY

SOURCES

Unpublished

SRO: SC 45/31/156, Inventory
      SC 45/34/116, Will

Published

The Daily Record, 13/10/1954
Directory of Directors, 1954
Evening Times, 13/10/1954
The Scotsman, 13/10/1954
The Times, 13/10/1954
Who Was Who

Harben James VALENTINE,

Greeting card/postcard manufacturer; b. 6/11/1872, Dundee, s. of William Dobson and Catherine Stone Young; m. Emily Elizabeth Sturrock; 4 s.; Ch, Valentine & Sons Ltd, Dundee; d. 13/3/1949, West Newport, Fife; g/v estate: £35,303 15s 3d.

In 1886, at the age of 13, Harben Valentine joined his father's photographic publishing business in Dundee, which had sidelines in studio portraiture and fancy goods. The firm was founded about 1825 by the subject's grandfather, John Valentine, who began printing on linen. It was then carried on and expanded by his grandfather, James, into lithography, engraving, stationery and fancy goods sales and in 1850 into studio portraiture, adding about 1860, seeking to emulate the success of G W Wilson in Aberdeen, landscape view publishing. This last line was vastly expanded by the subject's father, William Dobson Valentine, who in 1872 married Catherine Stone Young, a full cousin of Joseph Chamberlain. W D Valentine had raised the labour force to around a 100 and extended trade into the whole of the British Isles by the time his son joined the firm.

Harben Valentine's youthful interest was in developing the technical side of the firm's activities and after experiments over a number of years, persisted in owing to the encouragement of Sir James Caird, he had by the late 1890s mastered the collotype and photochrome printing processes, the latter hitherto the secret of a Swiss firm. The collotype process was used to develop a successful new line in photographic souvenir books. In 1898 the firm, in which Harben was taking, because of his father's ill health, a greater share in the day to day management, decided to enter the new field of postcard publishing. This market was to bring a period of incredible expansion as postcards were to become the focus of a worldwide collecting mania. Valentines with its newly developed printing processes was perfectly placed to take advantage of the opportunities and for many years claimed to be the only firm in Britain running the collotype process in a large way.

Harben became managing director in 1900, when the firm was changed from a partnership into a private limited company and the business grew so rapidly under his direction that by 1907, when it became a public company with a share capital of £130,000, the majority of which was controlled by the family, the employees numbered close on a thousand. Most were females, who were paid between 8/- and 12/- for a 50 hour week. Overseas branches were opened in Montreal, New York, South Africa and Australia. About 1900 Valentines Ltd had also taken over their main fancy goods supplier, D A P Anderson of Edinburgh. The Valentine premises in Perth Road, Dundee, originally a building in the garden of the family home, covered the whole site and also subsumed the property next door in a five storey factory building, Westfield Works.

The period of expansion and prosperity was short-lived. American tariffs were introduced to kill off all postcard trade with the USA and a price war developed with the German postcard publishers. Harben Valentine attempted to counteract these misfortunes by developing Christmas card publishing, but the Germans moved into this trade too. However the design of special cards, particularly for the Canadian market and the introduction of children's toy books brought success as did bids to become official postcard publishers to a number of the international trade exhibitions held in London before the First World War. In 1912 annual sales were nearly £100,000 and profits £10,000, but in 1913 no dividend was paid on the ordinary shares. The war years cut postcard production to a trickle and a period of 21 difficult years for the firm began. Although a modest profit on turnover was usually made, the payment of dividends to preference shareholders fell into arrears. The overseas branches were re-arranged on general merchandise lines and later sold off to local management in 1923 but trading connections with them were maintained. Calendar production was successfully introduced during the war and served to counter the catastrophic effect of the Post Office's doubling of postage on postcards in 1918. Harben, having brought his son Ranald into the business in 1919, adopted various stratagems over the next decade in an effort to attain profitability. As earlier new lines were added and in 1928 the birthday card department was opened. Small specialist publishing and stationery firms were bought over, the Simmath Press Ltd in 1923, Gillard, Willett & Co Ltd in 1928, Felix Macauley Ltd and Gold Nibs Ltd of Newhaven, Sussex in 1929. Many of these moves were not particularly successful. The Simmath Press, which published tourist guidebooks was disposed of to a newly reconstituted company in 1927 and the Valentine Pen Co, the successor of Gold Nibs Ltd, rarely made a profit until it was sold off about 1937 to the Parker Pen Co. A major adjustment of the share capital was undertaken in 1926 as part of the effort to overcome Valentine's difficulties, the end result of which was to raise the capital to £130,000. Gradually over the following years prospects improved. New warehouse space was acquired in 1927 as the calendar and greeting card trade developed. By 1932 prospects were bright and 1936, which was Harben Valentine's jubilee year with the firm, brought a record profit. In that year employees numbered 800 and the wages bill was £1,800 per week. In his jubilee celebration dinner speech he took particular pride in the number of long serving employees, but recognised that success and growth were bringing a challenge to the family control of the firm, although he still controlled the direction of the business despite the number of specialists who were having to be brought in. His sons Ranald and Douglas were now assisting him. The former had become a director in 1923 and was in 1940 appointed assistant managing director.

In 1937 a new factory was begun to replace the Westfield Works on the new Kingsway West industrial estate, the first to be started there. At the outbreak of war the Kingsway factory was taken over by the Ministry of Supply and the firm was restricted to producing patriotic greetings and postcards at its Perth Road premises. In 1938 sales had reached an all time record of £306,000 including the sale of some 40 million postcards, with a profit of £30,000. By this time Woolworths was accounting for about a quarter of the company's trade and Valentines claimed to be supplying a quarter of the entire British greeting card and postcard market.

Towards the end of the war, Harben's health began to fail and although he remained chairman and joint managing director until his death he was now taking little part in the ordinary running of the company. While he had an old fashioned paternalistic attitude towards his workforce, almost the last act of his association wih the firm was the setting up of a 'Joint Consultative Committee to discuss matters relating to human relationships'.

Unlike his grandfather, who was a staunch member of the Congregational church and inveterate espouser of public causes and his father, who involved himself in local Tory politics, he took little part in public affairs and concentrated his entire interest on his company. His early mastery of the printing processes for the mechanical reproduction of the photographic views, which were the firm's main product was the chief reason for its expansion and success. His development and introduction of various classes of greetings cards were the means by which he maintained the company's momentum. For 30 years until shortly before 1939 he holidayed every winter in Norway in order to indulge in the national sport of cross country skiing.

When he died almost two thirds of his personal estate of £35,303 was accounted for by his 9,771 shares, in Valentine & Sons Ltd whose total authorised capital was by this time £205,000 of which £175,000 was issued.

ROBERT N SMART

SOURCES

Unpublished

Cupar Sheriff Court:
  Register of Inventories, 1949
  Register of Deeds, Trust disposition, 1949
St Andrew's University Library:
  Valentine & Sons Ltd, View registers 1878-1967

Published

British Journal of Photography, 'A visit to Messrs Valentine & Sons printing works', 12/3/1886
Dundee Courier and Advertiser, 14/3/1949
Dundee Directory
Dundee Public Library: Newspaper cuttings books
Dundee Yearbook
Gernsheim, Helmut, 'Through five generations, Valentine & Sons Ltd, Dundee', *Functional Photography*, 1952
Glasgow Herald, 14/3/1949
The Photographic News, 'At Messrs Valentine & Sons, Dundee', Vol XXXV, 13/11/1891
Scotsman, 14/3/1949
Scrymgeour, Norval, *A Visit to Valentines*, Dundee, c 1907
Sobieszek, R A, 'Messrs James Valentine & Sons, Dundee', *Image*, 14, 1971
Sobieszek, R A, 'A further note on Messrs James Valentine & Sons, Dundee', *Image*, 14, 1971

Other Manufactures

The official designation of a group of activities as 'Other Manufacturing Industries' indicates that even a detailed classification system can be defeated by some lines of production which do not relate easily to major and easily identifiable manufacturing groups. Thus the production of brushes and brooms, toys, games and sports equipment, while important in themselves do not relate easily to metal manufacturing or to engineering, although metals and engineering techniques might well figure in their manufacture. Deciding how to describe a particular industry can therefore be quite difficult. The standard industrial classification, for example, includes linoleum, plastics and floor coverings in the other manufacturing industries group. In Scotland however since linoleum was based on a hemp backcloth, and floor coverings were dominantly carpets, these activities were surveyed in our textile group of entrepreneurs in Volume I of this study. Conversely, a welding manufacturer who might have been included in our engineering sector in Volume I has been surveyed here in the other manufacturing sector. This type of flexibility clearly shows that this group is a 'catch all' category, and products may be reclassified to other areas of activity for particular purposes.

When the linoleum and floor covering group is excluded from this sector, the remaining lines of production in Scotland concentrate on rubber, brushes and brooms, toys and sports goods, and other miscellaneous industries. As a group these have always been small employers. In Scotland in 1951 the sector provided jobs for only 15,145 persons. Rubber production alone provided for 10,836 jobs, and this overwhelming dominance is reflected in the biographies included in this set of studies. All other areas of employment were very small, even toys and sports equipment providing work for just over 1,000 persons.

It will be evident from these comments that this sector presents researchers with considerable difficulty in classification and selection. Anomalies exist even within particular groups of activities. Rubber products show this problem very clearly; the manufacture of golf balls can be classified as 'rubber products' and may be included therefore under rubber companies directly or within the group of sports equipment manufacturers. The matter is further complicated by the diverse nature of production among the rubber products firms. The Caledonian Rubber Works in Edinburgh made waterproof clothing, rubber belting, but also golf balls; similarly, M D Thornton & Co which patented and manufactured a rubber hot water bottle, also made rubber belting and waterproof garments, and not only manufactured golf balls but produced golf clubs in addition. Indeed all the rubber firms had quite a diversified production range, since rubber lent itself to many uses; most manufactured footwear and in addition had their 'mechanical departments' which concentrated on industrial belting, hoses and other products.

Rubber manufacture was indeed a significant Scottish industry, although it developed here largely through a loop-hole in patent law. It was an American, Charles Goodyear, who laid the foundation for the modern rubber industry. In 1839 he discovered that if he heated the gummy milky latex of the Brazilian tree, *Hevea Brasiliensis*, with sulphur, the latex coagulated into a stable substance now called rubber. A year later, in England, Thomas Hancock made the same discovery of the 'vulcanising' process. Hancock patented his process in England, but overlooked the fact that a separate patent was required to protect his process, or ones derived from it, in Scotland. Consequently, in Scotland, early experimenters with 'gutta percha' like the Dick brothers, were able to develop the manufacture of rubber footwear without hindrance from the Hancock patent. From that flying start the Dicks developed one of the most extensive rubber manufacturing businesses in Scotland, selling their products through a network of warehouses and depots in British and European cities.

The manufacture of rubber boots, rubber soled footwear, and rubber overshoes developed very rapidly both in Britain and in the United States. Indeed the business expanded so vigorously in the United States that promoters there saw the opportunity of entering both the British and European market by exploiting the loop-hole in Hancock's patent. Consequently in 1855, an American, Henry Lee Norris came to Edinburgh to establish the North British Rubber Company. This company exploited the Scottish patent for Charles Goodyear's vulcanising process. It was soon a major European manufacturer of rubber footwear and quickly attracted native Scottish investment. The American link was sustained when in 1869, William Erskine Bartlett, a relation of Norris, came to Edinburgh and soon took over the management of the business. He made a significant contribution in developing a patented system for fixing solid and pneumatic tyres to wheel rims. It was especially successful in being applied to bicycle tyres. The North British Rubber Company grew to being second only in size to Dunlop in Britain, and was among Europe's leading rubber companies as well as being among the largest manufacturing employers in Edinburgh.

The North British Rubber Company was in many ways the exception among the rubber product companies. Most others were relatively small in scale. Their relative smallness was in many ways related to the special uses made of the rubber itself. One of the most successful specialist applications proved to be in the manufacture of golf balls. Not surprisingly, St Andrews was a prominent centre for both the manufacture of balls and of clubs. The manufacture of golf balls in St Andrews dates from at least the early eighteenth century, and by the 1840s the town had an envied reputation in the manufacture of 'featheries', balls made by tightly packing feathers into a stitched leather cover. These were expensive products and in the 1840s the production of 'gutta percha' encouraged experimentation. The first balls manufactured from rubber were smooth, and while they were not seriously affected by wet weather, as were the featheries, they were erratic in flight. It was quickly discovered that notching the surface made it aerodynamically much superior, and it is reputed that Robert Forgan of St Andrews was the first to introduce the new rubber golf ball with a regular pattern of indentations on the surface. This was initially achieved by hand hammering. It was not long however before moulds were devised to transform the economy and performance of the golf ball. Brand names also soon appeared as rival makers sought to establish their position in a new and expanding market. Among the makers of golf balls there also were the specialist manufacturers of golf clubs; the Forgans, the McEwans, and the Patricks were leading makers in the nineteenth century. Of these only Forgan survived into the second half of the present century.

Somewhat later, a further development in the use of rubber for golf ball manufacture gave an opportunity to another enterprising man, John Letters. Rubber cored balls began to replace the solid rubber version around the turn of the century. John Letters was employed in Glasgow by Miller and Taylor and was the manager of the golf ball section, learning the new trade. After the First World War he set up a partnership in 1918 to exploit the expanding golf ball market. Once established he rapidly added golf club manufacture to the making of balls and other equipment. He was among the first in Scotland to concentrate on using steel shafts as distinct from hickory for his clubs, and later he began forging the heads for his own products. Letters also pioneered linking the clubs to the names of distinguished professional players; his 'Fred Daly' club was the first in a long line of such leading models.

John Letters Company was eventually taken over by the Dunlop Rubber Co and was ultimately closed by that organisation in 1983. However the family repurchased the name and re-established a new and smaller company John Letters & Co (1918) Ltd which today continues the famous name. As in so many other areas of Scottish business, the family remained a powerful force in the making of the wide variety of products and companies grouped within the 'other manufacturing' industries.

ANTHONY SLAVEN

William Erskine BARTLETT,

Rubber manufacturer; b. 1830, Chicopee Falls, Massachusetts, USA; m. Josephine Hoxie; 4 d.; MD, North British Rubber Company, Edinburgh ; d. 4/5/1900, Bridge of Allan; g/v estate: £51,795 12s 10d.

A relative of William Erskine Bartlett, Henry Lee Norris, was managing director of the North British Rubber Company from its foundation in 1855 by American businessmen. The firm was located in Edinburgh in order to use the Scottish patent for Charles Goodyear's vulcanization process which enabled the company to circumvent Thomas Hancock's control of the English industry. Although it was smaller than the Manchester-based Charles MacIntosh and Company, the Scottish firm was among the leading European manufacturers of rubber footwear. From the 1860s ownership moved steadily into Scottish hands but the American link was apparent when Bartlett arrived as Norris' assistant in 1869. Within a year Norris had retired and Bartlett became general manager and in 1872 he joined the board at the insistence of the remaining American shareholders for whom he acted as proxy at shareholders' meetings.

Between 1870 and 1898 Bartlett was the dominant influence on the daily operations and development of the company. He travelled widely in Europe and North America, particularly when the firm extended its agency system during the 1870s and 1880s. At the same time he supervised the expansion of the company's wholesale and retail warehouses in Glasgow, Manchester, Leeds, Liverpool, Newcastle and London. Bartlett represented the firm in the regular negotiations over prices and discounts among the leading European footwear manufacturers. Agreements were frequent but unstable due to the volatile price of rubber and the seasonal demand for footwear. The North British Rubber Company's sales increased from £164,000 in 1869 to £309,323 in 1887 when its capital of £195,000 was fully paid up. However the original constitution restricted the raising of further capital and in 1888 the company was voluntarily wound up with Bartlett acting as the liquidator. A new North British Rubber Company was formed with authorised capital of £350,000, of which £313,190 was paid up; Bartlett received an honorarium of £200 for his part in the reorganisation. Sales of footwear and mechanical goods increased and the refinancing also allowed the development of carriage and bicycle tyre production in response to the rapid growth of the bicycle industry.

In 1870 Bartlett patented a design for cushioning vibration within steel tyres on traction engines and he was one of many innovators working on tyre designs during the next two decades. The principal breakthrough was John Boyd Dunlop's rediscovery of the pneumatic tyre in 1888, but there were many problems in developing practical and reliable tyres. At first tyres were cemented in place or attached using wires and bolts and, with punctures a frequent occurrence, such methods proved cumbersome. In 1889 Bartlett patented a 'clincher' rim design for solid tyres and in the following year he improved the design and applied it to pneumatic tyres. This remains the basic bicycle tyre design: on each side the hard rubber bead dovetailed into an inturned metal rim of the wheel and, thus, the tyre was held in place under tension.

His patents placed Bartlett among the leading innovators in the European and American tyre industries and his subsequent career was largely concerned with exploiting the 'clincher' patent during the bicycle 'craze'. He had full control over the resulting litigation in Britain, France, Germany and the United States. The results were mixed. A German patent was invalidated in 1893. In Britain a successful suit against Charles MacIntosh and Co Ltd confirmed the 'clincher' patent in 1894. However the main rival patent was held by the Gormully and Jeffrey Company of Chicago. Between 1894 and 1898 a lengthy case against the American firm's British sales, culminating in a House of Lords judgment, confirmed the Bartlett patent in Britain. Meanwhile an American court gave precedence to the Gormully and Jeffrey Company, thus ending the North British Rubber Company's royalties from the USA. Bartlett's French patent was worked by Rochet and Company of Paris from 1891 to 1896 when the patent was transferred to the newly-formed Compagnie Francaise de Caoutchouc Manufacture. In the firm's assets the 'clincher' patent was valued at 800,000 francs (around £28,000) but attempts to sell the patent failed and it was invalidated by a French court in 1897. Subsequently the North British Rubber Company wrote down its shareholdings in the French firm which was wound up in 1900.

In April 1896, well before the House of Lords case, the British patent was sold to the Pneumatic Tyre Company, later the Dunlop Rubber Company, for £196,000. This purchase completed the Pneumatic Tyre Company's control over the principal British tyre patents and the firm brought numerous patent suits to establish its influence and royalty income. The 'clincher' patent expired in 1904 and in eight years the North British Rubber Company paid £173,316 in royalties to the Dunlop Rubber Company. In the short-term the sale of the patent was profitable and it was partly vindicated by the collapse of the bicycle 'craze'. Bartlett received an honorarium of £5,000 and his share of a 50% special dividend from the sale of the patent. However the sale reflected a cautious approach to tyre production compared to the Dunlop interests.

In 1897 the North British Rubber Company rejected proposals for a merger or take-over from the Morgan and Wright Company, a leading US tyre firm.

Bartlett's ill-health forced him into semi-retirement early in 1898 although he was still nominally the managing director. He died at Bridge of Allan on 4 May 1900 leaving a gross personal estate of £51,795 12s 0d which, after an annuity to his widow, was divided equally among his four daughters. The estate was rather small because of recent financial losses; his family continued as shareholders in the Edinburgh firm.

Bartlett's role covered all aspects of the company's affairs although he is most remembered for his technical contribution. Under his control the firm's sales increased to £723,372 in 1900 when the workforce was 3,000 and the firm remained among the industry leaders in Europe. Its sales were divided almost evenly between footwear, mechanical goods and tyres by 1900. The increasing competition in the industry was reflected in the firm's average profit/sales ratio which declined from 20.1% in the 1870s to 11.1% in the 1890s. However, dividends still averaged 18.2%, not including the special dividend, in the 1890s.

MICHAEL J FRENCH

SOURCES

Unpublished

SRO: SC 70/1/391, Inventory
  SC 70/4/322, Will
Springfield City Library, Massachusetts: 'Springfield Families'
Uniroyal Ltd, Newbridge: North British Rubber Company Records, (National Register of Archives, Scotland survey, no. 2196); now with Gates Rubber, Heathall, Dumfries

Published

British Library, Patent Office, London, *Index to the Illustrated Offcial Journal (Patents) Illustrated Official Journal (Patents)*, 1870-1900

Bremner, David, *The Industries of Scotland: Their Rise, Progress and Present Condition*, Glasgow, 1869, reprinted Newton Abbot, 1969

Burton, Walter E, *The Story of Tire Beads and Tires*, Maidenhead, 1984

Ducros, Arthur, *Wheels of Fortune - a Salute to Pioneers*, London, 1938

Harrison, A E, 'The Competitiveness of the British Cycle Industry, 1890-1914', *Economic History Review*, 2nd series, Vol XXII, No 2, August 1969

Jones, Geoffrey, 'The Growth and Performance of British Multinational Firms before 1939: The Case of Dunlop', *Economic History Review*, 2nd series, Vol XXXVII, No 1, February 1984

The India Rubber and Gutta Percha and Electrical Trades Journal, 14/5/1900

Payne, Peter, *Rubber and Railways in the nineteenth century*, Liverpool, 1961

Reports of Patent, Design and Trade Market Cases, Vols 3-17, 1886-1900

Thompkins, Eric, *The History of the Pneumatic Tyre*, Dunlop Archive Project, 1981

Woodruff, William, 'Early Entrepreneurial Behaviour in Relation to Costs and Prices', *Oxford Economic Papers*, new series, Vol V, 1953

Woodruff, William, 'The American Origins of Scottish Industry', *Scottish Journal of Political Economy*, Vol II, 1955

Woodruff, William, *The Rise of the British Rubber Industry in the Nineteenth Century*, Liverpool, 1958

William Ewing BIRRELL,

India rubber manufacturer, b. 31/12/1854, Lanark, s. of William Birrell, insurance broker and Sara Tenent Reid; m. c 1879, Christina Pender Mollison; 3 s., 1 d.; Ch, The Clyde Rubberworks Co Ltd; d. 24/10/1926, Glasgow; g/v estate: £36,107.

William Ewing Birrell's origins were far removed from the manufacture of rubber the activity which was to make his name in the Glasgow business community. His father was a partner in the insurance brokers business of William Ewing & Co in Glasgow. After schooling the young William Ewing Birrell entered the partnership in 1871 at the age of 16. Five years later his father died and in 1876 he himself became a partner in the insurance brokers business.

William Birrell's transition from insurance broking to rubber and asbestos manufacturing began in 1883. In that year in an agreement with William Jones and R B Black the Clyde Rubber Co was formed to carry on the manufacture of 'all goods of caoutchouc or India rubber, gutta-percha etc'. The capital was £25,000 in £10 shares. One thousand of these shares were issued of which William Ewing Birrell held 977 in his own name and his wife another 9. Jones and Black held 5 shares each. The office of the company was initially established in Bothwell Street in September 1883 but by the end of the year had removed to Clyde Street, Port Dundas, where the works were established. The company was named the Clyde Rubberworks Co.; William Ewing Birrell was the sole director, but initially he left the running of the works presumably to Jones and Black, while he continued in his business as an insurance broker. He did not withdraw from insurance broking till 1895 at which point he moved into the active management of his rubber company. Even then he remained a member of the Association of Underwriters and Insurance Brokers of Glasgow.

The Clyde Rubberworks Co was established to meet the growing demand on industrial Clydeside for sheeting, belting, tubing, valves, hoses, cord, packing and flooring materials. The combination of asbestos and the recently utilised India rubber, gave products which were robust, resistant to heat, and flexible. Another significant advantage was that India rubber did not harden in cold conditions and was therefore ideally suited for use in belts to drive all types of machinery in mills, mines and engineering shops, as well as being employed in agricultural activities. The company also supplied hoses and asbestos products to the shipyards and vacuum brake hoses for railway engines.

The Clyde Rubberworks Co Ltd was the first of its kind to develop these products in the Glasgow area. By 1900 Birrell had extended his markets for his products throughout Britain with offices in London, Manchester, Birmingham and Newcastle. Some entry

had also been made to the Australian market and Birrell had offices in both Sydney and Melbourne. Even so the scale of activity was not large. The valuation of the property and assets of the Clyde Rubber Co in 1908 was reported at £30,133. The annual average net profit between 1908 and 1912 was £3,325.

By 1912 the company had begun to outgrow the capacity of the original Port Dundas works and there was some thought of entering into the manufacture of rubber tyres. This was not taken up, but the company did plan to establish new and more extended premises at Renfrew. A site of over five acres was acquired at Porterfield Road in Renfrew and the new works were constructed with access to railway sidings. At that time a further 1,000 shares of £10 each were issued to help finance the construction; William Ewing Birrell took 752 of these while his general manager W McAdam Sharp took a further 234. In addition the company issued £15,000 worth of 6% first mortgage redeemable debentures, these secured by a trust deed over the works at Port Dundas and on the new plant at Renfrew. The new premises were built at a cost of some £17,000.

The establishment of the new works permitted the Clyde Rubberworks Co Ltd to meet the demands made upon it during the First World War. The management of the company remained firmly in William Ewing Birrell's hands and all the market demand of the company appeared to be satisfied through the new arrangements. By 1925 the Renfrew works were valued at £21,335 for machinery and fixed plant and the movable assets at £11,318. Throughout its existence the Clyde Rubberworks Co had remained as essentially a relatively small scale family business filling a specialised niche in the rubber products market. William Ewing Birrell had no technical expertise in this area of production, but he did have financial and managerial skills to place behind his technical staff. His interests in insurance and in investment extended to his taking shares in the British Borneo Para Rubber Co of which he became a director. He had lesser shareholdings in the Edinburgh Rubber Estates Ltd and in El Palmar Rubber Estates. One of the great problems in the natural rubber products industry was that supplies and prices of India rubber were greatly volatile. Birrell's involvement in these companies would at least to some extent have given him information on price movements necessary for the conduct of his manufacturing business.

In his public life William Ewing Birrell played a role on the executive of the committee which planned and ran the Great International Exhibition in Glasgow in 1901. In the following year he was appointed as a Justice of the Peace for the County of the City of Glasgow, and played an active role in this office. In recreation he was a yachtsman and a member of the Clyde Corinthian Yacht Club and of the Royal Clyde Yacht Club; he had been an active sailor since his boyhood and owned and raced his own yachts. When he died in 1926 William Ewing Birrell was 71 and had been ailing for many years with heart trouble. This, however, had not prevented him from keeping actively involved in his business. He was still chairman of his own company at his death leaving a personal estate of £36,107; £12,535 of this represented his shareholding in the company he had founded.

ANTHONY SLAVEN

SOURCES

Unpublished

The Clyde Rubber Co Ltd: Strathclyde Regional Archives, BT2/1283
SRO: SC 36/48/382, Inventory
SC 36/51/213, Will

Published

The Bailie, 21/1/1903
Directory of Directors
Glasgow Post Office Directories
India Rubber and Gutta Percha Trades Journal, 21/1/1900

William CURRIE,

India rubber manufacturer; b. c.1840, near Edinburgh, s. of John Currie, calico printer and Helen Sharpe; m. Catherine MacGregor Bryce; 5 s., 1 d.; Founder and proprietor of Wm Currie & Co, East India Rubber Manufacturers, Edinburgh; d. 2/11/1928, Edinburgh; g/v estate: £323,561 16s 1d.

William Currie was founder and proprietor of the Caledonian Rubber Works, Edinburgh, which at the peak of its development in the early 1900s was described by one commentator of the time as the 'second largest undertaking of its kind' in Scotland with 400 employees. The North British Rubber Co was considered to be the largest rubber manufacturer. The manufacture of rubber products in Scotland was carried out by both large and small firms depending on the scale of output and the range of products. The Caledonian Rubber Works diversified into many areas and thus represented many of the different facets of the rubber industry.

Little is known of Currie's early life apart from the fact that he was born about 1840 near Edinburgh and was educated there. His early business training is also unknown but he started out in his own business in 1859, founding the Caledonian Rubber Works in Dalry Road, Edinburgh, while still only a young man of 20. By 1872 the number of employees was recorded in the Census at 100, indicating the scale of expansion since the works were founded.

An extensive range of products was soon a hallmark of the company. The products were as diverse as waterproof clothing for shooting, fishing, etc., rubber belting for industry, and sporting requisites such as footballs and golf bags. In this last category, Currie's production of golf balls brought him fame and success.

The first type of golf balls to be generally produced was the Feather Ball, leather covered and filled with goose feathers and remained popular until the 1850s when the 'gutta percha' ball was developed. The 'gutta' was cheaper to produce, travelled farther and was more durable. In the early years it was smooth but when a ball press was introduced into the manufacturing process the 'gutta' soon became renowned for the variety of markings and designs produced by the various manufacturers. As well as specialised companies beginning to spring up to manufacture golf balls, and companies which already made golf clubs diversifying into golf balls, rubber companies also diversified into the new products. Wm Currie & Co was one such company. In 1877 William Currie patented the 'Eclipse', one of the very first composite 'gutta percha' balls. The 'Eclipse' was different from the 'gutta' ball because it was made from a mixture of India rubber, cork, leather and other items. This was a fairly soft ball with an indented surface and proved very successful for a number of years although the rival production of similar types of balls soon made the production of golf balls a highly competitive activity. Changing fashions and preferences amongst golfers also dictated the success or failure of a particular ball. The 'Silvertoun No 4' manufactured by the Silvertoun Company of London was one such example of a rival to the 'Eclipse'. Currie in fact took action against the Silvertoun Company in 1888 whom he believed had infringed his patent although this was in fact not true.

In the late 1890s the development of the rubber core golf ball also signalled the demise of the Eclipse and the 'Star', another Currie golf ball. The range of Currie's products, however, reduced the impact of the change in the golf ball market. Indeed throughout the firm's early years, trade rivalry did not hamper the successful course of Messrs Wm Currie & Co. Representation at international exhibitions in Paris in 1878 and 1889, Melbourne in 1888 and in Edinburgh itself in 1890, brought silver and gold medal awards for the firm's products. The international reputation of the firm was reflected in the setting up of a branch in London and agencies worldwide although much of the exports went to Canada and Australia.

William Currie was renowned for his commercial expertise and business acumen. He also set up a retail outlet for his products at 96a Princes Street, Edinburgh, similar to Thornton's (qv), another India-rubber (manufacturing) company in Edinburgh. In Glasgow, in partnership with Robert McEachern, the Currie presence was also to be found under the name, Currie, Thomson & Co at 45 Jamaica Street.

Currie had several sons but only two, Charles and Douglas, seem to have had any active family business involvement. By the turn of the century it was Charles who was being groomed for a management role. Douglas Currie was a chartered accountant and as trustee of the firm on his father's death played a more belated role in the running of the business. Indeed, by the time of his death in 1928, William Currie had little financial involvement in the firm.

It is hardly surprising that William Currie's leisure interests encompassed shooting, fishing and golfing, the three key outlets for his own manufactures. In politics he was a Liberal and a member of the Edinburgh Liberal Club.

William Currie was nearly 90 when he died in 1928. His last wishes were that his son Douglas should receive his investments of which there were many including railway stock and government bonds. Much of his share in the company had already been passed on to his family by the time of his death, although it is clear from his will that some of his sons predeceased him. Currie did not forget his employees and business associates, with numerous small legacies and bequests. The sum of £2,000 was bequested to the Royal Infirmary, Edinburgh, and £1,000 to the Royal Edinburgh Hospital for Sick Children.

An obituarist described Currie as being 'of a very retiring nature'. However, his lack of known non-business activities is a reflection perhaps of his devoted attention to the successful running of the Caledonian Rubber Works. The business was run by trustees and T A Torrance for several years before being sold in 1947.

SHEILA HAMILTON

SOURCES

Unpublished

SRO: SC 70/4/629, Will
SC 70/1/799, SC 70/1/866, Inventory
BT2 25150, Dissolved Co, William Currie & Co (Rubber Manufacturers) Ltd

Published

Henderson, Ian and Stick, David, *Golf in the Making*, Crawley, 1979
India Rubber Journal, Vol LXXVI, 1928, Vol CXII, 1947
Men of the Period, 1900
Olmar, John M and Olmar, Morten W, *The Encyclopedia of Golf Collectibles*, Alabama, USA, 1985

James DICK,

Gutta percha manufacturer; b. 1823, Kilmarnock, s. of John Dick, spirit merchant, and Barbara Simpson; m. 1886, Kate MacDonald; Proprietor, R & J Dick, Gutta Percha Manufacturers; d. 7/3/1902, Glasgow; g/v estate: £1,077,034.

New industries generally required new men of ideas; this was the circumstance that brought James Dick and his elder brother Robert into the gutta percha business. It was a most unlikely step for the brothers whose father John Dick was in business in Kilmarnock as a spirit merchant. The family was large, three sons and two daughters; James was the youngest of the sons. While still at school in Kilmarnock James' father died in 1832, when James was only nine. The family then removed to Glasgow where his mother opened a small shop in Crown Street on the south side of the river. After elementary schooling James was apprenticed as an upholsterer, and his brother Robert trained as a watchmaker.

The two brothers, in common with most people in Britain, were fascinated by the novelty of natural rubber - gutta percha - first brought back to Britain from Borneo around 1843. The new substance was proclaimed to be superior to leather for most purposes. An English company was set up to manufacture gutta percha selling quantities of it together with a solution and instructions for dissolving and applying the substance. The Dick brothers are reputed to have bought a pound of gutta percha for 3/- in 1846; they experimented with treating the soles and heels of boots with the new substance. They were sufficiently impressed with the results to open a small shop in the Gallowgate to sell the rubber soled footwear. While their initial success was encouraging, this soon waned in hot summer weather when the rubber soles and heels became soft and sticky, a problem to which the Dicks addressed themselves. When this problem was overcome they rented premises opposite the shop and began manufacturing gutta percha boots and shoes. Indeed they pioneered a composite footwear, combining leather uppers with a waterproof and resilient rubber sole.

The Dicks first offered their new composite footwear at 7/6d per pair. Customers however had become shy of the novelty product, and were resistant to buying it. The Dicks therefore took to price cutting to try to attract custom. Fortunately for the Dicks, the price of raw gutta percha was also declining as supplies increased. The Dicks manufactured their boots and shoes at a cost of 4/6d per pair; they finally adopted a selling strategy of pricing all their goods at 5/- per pair. Demand quickened, though margins were slender, and by 1848 business was so brisk that the brothers acquired a site at Bridgeton at the east end of Glasgow Green to erect their Greenhead factory, which as it was steadily extended, became the centre of their operations.

The Dicks not only manufactured rubber boots and shoes, but quickly established a chain of shops and outlets, promoting their products under the brand name of 'Lifebuoy'. They also supplied and manufactured other rubber products like pedal coverings, and in the 1860s they moved into the manufacture of casings for undersea cables. By 1871 their factory at

Greenhead was turning out upwards to 30,000 pairs of footwear per week and employed nearly 1,300 persons; about 500 of these were women and young girls. The products were distributed through a network of shops which at its peak numbered around 70. The Dicks were therefore among the first to pioneer the multiple shop, or chain of shops system, to reach a large market with cheap standardised products.

From the mid 1860s, as many new uses were found for rubber, particularly because of its insulating properties, the supply of natural rubber began to come under strain. This tended to drive up the price of rubber footwear, and from that stage onwards, the cable business began to play a greater part in the Dicks operations.

The two brothers, James and Robert, worked closely in partnership and indeed lived together, first with their mother and after her death in a house in Monteith Row. However, at the age of 63, James Dick married a young woman of 35, Kate MacDonald and effectively retired from the business. His business had made him prosperous and he was already well known for many acts of anonymous charity. On the occasion of his marriage he gifted to the City of Glasgow an area of 49 acres on Cathkin Braes to the south of the town; this area was to be known as Cathkin Park. The sole stipulation laid upon the gift by James Dick was that it should not be landscaped and tamed; he wished it to be left as an area of natural beauty for the public to enjoy. With that business settled, James Dick and his new wife set out on an extended tour of Europe, the Middle East, and especially of Australia where James Dick had already investments in gold mining.

Between 1886 and 1891 the business was substantially managed and operated by James' brother Robert. Robert Dick wrestled with the problem of the failing market for their shoes and boots as rising gutta percha prices took their product out of the mass market. The industrial uses of rubber, already developed by the firm for their deep sea cables, attracted Robert Dick; in 1888 he took out a patent for the manufacture of 'gutta percha canvas material' for use in driving belts for machinery. This was to become the Dicks' 'Balata' belt, which was to bring a new prosperity to the business. Balata was the juice of the Bully tree (Manilkara Bidentata), which gave an elastic gum. The gum had insulating properties and could also be used for, among other things, the making of golf balls. However for R & J Dick, Balata allowed them to develop a canvas impregnated product of great durability and resistance to heat. Their 'Balata belt' was markedly superior to, and cheaper than, traditional leather belts for all driving purposes, and came to have a widespread market especially in drive and conveyor belts in mines. Robert Dick patented the new material but died in 1891 before the company could fully introduce it. James Dick was overseas on one of his prolonged travels with his wife at the time of his brother's death. When he returned to Glasgow he was 68 years of age, but like his brother had a strong paternal sense of responsibility for the welfare of the employees at Greenhead and in the shops. Consequently, instead of selling up the business, he ploughed in the wealth his many investments in Australia and South Africa had made for him to re-tool and re-equip the factory principally for the manufacture of 'Balata belt'. This new responsibility occupied him on a regular basis till he died in 1902 in his eightieth year.

When James Dick died in 1902, the business of R & J Dick was extensive. It manufactured rubber soles, pedals, rubber boots and shoes, casings for deep sea cables, and belting for driving machinery. The factory was the very large works at Greenhead in Glasgow, but warehouses were also maintained in London, Belfast, and in many European cities. The products of the factory were distributed through an extensive chain of shops. R & J Dick in 1902 operated 13 shops in Scotland, 8 being in Glasgow; 20 in England, 6 in London; 9 shops in Ireland, 4 being in Belfast; and 20 shops in Europe, 2 in Denmark, 1 in Sweden, 6 in Belgium, 8 in Holland and 3 in Germany; 62 shops in all. Each of these was the centre of an extensive local network of customers in local industries drawing on Dicks' products especially in later years on their cables and industrial 'Balata' belting. By 1900 the Dicks were also introducing flexible hoses made of Balata and took out a preliminary patent in 1901. Although the Dicks had patents on their 'Balata belts', their rubber soles and on their flexible hoses, it is clear that these patents merely registered their own innovations in the business rather than establishing them as licensees or monopolists in the business. Their success lay in a formula which stressed good quality, innovative products, and good value linked to an unrivalled distribution system through their chain of shops and warehouses.

In his will James Dick made provision both for the reward of his employees and for the future of the business. Fourteen managers were left shares in the company and were offered the business as a going concern for the cash sum of £20,000. This was accepted and this early management buy-out operated the company between 1902 and 1908 as a copartnery, before converting it to a limited company form. Every manager of the extensive chain of shops was left £300, and all employees in the shops received £50. The female workers at Greenhead each received sums varying from £50 to £300 depending on length of service; the range for male workers was from £30 to £100. His household staff were handsomely rewarded with sums varying from £500 to £2,000.

This was not a late conversion by James Dick to munificence. He and his brother had been well known for extensive charitable donations throughout the years, often anonymously. In addition to donating Cathkin Park to the City of Glasgow, James Dick gave to Kilmarnock a free library and institute (The Dick Institute) at an outlay of more than £20,000.

He left contributions of £25,000 to Glasgow Technical College, ultimately to become Strathclyde University, securing thereby a matching £25,000 from Andrew Carnegie. In his will he left benevolent and charitable bequests to the total of £82,000; £20,000 went to each of the Royal and Western Infirmaries, £10,000 to the Victoria Infirmary and £10,000 to the Glasgow Old Man's Friendly Society and Old Women's Home. Sums of £5,000 went to the Blind Asylum, Kilmarnock Infirmary, and to the Association for the Relief of the Incurable in Glasgow. Lesser donations of £1,000 went to each of the Glasgow Samaritan's Hospital for Women and to the Glasgow Maternity Hospital.

James Dick was clearly a benefactor of very substantial scale throughout his lifetime. However he played no part at all in the public life of Glasgow, his adopted home. He and his brother Robert created large fortunes and left them to their family, their employees, and to the City. James Dick had a personal movable estate at death of £1,070,000; he was one of Glasgow's more anonymous and unassuming millionaires.

ANTHONY SLAVEN

SOURCES

Unpublished

Death Certificate, Kinning Park District, No 644141, 1902, No 97
Marriage Certificate, Blackfriars District, No 64415, No 147, 1886
SRO: SC 36/48/180, Inventory
SC 36/51/130, Will

Published

The Bailie, 24/4/1889, 14/12/1898, 13/2/1902
Chalmers, Thomas, *A Hundred Years of Gutta Percha*, Glasgow, 1946
Glasgow Chamber of Commerce Journal, R & J Dick, Clydeside Companies, No 43, 1956
Glasgow Herald, 8/3/1902
Glasgow Today, Messrs R & J Dick Ltd, 1909
India Rubber and Gutta Percha Trades Journal, 17/3/1902
The Scotsman, 8/3/1902
The Times, 8/3/1902

Robert FORGAN,

Master Golf Club Maker, b. 30/6/1824, St. Andrews; s. of John Forgan, Harbour Master and Janet Paterson; m. Elizabeth Berwick; 5 s., 1 d.; Founder, Robert Forgan & Son; d. 15/12/1900, St. Andrews; g/v estate: £10,272 7s 0d.

At the start of the nineteenth century, Scottish golfers were almost entirely dependent for supplies of clubs on the two firms of Peter McEwan of Bruntsfield, Edinburgh (late of Musselburgh) and Simon Cossar of Leith. St Andrews, although already recognised as the country's leading golf centre, had no clubmakers. The Society of St Andrews Golfers (which in 1834 became the Royal and Ancient Golf Club) paid McEwan's to send a representative to each of their spring and autumn meetings. This arrangement lasted until 1827, but in 1812 the Society had first advertised for a clubmaker to come and live in St Andrews, and then agreed to 'countenance and support' Hugh Philp, a local joiner and carpenter who set up as an independent clubmaker. Philp made only the wooden clubs which were used for almost all golf shots; iron clubs or cleeks were only used in hazards where there was danger of breaking a wood, and their manufacture was regarded as a separate trade. In 1819 Philp was appointed official clubmaker to the Society; by 1841, when he was still the only clubmaker in the town, he was recognised as the most skilful manufacturer, especially of putters, in Scotland. The other essential equipment for the game, golf balls, had been produced in St Andrews since at least the early eighteenth century. In 1841 there were ten ballmakers, led by the Gourlay family and champion golfer Allan Robertson, whose work involved packing goose or chicken feathers tightly into leather covers. The town produced some 10,000 'featheries' each year.

By this time St Andrews, a town with neither agricultural markets nor significant manufacturing industry, was dependent for prosperity on catering for education and leisure. The increasingly popular game of golf was one of the main attractions both for tourists and, more importantly, for families of independent means who the civic authorities hoped, would settle in the town. In 1835 the newly titled Royal and Ancient was joined by the Union Club, founded principally by retired East Indian army officer Hugh Lyon Playfair. The two clubs co-existed harmoniously, with increasingly overlapping membership, until in 1853-4 the Union Club built its new headquarters (now the Royal and Ancient clubhouse). Both sides then agreed on a merger, although final full amalgamation did not come until 1877. Playfair, a golf fanatic who had in 1827 laid out one of the first courses in India at Dumdum, was provost and virtual dictator of St Andrews from 1842 until his death in 1861, being knighted for his achievements in 1856. Under his regime golf in St Andrews received every encouragement to expansion.

Robert Forgan, son of the harbourmaster of Pittenweem and grandson of a farmer at Lathockar, near St Andrews, was born in St Andrews on 30 June 1824. After schooling at Madras College, he was apprenticed as a joiner, the trade which produced most of the early clubmakers. In 1849 he married Elizabeth Berwick, daughter of the St Andrews harbourmaster and, more significantly, niece of Hugh Philp. Three years later he became Philp's assistant. From 1854 his employer's illness meant that he was effectively in charge, and when Philp died childless in 1856 he took over the business.

Forgan's start in the trade coincided with two important technological changes. Feathery balls were expensive, costing from 2/6d to 4/- each, as a skilled man could only make three or four in a day. They were also inefficient in wet weather. In the late 1840s balls made of gutta percha appeared and, although details of the development are unclear, a popular and plausible version gives credit to the Paterson family, cousins of Forgan's mother. James Paterson, a St Andrews graduate and missionary in India, sent home

a statue packed for safety in gutta percha; from this packing either his brother John or his half-brother Robert made an experimental golf ball. The first smooth guttas did not perform well, but it was found that they flew better after being nicked and dented in play. Ballmakers then sold guttas with indentations already on them; Forgan was the first to introduce a regular pattern of hand-hammering, originally on hand-rolled balls and then on ones made perfectly spherical in moulds. The firm then introduced moulds which also marked the balls, although at the end of the century they still employed the last skilled hand-hammerer, whose work was sufficiently well regarded to command a premium over machine-made balls. The guttas could be used in all kinds of weather, and retailed at about one shilling each. Since 12 guttas could be made by hand in the time required for one feathery, this suggests a considerable increase in income for the ballmakers.

Forgan was possibly the initiator and certainly the principal developer of the other major technological change - the use of hickory for golf club shafts, instead of the traditional ash. Well seasoned hickory was springy, resilient, relatively light, and impervious to weather. Philp had once bought a hickory log with no expectation of ever using it all; by the end of the century Forgan was buying his hickory in loads of either 100 logs or up to 30,000 square-cut billets for shafts at a time, and at any given moment he held enough wood to make 100,000 clubs. Early supplies were obtained by persuading Dundee skippers trading to Quebec to bring back logs as ballast; later stocks were obtained from Tennessee by more orthodox trading. Since gutta percha came from India and Malaya, and clubs and balls were sent across the world as migratory Scots set up golf courses, international trade became an increasingly important part of the Forgan business.

Forgan initially employed one assistant clubmaker and one ballmaker (his brother James, 15 years his junior). There was now a rival clubmaker in St Andrews - James Wilson, Philp's previous assistant who had left when Forgan arrived - but relations beween the two men were so good that they bought timber together, divided it into two piles, and tossed for lots; Forgan later had a similar arrangement with Tom Morris, clubmaker and four times Open champion. He had inherited Philp's position as club-maker to the Royal and Ancient; in 1863 this led to a Royal appointment as clubmaker to the Prince of Wales, who was that year's captain of the Club. A steady growth of business, no doubt helped by the fact that the Royal and Ancient had three times the membership of any other British golf club, allowed Forgan to expand his premises in the 1870s, including the provision of storage facilities for customers' clubs.

Rapid growth came with the golf boom of the last 20 years of the century. The number of clubs and societies in Britain rose from 60 in 1880 to 2,330 in 1900. The firm, now Robert Forgan & Son since his third son Thomas became a partner in 1881, attributed much of its growth to its success in winning the top awards for both clubs and balls in the Edinburgh International Exhibition of 1886. A weekly production of 600 to 800 wooden clubs could not keep up with demand. At a time of generally falling prices, demand pushed the price of a club up from 4/- to 5/-; balls, now the composite 'gutty' (containing gutta percha, cork and metal filings) rather than the simple gutta, still sold for a shilling. The six employees of 1881 became 37 by 1895. More significantly, production was mechanised. Gas engines, and powered lathes and saws, meant that a shaft, which previously had to be sawn by hand out of a six-inch square hickory billet, could now be cut and shaped in 2.5 minutes. Shafts were still normally of hickory, although ash and lancewood were sometimes used, with 'unbreakable' clubs of dogwood being made for beginners. Clubheads were usually beech, which had largely replaced the traditional applewood, although in the 1890s experiments were made with imported persimmon. Quality control meant that one in six shafts and two-thirds of head blocks were rejected.

By the mid-1890s Forgans were claiming to be concerned about the extent of competition in the golf supplies business. The boom had brought new firms into the business, often marketing cheap if inferior clubs. Spalding clubs from the United States had appeared as early as 1878, Slazengers in 1881; the Army & Navy Stores, which in the late 1880s was selling Forgan clubs, subsequently marketed its own brand, and other department stores were following suit. But Forgans were secure at the quality end of the trade. Apart from a successful range of clubs and the excellent 'Forgan' and 'Acleva' brands of gutty balls, they had developed high-class specialities such as club copying and the new socket clubs. They were also well established in foreign trade, which took much of their production in the winter months. In spite of any misgivings, when Forgan died of heart disease on 15 December 1900 (less than a month after his wife) the firm had expanded further, and had 50 employees.

Of the six families which dominated British club-making in the latter part of the nineteenth century, three - the Morrises of St Andrews, the Parks of Musselburgh and the Dunns of London - owed their reputation as much or more to their feats as golfers than to the quality of their products. The others - the Forgans, the McEwans and the Patricks of Leven - were essentially manufacturing craftsmen. Of the six, only Forgan established a business which survived successfully into the second half of the twentieth century. His own golfing prowess was limited to a best Old Course score of 87, and to once tying for the scratch medal of the St Andrews Club; he had neither the ability nor the time to reach the top as a player. His assistants at various times, however, included Andrew Strath (Open champion in 1865), Jamie Anderson (1877 to 1879) and Willie Auchterlonie

(1893). In 1892 Auchterlonie and his brother David, also a former Forgan employee, set up the firm of Auchterlonie & Crosthwaite, which two years later became the extant firm of D & W Auchterlonie.

Forgan was a quiet, cautious, genial man whose private life centred on his religion. He joined the Free Church at the Disruption, and remained a member of Martyrs' Church congregation for the rest of his life, serving as an elder from 1873 until his death, and being active in church charity work. His other main recreation was rifle shooting; he shot several times in the national tournament at Wimbledon, and won several local championships. He was also active in the volunteer movement. His children apparently divided between his strong religious conviction and his business acumen. The first and fourth sons, John and Robert, became Free Church ministers, while his only daughter Wilhelmina married into the same vocation. His second and fifth sons, James and David, crossed the Atlantic to found a banking dynasty; at the time of their father's death they were respectively president and vice-president of the First National Bank of Chicago, the second largest bank in the United States. The remaining son, Thomas, joined his father not only in the clubmaking business but also in the eldership of Martyrs' Church. For a small craftsman in a relatively small and remote town, Forgan exercised considerable influence in his chosen trade - the one area in which his native town happened to lead the world. As the obituarist of the local paper concluded, 'To write the biography of Mr Forgan is to write the history of golf club-making, and of the transition from costly feather balls to the moulding of gutta percha'.

C J ALAN ROBERTSON

SOURCES

Unpublished

Martyrs' Church, St Andrews, Kirk Session Minutes
SRO: Census Records 1861-91 SC 20/50/83, Inventory
St Andrews Eastern Cemetery, Robert Forgan tombstone

Published

Anderson, J, 'The real inventor of the "gutta"', *Golf Illustrated*, 22/2/1901
Anon, 'A famous firm of clubmakers', *Golf Illustrated*, 15/3/1901
Anon, 'Messrs R Forgan and Son, St Andrews', *Golf Illustrated*, 28/11/1902
Dalrymple, W, 'The real inventor of the "gutta"', *Golf Illustrated*, 30/11/1900
Forgan, J P, 'Golf ball making in St Andrews fifty years ago', *Golf Illustrated*, 27/12/1907
Forgan, Jnr, R, *The Golfer's Manual*, 6th ed, London, 1897
Henderson, I T, Stirk, D I, *Golf in the Making*, Crawley, 1979
McPherson, J G, 'The Inventor of the gutta', *Golf Illustrated*, 24/1/1902
Miller, T D, 'Robert Forgan, Golf Club Maker', *Golfing Annual*, 10, 1896- 7
North British Daily Mail, 17/12/1900
Robertson, J K, *St Andrews, Home of Golf*, St Andrews, 1967
Salmond, J B, *The Story of the R & A*, London, 1956
St Andrews Citizen, 22/12/1900
St Andrews Directory, 1898
Tulloch, W W, *Life of Tom Morris*, London, n d, c 1908

Samuel Hunter GORDON,

Welding Equipment Manufacturer; b. 1878, Nigg, Easter Ross, s. of John Gordon, farmer; married, 1 s., 4 d.; MD, Rose Street Foundry & Engineering Works, Inverness; d. 1959.

Samuel Hunter Gordon was born in 1878, the son of a farmer John Gordon of Cullisse Farm, Nigg, and Balmuchy of Fearn, Easter Ross. It is interesting that his father's obituary (1917) makes a strong point of old Mr Gordon's 'prominence as an up-to-date farmer, particularly on the scientific side of agriculture'. Sam, the younger son, was educated at Tain and Elgin Academies, and was sent at the age of 16 to MacKay & Doig, farm implement manufacturers in Elgin, for two and a half years. He then went to serve an engineering apprenticeship at The Ross Street Foundry, Inverness, for three years, and to the Highland Railway workshops in Inverness for a further two. He then went to Stephens of Linthouse and for four years to Vicker Sons & Maxims Ltd, Barrow in Furness, where he became a fully qualified engineer and carried out original experiments with oxy-acetylene welding from his arrival there in 1904. In 1908 he was recalled to his early training-ground, The Rose Street Foundry and Engineering Company, Inverness, as Managing Director, a post which he held for 50 years, retiring a year before his death in 1959. His career there was remarkable for his inventive capacity and ability to adopt new outlets for the engineering skills which he fostered in a loyal work-force at Inverness. By his death, welding equipment from Rose Street was being exported worldwide, and Rose Street had made significant contributions to two wars.

When Hunter Gordon arrived, Rose Street was in the doldrums. Founded in 1872 as the Northern Agricultural Implement & Foundry Co, (there were ten similar competitors in Inverness alone at that time) the firm had successfully switched manufacture to heavy castings for the railways, which were only then reaching the Highlands. For a time the Foundry had contracts for railway equipment supply from Blair Atholl north to Wick: this included the supply of girders for many bridges. However, railways fostered the import of cheap agricultural machinery, and eventually the Highland Railway was bought by LMSR, who ran its own engineering workshops. At the point when Hunter Gordon arrived most of the local competing foundries were giving up. Immediately he arrived in 1908, the Rose Street Foundry opened Thornbush Shipyard in Inverness, constructing steam drifters, including their boilers and all machinery. He also at this time advocated the extension of the tiny port of Inverness to make a safe shelter for the then vast Moray Firth fishing fleet, but the Town Council 'lacked vision and turned it down.' In 1914 the Admiralty took over the whole works and shipyard, which were then employed on the conversion of hundreds of vessels commandeered by the Admiralty for auxiliary work with the Grand Fleet at Scapa, Invergordon and Cromarty. During this time Hunter Gordon was largely responsible for the design and building of boom defences for these Naval stations. He also patented a submersible pump for the Navy, taking out 'an unique patent', and went on experimenting with uses for flash-butt welding.

By 1921 the firm was again experiencing the prevailing slump: Hunter Gordon however made two crucial decisions in that year. Immediate employment and cash was secured by a contract with the Admiralty to maintain and dispose of about 100 trawlers and drifters which had been used for Atlantic approach mine-sweeping and were laid up at Halifax, Nova Scotia. Hunter Gordon, who had a sense of humour, later claimed this contract had made him one of the last of the buccaneers; as the Admiralty did not grant him the use of an ensign nor crewing facilities, he sailed the hundred vessels back under his own flag, and with a separate bargain made with each member of their crews. The other innovation of 1921 was to have more lasting results. He bought a nearly defunct business, AI Welding Company of Bradford, from Messrs Ashton and Ibbitson, 'A-I', and with them the patent for resistance-welding under the original process of Professor Elihu Thomson, a British-born American who had invented it in 1886. It had not been widely used, but Hunter Gordon foresaw the manifold applications of fast welding, and developed and patented many improvements to the original

process. The name of the new company was changed to AI Electric Appliances Company, and Hunter Gordon opened a London office at 61 Victoria Street, SW1, which between the wars made steady progress, though not spectacular. By 1939 A-I sold the products of three associated companies: Rose Street Foundry and Engineering Co of Inverness; SA Electromechanique of Brussels, and Thomson-Gibb Welding Co. The last supplied welding equipment in Britain and the Empire, and had been set up by the inventor, Thomson: the Belgian firm founded in 1904 handled continental business, and had extensive research laboratories financed by the King of the Belgians. Later the parent company in Inverness became registered as Resistance Welders, and after 1945 as A-I Resistance Welders, but in the common speech of Inverness still remains 'The Rose Street Foundry'.

During the 1930s work continued on the development and application of flash-butt welding, and Resistance Welders of Rose Street claimed the monopoly of supplying welding machinery for making smoke-tubes of the superheated steam-tubes of all British railway locomotives. At this time there were only nine British firms in the field of welding machinery design and manufacture, and it was a clear leader. In 1934 Hunter Gordon patented a new machine for John Brown, Clydebank, used for welding the steel flanges of the main steam-pipes of the *Queen Mary* and *Queen Elizabeth I*. For all this, there were lean times in the early thirties, and in the 16 years between 1922 and 1937 the gross value of all the machines sold was £227,000. It was recalled on his retirement that Sam Hunter Gordon had imposed a cut on his own salary, and had forgone it altogether for some years. He was a tough but fair employer, known to have used his fists to settle disputes on the shopfloor. His workers were cohesive and formed almost a hereditary caste of engineers in the market town of Inverness. Apprenticeships were sought after, and Rose Street trained engineers took their skills to all parts of the world.

At the beginning of the second world war, early in 1940, the Ministry of Aircraft Production asked A-I Resistance Welders to advise on a problem that even American experts had found intractable: how to make the aircraft propellor hub-caps for Spitfire aircraft. The original hubs had been forged of solid steel and then bored. Hunter Gordon produced machines which automatically welded two steel pressings to form a hub much lighter than the prototype. This was subsequently used for other propellor-driven aircraft, notably the Mosquito. In a hearing before The Royal Commission on Awards to Inventors in 1952, Counsel for A-I Resistance Welders stated that the company 'took a substantial risk in undertaking this new development' and that 'the price charge was very small, not a commercial price, their profits on this were considerably less than £2,000 ... through savings in special alloyed steel and in skilled labour quite apart from money savings it was clear that these machines were of extreme utility.' Technical evidence was given at The Claim hearing by Hunter Gordon, and a small award was made.

Undoubtedly the greatest triumph of Hunter Gordon's professional career was his part in the war time PLUTO, acronym for Pipe Line Under The Ocean, later described by Churchill as 'a wholly British system and a feat of amphibious engineering skill'. His welding machines contributed to the laying of 970 miles of steel piping through which petroleum was pumped across the Channel, following closely the advance of the Allied armies, until it ended in Dusseldorf. The problem of petroleum supply was early identified as crucial to invasion plans and inquiries were set on foot early in 1942 by the Ministry for Petroleum Warfare. The first scheme, after the initial reluctance of the experts, was one put forward by the Anglo-Iranian Oil Co. using the hosing-coating of marine electrical cables to provide a flexible and continuous pipe. This was made and used, (code name: *Hais*) but was never considered heavy enough for the massive requirements of armoured warfare. the second pipe line (code named: *Hamel*) was proposed by Stewarts & Lloyds & Co who offered 40 ft steel solid-drawn tubes of 3′ diameter, 3.5′ o/d. These tubes Hunter Gordon proposed to weld into the continuous pipeline required. The initial project was for an undersea line from Sandown, Isle of Wight, to Cherbourg, a length of 80 miles. A fracture in any one of the 14,000 welds necessary would have wrecked the operation.

Early in development two other factors had to be considered carefully. Firstly, the flexibility of the steel pipe, so that it could be coiled in its full overall length, and uncoiled under operational conditions. Secondly, could a flash weld stand similar treatment without losing the properties of the original metal, under fatigue stress. Exhaustive tests at Stewarts & Lloyds, at Resistance Welders in Rose Street and the National Physical Laboratory at Teddington gave highly satisfactory results. (The pipe fractured before the welds).

The first contract was placed with Resistance Welders in September 1942. Sixteen specially designed and constructed welding machines together with ancillary equipment were delivered by October 1943. This had been achieved by working 24 hour shifts for seven days a week throughout, at the Rose Street Foundry. (Only dire national emergency allowed for Sabbath day working in Inverness). Hunter Gordon had taken as technical partner J M Sinclair, MI, MechE, who had come as an apprentice to Rose Street in 1917 and was very skilled, and another partner on management, W H Millward, AM, MechE.

A special site was selected at Tilbury, and a welding factory set down. The 16 A-I Automatic flash-butt welders were installed and the steel pipes fed in by conveyors from a railway siding, enabling all 16 to work simultaneously. Each machine was rated 180

KVA, and was oil-pressure operated both in the clamp and upsetting mechanisms; control was fully automatic. The alignment of pipes was also automatic under a full clamping. Each weld took 15 seconds to complete, but a further unit had then to smooth off the resulting extrusion of impurities and oxydised metal at the weld. Externally a rotary cutting lathe worked rapidly and efficiently but the corresponding internal 'fin', 40 ft up the pipe, was more of a problem. It was however successfully solved by a cutting tool incoporating wire brushes and reverse-blowing nozzles mounted on a 45 ft long spindle which was positioned in the pipe before the weld began. This cleaned and blew down each 3 ft section and the weld extrusion. Consistency and control of the entire process was maintained and 5% of all welds tested by repeated flexions under stress, when the tube invariably gave out before the weld.

The resulting piping, in 4,000 ft lengths, was moved by 'transversers' and stored on huge ramps, before being wound onto a buoyant steel drum of 40 ft diameter, flash-welding each length to produce the required 80 miles continuous pipe. The combined weight of drum and piping was 1,600 imperial tons and this monster was towed off and eventually laid across the Channel by sea-going tugs of the Merchant Marine. The crews paid out the piping under the operational threats of Stuka dive-bombing attack. There was no significant hitch. A welding programme of 12 miles a day was maintained at Tilbury, and a second pipeline across the ocean was subsequently laid from Dover to Boulogne. Work continued in Tilbury until by the end of the war the pipeline reached Dusseldorf and approximately 970 miles, with 198,000 flash-butt welds.

The Royal Commission of Inventions also made an award to A I Resistance Welders for their part in PLUTO.

After the war, which had demonstrated the efficacy of flash-butt welding the market was very greatly increased. So was the competition. Sam Hunter Gordon, had been joined in the business by his son, Major Pat Hunter Gordon MC, MA, CEng, FIEE, recently retired from the Royal Engineers, and they set about finding new markets. The biggest outlets were the railway systems of the world, speedily converting their old tracks into continuous steel-welded rails. A I Resistance Welders supplied equipment to the newly formed British Rail and London Underground, and to railways from America, through Europe, Asia and Africa to New Zealand. J M Sinclair made tireless journeys.

For the home market the company appreciated the huge post-war demand for domestic consumer goods. Resistance Welders patented new machinery for the welding of aluminium spokes in wheels, and in 1952 claimed that 80% of the wheels rolling in Britain, from prams to bicycles to British Leyland cars and vans, to the new tanks of the army were spoke-welded by Resistance Welders. Stewarts & Lloyds Ltd installed up-dated versions of the PLUTO welders at their new works at Corby, to weld continuous piping in 1953.

Acting on the initial suggestion of Charles Thomson, one of the Rose Street engineers, Hunter Gordon at nearly 80, decided on another diversification, producing a new method of transporting heavy minerals by means of a conveyor-belt suspended from a pair of steel driving cables. The newly formed National Coal Board took an interest, and the prototype was installed in the Frances Pit in Fife in July 1951. This newly patented conveyor took the place of three conventional conveyors of the old type Thomas Ediston conveyor patented in 1891. It was claimed to reduce the risk of sparks through reduced friction, and to have a carrying capacity of 150 tons an hour with negligible spillage, and a great decrease in dust and risk of fire. *The Times Review of Industry* commented, in a long article, on its 'excellent characteristics in respect of an angle of lift, low power consumption and maintenance, and its promise to make practical many schemes of development.' Unfortunately there were many initial problems and Hunter Gordon did not live to see much development of this invention, the prototype of which had been put up, on the tennis court of his garden on the banks of the River Ness.

Hunter Gordon was a Justice of the Peace, and took a temperate part in the affairs of Inverness, but his main energies were always devoted to The Foundry, and his employees there, where he ruled as a patriach, and was held in affection, as was evinced by the tributes paid to him in 1958 at a celebration of his 50 years of management of Rose Street Foundry: 'He kept the Foundry going to the inestimable benefit of Inverness and of many families in the town ... and succeeded quite remarkably in replacing old contracts with new orders in other spheres.' Turnover for 1957 was disclosed to be £325,000. He was also devoted to his family. He married and they had four daughters as well as the son who joined his father at Rose Street, becoming managing director in 1958. Hunter Gordon was brought up in the United Free Presbyterian Church, and later became a quietly radical freethinker, but he followed his wife, an Ulsterwoman, into the Episcopalian fold. He was buried after a service in St Andrew's Cathedral, Inverness, on May 12th, 1959.

MONICA CLOUGH

SOURCES

Unpublished

Family papers and scrap book of Mrs V Hunter Gordon

Information supplied by Verson A I Ltd, Inverness, Specialist manufacturers of Resistance Welding Machines and Metal and Strip Jointing Equipment.

Published

Daily Express, 25/4/1952
Highland News, 20/5/1939
The Inverness Courier, 3/8/1915; 25/5/1945; 13/6/1952; 6/5/1958; 12/5/1959
Leven Mail, 25/7/1951
Scotland Magazine, February 1953
The Times, Review of Industry, January 1958
Welding Magazine, July 1945

John Alexander Edward JOHNSTON,

Accountant and rubber mfr; b. 15/5/1880, Kent, s. of John Johnston, barrister and Kate O'Flaherty; m. (1) Masel Fulton Allan Berry; (2) Hilda Jocelyn Christine Barr; 3 s.; MD, North British Rubber Company; d. 27/7/1979, Edinburgh; g/v estate £82,527.

The son of a London barrister, Alexander Johnston was educated at a Jesuit college and then at a Roman Catholic public school. After the death of his parents he was brought up by an aunt whose fondness for ocean voyages resulted in the young Johnston being widely travelled and receiving schooling in France, Belgium, South Africa and on board ship. From this rather unconventional background he trained as a chartered accountant and in this capacity became involved in the reorganisation of the Hyde Imperial Rubber company, near Stockport, and the formation of a new business, the Hyde Rubber Company. Indeed, in the early 1900s Johnston became secretary and then manager of the company and, with this experience, was appointed secretary of the North British Rubber Company in 1905. Johnston remained with the Edinburgh firm throughout his career and dominated its subsequent development. He became works manager in 1909, at the age of 29, and ten years later joined the Board; he was managing director from 1919 to 1950 and remained a director until 1966. Thus his career encompassed all aspects of the firm's operations.

In 1905 Johnston's first task was a reorganisation of the internal accounting system with the introduction of monthly returns from all departments.

North British manufactured a full range of footwear, mechanical goods, waterproofed products, tyres and moulded goods. Johnston regularly visited the firm's European agencies and represented the company in the regular negotiations, and rather fragile agreements, over prices with the leading footwear manufacturers of Europe. In 1910 the company obtained its first stock exchange quotation, established a French company, in which Johnston was a director, with a Paris factory and also acquired the Scottish Vulcanite Company. To accommodate this domestic and overseas expansion Johnston reorganised the firm's executive structure, although the volatility of rubber prices and a general increase in competition reduced profits from 1910.

The First World War forced the company to close its German and Austrian branches, but military production of tyres, boots and groundsheets increased rapidly. New buildings were added to the Castle Mills, Edinburgh, factory including a department for dirigible balloon fabrics. In order to retain the workforce, the plant was designated a controlled establishment in November 1915 and this, coupled with controls on rubber supplies, brought Johnston into negotiations about contracts and wage rates with the War Office and the Ministry of Munitions. The company's sales increased from £803,116 in 1913 to £2,382,821 in 1918, and the resumption of peacetime business was quite smooth in 1919 due to the demand for tyres. North British Rubber planned for expansion although the Board, which Johnston joined in 1919, was concerned about the level of wages.

In the event the inter-war years presented profound difficulties in the form of weak demand and competition from imported rubber footwear and the establishment of British factories by multinational tyre firms. The Edinburgh company's share of industry sales declined from 7% in 1924 to just over 4% in 1930. There were efforts to expand overseas business and Johnston was one of North British Rubber's directors in a joint venture with the Australian Dunlop Company between 1925 and 1929. In Europe North British Rubber agreed to restrict its exports to France in 1925 in a reciprocal arrangement with Hutchinson (Paris). European manufacturers and importers regularly sought higher prices and export quotas between 1929 and 1935 and Johnston participated in the European Rubber Footwear Conference. However these discussions were undermined by declining demand and competition from producers in Central Europe, Japan and South-East Asia.

Despite a reorganisation of the sales department, by 1931 North British Rubber was in a poor financial state and Johnston implemented a retrenchment involving a 10% cut in salaries, contraction of the London office and reductions in overhead costs. Most of the overseas branches were closed although an experimental mail-order business was introduced. The firm considered ending tyre production in 1932 and 1933 but a slight improvement in sales led the board to retain the tyre department. The footwear department closed for two weeks in 1932 with Johnston blaming competition from Japanese imports and demanding tariff protection. A year later Johnston assumed personal control of the Works and Technical Departments following a strike over a new wages system. Domestic business remained sluggish and the liquidation of continental branches continued. North British Rubber's only new investment was the acquisition of a plantation at Brazzaville in the Belgian Congo, in 1931, which Johnston persuaded the board to retain throughout the thirties.

Against this background of financial constraints and considerable competition, Johnston was involved in negotiations about the tyre business with representatives of the United States Rubber Company during 1937 and 1938. The American firm was seeking to develop its European business and in 1939 Johnston visited the United States to investigate markets, technology and the import quotas. However the war delayed further development. Military demand doubled North British Rubber's workforce to 9,000 and the Treasury financed half of the cost of a rubber reclaiming plant. A technical agreement was finally signed with U S Rubber in 1945 which included the manufacture of Dominion tyres in Edinburgh. After delays in obtaining permits for imported machinery, a new footwear plant was established at Dumfries with Johnston's son, Hugh, as manager. The link with the American firm strengthened when U S Rubber acquired half of the ordinary capital in North British Rubber and American managers were increasingly active in the production departments. In 1950 Alexander Johnston retired as managing director, handing over to American management, but he continued to be active as a director until 1966. He held other directorships with various subsidiaries of North British Rubber and with Robert Stuart (London) Ltd, a supplier of aeroplane parts. From 1948 Johnston was chairman of Galloways (Edinburgh) Ltd, an interior decorating and fabrics company, and he went to the shop daily until two weeks before his death.

The First World War had brought Johnston into a prominent role in the rubber industry. He was the first chairman of the British Rubber Tyre Manufacturers' Association (BRTMA) in 1916 and held the post until 1919. In this capacity he was a representative on the Joint Industrial Council of the Rubber Manufacturing Industry in 1918 and chaired its Edinburgh District Council. He represented the BRTMA on the executive council of the Federation of British Industries (FBI) in 1917 and served on an FBI committee on trade groupings. After the war Johnston led the BRTMA's unsuccessful campaign for the retention of import restrictions on tyres and participated in the creation of a Rubber Research Association. He was involved in the industry's general campaign for a tariff on tyres which resulted in a 33.3% duty in 1927 and in the associated campaign to 'Buy British' and to establish the labelling of the origin of rubber products.

In 1921 Johnston became a vice-president of the Federation of British Industries, a position which he held until 1965, and became president of the Institution of the Rubber Industry (IRI). The IRI was based on smaller firms and Johnston was active in promoting training and research and campaigning for tariff protection. In 1924 Johnston was chairman of the India-Rubber Manufacturers' Association and in 1925 he served on an FBI committee examining industrial subsidies as alternatives to unemployment compensation. The range of Johnston's industry activities point to his prominent role although the diversity of rubber products and firms handicapped the development of consistent industry policies, especially over prices.

Johnston's national activities continued with parliamentary lobbying in the early thirties as chairman of the British Rubber Shoe Manufacturers' Association and the honorary presidency of the 1938 Rubber Technology Conference. The footwear trade was the one sector of the industry which still experienced major import penetration after the introduction of tariffs from 1927. Johnston also served on several Safeguarding of Industries Committees, the Census of Production Advisory Committee, the Advisory Council to the President of the Board of Trade, the Board of the Imperial Institute and the Council of the Industrial Welfare Society. Between 1937 and 1949 he chaired the FBI's Scottish Regional Committee and in 1939 was appointed to the executive comittee, and chaired the footwear section, of the Rubber Export Group which liaised with the Board of Trade over the allocation of raw materials and exports. At the same time Johnston was a member of the Scottish Savings Committee, the Edinburgh and District Local Emergency Reconstruction Board and the Board of Referees under the Finance Act. Finally he was vice-chairman of the newly formed Federation of British Rubber and Allied Manufacturers' Association in 1942 and its president in 1944-45.

Alexander Johnston's local activities were scarcely less varied and extensive. He joined the Edinburgh Chamber of Commerce in 1905, was active on many of its committees and was president between 1924 and 1926. In the latter capacity he served as a trustee on several local charities and on the executive council of the Association of British Chambers of Commerce. He was part of a deputation to the Prime Minister urging that the Secretary of State be made a full cabinet post. In his presidential address in 1925, Johnston welcomed the return of the Conservative government, stressed the need for 'goodwill and hearty co-operation of all classes' and spoke in favour of T T Broad's scheme for an 'All-in' National Insurance Scheme. The following year he defended the return to the gold standard while advocating a renewed subsidy to the coal industry. He was a Justice of the Peace from 1916 and in 1939 was president of the East of Scotland Branch of the Institute of Secretaries.

Throughout his life Johnston was interested in sport including cricket, rugby and hunting. With his second wife he was involved in horse-racing and bloodstock breeding on a stud farm in County Galway. Their most successful horse was *Auralia* which won over £12,000 in the late 1940s including the Ascot Gold Vase, Doncaster Cup and Goodwood Stakes. During the inter-war years he lived in a number of substantial houses to the west of Edinburgh, but eventually retired to a flat in the city. He was keenly interested in the stock market and his estate of £82,527 included a sizeable portfolio of shares. On his death the estate was placed in trust to provide an annual income for Helen Anne Davidson, a fellow director of Galloways, for her lifetime and then to be divided amongst his sons or their children.

MICHAEL J FRENCH

WRITINGS

Writings

'The Price of Rubber Goods from the Manufacturers' Point of View', *India Rubber Journal*, December 1921

'Looking Forward', *India Rubber Journal*, August 1924

'Tyre Types and Tendencies', *The Motor Trader*, February 1926

'Distribution Costs in the Rubber Industry', *India Rubber Journal*, November/December 1931

'The Rubber Industry, Scotland's Place Among the Pioneers', *The Scotsman*, 29/4/1938

SOURCES

Unpublished

SRO: Inventory Will

Edinburgh Central Public Library: YTS 1885 N, B 26326, North British Rubber Company Ltd YHF 3530, Journal of the Edinburgh Chamber of Commerce, 1925-1928

National Register of Archives (Scotland): 2196, Uniroyal Ltd, Records of the North British Rubber Company; now with Gates Rubber, Heathall, Dumfries

Published

Babcock, Glenn D, *History of the United States Rubber Company*, Bloomington, Illinois, 1966

India Rubber Journal, 1905-1950

Mortimer, Roger; Onslow, Richard and Willett, Peter, *Biographical Encyclopaedia of British Flat Racing*, London, 1978
Rubber Age, 1922-1946
Rubber Journal, 1966
Uniroyal News, March 1966

John LETTERS,

Golf club manufacturer; b. 15/8/1888, s. of Robert Letters, galvaniser's labourer and Jane Lowrie; m. 21/10/1887, Gorbals, Glasgow; 5 s., 2 d.; Founder and Joint MD of John Letters & Co Ltd; d. 8/1/1957, Glasgow; g/v estate: £3,770 16s 10d.

John Letters was very much a self made and self educated man who left school at the age of 12 to work in the Glasgow farriers, Messrs Miller and Taylor, who also made golf balls. No doubt this gave him his first introduction to golf since he later became a founder member of the private golf club, Caldwell Golf Club at Uplawmoor in Renfrewshire, which was formed in 1903. One year later he emigrated to Canada where he worked on a farm. He returned to Glasgow to work for Miller and Taylor where he soon became manager of the section manufacturing golf balls, the rubber cored variety which since the turn of the century had superceded the 'Gutty' ball. This change produced one of the major milestones in the history of golf since the game became even more popular because the rubber cored balls could be hit much further and lower scores were thus possible for the ordinary golfers. The golf ball models which he produced at this time were 'The Little Model', 'the Black Spot' and 'the Superior Brown Spot'.

John Letters appreciated that golf was growing rapidly in popularity both at home and throughout the world. Although the first Canadian Golf Club, Royal Montreal had been established in 1873 it was 1881 before the first incorporated club appeared in the USA, the Shinnecock Hills Golf Club, At the turn of the century the game was really in its infancy in those countries, a fact which no doubt did not escape the young John while he was in Canada. This possibly influenced his decision to start his own business in golf club manufacturing. He began in 1918 as Logan and Letters, sports goods manufacturers and horseshoe pad merchants. Initially, golf clubs were assembled only from bought-in components and rubber pads were produced for the protection of horses' hooves, working from premises at 112-114 Broomielaw, Glasgow. There was only one other employee at this time but business expanded so rapidly that by 1923, when Mr Logan departed to continue business on his own account, the company, now John Letters and Co, was in new premises at 31 Anne Street and employed 15 craftsmen. Two machines were used, one for sanding and one for polishing. Iron heads were supplied rough from local drop forgers then hand ground, polished and sold to other retailers at 21/- per dozen. Other golf accessories such as golf bags were also supplied.

Another major change in the golf industry took place in the early 1920s with the introduction in the USA of steel shafts to replace the hickory which was becoming scarce. In 1929 steel shafts were made legal by The Royal and Ancient Golf Club of St Andrews for UK competitions, by which time John Letters had already foreseen the possibilities and was concentrating on manufacture using steel shafts. Since America was one of their major overseas markets they were quickly geared up to supply the new steel shafted clubs. Matched sets were being introduced at this time and their major selling point was that their top grade clubs were manufactured to produce scientifically graded and tested matched sets, which consisted at that time of 8 irons and 4 woods. It was the company's proud boast that their clubs could be supplied in any weight and with any shaft to suit personal requirements and they were 'made by men who play the game'.

1935 was an important milestone in the expansion of the company when they moved to more spacious premises in Howard Street, Glasgow. John Letters' eldest son John began working for his father at this time and a year later Mr J W R Murray, a chartered accountant, also joined the firm which then became a limited company. The company took a major step forward in their new premises by installing machinery for forging their own iron heads. Prior to this period clubs designed by John Letters had been stamped to customers requirements but now they introduced their autographed 'John Letters' models as their best sets and this became a symbol of the highest quality of golf club manufacture for many years after. Other models much in demand were the *Follothru, Sweet Shot and Bridge* clubs. The last had been sold since 1920, the bridge logo indicating that the head at least and most probably the entire club had been made by John Letters and Co, even although the name on the head could be the name of the golf professional or sports shop selling the clubs. The bridge logo was well chosen by John Letters since it represented the 'Swilken Bridge' on the 18th hole on the Old Course at St Andrews which was known to golfers throughout the world. The success of this logo must have had a considerable influence in the expansion of the company over the first 20 years.

The company exhibited at the Empire Exhibition in Glasgow in 1938 and many new orders were received as a result. New export markets were opening up but the company was meeting fierce competition in the USA. The first real setback came with the second world war when raw material supplies were almost non-existent and business orders virtually nil. This forced John Letters to diversify and he survived by buying and re-selling virtually anything he could get his hands on for several of the war years. When John Letters Jnr returned from the forces at the end of the war in 1945 the company was having difficulty in meeting demand. It was very much a family concern then since John Jnr had been joined by his four brothers after their demob. They brought a wealth of other skills to the company. Thomas, a fully qualified engineer, became manager of the iron section; Robert, a nautical instrument maker, became manager of the wood section; Hope Lowrie, who became a director and managing director, had been in shipping; and James, a director and office manager, was an accountant. Two sisters also worked in the firm to complete the family involvement.

Production gradually increased until 1947 when two important events heralded the rapid expansion into the international field in a really big way. The first was the winning of the Open Championship by Fred Daly which made all golfers want to play the same John Letters clubs as the Open Champion. The second was a visit by John Jnr to the United States with the Ryder Cup team. This opened his eyes to the advantages of advertising, autographed models, and modern production methods. In particular, he was impressed by the presentation of the glittering array of American clubs compared to the relatively dull presentation of British products. The result of this trip was a reorganisation of the company which saw the introduction of an advisory panel of leading professionals for discussion on design and other matters or criticism. John Snr agreed wholeheartedly with the new proposals and they were quickly implemented. Demand quickly outstripped supply so that at one time there was an eight month waiting list for the popular Fred Daly autographed models.

A further move was necessary in 1949 to Thornliebank Industrial Estate to meet the further expansion now under the joint managing directorship of John Letters, Snr and Jnr. The next move in 1954 to Hillington Industrial Estate proved to be the final one.

John Letters and Co Ltd was the first company in Britain to manufacture full sets of graded irons. Production was now down to a fine art. In the 'cleek' section the master model was made on the premises and the dies cut. A mould was then made and the iron heads drop forged in quantity. The heads were then hand ground for weight followed by milling of the faces to 1/1000 of an inch, stamping by hydraulic pressers, boring, sand blasting and polishing. The head was carefully examined at each stage to ensure high quality and finally a 'Delachrome' finish was added, this being the company's own patented finish. Another Letters Patent, the 'Delafit' process was used to fit the head to a shaft specially selected to suit the

head. The final stages consisted of polishing, insertion of rubber insert at top of shaft and the fixing of the grip.

Wooden headed clubs were also produced, necessitating the import of about 30,000 blocks, on average, of persimmon wood per year from Memphis, Tennessee in the mid 1950s. As with the irons, the heads were precision made with the craftsmen providing a master model in wood from which a replica was made in bronze. The master was fitted to a profiling machine whose revolving cutters cut several persimmon blocks at a time to the shape specified by the master. Further machines were used for refining and cutting recesses for insert, weight and sole plate and for drilling the socket. A special adhesive fixed the shaft into the socket. The final operation on the head involved the application by spray gun of a special moisture resistant finish evolved over the years by the company.

Sales were still booming due in no small way to the sales expertise of John Jnr and the modern advertising techniques. A typical gimmick was the development of an association with the Hollywood stars who were interested in golf. Danny Kaye had a special personal set of clubs made to order with his face and name on the heads and others with clubs made to order were Bob Hope and Judy Garland. The last order came as a result of her visit to the Hillington factory when she left with a special junior set for her daughter, now Lisa Minelli. Of recent years Frank Sinatra and Sean Connery have similarly maintained the Hollywood connection.

The success of the earlier decision to incorporate an advisory panel of professionals and the improvements in production methods and advertising had finally come to fruition by 1957 when the majority of European professionals were using John Letters clubs. The success of the British Ryder Cup team against the USA at Lindrick, Sheffield, in 1957, the first GB victory since 1933 and only the third in 30 years was noteworthy in that five of the ten British players were using John Letters clubs. In another year eight of the British Ryder Cup professionals were playing John Letters clubs. Unfortunately, John Letters Snr did not live long enough to see this success since he died on 8 January 1957 just one day after signing the largest balance sheet in the company's history, a gratifying and crowning reward for his earlier efforts. However, as the driving force in the firm he had seen the company develop to an extent that it was now producing 18 times more than in 1938 and 60% of output was now exported worldwide. The number of employees had increased to about 75 in total, including approximately 60 craftsmen. The largest markets were North America and Africa and sales even reached inside the Iron Curtain. In 1958 the company was completely inundated with orders and had great difficulty in meeting demand. Extension of the factory was necessary to increase production threefold to meet the demand fuelled no doubt by the publicity from the Ryder Cup success of the previous year.

Unfortunately the necessary cash was not immediately available from their own resources. The injection of the much needed investment capital for the rapid expansion came that same year when the company became a wholly owned subsidiary of Dunlop Rubber Co Ltd. This was followed by the gradual departure of four of the founder's sons. John started his own company, Craigton Golf Company, manufacturing golf clubs; Hope went to North Berwick to be works director for Ben Sayers; Robert left to work for Swilken Golf Company and then emigrated to Australia where he made clubs for Brosnam. Tom retired and Jimmy remained to run the company which still bore his father's name.

The story of John Letters would not be complete without recording the subsequent fortunes of John Letters and Co Ltd, under the guidance of his son, James. The basic principles as laid down by John Letters Snr were the foundation for the continued success of the business. High quality clubs were produced and contact with the leading professionals was maintained and widened to include the new breed of leading world class players such as Gary Player (South Africa), Arnold Palmer (USA), Bob Charles (New Zealand), Graham Marsh (Australia), Tony Jacklin (England), Lee Trevino (USA), Bernhard Langer (West Germany) and Bernard Gallacher (Scotland) who all (at some time in their careers) have played with clubs made in the John Letters factory. The relationship survived successfully with Dunlop until they announced, without any prior warning, that the John Letters factory was to close in March 1983. It appeared that the world famous name of John Letters was about to depart from the golfing scene. However the family name was retained when James Letters negotiated the re-birth of the company under the name of John Letters & Co (1918) Ltd with himself as managing director and a much slimmed down workforce of 11 men on production and 7 clerical workers. A model image of a modern small streamlined company emerged with the workers as shareholders, new agreed procedures, interchangeability of jobs, flexible hours and no unions. A production target of 1,500 clubs a week, modest by previous standards, was set with 35% of production going to the export market. Top quality 'Letters Master Model' forged clubs are produced as well as the cheaper cast models. The new Letters organisation prserves the old skills of hand forging their own high quality iron heads introduced by the founder in 1936, and are one of the few remaining companies to do so in Scotland.

In private life John Letters Snr devoted much of his spare time to social and political activities as well as being a keen golfer with a lowest handicap of 7. Socially he was chairman of the Clynder Holiday Home for children and president of the Old Folks Association of Tradeston, Glasgow. His political activities included serving for many years as chairman of the Tradeston Conservative Association. His sporting interest extended to football and he was chairman of the Benburb Junior Football Club. His stocky build was ideal for his other sporting interests of weight lifting and wrestling. He was much respected as a hard worker who gave his all for his business and the same dedication was put into all activities outwith business. A teetotaller, he was a devout evangelist, involved in the church throughout his life, and was a regular preacher in the Tent Hall in Glasgow. His dedication to religion can be gauged by the fact that his son James describes him as the only man he has known who could deliver a sermon with tears of emotion streaming down his face.

The world famous name of John Letters has been preserved from near extinction. Although John Letters Snr did not survive long enough to see the company reach its peak, he can take all the credit for laying the foundations of its success. From a very humble beginning he had the courage to start his own business, was a very hard worker and had the vision to see the growing worldwide demand for golf clubs. He did not hesitate to expand as demand increased and he must be admired for his tenacity which saw his company survive the war years and for his ability to move with the times and introduce modern machinery and production methods to keep pace with progress and maintain competitiveness.

JOHN M CUBBAGE

SOURCES

Unpublished

SRO: SC 36/51/414, Will
     SC 36/48/851, Inventory

Published

Glasgow Chamber of Commerce Journal, No 55, 1957

Glasgow Herald, 27/6/1983 and 9/1/1957

Henderson, Ian T and Stirk, David I, *Golf in the Making,* Crawley, 1979

Olman, John M and Olman, Morton W, *The Encyclopedia of Golf Collectibles,* USA, 1985

Watt, Alick A, *Collecting Old Golf Clubs,* Glasgow, 1985

United Publishing Company, *Industrial Enterprise 1938,* Glasgow, 1938

Patrick Millar MATTHEW,

Rubber manufacturer; b. 19/7/1858, Perth, s. of Patrick Millar Matthew, landed proprietor and Jane Crombie; m. 9/4/1895, Catherine White, d. of Andrew Stevenson, Fundholder; 2 s., 2 d.; MD, Victoria Rubber Company, Edinburgh; d. 8/3/1947, Edinburgh; g/v est.: £179,801 18s 11d.

Matthew's career was spent in the family waterproofing business in Edinburgh. His father, also Patrick Millar, and a partner formed and operated the Victoria Rubber Works between 1876 and 1880. Matthew Jnr managed the factory from 1877 and father and son were partners from 1890 to 1893. Then he purchased the plant from his father's estate for £4,019 and in 1894 incorporated the Victoria Rubber Company with a fully-paid up capital of £60,000. Although the family had significant holdings, ownership of the preference shares was quite widely distributed in the Lothians and Fife but Matthew owned all of the ordinary shares. He was managing director and, from 1895, chairman and retained these posts until his death in 1947. The Articles of Association stipulated that he did not receive any salary until 1901; his annual salary was £500 between 1901 and 1917 and then was increased to £1,000.

The company produced footwear and waterproofed fabrics with the latter accounting for two-thirds of total sales between 1898 and 1932. Victoria Rubber was a small firm and its sales averaged only 7% of the sales of the neighbouring and more diversified North British Rubber Company. Under the younger Matthew's management sales increased steadily, although profits fluctuated up to 1912, and an export business was built up. During 1908 and 1909 high rubber prices prompted him to visit Malayan estates and to invest in a rubber syndicate. The firm achieved rapid expansion and substantial profits during the First World War and paid 20% on its ordinary shares. Between 1914 and 1918 the company's sales increased more rapidly than those of North British Rubber and Victoria Rubber's profit/sales ratio averaged 21% between 1914 and 1918 compared to 8.5% during the previous decade. The Admiralty financed an extension to the waterproofing department and Matthew handled negotiations over government contracts including product quality and wage-rates. The post-war recession brought inventory losses and business fluctuated throughout the inter-war period although good dividends were maintained during the 1920s. However profits declined sharply after 1928 and in 1931 Matthew reported declining export sales and keen competition from imports. He reduced the workforce and in 1932 ownership was concentrated in his hands by the repayment of all of the preference shares. Nominal capital was maintained at £60,000 and Matthew owned three-quarters of the issued shares. Despite sluggish sales, high dividends were maintained. His son, Francis, became assistant managing director in 1934 and ten years later was joint managing director. The Second World War brought a further expansion and Patrick Millar Matthew remained active in the firm until shortly before his death. His estate was valued at £179,801 and consisted of a diverse portfolio of shares.

Subsequently Francis Matthew managed the firm until 1971 and supervised its increasing specialisation on printing supplies. After his death, his sister Jean owned 90% of the firm but in 1982 financial problems led to the winding-up of the company. Patrick Millar Matthew sustained and developed a family business over a 60 year period through reinvestment of earnings and specialisation on waterproofed goods. He patented several new techniques and products. The firm leased out shops and tenements around its factory and built a new tenement in 1903. In 1918 Matthew was admitted to the Worshipful Company of Patternmakers of the City of London.

Michael J French

SOURCES

Unpublished

GD 404, Records of the Victoria Rubber Company Limited
Register of Births, Deaths and Marriages
SRO: SC 70/1/1168, Inventory
    SC 70/4/878, Will

Published

India Rubber Journal, Volume CXII, 22/3/1947
Reports of Patent, Design and Trade-Mark Cases, Vol III, 1886, and Vol IV, 1887, London, HMSO, Patent Office, 1957
The Scotsman, 10/3/1947 and 11/3/1947

George Boyd THORNTON,

India Rubber Manufacturer and Merchant; b. c 1851, s. of George Thornton, India Rubber Merchant and Cecilia Purdie; m. 20/4/1881, Elizabeth K Galbraith; 3s., 1d.; MD Thornton & Co Ltd; d. 28/9/1908, Feddal, Perthshire; g/v estate: £37,457 9s 10d.

George Boyd Thornton was the second generation to head the Thornton family business. His father, George, was an India rubber merchant in Edinburgh and founded the business in 1848. Although the merchanting side of the business, both wholesale/retail, comprised the greater part of Thornton & Co's business, they also had a small manufacturing side. So unlike other India rubber companies, Thornton & Co had a much wider base.

When George Thornton Snr died in 1864, his wife, Cecilia took over the family business. Apparently his early demise did not leave the Thornton family very well off and Mrs Thornton set up business in Clerk Street, The Bridges, Edinburgh, selling amongst other things gutta percha golf balls. It was not long before George Boyd Thornton joined his mother. Educated at Edinburgh Academy, he left there in 1864, together with his brother John James. They both joined their mother to start their 'training' directly in the family business. She continued to operate the firm successfully for several years before she handed over the reins to George Boyd.

Although little is known of Thornton & Co's early fortunes, by the 1880s its development can be measured by its performance at international exhibitions, receiving the highest awards for excellence of manufacture at the Fisheries Exhibition in 1882 for their waterproof manufactures and the gold medal at the Edinburgh International Exhibition in 1886. By this time in the 1880s, George Boyd Thornton was clearly at the helm and the company was described in trade advertisements as 'patentees, manufacturers, and wholesale and retail dealers'. In the waterproof department it specialised in waterpoof clothing for shooting, fishing, riding and driving plus various other waterpoof goods including cart and lorry covers. In the mechanical department all kinds of India rubber belting were listed. In both the waterproof and mechanical departments it is not clear how much of these were made in their own manufacturies and how much was purchased wholesale from other companies, certainly contemporary advertisements did list manufactures in Edinburgh and Belfast.

The wholesale and retail side had expanded considerably in the late 1880s and 1890s, by which time, as well as the main retail outlet at 78 Princes Street, Edinburgh, there were also branches in Leeds, Bradford and Belfast. Thornton's had moved to Princes Street in 1888 when the Empire Theatre was built on the old premises in Clerk Street. George Boyd's brother, John James, interestingly founded and ran the Leeds and Bradford branches of Thornton & Co. He also founded an arcade in Leeds which contained a variety theatre. It was called Thornton's Music Hall then but is now better known as the Leeds City Varieties' Hall, home of the BBC 'Good Old Days' television production.

The wholesale side operated from 4 Hanover Street, Edinburgh. Thornton's acted as agents for Dunlop and the North British Rubber Company, selling bicycle and car tyres. Family recollections recall that the wholesale side was wide ranging and included ironmongery, toys and sports goods. They also employed many commercial travellers. Sporting items began to play a large part in Thornton's operations from the late 1890s. Golf articles were particularly important and Thornton's began to introduce their own balls and clubs. All golf balls had their own trade names and indeed Thornton's were no exception. Two gutta brands were traded in 1896 and were called the 'Thornton' and 'The Match'. A later ball was called the 'Flying Scotsman'. The balls were said to have been made by Sir William Currie (qv) and overstamped with the company name. Similarly it was only the finishing end of golf club manufacturing with which Thornton's were concerned, purchasing the basic clubs from Cochran's of Leith, golf club manufacturers, and finishing them by adding grips and so on in their workshop in Rose Street, Edinburgh. Because of the wholesale side it is important to note that George Boyd Thornton had a close relationship with many of the leading India rubber companies in Scotland including the North British Rubber Co, Curries, and Maclellan's in Glasgow. On the manufacturing side, at this time, Thornton's were reputed to have patented the first rubber hot water bottles.

Thornton & Co became a limited liability company with a capital of £100,000 on 8th July 1897. The capital was divided into 10,000 £5 ordinary shares and 10,000 £5 preference shares at 5% per annum. This change was in part a reflection of the growth in business in the 1890s and the need to consolidate and safeguard the company's position. Its first directors were George Boyd Thornton, James Tullo and Thomas Paul. George Boyd received £50,000 in shares and £90,000 in cash as part of the transaction. The stock in trade was valued at £47,666 in 1897.

By the turn of the century one of George Boyd Thornton's sons, Arthur Galbraith was involved in the firm. He was a first class sportsman and in particular a very good golfer and this was to become an asset to the firm when he won the British Amateur. George Boyd Thornton's eldest son George Muir became a lawyer and advocate and his third son Cecil Taylor entered the ministry. When George Boyd Thornton died in 1908 at the comparatively young age of 57 it was on Arthur's shoulders that the family business rested.

Apart from Thornton and Co Ltd, George Boyd Thornton held directorships in the Bukit Lintang Rubber Estates Ltd and Inch Kenneth Rubber Estates Ltd. He also held numerous shares in many other companies and was noted for his interest in the stock market. At his death in 1907 he held 5,540 ordinary shares of £5 in Thornton and Co Ltd. Described by his daughter as very well-off, Thornton's estate apparently was much lower than one might expect due to heavy losses in the rubber market.

In his lifetime, George Boyd Thornton had not played a prominent role in public life. His business interests consumed his attention. He was a Liberal Unionist in politics but declined to take public office on the Town Council. He was a founder of the now defunct Union Club in Edinburgh and served as a Justice of the Peace.

His leisure activities were linked very closely to that of his business interests. Shooting and fishing were his great love and every year from 1895 he rented and later owned a country house at Feddal, near Dunblane in Perthshire. In the long Easter and Summer vacations which he took, the family moved to Perthshire and there George Boyd Thornton could entertain his shooting and fishing parties. Needless to say there was considerable business benefit from this as well.

He was president of the Edinburgh Golf Club. He also founded the Carlton Cricket Club in Edinburgh. His town residence was at Grangepark, Dick Place, Edinburgh, and attached to the ground was a large park which was used as a cricket ground. He was supposedly more supportive to the Carlton Cricket Club than the previous incumbent of the park, the Grange Cricket Club which he felt was politically less desirable. He was a member of St Cuthbert's Church of Scotland, Edinburgh.

George Boyd Thornton was described by his daughter as the 'hard headed businessman and the very lovable genial companion'. To his obituarist he was 'retiring' but 'hospitable'. He was also described by his daughter as always 'determinedly right' and this trait in his character may well explain the hearsay explaining the lack of an obituary in the *Scotsman* with whose owners he had apparently quarrelled. Nonetheless, despite his early death George Boyd Thornton was a prime example of entrepreneurial drive and determination and the success and development of Thornton and Co was due entirely to his commanding presence in the firm. The company continued for many years after his death under the Thornton family name until its final dissolution in 1971.

SHEILA HAMILTON

Sources

Unpublished

McGowan, Dora May, 'I Remember'
SRO: SC 3562, Dissolved Co File, Thornton & Co Ltd
SRO: SC 70/4/404, Will
SC 70/1/488, Inventory

Published

Edinburgh Post Office Directories, 1880-1910
Glasgow Herald, 30/9/1908
Henderson, Ian T and Stirk, David I, *Golf in the Making*, Crawley, 1979
Henderson, Ian T and Stirk, David I, *The Compleat Golfer*, London, 1982

Gas, Electricity and Water

Gas, electricity and water are commonly regarded as 'public utilities', essential conveniences whose supply has in the past been thought of as a 'natural monopoly' and consequently most appropriately placed under public regulation.

It is easy to see why such a view should have been held. The supply of each of these commodities to individual households, public offices, commercial and industrial premises, requires extensive distribution networks of pipes and cables. In the early stages of development, if competition was to be effective as a control on cost and quality of service, then each company offering to supply the service was required to run pipes and cables to each establishment. The potential for waste and duplication was a powerful factor in promoting a public responsibility for the supply of these services.

Yet the 'public utilities' did not begin as public services; private provision was first undertaken and in the case of electricity and gas, private enterprise persisted through to nationalisation after the Second World War. Of the three it was water which first fell under public control and in the process its administrators and technicians passed largely into the anonymity of bureaucracy and have left no outstanding entrepreneurs to be included in these biographies. Nevertheless the stages in the development of a public water supply clearly illustrate the problems and pressures affecting the provision of services in this sector.

At the beginning of the nineteenth century every community had its own arrangements for the supply of water, this largely being determined by local geography. Supplies drawn from streams, wells, lochs and rivers were the norm, and in larger towns some mixture of private and municipal wells was common. In the early decades of the nineteenth century the rapid growth of industry and population quickly polluted such sources of supply and sparked off a search for improved provision. Private companies abounded, to supply fresh and clean water from ever changing wells and reservoirs, and frequently distributed it from wheeled carts. The generally poor quality of such supplies, and the growing problem of urban public health, induced a municipal intervention into the water supply business. Consequently, from the middle of the century, the dependence of communities on private water supplies was steadily replaced by extensive municipal provision. This involved substantial expenditure on reservoirs, pump and storage facilities, filtration beds, and the development of piped supplies from the mains into every household.

Water was the first and most extensive of the public utilities. From its municipalisation there grew not only the supply of drinking water, but water for cleansing, sewerage, and fire fighting, and also water for public baths and washhouses. Moreover, in the larger towns the local authorities also undertook the supply of high pressure facilities to provide hydraulic power for presses, winches, hoists and other commercial purposes.

The pressures and arguments which lay behind the growth of public ownership of water supply were also quickly brought to bear upon the provision of gas for lighting. The origins of the gas industry lie in the technology of the distillation of coal for the production of tar. In Scotland this was pioneered by Lord Dundonald (Archibald Cochrane) who established tar kilns on his Culross estate in 1781. The tar produced was in great demand by the Navy during the Napoleonic Wars, and was also used in a variety of ways to waterproof and preserve roofs, rope and cordage. The Dundonald process also produced coal-gas as a by-product of tar distillation, but little use was made of it at first. However, in establishing his British Tar Company in 1786, Dundonald extended his tar kiln business to Muirkirk in association with the ironworks there. It was in these works that a Lugar man, William Murdoch, first applied the waste gas for lighting the workshops in the late 1790s. He did not patent the process, though he later successfully exploited it in England.

Following upon this there was a small trickle of developments using gas for lighting, such as that by Professor Andrew Ure in his lecture theatre in the Andersonian Institution around 1805. As the demonstration effect gathered momentum private individuals began to form town gas companies to provide lighting, first in the streets, and subsequently in homes, offices and factories. By the 1830s even remote and small settlements were establishing their own gasworks, since the technique was self-contained, delivering supplies along pipes from a central production and storage facility.

Municipal involvement came quickly as competing private companies brought complaints about service, and disrupted the use of public thoroughfares by digging up the roadways to lay supply pipes. There were also fears of an abuse of monopoly supply power to force up prices, and the Government quickly limited the distribution of dividends to a maximum of ten per cent in an attempt to control this tendency. Private companies indeed dominated the development of the gas supply industry in the middle decades of the nineteenth century, but by the 1870s the larger towns were seeking powers through Parliamentary Bills to enable them to take over the private companies and make and sell gas on their own account. Thus Glasgow gained powers in 1869 to acquire the private companies operating in the city, and by the 1880s the Corporation gas department not only manufactured and supplied gas, but was selling and renting stoves, cooking devices, and fires for use in the home.

Gas had first been developed as an 'illuminating' service, but during the second half of the nineteenth century it was being more widely utilised in heating, and in industrial applications. In contrast to water, however, the municipalisation of gas supplies did not lead to the disappearance of individuals whose influence on developments can be readily discerned. The complex technology of gas production and supply sustained a brotherhood of engineers and technical men who worked as managers and consultants in the industry. They were constantly in search of improved efficiency and economy, and the complex family involvement in these endeavours is well illustrated in the biography of William Young.

The demand for gas grew relentlessly throughout the nineteenth century, yet by the end of the century it was being used more for heat and power than supply for illumination. In many premises it was even used to power engines which in turn drove dynamos to produce the new electricity for lighting. The possibilities were not lost on town councils, and many municipalities quickly began adding clauses to Parliamentary Bills designed to provide gas, to enable them also to undertake the supply of electricity. The town authorities were anxious that no private concern should gain a monopoly in supply, and with it a right to dig up streets and disrupt public highways and services. Glasgow took such early electricity powers in 1890, and the developments were initially placed in the charge of the Gas Department.

The provision of electricity, like gas and water before it, initially involved both private and public enterprise. The larger towns quickly established municipal companies, but around them grew significant private cocerns like the Clyde Valley Electrical Co, designed to bring the new source of light and power to concentrations of consumers outside the cities. Remote areas, however, presented a greater challenge with smaller populations and scattered centres of consumption. Supplies to these areas were only gradually provided through the development of the National Grid. Some areas like the North and West Highlands lay beyond even the National Grid, and only began to have provision made with the formation of the North of Scotland Hydro Electric Board in 1943. This of course built upon earlier pioneering work of companies such as the Grampian Electricity Supply Co which had been established in 1922 to develop a public supply. However it was the Hydro which finally brought a public electricity supply to the remoter localities, and its great work was heavily influenced by men of driving energy and ambition, notably Sir Edward MacColl who was at the centre of the developments.

Electricity was the youngest of the public utilities to be developed in Scotland. Indeed it is surprising how recent the creation of the National Grid is. Barely 60 years have elapsed since its design, and only 50 years from its inception. Moreover the nationalisation of electricity supply consolidating the former initiatives of municipal and private companies into the two groups - the South of Scotland Electricity Board, and the North of Scotland Hydro-Electric Board, dates only from 1947. The arguments for public ownership and provision of electricity, like gas and water before it, rested not only on the unreality of 'competition' in the industry, but also grew out of postwar demands in the managed economy for greater efficiency in the interests of economic growth and industrial development. It is an irony that 40 years later, the same arguments are being employed to de-nationalise and restore private enterprise in a sector where the concept of 'public utility' has long held sway.

ANTHONY SLAVEN

Sir Frederick C GARDINER,

Chairman, Clyde Valley Electrical Power Company; b. 10/1/1855, Kincardine, Tulliallan, s. of Rev Andrew Gardiner and Jane Guthrie; m. 15/9/1887, Elizabeth Morton Ritchie, d. of William Ritchie, wholesale stationer; Partner, James Gardiner & Co, Shipowners; Ch, Clyde Valley Electrical Power Co Ltd; d. 7/8/1937, Killearn; g/v estate: £542,910.

The early electrical supply industry was one in which small independent and larger municipal enterprises flourished in uneasy competition. The industry was one in which progress commercially was dependent upon technical change and innovation in generation, transmission, and in the development of electrical products. As with railways it was one of those industries in which there early grew a divide between the technical men responsible for developing the expertise, and those men of capital and influence who managed the resources and lent their public persona to the business. Sir Frederick Crombie Gardiner was in the latter group.

The early developments in the use and supply of electricity in Britain did not lie in Scotland, even though Lord Kelvin's house in the Professors' Square in Glasgow University was the first in Britain to be lit by electric light. The first serious phase of developing electricity supply began in the 1880s after the passing of the Electric Lighting Act, 1882, which permitted local authorities to dig up thoroughfares, or to give permission to private developers to do so, for the purposes of laying electrical supply cables from a central point of supply to customers in homes and in commercial and industrial premises. Municipalities who gave private enterprises the responsibility of developing electrical supplies in their towns were also given powers to buy out these private companies after a period of 21 years. The local authority could of course negotiate the purchase from the private company within that period and Glasgow Corporation exercised that right in 1892 to buy out the local company. The Corporation then set about extending supply and raised the output of its generating stations from less than one million kilowatt hours (one million kilowatt hours equals 1 gigawatt; ie one GWH) to 1.78 GWH in 1903 and to a spectacular 91 GWH by 1914. Glasgow went in for high voltage distribution within the city and in the nearby towns. The growth of its output, and the improving technical efficiency of equipment in this period, clearly lay behind a rapidly increasing demand and provided an opportunity for suppliers outside the immediate areas served by Glasgow Corporation.

It was this circumstance that lay behind the establishment of the Clyde Valley Power Co in 1901 with an authorised capital of £900,000; Bonar Law was the first chairman. Frederick Gardiner succeeded Bonar Law as chairman of Clyde Valley Electrical Power Co Ltd in 1920, having been a director since 1911. This involvement in the electrical supply industry was a late interest, for Gardiner had by then had a distinguished business career as a shipowner and shipbroker, and had also contributed substantially in public affairs.

Frederick Gardiner was born a son of the manse in 1855. His father was the United Presbyterian Minister at Kincardine, and later at Dean Street Church, Edinburgh. Frederick was one of a family of six sons and one daughter. His early education is not clear, but it is known that he went for some years to New Zealand, partly to train in shipbroking, but largely on account of his health. He was a chronic sufferer from asthma throughout his life. On his return, he and his brothers James and William established the firm of James Gardiner & Co in Glasgow about 1880. They were shipowners and shipbrokers, and built up a successful fleet of cargo steamers, finally disposing of the vessels and withdrawing from shipping at the end of the First World War. By that time Frederick Gardiner was an established and influential man of business, his public services gaining him the Honorary LLD from Glasgow University in 1920. He and his brother William had bequeathed £60,000 to the university to establish three professorships in bacteriology, organic chemistry and physiological chemistry. In 1921 his wartime services were recognised with the award of the KBE.

While active in shipping, Frederick Gardiner had played a fully involved life in the shipping industry, particularly in the shipping federation. He had been, for a time, President of the Clyde Steamship Owners Association, and represented the industry on the London committee of Lloyd's Register of Shipping, as well as holding the position of chairman of the Glasgow Lloyd's Committee. From 1908 to 1923 he served on the Board of Trade Advisory Committee on new lighthouse works, and became its chairman. During the war he was a member of the Advisory Committee on Shipping and also of the Food Requisitioning Committee.

In his public life in Glasgow Frederick Gardiner was elected as a member of the Chamber of Commerce in 1899, became a director of the Chamber in 1909 and president from 1919 to 1921. He was also Lord

Dean of Guild from 1922 to 1924, and became Deputy Lieutenant, both of the City of Glasgow and of Stirlingshire where he had his estate at Ballinkinrain, Killearn. He was also chairman of the West of Scotland Public House Trust, charged with the management of the liquor trade in Glasgow and district.

When Frederick Gardiner withdrew from shipping management and ownership in 1918 he was 63 years old; he did however continue to play an active role in the many bodies of which he was a member. His more direct involvement in the Clyde Valley Power Co dated from 1920 when he succeeded Bonar Law as chairman. Gardiner held the position of chairman of Clyde Valley in the very challenging years which saw the establishment of the Central Electricity Board, and the beginnings of the national grid. As a director of the Clyde Valley Electrical Power Co from 1911, Gardiner had worked with Archibald Page who had been the chief engineer and manager. However as Gardiner succeeded to the chairmanship Page was attracted from the Clyde Valley Co to become one of the new body of electricity commissioners established by the Electricity Supply Act of 1919. Page subsequently became chief engineer of the CEB and succeeded Sir Andrew Duncan as chairman of the CEB in 1935. However, it was in his position as commissioner from 1920 to 1929, that he came most closely in contact with Gardiner. In that period Page was charged with negotiating the plans for the establishment of a national grid. The first area scheme to be adopted was that for Central Scotland in 1927, and Page was influential in bringing agreement between the competing companies, including the Clyde Valley Electrical Power Co. Under Frederick Gardiner's chairmanship the Clyde Valley Electrical Power Co extended its capacity at both its main generating stations at Clydesmill, Cambuslang, and at Yoker. It had a third major thermal plant at Motherwell and extended its area of operation largely by acquiring the shares of smaller independent companies, By 1930 the Clyde Valley Electrical Power Co had raised its authorised capital to £2.9 million; it then owned all the shares in the Strathclyde Electricity Supply Co, the Lanarkshire Hydro-electric Power Co, the Kilmarnock Electric Lighting Co, and in Clyde Valley Accessories Ltd. By the time of Gardiner's death in 1937, the Clyde Valley Power Co and its subsidiaries provided power to some 130,000 consumers, distributing its electricity from its generating stations through 561 substations, over 974 miles of high tension overhead lines and cables, and 1,086 miles of low tension distribution networks. The two main generating stations at Clydesmill and Yoker were interconnected and were also linked to the Central Electricity Board's grid scheme. Outside Glasgow the Clyde Valley Electrical Power Co had become the dominant supplier of electricity to domestic and industrial consumers under Gardiner's chairmanship.

When Frederick Gardiner died in 1937 at the age

of 82 he had a substantial personal estate valued at over £500,000. He left many legacies including £3,000 to the research department of Glasgow Royal Cancer Hospital; £1,500 to the Western Infirmary to endow a bed, and £1,000 to the Royal Society For the Relief of Indigent Gentlewomen of Scotland. The residue of his estate, after all claims and legacies had been met, was divided equally among Glasgow University, the Scottish National Academy of Music, and the National Art Collection Fund.

ANTHONY SLAVEN

SOURCES

Unpublished

SRO: SC 36/48/516

Published

The Bailie, 12/2/1919
Directory of Directors
Glasgow Chamber of Commerce Journal, 2/2/1919, 6/6/1919
Glasgow Chamber of Commerce Journal, Vol 20, No 8, August 1937
Glasgow Herald, 'Clyde Valley Finances', 20/5/1937
Glasgow Herald, 9/8/1937, 11/8/1937
Hannah, L, *Electricity Before Nationalisation*, London, 1979
The Times, 9/8/1937, 11/8/1937
Transactions of the Institute of the International Engineering Congress, Glasgow, 1938, The Clyde Valley Electrical Power Co
Who Was Who, 1929-40

Charles KER,

Chartered accountant; b. 12/9/1860, Glasgow, s. of William Ker, merchant, and Caroline Paton; m. Florence Higginbotham; 3 s., 2 d.; Snr Partner, McClelland, Ker & Co, CAs; d. 8/7/1940; g/v estate: £100,187.

Charles Ker was a chartered accountant whose range of interests and activities was so wide that his biography could have been included in any one of several

sectors of industry. A Glasgow man by birth and education he nevertheless was one of a relatively small number of businessmen who divided their time, almost equally between Glasgow and Edinburgh.

Charles Ker was born into a long established Glasgow family and was educated at Glasgow Academy and Glasgow University where he graduated MA in 1880. His apprenticeship was served in the firm of McClelland, MacKinnon and Blyth and he became a chartered accountant in the Glasgow Institute in 1883 serving on the council of that body from 1896-99 and again from 1910-13. He was its president from 1924-26. He wrote many articles on matters of accountancy for the professional journals. He was made a partner of his firm in 1890 and in 1901 the name of the firm was changed to McClelland, Ker and Company. Charles Ker became the senior partner in 1909.

His extensive friendships and business contacts, with the Gairdner and Blackie families amongst others, brought him invitations to serve on the board of directors of many companies. Amongst those which he accepted were the City of Glasgow Life Assurance Co Ltd, the Dalmellington Iron Co, the Steel Co of Scotland, the National Bank of Scotland, Lloyds

Bank, North British and Mercantile Insurance Co, Baird & Dalmellington and the London, Midland & Scottish Railway. He was chairman of the Scottish committee of the LMS.

Ker's first experience with the electricity industry was as a director of the Huelva Gas and Electricity Company, a Spanish company whose registered office was in Glasgow. It was one of the earliest directorships which he held. He served on the board of the Clyde Valley Electrical Power Company during the First World War and became its chairman in 1932. He was therefore in at the beginning of the electricity industry and well placed to make a contribution. The electricity industry, however, did not have a painless birth and there was something of a rivalry between the private sector and the public sector. In Glasgow, for example, the Corporation was responsible for electricity generation and distribution but elsewhere in central Scotland private companies such as Clyde Valley did the job. The difficult tasks, in building the national grid during the inter-war years were done by the engineers but accountants such as Ker had a vital role to play in ensuring that the heavy demands for investment did not outstrip their company's ability to pay.

Not unnaturally such a man found himself invited to serve on various public and private bodies and Ker did not shirk from such duties. He was a Deputy Lieutenant for the county and city of Glasgow, a Scottish Ecclesiastical Commissioner under the Church of Scotland (Property & Endowments) Act 1925, honorary governor of Glasgow Academy, chairman of the Merchants House of Glasgow, Dean of Guild, chairman of the Glasgow Convalescent Home and of the Institute for Orphan Girls. He also served on the commission on state control of the liquor traffic.

In 1928 Ker was awarded the honorary degree of Doctor of Laws by Glasgow University. He was a member of the Western Club, the Carlton Club and the University of Edinburgh Club. His recreation was hill-walking.

CHARLES W MUNN

SOURCES

Unpublished

SRO: SC 36/48/561, Inventory
  SC 36/51/274, Will

Published

The Accountants' Magazine, September 1940
Directory of Directors

Glasgow Herald, 9/7/1940
Official Directory of Scottish CAs
Scottish Biographies, Glasgow & London, 1938

Sir Edward MacCOLL,

Electrical engineer; b. 8/7/1882, Dumbarton, s. of John MacColl of Kilmelfort, Argyll; m. Margaret McDiarmid, d. of Andrew Donald of Kirkton Hill, Dumbarton; 1 s., 1 d.; Deputy Ch and Chief Executive, North of Scotland Hydro-Electric Board; d. 14/6/1951, Edinburgh.

Sir Edward MacColl was born in Dumbarton on 8 July 1882, the son of an English mother and a Highland father, John MacColl of Kilmelfort in Argyll. His father died when he was still a child and he and his mother went to live with his maternal grandfather, Albert Edward Johnstone, an exceptionally skilled model maker at Denny's shipyard. MacColl was greatly influenced by his grandfather to whom he ascribed his love of craftsmanship. His other passionate interest, music, he owed to his mother who, following her husband's death, was forced to turn her considerable musical accomplishments to account by taking in pupils. The family was able to provide MacColl with a formal education at a private school for Scots Episcopalians, but this came to an abrupt end when his grandparents died in the great influenza epidemic of 1895. At the age of 14 MacColl was apprenticed to John Brown's at Clydebank, a rigorous training which he supplemented by attendance at Glasgow Technical School and, later, some classes in electrical engineering at the University of Glasgow. MacColl's apprenticeship at Clydebank was terminated in 1901, ostensibly on the grounds of bad timekeeping, but essentially because the harsh, 12 hour day had become increasingly irksome to him, and his rebelliousness had become evident to his employers.

From Clydebank he went to Glasgow Corporation Tramways as a sub-station chargeman and, when his practical ability was recognised, to the test room and then to Pinkston power station. He remained with the Tramways Department until 1919, when he became chief technical engineer of the Clyde Valley Electric Power Co. By the end of the First World War the Clyde Valley Co had become the largest generator and distributor of electricity in Scotland, with thermal stations at Yoker, Clyde's Mill and Motherwell. To undertake the post-war reorganisation that their growing system demanded, the company had appointed G T Goslin their general manager. Goslin had previously been with the Glasgow Corporation Electricity Department where he had become aware of MacColl's driving energy and inventive skills. It was at Goslin's insistence that MacColl was invited to join the Clyde Valley Co.

Within a few years, MacColl had devised a range of equipment for the control of high voltage transmission lines, electrical generators and transformers, and had so mastered the problems of thermal generating stations that he had been able to secure a significant reduction in fuel costs. A man so receptive to new ideas could hardly fail to support a scheme to harness the latent powers of the Falls of Clyde. First suggested in 1909, the original proposals had foundered on the twin rocks of the inadequacy of demand for the electrical energy that such a scheme was capable of producing and the problems of storing sufficient water to ensure continuous operation. When similar difficulties threatened the viability of the post-war proposals of the Power & Traction Finance Co - a consortium of Sir William Arrol, John Brown, Cammell Laird, English Electric and the Prudential Insurance Co - MacColl's advice was sought. Indeed, because the Clyde Valley Co were the 'authorised undertakers' for the area surrounding the Falls, the Power & Traction Co had no alternative but to approach MacColl's employers.

With his customary energy, MacColl carried out a detailed investigation of the technical, economic and legal features of the scheme. This revealed that with a very large catchment area of over 400 square miles providing the assurance of reasonably continuous water supplies, the Falls of Clyde were capable of development by a run-of-river scheme that required no storage facilities. All that was needed was the diversion of the waters of the Clyde by means of regulating weirs equipped with automatic flood gates to two stations, three miles apart, at Bonnington and Stonebyres. MacColl's careful assessment greatly encouraged the promoters, and in 1924 the Clyde Valley Co established a subsidiary, the Lanarkshire Hydro-Electric Power Co, to undertake the schemes. It was completed within three years, the stations being specifically designed to work in conjunction with the Clyde Valley's thermal stations. The Falls of Clyde scheme marked the emergence of Edward MacColl as a pioneer in the use of hydro-electric power for supply in Scotland. 'MacColl's Folly', the coal lobby called it, but its capital cost per k/W installed (£27.2) was the lowest of all the pre-war hydro schemes; the scheme neither offended against scenic beauty nor, because it provided a generous quantity of compensation water, did it destroy the attractions of the famous Falls.

In 1927 MacColl left the Clyde Valley Co to become engineer of the Central Scotland District of the Central Electricity Board (CEB), where he created the first regional grid in Britain. His previous employers - Glasgow Corporation and the Clyde Valley Co - had established supply systems which employed a frequency of 25 cycles per second, whereas 50 cycles was standard for the rest of Scotland. One of the most important objectives of the CEB was to standardise the frequency of 50 cycles throughout Great Britain. This would permit all generating stations to be interlinked in a national grid. MacColl's initial responsibility as district engineer for Central Scotland was to organise the change of frequency in his area. This was accomplished so successfully that the methods adopted were later applied throughout the country. Later he was involved in the construction of the 132 kW grid lines and sub-stations not simply for the Central Scotland District but for the whole of Scotland, for in 1931 he had been appointed CEB's Scottish manager. The fact that the administrative and maintenance costs of the Scottish section of the grid, which by 1933 had been extended to the South of Scotland, were the lowest in the country was largely credited to MacColl's technical expertise.

MacColl's interest in the development of water power was sustained during his early years with the CEB by his negotiations with the Grampian Electricty Supply Co, from whom the CEB purchased bulk hydro-electricity, and the Galloway Water Power Co, whose generating capacity was linked to the national grid in 1936. It is in that year when MacColl, engaged in working out the details of the possible hydro development of Loch Sloy conceived the idea of going beyond his remit and proposing, not an orthodox scheme utilising the latent power of the waters of Loch Sloy, 800 ft above Loch Lomond, but a massive pumped storage scheme. This would have drawn electricity from the grid to pump water from Loch Lomond up to Loch Sloy during the night, when surplus power was available, and used this water - now flowing in the reverse direction - to feed eight generators installed in a power station on the banks of Loch Lomond during the hours of maximum daytime demand. This was a remarkably bold conception for its time. It proved to be too bold. The technical committee of the CEB refused to sanction the scheme and MacColl was told to abandon it.

The survey of the water power resources of Scotland prepared by MacColl in collaboration with J Henderson and James Williamson, the distinguisihed civil engineer, for the Scottish Economic Committee (the Hilleary Committee) in 1938 received a similar rebuff. When the original report, together with its recommendation for a co-ordinated system of generation and transmission, was submitted to the CEB it was rejected immediately. These setbacks greatly disappointed MacColl. He had always found control from above frustrating; intervention from London was intolerable. He became increasingly fretful. Now that the Scottish grid had been 'completed' (although no attempt was to be made to extend it to the Highlands), he felt that his work for the CEB had become a matter of routine, completely unsuitable for a creative engineer. This partially explains the energy with which he conjured up plans for exploiting the water power of the Highlands. Thus, when the North of Scotland Hydro-Electric Board came into existence in 1943, he eagerly accepted the call to become the Board's deputy chairman and chief executive.

Gathering together a group of committed engineers and a panel of technical advisors drawn from consulting firms with experience in hydro-electricity, he made it abundantly clear that he intended 'to drive ahead at full speed and produce electricity in the North of Scotland at a much earlier date than anyone had visualised'. The Board's first duty was to produce a Development Scheme showing the water resources in the area under its jurisdiction which might be the subject of more detailed and operational 'constructional schemes'. Almost unbelievably, the Development Scheme was completed within three months. Drawing heavily on the report which he himself had prepared for the Hilleary Committee, MacColl drew up a list of 102 possible areas of water power development. Every possible site, however small, was listed. One of his technical advisers, J Guthrie Brown, was astonished by MacColl's 'detailed knowledge ... It seemed as if he had walked over all the areas himself and assessed their potentialities'.

It was almost inevitable that of the projects enumerated in the Development Scheme, the first to be the subject of a constructional scheme was Loch Sloy. Abandoning the grandiose 'reversible hydraulic features' of the 1938 proposals, MacColl pushed it forward as a conventional scheme. It was still very big, practical and potentially highly 'profitable', in the sense that most of its output could be sold to the CEB on terms that would provide the revenue necessary to fulfil MacColl's primary objective: the provision of electric power in those parts of the Highlands where there was little or no prospect of covering the costs of generation, transmission and distribution. In effect, Loch Sloy would subsidise much of his ambitious development programme. But *one* such major scheme was not enough to attain this goal. It had to be supported by a second, similarly profitable scheme. It was for this reason that MacColl insisted that the Board should follow Loch Sloy with the Tummel-Garry scheme. This was a typically courageous decision, for it was always recognised that his plans to impound the waters of the upper tributaries of the River Garry and the River Tummel would create such a storm of indignation that the activities of the Board might be severely circumscribed. To MacColl the risk was worth taking. Not only was Tummel-Garry vital to his long-term plans but he believed that if there was to be a fight to enforce the principles underlying the Hydro-Electric Development Act of 1943, the Board should go all out and settle the issue once and for all. After months of bitter argument Tummel-Garry was finally approved and, following acrimonious debate, sanctioned by Parliament.

In promoting Sloy and Tummel-Garry the Board had argued that the construction of these two great schemes promised to alleviate the critical power shortage that was anticipated in the near future. It was stated that they would both be able to feed significant amounts of power into the national grid by 1947, but within a few months of the beginning of their construction in 1945, it was already apparent that this timetable was impossibly optimistic. Everywhere MacColl and the contractors encountered shortages: of steel, cement, heavy mechanical and electrical plant, timber and men. Not until February 1950 were the first of Loch Sloy's generating sets put in motion; not until two months later did the first of Tummel-Garry's massive turbo-alternators begin to make its contribution to the grid. In little more than a year, on the very eve of the formal opening of the latter scheme, MacColl was dead, exhausted by over-work (he did not delegate easily), racked by assuming personal responsibility for the embarrassing delays that made it impossible for Sloy and Tummel-Garry to contribute to the national supply of electricity during the fuel crisis of 1947-48, and increasingly conscious that the inflationary pressures, which were making nonsense of his earlier cost estimates, might be used not only as a reason for limiting the Board's programme of rural electrification but even as an excuse for ending the Board's very existence.

He could not know that the Board would not only survive, but that by the mid-1960s many of his dreams would be realised. Others played vital roles in the attainment of the board's objectives - Tom Johnston, Lord Airlie, the board's senior officials, the contractors, and the members of the board's panels of civil and electrical engineering consultants - but it is generally acknowledged that in the last eight years of his life, MacColl had fashioned the future course of the North of Scotland Hydro-Electric Board. He was knighted in 1949.

Everything he did was done with enthusiasm. While others counselled caution, MacColl was an inspired innovator. Not content with hydro schemes, he experimented with harnessing wind power, exploiting Scotland's reserves of peat, and investigating the possibilities of the closed-cycle gas turbine as a source of thermal generation. By clothing the Board's power stations with local stone not only did he attempt to make these potentially unsightly boxes blend with their environment, he did much to resuscitate stone quarrying in the north of Scotland. While many were disappointed with the refusal of industrialists to establish themselves in the Highlands, thereby stemming the outward flow of migrants, MacColl was more concerned to concentrate on measures which he believed would increase the comforts and raise the living standards of the crofters. They were his major concern.

Among his many interests outside engineering were his love of music, inherited from his mother, reading, tramping the hills, and actively supporting the MacColl Society, of which he was sometime president.

But all these took second place to his work. As his wife wrote soon after his death, 'perhaps his biography is written in Sloy, Pitlochry and Affric, the perceptible evidence of his vision'.

PETER L PAYNE

WRITINGS

Writings

'Hydro-Electric Development in Scotland', *Transactions of the Institution of Engineers and Shipbuilders in Scotland* Vol 89, 1946
'From Paraffin and Sod peat to the All-Electric Age', *Electrical Age,* October 1946

SOURCES

Unpublished

Archives of the North of Scotland Hydro-Electric Board
'Report of the Water Power Resources of Scotland', undated, c 1937

Published

Fraser, Norrie, (ed), *Sir Edward MacColl: A Maker of Modern Scotland,* Edinburgh, undated, c 1956
Johnston, Thomas, *Memories,* London, 1952
Paton, T A L and Brown, J Guthrie, *Power from Water,* London, 1960
Payne, Peter L, *The Hydro: A Study of the development of the major hydro-electric schemes undertaken by the North of Scotland Hydro-Electric Board,* Aberdeen, 1988

William YOUNG,

Gasworks Manager and Consultant Engineer; born 1841, Selkirk; s. of John Young, gasworks engineer; m.; 1 s.; Manager, Messrs Taylor, oilworks, Musselburgh; d. 1/3/1907, Priorsford House, Peebles; g/v estate: £13,726.

The coal-gas and petrochemical oil-shale industries in Scotland collaborated intermittently, yet most advantageously during the late nineteenth century, as exemplified by the successes of William Young. Horizontal cast-iron retorts in which Ayrshireman William Murdoch heated coals for the first economical application of coal-gas to illumination in 1792, were direct progenitors of those used by James 'Paraffin' Young to distil oil-shale for mineral oils in 1850.

William Young was unrelated to James, with whom he is often confused, as in a 1924 *Glasgow Herald* article about their mutual colleague George Beilby. From the 1860s William applied to gasworks the new technological advances made by shale-oilworks in response to increasingly poor shales and competition from natural liquid petroleum imports.

William was a second generation gasworks engineer with a technological and entrepreneurial flair which gave him a pre-eminence in the industry and a widespread practice as a consultant engineer. A brilliant industrial chemist whose work was his hobby, William had no time for frivolities or outside interests. His retiring nature shunned the publicity that would have dispelled his obscurity. Despite this disposition, technical editor Walter King found him a 'very human, warm hearted, true friend, and transparently honest of purpose.' Enthusiasm, a piercing intellect and remarkably retentive memory kept William at the forefront of developments. One of the greatest authorities on destructive distillation of coal and shale, he also specialised in by-product recovery and fractional distillation and gasification of oils. From 1893 until his death he was a close adviser to the Government Alkali Inspector, R F Carpenter.

The investment pattern in the Scottish gas industry left little scope for talented engineers to profit from their skills by direct ownership. Like waterworks, heavy investment in immovable distribution pipes made monopoly supply the most cost-effective and inhibited rivalry or forced competitors into price-fixing agreements. Monopoly was normal, but was only tolerated uneasily by consumers, from companies owned largely by numerous resident consumer-investors, or municipal authorities. William had other ideas.

Bright gas engineers profited mainly as consultants, employed to plan and perhaps supervise construction or alteration of gasworks elsewhere in Britain or abroad. Some also patented equipment, manufactured by ironworks for sale to the industry. William gained from both fields, and went further by promoting a company to supply under licence the oil-gas process he invented.

William was born in Selkirk in 1841, shortly after his father John became manager of the first, new gasworks there. His earliest childhood recollection, perhaps due to the smell, was of his father experimenting with a water-gas process carburetted with fish-oil. John (1815-1886), known locally as 'Jock the Genius', imbued William with his questing mind. Self taught in the library of his Galashiels shoemaker uncle, to whom he had been apprenticed, John entered the industry the same way as many of the first Scottish managers. After reading newspaper descriptions of London gasworks, he turned a domestic kettle into a retort to hold hot coal, and inverted a butter firkin over a water-filled tub as a gas-holder to supply gaslights in the shoeshop.

William spent his later childhood in Dalkeith with his five brothers and sister Mary. John became manager of that larger town gasworks, closer to Edinburgh, in 1852 on the basis of his growing reputation as a coal and water analyst as well as consultant gas and water engineer. He won a silver medal from the Scottish Society of Arts for improved gas apparatus, and exhibited a model gasworks at the 1851 International Exhibition in London.

The lives of all John's family came to revolve around the new gas and oil technologies, especially Dalkeith gasworks where he became a director. Mary married a former schoolmaster, George Frith Cusitor (d. 1874), who was manager at Dalkeith from 1868 to 1874. When William then declined the post, it went to his brother David who was dismissed for mismanagement and inebriation in 1889, and thereafter until 1910 to William's friend Alex Bell Snr. Of William's other brothers, Robert became manager of Uphall Oil Works, John Jnr was manager at Oakbank Oilworks and eventually a fruit merchant in Edinburgh, while Thomas became a contractor at Emmetsburgh in Iowa, USA.

In youth William assisted his father's extensive practice of analysing the gas potential of coals, and paraffin oil in shales, for industrialists. He may also have helped in experimental projects and with planning the improved water-supply for Dalkeith. Science was an exciting novelty in the household. John was one of the first Scots to make artificial carbons for electricity, and gave public lectures on electricity, chemistry and optics. William certainly assisted with winter evening-classes in science which his father ran at home for young Dalkethians. William was an idealist and hater of waste. Brought up under Puritan influences, and suffering moderately weak health throughout his life, he later rejected religious dogma yet was considered extremely high principled and a friend to many in need.

During the mid 1850s, William gained the patronage of Peter Brash a soap, candle and oil manufacturer with Messrs Wm Taylor & Co of Leith. Brash had an eye for chemical technology, lent him science books, and encouraged William to attend public lectures in Edinburgh given by Dr Lyon Playfair and other scientists.

He then became an apprentice gasfitter or 'plumber', under Lasswade gas manager Alexander Bell (1836-1910). Bell had trained the same way at Dalkeith under William's father before building Lasswade gasworks to John's designs. Bell's son, Alexander Jnr, later assisted William's experiments. Apprentice William was an innovator, often castigated by Bell for disturbing the conservative workshop routine. As a journeyman fitter he quickly introduced a new system of rolling lead for pipes, which trebled productivity.

In 1863 Bell left to manage Gibraltar gasworks, and William at 21 became manager at Lasswade, with a tied-house and annual salary of £75. He soon experimented with bituminous blind-shale and blaes being discarded as waste by a re-opened Bonnyrigg colliery, and obtained 9,000 cu ft of gas per ton. Then, from oil shales came a rich 30 candle power gas and good paraffin.

Unable to persuade his Lasswade directors to permit large-scale low temperature distillation in improved retorts, for both paraffin and gas, William obtained space from Bonnyrigg colliery to build a small crude-oil works. Without a market for the gas, some was burned as fuel to heat the horizontal retorts but most was wasted. This inspired William's attempts to minimise gas production and maximise oil, and led to the study of retort design which remained central throughout his life. Improvements came with deep 'charges' of shale reducing air-spaces, and false-bottomed retorts to prevent the furnace gasifying oil droplets. Real success only came with vertical retorts and the replacement of steam-injection by 'exhauster' fans blowing incondensible gas down the retort to flush all oil-vapour out through its base.

About 1866 William left Lasswade gasworks, to become Brash's manager at Messrs Taylor's oilworks in Musselburgh, and Oakbank, Straiton. Oil companies proliferated after the expiry of 'Paraffin' Young's exclusive patent (1850-1864) and stiff competition was increased by the scarcity of good quality oil shales which rapidly rose in price. Moreover, imports of North American crude oil, exploited since 1859, pushed British oil prices down heavily in 1866. The industry still used horizontal retorts which baked and discoloured the oil, making it unattractive to customers. Retorts were small and furnaces large, wasting fuel, causing rapid deterioration of retorts, and preventing the recovery of ammonium by-products which were increasingly profitable at gasworks.

Unsuccessful vertical retorts had been tried much earlier, for coal gas by Murdoch, and by Barnet in 1829, and for oil by 'Paraffin' Young in 1854. Interest in them increased in the 1860s, and William's design successfully reduced the charring of oil although, like others, uneven heating caused retort damage. Vapour and tar were recycled to the retort for re-distillation, the first step in fractional-distillation methods which William later developed extensively.

Brash financed further development in return for half of the profits, and became joint patentee with William in 1866. William soon sold his share of the retort patent for £3,000, but Brash later made more when it was quite widely adopted. William's new retort of 1868 achieved the ideal uniform low red heat which 'Paraffin' Young had advocated 20 years earlier but had been unable to maintain. Some, with an expensive double-casing, were erected at Oakbank in 1871. George Beilby, works chemist there from 1869, recalled fierce controversy between proponents of horizontal and vertical retorts. In 1872 William patented a better, single-casing design using 'spent shale' at the bottom as fuel to heat the top. By burning residual carbon this curtailed the public nuisance of smouldering shale-bings. Retort labourers found it too complex and William lost his rewards to a similar but simplified version by N M Henderson in 1873, which swept the industry.

At Oakbank, Beilby was obliged to operate both types and from 1878 began improving William's design. A gifted pupil of 'Paraffin' Young's chief chemist, John Galletly, he was well equipped for the task, and later became wealthy through his Cassel chemical company.

William joined Clippens Oil Company of Paisley in 1874 and ran their experimental plant at Straiton, using low temperatures to recover ammonia. Later, with Alex Bell Snr, who became its chief engineer, he designed a large new oilworks at New Pentland. William explored new possibilities for emolument. In 1877 he patented a process to manufacture petrol, then called gazolene, but in the absence of petrol-engines its main use was to make an illuminating gas called carburetted air, using a small apparatus suitable for private houses. William lit his own and adjacent houses this way.

Against the entire trend of investment patterns in the Scottish gas industry, William organised inter-industry investment by restricted membership groups to profit directly by improved management. With four partners in 1878 he acquired and revitalised the 1829 Falkirk gas company, which had competed with a Consumer's company since 1845. William held 290 of the 900 shares, and his partners included gasworks managers from Dumbarton (200) and Greenock (50), Alex Young of Musselburgh Oilworks (10) and W S Brown iron-tube maker of Glasgow (50). They sold out to the rival in 1887, but meanwhile they had in 1883 purchased West Kilpatrick gas company from its 22 shareholders, followed in 1887 by companies at Dunblane and Earlston (re-sold in 1894). William and Brown formed a similar group of eight partners, including five gasworks managers, to acquire Busby gas company in 1886.

Throughout his career, William encouraged Scottish gasworks managers to use the knowledge gained by shale-oil works, and upheld the aims of technical co-operation and efficiency propounded by the North British Association of Gas Managers. His father had helped to found that Association in 1861 after strongly refuting claims of incompetent management and profit concealment made against the gas industry, by G.R. Flintoff and his Cheap Gas Movement which promoted rival Consumers' companies.

Many of William's researches took decades to reach fruition. To assist his brother-in-law George Cusitor, a Committee member of the Association, William tested paraffin-oil anti-freeze for consumers' water-filled gas-meters after the havoc of severe frosts in 1860/61 and showed these light oils were unsuitable. They absorbed some illuminating constituents, but because these could be released again by volatisation, oil-washing became valuable for by-products recovery from waste shale-oil gas.

Virtually all coal-gas in Scotland until the 1880s was used for illumination from open-flame burners. Its 'candle power' required a carefully balanced mixture of heat-generating and of soot-generating hydrocarbons. Fine carbon soot became incandescent momentarily before burning away. The development of Welsbach gas-mantles using incandescent minerals permitted the soot chemicals to be phased out, and great improvements made in calorific value for cooking and heating only after 1885.

William's first marketable gasworks equipment, for improved 'candle power', was the 'Analyzer' developed in 1874-5 with Henry Aitken (1838-1903) of Falkirk, a coal-mine owner and experimentalist at Almond Ironworks. Used at Hamilton and Dalmarnock, it released illuminants by rewarming tar, but was uneconomical. William's water-washer, tried at Lanark in 1880, enabled small gasworks to produce ammoniacal liquor for the boom market in sulphate fertilisers, and was very widely used.

In 1874 a full scale experiment to produce coal gas in four large vertical retorts was made at Musselburgh gasworks, managed by family friend Andrew Scott. Non-caking Scottish coal suited vertical retorts with great potential advantages, particularly reduced heat loss and deterioration, and automatic gravity feed instead of slow and skilful manual emptying and re-charging. Failure resulted from water-gas dilution, and inadequate heat without C W Siemens' revolutionary producer-gas furnaces and heat- regenerators.

At Straiton, with Alex Bell Jnr, William developed a radically improved two-phase version of his shale-oil retort, with steam injection to recover ammonia. Beilby also had devised improvements and in 1881 they collaborated to make the famous Pentland Retort, with producer and regenerators. This doubled ammonia recovery, improved paraffin yield, resuscitated the industry, and made William wealthy. He retired to Priorsford House, Peebles, as a consultant engineer.

For John Fyfe of James Young's Paraffin Co he sought methods of making permanent oil-gas from low value heavy-oils. Helped again by Alex Bell Jnr, then gas manager at Peebles, his very successful 'Peebles Process' of high-candle power enrichment for coal-gas found an eager market since best cannel coal used for enrichment had become very scarce and expensive in 1892. To market it, William formed the Oil Gas Enrichment Co in 1893 with a nominal £30,000 in £1 shares. He held 900 shares, and fellow directors were G T Beilby (1,400), James Milne (500) gas-meter maker, Hugh Brown (500), G Harrison (700) and W Thorburn (400) MP. Sixteen oil and gas engineers held a further 1,650 shares. The process was used at 30 gasworks by 1896, including the main Scottish towns, but William's work on an improved version in 1893 permanently damaged his health.

Behind his triumphs, William concealed a personal tragedy over his only child, John Alison Young, born in 1877 with poor mental and physical health. To separate John from 'several undesirable women' in Edinburgh, William sent him to a London aunt after his wife's death in 1897, but John thereupon married one of the women, Isabella Gloag. William became estranged, and threw himself back into his work.

Many gasworks had adopted horizontal 'regenerative' retorts with higher temperatures causing unwanted naphthalene deposits. Samuel and Thomas Glover, who had used the Peebles Process at St Helens gasworks, visited William for advice about this and with him visited several oil works. They were so impressed with vertical retort efficiency that they persuaded him to help them design vertical gas retorts. The first Glover-Young retort of 1905 gave high calorie gas, coke and by-products, and became a market leader.

At his death in 1907 Wiliam Young left an estate of only £23,007 (actually worth £13,726) including £9,281 invested abroad. It included £1,003 in Lewes Gas Co, £1,391 in Dublin Consumers Gas Co, £4,861 in Melbourne Metropolitan Gas Co, £2,643 in the Australian Gas Co of Sydney, and £2,687 in the South Australian Gas Company of Adelaide. An annuity was granted to his son, and Harehope Farm at Eddlestone with its stock of £2,000 was donated to Peebles Town Council for use as a sanitarium.

MICHAEL S COTTERILL

WRITINGS

Young, W, 'Vertical Retorts', *Journal of Gas Lighting*, Vol 93, pp 305, 560; Vol 94, p 95, 1906

SOURCES

Unpublished

Cotterill, M S, 'The Scottish Gas Industry up to 1914', University of Strathclyde PhD Thesis, 1976
SRO: BT2/2544, Oil Gas Enrichment Co Ltd
SRO: SC 42/20/17, Testament and Inventory

Published

Beilby, G, 'Shale Oil Industry', *Journal of the Society of Chemical Industry*, Vol 16, p 878, 1897
Beilby, G, 'William Young', *North British Association of Gas Managers Transactions*, p 76, 1912
Carpenter, R F, *44th Annual Report of Alkali Commissioners*, Vol 11, p 218, 1908
King, W, 'William Young', *Journal of Gas Lighting*, Vol 97, pp 589, 593, 1907
Dalkeith Advertiser, 7/3/1907
Scott, A, 'Distilling Coal', *Journal of Gas Lighting*, Vol 24, p 93, 1874

Transport and Communication

Despite its title, this section deals with transport rather than communication. In the twentieth century, communication has mushroomed with the expansion of mass and specialist publications and the further rise of marketing, education, advertising and the electronic gadgetry of radio, television and the computer. Even in the last quarter of the nineteenth century, modern advertising and the mass press were emerging with the telegraph being supplemented by the telephone. This 'communications revolution' was an important area for enterprise. It is touched on, briefly, in Andrew Weir's biography within this section and in several of the publishing biographies but radio and television was deliberately excluded from the sector remit. Essays are therefore confined to the more traditional role of transport as a means of goods, mail and passenger movement. Another convention which is followed is the exclusion of such not unimportant matters as water supply, drainage, other pipelines (primarily gas and oil) and electricity distribution. This is covered in the section on Gas, Electricity and Water. Post Office employment is also excluded as a special type of transport employment which was within the public sector and, of course, extending its role into a large extension of telephone systems. Employment in road provision and maintenance appears as part of general employment in local and central government.

Within these qualifications, Table 1 suggests that transport employment in Scotland doubled between 1871 and 1901, attained some further modest growth to 1931 and thereafter stabilised more or less in line with the stagnation in total Scottish population and employment.

Though the table shows a substantial rise in the share of Scottish employment in transport, the extent of the actual rise between 1871 and 1901 must be queried. Some of this growth is certainly due to a re-categorisation of general workers of 1871, particularly port workers, as transport specific workers by 1901. On the other hand, strong growth in the volume of goods movement and in the sophistication of services offered required extra labour despite some improvements in productivity. Rail employment also gained from buoyant passenger demand encouraged both by service improvements and by rising real incomes. Most road passenger workers were still cabmen and grooms in 1901 but local demand for mass transit was already reflected in over 3,000 urban tramway employees.

Between 1901 and 1961, the almost stationary share of transport employment conceals significant structural changes. Rail employment peaked in the 1920s but fell away very slowly with a loss of only 10% of jobs between 1931 and 1961. The sharpest fall in employment, and in the rail share of traffic, did not come until the 1960s. Sea employment fell much more quickly from 1931 reflecting some gains in productivity but influenced by such factors as the relative decline of the Scottish economy, some increases in the use of English ports for Scottish imports and exports and a reduced involvement of Scottish-based sailors in world merchant shipping. Perhaps surprisingly, road goods employment also dropped sharply between 1901 and 1931 with only a mild increase to 1961. The initial fall may be related to a replacement of workers in carting firms by workers within other non-transport firms developing 'own account' operations in supplying their own transport. 'Own account' motor-vans and lorries began to replace the local carter and generate new traffic not picked up in the census categorisation of transport. At the same time, motorisation must have allowed one lorry driver to replace two or more carters. From 1931, shifts to larger lorries reduced the need for extra drivers but this factor was more than compensated by the explosive growth of road freight movement. Hence the rise in road freight employment to 1961.

Turning to passengers, the coming of the motor bus, allied with the continued growth of real incomes and a strong desire for mobility, brought a more dramatic explosion of demand which

Table 1 *Transport Employment in Scotland, 1871-961 (thousands)*

	1871	1901	1931	1961
Sea	20	21	27	11
Ports	—	11	13	12
Rail	12	43	60	54
Roads: Goods		39	17	21
Passengers	21	15	26	37
Air	—	—	⋆	3
Other	21	23	34	36
Total	74	152	177	174
Total Scottish Employment	1464	1983	2221	2200
Transport as share of Scottish employment	5.1%	7.7%	8.8%	7.9%

Sources: C H Lee, *British Regional Employment Statistics, 1841-1971*, Cambridge
      University Press, 1979, for totals and relevant Decennial Censuses for sea,
      ports, rail, road and air.
  ⋆ The 1931 census records a total of 18 persons empoyed in air transport.

could not be met without large increases in the number of drivers. The bus brought new travel opportunities to tramless suburbs and all of rural Scotland. Bus employment exceeded tram employment around 1928 and, by 1961, road passenger employment was dominated by the bus with 33,000 workers, less than 1,000 in trams (the last system, that of Glasgow, finally closed in 1962) and some 3,000 in taxis and private hire. Car use had become a serious threat to bus traffic growth by the 1950s but, as on the railways, a massive impact on bus employment did not become apparent until after 1961. The sales and maintenance requirements of motor vehicles produced fresh areas for private enterprise, notably from the 1920s. The 1931 Census included such workers (some 9,000) in its transport category but they were transferred to miscellaneous services in subsequent censuses and are *not* included in the 1931 and 1961 figures given in Table 1. By 1961, 34,000 jobs were listed in garages, filling stations and motor distribution. Air traffic, overwhelmingly related to passengers and mails, accounted for just over 3,000 jobs by 1961.

One final comment must be made on what is omitted from statistics of Scottish transport employment. Only by implication do they tell us anything about profitability and they conceal the role of Scottish-based entrepreneurs in developing worldwide transport services, particularly in the heyday of British shipping between the 1850s and 1914.

THE DIMENSIONS OF TRANSPORT: VOLUMES OF MOVEMENT

Rail

No official data is available on rail passenger miles and freight ton miles are not recorded until 1950. Inter-war information is also missing for most types of rail statistics but passenger and goods traffic was clearly rising much faster than both population and route length from 1870 (Table 2). Freight tonnage did fall after the First World War, influenced initially by recession in coal mining and the heavy industries. High levels of traffic loss to the road sector did not begin until the later 1950s. Passenger trips shot up between 1860 and 1900. Many of these trips were short-distance urban journeys soon to suffer from electric tram competition. The bus took away more shorter-

Table 2   *Scottish Rail Statistics*

	Route Length (Miles)	Mineral and General Freight (Million Tons)		Ton Miles (Millions)	Passenger Trips (Millions)	Gross Receipts (£ millions)	Operating Ratio
1860	1486				16.5	£2.9	45%
1870	2519				27.1	£4.7	51%
1880	2907	31.3			46.0	£7.0	51%
1890	3162	39.7			75.1	£8.6	52%
		Mineral	*Other Freight*				
1900	3485	48.0	12.3		108.4	£11.1	57%
1910	3838	54.1	13.2		89.0	£11.9	57%
1938	3652						
1950	3549	27.2	7.7	2328	63.6	£35.0	
1960	3364	24.9	4.9	1629	64.9	£43.9	

Sources: Annual Statistical Abstracts of the United Kingdom (to 1910) and Digest of Scottish Statistics. Season Ticket Trips are not included before 1950 and trips on the Glasgow Circle Underground (opened in December, 1896) have been allocated to Table 3.

distance rural passengers from 1919 but continuing growth in longer-distance trips and in suburban trips where rail offered significant time advantages resulted in a stabilisation of total rail trips in the 1950s. Total miles travelled rose due to increases in average trip lengths. Railway operating ratios (working expenses expressed as a percentage of gross receipts) worsened from the 1890s. By the late 1950s, the Scottish operating ratio must have risen to 90% or higher, leaving little margin for any return on capital. Many services had become serious loss-makers.

Road and Air

Collated information on road motor vehicles registered in Scotland is not available before 1938 nor are there any official estimates of passenger and goods volumes by car and lorry. Apart from doctors, vets and some business vehicles, most cars were used primarily for leisure purposes before 1938 and general use for travel to work and shopping did not become common till after the abolition of wartime petrol rationing in 1953. Buses were a common sight by the mid-1920s but large lorries, and lengthy trips by lorry remained unusual before the 1950s. Mass air travel did not appear until the same decade. The long delay in the motorisation of farming is also apparent from Table 3. Information on tram and bus usage is much better and the table confirms the absolute peak of the early 1950s followed by decline brought on by increased car usage and other changes such as the effect of television on reducing evening trips.

Sea

The Annual Statements of Navigation and Shipping, supplemented by surviving port records, provide voluminous data on shipping yet a comprehensive study of Scottish coastal and overseas trade since 1870 has still to be undertaken. Tonnage registered at Scottish Ports is another indicator of activity but poses two problems. Much of this tonnage seldom visited Scotland while ships registered elsewhere did make frequent visits. For these reasons, Tables 4 and 5 focus on ships

Table 3   Movement by Road and Air

| | Tram Route (Miles) | Passenger Trips Millions | | | Tram and bus Receipts (£ millions) | Cars | Motorised Goods Vehicles (Thousands) | Motorised Farm Vehicles |
		Tram	Bus	Air				
1880	50	42.6						
1890	84	76.0			£0.2			
1900	107	189.4			£0.4			
1910	295	398.8			£0.7			
1920	317	828.0			£1.7			
1938	(222)		(100)			150	40	5
1950	(225)	(850)	(1350)	0.4	£25.0	170	73	43
1960	(50)	(90)	(1650)	1.4	£39.0	410	107	68

Sources: Annual Statistical Abstracts of United Kingdom (to 1920) and Scottish Digest of Statistics. Tram trips are adjusted to include circle underground trips in Glasgow and figures in brackets include elements of estimation. Receipts before 1950 are for trams only while combined tram and bus receipts for 1950 and 1960 include a small increase on the official figures to take account of residual private bus companies.

arriving in Scotland as an indicator of the volume of port through-put. Table 6 utilises Flinn's figures for trade values.

These figures show a substantial increase in the volume of overseas trade handled at Scottish ports between 1880 and 1910. In relation to population already growing more slowly than that of England and Wales, Scotland secured a marked strengthening of its physical involvement in overseas trade over this period. Apart from the aberrant post-war position in 1920, Table 4 indicates that this strength was well maintained in the inter-war period but the subsequent performance to 1960 was much weaker with clear signs of relative deterioration in the 1950s. This change from strength to weakness is also confirmed in the trade values of Table 6. In 1900 and 1910 Scottish ports had a much better export to import ratio than the rest of the UK. This ratio remained comparatively favourable to 1938 but then fell sharply to 1960.

Table 4   Net Tonnage of Vessels Arriving at Scottish and Other UK Ports from Overseas with Cargoes and in Ballast (Million Tons)

	Scotland	UK	Scotland as % of UK	London	Liverpool	South-ampton	Glasgow	Leith	Other Principal Scottish Ports
1860		12.3							
1880	2.5	29.3	8.5%	6.0	4.9		0.8	0.6	1.1
1890	3.7	37.2	9.9%	7.7	5.8		1.1	0.7	1.9
1900	5.4	49.2	11.0%	9.6	6.0	1.6	1.5	1.1	2.8
1910	8.9	66.7	13.3%	13.3	11.0	5.1	3.1	1.6	4.2
1920	5.4	55.7	9.7%	11.8	9.3	3.9	2.6	0.8	2.0
									5.5
1930	11.2	97.5	11.5%	22.6	14.3	11.4	4.3	1.4	5.7
1938	11.9	91.9	12.9%	22.5	14.6	11.5	4.9	1.3	5.0
1960	12.4	142.7	8.7%	34.2	17.3	20.0	6.5	0.9	

Table 5 *Net Tonnage of Vessels Arriving at Scottish and Other UK Ports in Coastal Trade with Cargoes and in Ballast* (Million Tons)

	Scotland	UK	Scotland as % of UK	London	Liverpool	South-ampton	Glasgow	Leith	Other Principal Scottish Ports
1890		47.7							
1900		55.8							
1910	6.7	61.8	10.8%	6.5	3.3		2.6	0.8	3.3
1920	4.5	50.3	8.9%	4.7	3.5		1.9	0.3	2.3
1930	7.0	55.0	12.7%	6.7	2.6		1.9	0.8	4.3
1938	7.2	63.1	11.4%	3.3	3.0		1.7	0.8	4.6
1960	8.0	75.7	10.6%	10.0	3.7	5.9	2.1		5.9

Flinn recognised that the overseas import/export position of the Scottish economy was complicated by changes in the proportion of Scottish imports and exports handled via English ports. Some English imports and exports may also have proceeded via Scotland. There has been no systematic analysis of Scottish trade between 1870 and 1938 in relation to these questions but the impression has been of a small net diversion away from Scottish ports, somewhat larger if measured on a value basis. For 1948, Murray estimated that the value of Scottish exports should be increased by 30%, and imports by 27%, to allow for the use of English ports. Though this use of English ports increased in the 1950s, the principal manifestation of this trend, especially on a value basis, has been a post-1960 development. In other words, the relative decline of Scottish ports in UK aggregates prior to 1960 has more to do with the diverging economic performance of the respective port hinterlands than with a shift of Scottish traffic to English ports. Even within England, Table 4 shows the much higher growth rate of Southampton and London compared to Liverpool between 1910 and 1960. In Scotland, Glasgow increased its dominance over Leith, the only other major port dealing with general merchandise.

Coastal trade grew less rapidly than overseas trade (Table 5) but was far from negligible. Geographical factors such as proximity to Northern Ireland and a long and multi-islanded coastline sustained UK coastal trade from Scottish ports at significant proportion of the UK total between

Table 6 *Imports and Escorts At Scottish and UK Ports* (£ millions)

	Imports		Scotland as % of UK	Exports		Scotland as % of UK
	Scotland	UK		Scotland	UK	
1900	£38.7	£523.1	7.5%	£32.2	£291.0	11.0%
1910	£43.6	£678.3	6.5%	£44.4	£430.4	10.3%
1920	£138.6	£1932.6	7.2%	£125.6	£1334.4	9.4%
1930	£64.4	£1044.0	6.1%	£58.6	£570.8	10.3%
1938	£62.2	£919.5	6.7%	£44.0	£470.8	9.3%
1950	£174.1	£2608.2	6.7%	£156.0	£2171.3	7.2%
1960	£267.1	£4540.7	5.9%	£230.9	£3554.8	6.5%

Source: M. W. Flinn, "The Overseas Trade of the Scottish Ports, 1900-60; *SJPE*, June 1966.

Anchor Line Ships at Yorkhill Quay, 8 September 1950   COURTESY OF GLASGOW UNIVERSITY ARCHIVES

1910 and 1938. Data from 1960 is not available in the same form as for 1938 but the best estimates suggest a much smaller fall in the Scottish share of UK coastal trade than was the case for overseas trade. Oil in particular helped to boost coastal volumes and compensate for the loss of more traditional traffics.

The Parameters of Enterprise

Transport entrepreneurship was influenced by three factors - technological opportunities, the state of the Scottish, British and world market and changing political preferences. These are considered in turn in the sections which follow.

Technology

Technically, the years 1871-1961 can be split into two periods with a substantial overlap between 1910 and the 1930s. In the first period from the 1860s to the early twentieth century, railways and steam shipping offered the most exhilarating opportunities though always within the confines of a trade cycle which could affect year-to-year returns and the timing of major investments. The First World War brought its own special problems. So too did motorisation from the 1900s but, for three decades, road motor vehicles seemed entirely complementary to shipping and substantially complementary to rail. Motor vehicles soon threatened the horse's role in local transport (though fair numbers of horses continued to be used until 1945-55, especially in the farming sector) but they had a limited influence on the major rail markets in bulk, longer-distance and suburban movement sectors compared to Scotland's weakening economic performance in the inter-war years and the more severe international recession of the 1930s. The Second World War revival of the heavy industries and their comparative economic strength in the early post-war years, coupled with petrol rationing, delayed a more fundamental rail response to powerful competition from the roads until the 1960s.

While rail and shipping dominated the technical opportunities of the later nineteenth century, there were differences in organisation. By 1871, the Scottish rail network was well developed, reliant on previous capital from a wide variety of shareholders rather than a few individuals and rapidly shaking down into a corporate organisation of five main companies - the Caledonian and the North British being the 'Big Two' with the Glasgow and South Western, the Highland and the Great North of Scotland having subsidiary roles. Though there was competition between these

M V *Elysian*, Anchor Line Ship

companies and though the 2721 route miles of 1875 had increased to 3882 by 1915, the main Scottish market was already well served and its growing needs could continue to be served by the five railway companies of 1875. The character of the market and of railway operations left no room for significant new entrants. Given this position, there was no scope for making vast personal fortunes in railway enterprise.

In contrast, the shipping market lay wide open for individual enterprise to play a major role in sharing new patterns of family firm expansion and corporate organisation. Steam technology was at last coming into its own as a commercial asset in longer-distance shipping and Scottish shipowners could turn their attention to the world market. Here lay the possibility of substantial personal gains and extensive shareholdings in the emergent corporate organisation of shipping. Here too lies the justification for the dominance of shipowner biographers.

Before 1900, the road sector offered few prospects for radical initiatives. There were some opportunities in horse trams and cable trams as the biographies of Duncan and Pitcairn show but roads could not attract the attention of the more technically flamboyant rail and shipping sectors. There was, in fact, considerable managerial skill in the organisation of carting to meet new volumes of traffic, in the provision of specialist road traction engines, in dock and harbour development and in the improvement of road surfaces and local road capacity but none of these areas offered prospects for substantial profits.

From 1900, and more especially from the 1920s, this situation changed. Electric traction transformed the commercial potential of trams while the motorbus, itself a challenge to the urban tram, widened this potential to the whole of Scotland. The technology of tarmac with improved roads and road surfaces extended this process, benefiting goods as well as passenger movement. Motor vans and lorries could substitute for the horse and, more importantly, generate greater volumes of movement and factory locations more favourable to road use. At the margin, there was also the hope of attracting remunerative traffic from rail; a hope which was to be fully realised with the triumph of the larger lorry and the more economical diesel engine after 1945. These conditions helped produce a new wave of enterprise in the road sector (see the biographies of Hastie, Barrie, W Alexander, W J Thomson and J C Sword). Unfortunately, but not unexpectedly, the records of the embryonic years of new firms are often poor and, in the motor sector, our understanding of the process of change is also hampered by the large numbers of small firms which existed in the early years. Air technology is represented in Freeson's biography and also in one of the episode's in Sword's life until he was ousted by the interest of the London, Midland and Scottish Railway in rail air services in the 1930s. Shipping began to make some use of diesel engines, bulk and specialist carriers in the inter-war years but the much greater influence of super-tankers, containerisation and roll-on/roll-off ferry services was only just beginning to be felt on shipping and ports in the 1950s.

Markets

Expansion of aggregate demand was a prominent feature of the British economy in the nineteeneth and twentieth century. The trade cycle and two major wars caused fluctuations but the underlying strength of demand, and the need to adjust services to new sources of supply encouraged transport enterprise. Technology also permitted reductions in the real costs of transport, further increasing demand for freight and passenger movement. Transport volumes rose faster than rates of economic growth and one of the most outstanding features of the period was the huge expansion of internal passenger movement and the commonplace use of mechanised local transport as an alternative to walking (see Tables 2 to 5). This would have been impossible without the strong growth of real incomes per head. Such growth, paralleled by increases in leisure time, became evident for the mass of the population in the last quarter of the nineteenth century. War and recession halted progress in some years but even the intensity of unemployment in the early 1930s had no more than a fleeting effect in slowing the upward spiral of passenger mobility. Average real incomes per head rose faster than ever in the inter-war period only to be surpassed by the new affluence of the 1950s.

Scotland shared in this British pattern but its economic performance was faltering compared to Britain as a whole. Real incomes rose at not much less than the British rate but it proved impossible to maintain Scotland's share of the British population. This was true of 1871-1914 as well as of the subsequent period but relative decline was more pronounced from the 1920s and a major political issue by 1961.

Of the growth which did occur to 1914, Clydeside accounted for by far the largest proportion though the east of Scotland (Lothians, Fife and the Upper Forth) gained from the service resilience of the Edinburgh economy and the shift of coal production from the west to the newer mines opening up in the east. These conditions account for many major initiatives by the Caledonian, North British and Glasgow and South Western Railways and the more modest ventures of the Highland and the Great North of Scotland. The latter two companies could hope for some gains from incoming tourists from England and Central Scotland but their market situation was peripheral (see Sir Alexander Matheson and William Ferguson). Central Scotland was a riper field for enterprise in access to docks, coalfields and manufacture, in suburban traffic and in Anglo-Scottish trunk traffic (see D Cooper, P Caird, D Matheson and Sir James Thomson for rail and J Duncan and J Pitcairn for trams).

Shippers had the choice of concentrating on the Scottish and United Kingdom coastal market (see David MacBrayne and Thomas Aitken) or of using Scottish overseas trade as a means towards strong representation in the international shipping market with routes and service patterns responding to international needs. The biographies provide repeated confirmation of this extension beyond Scottish horizons. Examples include Sir William McKinnon's interests in India, the Far East, Australia and Africa, John Burns' (Lord Inverclyde) shift from his father's involvement in the Irish trade to Cunard transatlantic traffic, the Galbraith/Kennedy shift from the Italian trade to the Far East and the famous Irrawaddy Flotilla in Burma's development and Sir William Burrell's success in tramp shipping and the timing of ship sales. Other successes were Lyle shipping and the Donaldson, Anchor, Clan and Ben Lines. The only contrary examples of growth unrelated to the international carrying trade were the shift of Salvesen from Scottish-Norwegian shipping into whaling and the growth of interest in steam powered and motorised fishing.

The mainstream expansions and company creations were facilitated by Britain's special position in international shipping at a time of great extension of international trade. The core traffics of export manufactures and export coal from Britain and near balancing imports of raw materials provided a good revenue and organisational base for further growth in earnings from international shipping. Competing with other British firms and seeking the right contacts in Liverpool, London and overseas, Scottish entrepreneurs were able to take advantage of this favourable market situation and, in so doing, helped channel more orders for new ships to Clydeside.

From 1918, a different scenario was in place. Britain's financial dominance in world currency markets and world trade was now gone and the incipient mercantilism and trade tariffs of 1870-1914 changed to full-blown economic nationalism. Reduced demand for export coal from Britain eroded the relative shipping advantage of Britain while the collapse of foreign trade growth brought economic crisis to shipping companies as well as shipbuilders. Weighed down by the costs of misplaced expansion in the early 1920s, Henderson's Anchor Line was in deep financial trouble by 1930 and in liquidation by 1935. More cautious policies and selective innovation helped Lyle shipping and the Donaldson and Ben Lines to survive but the element of Scottish control in British shipping was reduced through mergers and the larger share of trade growth handled by non-Scottish ports after the Second World War. This reflected the declining importance of Scotland as a market and, to a lesser extent, the attraction of Scottish overseas trade to the better facilities of

Hull and the channel ports, for access to and from strong European markets, and of Tilbury, Southampton and Liverpool for extra-European trade.

Politics

The general shift from international free trade to stronger economic nationalism in the inter-war years was itself a factor which influenced the market framework. Shipping profitability suffered but the increasing cheapness of imports had the effect of allowing an increase in internal British demand with favourable repercussions on passenger growth and on consumer factories more suited to lorry distribution. Because of its lower involvement in the newer industries, Scottish transport did not receive the full impact of this change but it worked in the direction of increased lorry and passenger movement. Freer trade attitudes were to revive from 1945 but, since Scottish manufacturers were not able to take sustained advantage of the new opportunities in world and European markets, more sluggish economic growth in Scotland restrained transport enterprise. A new phase of higher road spending was ushered in by the 1956 transfer of road responsibilities from the Department of Transport to the Scottish Office. The rise of regional policy in the late 1950s and early 1960s produced another escalation of road spending in Scotland but the impact of this had hardly been felt by 1961.

Mention of road spending provides a striking example of the role of public enterprise in the transport sector. Before the nationalisation programme of Attlee's 1945 Labour government, transport had the heaviest public involvement of any sector of the economy. The Attlee legislation increased an emphasis on public enterprise which was already dominant in roads, ports and local transport. Such features also help to explain the preponderance of shipowners in the attached biographies. Other key individuals - such as James Dalrymple of Glasgow Corporation Tramways, senior port and road officials and post-nationalisation rail managers - exhibited enterprise within a public sector framework and so do not come within the terms of reference of the present biography.

Private enterprise rail and shipping was never free from political factors. William Ferguson's biography is a reminder of the wider area of political lobbying associated with the success or failure of railway company parliamentary bills and contacts in London were even more important for leading companies like the Caledonian. Strong government control over rail freight rates applied from 1894. In the Highlands and Islands, government and county council capital grants or guarantees also became more important for new lines from the 1890s though the eventual outcome by the 1920s was the transmutation of most rail proposals into road improvements. The Roads Board began to supplement local government sources of road funding with grant aid after the Development and Roads Improvement Act of 1909. The Ministry of Transport was established in 1919 and soon had strong interests in the road sector. Partly looking to the relief of unemployment, it accelerated the Scottish roads programme in the 1920s. The conversion of key routes to trunk roads directly financed by the state followed from 1936.

Local shipping, and fishery development in the Highlands and Islands, also came to depend on harbour grants, mail subsidies and other government help from the 1880s with MacBrayne's services among those benefiting. Beyond Scotland, Sir William Mackinnon provided a classic example of the value of London-based government contacts to secure mail contracts of a scale and nature to underwrite the expansion of services. Though some ports were in the private sector (including railway company ports such as Troon, Grangemouth, Burntisland and Methil), most of the leading Scottish ports - together with Liverpool - were operated by public trusts before, and after, 1871. Ports in this category included Glasgow, Greenock, Leith, Dundee and Aberdeen. It was the Clyde Navigation Trust, not private concerns, which carried through the great improvement of the River Clyde and created the large new docks to supplement outmoded and inadequate quay space. Shipowners could be elected to such Trusts and we find that Thomas Aitken of the London and Edinburgh Shipping Company was also a Leith Dock Commissioner.

Business preferences, flavoured by municipal self-confidence and the local voter, gave increasing support to selective municipal enterprise and public trusts. Earlier experiences with streets, water supplies and road/tram infrastructure led on to extensive municipalisation of gas, electricity and tramway operation. Glasgow was regarded as a paragon of municipal enterprise and, in the early 1920s, this was still being extended through the acquisition of the Subway Railway Company and the tramways of Paisley and the Monklands. Turnpike trusts and other local road trusts were replaced with increasingly professional city road engineers and countrywide road administrations. Similar beliefs in planning and economies of scale in rail provision almost produced a compulsory government merger of all the Scottish rail companies in the early 1920s. The eventual solution, affected by the view that the weakened Scottish rail system required some cross-subsidy from south of the border, merged the 'Caley', the Highland and the Glasgow and South Western with the London, Midland and Scottish (LMSR) and the North British and the Great North of Scotland with the London and North Eastern (LNER) in 1923. Headquarters control moved out of Scotland and this situation continued after rail nationalisation in 1948. The extensive railway interests in bus companies (dating from 1928) and in shipping also meant that most Scottish bus services (except for the municipal undertakings of the four cities) and Highlands, Clyde and Islands shipping came into majority government ownership. The nationalisation of all scheduled air services followed in 1949. British government policy extended detailed regulatory control from rail services to all bus and lorry services in 1930 and 1933 respectively with the open intention of channelling enterprise towards cross-subsidy, larger firms and zonal areas of operation. Aided by the pressures of recession, competition was out of fashion and anti-competitive attitudes continued to have a strong influence on post-war transport. There were only two exceptions to the spread of public ownership. Beset by bus competition and conscious of their own boundary limitations, four town councils (Ayr, Kilmarnock, Kirkcaldy and Perth) discontinued municipal operation in favour of private buses in the inter-war years. Privately owned bus companies expanded rapidly from 1919 but most of these buses were soon back in public ownership via railway company acquisition of majority interests and subsequent rail nationalisation. The other example was a more lasting success for the private sector. From the start, lorry operation had been a stronghold of private entrepeneurship. The 1933 public controls were less onerous than those imposed on buses and encouraged the expansion of 'own account' haulage since this was virtually free of regulation. Upsetting these arrangements by wholesale nationalisation of road haulage would have been unthinkable and the 1947 Transport Act went no further than establishing public ownership of trunk road haulage. This caused far deeper business resentment than the associated rail, coal, gas and electricity nationalisations. From 1953, the new Conservative government was making provision for the return of trunk haulage to private ownership.

Conclusions and Speculations

The most interesting issues raised by the biographies are the relative importance of transport enterprise in Scotland's development and the problems of separating entrepreneurship in Scottish transport from the enterprise shown by individual Scots in the transport sector.

Taking first the importance of transport for Scottish development, can transport be seen as having a vital role in promoting new enterprise in other sectors of the Scottish economy or is transport's role more one of response to emerging market requirements and enterprise outwith transport? Prior to 1830, it is possible to argue that transport enterprise and investment did indeed play a large role in creating the conditions for other sectors of the economy to expand. Landowners and merchants alike appreciated that reductions in transport costs offered more scope than cuts in production costs to open up regional and international markets. Subsequently, however, further substantial and successful enterprise in transport had to be more closely related to the specific requirements of expanding industries. Perceptions of growth prospects in the Scottish, British and world economy were to provide the main basis for post-1860 transport initiatives even though changing transport technology provided a powerful secondary impetus. Had there been no evidence of rising real incomes, urbanisation and products able to compete in British and world markets, late nineteenth century transport enterprise in Scotland would have been severely restricted.

Land transport enterprise, and a large part of post-1860 shipping expansion, arose from the favourable condition of the Scottish economy of this period. The main prospects stemmed from the powerhouse of the Central Belt with financial returns to enterprise being much poorer in the Borders, Galloway and the Highlands and Islands. After 1910, motorised road transport provided opportunities for significant shifts in modal shares but these opportunities developed gradually and against a backcloth of a declining British share of world economic growth and a declining Scottish share of British growth. Coupled with the extension of public regulation and public ownership in transport, this placed a heavy damper on expansionary private enterprise. Road haulage, bus services (until the 1950s) and garage/car sales operations did provide profit prospects but to a lesser extent than in England and in no way comparable to the shipping prospects of the later nineteenth century.

Shipping merits the final and more speculative part of this conclusion. In the case of rail and road transport, Scots showing enterprise outwith Scotland can be easily identified and excluded from biographies of entrepreneurs operating primarily from a base in Scotland (including non-Scottish born such as Christian Salvesen and E E Freeson). Shipping raises greater difficulty as some of the leading 'Scottish' shipowners - Sir C W Cayzer, F C Kennedy, Sir W McKinnon and Andrew Weir spent large amounts of time in Liverpool, London or overseas. Their companies also had various degrees of ownership in non-Scottish hands. It becomes harder to identify mainly Scottish companies after 1918 and, even more so, after 1945. The share of British trade handled in non-British ships also rose from just under 30% in 1890 to 45% in 1910, staying at this level until increasing to over 50% in the late 1950s. Between the wars, however, the share of non-British shipping carried in British ships fell with increasing competition, especially from Scandinavia, the Mediterranean and Japan. Overall prospects for British shipping were therefore deteriorating from the 1920s despite an ability to hold on to a substantial share of British trade.

Just how successful were companies based on Scotland in expanding their share of the total world shipping market between 1870 and 1910? To what extent did they remain under control from Scotland and did they have more, or less, success than other British firms in responding to competition from foreign shippers? Did Scottish based firms have a significantly greater multiplier impact on the Scottish economy than other firms? All of these questions are crying out for further research, especially in the period since 1918.

From the biographies and the statistical tables, it is evident that Scottish shipping firms have an impressive record to 1913. They became heavily involved in international trade on the expanding liner routes and tramp services that characterised the period to 1914, moving from the limited horizons of the coastal, Baltic and Mediterranean trades to the North Atlantic and the rapidly emerging potential of India, the Far East, Australia, Africa and Latin America. As well as securing a large share of Scottish trade, substantial earnings were gained from 'third party' traffic never touching Scottish shores. There was a close relationship with Scottish shipbuilders in ordering new ships for these trades. London-based firms such as Peninsular and Orient had established Scottish offices by 1880 yet Scottish firms were aggressive in establishing contacts at key English and overseas ports. North of the border, coal exports boosted ports like Burntisland, Methil and Ayr but higher-value general merchandise trade shifted to Glasgow. Lyle Shipping, for example, moved from its Greenock base to Glasgow in 1906. Yet, even in this period the centre of gravity of shipping firms could move away from Glasgow. Alexander Allan's biography illustrates this process.

The Allan Line moved from Greenock to Glasgow in 1846 and was the seventh largest shipping concern in the world by 1880, deeply involved in the Canada trade. The Montreal Office was soon to overshadow the Glasgow base and the Allan Line was firmly in the control of the Canadian Pacific Railway Company by 1909.

In tonnage handled, Glasgow lagged far behind Liverpool (Table 4) but tonnage handled at Glasgow did not reflect the heavy involvement of that city in world shipping by 1910. Lloyds Register treated Glasgow and Liverpool as the only UK ports outside London with the status to require a General Committee of Shipowners. The records of ship managing companies for 1930/31 still show Glasgow with 76 companies compared to 80 in Liverpool. For the most part, these Glasgow companies had offices in the city centre with concentrations on St Vincent Street, Renfield Street, Hope Street and Bothwell Street. Twenty companies (28 in Liverpool) managed ten or more ships. This group included the Anchor Line, J & J Denholm, Donaldson Line, Glen Line, H Hogarth and Sons, David MacBrayne and the Irrawaddy Flotilla (of 66 Glasgow registered vessels operating in Burma). At this time, Leith had only two major firms - Christian Salvesen and W Thomson and Co (Ben Line).

Excluding the Irrawaddy Flotilla, Glasgow's 1930 total of 341 vessels in firms with ten or more ships compared badly with Liverpool at 763 and with London at 1794. Glasgow was already in relative decline with the biggest firms focussed on London, Southampton and Liverpool. British, rather than Scottish, firms also dominated the new market for international and coastal tankers. For a time, the post-1945 world trade boom disguised the weaknesses of remaining Scottish firms but pressures to join larger groups and to shift away from the Clyde were increasing rapidly by the late 1950s. Considerations of efficiency were undermining the automatic ordering of new ships from Scottish shipbuilders while, following the earlier growth of competition from Scandinavian, German, Mediterranean and Japanese shipping competition, competition was spreading to ships of Liberian, Panamanian and Soviet registration.

Decline was poised to become more precipitate from 1960 yet further research and analysis is necessary to probe the causes and to date more precisely the origins and scale of earlier relative decline from 1913. Is this explicable by market changes with specially adverse effects on Scottish shipowners or did internal failures of enterprise become more pronounced? The period of growth to 1910 also requires re-examination. The outstanding personal successes such as John Burns (Lord Inverclyde), Sir C W Cayzer, and Sir William McKinnon may have contributed far less to the Scottish economy than to other parts of Britain, America, Africa and Asia. In a *Scottish* business biography, these shipowners may deserve downgrading relative to less well-known entrepreneurs whose activities produced greater benefits for Scotland. On the other hand, much of the period since 1860 can be seen as one in which Scotland could anticipate, and rival, Norway and Greece in entering the stage of world shipping and fisheries to secure personal fortunes and greater national economic benefits than enterprise channelled in other directions. With the increase of inter-war competition and the growth of economic nationalism and an international recession hitting Scotland harder than Britain, it seems probable that Scottish shipping retained a surprising resilience compared to the more substantial shipping firms based on England. Sharp, relative decline, only became more evident from 1960. In themselves the biographies cannot resolve these speculations because of their bias to pre-1918 shipping entrepreneurs but they provide a stimulus for much future work on the inter-war and post Second World War periods.

TOM HART

Thomas AITKEN,

Shipping manager; b. 1821, Culross, Fife, s. of David Aitken, ship agent and Janet Kemp; m. (1) 17/6/1860, Margaret Croall, (2) Frances Sarah Turrill; 1 s.; Manager & MD, London & Edinburgh Shipping Co Ltd; Ch, Fife Coal Co Ltd; d. 29/1/1907, Nivingstone, Kinross; g/v estate £118,685 15s 9d.

Thomas Aitken had two parallel business careers. As manager and later managing director, of the London and Edinburgh Shipping Company in Leith he played an important role in the shipping world for over half a century. The Leith connection was crucial for the second of his business activities, namely the chairmanship of the Fife Coal Co Ltd from 1884 to 1907. Leith had been the location of the Fife Coal Co's first office and there remained a close association between Leith shipping interests and the Fife Coal Co.

Coincidentally, there were in fact two Leith personalities called Thomas Aitken. The other Thomas Aitken was a businessman in his own right as senior partner in the firm of Aitken and Wright, provision merchants, Leith and as chairman of the Leith Printing and Publishing Co. He was, however, more politically oriented and involved in public office, being a Justice of the Peace for Midlothian and for Edinburgh City and Deputy Lieutenant for the City of Edinburgh. This culminated in his election as Lord Provost of Leith from 1887 - 1890. As both men served on the Leith Dock Commission a cautionary note should be sounded to any future biographer over possible mistaken identity.

Thomas Aitken the shipping manager, was born in Culross in what was then the County of Perth. He received his early education there but completed his education at the Edinburgh High School. Very little is known of his family's movements at this time. In 1837, on leaving school, Aitken was apprenticed to a leading firm of shipbrokers in Grangemouth. He moved to another shipbroking firm in Leith in 1842. After a year there he was taken on by the London and Edinburgh Shipping Co, as book-keeper.

When Aitken joined the firm it had already been in existence since 1809. The firm had been founded by a group of local merchants and shipowners in Edinburgh and Leith whose purpose was to establish a sea route between London and Leith for the transportation of goods and passengers which would facilitate communication between the two ports and which would prevent 'injurious monopoly'. Indeed the aim of the new operation was to provide a superior sailing fleet to customers at competitive rates.

The organisation of the firm remained largely unchanged for a century. On 1 December 1809 a contract of copartnery was signed which would endure for 99 years. The capital was then £35,000 in 700 shares of £50. These shares were divided amongst some 200 'partners', the maximum holding of each partner being ten shares. From these partners, a group of 12 were chosen to be directors of the London and Edinburgh Shipping Co. Each partner had to be involved in shipping goods between Leith and London. Special resolutions in 1863 and 1877 increased the fully paid up capital to £70,000 and £140,000 respectively. The firm was registered as an unlimited company in 1863 but it was only in 1908 when the Contract of Copartnery expired that it became a limited liability company, the capital was rearranged and the 'antiquated constitution' was altered. However the structure of the firm was no hindrance and its reputation soon brought success and development to the port of Leith, contributing to the legendary seafaring tales of the time.

Their early fleet consisted of vessels called 'Leith smacks' which combatted the perils of high seas and foreign privateers. From 1841 onwards the 'Aberdeen clippers' formed the next generation of the fleet, swift, sleek sailing craft which retained their position despite the advent of steam power. However in the 1850s the London and Edinburgh Shipping Co bowed to the inevitability of steam and replaced their clippers with steamers which served both traveller and cargo alike.

When Aitken was appointed general manager in March 1855 the fleet consisted of one steamer called *The Prompt* and two clippers *The Dart* and *The Nonsuch*. A regular service between London and Leith was well established and in addition a small steamer of 250 tons sailed to the wine growing regions in France, Spain and Portugal. This side of the trade as wine carriers from Mediterranean ports expanded to make full demand on the firm's fleet by the turn of the century; by 1906 ten steamers operated regularly on the coastal and continental routes.

The success and development of the London and Edinburgh Shipping Co was always attributed by contemporaries to the driving force of Thomas Aitken. He appeared to some as a 'careful administrator' and a 'shrewd, sensible talker'. To others he earned the description of 'a stern disciplinarian' and someone who had a rather blunt and direct manner underneath which lurked a kind and considerate personality. The manager's role in the company had always been clearly laid down. Under the supervision of the directors, he was to attend to the shipping and delivery of goods, the accommodation of passengers and the purchase of stores. Yet there is no doubt that Aitken fulfilled much more than this and that he was at the centre of the building up of the business. He took on the position of manager just at the time when the firm was undergoing a transition to the steamer fleet. His was an era of progress and expansion and his business acumen helped him to respond to the challenge.

Thomas Aitken's name was always synonymous with the London and Edinburgh Shipping Co. He became a major shareholder and he also was elected a director. He also combined the roles of manager and director with that of chairman from 1900 to 1906. After 50 years service in 1893 Aitken's fellow directors presented him with his portrait, painted by Sir George Reid, RSA. He was to remain another 15 years until he resigned as managing director due to ill health in 1906. While Aitken did not create the company, his business skills made him a necessary participant in all facets of the firm's organisation. His peers in the early days and latterly his fellow management were all figures in the background. James Taylor of Starleyhall was chairman for several years, including 1878-1889. He also held shares in the Leith, Hamburg and Rotterdam Packet Co. John Cowan of Beeslack was chairman in the 1890s. Prominent among the other directors were representatives of the brewery and distillery trade who shipped their products to London via the company's fleet. 'Brewer' directors included Thomas Usher (1821-1896) and from 1907 to 1951, Harry George Younger (qv) who was also company chairman.

Aitken widened his commercial interests and one of his principal activities outwith shipping was in the Fife Coal Co. From its inception in 1872 Aitken was vice-chairman and on the death of William Lindsay in 1884 he became its chairman. The Aitken era in the Fife Coal Co was one of the most important in its history. It was a time of rapid expansion. Under Aitken's chairmanship the company nurtured the young Charles Carlow (qv) to become a leading, dynamic force in the running of the company. Pits were opened at Kelty, Hill of Beath, Dalbeath, Leven, Pirnie, Durie and Wellsgreen and one was named after Aitken in 1893, a colliery which was to become the largest of the Fife Coal Co Aitken's fellow directors reinforced the Leith shipping connection. Sir William Miller, director from 1872 to 1880, was a well known Leith merchant and Member of Parliament. William Lindsay, chairman from 1872 to 1880 was Provost of Leith from 1860 to 1866 and had close connections with Leith mercantile affairs and John Jordan, a Leith shipowner, a director from 1886 to 1914 completed the Leith shipping network. Coal connections led to Aitken's directorship of the Longrigg Coal Co. However, Aitken's first interest was always shipping. He became a director of other shipping companies including the Irrawaddy Flotilla Co Ltd whose manager, F C Kennedy (qv), had been an apprentice of Aitkens, the Galloway Steam Packet Co and the British and Burmese Steam Shipping Co. He extended his directorships from time to time. He was a director of the Reversionary Association of Edinburgh, the British Law Fire Insurance Co, the North British Investment Co Ltd, the Scottish New Zealand Investment Co and the Scottish Wharf Co Ltd which sold their Hermitage Wharf, London, to the London and Edinburgh Shipping Co. He was also an extraordinary director of the Royal Bank of Scotland and briefly chairman of the Scottish Cyanide Co Ltd. He was involved in John Croall & Son, Edinburgh coach

proprietors, through his marriage to Margaret, daughter of John Croall, at the comparatively late age of 40.

Aitken's career was therefore of a diversified nature in the business sense. While not aspiring to the public duties of his namesake, Thomas Aitken did serve the community well as a Leith Dock Commissioner, and as a member of the Chambers of Commerce of Edinburgh and Leith. He was also an assistant in the prestigious Merchant Company of Edinburgh and became a director of the new Nautical College. As well as his contribution to local activities, Aitken was for many years chairman of the Mercantile Marine Board and a director for 30 years of the Scottish Trade Protection Society. He was also an associate of the Scottish Shipbuilders' Association at the time of its incorporation as an Institution in 1865.

Politics were not a strong force in Aitken's life and this is reflected in his low key approach to local political affairs and municipal office although he did espouse the cause of the Liberal Unionists. In religious affiliation he was an elder of St Cuthbert's Church of Scotland, Edinburgh, for many years. He was a Fellow of the Royal Scottish Geographical Society and his main recreational pursuit was angling.

If contemporaries were in any doubt about his generous nature behind the brusque business image, Aitken's philanthropic and benevolent contribution would have dispelled any fears. Aitken married twice but both wives died, Margaret first in 1882 and Frances in 1899. In their memory he gave £40,000 to the Royal Infirmary in Edinburgh in 1900. He also donated generously to the Royal Hospital for Sick Children, Edinburgh and to the Longmore Hospital for Incurables, Edinburgh. His interest in the Royal Hospital for Sick Children involved him in its organisation as director and he also found time to act as honorary treasurer to James Gillespie's hospital. Neither did he forget these charitable institutions in his will with legacies of £1,000 each to Leith Hospital, Longmore Hospital and the Royal Hospital for Sick Children. A further £1,000 was bequested to the deserving poor in Culross. His shares in the London and Edinburgh Shipping Co went in part to Thomas Reekie, the cashier and James Herd the book-keeper, who also received legacies of £1,000 each. Aitken gave alimentary provision from the revenue of his estate to his grand-daughter, Margaret Theodor Aitken. She received no capital as she was to benefit from her great grandfather's estate, John Croall, on Aitken's death. His son, Percy, had predeceased him some years before his death. Aitken had purchased the country estate of Farraline, Inverness-shire and he instructed his executors to sell this along with his Edinburgh residence at 5 Grosvenor Crescent. He asked his trustees to retain his country seat, Nivingstone, near Cleish, Kinross and also to hold on to his Fife Coal Co shares. Aitken's portfolio of shareholdings reflected the diversity of his business interests and included for example substantial holdings in

Edinburgh Collieries Co Ltd, Wemyss Coal Co Ltd, Fife Coal Co Ltd, the Irrawaddy Flotilla Co Ltd as well as the London and Edinburgh Shipping Co. In addition to his specific bequests to charitable institutions already mentioned, Aitken instructed that any undisposed residue should be distributed to charities, especially to those in Edinburgh and Leith.

Aitken was connected with the London and Edinburgh Shipping Co for 60 years and manager for over 50 years. When he died in 1907 for many people he had earned the title of one of 'the makers of Leith' and he was certainly held in high esteem in the commercial world. The characteristics of sheer effort and ability combined to make Thomas Aitken's career the success it was. It also spanned three quite different types of activity: that of manager to a coastal shipping company, multiple director, and chairman of the Fife Coal Co Ltd.

SHEILA HAMILTON

SOURCES

Unpublished

SRO: GD 301, GD 301/8, 301/14, 301/58, 301/74, 301/119, Records of London and Edinburgh Shipping Co
SC 70/1/466, Inventory
SC 70/1/509, Additional Inventory
SC 70/4/385, Will

Published

Directory of Directors, 1880-1900
Edinburgh and the Lothians at the Opening of the Twentieth Century, Edinburgh, 1904
Glasgow Herald, 30/1/1907
Irons, J, *Leith and Its Antiquities*, Vol II, Edinburgh, c 1897
Leith Observer, 2/2/1907
Leith Pilot Annual, 1890
Men of the Period, London, n d
Muir, A, *Fife Coal Company Ltd. A Short History*, Cambridge, 1951
TIESS, Vol 1906-7

Walter ALEXANDER, Snr,

Bus operator; b. 2/5/1879, Bonnyside, Falkirk, s. of Robert Alexander, carter and Elizabeth Stirling; m. (1) 16/11/1898, Denny, Isabella Daly, tablemaid, d. of Thomas Daly, coalminer; (2) 2/10/1936, Glasgow, Clarissa May Brookes, d. of George Henry Brookes, mechanical engineer; (3) 12/10/1953, Dollar, Ann Cooper Elder or Strachan, d. of John Elder, master painter; 2 s., 1 d., 1 step-d.; Founder of Walter Alexander & Sons Ltd, Dir, Scottish Omnibus Ltd, Ch, Falkirk Football Club; d. 19/6/1959, Edinburgh Royal Infirmary; g/v UK estate: £162,263 16s 6d.

The growth of motor transport marked a revolutionary development in the area of transport in the first half of the twentieth century. A wide range of new opportunities was created with the increasing use of motor vehicles, from the motor car to omnibus services. Motor omnibus services began on a small scale before 1914, run by a number of private operators. When war broke the service was still in its infancy. It was after World War I that a more rapid development of bus services occurred.

There was no shortage of enterprise in the early days. One pioneer in the development of motor bus services was Falkirk man, Walter Alexander Snr. Walter Alexander was born in Bonnyside, Falkirk, on 2 May 1879. His father, Robert, was a carter by trade. Alexander worked by day as a grate fitter in a Bonnybridge foundry and at night he spent his spare time repairing and selling bicycles in Camelon, Falkirk, with his two brothers. He managed to save up enough money to open a bicycle shop in Camelon. While Alexander was working in his shop he became aware of the opportunities arising from motor transport. It was this recognition that led Alexander to his first venture into road passenger transport before the outbreak of World War One. He bought a Belhaven charabanc which was chain-driven and had been made in or assembled in Wishaw. With this vehicle Alexander operated a passenger service on Saturdays and Sundays between Falkirk and Bonnybridge for a fare of a penny. During the week the charabanc body was removed and a platform body was fitted and the vehicle became a goods lorry, except on the frequent evenings when the charabanc was needed by private parties, when the transformation was repeated. This was the beginning of a vast concern.

During the war the lorry still ran and was used to transport ammunition from the factories of Falkirk. In 1916 and in 1918 two more Belhavens were acquired by Alexander. In 1919 the first Leyland chassis, from Royal Air Force surplus supplies was bought and fitted with a Belhaven body and solid tyres. In the same year Alexander drove the Leyland to John O'Groats with a private party and so far as is known it was the first charabanc to make such an excursion tour. By 1920 a regular daily service to Denny was being operated in a new Leyland. This bus was regarded as a luxury vehicle at the time because it had glass sides and was known as the 'Glass Bus'. The seats were also softer than the hard wooden forms of the old lorry. Timetables had been printed and by the summer of 1920 six-day tours from Falkirk to Inverness and Aberdeen were running. In 1921 services to Kilsyth were introduced, the bus driven by Alexander's son, Walter, and weekend excursions to Glasgow were also introduced. By 1922 the fleet had grown to 15 - though the number 13 was missing! - and a new garage had to be built. A brick garage was built in Brown Street, Camelon, to replace the old wooden one. The concern continued to expand and in May 1924 the business was incorporated as a private limited company, W Alexander and Sons.

Extension of existing and introduction of new services continued and the company were soon running over 20 buses on various local routes, as well as buses running to Glasgow, Stirling and Dundee. An experiment with an open topped vehicle was tried. A double-deck vehicle with an open top was used between Glasgow and Stirling but the inclement Scottish weather compelled its withdrawal. By now W Alexander and Sons had emerged as substantial operators.

While Alexander continued the development and expansion of his services the ill-effects of unrestrained competition were becoming obvious throughout the country. There had been no shortage of people who had hoped to take advantage of motor passenger transport. Competition was fierce and many small scale and inadequately equipped operators, hopeful of making a fortune, went to the wall in the process. Many of these operators failed partly because of high operating costs, especially as many started out with very little capital, and because of technical problems of earlier vehicles which meant breakdowns were a frequent occurrence. Thus many did not have the money to repair their vehicles. It was also lack of experience in provision of a passenger service. Conditions were chaotic; many small operators with poor vehicles and no proper service schedules competed fiercely against each other for traffic. There was almost no attempt made to co-ordinate these services. This encouraged speeding, jockeying for position on the streets and inadequate vehicle maintenance, all of which lowered the quality of service provided to the public. Up until 1930 road transport was unfettered by statutory restrictions and conditions were such that there was growing feeling that some greater degree of control over the passenger transport industry was urgently required. This resulted in the Road Traffic Act of 1930 which brought in a fairly rigid form of control which regulated the conditions in and entry into the passenger transport industry.

About this time a very important development took place for W Alexander and Sons, The Railway (Road Transport) Acts, 1928, authorised railway companies to invest in road motor transport enterprises. In 1929 the Scottish Motor Traction Company, in conjunction with the LMS and LNER railway companies acquired a financial interest in Messrs W Alexander and Sons. The bus subsidiaries of the Fife Tramway, Light and Power Company and the Balfour-Beatty group were also purchased by the group and operation was vested from June 1930 in W Alexander and Sons. Within 12 months services had been re-organised and rationalised to avoid competition and the blue Alexander buses ruled the roost in the East. The Road Traffic Act, 1930, encouraged an amalgamation of the bus interests of SMT with those of W Alexander and Sons, J C Sword (qv) and R B Dick, along with others in the control of the LNER and LMS, who in due course became part owners of the new group. The holding company for the combine became SMT itself, which also remained an operating unit, covering most of Eastern Scotland south of the Forth. Its subsidiaries were the Central SMT Company Ltd in the Clyde Valley, the Western SMT Company Ltd based in Kilmarnock, and W Alexander and Sons Ltd occupying eastern Scotland from the Forth to Inverness. The Alexander, Sword and Dick families were all represented in the group.

By 1929 Alexanders owned over 150 buses and a new garage was opened - Stepps garage. The 1930s saw the absorption of other companies by the business. In 1930 D Shields of Laurieston was bought out. In March 1930 they acquired Messrs Wilson, Marshall and Co, Avonbridge. In 1933 the company of William Scott, New Market Street, was acquired, and in 1937 the company of William Blaylock, Falkirk, was taken over by Alexander. By 1937 the company had over 1,000 motor coaches and had taken over the municipal transport services of Perth, Kirkcaldy, Falkirk and Dunfermline. The company became part of the British Transport Commission in 1948 following nationalisation of the railways and their bus interests.

Walter Alexander's also operated as coachbuilders and private car hirers. The coachbuilding venture began around 1924, at Brown Street, Camelon, with the aim of building bodies for their own bus fleet. The coachbuilding side of the business expanded rapidly. The company's fleet of buses grew at such a rate that in 1930 the decision was taken to move the coachbuilding department from Camelon to premises at Stirling to give greater scope for the increased work which had to be undertaken. There was some outcry at the time by the people of Falkirk at the loss of the industry to Stirling. Once in Stirling the business considerably expanded. Now the works not only produced the bodywork for their own buses but were undertaking similar work for other bus operators. The two sides of the business - bus services and coachbuilding - continued to develop and expand and it was not until after World War II, with the coming of nationalisation, when the bus services of Alexander passed into sole ownership of the British Transport Commission, that it was decided to form a separate private company for the coachbuilding part of the business. In February 1948 the firm of Walter Alexander and Co (Coachbuilders) Ltd was incorporated with a capital of £100,000.

The coachbuilding business continued to flourish and such was the increase in demand and in production that the size of the Stirling premises proved inadequate. This led the firm to return once more to Camelon in the 1950s to a site in Glasgow Road which became available and which covered an area of nine acres. It was a modern and well-equipped factory building, and there was room for further expansion, which was just as well because within a year of production starting in the new site, work was under way on extensions for various departments including a repair and experimental shop and a chassis store. A diversity of trades were necessary for building coach bodies, from fitters and welders, sheet metal workers, wood machinists to electricians, coachbuilders and painters. The factory employed 500 workers. A large capital outlay was necessary to build and equip the new factory which indicated the company's faith in its future expansion. Some of the departments within the new factory reflected developments in new methods and materials used in coachbuilding. For example, in the plastics department there was increasing use of fibreglass. The new works were claimed to be 'the largest of their kind in Scotland'. Much of this new development occurred shortly before Alexander's death in June 1959, and the importance of his coachbuilding works was recognised on 22 September that year when representatives of the Municipal Passenger Association visited the factory during their annual conference in Edinburgh.

Little is known about Alexander's personal life. Walter Alexander married three times. His third wife Ann Cooper Elder and two sons, Walter and Robert, and his daughter Isobel and step-daughter Margaret all survived him. He had little time for outside interests but took a deep interest in local activities. He was very interested in Falkirk Football Club. He was appointed to the board of the club in 1931, and in 1951 he became its chairman. It was during his chairmanship that Falkirk won the Scottish cup, in 1957, for only the second time in their history. He took an interest in his native town, providing a lorry for the carnival each year for Camelon Mariners Day, and the Mariners' Committee received donations from him until the event was indefinitely postponed in 1958 due to lack of public support.

Walter Alexander Snr died of heart failure in the Royal Infirmary, Edinburgh, on 19 June 1959. He was 80 years of age. He left an estate of £162,263 16s 6d. His son, Walter, carried on the business. Walter Alexander Snr was well-known and much respected for his modesty and fair dealings, but he will be best remembered for providing the ubiquitous blue buses of Walter Alexander and Sons and achieving a position of pre-eminence in the industry.

THERESA BARTON

SOURCES

Unpublished
SRO: SC 22/44/31, Inventory and Will

Published
Brotchie, Alan W, *The Tramways of Falkirk*, West Yorkshire, 1975
Dyos, H J and Aldcroft, D H, *British Transport*, Surrey, 1971
The Falkirk Herald, 26/9/1959
Glasgow Herald, 20/6/1959
Hibbs, John, *The History of British Bus Services*, Newton Abbot, 1968
Motor Transport, 26/6/1959
Rennie, T C and Gordon, T Crowther, *The Third Statistical Account of Scotland, The Counties of Stirling and Clackmannan*, Glasgow, 1966
Strong, L A G, *The Rolling Road*, London, 1956

Alexander ALLAN,

Shipowner; b. 1825, Greenock, s. of Alexander Allan, shipowner, and Jean Crawford; m. 1854, Jane Smith, d. of Robert Smith, shipowner (City Line); 5 s. 2 d.; Snr Partner, James & Alexander Allan, The Allan Line; d. 2/4/1892, Kirkmuirhill, Lanarkshire; g/v estate: £519,022.

Alexander Allan was the youngest of five brothers who together with their father formed the great shipping dynasty, the Allan Line. This company came to play a leading role in the development of the United Kingdom and Canadian trade in the second half of the nineteenth century. The success of the company owed a great deal to both the drive and the fecundity of the father, Alexander Allan Snr. His enterprise laid the foundation of the small shipping business engaged in the trade from the Clyde to the St Lawrence; his five sons then provided the family network which was to prove capable of operating a far flung business without the necessity of taking in non-family members.

Alexander Allan Snr was a Saltcoats man born in 1780. He trained as a ship's carpenter and made some small initial capital in supplying victuals to the British army in Spain during the Peninsular Wars. By the end of the Napoleonic hostilities, the ship's carpenter turned ship's captain, had made sufficent money to enable him to think of engaging in wider shipping activities. In 1819 he acquired one small wooden brigantine naming it *The Jean* after his wife Jean Crawford. With this small vessel he began making the trip from Greenock to Quebec in the spring and autumn of each year. In this enterprise he was both ship's captain and merchant, buying and selling both outward and inward cargoes on his own account. He took out cargoes of coal, iron, herring and sugar, and brought home wheat, peas, flour, potash and timber, supplying the needs of the Clyde and Ayrshire coastal towns.

Greenock was the obvious home base for this trade, and the Allan family moved there shortly before Alexander was born in 1825. All five brothers automatically went into business with their father. James, the eldest son, became the father's right hand man in Greenock, while Hugh, the second son, was located in Montreal from the late 1820s. Hugh headed the Canadian side of the business and as the fleet expanded it became necessary for the Allans to strengthen their agencies. Andrew Allan, a younger son, joined Hugh in Canada, while Bryce Allan, the fourth son, was sent to take care of the family interest in Liverpool. These four brothers not only operated the business on shore but frequently sailed as ship's captains. By the 1840s however the shipping business was so extensive that James Allan, the eldest son, was forced to come ashore to take management of the Scottish end of the business as his father, Alexander, began to withdraw from active day to day involvement. About this time, with the improvement in the River Clyde above Greenock, Glasgow was coming to be the main port; consequently the family moved its base operations from Greenock to Glasgow in 1846. This was the occasion for Alexander Allan, the youngest of the five brothers, to join his father and his brother James in the shipping business based in Glasgow. Unlike his brothers, the young Alexander does not appear to have gone to sea, but to have directly entered the onshore management of the firm under the direction of his eldest brother James.

It is clear that the Allans based the organisation of their company on close and strong family ties. They secured its shipping success by obtaining mail contracts which were subsidised by the Canadian provincial government. Hugh Allan was instrumental in making this connection and the Montreal end of the business became so important that it began to dominate and lead the development of the Allan shipping business in the middle decades of the nineteenth century. This in part reflected the different personalities of the two eldest brothers James and Hugh. James was at the head of the Glasgow business and by nature was modest and retiring. This gave great scope to his brother Hugh who had a driving restless energy. It was Hugh who took the lead in persuading his brothers and his father to build steamers for the transatlantic service. His father was rather sceptical of this development but Hugh was

impressed with the potential of steam and screw propulsion on longer ocean voyages. Consequently in 1854, the year in which the father Alexander Allan died, the brothers introduced their first steamer on the Glasgow to Montreal route; this was the *Canadian* built by Denny at Dumbarton. The father's death in 1854 was also the occasion for a reorganisation of the company. The shipping business was reorganised in two firms; in Canada Hugh Allan headed the Montreal Ocean Steamship Company, while in Glasgow the business was reformed as James & Alexander Allan, the oldest and youngest brothers coming together as the main partners. These two companies together formed the business that was later to become the Allan Line, with branches in Glasgow, Montreal and Liverpool; the firm also established offices in London, Boston, Philadelphia, Baltimore and Buenos Aires.

While Hugh Allan came to drive the business forward in these middle decades of the nineteenth century, ultimately earning himself a knighthood for services to the colony, it was the young Alexander Allan who gradually emerged as the main influence on the business in Glasgow. As the Allans developed their steamer services from 1854 it was Alexander who increasingly took the major part in management in the Scottish end of the business. This decision to move into steamers gave the Allans a lead in the shipping services between the United Kingdom and Canada. While other lines quickly followed them, as did the Donaldsons, the Anchor Line, the Furness Line, and the State Line, it was the Allans who held the leading position and consolidated that leadership until it met serious competition from the Canadian Pacific Railway Company near the end of the century.

When the Allans inaugurated their steamer services from the Clyde to the St Lawrence the frequency was fortnightly in summer and monthly in winter. However by 1860 they had developed a weekly service throughout the year. It was this frequency which enabled the Allans to take their next major step. This was the inauguration of their emigrant services from Glasgow to Canada in 1861. This was to become a major part of the Allan Line business for the remainder of the nineteenth century.

With Alexander in Glasgow and Hugh in Montreal, the Allan business prospered. By 1880 they were operating 39 vessels this making the Allan Line the seventh largest in the world and probably the first among the private family shipping firms as distinct from those operated by public companies. The Allans pursued a vigorous building policy adding 11 vessels in the 1860s and another 19 to their shipping line in the 1870s. At that stage only three of their vessels were more than 20 years old. Even though the Allans were pioneers in developing steamers on the Canadian trade they still built and operated many iron sail ships; seven of the 11 vessels built in the 1860s were of this type as were six of the 19 constructed in the 1870s. These vessels were employed on the longer trade routes to the East. In all of these developments it was

Hugh more than Alexander who was the innovator. Alexander was the competent manager implementing the decisions and new developments pioneered by his older brother.

While Alexander was in some ways in the shadow of his brother Hugh in terms of leading the business he nevertheless came to develop a distinctive niche for himself in other directions. In 1854 he had married Jane Smith, the only daughter of Robert Smith of the City Line. This had a profound influence on his life since Robert Smith and his daughter were staunch members of the Scottish Temperance League; Robert Smith had been president of the League for 21 years. Alexander Allan joined the League in 1854 and through his influence the Allan vessels gradually came to be manned by Masters who were themselves mainly abstainers. Indeed the Allan Line vessels were liberally supplied with the literature and tracts of the Temperance League as reading material for their passengers.

Alexander Allan and his wife Jane shared a life-long commitment to the temperance movement. He was wealthy and his wife independently so; consequently they could afford to indulge their beliefs. The Allans were also evangelically inclined, and both were active members of the United Free Presbyterian Church, attending the Wellington Church in Glasgow.

While Alexander Allan was reputed to be a man who liked doing things more than speaking about them, he nevertheless played an active part in the affairs of his church and of the Temperance League. He attended the annual meetings of the Synod, and he actively promoted the Home and Foreign Mission work of the church. Wherever he was in residence during the summer months he quickly gravitated to the nearest United Presbyterian Church and 'endeavoured to encourage and strengthen its minister by his presence and sympathy'. He was one of the main supporters of the Glasgow United Evangelistic Association, and was its first president. He had been very much influenced by the work of Moody and Sankey during their evangelical visit to Glasgow in 1874. He and his wife were heavily involved in good works, providing free breakfasts and other assistance to orphans and to the Glasgow Seamen's Friends Society. He gave liberally to all of these on a regular basis and through his commitment to the Mission work of his Church he provided Wellington Church with £7,000 to build its Home Mission at Cranstonhill.

Although Alexander was active in all these ways it was his role in the Temperance League which took most of his time. He had become a member of the League in 1854; he was a director for a period of nine years and a vice president of the League for 25 years. He undertook, at his own expense, the cost of publishing thousands of Temperance Tracts and frequently presided over the annual meetings and other important occasions of the League. In this activity he was strongly supported with his wife and by his family of five sons and two daughters all of whom adopted lifetime abstinence. He was able to undertake this activity not only because of his great wealth but because the family structure of the business, with extensive networks of second and third generation Allans available, could fill the managerial posts in the firm.

Although Alexander Allan led a busy life it is clear that he did not enjoy good health. Consequently in 1890 he and his wife planned for and set out upon an extensive world tour in the hope of improving his health; they combined this with plans to visit the Foreign Missions of the Church. Unfortunately serious illness struck him while in Ceylon and he returned home after only six months. He was never to recover his health from this occasion, but surprisingly it was his wife Jane, who caught a chill and pre-deceased him by six weeks in February 1892. Alexander himself died in his sixty-seventh year on 2 April 1892 at his country residence, Blackwood House, Kirkmuirhill. Between them, the Allans left an estate valued at over £1 million; Mrs Allan, independently wealthy from her father's City Line, left a gross personal estate of £583,163 while Alexander Allan himself left £519,022. Alexander and his wife both left extensive bequests to the United Free Presbyterian Church and to the many charitable interests they had supported in their lifetimes. The main beneficiary of Alexander Allan's estate was Wellington Church, over £6,000 being donated to it for investments to support a range of its activities. His wife made similar provision but also left extensive bequests to Glasgow hospitals.

When Alexander Allan died in 1892 the Allan Line comprised 37 steamers and 9 sailing vessels. Alexander's personal holdings in these vessels was valued at £102,862. The Allan business had acquired the State Line of Glasgow in 1890 for £72,000, thus adding to the strength of the Allan Line in the Canadian trade. However with Alexander Allan's death, the last of the second generation of Allan brothers was gone, and the Allan Line was not to retain its lead or its independence for long. By 1909 the Allan Line had effectively been purchased by the Canadian Pacific Railway Company for $8.5 million, though it still traded under the Allan Line name. It was formally absorbed into the structure of the Canadian Pacific Railway Company in 1916 and the Allan Line was finally dissolved in 1931.

ANTHONY SLAVEN

SOURCES

Unpublished

SRO: SC 36/48/137, Inventory of Estate of Alexander Allan

SC 36/51/105, Will of Alexander Allan
SC 36/48/136, Inventory of Estate of Jane
Smith or Allan

Published

Allan, James, *One Hundred Glasgow Men,* Vol 1
Glasgow Herald, 4/4/1892, 7/4/1892
*The League Journal: Organ of the Scottish Temperance
    League,* No 536, 9 April 1892
North British Daily Mail, 25/2/1886
United Presbyterian Magazine, Vol 9, May 189

James BARRIE,
FCIT, AMITA, F.Inst M.,

Road haulier; b. 27/3/1902, s. of John Barrie; m.
Alice Milne Methven; 1 s., 1 d.; CH/MD, John
Barrie (Contractor) Ltd; d. 16/3/87.

The Barrie family were closely connected with the
road haulage industry in Glasgow and the West of
Scotland. James Barrie was the son of John Barrie,
the founder of John Barrie (Contractor) Ltd. Both
John and his son, James, made important contributions to the development of the industry.

John Barrie was born on 16 January 1879 and
started in business aged 15 as a message boy for
William Crockett's, the Glasgow ironmongery firm
before joining John Law and Co, a Glasgow Foundry
business. He then set up on his own as a carter with
one horse. This was in April 1895. The contracting
business was not new to him however since his father,
also James, had carried on a cartage business and
when he died John's brother Isaac had taken over the
family business. Isaac was also to become an important
figure in the road haulage trade. He also joined his
brother John in his new venture.

John Barrie started his business from his grand-
mother's home in Pinkston Road, Glasgow, where
she had a farm. His first contract was with Wm
Holmes & Co, wholesale newsagents in Glasgow,
which entailed a 1.30 am start. His business went
from strength to strength as new contracts were won,
including those with many of the Glasgow bakeries,
Wm Arrol, Stewart & Lloyds and the newspapers and
newsagents.

John Barrie was the mainstay of the business which
at its peak was one of the largest independent cartage
contractors in Glasgow with 500 horses and 200 motor
vehicles. The company operated from eight depots
across Glasgow. John Barrie's firm operated by undertaking contracts to carry goods and also by hiring

men and horses, later motor vehicles, to specific
companies. The firm does not appear to have undertaken longer distance operations nor did it become
greatly involved as agents for the railways. However
it did take over several companies in Glasgow including the Glasgow Hiring Co Ltd (incorporated as a
limited company in 1909) in 1919 and Barrie's
nephew, James Barrie Hastie (qv) took charge there.
This company also operated in a similar way hiring
on an annual contract basis or by time, mileage and
tonnage.

This was the background then to James Barrie's
entrance into the business world. Born in 1902, he
was educated at Allan Glen's School, the West of
Scotland Commercial College and Glasgow University. He entered his father's business in the 1920s and
became closely involved with the running of the
company. His father died in 1940 after an accident
near the Milngavie Waterworks. The firm then
became a limited company in 1941 and the directors
at that time were James Barrie, James Barrie Hastie,
Isaac Barrie, John Barrie CA and L Sangster CA.
James Barrie remained chairman and managing director until 1978 when he resigned. James' son, John
Bruce Barrie, had been involved in the firm for several
years as a director and developed meat transport and
long distance operations. He remained to continue
the family name but by the late 1970s the firm of
John Barrie (Contractor) Ltd was under the holding
control of the Macfarlane Group (Clansman) Ltd.

James Barrie's involvement outside the business
was limited to a directorship of United Dominion
(Denationalised Transport) Ltd. However he also
made a significant contribution to the road haulage
industry. From 1954 to 1956 he served as Chairman
to both the Road Haulage Association and to the
National Road Transport Federation. He was also
chairman of the Institute of Transport (Scottish Area)
from 1957 to 1958. He chaired the Road Haulage and
West of Scotland sub-area committee from 1956 to
1958. He served as chairman of the Road Haulage
Association's Wages Council and was also the Scottish
chairman of the Civil Defence Commercial Vehicles
Unit.

James Barrie was a member of the Glasgow Conservative Club and actively involved in the Rotary
Club, being its chairman from 1947 to 1948. He also
retained his school connection as president of Allan
Glen's Old Boys Club from 1944 to 1948.

SHEILA HAMILTON

SOURCES

Unpublished

SRO: SC 21884, John Barrie (Contractor) Ltd Company file

Published

The Business Who's Who 1974-1975

John BURNS,
1st Baron Inverclyde,

Shipowner, b. 1829, s. of George Burns, ship-owner, and Miss Clelland; m. 1860, Emily, d. of G C Arbuthnot; 2 s., 3 d.; Ch, G & J Burns and the Cunard Steamship Co.; d. 12/2/1901, Wemyss Bay; g/v estate: £886,545.

The name of the Burns family is inextricably bound up with the development of steamship services in both coastal and ocean shipping; the family firm of G & J Burns dominated the Irish Steam Packet Services while the partnership that was to become the Cunard Line was the most famous of the great nineteenth century transatlantic liner services. Two generations of the Burns family brought these enterprises to full development, and two individuals, John Burns, and his father George, were the leading players in the family involvement.

John Burns father, George Burns, came from a distinguished professional Glasgow family. George's father was Dr John Burns, minister of the Barony Parish, Glasgow, for a period of 72 years; both his brothers were surgeons of distinction. Perhaps surprisingly the professions did not attract George and his younger brother John, who set up in partnership in Glasgow in 1818 as general merchants. By 1824 they had joined with Hugh Mathie of Liverpool to jointly own and manage six sailing vessels trading between Liverpool and Glasgow. In the same year they built their first steam vessel to ply on the Glasgow to Belfast route. The Liverpool connection of the Burns brothers was strong from the outset, and in 1830 they joined with two Liverpool based Scots, David and Charles MacIver to form the City of Glasgow Steam Packet Co, which developed services running between Glasgow and Liverpool, Belfast, and Londonderry; a West Highland service was acquired by G & J Burns in 1845 when they bought out the Castle Line, but this was quickly sold off again in 1848 to a partnership comprising David Hutcheson, their shipping clerk in Glasgow, his brother Alexander, and David Mac-Brayne (qv) the Burns' nephew.

George Burns joined with the MacIvers in 1830, the year following the birth of his first son John. By the time young John was ten years old, his father was establishing the transatlantic bridgehead in their shipping interests, linking with Samuel Cunard, and David MacIver in 1839, to take up a seven year government contract to deliver mail once a fortnight from Liverpool to Halifax and Boston. This was to be the origin of the Cunard Line. George Burns had been instrumental in putting together the funding of £270,000 needed by Samuel Cunard to establish the new transatlantic service. The new line made its first voyage in July 1840, and the first four Cunard vessels were built on the Clyde by Robert Napier.

With this development the Burns family now had two major enterprises. The partnership of G & J Burns operated out of Glasgow on the Mersey and Irish routes; the partnership with Cunard and MacIver pioneered the transatlantic services. In this latter partnership Samuel Cunard made his head-quarters in London; David MacIver ran the shipping interest in Liverpool, and George Burns ran the Glasgow end of the business though spending much time in both Liverpool and London.

While his father pioneered these ventures, the young John Burns pursued his education taking an arts degree at Glasgow University, and only then joining the family business about 1850. Ten years later his father, then 65, retired from active business, and John Burns entered upon a period of 40 years in control of G & J Burns, and as a leading influence in the development of the Cunard Line. Like his father before him he initially gave most of his time to the coasting business of the family firm, but he was also increasingly drawn into the management of Cunard. David MacIver had died in 1845 and his place in Liverpool was taken by his younger brother Charles, who remained in that position for nearly 35 years. In the 1860s, under the influence of John Burns, Cunard moved steadily to replace its fleet of wooden paddle steamers with iron hulled vessels, first with paddle boats and then with screw steamers. The *Persia*, in 1860, was Cunard's first iron paddle boat, and in 1862 they completed that type of vessel with the *Scotia*. In the same year they inaugurated their first screw steamer with the *China*. John Burns' view of what kind of vessels his Lines should build had no doubt been influenced by his father's long connection with the pioneering Robert Napier. Consequently he always pressed for Cunard to build the soundest and most advanced steamers. Compound engines were quickly adopted from 1870 in the *Batavia*. When steel appeared as an alternative to iron, Cunard was also quick to adopt it, bringing it into service in 1881 in the *SS Servia*. This was Cunard's first steel vessel and apart from the *Great Eastern* it was the largest ship in the world. It was also one of the first vessels to adopt automatically closing watertight doors in the bulkheads. The *Servia* was built by J & G Thomson at their new Clydebank yard.

By 1880 the Cunard business had been restructured. In 1878 the partnership was transformed into a limited company with a capital of £2 million, the three founding families holding £1.2 million. Shares and a prospectus were eventually issued in 1880, the prospectus indicating that 'the growing wants of the company's transatlantic trade demand the acquisition of additional steamships of great size and power involving a cost for construction that might best be met by a large public company'. The shares were quickly taken up and John Burns was elected chairman of the new Cunard company. Under his chairmanship the Cunard Line pursued a very active policy of constructing ever larger, more powerful, and more luxurious liners for the transatlantic service. Following the *Servia* in 1881 came the *Umbria* and *Etruria* in 1884, and then the *Campania* and *Lucania* in 1891. In this period Cunard extended and consolidated its reputation for quality, reliability and safety. Its ships were built to the highest standards, its officers and crews well-trained and subject to strict discipline and procedures. John Burns was rightly proud of Cunard's reputation for never having lost a passenger through accident.

In the 1880s John Burns was not only deeply immersed in the management of G & J Burns and the Cunard Line, but was much involved in all maritime affairs. He was long an advocate of building merchant vessels so that they could be quickly adapted for war purposes; indeed he wrote and published a volume in 1887 entitled 'Adaptation of Merchant Steamships for War Purposes'. His views on this had no doubt been influenced by his being present in 1855 at the Fall of Sebastopol during the Crimean War. He was also an advocate of coastal defences, and the later plans for defences on the Clyde owed much to his thinking. While he was active in business he also travelled widely, notably in Europe, America and Syria; indeed his interest in travel involved him in the Royal Geographical Society of which he became a Fellow.

When John Burns succeeded his father to be head of the family business in 1860 he also in that year married Emily Arbuthnot who bore him two sons and three daughters. Both his sons, George A Burns and James C Burns, followed him into the business in the 1880s. As their experience grew John Burns clearly allowed more and more of the day to day business of G & J Burns to pass into their hands. In the 1890s the elder son, George A Burns, concentrated on the Scottish and Irish mail services, while his young brother played a more active role in Glasgow shipping circles. James C Burns became chairman of the Glasgow Shipowners' Association at that time. The 1890s indeed, were a transition period as the first and second generation Burns passed out of major influence in the business. The founder of the enterprises, Sir George Burns, had retired from active involvement in 1860 and his influence had gradually diminished. He was raised to the Baronetcy in 1889, the year before he died in 1890 at the age of 96. His son Sir John Burns, came into the title and the estate at Wemyss Bay and was created a Baron in 1897 on the occasion of Queen Victoria's Jubilee. By then the third generation, his sons George and James ran the Glasgow business, while in Liverpool the deputy chairman David Jardine bore the brunt of running Cunard.

In addition to his extensive business interests, John Burns also enjoyed a full public life. He was a Justice of the Peace and a Deputy Lieutenant of Renfrewshire, Lanarkshire and the County of the City of Glasgow. In addition he was an honorary lieutenant in the RNVR, and through his great recreational interests in yachting he was a member of all the leading yacht clubs on the Clyde. He also had a particular interest in youth training, and largely through his efforts, the training ship scheme was established, the first such vessel on the Clyde being the *Cumberland*. Like his father before him he was a Liberal in politics and an episcopalian in religion. He was in his life time an extensive benefactor of welfare and other activities and at his death he left generous payments to all his household retainers and a long list of bequests. These included £500 to each of the Clyde Industrial Training Ships Association, the Eastpark Children's Home, the Training Home for Nurses in Glasgow, and the St Silas English Episcopalian Church. The gross value of his estate amounted to £886,545, of which £220,000 represented the valuation of his fleet of 14 steamers in the firm of G & J Burns, of which he was sole partner. He also held shares in the Cunard Steamship Co to the value of £67,713. Tragically his wife died only two days after him on 14 February 1901. This ill fortune continued, for four years later his eldest son George, second Lord Inverclyde, died at the early age of 44. Control of the business then passed to his younger brother James Cleland Burns. Like his father, his grandfather, and his brother, James C Burns became chairman of G & J Burns, and also became a director of Cunard. But with the death in quick succession of John Burns and then George A Burns, the controlling influence of the Burns family in the Cunard Line dwindled and the family then concentrated more on the traditional family business of G & J Burns.

ANTHONY SLAVEN

SOURCES

Unpublished

SRO: SC 53/41/11, Inventory
     SC: 53/47/8, Will

Published

The Engineer, 15/2/1901
Engineering, 15/2/1901

Glasgow Contemporaries at the Dawn of the Twentieth Century Glasgow, 1901
Glasgow Herald, 13/2/1901
MaGinnis, A J M, *The Atlantic Ferry*, London, 1893
Pollock, D, *Modern Shipbuilding and the Men Engaged in it*, London, 1884
The Times, 15/2/1901

Sir William BURRELL,

Shipowner; b. 9/7/1861, Glasgow, s. of William Burrell, shipowner and Isabella Duncan Guthrie; m. 10/9/1901, Constance Mary, d. of James Lockhart Mitchell, merchant; 1 d.; Partner, Burrell & Son, Shipowners, Glasgow; d. 29/3/1958, Hutton Castle, Berwick-on-Tweed; g/v estate: £312,035 1s 9d.

Sir William Burrell is best remembered for his activities as an art collector and for the gift of his extensive collection to the City of Glasgow in 1944. He continued to add to the collection, so that at the time of his death in 1958 there were over 8,000 objects, valued at almost two million pounds. For nearly 50 years the annual expenditure averaged £20,000, with several years far in excess of this average, for example, £80,000 in 1936 and £60,000 in 1948. Besides the gift of the collection, Sir William also gave Glasgow £450,000 to help meet the cost of building a facility to house the collection and a substantial trust fund to use for additional acquisitions.

Burrell acquired his fortune from his association with the Glasgow shipping firm, Burrell & Son, established by his grandfather, George, in 1856. Sir William's father, William, entered the business in 1857, whereupon it became Burrell & Son. Operations in the initial years were confined to acting as shipping and forwarding agents on the Forth & Clyde Canal. It was an interesting time to be involved in canal shipping for the transition from horse drawn barges to steam powered boats was underway and the new firm took full advantage of the changes. Despite the fact that the railway posed an increasing threat to profitability, in the form of tariff wars, Burrell & Son maintained an interest in Canal operations until 1903, using a small and diminishing fleet of 'puffers'. The firm also owned a yard at Hamiltonhill from at least 1875 until 1903, where they constructed and repaired puffers for canal and intercoastal shipping; at least 46 puffers were constructed at the yard.

An alternative to canal shipping had to be found and Burrell & Son's first known venture into deep-sea vessels was made with the purchase of a quarter share of *Suffolk* in 1864. At the time of William Snr's death in 1885, Burrell & Son had had ownership shares in and managerial control over 27 ocean-going vessels, most having the prefix *Strath*. William Snr was the sole proprietor at the time of his death in 1885, and the value of the firm was £80,000. According to the terms of his will, his sons, George and William were to be allowed to buy the business from the trustees for £73,000. This they did, largely financing the purchase by mortgages issued to their mother at 4.5%. All the mortgages were discharged before or during 1889. Both sons had practical experience with the firm; George as a shipbuilder when the firm owned a yard at Dumbarton from 1881-4 (14 ships and 6 barges were built at this yard); William entered the office at 14 years of age in 1876 straight from boarding school in St. Andrews and received commercial training. This training served them well, as George looked after the technical aspects of the business, while William was in charge of the commercial aspects.

Burrell's responsibility for the commercial side of the business involved him in extensive travel abroad, for the firm came to rely on an extensive network of agents in the main ports to get cargoes rather than depend on the captains of their ships to obtain business. His job was to appoint the agents and to liaise with them about cargoes. This was found to be a more efficient way of doing business for it enabled the partners in Glasgow to plan ship journeys with a greater degree of certainty than would otherwise have been possible. Several friendships were cemented by Burrell on his trips. Of particular importance was the friendship with Gottfried Schenber whose firm had premises in Vienna, Budapest and Fiume (now Rijeka). In 1879 Schenber and Co and Burrell and Son set up the Adria Hungarian Steam Navigation Co to ply the route between the Adriatic and Scotland, and in 1895 they formed the Austro-Hungarian Steamship Co to serve the US-Adriatic route. This close connection led to Burrell being appointed Austro-Hungarian vice-consul for Glasgow in 1888. The maintenance of contact with the agents, of whom Schenber was only one of a large number, made it necessary for William to visit the continent two or three times a year.

Burrell also developed a large business with the Far East and in 1880 a cargo of frozen meat was brought to Britain from Australia but, for some unexplained reason, the firm failed to develop the potential of this rich new commerce.

Almost immediately after William Snr's death in 1885 the nature of the firm changed dramatically. There was a period of rapid expansion, with 34 ships being added to the fleet between 1888-1898. The method of financing the ships changed. During this period most ships were owned on a 64 share basis. Before 1885 William Snr either was sole owner or held at least half of the 64 shares for most of the ships in which he had a financial interest; moreover, few mortgages were issued against the ships. After 1885 Burrell followed a different practice. Shares were sold to a wider number of people, with Burrell & Son frequently not holding a majority, being content to be managing owners. Ownership of shares were, however, restricted to a few people, mainly relatives and close business associates. Numerous mortgages were issued against the ships. Such practices allowed rapid expansion of the fleet by allowing the Burrells to invest their capital in more vessels, reducing risk of loss from shipwreck, and enjoying increased profits from an expanded number of voyages. By concentrating on tramp operations, the firm was able to seek the most profitable cargoes. Burrell ships in this period normally provided annual rates of return of 45 to 64%. Burrell gained a reputation of being a successful investor for the ships were purchased cheaply when markets were depressed. Moreover, the firm's activities were diversified, expanding its role as shipping agent, shipbroker, and insurance agent. Then, beginning in 1898, the Burrells started selling their fleet. It is interesting to note that instead of selling their shares, they purchased all 64 shares for each ship, then sold all 64. The reason being, of course, that the market value of the ship was higher than the market value of the individual shares. The entire fleet was disposed of by 1901. As the market was quite buoyant when the ships were sold the prices were generally much higher than when the ships were purchased, so in addition to several years operating profits the Burrells were also able to pocket a sizeable capital gain on their vessels.

Considerable speculation exists as to the reasons for Burrell leaving the shipowning business at this stage in his life. Some argue it was for altruistic reasons, as he became a member of the Glasgow Town Council in 1899, representing the Exchange Ward. He was a magistrate from 1903 to 1905. He quickly turned his attention to the severe housing problem then existing in Glasgow, and he made numerous attempts to expand the city's housing programmes. He even argued that landlords should not be compensated for the tearing down of back-land housing, as these were considered to be uninhabitable and landlords were not willing to pay for improvements. Little progress was made, so he resigned in 1906. During these years, he enjoyed income from numerous investments and from the ship agent and insurance activities of Burrell & Son.

In 1905, a depressed period for the shipping industry, Burrell & Son started to acquire a new fleet, with impressive speed and scale; 8 in 1906, 13 in 1907, 6 in 1909 - 32 in all between 1905 and 1912. Clearly the firm's policy was to buy low and sell high - a strategy which required ice cool nerves and an intimate knowledge of the shipping and shipbuilding industries. Again there was a radical departure from previous ownership practices. By now the common method was to form single-ship companies and to sell shares in the company. Burrell & Son arranged a

contract price for construction of a ship, issued £100 shares for half its value and a mortgage to the builder for the other half. A portion of the profits for each voyage went towards paying off the mortgage, the balance to the shareholders. Burrell & Son acted as managers of the ships, receiving a fee for this service, besides the annual return on their investment. Ships from the fleet could be found all over the world, carrying such diverse cargoes as grain, coal and lumber. In 1915 and 1916 the fleet was sold, with the exception of one which was kept until its sale in 1930. Ten ships were sold to the Australian government for about £140,000 each; they had cost about £40,000 each. With their sales, the 21 surviving steamship companies (the others were war losses), distributed to the shareholders a total of £604,968 from a special capital reserve account and accumulated profits. Of this amount Burrell received £112,042.

After 1916 Burrell was in semi-retirement and the firm of Burrell and Son continued in a rather perfunctory way as shipping and insurance agents until 1939. His time was spent largely in touring for the purpose of adding to his growing art collection. He had inherited his love of art from his mother, although he had not been encouraged in this by his father. His collection had been started when he was still a young man and in his retirement it consumed most of his time and interest - and not a little part of his fortune, for between 1911 and 1957 his annual expenditure on it averaged £20,000.

In 1916 Burrell bought Hutton Castle in Berwickshire and spent the next decade restoring and altering it before he and his wife moved themselves and their art collection into it in 1927.

Burrell's reputation as a connoisseur and collector gained public recognition in 1923 when he was invited to be one of the Trustees of the National Gallery of Scotland - a post which he held until 1946. From 1927 to 1934 he was also a Trustee of the National Gallery of British Art (now the Tate Gallery). About 1930 he seems to have made up his mind to give his collection away, although the decision to give it to Glasgow was not made until 1943. He was awarded the Freedom of the City in 1944 and received the St Mungo Prize two years later. Burrell was knighted in 1927 for services to art in Scotland and for public works. But that year was marred for him by the death of his brother George. Thereafter the premises occupied by Burrell and Son in George Square, Glasgow were given up and the firm moved to Buchanan Street where it remained in business for 12 years, but Burrell himself took little interest in it.

The works in his art collection perhaps reflect the nature of Burrell, as all are traditional in subject matter and approach, meticulously executed examples of technical excellence. Burrell was a conservative buyer, purchasing only sure investments, always making a wise and well-researched buy. The same can be said of his shipping interests. New ships were ordered at favourable prices when yards were experiencing slumps, and sold at opportune moments, reaping tremendous wind-fall profits. Even though he was a successful and extremely skilled businessman, Sir William Burrell made no lasting contribution to the British shipping industry.

R A CAGE

SOURCES

Unpublished

SRO: SC 60/41/70, Inventory
SC 60/47/14, Will

Published

The Bailie, 17/6/1925
Clark, K, 'Sir William Burrell. A Personal Remi-niscence', *The Scottish Review*, 1977
Glasgow Herald, 7/12/1906, 31/3/1958
Leslie, P S, *Notes on Hutton Parish*, Berwick upon Tweed, 1934
Marks, R, *Burrell: Portrait of a Collector*, Glasgow, 1983
Scottish Art Review, Vol XIV, No 4, 1975
See Breezes, Vol 49, 1975
Wells, W, 'The Burrell Collection - five years on', *Museums Journal*, Vol 72, No 3, 1972

Patrick CAIRD,

Engineer and railway company chairman; b. 1868, Greenock, s. of James T Caird, shipbuilder, and Elizabeth McArthur; m. Jane Neilson; 1s., 3 d.; Ch, Messrs Caird & Co, Engineers & Shipbuilders; Ch, Glasgow & South-Western Railway Co; d. 7/1/1933, Greenock; g/v estate: £309,239.

Patrick Caird was educated in Scotland and Germany before beginning a five year engineering apprenticeship in 1865 in his father's shipbuilding and engineering firm. Promotion was rapid for, almost as soon as the apprenticeship was concluded, he was appointed engineering manager and soon after that he became a partner in the firm. When his father died, almost 20 years later, he became chairman of the company (by then registered as a limited company). Caird remained in this position until he sold the business to Harland & Wolff in 1916.

Caird & Co built ships for many of the world's major shipping lines such as P & O, British and Continental and the Pacific Steam Navigation Company. They also built for many of the not so famous lines. Technologically Caird & Co kept up to date and Patrick Caird was closely identified with the various developments in the reciprocating marine engine, from simple to compound and from triple to quadruple expansion.

These interests, however, were not enough to consume all his energies and interest and in 1891 he became a director of the Glasgow and South-Western Railway Company. He was appointed deputy chairman in 1897 and three years later he succeeded Sir Renny Watson as chairman. He retained this position until he retired in 1915. This was an exceptionally active time for the railway which expanded greatly under Caird's chairmanship and David Cooper's (qv) management. After Caird joined the board in 1891 the Glasgow and South Western embarked on a period of expansion both by acquisition and new building. The Ayrshire and Wigtownshire Railway Company was acquired giving the company access to Stranraer and therefore to the Irish crossing. Harbours were acquired at Largs and Troon and an extensive steamer fleet was built up. Indeed all departments of the company's business took a firm upwards turn in this period.

Caird was an enthusiastic Unionist in politics but he was more interested in matters which affected him closely. He took a particular interest in social and labour questions and he served for a time as chairman of the Institution of Clyde Engineers and Shipbuilders which he joined as a life member in 1896. At one time he was an active member of the Federation of Employers.

Throughout his life Caird was an enthusiastic reader of the popular literature of his day. Indeed he thought so much of his collection as to make specific bequests of his books in his will.

CHARLES W MUNN

SOURCES

Unpublished

SRO: SC 53/41/41, Inventory
SC 53/47/25, Will

Published

The Bailie, 20/8/1933
Glasgow Herald, 9/1/1933

The Scotsman, 10/1/1933
The Times, 23/3/1933
Transactions of the Institution of Engineers and Shipbuilders in Scotland, Vol 76, 1932-3

Sir Charles William CAYZER,

Shipowner; b. 15/7/1843, London, s. of Charles William Cayzer, gentleman and Mary Elizabeth Nickin; m. 16/5/1868, Agnes Elizabeth, d. of William Trickey, Bristol mariner; 6 s., 4 d.; Founder, Cayzer, Irvine & Co, Glasgow & Liverpool; Partner, Clan Line Association, Glasgow; d. 28/9/1916, Gartmore, Stirlingshire; g/v estate £2,183,823 9s 3d.

Charles Cayzer was born on 15 July 1843, son of a Cornish schoolmaster in Poplar, London, who gave his son a sound education. At the age of 15 Cayzer shipped as master's clerk on a sailing ship bound for Nagasaki. In 1861 he obtained a shore job in Bombay with an established Scottish agency house, Wm Nichols & Co under James Nichol Fleming. Cayzer went into their shipping department and became store-keeper of the Agency for Wm Mackinnon's (qv) new British India Steam Navigation Co. Cayzer quickly gained a reputation for hard work and probity. He married Alice Trickey, daughter of a master mariner, in Bombay. In 1871 he sent her and two infants back to Britain, in a rat-infested ship round the Cape, conditions which made improved passenger accommodation one of his ultimate objectives. He followed in 1873 via the new Suez Canal, grasping its immense significance. He left Nichols in 1874 and was engaged by Gray, Dawes & Co, London, agents for BISNC, as cashier. His later demand for a partnership was rejected and he left. He had no capital, but opened a small office in Liverpool as ships' chandler, and he joined the Masons there, becoming Master of a new Lodge. He observed that the bulk of British exports to India were from Lancashire or Clydeside. He made his way to Glasgow in 1877 to see if he could raise capital to realise his vision of the first fast regular cargo line to Bombay, ex Glasgow and Liverpool. Competitors only sailed from London. He got introductions to Alexander Stephen (qv) of Linthouse, shipbuilder, and to John Muir (qv) of James Finlay & Co, East India merchants. The partnership they soon agreed upon was profitable to all three but they remained mutually hostile for many years. Stephen was to build the ships, Muir finance them and Cayzer manage them. Agreement was signed

on 30 January 1878 and the keels of the first two ships were laid in February. Muir paid cash down for one third of building cost, Stephen (building his way out of depression) bore two thirds on three-year bills and Cayzer had to raise an additional £22,000 in cash. He did this by selling one sixty-fourth shares in the ships he was proposing to build in Liverpool. His advertisement anticipated an annual profit of 15% on the basic cost of each steamer. In 1878 Cayzer took Captain Irvine into partnership. A former BI skipper, he died in 1879 leaving only his name.

Clan MacAlpine, the first vessel, sailed on 26 October 1878 freighted with Glasgow railway stores and Liverpool textiles. Cayzer had decided to register in Glasgow, moved his family north and became an enthusiast for things Scottish. His use of the flag of the monarchs of Scotland had to be modified, but the Clan Line continued to have vessels named for Scottish families and to sport a wealth of tartan in their fittings. Cayzer and Muir decided to have good passenger accommodation for 12 passengers in each ship. Six ships were added to the fleet and Muir had secured the sole agency for all ports east of Suez. Cayzer set up as his own underwriter. The line prospered, but by the time *Clan Lamont* went on trial in 1879 Cayzer owed Stephen £23,000 and Muir held mortgages on all ships which he refused to surrender until he was completely paid off. The liquidity of Cayzer, Irvine & Co was long doubtful. Then, in 1881 Muir produced a surprising scheme for 'Clan Line Association Steamers', a company having no financial connection with the six existing Clan ships, but managed by Cayzer, Irvine & Co the Association partners were John Muir, T P Coats and James Arthur; six major Scottish banks backed them. Muir thus showed his appreciation of Cayzer's brilliant grasp of shipping. Cayzer opened his head office in Glasgow in 1880 moving from St Vincent Street to 110 Hope Street in 1881. The Association bought or built six vessels, paying in cash not bills and the Bombay run was soon extended. Cayzer had ambitions to enter the Cape run in opposition to the established mail carriers, Union and Castle, and offered regular sailings once a month. His rivals did all they could to make this venture unprofitable, but during the rush to the Gold Fields general stores shipped by Arthur & Co were profitable outward cargo. Then a possible entry to the Bengal trade was seen by Muir, in the demise of the London Queen Line, trading to Calcutta, Madras and Colombo. Cayzer agreed and temporarily took ships off his new South African run. The prize from Bengal was carriage of the expanding jute and tea trades. After much argument over 'clean' ships, Muir agreed to ship his teas by Clan vessels. He also warned Cayzer not to engage in a freight 'war' in Bombay, the outcome of which was the first West India Liners' Conference agreeing rates. Cayzer became a staunch supporter of the conference cartel system.

By 1885 only Muir and Cayzer of the original

Association's six partners survived, and the Association was in trouble through over-investment in new steamers, and under pressure for repayment from the banks who had funded their start - Muir complained that Cayzer in times of cargo shortage preferred his own ships to the Associations', who now owned 18 ships valued at £600,000. Cayzer had meantime been accumulating his own capital and by 1888 the Association came under legal arbitration and the partnership was dissolved in the following year. Cayzer reverted to an earlier scheme, and formed a limited company, Clan Line Steamers Ltd. He repaid his indebtedness to the Association; in 1888 he paid £26,000 from his own funds; in 1889 he had to liquidate his big share of the original sixty-fourths. He managed to find over £60,000 in a short time, helped by bankers of the Commercial Bank of Scotland and the Capital & Counties Bank, London. By then he was making large operational profits. The Association retained six ships. Shareholders in Clan Line Steamers Ltd were invited to invest in the Bombay and South African trades from Glasgow and Liverpool. Later Australia was added. The Bengal trade was reserved for the Association ships, of which Cayzer, Irvine & Co remained the sole administrator and Finlay Muir Owner's Agent. Ahead of formal flotation in June 1890, Cayzer refitted his existing fleet and those bought from the Association, with compound triple expansion engines, effecting a big economy in coal. Clan Line Steamers' authorised capital was £500,000, in addition £125,000 of 5% mortgage debentures were issued. Cayzer personally owned a majority of shares, two of Muir's nominees served on the board, Muir himself being trustee for debenture holders. Further ships were ordered.

Ships' masters served long spells with the Clan Line: in 1889 at £20 per month but, for a short period while the Line expanded rapidly, they were paid as much as £25 per month plus bonus. However, when Cayzer was well-established new masters had to start at £18, not reaching £25 until their ninth year. Lascar seamen, at the bottom of the scale, were recruited in East India and paid £3 per month, compared with the Fourth Officer at £5 and the British quartermasters at £4 per month. Cayzer's passenger accommodation was adequate but austere.

As he prospered he moved to a mansion house, Ralston in Renfrew, and also in 1886 bought a family holiday house near Cove, up Loch Long where he installed his aged parents. He began investing in land and estates for his large family. He also began his public career in Cove, becoming Provost and elected to Dumbarton County Council. He was adopted and won the parliamentary seat of Barrow-in-Furness for the Conservatives in 1892. He only spoke on maritime matters but did advocate a Ministry of Labour, more than 20 years before it was set up. He is said to have had a genuine understanding of working men's interests. Barrow yards got orders for Clan ships. He also founded the Seamens' Children's Orphanage in Kilmacolm. By the 1890s trade with South Africa had expanded and Clans called at the new ports of Beira, Port Elizabeth and East London and started a refrigerated run to Australia and New Zealand. Cayzer invested privately in South Africa and in gilt-edged. Cayzer then expanded into the Persian Gulf, also extending the Bombay run southwards to Malabar. The growth of the tea trade in North India had created a bottleneck at Calcutta. Muir strongly advocated the tiny unknown port of Chittagong as an alternative and took on a coal agency. The Clan Line followed. This may be said to have created that port.

Cayzer was knighted in 1897. In 1899 Clan Line made a record 58 sailings to place stores and munitions in South Africa where the Boer War had broken out. Cayzer's private fortune was accumulating once he became financially independent of the Association and secure enough to delegate some of his work. Up to this time he had personally scrutinised all the voyage accounts, the resultant division of profit or loss, and the intricate bank accounts: banks had been allocated named vessels as security. Cayzer interviewed masters, pursued new cargoes and encouraged old customers to re-ship, and trained his sons. Muir and Cayzer remained mutually necessary to one another, as Clans carried the tea shipments of Finlay, Muir and Co's India and Ceylon properties, while Finlays were Agents in Bombay, Karachi and Calcutta, later Colombo and Chittagong. Muir's private company, Steel, Murray & Co were Agents in Natal. Between 25 and 30 Clans were at sea. By 1903 Muir was dead, though his sons carried on business on the same terms.

Charles Cayzer was 71 years old when war broke out in 1914. His four sons immediately joined up; two daughters had married Naval officers, Admirals Jellicoe and Madden. Clan ships became targets, two being sunk by the cruiser *Emden* almost without knowing the war had started, as they were without radio. RNVR Masters were recalled to the Navy. Eventually Cayzer's second son was released by the Army to help his father. Jellicoe's private advice to the Masters was to 'Go full steam ahead and zig-zag'. *Clan Macgillivary* was commandeered for Gallipoli, taking 600 wounded back on board whilst still discharging troops. After demands from Government that all losses should be replaced by unsubsidised shipowners, Cayzer felt like giving up and made tentative plans to sell the Clan Line which, however, his sons actively discouraged. By April 1916 an average of one Clan every eight weeks had been lost, with 300 men. Cayzer developed kidney failure and died at Gartmore, his estate in Stirlingshire, in September 1916. He left £2.8 million divided between his much-loved wife and his family, commending the management of the Clans to his sons. By the end of the war, the gross tonnage of Clan Line was greater than in 1914 although a total of 28 vessels had been lost.

MONICA CLOUGH

SOURCES

Unpublished

SRO: SC 70/1/589, Inventory
SC 70/4/491, Will

Published

The Bailie, No 1215
Directory of Directors, 1888-1917
Fairplay, Vol LXVI, No 1743, 5/10/1916
Glasgow Herald, 29/9/1916, Obituary
Muir, A & Davies, M, *A Victorian Shipowner, a Portrait of Sir Charles Cayzer, Baronet of Gartmore*, London, 1978
Shipbuilder and Shipping Record, Vol 8, 5/10/1916, Obituary
Shipping World, 7/10/1916, Obituary
The Times, 2/10/1916, Obituary
Who's Who in Glasgow, Glasgow, 1909

David COOPER,

Railway manager; b. 3/7/1855, Waterside, Dalmellington, s. of John Cooper, iron miner and Margaret Alexander; m. 1885, Betsy Mathieson, d. of John Mathieson, crofter; 3 s.; General manager, Glasgow and South Western Railway Co; d. 28/10/1940, Glasgow; g/v estate: £37,006.

David Cooper was the longest serving of the late nineteenth century Scottish railway managers. In his period of service he saw many changes in the sphere of operation of the railway companies and he initiated many of these changes himself. He was a professional manager and, as such, is a good example of the growing separation of ownership from control in British business. He held a few shares in the company which he managed but he could never aspire to owning it completely.

Cooper's origins were modest. He was born and raised in Waterside, Dalmellington in Ayrshire, the sixth child of his parents. Evidently he was a bright boy for he was dux of the village school. Despite this his formal education ended at age 12 when he took up employment as a parcels clerk with the Glasgow and South Western Railway at the local station. Five years later he moved to Maybole where he gained experience of all departments of railway management. From there he moved in 1885 to Glasgow, to the general manager's office where he worked as chief assistant. Only young men destined for greater things filled such posts. Four years later he was promoted to the responsible post of superintendent and in 1889, aged only 39, he was appointed to be general manager. He retired from this post in 1922 but his influence did not cease for he served for another ten years as director of the London, Midland and Scottish Railway Company.

His period of active service was therefore one of mixed fortunes for the railways. The expansion of the late nineteenth century gave way to more difficult years before the war and to a period of rationalisation immediately afterwards.

In the expansive phase Cooper took a leading role in the improvement of rolling stock and accommodation and in the building of new lines such as the Paisley to Barrhead line, the Renfrew and District line and the Catrine branch line. By the time of his retiral the company controlled almost 500 miles of track. Perhaps the most enduring testimony to his work, however, is not the railway but the Turnberry hotel and golf courses which were opened in 1906. This event could be said to mark the peak of expansion for the company.

The years immediately before the First World War were marked by acute labour problems in the railway industry although the Glasgow and South Western suffered much less than many other companies. It was said that this was due to the 'tact and understanding of working conditions displayed by the general manager'. This may not have been the whole explanation but there is undoubtedly some truth in it. It was well known that Cooper had risen from the ranks and his 'hands on' approach to management meant that he was not seen as aloof and remote.

During the war the railways were taken into public ownership and Cooper became, in effect, a civil servant. As part of the war effort the Engineer and Railway Staff Corps was formed with the task of arranging the rapid mobilisation of troops in the event of an invasion. Cooper held the rank of Lieutenant Colonel.

When peace was restored plans were made to return the railways to private ownership but the financial difficulties which many companies had faced before 1914 made it impractical to return them to their original form. Four large regional railway companies were formed and the Glasgow and South Western became part of the London, Midland and Scottish. Cooper played a major part in the negotiations. He was then 67 years of age and decided to take the opportunity to retire from active management. He became Scottish director of the new company and served for a further ten years before retiring in 1932.

Throughout his adult life David Cooper took an interest in the St Andrew's Ambulance Association and from 1885-89 he was secretary for Scotland of the Railway Benevolent Institution. In 1893 he served as chairman of the General Managers' Conference of the Railway Companies of Great Britain.

Cooper was a Justice of the Peace for Glasgow and Renfrew and in 1929 he became Deputy Lieutenant of the County of the City of Glasgow. When he died in 1940 his collection of jewellery and paintings, together with his financial resources were divided amongst his three sons. Several bequests were made to servants.

CHARLES W MUNN

SOURCES

Unpublished

SRO: SC 38/51/275, Will
SC 36/48/564, Inventory

Published

Glasgow Contemporaries at the Dawn of the Twentieth Century, Glasgow, 1901
Glasgow Herald, 29/10/1940
Railway Gazette, 1/11/1940
The Scotsman, 29/10/1940

William Betts DONALDSON,

Shipowner, b. 27/2/1872, Glasgow, s. of William Falconer Donaldson, shipowner, and Henrietta Maria Betts; Ch, Donaldson Brothers Ltd, Donaldson Line Ltd, Donaldson Atlantic Line Ltd; d. 4/4/1945, Glasgow; g/v estate: £505,427.

William Betts Donaldson was born into the shipping business. In 1854 his father, William Falconer Donaldson, and his father's two younger brothers John and Archibald, formed the partnership of Donaldson Brothers who worked as shipbrokers, charterers, and insurance agents. Ship owning was quickly added to these activities when in 1858 the Donaldson brothers bought their first vessel a 299 ton wooden sailing vessel the *Joan Taylor*, which inaugurated their trade from Glasgow to South America, plying between the Clyde and the River Plate. In the second half of the nineteenth century South America was a growing market for Britain, especially in grain, hides and latterly in refrigerated beef. The Donaldsons entered early into this trade and within ten years of estab-

lishment the brothers were operating 12 vessels, owning six of them, and were employing them chiefly on the South American routes. Initially their business was conducted in vessels of wood and sail, but the Donaldsons then added composite vessels in the early 1860s and then began to have built for them iron sailing ships from 1867. By 1870 the Donaldsons had purchased their first steamer, and just as William Betts Donaldson was born in 1872, his father and his uncles were quickly converting their fleet to steam and iron vessels. Four years later the Donaldsons turned their eyes northwards and inaugurated routes to Canada and the USA, where in competition with the Allan Line, they moved into the emigrant business. As heavy industry came to dominate Clydeside, coal, iron, and men and women, flowed outward from the Clyde to Canada and the USA; the main return cargo was cattle for the table of the growing urban population of Scotland.

By the time the young William Betts Donaldson went to school at Kelvinside Academy, his father's company was well established in the South American and North American routes. When William was aged eight his father, the senior partner in the business, died, leaving his two younger brothers in control. The young William was therefore automatically trained to fill his father's shoes. In 1888 at the age of 16, he entered the shipping office of Donaldson brothers under the tutelage of his uncles John and Archibald. As was common in family firms, the sons of the partners were given experience in each of the branches of the business, equipping them with general experience rather than specialised skill. The year after William joined the business his uncle John died, and in 1895, after seven years general training William was brought into partnership at the age of 23. His younger brother Norman P Donaldson also joined the business about this time. His older cousin William Cattanach Donaldson was also in the firm.

When William Betts Donaldson joined the business it was a thriving shipping line with a strong involvement in both South and North America. By the turn of the century however, the emigrant market was so buoyant, that in 1904 the Donaldsons introduced their first exclusively passenger ship the *Athenia*, designed specifically for the emigrant trade. The emigrant traffic then became a dominant influence in the Donaldson business before the First World War, and the South American interests became less important. Even so the Donaldsons' involvement in general commodity trades still continued, and in 1912 they began carrying Canadian paper back to Scotland, as well as grain, hides and cattle.

In the middle of this busy pre-war decade, Archibald Donaldson, the last surviving founding partner, died in 1907 and William Cattanach Donaldson became the senior partner. In 1913 the partnership was voluntarily dissolved and two new companies were formed. The individual ship companies were combined to form the Donaldson Line Ltd, while

Donaldson Brothers Ltd was formed as the managing agency. William Betts Donaldson became chairman of Donaldson Brothers Ltd while his cousin Charles was chairman of the Donaldson Line. The second generation Donaldsons, William Cattanach, William Betts, and Norman P Donaldson, were now firmly in control. The Donaldson Line was set up with a nominal capital of £560,000. The two brothers and their cousin held shares to the value of £200,000 and the remaining shares were mainly in family hands. At its establishment the company operated 14 vessels. Quite suddenly in the year following the formation William Cattanach Donaldson died. He was succeeded by William Betts Donaldson then aged 42. William retained the chairmanship of the Donaldson Line till 1941, and of Donaldson Brothers Ltd till his death in 1945.

As chairman of both the Donaldson Line and of Donaldson Brothers Ltd William Betts Donaldson headed the companies through two wars and the difficult decades between. The Donaldson vessels were hard hit by the U boat campaign in the First World War but wartime earnings of some £2.5 million enabled the company to rebuild quickly at the end of the hostilities. During the First World War the Donaldsons also joined with Henderson Brothers, operators of the Anchor Line, to form Anchor-Donaldson Ltd to share the Canadian business and help to minimise competition. In 1919 a further company, the Donaldson South American Line Ltd, was also incorporated with John A Black as chairman. William Betts Donaldson and his brother were on the board. His brother Norman succeeded to the chairmanship in 1927.

This restructuring of the business reflected both a growing scale of operations and a more specialised form of business. In 1919 the Donaldsons had won a meat contract and the new Donaldson South American Line was formed to operate refrigerated vessels. Five such new ships were constructed between 1920 and 1923, Scotts at Greenock and Lithgows at Port Glasgow built one each of these new vessels, a third was constructed by Vickers Armstrong and the last two by Short Brothers. In addition the Donaldsons also had eight new vessels built for the Donaldson Line, and a further two for the Anchor-Donaldson business. In all 15 new vessels were built for the Donaldsons between the wars. This busy period also saw the third generation of the Donaldson family come into the business in the 1920s.

In the period between the wars all the vessels built for the Donaldson line and for the Donaldson South American line were cargo vessels; but the two ships built for the transatlantic services of the Anchor-Donaldson line were liners. The *Athenia* and *Letitia* were built by Fairfields in 1923 and 1925 respectively. The *Athenia* was to be the first victim of the U boats on the 3 September 1939 on the outbreak of the Second World War.

During the 1920s and the 1930s the emigrant traffic ceased to be important while the passenger services to North America were only a small part of the Donaldsons' business. In the South American trade meat remained as the most important commodity but in the 1930s the Donaldsons also began to carry fresh oranges from Brazil to Britain. Also in the 1930s the link with the Anchor Line was severed, when in 1935 the Anchor Line was liquidated, and Donaldsons established the independent Donaldson Atlantic Line. With these developments the Donaldsons entered upon the Second World War with 18 vessels of 150,000 grt. By 1944 only seven of their vessels had survived the U boats.

Although William Betts Donaldson was chairman of Donaldson Brothers from 1914 to 1945 and of the Donaldson Line till 1941 it is not clear how much time he continued to give to the business in his later years. By the 1930s he was in his sixties, and the third generation of the Donaldsons all held managerial positions. Since William Betts Donaldson had extensive interests outside the shipping sector this does suggest that he gave over much of the day to day operation of the business to his younger nephews while he himself enjoyed his other activities.

Both William and his younger brother Norman were keen yachtsmen. They sailed competitively in both the six and eight metre classes. William was a fine helmsman, and sailed in the team races for the British America Cup on the Clyde in 1936. He was vice-commodore of the Royal Clyde Yacht Club, and was on the committee of the Royal Northern Yacht Club. But although he was an enthusiastic yachtsman his passion was farming and stock rearing. He lived on his estate and on his model farm at Auchenedin in the Blane Valley. There he bred prize Galloways and won prizes at all the leading shows in Scotland and England. In addition he bred Clydesdales and Black Face sheep. When he inherited his friend W J Thomson's farm, Brae of Auchendrane at Alloway, he continued Thomson's passion for breeding Ayrshire cattle.

William Betts Donaldson was deeply involved in agricultural activities throughout his adult life. He was president of the Glasgow Agricultural Society and a long time member of the Council of the Galloway Cattle Society. He was ultimately president of the society. In addition he was a governor of the West of Scotland Agricultural Society and of the Glasgow Veterinary College. Almost inevitably he had interests in horse racing and was a regular rider with the Lanarkshire and Renfrewshire hunts. He was also a keen fisherman and enjoyed shooting. It is notable that William Betts Donaldson's positions in public life virtually all stemmed from his involvement in his agricultural pursuits, rather than emerging from his shipping business. There he served only as a director of the Glasgow Steamship Owners' Association and of the Clyde Steamship Owners' Association.

William Betts Donaldson never married; when he

died he left a personal movable estate of over £500,000. He made some small benefactions of £2,000 to Yorkhill Sick Children's Hospital, and of £500 to each of the Royal, Western, and Victoria Infirmaries in Glasgow. The remainder of his wealth went back to the family. William Betts Donaldson exercised cautious stewardship over his inherited business and its activities; he and his brother and his cousins shared in its responsibilities and in its benefits. However William Betts Donaldson's real imaginative contribution and commitment lay in his agricultural and breeding interest; indeed it is appropriate to see him as a successful man of business in these two quite different fields of enterprise.

ANTHONY SLAVEN

SOURCES

Unpublished

Birth Certificate, Partick, 6463, No 216, 1872
Death Certificate, Killearn, 482, No 30, 1945
Donaldson Bros Archives, TD 49, TD 482, TD 520

Published

The Bailie, 8/3/1922
Dunnett, A, *The Donaldson Line*, Glasgow, 1960
Fairplay, 12/4/1945
Glasgow Herald, 5/4/1945
The Scotsman, 5/4/1945
The Shipbuilder and Marine Engine Builder, Vol 52, No 434, May 1945
Shipbuilding and Shipping Record, 12/4/1945

John DUNCAN,

Tram and bus company manager; b. c. 1842, Kinross-shire, s. of James Duncan, farmer and Mary Finlay; m. Annie Brown Allan; multiple issue; MD, Glasgow Tramways Co, Founder of Carriage Hire/Undertake Co; d. 20/8/1908, Pollokshields, Glasgow; g/v estate: £1,758 18s 10d.

John Duncan was born of east of Scotland farming stock c 1842 and started work as a junior in the office

of the local lawyer and banker in the small county town of Kinross in 1854. He proceeded to further legal work in Glasgow, and briefly in Edinburgh, from 1859. Formal legal training was taken at Glasgow University but his interests turned to administration rather than the practice of law. In 1870, he was appointed secretary of the Glasgow Tramway Company, about to be set up as the lessor for 23 years of the horse-tram routes being built by the Corporation of Glasgow. The first services began operation in August 1872.

In effect, he was the manager and chief organiser of the company, taking early steps to establish stables and to acquire the pre-existing horse buses. Setting-up costs amounted to £180,000. No dividends were paid for three and a half years but, against expectations, dividends built up to 11% in the 1880s. This was one of the highest returns on the expanding horse-tram systems of European cities. By 1894, the enterprise employed 3,600 horses, and 1,800 men, carrying 43,000,000 passengers a year on 32 miles of route and earning £250,000. Further expansion of the company was prevented by the refusal, after protracted negotiations, of Glasow Corporation to extend the lease beyond 1894 and Duncan was forced to switch the emphasis of the company activity to

COURTESY OF THE MITCHELL LIBRARY

cab and carriage hiring, funeral undertaking and contracting. Corresponding expansion began beyond Glasgow in Paisley, Greenock, Ayr, Leith and Edinburgh. Duncan became Managing Director of the reorganised company but employment had fallen to 1,800 horses and under 1,400 men by 1901.

Well known as a hard worker, discipliarian and ambitious organiser, Duncan was the driving force behind the expansion of the tramway company but he could not come to terms with municipalisation. His high hopes of an extension of the tramway lease were dashed by the decision of Glasgow Corporation in 1891 to take on the responsibility of operating the services from 1 July 1894. In 1891, Duncan's company had applied unsuccessfully for the tramway lease being put out to tender by Edinburgh Corporation and there then developed a costly dispute with Glasgow Corporation. Duncan made plans for new horse buses to compete with the municipal corporation trams from 1894 while the Corporation refused to buy the depots and vehicles of the tramway company. Company finances were doubly hit by loss of the sale value of its horse trams and stables and by the high cost of competing with the new municipal services. Duncan soon found himself forced to reduce the scale of his operations. Opportunities outside Glasgow failed to compensate for the loss of business in Glasgow itself. By the late 1890s, the company was in severe financial difficulties with Duncan very bitter about the impact of municipalisation on the value of company assets which formed a major part of his own personal wealth. The company was in liquidation at the time of his death and he had become insolvent. Despite his administrative abilities in organising Glasgow's first tramway system in an age of rapid urban growth and improving incomes, his judgment was misguided in seeking confrontation with the determination of a powerful city council to move from the ownership of tramway route to direct operation. After 1894, Duncan was no longer an important and credible figure in the business community.

TOM HART

Sources

Published

The Bailie, 21/1/1885
Cormack, I L, *Glasgow Tramways, 1872-1962*, Railway Transport League, 1962
Glasgow Herald, 1/8/1909
Glasgow Tramways Jubilee, 1872-1922
Oakley, C A, *The Last Tram*, Glasgow Corporation Transport Department, 1962

The Tramway and Railway World, Vol 24, October 1908
Who's Who in Glasgow, 1909

Alexander ELDER,

Shipowner; b. c 1834, Glasgow; s. of David Elder, engineer; married; no issue; Partner, Elder, Dempster & Co; Dir, British & African Steam Navigation Co; Dir, Pacific Steam Navigation Co; Ch, Liverpool Steamship Owners Association; d. 25/1/1915, Southport, Lancaster; g/v estate: £309,068 19s 11d.

Alexander Elder was born in Glasgow in 1834. His father was David Elder who for many years acted as manager of Robert Napier and Sons, the well known firm of engine and ship-builders. One of Alexander's elder brothers was John Elder who, after serving an apprenticeship with Napier's, became chief draughtsman of that firm at the early age of 24. Four years later John formed a partnership with Charles Randolph (qv) and together they established a business at Govan which was first known as Randolph, Elder and Company, then as John Elder and Company and, eventually, as the Fairfield Shipbuilding and Engineering Company.

With this background it is not surprising that after completing his education at Glasgow High School, Alexander Elder decided to serve his time as an apprentice engineer. This was a time of great technological innovation and in 1853 Randolph and Elder took out a patent for a compound engine and the following year they fitted the first practical machinery of this type to the *BRANDON*, an iron, screw vessel of 764 tons. This ship was constructed for the American trade and, although only 20, Alexander sailed as chief engineer on her maiden voyage. This may have been solely due to his brother's influence but it should be remembered that marine engineering was still in its infancy and men specially trained for this work were hard to find. It also seems possible that Alexander had gained extensive knowledge of this particular engine during his apprenticeship, and this experience would naturally have strengthened his claim for the job. Support for the view that Alexander obtained the situation on merit is provided by his subsequent appointment to a similar position in *COLUMBIAN*, an iron barque of 2,189 tons that had been fitted with a 400 horse power auxiliary engine. This vessel, built for the Australian trade, was chartered by the French government for service in the Crimean War and Alexander spent some hours in Sebastopol on the day of its fall in 1855.

After further experience at sea, Alexander Elder was attracted to Liverpool to act as marine superintendent for the African Steam Ship Company (African). He held this situation from 1859 to 1866 and in the course of his duties learned a great deal about the West African trade. He also came into contact with John Dempster who at that time was working for the 'African' on the clerical side and no doubt their common Scottish heritage (Dempster was born in Dumfriesshire) did much to cement their relationship. Elder then moved to the Board of Trade and acted as its engineering and shipwright surveyor for the Merseyside area for the next two years. During this period he undoubtedly heard much of the inadequacy of the services provided by the 'African' which was failing to increase its tonnage in line with the growth of West African trade. One effect of this omission was that the peripheral business from outlying ports (which had to be trans-shipped at Liverpool) tended to be neglected and certain firms - including Coats of Paisley - felt that a direct line would be beneficial to their interests.

The combination of Elder's special knowledge and the promise of support then led him to establish the British and African Steam Navigation Company with a nominal capital of £200,000 of which £68,400 had been called up by 1870. The new firm was registered in Scotland and it was partly financed by Scottish investors but much was also contributed from Merseyside. Elder quickly learned that although the idea of a direct link between Glasgow and West Africa was attractive to the local merchants they could not generate sufficient trade to make this a viable proposition. This made a Liverpool office a necessity so he approached his old friend, John Dempster, who was still working with the 'African', and together they formed the firm of Elder, Dempster and Company.

Apart from its initial task of acting as its Liverpool Agents, Elder Dempster almost immediately acquired the entire job of operating the 'British and African'. John Elder died in 1869 just when these arrangements were coming to fruition but this was not before his company had arranged to build the seven vessels that were to form the basis of the new fleet. In many ways these were superior to those of the 'African' and this was a major factor in enabling the new line to survive a period of sharp competition with the old. 'Elder Dempster' then negotiated the first of a series of agreements with the 'African' that was eventually to pave the way for an extensive system of co-operation between the two lines.

The consequence of these actions was that the 'British and African', the 'African' and 'Elder Dempster' made reasonable profits throughout the seventies although the West African trade was under constant threat from other shipping lines and individual vessels. One potential danger was eliminated when Alfred Lewis Jones, formerly with the 'African's' Liverpool agents, who had set up on his own account in 1878 was persuaded to join 'Elder Dempster' as a junior partner. However, Jones was not content to remain in an inferior position and when, by 1884, he felt that he had a complete grasp of the business he successfully ejected both Alexander Elder and John Dempster from the firm they had created.

The terms on which this was achieved are not known but clearly there must have been a satisfactory financial settlement. In any event 'Elder Dempster' continued to manage the 'British and African' and, in 1891, also became the managing agents for the 'African'. In spite, or because, of these events Alexander Elder and John Dempster continued to be major shareholders in the 'British and African' and the former acted as a director of the line until it was re-constituted in 1900. He was also a director of the Pacific Steam Navigation Company and filled the position of chairman of the Liverpool Steamship Owners Association in 1890.

Throughout his career in business Alexander Elder lived in Southport travelling to his office each day by train. Although happily married he had no children and he and his wife appear to have devoted much of their time and money to the re-building of Holy Trinity Church. Alexander also appears to have been a generous contributor to all local charities and he was a keen supporter of the Southport Division of the Conservative and Unionist Association. In 1909 he contributed £12,500 - subsequently increased to £20,000 - for the establishment of a Chair of Naval Architecture at the University of Liverpool.

Alexander Elder was awarded the bronze medal of the Royal Humane Society for bravery having dived into Sandon Dock to rescue a man who had fallen in during thick fog. In 1903 he became a Justice of the Peace for Southport and was subsequently offered the position of Chief Magistrate, an honour he felt obliged to refuse because of failing health. However he continued to take an active interest in local affairs until within a few weeks of his death on 25 January 1915, at the age of 81. He and later his wife, was buried at the Necropolis in Glasgow, in the grave of his parents.

Elder's estate amounted to £309,068 and after making provision for his wife and for many individual charities, he arranged for the balance to be expended on the provision of a new hospital at Girvan, and for an additional wing at Glasgow Western Infirmary.

P N DAVIES

SOURCES

Published

The Bailie, 'Men You Know', 24/6/1885
Davies, P N, 'The African Steam Ship Company', *Liverpool and Merseyside,* London, 1969, Harris, J R (ed)
Davies, P N, *The Trade Makers: Elder Dempster in West Africa,* London, 1973
Glasgow Herald, 26/1/1915, 27/1/1915
Journal of Commerce, 26/1/1915
Shields, J, *Clyde-Built,* Glasgow, 1949
Smith, E C, *A Short History of Naval and Marine Engineering,* 1939
Southport Visitor, 26/1/1915, Obituary
Wilson, C and Reader, W, *Men and Machines. A History of D Napier and Son, Engineering Ltd,* London, 1958

William FERGUSON,

Landed proprietor; b. 20/12/1823, Kinmundy, Mintlaw, s. of James Ferguson, landed proprietor, and Emily Chalmers; m. 22/7/1856, Eliza, d. of Andrew Williamson, wine merchant; 2 s., 1 d.; Ch, Great North of Scotland Railway Co Ltd; Dir. Robert Benson & Co; Dir, Cropper, Ferguson & Co; Dir, North of Scotland Bank; Dir, Ocean Accident & Guarantee Corporation; d. 11/9/1904, Kinmundy; g/v UK estate: £47,709 16s 4d.

Ferguson, the third son of James Ferguson and his wife Emily Chalmers, was born on 20 December 1823 on the estate of Kinmundy, near Mintlaw, which had been in the family since 1723. In 1838 he entered Marischal College, Aberdeen, with the intention of becoming a minister, but left without a degree after two years, partly because of family financial problems and partly because the death of his only surviving elder brother left him heir to the estate. He worked first in the office of Leith timber mechants, Ferguson, Davidson & Co (presumably a family connection), and then for various Glasgow and Liverpool firms connected with the eastern trade. In 1854 he went from Liverpool to London as a partner in Robert Benson & Co, American bankers and general merchants, whose interests included railway finance; Robert Benson was for 30 years a director of the

London & North-Western. During the American railway crisis of the mid-1850s Ferguson was sent across the Atlantic on behalf of the holders of some £2,000,000 worth of railway stock, with power of attorney to do as he thought fit; his mission was accounted a considerable personal success. Back in Liverpool Bensons, who were agents for the East India Company there, were closely connected with the Croppers; both families had been active among the promoters of the Liverpool & Manchester Railway, and James Cropper was a London & North-Western representative on the board of the Lancaster & Carlisle. In 1862 Ferguson was back in Liverpool as a partner (later sole managing partner) in Cropper, Ferguson & Co. In the same year he inherited Kinmundy.

The attraction to the Great North of a local man with Ferguson's business experience was obvious, but during John Duncan's five-year chairmanship he was an infrequent attender at meetings. In 1872 he retired from business to settle at Kinmundy and became an extremely active member of the board, now under ex-provost William Leslie of Aberdeen. For a decade or more after the general financial crisis of 1866, however, there was little that the company could do beyond following a policy of strict economy. Within these limits, some success was attained. Local conditions of capital spending ahead of revenue prospects aggravated the position of the Great North of Scotland Railway. By 1875 the money raised without sanction and the floating debt were paid off, preferential dividends were being paid in full, and a small dividend reappeared for ordinary shareholders - the company's capital structure, by which almost exactly half the issued capital was in preference or guaranteed shares and a further 22% was in loans and debentures, meant that ordinary dividends came well down the pecking order if there was a profit to divide. Between 1867 and 1879 gross revenue on current account increased by 57.6% while expenditure fell by 15.5%, so that net revenue rose tenfold. Some of this was achieved by transferring some items from current to capital account; the rest was at the expense of high fares and rates, minimal maintenance and virtually no replacements of track or rolling stock, a stop to further extensions of the system, and no improvements to the services provided.

In 1879 Leslie died and Ferguson, who had become deputy chairman in 1877, succeeded to the chair. In the same year both the general manager Robert Milne and the secretary William B Ferguson retired for health reasons, followed the next year by passenger superintendent Forbes Morrison. The posts of general manager and secretary were combined - according to Ferguson, 'on a line of our limited extent there is no need for a secretariat as a separate department' - and given to William Moffatt, a 43-year old native of North Shields who had in the previous 26 years worked his way up through the North Eastern Railway hiearchy from ticket boy to manager of the Tyne docks railways. A North Eastern colleague, Alexander Reid, became the new passenger superintendent. The team was in place which would reform the company.

Company policy changed almost immediately, as money was spent to improve the service and image of the railway. This might not please the shareholders - the ordinary dividend, which had briefly reached 21% in 1876, disappeared from 1881 to 1883 and remained below 2% until 1891 - but it did suit the customers, and the Great North had a substantial overlap between its users and its shareholders. In 1880-84 some £250,000 was spent on improvements to the permanent way, the stations and the signals. The main line, originally double for only the 6.25 miles to Dyce, was doubled for a further 12.25 to Inveramsay (by the end of the century doubling had reached Keith), and 142 miles of track were relaid with steel rails. Manson's automatic tablet exchanger, invented by the company engineer, was installed on the single track network, allowing faster services and cutting out risk of injury to staff. At last a policy of rolling stock renewal and replacement was undertaken, with economical locomotives built to a standard pattern and coaches which 'would do credit to any line in Great Britain', including the first in the country to have electric light. Moffatt and Reid followed with improvements in the speed and frequency of passenger services. The 1,095,000 train-miles (including goods) of 1878 became the 1,752,000 of a decade later, and 2,542,000 in 1898. In 1884 third class fares were reduced to 1d per mile, encouraged by the agreement of the Inland Revenue that all such fares should be free of passenger duty. In 1885 the company started suburban services to Dyce, building several new stations; by 1894 similar services ran to Culter on the Deeside section. According to Acworth in 1890, 'the Great North has turned over a new leaf of recent years, and resolutely set itself to live down the reputation acquired by long and patient continuance in ill-doing ... Perhaps no line can boast of more rapid improvement in recent years'.

It is impossible to determine the balance of credit for the improvement between Ferguson and Moffatt. Of writers about the company, Barclay-Harvey and O'Dell credited Ferguson while Scott and Nock inclined towards Moffatt; Vallance hedged his bets. Ferguson was certainly not a figurehead chairman. He was an active creator of company policy and practice. According to a supporter, he was 'a gentleman of position and standing, of thorough business habits ... and of a kind and courteous manner'; according to an opponent he was 'one of the greatest diplomatists in the country'. He deserves much of the credit for the company's improved image in terms of public and industrial relations, which culminated in the diamond jubilee celebrations of 1897 when the directors gave four elaborate receptions for the entire staff of the railway. Moffatt was more than a mere executor of other men's policies. Much of the correspondence between the two men has been lost; what

survives suggests that they corresponded cordially and copiously on matters of both great and minor significance, and generally achieved a remarkable measure of agreement. Moffatt was a man who commanded respect if not always affection. The *Times* obituarist summed him up: 'his somewhat imperious character did not commend itself to everyone. He could be a formidable antagonist, a difficult witness before a Parliamentary Committee; as a master, if just, he was rather awe-inspiring; worse, he could be a painfully candid friend. To the *Aberdeen Bon-Accord,* he 'won for the Great North of Scotland Railway the title of "Little and Good"'; to Ferguson, he was 'the right man for the right place'. He was also, though fully supported by his chairman, the company's front line in the prolonged and often rancorous battle with the Highland.

Like the Caledonian and the North British, Scotland's two northern railways conducted a prolonged feud broken by uncertain truces. The Great North professed two main grievances against the Highland. In 1865 it had been agreed that through traffic between the two companies should be exchanged at Keith. In 1881 the Great North took over the Morayshire, giving it an alternative route to Elgin via Craigellachie; five years later it opened a third route to Elgin via the Moray coast. Although the Highland's line was shortest, both Great North alternatives passed through more populous districts, and the company demanded that traffic should be exchanged at Elgin, or at least at Elgin equally with Keith. The Highland refused, although it was not averse to handing back empty and therefore unprofitable wagons at Elgin. Secondly, the Highland treated its Forres to Elgin section as a branch of the route to Perth, with its timetable subordinated to the main line trains rather than co-ordinated with the Great North. Underlying everything was the intense desire of the Great North to run its trains through to Inverness, and the equally fierce determination of the Highland to prevent them.

The war lasted, with varying virulence, until 1897. Aggression on the Highland's side was mainly limited to avoiding any possible co-ordination of through timetables with the Great North. Great North tactics appeared in a series of manoeuvres designed to gain access to Inverness. In 1883 the Highland, worried by a North British-supported plan for a line from Glasgow to Inverness by Fort William, promised to reduce the length of its main line by building a direct link from Aviemore to Inverness by Carr Bridge. The Great North optimistically put forward a bill to make this a joint line, and also gave moral and a little financial support to an apparently improbable scheme to connect Deeside and Nethybridge via Tomintoul. Underlying this was an ambitious Great North hope for a line from Dundee to Inverness, of which the Tomintoul scheme would form part, and which in secret discussions attracted the interest of John Walker of the North British. The plan was never made public, and considered in isolation the Tomintoul line had no chance before Parliament. The Carr Bridge line was authorised, but the Great North did get an agreement for unrestricted through bookings, no unnecessary delays, and the possibility of exchanging traffic at any junction. In 1886 it was agreed to pool receipts in the disputed area between Elgin and Grange Junction, however the traffic travelled (thus making it advantageous to push traffic on to the opponents' trains), while James Grierson, manager of the Great Western, was appointed arbiter in disputes between the companies. On his death two years later, he was replaced by Henry Tennant, manager of Moffatt's old employers, the North Eastern, although there is no evidence that he unduly favoured Moffatt in the 150 or so complaints brought before him in the following five years.

Reaching Inverness remained an *idée fixe* with the Great North. Among their schemes rejected by parliament was an 1890 plan to build another Elgin-Inverness line parallel to the Highland; plans to finance and work locally projected lines in the far north-west, in 1890 from Garve to Ullapool and in 1893 from Achnasheen to Aultbea, providing they got running powers from Elgin through Inverness to connect with their new protégés; and in 1895 a simple bill for running powers over the Highland to Inverness, withdrawn when it became clear that this would overcrowd the single line. By the time the Great North brought their bill back in 1897, with an additional offer to pay for doubling the line, two things had changed. Crucially, Andrew Dougall, the Highland general manager and secretary whose service went back to the days of the Inverness & Aberdeen Junction, and who had been the immovable object against the irresistible force of William Moffatt, had resigned in considerable disgrace, and had been succeeded by yet another former North Eastern man, the more conciliatory Charles Steel. And in 1897 the Railway and Canal Commissioners, appointed two years before to adjudicate between the companies, suggested a compromise by which traffic would be exchanged equally at Keith and Elgin, through time-tables would be co-ordinated, and either company was bound to maintain the average speed of any train handed on to it for through traffic; as the Great North by now had, at least as far as Huntly, some of the fastest scheduled services in Britain, this allowed for some impressive through trains. The fastest train from Aberdeen to Keith, which in 1867 had taken 2.75 hours for 54 miles, was from 1888 only allowed 65 minutes. The new 'commissioners' services' brought peace at last; in 1905 Great North shareholders even approved the idea of a merger, but substantial opposition and abstention among Highland share-holders prevented further progress.

Some of the Ferguson-Moffatt improvements at the end of the century were over-ambitious. The purchase of the Palace Hotel in Aberdeen in 1891 was a success, but the attempt to develop the tourist potential of Cruden Bay with a hotel, a golf course, and a new

line past them to the fishing village of Boddam was not. Both Ferguson and Moffatt had some doubts about the scheme, but they still went ahead with what turned out to be a financial disaster. The old locomotive works at Kittybrewster were inadequate, but the new works at Inverurie, built from 1898 to 1902 and, according to the *Railway Times*, the best equipped in Scotland, did not really generate enough work for the extra 1,200 people added to the town's population; Ferguson, however, received the freedom of Inverurie in 1902. It was necessary, if expensive, to undertake the reconstruction of the cramped joint station in Aberdeen from 1899, and perhaps also to construct elaborate new railway offices beside it from 1894. It was also necessary to replace Elgin station in 1902, since it had been built as a temporary structure 40 years before, but the distinguished new building would have graced a very much more important terminus. At the end of the century traffic growth slowed down; gross revenue, having climbed steadily and almost without interruption from £278,326 in Ferguson's first year as chairman to £484,544 in 1899, then stagnated. Working expenditure rose to be consistently over 50% of revenue; the price of coal, in particular, having fluctuated around 9/- to 11/- per ton for two decades, rose to 17/- in 1900 and stayed over 12/- thereafter. The company was forced back to some measures of economy and reduction of services.

The Great North leadership broke up at the start of the new century. Alexander Reid left in 1900 to become manager of the Dublin, Wicklow & Wexford, having previously refused several offers from other companies. William Moffatt retired in 1906, eventu-ally dying in 1929 at the age of 92, in the Wimbledon house which he shared with two unmarried daughters; his wife and only son had predeceased him, while two other daughters also lived on. Meanwhile William Ferguson had died at Kinmundy of uraemia on 11 September 1904, after serving the railway for 37 years as a director and 25 as chairman.

Ferguson's activities ranged widely. In particular he was prominent in the Free Church. Religion ran in the family; the Fergusons had been enthusiastic members of the Secession Church from the 1730s and had founded the church at Clola, near Kinmundy, in 1769, while his maternal grandfather, Robert Chal-mers, was a founder of that fissiparous group the Auld Licht Anti-Burghers. Ferguson, for long a Free Church elder, became a leading layman in the church's assemblies and a prominent advocate of the 1900 union with the United Presbyterian Church. While in Liverpool he had helped found Hamilton Presbyterian Church, Birkenhead; at Clola he found time to be session clerk for 30 years. He was noted for charitable effort, for his advocacy of Sunday schools, and for his work for Heathfield House reformatory school. His intense religious convictions also ensured that no Great North trains ran on Sundays.

He was also a considerable amateur scholar, par-ticularly in geology. He was a Fellow of the Royal

Society of Edinburgh, the Royal Geographical Society, and the Linnean Society. He was a founder of the Glasgow Natural History Society, chairman of the business committee of the New Spalding Club, and an active member at various times of other institutions ranging from the Buchan Field Club to the Glasgow Geological Society and the Birkenhead Literary and Philosophical Society. A copious writer, his 54 known books, pamphlets, tracts and articles reflect the tripartite nature of his interests. Smallest in number but weightiest in bulk are the books connected with railways, notably *America by River and Rail*, *The Illinois Central Railroad: a Historial Sketch*, and *The Great North of Scotland Railway: a Guide*, which contained a comprehensive survey of the history, folklore and natural history of north-east Scotland. Secondly, making up more than half of the total number, are articles, tracts, printed speeches and notes for teachers on a wide range of religious subjects. And thirdly, there are 18 geological articles in various journals, mostly concerned with features or finds in Aberdeenshire. In 1895 Aberdeen University awarded him an honorary LLD.

Kinmundy in 1883 was an estate of 4,068 acres, with a gross annual value estimated at £3,900. A well-known and active proprietor of this sort of estate was liable to be in demand for local office; at various times Ferguson served Aberdeenshire as Commissioner of Supply, County Councillor, Justice of the Peace and Deputy Lieutenant. At lower levels he chaired both parish and school boards. His commercial acumen brought him directorships in the North of Scotland Bank, and the Ocean Accident and Guarantee Corporation. In 1856 he married Eliza Williamson, daughter of an Ayr merchant, who died in 1881. He was survived by one son, James, who at the time of his father's death was Sheriff of Argyll, and by an unmarried daughter Agnes; a second son had died at the age of four. His personal estate was valued at £47,710, of which £15,289 was in life asurance and £28,633 in shares, dominated by a £21,412 holding in the Great North; his personal debts, however, were £55,914. The heritage was valued at £76,864, but encumbered by debts of £59,000. After the payment of debts and a £12,000 settlement to Agnes, the residue would not have made James a rich man.

Ferguson and Moffatt left as their monument the 'little and good' Great North of Scotland Railway. They created managerial efficiency out of a notoriously chaotic system, and provided north-east Scotland with cheap fares, logical goods rates, well maintained stock and, for a largely single-track railway, remarkably speedy services. Even the shareholders were tolerably pleased; the 3% dividends of the early 1890s were not exciting, but they were better than anything seen since the opening of the Highland. When Ferguson died, the dividend was still 3%. During his chairmanship, the mileage of the railway had risen from 289 to 335, the issued capital from £3,623,521 to £6,773,478, and the net revenue from £140,170 to £237,461. In 1867 it had looked as if survival would be an achievement; the Great North had done much better than that.

C J Alan Robertson

WRITINGS

America by River and Rail, London, 1856
The Great North of Scotland Railway: a Guide, Edinburgh, 1881

SOURCES

Unpublished

Information from Dr S Chapman

O'Dell Collection, Aberdeen University: OD MISC 2, 5, 7, 74, Great North of Scotland papers and correspondence

SRO: BR/GNS/1/10, 1/11, Great North of Scotland minutes
BR/GNS/4/13, Great North of Scotland revenue accounts
BR/RAC(S)/1/15, 1/16, Great North of Scotland reports
BR/PYB(S)/1/85, Great North of Scotland dividends
Cen 1861-91, Census Records
SC 1/36/150, Inventory
SC 1/37/124, Will

Published

Aberdeen Daily Journal, 13/9/1904
Acworth, W, *The Railways of Scotland*, London, 1890
The Bailie, 26/11/1902
Barclay, M Harvey, *A History of the Great North of Scotland Railway PS*, London, 1949, 2nd ed
Bateman, J, *The Great Landowners of Great Britain and Ireland*, Leicester, 1971, reprint of 1883 edition
Bon Accord, 15/9/1904, 5/4/1906, 21/9/1929
Burke's Landed Gentry, 1871
Ferguson, James, *Records of the Clan and Name of Fergusson, Ferguson and Fergus*, Edinburgh, 1895
Fleming, J, *The Church in Scotland 1875-1929*, Edinburgh, 1933
Nock, O S, *Scottish Railways*, London, 1950
O'Dell, A C, 'Pioneer railways of the LNER', *Scotland's SMT Magazine*, January, 1948
Pratt, J B, *Buchan*, Aberdeen, 1901
Railway News, 7/4/1906
Railway Times, 3/4/1880, 12/3/1904, 7/4/1906
Report of Committee of Investigation to the Shareholders of the Great North of Scotland Railway, Aberdeen, 1865

Robertson, G B, 'William Ferguson of Kinmundy', *Great North Review*, Aberdeen, 1981

Scotsman, 13/9/1904

Scott, W J, 'Little and good. The Great North of Scotland Railway', *Railway Magazine*, January, 1898

Sinclair, N T, 'The Aviemore Line: railway politics in the Highlands 1882–98', *Transport History*, 2, 1969

Stephenson Locomotive Society, 'Little and good': The Great North of Scotland Railway, Durham, 1972

The Times, 13/9/1904, 18/9/1929

Vallance, H A, *The Great North of Scotland Railway*, Dawlish, 1965

Ernest Edmund FRESSON,

Aviator; b. 20/9/1891, Essex, s. of Ernest Mitchell Fresson, stockbroker and Kathleen Robins; m. (1) 1919, Dorothy Cummings; 1 d; (2) Gwendolyne Holloway or Symons, 1934; 1 s.; MD, Highland Airways Ltd; N. Divisional Director, Scottish Airways Ltd; Manager, British European Airways Corporation; d. 25/9/1963, Inverness; g/v estate: £14,168 16s 2d.

Captain E E Fresson, OBE - his title reflecting his substantive rank in the early Royal Air Force as well as his status as a senior airline pilot - was the founder of the first regular air service in the Highlands and Islands. The inaugural flight of his company, Highland Airways Ltd, took place on 8 May 1933 between Inverness, Wick and Kirkwall, with Fresson himself piloting the firm's sole aircraft with three passengers and 60 pounds of freight. From this small beginning, the airline Fresson had built up was by 1946, the year before its nationalisation, flying scheduled services covering some two million miles per year with some 30,000 passengers. By that time, Fresson had become a household name throughout Scotland. His renown rested not only on his reputation as the entrepreneur who had developed the air services to overcome the tyranny of distance under which northern communities laboured, nor yet on his role as hero of numerous incidents that demonstrated his considerable skills as a pilot and navigator (to say nothing of publicist). He was also known as a man imbued with a genuine concern for the small and often very isolated communities that his enterprise served on a basis transcending the narrowly commercial, and he was willing to put himself at risk in the process.

Fresson was educated at Framlingham College, Suffolk. Like many boys of his generation, Fresson was much taken with the pioneer aviators like Blériot and Graham-White. The Great War of 1914-18 gave such lads the chance to turn this casual interest into something more. Fresson had gone to China in 1911 as a trainee engineer with Jardine Engineering Co, Shanghai and illness frustrated his attempts to return to Britain to enlist before 1917. In that year, travelling east *via* North America, he eventually joined the Royal Flying Corps in Toronto. Pilot training in Ontario and Texas was followed by assignment to a squadron flying anti-submarine patrols over the North Sea, and then by a posting to RAF Duxford as a flying instructor. As a military career, it lacked the glamour of active service on the Western Front, but Fresson may have benefitted in the long run by the training and experience he gained in actual flying technique and air navigation, so necessary to his later exploits in the Highlands.

In 1919, the newly-married Fresson returned to his old occupation in Shanghai, where tragically his wife died of typhoid the following year. In 1923, he gave up his job with Jardine Engineering and spent the years until 1927 catering to the interest in aviation shown first by Yen Hsi-shan, warlord of the northern province of Shansi, and later by the great Manchurian warlord, Marshal Chang Tso-lin. In both cases, however, Fresson was cut out by larger and better-organised European interests, German in Shansi and French at Mukden. Disappointed, he came back to Britain in March 1927.

At that time, wartime RFC pilots could still make a kind of living by meeting the demand from holiday crowds for the exhilaration provided by a short flight in the open cockpit of some superannuated wartime training aircraft - usually the docile and durable Avro 504K. The 'joy-ride' or 'five-bob flip' remained a popular diversion at seaside resorts and fairgrounds, and it was to this seasonal and uncertain occupation that Fresson now turned. After a short spell in the employ of Berkshire Aviation Tours, he set up with another ex-RFC pilot a 'joy-riding' outfit grandiosely named the North British Aviation Company Ltd at Hooton Park near Liverpool, equipped with two third-hand Avro 504's bought cheaply from a defunct Scottish flying school. It was not a very safe existence, given the type of flying it involved - the maximum possible number of flights in the shortest possible time out of makeshift airfields in old and fragile aircraft. On one Saturday afternoon at Renfrew in 1928, Fresson had made no fewer than 114 such flights, the proverbial risks of take-off and landing being separated only by a couple of minutes in the air in a ten year old bi-plane with a notoriously temperamental rotary engine. But again, it was superb training for flying in the Highlands.

What gave Captain Fresson the opportunity and inspiration to make his name as something more than just another ageing ex-RFC pilot eking out a precarious living with a battered and obsolete plane was a 'joy-riding' expedition he made in the summer of 1931 into Scotland's most northerly reaches, in search of communities where intrepid aviators were still an exotic novelty. In his trusty 504K, he flew 'joy-riders' out of patches of grazing land on the outskirts of Inverness, Thurso, Wick, Kirkwall and other northern towns where aeroplanes had hitherto been almost unheard of. Occasionally, his services were chartered for less frivolous flights, by local businessmen who preferred the 20 minute flight from, say, Wick to Kirkwall to the rigours of a four hour sea voyage across the Pentland Firth. In the process, Fresson and some of his passengers came to recognise the potential the Highlands and Islands offered for the development of air transport services on a regular commercial basis. The benefits to passengers of air travel between localities otherwise widely separated in time and space were obvious enough. So were the advantages of transporting by air time-sensitive or small-bulk/high-value commodities like newspapers or the mails. Air transport could do much to offset the tenuous nature of road, rail and sea communications in the Highlands and the Northern Isles.

To exploit the opportunities he had spotted, Fresson had to buy an aircraft more suited than the Avro 504 to the operations of a properly-constituted airline; something that could operate from small, improvised airfields with a worthwhile commercial payload and a certain basic standard of passenger comfort. Airfields of a standard acceptable to the Air Ministry's licensing department would also have to be created. Fresson calculated the cost of providing these basic essentials at £3,000, and that he would need another £7,000 to cover the costs of his first year's operations - an optimistic figure based on the assumption that he would be able to obtain contracts for the carriage by air of both mail and newspapers.

Highland Airways Ltd was formally constituted in April 1933, with Fresson as managing director and financed by himself and members of the medical and legal professions and of the motor trade in Inverness and Elgin. Its main asset was a brand-new General Aircraft Monospar ST4, a twin-engined monoplane airliner in miniature with four seats and a tiny freight compartment just big enough to hold the 60 pounds of newspapers which Fresson had contracted with *The Scotsman* to fly from Inverness to Kirkwall. The one year contract gave *The Scotsman* exclusive use of Fresson's service for £500 and 3d per pound freight-age; in return, *The Scotsman* gained the advantage over its mainland daily rivals of going on sale in Orkney on the morning of publication rather than the afternoon. The hoped for mail contract, however, did not materialise: all Fresson got from the Post Office was an undertaking to consider the granting of such a contract after his service had proved itself for a year. He had better luck with other public authorities. Inverness town council built a municipal airport at Longman to accommodate Fresson's service, and the town council at Wick helped with the construction of an airfield there. Kirkwall was less co-operative, perhaps, as Fresson suspected, because the Provost and some councillors had shares in the North of Scotland Shipping Company with whom he would be competing. He had to build his own airfield for Kirkwall by leasing land from a local farmer.

The inaugural flight of 8 May 1933, attended by due civic ceremony both on departure from Inverness and arrival at Kirkwall, was very much a culmination to Fresson's own efforts. As Highland Airways' moving spirit and managing director, most of the preparatory spade-work had fallen to him. And to him fell much of the responsibility for the rapid development of the enterprise thereafter. An early mishap in July 1933 nearly put a premature end to the whole affair: Fresson crashed in fog near Kirkwall and nearly wrote off his only aircraft. Hired planes kept the service going while repairs were effected, and by August business was good enough for Highlands Airways to add to its fleet a new De Havilland DH84 Dragon - much larger than the rebuilt Monospar and capable of lifting eight passengers and 400 lbs of freight. From then on, Highland Airways never looked back. New and even better aircraft were purchased, notably the DH89 Dragon Rapide. New routes were developed, the original Inverness-Kirkwall service being extended at both ends to Aberdeen and Sumburgh (Shetland). Eventually, links were forged between Inverness, which was the hub of Highland Airways route system, and Glasgow, Perth, Edinburgh and the Western Isles. New services were pioneered, like the mail service awarded by the Post Office in May 1934 which *The Scotsman* proclaimed to be 'the first regular air mail service in Britain at ordinary letter rates'. Fresson himself was equally proud of the air-ambulance service that he introduced on contract to Orkney County Council, to fly the seriously ill or injured from outlying communities to the Balfour Hospital in Kirkwall. New airfields were created on Fresson's initiative, and sometimes at the airline's own expense, at Aberdeen, Sumburgh, Stornoway and other places. Highland Airways played a leading part in the provision of radio-aids to navigation over the difficult terrain and in the appalling weather that frequently characterised its routes. Indeed, by late 1936 Fresson was so tied up with the administrative and technical aspects of running the airline that he ceased to fly regular scheduled flights. There is no doubt, however, that he preferred flying to administration, though he was effective enough as a manager in a concern of such intimate scale, and he continued to take charter and route-development flights whenever he could.

Expansion meant the need for more investment, and from 1934 Highland Airways was able to attract finance from larger organisations, such as *The Scotsman*, the North of Scotland Shipping Company, and the English investment-house Whitehall Securities Ltd, run by Clive Pearson. In 1935, indeed, Pearson's creation, United Airways Ltd, took over Highland Airways in a deal that worked very favourably for Fresson's shareholders and which allowed him to retain operational control as managing director and to preserve the distinctive identity and operating autonomy of Highland Airways.

The activities of United Airways (known from October 1935 as British Airways) were the cause of much concern among the railway companies, which initially tried to block airline competition by forbidding their agents from handling airline bookings and then tried themselves to get in on the airline's act by setting up Railway Air Services Ltd. Both British Airways and RAS, however, recognised that a war of attrition was in neither's interest, and in August 1937 they merged. In the process, Highland Airways was amalgamated with Northern and Scottish Airways of Renfrew to form a new organisation called Scottish Airways Ltd, in which Fresson was the director with responsibility for managing the services previously operated by Highland Airways.

Fresson was not initially enthusiastic about the new set-up. He recognised the financial benefits but, as he later wrote,

'It was clear that they had a very different outlook on operational methods from my own. Moreover, I did not wish to lose my identity and authority to possible bureaucracy, restrictions and planning unsuitable to our part of Britain.'

And there were initial problems: Fresson found, for example, that decisions with which he disagreed were being made by the main British Airways board, without consulting him, which affected the services for which he was responsible. Fortunately, the difficulty was amicably resolved, but the incident was indicative of Fresson's intolerance of bureaucrats and London management interfering with the Highland air-routes that he regarded as his particular preserve. It was an attitude that eventually, in 1948, was to put an end to his career as an airline pilot and manager.

Fresson's dislike of big organisations and remote direction may have been overcome by his enthusiasm for the possibilities which the new arrangements opened up. He played a major part in the initiation of a through service in August 1938 between Glasgow and Shetland, *via* Perth, Inverness and Kirkwall. And in the spring of 1939 it became possible to open up a through service from London to Kirkwall. His misgivings about the new set-up might also have been diverted by the fact that he was having to meet some competition. Until 1936, Fresson had had things very much his own way as far as Highland air services were concerned, but in that year he was challenged by the upstart Aberdeen Airways (later Allied Airways) founded by E L Gandar Dower, which started to operate over routes that Fresson had pioneered and to threaten his monopoly of the mail-service. Fresson professed to be furious, but it is clear that he rather enjoyed the contest, and he certainly later enjoyed the friendliest relations with his rival.

The outbreak of war in September 1939 temporarily put an end to the rivalry between Fresson and Gandar Dower, as all regular civil air services were immediately suspended and the use of ground-radio and navigation-aids denied to civil aircraft. Some of the airfields Fresson had developed, such as Stornoway and Sumburgh, were commandeered by the RAF and the Fleet Air Arm and closed to civil traffic. Normal peacetime flight-paths were shut down, especially in Fresson's area of operation where Home Fleet anchorages and exercise areas abounded. But it rapidly became apparent to the authorities that, north of the Highland Line, air transport was as much of a boon to the military as it had been in peacetime to the civil population. Fresson was allowed to restore some of the services flown by Scottish Airways, but this time under direct Air Ministry control.

The recruitment of younger pilots into the RAF and Navy meant that with the outbreak of war Fresson was obliged to return to regular flying duties. He had always enjoyed any challenge to his very considerable skills as a pilot and navigator, and peacetime flying in the Highlands and Islands had provided many such challenges in the form of landing-strips with blind approaches or cliffs at the end of the take-off run, to say nothing of the frequent gales, fogs and blinding snowstorms. Fresson, however, was strongly imbued with the belief that the mail must go through, and in conditions that halted other forms of transport his De Havilland Dragons and Rapides - aircraft of the flimsiest appearance but great structural strength - would still fly as scheduled. Between 1933 and 1939, Highland Airways and the Highland services of Scottish Airways maintained an enviable record of regularity, with never less than 97% of the flights scheduled actually being flown and in some years a 100% service being achieved. Much was made of this record for publicity purposes, and Fresson always made sure that the press was informed of any particularly notable flight. The advent of war, of course, added to the hazards. At least one of Fresson's aircraft, with a full load of passengers for Kirkwall, was menaced by a German intruder. And Fresson himself, flying Clement Attlee to Kirkwall, was fired upon by Royal Navy anti-aircraft gunners, who proverbially shot first and identified the aircraft later. Yet the aircraft under Fresson's wartime management (for he continued to exercise his full managerial responsibilities despite his return to regular flying) maintained between 1939 and 1945 their excellent safety and regularity records. In recognition of this achievement Fresson was awarded the OBE in 1943.

The war had increased 'air mindedness' quite dramatically in Scotland and elsewhere, and great things were expected of the return to peace by Scottish Airways and its financial sponsors (who now included David MacBrayne Ltd and Coast Lines, as well as the LMS Railway). But peacetime was to be far from kind to either Fresson himself or the airline he had built up. The return of a Labour government committed to the nationalisation of internal air services in the 1945 General Election ensured that any resumption of peacetime services by private airlines like Scottish Airways would be merely temporary, a stop-gap until the new state corporation was established. Operations were nevertheless resumed, and the first nine months of 1946 saw Scottish Airways fly some 28,000 passengers on scheduled services covering two million miles, at the modest profit of £8,000. It was hoped that these figures might be doubled in 1947, but instead that year saw the dissolution of Scottish Airways and the absorption of its assets and personnel by the British European Airways Corporation based at Northolt. Fresson was retained as manager of the northern sector of BEA's Scottish Division, but was most unhappy about the new arrangements. To him, BEA represented all the things he had feared in 1937 - a remote and uninformed management, the stultifying bureaucracy of the large-scale undertaking, the narrow-mindedness of organised labour, and so on. His London overlords made decisions about north of Scotland operations without consulting him. He was prevented from rebuilding services which his pre-war experience had shown to be viable. He was allocated aircraft like the Junkers JU52/3M which were manifestly unsuitable for service on Highland and Island routes, while the De Havilland Dragons and Rapides which had proved their worth in this service were sold off or re-assigned elsewhere. Above all, perhaps, Fresson found the chief executive of BEA, Gerard d'Erlanger, totally uncongenial and unsympathetic to work for. A clash was bound to come, and when it did d'Erlanger would have all the big battalions within BEA and in the Air Ministry on his side.

In February 1948, Fresson made an ambulance flight from the island of Stronsay to Kirkwall with a small boy who had been crushed by a tractor and who urgently needed surgery at the Balfour Hospital. For doing so without authority and without financial guarantees, he was reprimanded by the Scottish Divisional Director of BEA. After challenging the reprimand, Fresson was called south to Northolt and told that there was no place for him in the corporation's future activities. His dismissal provoked a storm of protest throughout Scotland, where there was already widespread dissatisfaction with the air services offered by BEA compared to those previously available under the old private airlines. But for all the support Fresson received from the Scotish press, local authorities, chambers of commerce, Members of Parliament and the public at large, he was not reinstated. In November 1948, he went to Kenya to take up a managerial post with the local subsidiary of one of the large Scottish breweries.

Fresson's memoirs end with his flight to Kenya, and indeed he seems to have done nothing of note from then on. He returned to Inverness in the 1950s and ran a small air-charter company for a few years, but compared with what he had done in the thirties and forties this must have been a sad anti-climax. He died in Inverness, shortly after his 72nd birthday, in 1963. At the time of his dismissal, the *Highland News* had praised Fresson's service to the people of the Highlands and Islands in having 'brought the world to their door'. It seems a fitting epitaph.

ALEX J ROBERTSON

WRITINGS

Air Road to the Isles; the Memoirs of Captain E E Fresson, OBE, London, 1967

SOURCES

Unpublished

SRO: SC 29/44/148, Inventory

Published

Aldcroft, D H, *Studies in British Transport History, 1870-1970*, Newton Abbot, 1974
The Highland News, 27/4/1948
House of Commons Debates, Vol 451 (1947-48), col 646
The Scotsman, 30/5/1934, 26/9/1963
The Times, 19/3/1948, 28/9/1963

James GALBRAITH,

Shipowner; b. 30/6/1818, Strathaven, Lanarkshire; m. 1859, Margaret Nelson, d. of Alexander Kirkwood; 1 s., Partner, Messrs P Henderson & Co; Dir, Irrawaddy Flotilla Co; d. 4/3/1885, Versailles; g/v estate: £246,388 15 11d.

In 1844, when James Galbraith joined the firm of Patrick Henderson and Company in Glasgow, three Henderson brothers were firmly in control of the business founded ten years before by their late brother Patrick. George, the master mariner, and Robert were in Glasgow and Thomas (qv) at Leghorn in Italy. Their business had been established on trade between the two ports, gradually introducing their own ships;

and now they were beginning to see beyond the bounds of the 'middle sea' as shipowners. They decided to look for a man with wide shipbroking experience and their choice fell on Galbraith.

James Galbraith was born on 30 June 1818 in the Lanarkshire village of Strathaven. In his early childhood his father secured an appointment with the Inland Revenue in Glasgow and it was there, at St John's Parish School, that the young James went first to school at the age of four under the care of an elder sister. Later he attended a private school in North Frederick Street, where his father felt that his bright son would receive the best education and would be able to study Latin, Greek and French. The boy was undoubtedly clever and took every prize within reach. He was also a devoted son and revealed qualities of patience and kindness which were to be equally important in later years.

Plans that he should read for the Bar or follow an uncle into medicine were abandoned when his schooling was over, no doubt for financial reasons, and the first six months of his working life were spent in a Glasgow drysalter's office. Then a promising opportunity was presented by his appointment to a clerkship in the office of John Cree, the principal shipbroker in Glasgow. In eight years with Mr Cree

he acquired wide experience of shipbroking and his keen mind made him a valuable member of the staff. But Mr Cree had sons to follow him and Galbraith saw no chance of fulfilling his ambitions there. He decided to offer his services elsewhere. A disastrous year was to follow.

He joined a Glasgow insurance broker who within a few months went out of business, then tried to set up on his own with a fellow clerk. This did not work out at all and at that time James Galbraith may well have been lost to obscurity had not the keen eyes of George and Robert Henderson spotted him. In 1844 they engaged him as their chartering clerk. Within four years, at the age of 30, he was made a partner, the first outside the Henderson family, and by then the business was concentrating more and more on shipping.

Captain George Henderson died in 1852 and Thomas, the brother in Leghorn, in 1854. The Leghorn business was sold and the last Henderson, Robert, with James Galbraith, continued the Glasgow business in the name of P Henderson and Company entirely as shipowners and shipbrokers, later to add insurance broking. Robert Henderson and James Galbraith were both strong personalities in the mould of that generation of Victorian merchant adventurers who were ready to pioneer and trade in any part of the world. They proceeded to embark on a number of shipping ventures with remarkable energy, but soon their interests were concentrated on regular sailing ship services to New Zealand and Burma. During the remainder of Robert Henderson's lifetime (he died in 1868) it is apparent that the mantle of leadership gradually fell on Galbraith.

The part played by James Galbraith in the early development of the British settlement of New Zealand was recognised in a tribute later paid to him by the New Zealand Government. Sailing ships chartered by P Henderson and Company had been carrying settlers out mainly to Otago in the South Island since the Otago Association was formed by the Free Church of Scotland in 1843; the first settlers were landed to establish Dunedin in 1848. But the real impetus of this emigration from Scotland began in 1856 when the first ship jointly owned by Robert Henderson and James Galbraith sailed out from Glasgow, the forerunner of a fleet of fine sailing ships. The Albion Shipping Company was formed in 1864 to carry on this trade, Henderson and Galbraith being joined by a number of other smaller shareholders. By then, many shipowners were building steamships, but even when the Suez Canal was opened in 1869 the Albion Line and their rivals the Shaw Savill Line of London continued with their sailing ships. Bunkering on such a long voyage was a problem resolved only well into the 1880s and even in 1882 the epoch-making voyage which brought to Britain the first frozen meat cargo from New Zealand was made by the Albion Line's clipper *Dunedin* equipped with steam generated refrigeration.

The Albion fleet had grown to 16 ships when in 1877 the need for more capital resulted in the Albion Shipping Company being converted to a limited liability company. Galbraith had been joined in this and other ventures by another enterprising Scot, Peter Denny (qv) of the Dumbarton shipbuilding family, who became chairman of the new Company. Galbraith was managing director.

The triumphant voyage of the *Dunedin* took place close to the end of the independent days of the Albion Shipping Co Ltd. Later in 1882 a merger was arranged with Shaw Savill and the Shaw Savill and Albion Line of twentieth century fame came into being with headquarters in London. Galbraith and Peter Denny were appointed to the Board of Directors and P Henderson and Company as managers and agents in Glasgow.

Back in the early days when the New Zealand trade was in its infancy homeward cargoes were hard to come by and the ships frequently returned from New Zealand by way of Burma, filling up there with cargoes of teak and rice. British annexation of Lower Burma in 1852 presented an opportunity which P Henderson and Company were not slow to grasp and Galbraith opened a regular service from the Clyde to Rangoon and Moulmein in 1860 with the 'beautiful Clyde-built clipper ship '*Lady Douglas*'. Steam took over here much faster than in the New Zealand trade and by 1873 Galbraith and Peter Denny were forming the British and Burmese Steam Navigation Company Limited, along with fellow Scots and Rangoon merchants, to provide capital for the costly steamer fleet required to maintain the rapidly growing trade. Already they had five steamers in the service, built with their own and other private capital between 1870 and 1873 (the Suez Canal, opened in 1869, is a pointer to that development) and these were taken over to form the nucleus of the new Company.

James Galbraith never went to Burma or to New Zealand. His health was never robust, but his qualities of leadership and business acumen enabled him to conduct affairs from Glasgow, and later from London also, depending on his ability to select the right men for overseas appointments and to form the right associations for supporting investment. It was through his friendship with T D Findlay, a Glasgow merchant who was trading in Burma in rice and timber, that he became the prime mover in setting up the Irrawaddy Flotilla Company Limited in 1865.

By then the Henderson Line to Burma was well established and a river Company to carry the trade into the heart of the country was a venture which required the courage and enterprise so amply possessed by James Galbraith. For 20 years, until his death, he guided the destiny of the Irrawaddy Flotilla, choosing the men to conduct the business in Burma and managing the financial affairs of the rapidly growing Company. Peter Denny became involved and built many of the river steamers which were sent out in the Henderson ships to be re-erected in Rangoon.

At an unbelievable speed the fleet grew in numbers, and the great river paddlers in size; when they were all needed in the Third Burmese War of 1885 to transport the British Expeditionary Force up the Irrawaddy, a campaign which ended with the annexation of Upper Burma, there were over 100 steamers and barges in the fleet. They embarked some 17,000 men, pack animals and artillery on their spacious decks.

This was not all, by any means. While the Albion Shipping Company traded to New Zealand, the Henderson Line to Burma and the Irrawaddy Flotilla was taking these first steps to becoming the greatest river fleet the world has ever known, James Galbraith had been establishing a strong foothold in London. Much of both the New Zealand and Burma homeward cargoes was being discharged at the Port of London and the City was, as it still is, the world centre of shipbroking, conducted on the Baltic Exchange. Galbraith had acquired in 1869 a partnership in the firm of Stringer, Pembroke and Company, a well known London shipbroking business. In 1877 he became the senior partner and the name was changed to Galbraith, Pembroke and Company. Now, in the 1980s, Galbraith, Wrightson & Co Ltd is one of the leading shipbrokers on the Baltic Exchange.

In 1871 Galbraith also briefly entered the world of oil. He promoted the Rangoon Oil Company Ltd registered in Edinburgh in that year. The Burma oilfields were situated by the Irrawaddy River and his Flotilla Company steamers could take in cargoes at Yenangyaung, mid-way between Mandalay and Rangoon, and transfer them to the Henderson steamers at Rangoon for Europe. Unsuccessful attempts had earlier been made to exploit these oil resources in Burma and it appears that Galbraith could have been successful but for arbitrary actions by the king's government in Upper Burma. A ready market was established in India, not in Europe, but shady dealings in Upper Burma denied a regularity of supplies at the oilfields where Galbraith had invested some £30,000 in a refinery. This enterprise lasted only five years; the Rangoon Oil Company was put into voluntary liquidation in 1876.

James Galbraith had inherited the whole business of P Henderson and Company when Robert Henderson died in 1868, the firm having been established by the Henderson brothers as a life and death partnership. However, he adopted partners thereafter, yet always keeping in his own lifetime a controlling interest. It is not surprising to know that his numerous ventures left him little time to become involved in public life. He was a member of the Clyde Navigation Trust for a time and chairman of the Clyde Training Ship *Cumberland* Executive Committee where he maintained a keen interest in boys' training for careers at sea. He was the complete shipowner and undoubtedly one of the greatest of his generation.

Having accumulated considerable wealth he had purchased a large house at Wemyss Bay on the Clyde and kept an ocean-going steam yacht which took him, his family and friends to the Mediterranean and the Norwegian Fjords, when time for relaxation was found. He was a devoted husband and father; his son, Charles Edward Galbraith, did not follow him into the Henderson business but later became a director of the British and Burmese Steam Navigation Co Ltd and of the Irrawaddy Flotilla Co Ltd.

James Galbraith died in Versailles in 1885 at the age of 66. He had gone to Paris for an operation, then to Versailles to recuperate, but much of his strength had been impaired by failing health. In his will his family were his first concern but he had made provision also for charitable institutions. The part played in his life by business friends is clearly shown by his choice of executors who included one of his Henderson parters, Peter and William Denny, and Edward Pembroke of the London shipbrokers.

ALISTER McCRAE

SOURCES

Unpublished

SRO: BT2/181, Albion Shipping Co
BT2/188, Albion Shipping Co
BT2/188, Irrawaddy Flotilla & Burmese Steam Navigation Co Ltd
SC 6/44/46, Inventory
SC 6/46/17, Will

Published

Biographical Notices of Glasgow Men, Vol V
The Scotsman, 5/3/1883

James Barrie HASTIE,

Road haulier; b. 11/8/1891, s. of John Kerr Hastie, customs officer and Agnes Barrie; m. 28/6/1919, Thomasina H Allison; 2 s., 1 d.; MD, Glasgow Hiring Co Ltd; d. 15/8/1968; g/v estate: £39,759 7s 0d.

The road haulage industry in Scotland is one part of the transport and communications sector which is rarely documented in the annals of business history, largely being overshadowed by its other counterparts, namely railways and shipping. Further little is known about the careers of the road hauliers themselves.

The history of road haulage goes back to horse-drawn vehicles and the numerous small carters and carriers which operated throughout Scotland and beyond. The growth of other forms of transportation like railways and shipping in the second half of the nineteenth century also saw a parallel expansion in road transport. One part of this was of course the development of passenger transport like tramways and buses. However the haulage section was also of importance to the transport network. Essentially there were two types of hauliers. Firstly there were the carriers who operated a service carrying goods anywhere both locally and long-distance. Secondly there were the carting contractors who either undertook contract work for specific firms or who supplied the horses and men and later motor vehicles to companies on a hiring basis. Many firms specialised as railway carriers undertaking contracts for the likes of the North British Railway. Others had more varied contracts.

James Barrie Hastie was the Managing Director of one such company, the Glasgow Hiring Company which serves as a useful illustration of the second type of haulier. He also became divisional manager of British Road Services after the nationalisation of road haulage after the Second World War. Thus his career spanned the period of the early developments of road haulage which saw the transfer from horse drawn to motor vehicles and through to nationalisation.

The Barrie family name was synonymous with carting contracting in Glasgow and Hastie was linked to this family through his mother. His uncle, John Barrie ran the successful firm John Barrie (Contractor) Ltd together with his son James Barrie. John Barrie was to be an influential figure in the career of J B Hastie.

Hastie was born in 1891, his mother being a sister of John Barrie. He was educated at Kent Road School, Glasgow, and later in Grangemouth before his family moved to Liverpool. Hastie however remained in Glasgow and joined his uncle's firm as a clerk and there under his uncle's guidance he learned the business of road haulage.

His career was interrupted by the First World War when he joined the Yeomanry in 1914 as a dispatch rider in Egypt and the Dardanelles. He came home after the war to marry in June 1919 and also to rejoin, briefly, his uncle's business as manager. In that same year John Barrie took over the Glasgow Hiring Co Ltd and installed Hastie as director and secretary. The company retained its name although under the wing of John Barrie.

Like many of the other hauliers the Glasgow Hiring Company was not highly capitalised. In 1909 its nominal capital was £1,000 increased in 1912 to £6,000. Its registered office was at 138 Bath Street but at that time it operated from its two depots at Sharp's Lane, Anderston, and 19 Otago Lane.

Some features of the company development with which James Barrie Hastie was associated were the introduction of motor vehicles, the growth of contract hire and, the introduction of contract hire in the companies own liveries, the first hiring company to do so. James Barrie Hastie also linked up his own interests when the Glasgow Hiring Company supplied vans for the Territorial Army in the 1930s. He had been a member of the 51st Territorials. Another useful contract was one with the Royal Mail.

Hastie remained managing director until the Second World War when he was seconded to the Ministry Unit Controller for Ministry of War Transport Service. In recognition of his war-time service he received the OBE. He was also a director of John Barrie (Contractor) Ltd after its registration as a private company in 1941.

Nationalisation of the longer-distance road haulage sector followed the end of the war. Trunk services were organised as British Road Services and Hastie became divisional manager for Scotland. Independent hauliers continued to operate in local transport as did a large number of C licence holders entitled to use lorries to carry their own goods anywhere in Britain. The trunk sector was gradually restored to private ownership after the Conservative Government legislation of 1953.

Hastie was typical of many hauliers in that he remained a shadowy figure, well known within the haulage industry but unlike many other entrepreneurs not more widely recognised outwith it. His low profile was reflected in his lack of involvement in other non-business activities. As far as is known he was not a director of any other companies. He was a member of New City Road Congregational Church, Glasgow, and supported the Conservative party.

Until his death in 1968 Hastie retained an interest in the Glasgow Hiring Company which was by then a wholly owned subsidiary of the Transport Development Corporation Ltd. He was survived by his wife and family to whom he left his estate.

SHEILA HAMILTON

SOURCES

Unpublished

SRO: SC 65/36/98, Will
      SC 65/38/89, Inventory

Published

Cunnison, J and Gilfillan, J B, *Third Statistical Account*, Glasgow, 1958

Algernon C F HENDERSON,

Shipowner, b. 1882, s. of Francis Henderson, shipowner; Managing Dir, Anchor Line; d. 14/2/1934, London; g/v estate: £15,009.

A C F Henderson was a third generation member of the Henderson family, founders of the Anchor Line, and owners for a time of the Clyde shipyard of D & W Henderson Ltd at Meadowside. He demonstrated very clearly the demands made on shipping families based on the Clyde who wished to be in the front rank of British shipping. Some like Andrew Weir (qv) abandoned his base on the Clyde to locate in London in order to secure this end; in contrast George Burns and the Burns family (qv) formed partnerships with the MacIvers in Liverpool and Samuel Cunard in London for the same reason. For these men the Clyde and its Glasgow hinterland was too small a base for the entirety of their business. The Henderson answer to this dilemma was not partnership with Liverpool or London families nor a permanent removal to one of the larger ports. Instead a personal nomadism was chosen as Algernon Henderson migrated from Liverpool to Glasgow and then back to Liverpool at different stages in his business career.

The origins of the Anchor Line lay in a Glasgow partnership of Messrs Handyside & Henderson formed in 1852 to operate some small sailing vessels. In 1856 they inaugurated their first transatlantic service with the *Tempest*, a former East Indiaman converted to steam. The success of this venture saw the Anchor Line established with a weekly service between Glasgow and New York; services were later added from Liverpool, and from both these home ports to Karachi, Bombay and Calcutta. A Mediterranean service was also developed. Late in 1872 Messrs Handyside & Henderson acquired the Meadowside yard of Tod & MacGregor and it was operated from 1873 as the shipyard of D & W Henderson. The Henderson brothers were another branch of the Henderson family of the Anchor Line. In 1899 the Handyside & Henderson partnership was brought to an end and a new limited company, Anchor Line (Henderson Brothers) Ltd was formed.

It is clear that from its earliest days the Anchor Line had close connections with Liverpool. By the time Algernon Henderson was born in 1882 the Henderson family was already firmly based in both Glasgow and Liverpool. His father, Francis Henderson, ran the Liverpool end of the family business for some time and Algernon Henderson went to school in Liverpool and then to Rugby; an education far removed from the typical Scottish parish school.

In 1900, aged 18, A C F Henderson entered the family business, the Anchor Line, at its head office in Glasgow. His first three years were spent in the usual way moving from department to department to gain experience of all aspects of the business. In 1903 he was sent out to New York and for the next two years learned the American end of operations. From there his footloose training took him to India, and between 1905 and 1906 he worked in the offices of the Anchor Line agents in both Calcutta and Bombay. At the end of 1906 A C F Henderson's apprenticeship was over and he returned to Liverpool to join the staff there. Two years later in 1908, at the age of 26, he became a director of the Anchor Line; two years later he was managing director, an accelerated promotion possible only in family owned businesses.

A C F Henderson spent the period from the end of 1906 to early 1912 in Liverpool. During that period of activity he became well involved in Liverpool life. In 1910 he was elected to Liverpool's city council and also became chairman of the Bombay Steam Trade Conference. The following year he was a member of the Mersey Docks & Harbour Board.

1911 also brought a significant change in the Henderson family position in the Anchor Line. In that year the ordinary shares of the Anchor Line were purchased by the Cunard Steamship Co. Thereafter, although the Hendersons played a significant management role, the Anchor Line was effectively controlled by Cunard through a board of directors who were effectively Cunard's nominees. As part of this arrangement Algernon Henderson became a director of the Cunard Steamship Co in 1912. Also in 1912 the Anchor Line acquired shares to the value of £100,000 out of the £250,000 ordinary capital in T & J Brocklebank Ltd. The balance of £150,000 in ordinary capital was taken up by Cunard. As a consequence of this further takeover Algernon Henderson joined the board of Brocklebank Ltd in 1912.

From 1912 Algernon Henderson remained managing director of the Anchor Line, but clearly subject to Cunard policy. In that year he left Liverpool and returned to Glasgow where he remained for the next nine years. While in Glasgow he succeeded his father as a ratepayer's member on the Clyde Trust and through his involvement in the shipping life of the port, he became a member of the Glasgow Steamship Owners' Association and chairman of the Glasgow Committee of the Seaman's National Insurance Society. Although these were busy years in Glasgow, especially in the war, Henderson followed the usual shipping fraternity relaxation of yachting; he quickly became a member of the Royal Northern, Royal Clyde, Royal Highland, and Gareloch Yacht Clubs. His spell of nine years in Glasgow was only broken for a few months in 1918 when he went to Malta as a representative of the Ministry of Shipping. During this period in Glasgow he negotiated the link with the Donaldson Line to form the Anchor-Donaldson Line in 1916 to share business on the Canadian services. The Anchor Line held half the paid up capital of £410,000 the other half being held by the Donaldsons (qv).

The First World War was hard on the Anchor

Line. At the beginning of hostilities the Anchor Line was a profitable company with a fleet of nine large modern vessels and a number of smaller craft. Only one survived, seven being sunk by U boat activity and one foundering in the ordinary course of trade. As an emergency measure the Anchor Line resumed business at the end of the war by purchasing ex-enemy steamers confiscated and sold off in reparations.

The policy for the company in the 1920s lay essentially with the Cunard board rather than with the Henderson family and the Anchor Line itself. In the early 1920s the Anchor Line ordered six large new vessels totalling nearly 120,000 grt. Three of these were constructed by Stephens of Linthouse, two by the Fairfield yard, and one by Beardmore at Dalmuir. Two further vessels were ordered from Fairfield for the Anchor-Donaldson Line. The contracts for the six Anchor Line vessels were taken at the peak prices in the immediate postwar boom. The vessels cost £7.3 million though this outlay was partly offset by the Anchor Line receiving £2.65 million in insurance payments for wartime losses. The net cost to the company was consequently £5 million. In order to pay for this the company had to anticipate high levels of trade. The collapse of trade in the second half of 1921 and the reduction in prices that followed meant that throughout the 1920s it was difficult for the Anchor Line to earn sufficient revenue to pay off the debts incurred in these contracts. The building of the vessels was partly funded by Treasury loans some £1.6 million being made available to the company through the Trades Facilities Acts. The remainder was underwritten by mortgages. As a consequence when the Anchor Line ran into difficulties in meeting its payments following the 1929 crash, the company still owed £850,000 to the Treasury, £300,000 in overdraft to the Union Bank of Scotland, a further £160,000 to Alexander Stephens & Co and £145,000 to the Fairfield Shipbuilding Co. In addition to these mortgages the Union Bank of Scotland held shares belonging to the Anchor Line and in the Anchor-Donaldson Line as security.

The poor trading conditions in the 1920s clearly saw the Anchor Line being burdened by a heavy load of debt. Although the Anchor Line was part of the Cunard empire it is clear that the Cunard company pursued its own interests and indeed drew considerable resources from the Anchor Line to contribute to meet its own American expenses. The Anchor Line was largely left to sink or swim on its own.

These complexities were largely beyond the control of Algernon Henderson himself; he had returned to Liverpool at the end of 1921 as managing director of Anchor Line and joint manager of the Cunard Steamship Co. By 1932 however his health had failed, and he retired from the business and removed to London. His company, the Anchor Line was then very deeply in debt and seemed likely to fail. Two years later Algernon Henderson was dead at the early age of 52. His company's difficulties were not finally resolved till 1935, by which time the Henderson family connection had been completely broken. He and his father Francis, died within three weeks of each other in 1934, bringing the Henderson family shipping enterprise to an end after some 82 years.

ANTHONY SLAVEN

SOURCES

Unpublished

Bank of England Archives:
  SMT 3/273, Anchor Line
  SMT 3/282, Fairfield Shipbuilding and Engineering Co
  Shipbuilders Repairers National Association Records, 'Merchant Shipbuilding in Great Britain and Ireland', Vol 1, 1920-1938

Published

Anon, *The Book of the Anchor Line 1852-1931*, London, 1932
Glasgow Herald, 16/2/1934
McLellan, R S, *The Anchor Line 1856-1956*, 1956
Shipbuilding and shipping Record, 22/2/1934
The Times, 16/2/1934

Hugh HOGARTH,

Shipowner, b. 1840, Stevenson, Ayrshire, s. of Robert Hogarth, painter and Ann Barclay; m. Mary McFee; 3 s., 4 d.; Ch, Hugh Hogarth & Sons and Hogarth Shipping Co Ltd; d. 28/4/1904, Ardrossan, Ayrshire; g/v estate: £126,449.

Hugh Hogarth, like Andrew Weir (qv), found that the declining sailing ship presented the easiest and cheapest entry route into shipping circles in the west of Scotland in the last quarter of the nineteenth century.

Hogarth was born in Stevenson in Ayrshire in 1840, just as the River Clyde was moving rapidly into constructing steam boats, and as firms like G & J

Burns (qv) and D & A Hutcheson, were opening up the coastal and Highland and Island services. His family origins were not in shipping; his father Robert Hogarth, was a journeyman painter, and could offer no springboard into business for his son.

While there is no evidence of Hogarth's schooling, it is likely that he completed his elementary education at the local parish school, and then began work in nearby Ardrossan as a ship chandler's assistant. Here Hogarth learned all there was to know of the fitting out needs of sailing ships, and by 1862 at the age of 22, he was in business in the partnership of Goodwin & Hogarth as ship stores merchants. This enterprise lasted for some ten years after which it appears that Hogarth continued in business on his own. Inevitably in this line of work he was able to take some shares in vessels; by 1878 he had established himself as an owner and operator of sailing vessels in the Hogarth Shipping Co, based at Clyde Street, Glasgow. In 1884 he added his first steamer, the *Baron Ardrossan*, and from this emerged the Baron Line of steamers and sailing vessels owned and managed by Hugh Hogarth. Hogarth, like Andrew Weir and others, found a blend of sailing vessels and steamships a viable and profitable investment in long distance carrying trades from the Clyde towards the end of the nineteenth century.

Although Hogarth removed his business to Glasgow he still lived in Ardrossan, and was deeply involved in local affairs, including being a director of the Ardrossan Harbour Co. He had interests in marine insurance and became chairman of the North of England Protecting and Indemnity Association. The welfare of fellow shipowners and brokers also attracted his attention, and at the time of his death in 1904 he was vice president of the Glasgow Shipowners and Shipbrokers Benevolent Association.

Throughout his career as a shipowner Hogarth remained committed to the utility of sailing vessels; when there was an attempt to form an international sailing ship union, he registered his sail ship tonnage with the movement. In 1901 he changed the name of his business to Hugh Hogarth & Sons, Shipowners, signifying the admission of his sons to partnership in the business. This was the managing company for the Hogarth Shipping Co Ltd.

This step was barely accomplished when on 28 April 1904, Hogarth was taken ill at evening church service in Ardrossan and died that night. Hugh Hogarth's shipowning career spanned some 40 years, and from modest beginnings he left a gross estate valued at £126,449. His share in the partnership then stood at £41,583. In addition he had substantial shares in the Kelvin Shipping Co Ltd, the Irrawaddy Flotilla Co Ltd, and in the Burmah Oil Co Ltd. His estate passed to his sons to secure the future of the business and thereafter it was managed and owned by them.

ANTHONY SLAVEN

SOURCES

Unpublished

SRO: SC 7/28/1, Inventory
　　　SC 7/30/1, Will

Published

Glasgow Herald, 26/4/1904
Orbell, M J, *From Cape to Cape: A History of Lyle
　　Shipping Co*, Edinburgh, 1978
The Scotsman, 26/4/1904
Shipping World, 4/5/1904

Frederick Charles KENNEDY,

Shipping Company Manager; b. 1848, Edinburgh, s. of Peter Cumming Kennedy, Tweed merchant and Eliza Johnston; m. 8/7/1881, Mary, d. of John Cuddie, leather merchant; no issue; Manager & Dir, Irrawaddy Flotilla Co; d. 17/4/1916, Edinburgh; g/v estate: £251,214 4s 1d.

Frederick Kennedy was born and bred in Edinburgh and from all accounts had no ideas in his youth of seeking his fortune in Britain's flourishing Empire overseas.

Peter Kennedy, his father, was a tweed merchant and the young Frederick was brought up in good middle class circumstances and well schooled in the Scottish tradition. On leaving school he joined the Edinburgh head office of the London and Edinburgh Shipping Company as a junior clerk and we find records recognising his ability by increases in his salary. It is a fair assumption that the company were sorry to part with him in 1877 when he seized an opportunity for which his experience and good character well suited him.

The Thomson shipowning family of Leith were friends of his father; they also had a close relationship with Glasgow shipowners Patrick Henderson and Company, particularly with the senior partner James Galbraith (qv). Thus Frederick Kennedy learned of and applied for the important position of assistant manager in the Irrawaddy Flotilla Company in Burma. Just two years before, in 1875, the Irrawaddy Flotilla had ceased to be run by a managing agency in Rangoon and had set up its own management under another Scot, George Swann, a protege of James Galbraith.

By 1877 Swann had three assistants, recruited in Scotland by Galbraith. The senior, his assistant manager, died suddenly and Swann cabled for a replacement of similar age, deeming that his other assistants were too young for such an important post. Frederick Kennedy was 29 and when Galbraith interviewed him he judged him to be the man they wanted. Before the year was out Kennedy had sailed on the first Henderson Liner and arrived in Rangoon. Galbraith's judgement had not faltered. George Swann became a name to be reckoned with: Kennedy followed his footsteps and far surpassed him.

It is necessary to draw comparisons between these two men to emphasise the great contribution which Frederick Kennedy made to the development of the Irrawaddy Flotilla Company and in consequence to the economic development of Burma under British rule. James Galbraith had sent George Swann out to Rangoon in 1868 as a book-keeper, having first trained him in Henderson's office in Glasgow.

He joined the managing agency of T D Findlay & Company who had been appointed on the formation of the first Irrawaddy Flotilla Company in 1865. Four elderly river steamers were taken over from the Bengal Marine and commercial operations began with a share capital of £60,000, raised by the directors in Glasgow, behind the new enterprise. Within three years Swann had shown his mettle and at the age of 31 became manager of the steamers within the Findlay Agency. When in 1875 T D Findlay resigned Swann was appointed manager in full control in Burma of a new Irrawaddy Flotilla Company with share capital of £300,000. By then the fleet comprised 11 fine new paddlers and 32 flats (covered barges). Profits were being ploughed back and only small dividends spared to the Scottish shareholders.

Into this well established scene came Frederick Kennedy in 1877. Swann was soon impressed by his new assistant manager's ability and vigorous approach to his own progressive plans for expansion. When Kennedy returned to Scotland in 1881 for his first home leave it had already been decided that Swann would become general manager of the company, spending most of his time in the UK where there was much to do in the company's interests, and visiting Burma every winter. Kennedy became manager in Burma and gathering up the momentum of Swann's expansionist plans, he was to be the moving spirit for the next 35 years in making the Irrawaddy Flotilla the greatest riverine fleet the world has ever known.

That George Swann went along with Kennedy's immense plans for development and had the major task of taking the board of directors with them reflects great credit on both men. But it was Frederick Kennedy who had the ideas and made the running; and he was on his own after Swann retired in 1894. Then Kennedy became general manager and in 1902 he was appointed a director of the company. His dominating influence over the company's progress continued until his death in 1916.

George Swann was a bachelor, not an uncommon state for men working in the East in those days. Kennedy, however, married in 1881 during his leave, his bride being 21 year old Mary Cuddie, daughter of a leather merchant in Falkirk. She did not go to Burma until later years for at the time of Kennedy's return from leave in 1881 the country was too unsettled with the despotic rule of King Thebaw in Upper Burma; and it was there that Kennedy required to spend much of his time. He had already made a pioneering expedition on the Chindwin River in Upper Burma early in 1881 and now preparations for the opening of a steamer service had to be made. The shallow draft sternwheelers which he introduced to the Chindwin were the first Kennedy innovation. There were to be many more.

Inevitably, Kennedy became involved in the political problems which beset the Government of British (Lower) Burma. Swann had been on good personal terms with the Burmese King Mindon and Kennedy had endeavoured to continue this relationship with Mindon's successor Thebaw, who came to the throne in 1878. The steamers were running through Upper Burma right up to Bhamo on the Chinese frontier, a thousand miles from Rangoon, and now the Chindwin Service also required the royal approval. This was obtained and Kennedy frequently paid respects to King Thebaw to ensure that there was no hindrance to the smooth running of his services. But relations between Thebaw and British Burma were deteriorating and by 1884 Kennedy was worried. His letters to the Chief Commissioner of British Burma pointing to the dangers being run by the captains and crews of the steamers when plying in Upper Burma waters alerted the Commissioner to the growing insecurity for British subjects in the King's territory.

The tension did not diminish and late in 1885 the British delivered an ultimatum to King Thebaw. That historic document was carried to Mandalay by an Irrawaddy Flotilla steamer Captain, and the Burmese rejection carried back. Kennedy and his Flotilla then became the key to the invasion and taking of Mandalay. War was declared and the Chief Commissioner ordered 'in the matter of taking up flotilla vessels we must ask Mr Kennedy to undertake the fittings for us'. From a fleet then numbering 35 steamers no fewer than 26 were prepared, each with one or two flats in tow, for the transport from Rangoon of some 17,000 soldiers and followers, mules and artillery up river the 650 miles to Mandalay. They were embarked as ocean steamers brought them in from Madras and Calcutta and proceeded to muster at the frontier. After some short sharp engagements on the way Mandalay was taken, the King exiled and Upper Burma annexed in January 1886.

George Swann arrived in Rangoon on his annual visit in time to accompany the Viceroy of India, Lord Dufferin, by steamer to Mandalay the following month, the whole of Burma then having become a Province of the Indian Empire. Viceregal gratitude to the Irrawaddy Flotilla Company was expressed by the conferring on both Swann and Kennedy the honour of Commander of the Indian Empire (CIE).

Unsettled conditions in Upper Burma following the annexation, depressed trading world-wide and a period of instability for the Indian rupee were all hindrances to Kennedy's expansionist plans for the next few years. But he pressed on and began opening up the vast delta of the Irrawaddy with double-decked screw driven steamers of around 100 feet in length capable of carrying some 300/400 deck passengers and small cargoes. The delta had few of the problems of navigation presented by the main river and the Chindwin, where draft restrictions required the employment of side paddlers in the former and sternwheelers in the latter.

By the 1890s the economy was on the move again and more and more fine paddy land was being cultivated in the Irrawaddy delta as Burma became the rice-bowl of the world. The delta population grew and the only transport possible was by river: the fleet increased rapidly in numbers and by 1910 there were more than 100 steamers serving the townships and villages throughout the great maze of creeks. As rice mills sprung up all over the delta the company introduced a fleet of tugs and barges to bring rice cargoes to ocean steamers at Rangoon and Bassein. On the 1,000 miles of the Irrawaddy up to Bhamo, on the Chindwin and on the rivers further east at Moulmein new ferry services were opened. But the greatest step forward came in 1903 when Denny of Dumbarton, who had been much involved in the whole venture from the start, built seven double-decked side paddlers 326 feet in length for the Rangoon to Mandalay mail service. Kennedy was much concerned with the design of these leviathans of the Irrawaddy, the largest shallow draft side paddlers ever to exist and capable of carrying 4,200 deck passengers and with flats at each side 2,000 tons of cargo. When the present writer joined the Flotilla Company 30 years later these fine 'queens of the river' were still in service and continued until the Japanese invasion in 1942 precipitated their end along with the rest of the fleet.

With the rapid expansion of the fleet Kennedy had made sure that technical services were adequate to ensure their efficient running. The Dockyard at Dalla on the Rangoon river opposite the city was extended, another yard acquired and slipways and dockyards established at Mandalay and Moulmein. Some 5,000 men were employed in these establishments and as the fleet grew a similar number were required to man the ships, flats and barges. British officers and engineers for the larger steamers were recruited in Glasgow and many of the managers and foremen for the dockyards came from Denny's yard in Dumbarton. The crews were almost entirely Chittagonian, the Burmese having little inclination for the disciplines demanded. It became an immense undertaking and required men of high calibre at the top. It is not difficult to contemplate the quality of Kennedy's leadership.

From 1890 also the shareholders began to reap the benefit of their investment. Prudent provision for depreciation and reserve continued to be the first priority but net profits in excess annually of £300,000 enabled the Board to pay dividends of 10% to 15% free of tax. By a capital distribution from reserves the share capital was increased in 1904 to £720,000.

When Frederick Kennedy had taken over completely on George Swann's retiral in 1894 the fleet had comprised some 200 units. When Kennedy died, still in harness, in 1916 the fleet exceeded 500 units: there were close on 200 powered vessels from the large paddlers to the little fleet of buoying launches, and 320 flats and barges. Undoubtedly, the field for men of enterprise was wide open and Kennedy's success was not achieved single-handed by any means, but the evidence is there that he was a quite outstanding businessman of great acumen.

Here we had a man, happily married but with no children, who after some 17 years almost continuous living in Burma returned to set up home in Palmerston Place in Edinburgh in 1894, travelling to Glasgow to conduct the affairs of the great Company in far off Burma. Every winter he went out to Rangoon for two or three months and travelled over the steamer routes, keeping up to date and considering the next moves with the Rangoon managers; no less than four served under his general management in the 22 years until his death in 1916.

In 1901 he also became a director of the London and Edinburgh Shipping Company and for a period was managing director. He was a director of a number of other Scottish Companies and had investments in a wide variety of enterprises. He died leaving a large portfolio of shareholdings and the traditional sixty-fourths in several ships. That his skills and acumen were not confined to his major role in the making of the Irrawaddy Flotilla Company is evident by the fortune he left of £250,000, a huge sum in those days. It could be said that he was one of the great Nabobs.

ALISTER MACRAE

SOURCES

Unpublished

Glasgow University Archives: GD 301
GD 301/4
SRO: SC 70/1/582, Inventory
SC 70/4/486, Will

Published

Directory of Directors, 1901-1916
McCrae, Alister and Prentice, Alan, *Irrawaddy Flotilla*, Paisley, 1978
McCrae, Alister, 'The Irrawaddy Flotilla Co', *Business History*, Vol XXII, No 1
The Scotsman, 19/4/1916
The Times, 21/4/1916, 1/9/1916
Who Was Who, Vol II

David MacBRAYNE,

Shipowner; b. 1818, Glasgow, s. of David MacBrayne, registrar of births, Barony Parish, and Elizabeth Stevenson Burns; m. 1860, Robina Eckford Robertson, d. of Lawrence Robertson, manager of Royal Bank of Scotland, Edinburgh; 2 s., 1 d.; Partner, David & Alexander Hutcheson & Co; Sole Proprietor, David MacBrayne & Co; d. 26/1/1907, Glasgow; g/v estate: £79,004 14s 2d.

Family connections, as in so many successful businesses in Scotland, were to be the stepping stones on which David MacBrayne was to found his career as a successful shipowner. David MacBrayne's mother was Elizabeth Stevenson Burns, sister of James and George Burns, founders of J & G Burns Steamship Co Ltd and through George Burns the founder of the Cunard Shipping Co together with Samuel Cunard and David MacIver. Shipping was therefore in the family blood. It is somewhat surprising then to find that after schooling, presumably in the local parish school, the young David MacBrayne entered an apprenticeship as a type founder. This, however, did not last long and he soon entered a shipping office to train as a clerk. It is not clear what office he entered but it seems likely to have been in the firm of David & Alexander Hutcheson, shipowners, with whom he was ultimately to become a partner. The Hutchesons were also related to the Burns family.

The opportunity for David MacBrayne and the Hutchesons to secure a place for themselves in west coast shipping in Scotland came more from the enterprise and ambition of J & G Burns rather than from their own activities. In 1845 J & G Burns had broken into the Clyde and west coast steamship trade by buying out the old Castle Line of steamers which had been established in 1842 by a group of Glasgow merchants including W Campbell of Tilliechewan, J Hunter of Hafton and A S Finlay of Castle Toward.

However, the attention of the Burns's was soon diverted to developing the Atlantic trade and the company was passed to their relatives David and Alexander Hutcheson and the young David Mac-Brayne in 1848. MacBrayne was only 30 years of age and clearly the junior partner in the new company.

The opportunity confronting the new company of David & Alexander Hutcheson was considerable. Access to and from the Highlands and Islands had always been difficult but the improving efficiency of steamboats in conquering tide and weather brought the promise of regular and economic services to distant places. The Highlands and Islands offered both an active cargo and passenger trade. One stream was emigrants pouring southwards to the Clyde to trans-ship to the Americas. Grain, cattle, hides and fish also came south to urban markets and all the necessities of the scattered Highland and Island communities could be transported more easily by steamer than by any other means. Moreover the 1840s saw the early beginnings of the seasonal tourist trade especially as the growing urban middle classes sought rural idylls in imitation of Queen Victoria. Victoria had made the trip to the Highlands and Islands by the west coast route in 1847. She had travelled by track boat through the Crinan Canal and then by

steamboat onward to Oban. This route and onward journey by Loch Linnie, Fort William and Caledonian Canal to Inverness became known as the Royal Route and was a busy summer attraction for visitors and holidaymakers.

The Hutchesons and MacBrayne were well aware of this opportunity and rapidly set about capturing the west coast traffic. They expanded their fleet first by acquiring steamers already in service. They purchased those formerly operated by Thomson and McConnell and extended their services quickly to the western isles. In 1855 they began to build purpose designed vessels with the *Iona*. This was the first of the Hutcheson's 'crack' steamers. These vessels combining luxury, speed, regularity and economy. The hand of David MacBrayne was evident in this policy. He was a first class administrator with a clear eye and sharp memory for detail. He built the company's reputation on service and quality.

In the 30 years from 1848 to 1878 the two Hutchesons and David MacBrayne developed a fleet of 15 vessels and became the most important influence in shipping services to the western isles and islands. The two Hutcheson brothers retired within two years of each other in 1876 and 1878 leaving David MacBrayne, then aged 60, as sole proprietor. Mac-Brayne renamed the company as Messrs David Mac-Brayne & Co and immediately set about expanding the fleet. In the decade from 1879 he added ten new vessels to the fleet commencing with the *Columba*, his first all steel paddle steamer. In 1881 he added the *Claymore*, the first screw steamer in his fleet. This was followed in 1883 by the *Cavalier*, in which MacBrayne had installed the first electric light on any vessel plying the Clyde routes.

Throughout these years the major challenge to MacBrayne's supremacy on the services to the west coast were the railway steamers. But in effect the penetration of the railways to remote points on the western seaboard created more trade rather than simply diverting trade from MacBrayne to railway controlled services. Consequently, in this growing market, MacBrayne prospered. By the end of the 1880s he had a fleet of 28 vessels and employed more than 750 men afloat together another 700 men onshore as agents, clerks and storemen. As well as having regular services to the western isles and west coast, Thurso, and Inverness, MacBrayne specialised in daily and longer circular tours in the summer season. Indeed in 1878 he had published a booklet, handsomely illustrated and fully descriptive of all the tourist attractions offered by his fleet of high quality vessels with their distinctive red funnels. The importance of MacBrayne and his steamers to the Islands and Highlands was reflected in the fact that the GPO employed three persons on the the *Columba* to operate a floating post office. The *Columba* plied daily between Glasgow and Ardrishaig via Rothesay, Kyles of Bute and East Tarbert. The floating post office was reputed to handle some 95,000 letters each month.

David MacBrayne was in many ways the model of the successful Victorian self-made businessman. He is reputed to have worked long hours, and clearly had only a little time for activities outside his business. He did not marry till 1860 when he was then 42 years of age. In the 1860s he sat as a ratepayers member of the Clyde Navigation Trust. His longest standing involvement was with one of the Glasgow Volunteer Regiments in which he rose to the rank of major. He was in addition a Justice of the Peace but was not further involved in local affairs. In business he emphasised service and a close personal attention to detail. He is said to have known most of the staff by name, and indeed he seems to have generated a considerable loyalty; most of his officers were long serving members of the company having joined it in its first expansion in the 1850s and 1860s.

Yet while David MacBrayne had developed a near monopoly of services to the western isles and Highlands by the 1880s, he effectively watched over his company rather than actively expanded it in the latter years of his life. After the burst of building eight new vessels in the 1880s MacBrayne added only another five in the 1890s. Further extension of the fleet had to await the involvement of MacBrayne's two sons David Hope MacBrayne and Lawrence MacBrayne, who joined the business as partners each with a quarter share in 1902. Both had engineering and commercial experience and actively engaged in new acquisitions in the early years of the twentieth century. It is clear that although David MacBrayne devoted long hours to the business, his drive waned in the 1880s, and his sons progressively took more and more of the responsibility onto their own shoulders. Even so David MacBrayne still dictated policy and when he died after a long deterioration in 1907 his fleet stood at 31 vessels and he then employed over 1,000 men afloat. The evidence of his waning involvement can be seen in the age of the vessels, 11 of them dated from the Hutcheson era and were over 30 years old. A further 11 were over 15 years old and only 7 vessels constructed once the sons entered the business were less than five years old.

The ageing MacBrayne finally relinquished control of the business in 1905 at which point the partnership was converted into a limited company. His elder son, David Hope MacBrayne, became chairman and managing director. Even then David MacBrayne Snr kept constantly in touch with the affairs of the business. Even though the company had taken a Limited form it essentially remained a family business. Half the capital had already gone to the sons in 1902 when they came into the partnership, and in his will David MacBrayne provided that the remainder should go to them. His daughter was given a life-rent of one-fifth of the value of his estate; but he specifically stipulated that this should be provided for from his resources, other than those tied up in the business. He indeed acted to preserve the capital of the company. When he died in his ninetieth year David

MacBrayne had outlived all his competitors, and had come to dominate all the cargo and passenger trade to the western isles and Highlands. In the 1980s the company still survives in public ownership, though merged with the Caledonian Steam Packet Company as the Caledonian/MacBrayne subsidiary of the Scottish Transport Group.

ANTHONY SLAVEN

SOURCES

Unpublished

SRO: SC 36/48/207, Inventory
     SC 36/51/44, Will

Published

The Bailie, No 303, 7/8/1878, No 819, 27/6/1888
The Engineer, 1/2/1907
Glasgow Herald, 28/1/1907
Glasgow Today, 1888
The Scotsman, 28/1/1907
Stratten, *Glasgow and its Environs*, London, 1891
Who's Who in Glasgow, 1909

Sir William MACKINNON,

Shipowner, b. 31/3/1823, Campbeltown, s. of Duncan Mackinnon, excise officer and Isabella Currie; m. 12/3/1856, Janet Colquhoun, d. of Robert Jameson, solicitor; no issue; Founder, British India Steam Navigation Co Ltd; Partner, W Mackinnon & Co, Glasgow and Mackinnon, Mackenzie & Co, Calcutta; d. 22/6/1893, London; g/v estate £560,563 7s 10d.

William Mackinnon was an outstanding figure within the West of Scotland's overseas trading community during the middle and later decades of the nineteenth century. Unlike many of the expatriate Scots who left home to seek new opportunities, he retained his links with Scotland, and his enterprise in the fields of commerce, finance, and above all shipping, served as one of the important strands which connected industrial Scotland to the wider world economy. His leadership of a group of businessmen connected by ties of family and friendship resulted in the creation of a loosely-knit cluster of companies (today forming part of the Inchcape Group) the operations of which spanned the entire Indian Ocean maritime region. From its initial twin bases in Calcutta and Glasgow, the Mackinnon group's activities eventually extended to Australia, the Netherlands East Indies, the Straits Settlements, Burma, India, the Persian Gulf, the Red Sea and East Africa. This was probably the most far-flung business empire ever created by Scottish entrepreneurship, and it owed its expansion not only to the commercial acumen of Mackinnon and his associates but also to its role in serving the needs and interests of British imperial authority east of Suez. The economic growth of Clydeside and the expansion of the British Empire were inter-twined in the career of William Mackinnon.

The young William Mackinnon, fourteenth child in a family of modest means, first tried his hand in the grocery trade in Campbeltown and as a silk-merchant's clerk in Glasgow before going out to India in 1847 to join another Campbeltown man, Robert Mackenzie, in a general mercantile business in Bengal. In 1849 the partnership was joined by Mackinnon's school friend, James Macalister Hall. Following Mackenzie's death by drowning in 1853, Mackinnon

and Hall reorganised their interests into two companies, Mackinnon, Mackenzie & Co, Calcutta, and W Mackinnon & Co, Glasgow. The two firms (with some assistance from Mackinnon's brother, Peter, of Mackinnon, Frew & Co, Liverpool) conducted jointly those activities in which the partnership had come to specialise - first, the shipping of cotton goods from Glasgow and Manchester for sale in Calcutta; second, a trade in general goods between Calcutta and Australia; and third, the running of a few sailing ships on the Glasgow-Liverpool-Calcutta and Calcutta-Sydney-Melbourne routes.

Until 1855 there was probably little to distinguish the Mackinnon-Hall partnership among Glasgow's colonial traders or within the ranks of the expatriate houses of Calcutta. In that year, however, William Mackinnon returned to take charge of the Glasgow firm. Other than two short but important tours in India, during 1861-63 and 1872-73, his primary function was to develop the UK end of the Mackinnon-Hall interests. In particular, his skilful cultivation of business contacts in Clydeside, Lancashire and London laid the financial foundations for an entry into steam-shipping and the subsequent growth of what became by the 1880's one of the world's largest and most diverse assembly of steam-ship enterprises.

The key to success lay in obtaining government subsidies, principally mail contracts, which made it possible to operate steamers in distant waters where, until the mid-1870s at least, high costs of coal, engine repairs and skilled manpower rendered commercial steam-shipping relatively unprofitable. In 1856 Mackinnon and Hall promoted the tiny Calcutta and Burmah Steam Navigation Company to secure a contract from the Government of Bengal to carry mails from Calcutta to the Burmese ports. Further postal contracts, negotiated by Mackinnon while in India in 1861-63, enabled the company to inaugurate a series of lines from Calcutta eastwards to Burma and Singapore, from Calcutta round the coasts of India to Bombay, and from Bombay to the Persian Gulf. The paid-up capital of the company, renamed the British India Steam Navigation Company in 1862, rose from £39,800 in 1857 to £342,685 in 1865. The holdings of the Mackinnon and Hall families represented only some 16% of the total shares, but William Mackinnon could count on the support of friends among the expatriate Scottish merchants of India and London, and the cotton merchants and manufacturers of Glasgow and Lancashire, who were the other large shareholders, as well as the many small shareholders in Campbeltown, in retaining control of the company's direction. In 1864 Mackinnon took over a contract from the Government of the Netherlands East Indies for a steam packet service along the coast of Java, and from Java to other islands in the archipelago, and floated the Netherlands India Steam Navigation Company. The shareholders and directors were virtually the same as in the British India S N Co, but the two companies were managed as distinctly separate entities, B I with its head offices in Glasgow and N I in London. The ships of the N I were required by Dutch law to fly the Dutch flag and to be under the command of Dutch captains, but in most other respects the company was a smaller, parallel version of B I.

Investment in coastal steam-shipping in Asian waters, together with the development of a small line of sailing vessels for the UK-India trades which was managed by Mackinnon, Frew & Co, taxed the capital-raising powers of the Mackinnon group. One source of finance was the profits made by Mackinnon, Mackenzie & Co in Calcutta during the boom in Indian trade in the years of the American Civil War, and the group as a whole enjoyed access to credit from the City of Glasgow Bank. Mackinnon, Mackenzie & Co. became Calcutta agents for the City of Glasgow Bank early in 1857, and William Mackinnon's significant part in rescuing the bank from closure during the crisis later that year led to his appointment as a director in 1858. While the extent of the group's financial reliance on the bank is obscure, the relationship would appear to have been important during the expansion of shipping activities in the early and mid-1860s. In 1870 Mackinnon, who had never been happy about the competence of his fellow board-members, felt able to loosen the ties and resign his directorship. By the time the bank finally collapsed in 1878 he had been able to distance himself from its affairs. An attempt by the liquidators to sue him for alleged malpractices during the period of his directorship, a case hinging upon the propriety of lending to an unsuccessful railway in the American Mid-West, was dismissed in the Edinburgh court of session in December 1881.

By 1881 the Mackinnon group's overseas ventures were in a flourishing condition. Two decades of growth in the foreign trade of South and Southeast Asia, and improvements in internal transport and communications in India and the Dutch East Indies, had generated a demand for coastal shipping services to which the B I and N I companies, backed by contracts for the conveyance of mails, government passengers and stores, and troops, were well placed to respond. In 1880 their paid-up capital amounted to £564,200 and £250,000 respectively. The B I fleet, enlarged by continuous plough-back of profits into fresh tonnage and engine refits for older vessels, had grown to a total of 60 ships and a gross tonnage of 58,930 tons. The N I's expansion was more modest, in consequence of a higher level of dividend payments to shareholders. Its fleet amounted to 15 ships with a gross tonnage of 24,383 tons. Mackinnon's function as chairman was especially significant in the ordering of vessels from Clyde shipbuilders, increasingly over the years from Dennys of Dumbarton, and in negotiating contracts with colonial and metropolitan governments. Day-to-day control of the steamers was left, always subject to Mackinnon's close scrutiny, to Mackinnon, Mackenzie & Co as managing agents for

B I and to Alexander Fraser of Batavia as local manager for N I. The creation of a network of agents at the various ports served by the lines was equally crucial to the success of dispersed shipping operations over such wide areas and so far from the seat of central management. The agents were selected from the expatriate Scottish houses scattered around the Indian Ocean, or were members of the Mackinnon-Hall families or trusted former employees placed in particular locations.

The 1860s and 1870s were also decades of diversification. As well as participating in a fruitless effort to introduce jute manufacturing to Glasgow, Mackinnon and Hall established a Scottish-registered company in 1866 for jute-making in Calcutta. Out of the profits of Mackinnon, Mackenzie & Co, in which William Mackinnon became sole senior partner after James Hall's retirement in 1869, came investment in a Calcutta cotton mill and several tea companies. Younger members of the Mackinnon and Hall families were coming to the fore in the management of the group's Indian ventures and in the development of associated businesses. In 1872, for example, two of Mackinnon's several nephews set up the firms of Macneill & Co, Calcutta, and Duncan Macneill & Co, London to engage in the tea trade and to become managing agents for some of the group's Indian investments, most notably the Rivers Steam Navigation Company which ran a line of steamers on the Brahmaputra between Calcutta and the tea districts of Assam. Another nephew was a founder of Gray Dawes & Co, London, which acted as London agents for B I, handled the group's marine insurance, and looked after its interests in the Persian Gulf through its associated firms of Gray, Paul & Co, Bushire, and Gray, Mackenzie & Co, Basra. The emergence of the younger men in turn freed William Mackinnon to concentrate on the two issues which dominated his later years - the development of a 'home line' of steamers, from the UK to the Indian Ocean, and his involvement in the affairs of East Africa.

The innovation of a 'home line', partly to replace the group's sailing ships, followed the opening of the Suez Canal in 1869. Rather than challenge P & O on the UK-Bombay routes, Mackinnon and his associates decided to operate between the UK and the Persian Gulf, calling at Karachi. Sailings began in 1872. A London-Calcutta route was added in 1876. On neither of those routes was any mail subsidy available, but in 1881 Mackinnon achieved a long-standing ambition by securing contracts from the Government of Queensland for the conveyance of mails and emigrants via the Torres Straits, which led to regular UK-Queensland sailings. Initially the 'home line' employed a few of the newer B I steamers, but in 1874 the syndicate known as British India Associated Steamers was created to supply larger and more specialised ocean-going vessels. B I Associated, at first a joint venture between the Mackinnons and Peter Denny (qv) of Dumbarton, gradually attracted other participants and in 1885 was converted into a public company. From the entry into Queensland stemmed further initiatives by the B I and B I Associated interests, including the pioneering of the frozen meat trade from Queensland, investment in a meat-freezing plant, and in 1882 the establishment of a coastal shipping firm, the Queensland Steam Shipping Company. In 1887 the Queensland S S Co amalgamated with a local rival into the Australasian United Steam Navigation Company. The group's shipping activities were now at their peak, embracing five companies which owned a total of 181 steamers with a book value of almost £3 millions.

The group's deep-sea operations never achieved the spectacular growth and substantial profits which had previously accrued to coasting in India and the Dutch East Indies. Conditions were much more competitive on the long-distance route to the UK, especially during the shipping depressions of the mid-1880s and early 1890s. During these decades, however, competition was also growing in the coastal trades and Continental governments began to take a more nationalistic attitude to shipping in their colonial empires. In 1888, in particular, the Dutch government changed the law on shipping in the Netherlands East Indies in such a way as to exclude N I from tendering for public contracts. The Netherlands India Steam Navigation Company therefore went into liquidation in 1890. It is against this background of an emerging struggle between longer-established British shipping concerns and newer, state-promoted Continental lines that William Mackinnon's role in the scramble for colonial territories in Eastern Africa should be seen. There, from the mid-1880s, a B I pre-eminence in coastal shipping was threatened by German, French and Portuguese rivals at a time when Britain's political influence in the region also came under challenge.

Mackinnon's connections with Eastern Africa initially developed out of B I's role as an agency for the extension of British-Indian and British political authority in the Persian Gulf and Red Sea areas, and in the Sultanate of Zanzibar. In 1872, hard on the heels of a renewed British commitment to the eradication of the East African maritime slave trade, B I commenced an Aden-Zanzibar line with the aid of a mail subsidy from Britain. Smith, Mackenzie & Co, associates of Gray Dawes & Co, became the B I agents in Zanzibar. A second factor was Mackinnon's long membership of the Free Church of Scotland and his support for its missionary endeavours in India. When, in 1878, the Free Church turned to Eastern Africa, establishing its mission at Livingstonia on Lake Nyasa, William Mackinnon was one of its principal backers. A complex inter-twining of commercial and humanitarian motives, for which the abolition of the slave trade within Eastern Africa was both an end and a means, drew Mackinnon into the schemes of John Kirk, British consul at Zanzibar, who was seeking to extend his influence within the Sultan's territories. A plan devised in 1877 for the formation of a company to lease the mainland from the Sultan, failed to come to fruition, but in 1882 B I became the instrument of Kirk's 'closer administration' of the mainland by the introduction of regular sailings to a number of East African ports at which consular agents were established. However, this 'informal imperialism' was transformed by Germany's bid for colonial possessions in 1884, which resulted in the division of East Africa into German and British 'spheres of influence' and the revival of the idea of a company to administer the British sector. The company, chartered in 1888 as the Imperial British East Africa Company, raised within its first year a paid-up capital of some £500,000, largely subscribed by the Mackinnon group. In return, Mackinnon obtained a mail subsidy from the British government for a direct London to Zanzibar line, to compete with the German East Africa Line.

This attempt to defend the group's shipping and trading interests, in what was merely a 'frontier' of its extensive business empire, proved unsuccessful. The IBEA Co over-extended itself financially in securing control of Uganda, a subsidy for railway-construction from the British government, on which Mackinnon pinned his hopes of raising further capital, was not forthcoming, and early in 1893 the Treasury withdrew the postal contract. Failure in these East African ventures, although having few repercussions on the rest of the group's activities, was a bitter personal blow to William Mackinnon, and it coincided with a recurrence of the lung infection which he had first contracted as a young man in India. He died in his personal suite at the Burlington Hotel, London, on 22 June 1893.

Two facets of William Mackinnon's entrepreneurship perhaps stand out above the others. First, he was principally a public contractor, operating at the interface between the state and the economy where, for the businessman, the cultivation of contacts with civil servants and politicians, and the skilful reading of their nods and winks, was essential to the promotion of the firm's interests. His mid-career success in liaising with the governing circles of India, in pursuit of mutual goals, contrasts markedly with his later failure to interpret correctly the signals emanating from the uncertainty and confusion of British policy towards East Africa. Second, his group's organistion was patriarchal and decentralised, rather than hierarchic and tightly-controlled, and Mackinnon's leadership rested upon the authority and respect which accrued to seniority within a family or kinship pattern of relationships. Whether such a structure could survive the death of its founding figure, in a world economy much more closely integrated by improved communications, and in the absence of a clearly-designated successor, was the major problem facing the Mackinnon group in the depression year of 1893.

J FORBES MUNRO

SOURCES

Unpublished

Orchardson, I K, 'Sir William Mackinnon, Ship-owner, 1823-1893', Unpublished PhD thesis, University of London, 1970

SRO: SC 51/32/43, Inventory
     SC 51/32/43, Will

Published

The Bailie, No 448, 18/5/1881

Blake, G, *Bicentenary 1856-1956: The British India Steam Navigation Co,* London, 1956

The Concise Dictionary of National Biography, Vol I

Galbraith, J S, *Mackinnon and East Africa,* London, 1972

Glasgow Herald, 23/6/1893

Griffiths, Sir Percival, *A History of the Inchcape Group,* 1977

Munro, J F, 'Scottish Business Imperialism: Sir William Mackinnon and the Development of Trade and Shipping in the Indian Ocean', ESRC Report HR 87001, British Library, 1984

Munro, J F, 'Shipping Subsidies and Railways Guarantees: William MacKinnon, Eastern Africa and the Indian Ocean, 1860-93', *Journal of African History,* Vol XXVIII, 1987

Munro, J F, 'Scottish Overseas Enterprise and the Lure of London: The MacKinnon Shipping Group, 1847-1893', *Scottish Economic and Social History,* Vol 8, 1988

The Times, 23/6/1893

Sir Alexander MATHESON,

b. 1805, Attadale, Ross-shire, s. of John Matheson and Margaret Matheson; m. (1) 1841, Mary McLeod; (2) 1853, the Honourable Mary Lavinia Stapleton; 1 s.; (3) 1860, Elenor Irving Percival; 3 s., 4 d.; Partner, Jardine, Matheson & Co; Ch, Matheson & Co; Ch, Highland Railways; d. 26/7/1886, London; g/v estate: £643,759.

The chairmen of railway companies only rarely came from the ranks of engineers and managers. Sir Alexander Matheson had no backbround in either railway operation or construction, but he did bring to the job experience, wealth and influence, achieved in other fields.

Alexander Matheson was born in 1805 in Attadale, Ross-shire. He attended the local school and then went on to Edinburgh University to take an Arts degree. In 1832 at the age of 27 he was called to Canton to become assistant to his uncle James Matheson. James Matheson together with Andrew Jardine were the founding partners in the great company of Jardine, Matheson & Co, established in July 1832.

Alexander Matheson was to play a significant role in the early development of Jardine, Matheson. In 1833 the East India Company's China monopoly was revoked, and between then and the 1840s there was great uncertainty in the China trade; in particular there was growing conflict over the importation of opium into China. As his uncle's assistant Alexander Matheson frequently had responsibility for the Jardine, Matheson ships conveying the opium to the Chinese ports.

The firm of Jardine, Matheson & Co was in the forefront of putting pressure on the British government to force concessions from the Chinese authorities to open up trade. Alexander Matheson indeed returned to Britain in 1840 to give evidence to the Parliamentary Committee on the China question. This coincided with the retiral of Andrew Jardine who withdrew from the business in 1839; James Matheson, his uncle, also retired in 1842. The original partners having retired, the fortunes of Jardine, Matheson then lay in the hands of the nephews. Alexander Matheson then became senior partner running the business in the East based in Macao. After the Treaty of Nanking of 1842 ceded Hong Kong to Britain, Jardine, Matheson & Co built up their base there, established in 1841, and moved their headquarter staff to Hong Kong from Macao in 1844.

During the 1840s, in which in a series of opium wars Britain forced open treaty ports for her traders, Alexander Matheson controlled the overall operation of Jardine, Matheson in Canton, Macao, and Hong Kong. By reputation he was an impatient and irritable man, his temper not being improved by recurring bouts of illness. Indeed he returned to London 1847 at a time of financial crisis and did not go back to China. On his arrival in London he found that the London agency, Magniac Jardine, was in financial difficulty. Only his skill and the financial resources of the two families prevented the firm from going under. As part of the reorganisation Magniac Jardine was wound up to be replaced by a new company Matheson & Co of which Alexander Matheson was chairman. His influence in the China trade was now so significant that he was then also appointed a director of the Bank of England.

The years from 1832 to 1847 saw Alexander Matheson travel frequently between Britain and China. His work with Jardine, Matheson brought him great wealth. From 1847 he was to use that wealth to create a new career from himself in Britain. His first step was to be elected as Liberal MP for Inverness in 1847. He held that seat till 1868 and on its dissolution became MP for Ross & Cromarty from 1868 to 1884. His new wealth also allowed him to purchase the estate of Lochalsh in 1851, land which had been forfeited by a member of his family in the fifteenth century. He later acquired Ardross Castle, though much of his life was to be spent in his London home in Berkeley Square. His new life style also saw him once more enter matrimony. He had first married Mary McLeod in 1841, but she had died tragically within a few months of the wedding. In 1853 he married for the second time, this time to a sister of Lord Bowmont, the Honourable Mary Lavinia Stapleton.

With these achievements behind him Sir Alexander Matheson now had all the attributes which railway companies required to give investors confidence. He had wealth, position and influence. In addition he had extensive landholdings in the Highlands where his ownership gave him great authority. In 1856 he became chairman of the Inverness & Aberdeen Junction Railway; in 1860 he added the chairmanship of the Inverness & Ross-shire Railway, and in 1865 the Dingwall & Skye Railway. 1865 also saw him become chairman of the Highland Railway, this being created by the amalgamation of the Inverness & Aberdeen Junction Railway and the Inverness & Perth Junction Railway. Matheson then retained his position as chairman of the Highland Railway for 20 years, only withdrawing from that position in 1884 when he gave up his parliamentary seat.

During his years as a landowner and a member of parliament, Alexander Matheson's career followed familiar paths. He continued as a partner in Jardine, Matheson & Co and acted still as chairman of Matheson & Co. He held his directorship of he Bank of England for many years and additionally became a director of the East & West India Dock Co. In addition to his role as a member of parliament, his public service saw him become a magistrate and a Deputy Lieutenant for Ross, Cromarty & Inverness, and also for the city of London. His wide ranging contributions brought him a baronetcy in 1882.

Although Sir Alexander Matheson occupied the position of chairman of a variety of railway lines for nearly 30 years, and as chairman of the Highland Railway for some 20 years, there is little evidence to suggest that he played any significant role in the development of their operations. Indeed his business interest remained firmly in his company in London, Matheson & Co. When he died in 1886 at the age of 81 he left a personal estate of £643,759. Much of this was tied up in Matheson & Co and he empowered his trustees to withdraw his funds slowly from that company leaving £100,000 there until such time as it was decided whether one or other of his sons would enter the business in his wake. His concern at his death was to retain the Mathesons' involvement in the China trade rather than in his railway activities.

ANTHONY SLAVEN

SOURCES

Unpublished

SRO: SC 70/1/260
    SC 70/6/33

Published

Keswick, M (ed), *The Thistle and the Jade*, 1982
Vallance, H A, *The Highland Railway*, 1943
The Scotsman, 28/7/1886
The Times, 28/7/1886

Donald Alexander MATHESON,

Railway engineer and manager; b. 5/11/1860, Tulliallan, Perthshire, s. of Donald Matheson, gardener, and Emma Nivette; m. 1891, Agnes Sim; 1s. 2 d.; Gen Manager, Caledonian Railway; Deputy Gen Manager, London, Midland & Scottish Railway Ltd; d. 10/12/1935, Glasgow; g/v estate: £43,332.

Railways, because of their scale and complexity, were organised as public companies virtually from the outset; consequently their operation required a professional and skilled management. Railways were therefore organisations which provided a career for able men and offered a route to senior management which depended largely upon ability and experience. D A Matheson is a classic example of the railway professional manager.

Born in 1860 it was Matheson's scholastic ability that took him from Perth Academy first to Watt College in Edinburgh to pursue his engineering studies. This was added to by further study at the Owens College in Manchester. Appropriately armed with paper qualifications, Donald Matheson then sought practical experience and gained his first post as an apprentice civil engineer with John Young of Perth. Various posts as assistant and consulting engineer followed; first on the Edinburgh suburban railway and then to England to join the staff of the London & North Western Railway where he was chief assistant to the engineer for the Lancashire & Yorkshire District. By 1890 he was back in Scotland as contractor's engineer and agent for the construction of the Lanarkshire & Ayrshire railway.

It was in this 'contractor's' capacity that he first

gained employment with the Caledonian Railway which took him on as resident engineer on the construction of the Glasgow Central Underground Railway. This was a line requiring five miles of tunnels beneath the city and cost some £2 million. His skills obviously impressed, for on completion of the project he was taken on to the permanent staff of the Caledonian Railway in 1896 as engineer for the western district. This was a stepping stone to more senior positions, for in 1899 he became engineer in chief and consultant engineer for the entire Caledonian Railway in succession to George Graham.

The next decade saw Donald Matheson make a considerable contribution to the Caledonian system. Under his guidance the second major extension of Glasgow Central Station took place between 1900 and 1906, including the building of the new bridge across the Clyde to carry another nine lines into the station. At a more modest level he designed and supervised the construction of Wemyss Bay Station for the Caledonian's steamer services. His effectiveness was well demonstrated in these ways, and when Guy Calthrop resigned as general manager in 1910, Matheson was appointed to replace him. He held the top position till the Caledonian became part of the LMS Railway in 1922. Thereafter Matheson was deputy general manager of LMS in Scotland; he was in that capacity the manager of the Scottish division comprising the Caledonian, the Glasgow & South Western Railway, and the Highland Railway. He retired from this position in 1926 at the age of 66.

Matheson was general manager of the Caledonian Railway in a period in which there was a constant demand for improved services. As an engineer he was much involved in promoting improved design and construction, and his many papers on technical matters won him both the James Watt and George Stephenson gold medals from the Institution of Civil Engineers. His ideas were influenced to some extent by North American practice; he had visited the USA and Canada in 1903 to investigate their technology and operations on behalf of the Caledonian. He was always keen to create a position of leadership for the Caledonian, and it was Matheson who was behind the idea and design of the Gleneagles Hotel and golf courses as a kind of railway country club holiday resort. This grandiose project was interrupted by the First World War, but Matheson pushed for its completion and he was rightly proud of his achievement.

The war also involved Matheson in extended public service. He had long been a member of the Engineers and Railway Volunteer Staff Corps, rising to the rank of major in 1900 and to lieutenant-colonel in 1910. However, it was his managerial skills rather than his role as a volunteer officer, that was taken up in wartime. In 1912 he had become a member of the Communication Board attached to the War Office and the Board of Trade. This was a body charged with planning a railway system capable of meeting both the needs of military movements and civilian requirements in times of war. This body became the Railway Executive Committee during the war and its plans were implemented. Matheson worked on this committee and in 1917, as chairman of the General Managers' Conference of the Associated Railway Companies of Great Britain, he visited the front in France to collect information for advising the government on military needs relating to the movement of personnel and materials.

At the end of the war Matheson gave his full-time to running the Caledonian which by then was a system of over 1,100 miles, employing a capital in excess of £50 million, and earning a gross annual revenue of around £12 million: its employees then numbered about 26,000. At the end of the war new arrangements were made to attempt to settle wage disputes in the railway industry, especially as the country attempted to come to terms with deflationary policies from 1921. A Central Wages Board was established to try to resolve wages questions; if unable to do so the matter was then taken to the National Wages Board which included six representatives from each of the employees and the trades' unions, together with an independent chairman. The vexed negotiations over wage reductions occupied a good deal of this body's time; Matheson represented the Scottish railways' case on wage reductions to the National Board. His advocacy carried the day and it was largely his ideas on the pattern of wage reductions and changes in the hours of work which were accepted by the board.

Matheson was one of the last of the breed of regional railway managers, who came to control the fortunes and business of particular lines for long periods of time. The opportunities for this kind of influence diminished with the railway amalgamations of 1922. During his career Matheson became an influential engineer and manager, and was a regular speaker and delegate to international railway congresses. He was a professional member of the main engineering societies, namely, the Institution of Civil Engineers and the Institution of Engineers and Shipbuilders in Scotland; he was also a member of the American Society of Civil Engineers. At various times he occupied the position of chairman of the Railway Engineers' Association of the United Kingdom, and was a past president of the Glasgow Association of Students of the Institution of Civil Engineers.

When Matheson retired in 1926 it was not to take a quiet life. He continued to be active in many charitable bodies in which he had had a long time interest. He was involved on the boards of the Royal Infirmary, the Glasgow Eye Infirmary, and the Broomhill Home for Incurables. In 1927 he was awarded the MVO for his public services, while his military volunteer work had previously brought him the TD. His MVO must at least in part have reflected the fact that for 28 years he travelled on every Royal train carrying the Royal family over the Caledonian section of the line between Carlisle and Aberdeen.

As was the case with so many distinguished businessmen Matheson also became a Justice of the Peace for the county of the city of Glasgow. In his retirement in 1928 he was also elected as a director of the Glasgow Chamber of Commerce, serving as a member of the Home Affairs and Railway Transport committees. He also represented the Chamber on the Scottish Rating Reform Association. In 1930 he became a member of the Scottish Committee of Investigation under the Coal Mines Act. This committee investigated complaints by coal owners, and others, concerning the operation of the scheme for regulating the production, supply and sale of coal.

Donald Matheson pursued a very busy life both in work and in retirement; he only withdrew from his active involvement for a few months, in ill-health, before his death in 1935. His long career as a distinguished civil engineer, and a successful railway general manager, had made him comfortable rather than wealthy. Of his gross estate of £43,332, over half was in the form of life insurance policies; some £10,000 was held in government stocks, and the remainder was not surprisingly made up of small investments in railway debentures.

ANTHONY SLAVEN

SOURCES

Unpublished

Calendar of Confirmations, 10/2/1936
SRO: SC 36/48/493, Inventory
         SC 36/51/253, Will

Published

The Bailie, 4/7/1906, 1/2/1922
Glasgow Herald, 11/12/1935
The Railway Gazette, 13/12/1935
The Scotsman, 11/12/1935
The Times, 12/12/1935
Stothers, *Glasgow, Lanarkshire and Renfrewshire*, 1917
Who Was Who, 1929-40
Who's Who in Glasgow, 1909

John Erskine PITCAIRN,

Tramway company manager; b. 1850, Glasgow, s. of William Pitcairn, warehouseman and Janet Erskine; m. (1) 22/08/1881, Amelia McGlashen; (2) 18/08/1900, Margaret Ellen Butter; 4 s., 2 d.; d. 1/11/1909, Edinburgh; g/v estate: £1,282 3s 9d.

John Erskine Pitcairn was born in Glasgow and educated at the Freelands School there, and in Edinburgh. He trained on the North British Railway as a traffic superintendent and then moved into the general manager's office. He became general manager of the Edinburgh Street Tramways Company in 1884 and of the Edinburgh and District Tramway Co Ltd from 1893, retaining that office until retiring on a special allowance in 1906. His period as manager coincided with the principal expansion phase of the Edinburgh tramway system, with traffic growing from 10.9 million passengers in 1884 to 51.7 million by 1905.

Quoted as having a bright and genial temperament, he was involved outwith his work as a Justice of the Peace. Golf was a leisure interest and he was a member of the Scottish Liberal Club, the Edinburgh Merchant Company and the Edinburgh Chamber of Commerce.

Edinburgh was unusual in moving from horse to cable trams rather than to electricity. Coming from the North British Railway, which utilised cable traction on the incline out of Queen Street station in Glasgow, Pitcairn had some prior experience of cables but it is unlikely that this was a factor in the adoption of this form of traction in Edinburgh. The steep gradients of Edinburgh's north/south streets and strong objections on amenity grounds to electrical overhead wiring were the predominant considerations influencing the adoption of cable traction.

The Dick Kerr engineering company of Kilmarnock was the prime force in introducing cables to Edinburgh on the streets leading down from the city centre to the Forth at Granton. Dick Kerr formed the Edinburgh Northern Tramway Co in 1884 to construct this cable system while Pitcairn, in the same year, became manager of the entirely horse-based Edinburgh Street Tramway Co.

Like James Duncan in Glasgow, Pitcairn was caught up in the desire for municipalisation. Edinburgh differed from Glasgow in that the original tramway companies owned the track and operated services under a 21 year lease. By 1891, just before expiry of the first lease, Edinburgh Corporation was determined to acquire ownership while continuing with a policy of leased operation.

The old Edinburgh Street Tramway Co failed in its bid to become lessee and the contract went instead to Dick Kerr in October, 1893. It was at this point that Pitcairn transferred from being manager of the Edinburgh Street Tramway Co (which continued to own and operate services in the Burgh of Leith) to become manager of the Edinburgh and District Tramway Co Ltd which had been formed by Dick Kerr to operate the leased system. The Dick Kerr inspired Edinburgh Northern Tramway Co was itself acquired by the Corporation in 1897 and operations absorbed in the Edinburgh and District lease. From now on, the momentum for a general conversion to cable traction increased and Dick Kerr secured the contract for the conversion work in 1896. Protracted negotiations also took place with the Burgh of Leith but these eventually failed in 1904 and led to the introduction there of municipally owned and operated electric trams in 1905.

The planning and implementation of cable conversions on top of the time given to discussions with Leith must have placed a heavy burden on Pitcairn which probably contributed to his early retirement in 1906 and death from heart failure three years later, aged 59.

Pitcairn was highly regarded by staff and directors and he was able to adapt to municipalising pressures in contrast to his fellow manager, James Duncan, in Glasgow. The high costs and poor quality of cable traction became an increasing liability. The whole system was electrified, and the Leith routes incorporated, by the early 1920s. It is questionable, however, whether Pitcairn should be blamed for the choice of cable operation. The precise relationships which he had with Dick Kerr, and with Edinburgh Corporation, remain shadowy but it seems likely that the prime initiators of policies were Dick Kerr and the Corporation with Pitcairn having a subsidiary role. He was a manager rather than an owner-businessman. He had no great personal wealth and all his moveable property was assigned to the Bank of Scotland following his death.

TOM HART

SOURCES

Unpublished

SRO: SC 70/1/496, Inventory
SC 70/4/411, Will

Published

Glasgow Herald, 2 November 1909
Hunter, D L G, *Edinburgh's Transport*, Huddersfield, 1966
Pike, W T, *Edinburgh and the Lothians*, Edinburgh, 1904

Salve Christian Fredrik SALVESEN,

Shipowner; b. 8/3/1827, Mandal, Norway, s. of Thomas Salvesen, shipowner and Johanna Ross; m. 7/7/1853, Amalie Georgine Salome, d. of Gulow Andorsen, ship repairer; 4 s., 3 d.; Prop, Christian Salvesen & Co, Leith; d. 15/1/1911, Leith; g/v estate: £254,417 19s 0d.

Salve Christian Fredrik Salvesen, the eighth child of a family of nine, was born in Mandal, Norway in 1827 and was educated there at his maternal uncle's private school. At 16 he left Norway to gain experience with shipbrokers in Glasgow, working also at his brother Theodor's, Grangemouth shipbroking and shipping agency, before moving on to similar work in Stettin. In 1846 he returned to Mandal and for five years worked in his father's business of timber-exporting and small scale shipowning.

It was also in 1846 that Theodor formed the Leith based partnership of Salvesen & Turnbull with George Vair Turnbull, a local merchant, as an adjunct to the Grangemouth enterprise. A third partner was added in 1848 when J O Lietke took a one-fifth share: as Lietke already operated a shipping agency in Glasgow with W D Bankier, his inclusion gave the partners a foothold in the West of Scotland. As his Grangemouth business prospered, Theodor had less time to devote to the Leith office and in 1851, shortly after his marriage to Amalie Andorsen, daughter of one of Mandal's leading citizens, Christian returned to Scotland to become a manager in the Leith enterprise. Two years later the Leith partnership was dissolved and Theodor financed Christian's entry into a new partnership with Turnbull which traded as Turnbull, Salvesen & Co. Leitke had no financial interest in the firm, but acted as its Glasgow associate until 1867.

Shipbroking provided the bread and butter for Turnbull, Salvesen & Co and Christian worked hard to secure contracts. His languages and commercial knowledge helped, but his major contribution was the hours he spent making the acquaintance of ship's masters in the hope that freights would follow friendship. Agency work was also ensured by taking small shareholdings in vessels, principally sailing boats owned by German and Norwegian firms in the Scandinavian and Baltic ports. Nevertheless, the early years of the new partnership were not profitable and without financial assistance from Theodor and commission work secured through his influence it might have foundered.

From the late 1850s Turnbull, Salvesen & Co ventured successfully into the Scottish-Norwegian trade as coal exporters and timber importers, the former being assisted by Christian's father-in-law in Norway and the latter making use of Turnbull's father-in-law, a Leith timber merchant, and Christian's brother Emil who owned timber mills in Norway. A less successful enterprise was the Paraffin Oil Company of Mandal designed to circumvent James Young's (qv) British patent on the conversion of bituminous coal into mineral oil by shipping the coal to Norway for processing.

In 1865 Theodor died of tuberculosis. At this time he was standing cautioner (guarantor) for a £5,500 cash credit given to Turnbull, Salvesen & Co by the National Bank of Scotland. Additionally he had made substantial personal loans to the firm. Fortunately Theodor had instructed the trustees of his estate to continue such assistance and Christian was able to persuade them to grant an additional loan of £5,000. In 1870 £2,000 was repaid and the rest five years later.

Meantime, following an argument over losses incurred on Australian business introduced by Turnbull's brother, Christian and Turnbull dissolved their partnership in 1872. Now at the age of 45 Christian, as head of Christian Salvesen & Co, was at last commercially independent, free to rise or fall by his own entrepreneurial talent. He did not bring in any partners until 1883 when his eldest sons, Thomas and Fred, each obtained a one-sixth share in the firm. Despite his desire to run a family firm, Christian had no intention of granting his offspring sinecures. Both the elder boys were sent abroad in 1870 to Rostock, the port of registration of many of the vessels in which Christian had a small shareholding. Thomas then proceeded to Stettin, as his father had done before him, and worked as a clerk in a shipbroker's office, finally returning to Leith to occupy a similar position in his father's firm. Fred stayed abroad for three years in Germany and Norway then he too came back to be a clerk with Christian Salvesen & Co. The commercial training of Theodore, Christian's fourth son but the third to enter the firm, was both longer and broader. In 1879 he attended the Commercial Academy at Christiania and graduated from there in 1881, the first non-Norwegian to do so. Then came a couple of years as clerk in the Leith enterprise, followed in late 1883 by work with the shipowning and broking concern of Edward Carr of Hamburg, with which Christian Salvesen & Co had built up considerable business connections. He remained there for two years and then spent a further year in Paris as head clerk with the French chartering agency of Renaud & Battandier. After declining a partnership with Carr he returned to Leith in 1887 and two years later he too became a partner in the family firm. Initially he obtained only a one-eighth interest but in 1891 he was given equality with his brothers. Christian's other son, Edward (later Lord Salvesen) was encouraged to take a law degree and ultimately had a distinguished legal career.

After Christian was joined by his sons the business gradually became more departmentalised. Thomas was responsible for the deep-sea fleet and also super-

vised the firm's investments and securities. Fred attended to most of the short-sea vessels, especially those on the Baltic and Norwegian routes, and from 1890 he was also responsible for the coal export trade. Timber was Theodore's prime responsibility in the early years, but later he was the prime mover in launching the firm into whaling. In 1895 Christian, aged 68, decided to become less involved in management and increased the shares of each of his sons to one-fifth in compensation. Nevertheless he continued to influence policy almost to the day he died on 15 January 1911.

Christian Salvesen & Co became one of the largest shipping agents and shipbrokers in the east of Scotland. It also became one of the leading shipowners as the firm increasingly took full ownership rather than partial shares in vessels: indeed between 1872 and 1910 the partnership held the major share or had sole ownership in 30 merchant vessels. Although Christian made some innovations such as the introduction of a cargo liner service to Norway, his shipping policy was essentially conservative and concentrated upon the fields initially established by Turnbull & Salvesen, coal exports, timber imports and the Scandinavian trade in general. Nevertheless these were expanded significantly as witness the coal trade which increased from an annual average of 53,600 tons exported in the 1870s to 195,100 in the 1900s. The Salvesen fleet reflected Christian's conservatism in shipping matters; new vessels were rarely purchased and in 1911 the average age of the 16 ships was 24.4 years. One reason for the relative lack of modernisation was that many of the vessels had guaranteed cargoes from other Salvesen enterprises for Christian diversified into a variety of activities, predominantly in Scandinavia, including timber mills, coal mines, a tourist hotel, and above all, whaling.

From the mid-1860s Christian had been involved in selling marine oil, initially this was mainly herring and seal oil but soon sales were dominated by whale oil from several of the leading Norwegian whaling companies. The agency work made Christian aware of the profit potential of the industry, but he was reluctant to enter whaling as a principal as he feared, rightly as it turned out, that it would lead to the loss of commission work from existing participants. It was pressure from Theodore, eager to find an outlet for his commercial energies, which eventually caused Christian to relent. After some initial failures, due mainly to declining stocks, successful enterprises were established in Iceland and in the Shetlands. In 1907 the focus of the company's whaling activities was switched south to the Falklands and two years later the South Georgia Co was set up to exploit the whaling stocks around that island and later in the Antarctic. By 1911 Salvesen was the largest whaling group in the world with a catch of 2,350 whales and an oil production of 66,510 barrels.

Until late in his life Christian took little part in

public work. In 1859 he did become Hanoverian Vice-Consul in Leith, but this brought benefits to his firm through contracts with German ship's masters seeking return cargoes. In the mid-1880s, when Christian Salvesen & Co was well established, he accepted a term as chairman of the Leith Chamber of Commerce and also served on the Leith Dock Commission.

Although Christian had become a naturalised Briton in 1859, Norway remained dear to his heart. Young men from his homeland were often given employment; he was one of the founders of the Scandinavian Lutheran Church for Seamen in Leith; and he contributed generously to many Norwegian charities. For this he was awarded the Order of Knight Bachelor of St Olav, First Class in 1891.

WRAY VAMPLEW

SOURCES

Unpublished

Edinburgh University Business Archives: Records of Christian Salvesen & Co (uncatalogued)
SRO: SC 70/1/517, Inventory
SC 74/4/429, Will

Published

Andorsen, H F, *Memoirs of Lord Salvesen,* Edinburgh, 1949
Leith Observer, 21/1/1911
Neilsen, A W, *Mandals Sjofartshistone, fra 1850,* Oslo, 1941
Salvesen, J, *Siekten Salvesen,* Oslo, 1930
Salvesen, T E, 'The Whaling Industry of Today', *Journal of the Royal Society of Arts,* 29/3/1912
The Scotsman, 16/1/1911
The Times, 18/1/1911
Tonnessen, J N, *Den Modern Hvalfangsts Histories,* Sandefjord, 1967
Vamplew, W, 'The Paraffin Factory at Mandal: A Study in Business Enterprise', *Scandinavian Economic History Review,* 1970
Vamplew, W, *Salvesen of Leith,* Edinburgh, 1975

James SHEARER,

Shipowner; b. 21/1/1877, Gourock, s. of Thomas Shearer, coal merchant and Christina Thom; m. Katherine Adam, d. of James Shearer, Shipowner; 1 s., 1 d.; MD Lyle Shipping Co; d. 29/12/1964, Glasgow; g/v UK estate: £37,233 11s 0d.

James Shearer Jnr was a noted shipowner and ship manager, spending most of his career with the Lyle Shipping Co Ltd of Glasgow. Born at Royal Street, Gourock in 1877, he was the son of Thomas Shearer, a coal merchant and formerly master mariner, and Christina Shearer (nee Thom) who had been a domestic servant at the time of her marriage in 1870.

Few details of James Shearer's education are known. He attended Greenock Academy and his formal education probably ceased on leaving that institution. His business career began in the Greenock office of Thomas Skinner & Co, shipbrokers of London, Glasgow and Greenock, and he later moved into ship management with the Clyde Shipping Co, where he was employed for about ten years. Subsequently he joined Bell Brothers, a Glasgow company operating ten ships in the River Plate and South American trades.

He joined Lyle Shipping Co in 1913 at the age of 35 as assistant manager and in 1918 married Katherine, daughter of James Shearer Snr, a second cousin, the company's manager and an important minority shareholder. Lyle Shipping had operated at Greenock for over a century and moved to Glasgow in 1906. It was then a private company controlled mainly by the Lyle and Macfarlane families. The former were founders of the famous sugar refining business which had transferred from Greenock to London in 1881. Shortly afterwards the shipping business became a quite separate entity.

Shearer was appointed to the Lyle Board as managing director in 1925 on the retirement of James Shearer Snr then his father-in-law, and remained with the company for the rest of his life. Lyle Shipping was little different from a score of other West of Scotland tramp shipping concerns. In 1919 its paid up share capital was £250,000 when it owned just two ships totalling 8,768 tons, having suffered heavy losses during the First World War. However, it also had very considerable cash resources as a result of government compensation for war losses. James Shearer masterminded his company's expansion in the inter war years so that in 1939 it owned six ships and either joint owned or managed a further four, in all totalling 43,318 tons.

This expansion took place against a steady decline in freight rates and shipping company profits when many similar companies failed to survive. Expansion was achieved despite the operation of old or middle aged tonnage, often purchased second hand and not to modern design. Shearer's success supports the basic importance of sound financial management, tight cost controls, high motivation and close supervision of ship captains and managers, and a sound knowledge of ship and freight markets.

Lyle directors were largely non executive so Shearer dominated day to day decision making while at board level he was the key architect in formulating policies. The strength of his personality meant he was feared and respected in equal quantities and his stream of telegrams and letters to ship captains kept them on their toes even if on the other side of the globe. His penetrating inquests into even the smallest items of expenditure he regarded as unnecessary, were legendary. He was a proficient shorthand writer and made a record of almost every telephone conversation.

His opportunist purchase of four modern steamers in 1934 which would have cost almost half as much again a year later, and his early recognition of the importance of long term charters which had meant that most of the Lyle fleet was at work even in the darkest days of the slump, speak for his abilities. But Shearer benefited greatly from his friendship with Sir James (qv) and Henry Lithgow who controlled an empire of well run shipyards and heavy engineering plants in the West of Scotland. Mutual confidence caused Lyle to order all their ships from Lithgow yards during Shearer's management, and the Lithgows reciprocated by providing finance by way of loans, by taking an equity interest with Lyles in single ship companies - a device used to share the risk in acquiring the fleet's first motorship in 1924 - and by placing under Lyle management speculatively built ships for which owners could not be found. This association reflects the web of connections between members of the West of Scotland business community of the time.

In 1953 Lyle Shipping was floated as a public company but with the Lyle, Macfarlane and Shearer families retaining control, holding 328,440, 240,880 and 74,200 ordinary shares respectively. By 1953 the fleet totalled some 13 trampships with two other ships under management. Shearer masterminded this expansion by ordering new tonnage to replace war losses and by acquiring war built tonnage often at bargain prices. The task was facilitated by buoyant freight rates which would have permitted greater expansion but Shearer had probably been less cautious than many other British shipowners. Expansion had also been helped by the continuing association with the Lithgow brothers.

In the 1950s radical changes were taking place in the character of the freight market and in ship design. Further conventional tonnage was ordered in 1953 when overseas owners were benefiting from operating ships with engines and superstructure in the stern. More tonnage of the old type was ordered in 1956, although Shearer was apparently quick to see in 1956-57 the advantages of ordering three ore carriers of modern design for long term charter. These enabled the company's survival in the early 1960s.

The fall in freight rates in the late 1950s put the company's profits under considerable pressure, especially as several of the modern ships had not proved successful to operate. The company experienced great difficulties until new ships and improved trading conditions restored prosperity in the mid-1960s.

Dogged by ill health, Shearer retired as managing director in 1958 at the age of 78, although he remained a director until shortly before his death in 1964. Until his retirement he had continued in firm control of the company.

From 1912 Shearer devoted the whole of his business career to Lyle except for two years, 1917 and 1918, when he was seconded to the Ministry of Shipping in London where he headed a department concerned with the operation of ships controlled by the Government. He was awarded an OBE for this work. He held a number of appointments with the Chamber of Shipping, culminating in the presidency of the Deep Sea Tramp Section and the offer of the Chamber's vice presidency in 1942 (with a view to becoming president a year later) which he declined. For ten years he was chairman of the Glasgow Committee of Lloyds Register of Shipping. He was especially concerned with the welfare of seamen through his support of the Glasgow Seaman's Friendly Society.

On his death in 1964 he was survived by his wife, daughter and son, who was a director of Lyle. He left estate of £37,233 0s 11d.

JOHN ORBELL

SOURCES

Unpublished

Inventory, Lodged 12/2/1965, Glasgow Sheriff Court
Will, Lodged 16/1/1965, Vol 494, Edinburgh Sheriff Court

Published

Crowdy, M, *Lyle Shipping Co Ltd 1827-1966*, Kendal, 1966
Glasgow Herald, 30/12/1964
Orbell, M J, *From Cape to Cape: A History of Lyle Shipping Company*, Edinburgh, 1978

John SWORD,

Motor engineer; b. 1892, Airdrie, s. of William Sword; m. 1918/19, Christina, d. of James Taylor, master baker; 4s., 1d., MD, Western SMT Co Ltd; d. 27/3/1960, Prestwick.

John Sword left school at the age of 14 with an insatiable capacity for hard work and a determination to make good, although he later claimed that he had burned his school books on his birthday to avoid being sent back to school. His first employment was in the Airdrie business of his father who was a master baker. In the 1914-18 war he enlisted into the Royal Flying Corps where he served as a mechanic in the department providing road transport for the infant branch of the army which subsequently became the RAF.

It was his service in the RFC/RAF that stimulated a love for machinery and flying. After the war he set up business as a motor engineer and haulier with one vehicle. Using former military vehicles to transport the products of the nuts and bolts side of engineering which was centred on Airdrie, to Glasgow where he collected flour for the family bakeries for the return journey, the business quickly expanded.

In the early 1920s, he extended his activities to bus operation between Airdrie and Glasgow and later onto Paisley, eventually in 1924 forming Midland Bus Services Ltd of Airdrie. Over the ensuing five years, the company grew considerably under his leadership in which he exercised drive, imagination and total dedication. Some competing bus companies were acquired, thus extending the areas of influence into Ayrshire and Renfrewshire while innovative new services were introduced including express coach services from Glasgow to Blackpool in 1927 and to London in 1928. At the same time, there were some agreements on sharing traffic on Scottish routes with competitors, in particular William Thomson's Edinburgh-based Scottish Motor Traction, Alexander & Sons (qv W Alexander) of Falkirk and R B Dick's Glasgow General Omnibus.

Sword was fiercely proud of his company's independence but when the railways obtained road powers in 1928 and the government proposed to introduce quantity licensing, he helped to persuade Dick of Glasgow General Omnibus and Alexander to agree to Thomson's proposals for a merger of the groups. The exact sequence of events is not clear but before there could be a merger, the London, Midland & Scottish Railway Company and London & North Eastern Railway Company secured control of SMT. Sword may not have welcomed the intrusion of the railways but he remained pragmatic and in December 1929 agreed to sell his company to the re-constituted SMT - the alternative could have been direct involvement in the bus industry by the railways. The negotiations were complicated by the presence in Scotland of bus interests of the British Electric Traction Company.

Following agreement with BET, SMT acquired control in November 1931 of its Scottish General Transport bus group; and on 1 April 1932 Sword's Midland Bus Company was vested in Scottish General Transport. In return Sword received 250,000 shares of £1 each. In June 1932 the combined company was re-named Western SMT Co Ltd with Sword as the managing director at a head office in Kilmarnock, although the registered office was in London on account of SGT's origin.

The SMT combine was interesting in that both Western SMT and Central SMT were allowed to function with the minimum of control by Edinburgh which was the head office of the group. At the same time, any major expansion or change of policy would have to be sanctioned by the railways whose nominees now sat on both SMT in Edinburgh and on the Western and Central companies. Sword also sat on the main board of SMT and on the Central and Alexander subsidiaries as did Thomson, Dick and Alexander.

Nevertheless, the railways did not attempt to reduce the activities of the company and under Sword's leadership it had by the late 1930s, a fleet of 495 vehicles operating on 67 routes in the South West of Scotland plus some long-distance coach services and various excursions and tours.

In the year Western SMT company was formed, there was no dividend for the shareholder but 5% was paid in 1933 and 10% in 1936. Bus and coach operations were by no means his only business activity and during the early 1930s, he purchased a potato crisp business in Manchester and opened a second factory (Crimpy Crisps) in Airdrie, thereby becoming one of the biggest employers in the town. This action could not be described as a sound business investment in that Sword thought that once one had a potato field and factory, the course was easy. Sword may also have been motivated by a desire to help the economy of his home town. In the event, the crisp business was always a loss-maker, although he started another factory near Reading after the 1939-45 war. Both factories were managed by Sword's sons, the Airdrie operation coming to an end in a disastrous fire. Another post-war diversification was the restaurant business of Skinner's of Glasgow.

Sword's farming activities were also loss-making and his ownership of five farms in the Irvine district of Ayrshire was only because of his love of horses, at one time owning over 200. On one farm he bred hackneys and on another Arabian horses, although there was dairy activity on three of them. During the early 1950s he became president of the British Hackney Association. He also built up an extensive collection of saddlery.

Sword also became the first director outside of Edinburgh on the board of the Scottish Amicable Building Society in whose development he played a full part. But it was in air transport that John Sword had the greatest opportunities and, through no fault of his own, the greatest disappointments. It was his military service in the RFC/RAF in the Great War that left him with a desire to enter air transport but civil aviation did not have suitable aircraft for scheduled services in the 1920s. The appearance of more economic and efficient aircraft and the greater availability of aerodromes in the late 1920s stimulated interest in scheduled services in the early 1930s. Exactly what awoke Sword's latent interest is not clear but it is believed that he formulated ideas on operating air services early in 1931. In 1932 he carried out exploratory investigations into routes and reconnoitred suitable landing fields in Scotland. One of these landing fields was later to be better known as Prestwick International Airport. It is believed his surveys were undertaken in a hired Puss Moth aircraft.

In the meantime, SMT itself had in the summer of 1932 entered civil aviation with the purchase of two small aircraft which were subsequently used to offer joy rides on the sands at Ayr and elsewhere. The motive of SMT in entering air transport at the very time that Sword was about to enter the industry is not entirely clear but it did not inhibit Sword who at the end of 1932 purchased a ten seat Airspeed Ferry aircraft. On 20 February 1933, Sword inaugurated his first air service in the name of the yet to be incorporated Midland & Scottish Air Ferries. This service was not itself in Scotland; it operated from Hooton in Cheshire to Castle Bromwich near Birmingham in connection with the British Industries Fair in the city. A connecting service was also provided between Hooton and Liverpool's new airport at Speke across the Mersey but it was only for the duration of the week-long exhibition. The new aircraft was purchased from the manufacturer in part exchange for a Bentley car! The second aircraft, a Fox Moth, was similarly purchased from a retailer. Sword subsequently purchased additional aircraft.

One of Sword's plans was for a service from Liverpool to Dublin and he arranged representation in Ireland to liaise with the authorities but the politics of Irish economic nationalism proved difficult to penetrate. In the meantime, Sword registered on 10 March 1933 a private company in Edinburgh. This was called Midland & Scottish Air Ferries Ltd with a nominal capital of £20,000 in £1 shares. It was based at Renfrew Aerodrome. Sword and his wife were the sole subscribers. More aircraft were ordered, all new and of a high proven standard. The chairman of SMT, William Thomson (qv) reacted by trying to dissuade Sword from developing his airline. Unsuccessful, Thomson ordered aircraft without his board's authority while Sword, at the beginning of June, opened scheduled services from Glasgow to Islay and to Belfast. Irish politics continued to frustrate Sword's Dublin plans until August when he struck out without official approval with a service between Liverpool and Dublin. The Dublin service was not particularly successful and only lasted about six weeks but the following April Sword opened a service between

London and Liverpool with linking services to the Isle of Man and to Belfast. This proved to be the final straw for the LMS board which was developing its own air services. Sword was forced to agree to dispose of his airline interests by the end of September. The agreement also stipulated that if Sword sold the airline, the name Midland & Scottish Air Ferries would not be part of the sale.

It was a bitter pill for Sword to swallow but swallow it he did. It was partially sweetened by a compensatory payment of £13,312 10s which was paid to Sword by Western SMT. These events more than anything else embittered Sword towards the LMS railway, in particular its chairman Sir Josiah Stamp whom he personally blamed - he always described Stamp's action as something honourable people did not do. Sword could of course have declined to withdraw but the railways would almost certainly have forced his withdrawal from SMT, an action which could not have appealed to him after losing a lot of money on his airline.

The agreement to withdraw from his airline also covered Sword's subsequent relationship with Western SMT. From 1 October 1933 until 30 September 1939, he was to receive a salary of £2,000 per annum payable monthly in arrears and commission at a rate of 10% of the share capital of the company ranking for dividend in the year in which the commission fund was being ascertained. Sword was also to remain the proprietor of the 53,250 shares which were registered in his name; and he was to receive interest at the rate of 5% per annum on this £53,250 until 1939. Thereafter he was to draw the dividends on his shareholding as long as he retained it.

The railways maintained that Sword was neglecting his duties as manager of Western SMT as long as he was managing his airline. Certainly he could not have concentrated all his energies into managing Western SMT when a lot of his time was taken up with airline policy which sometimes took him to Ireland. At the same time, it is doubtful if the direction of Western SMT suffered in this period as Sword was very dedicated and hard working. When the railways were nationalised in 1947, SMT and it subsidiaries also became state-owned. After piloting the change of ownership, he relinquished the position of General Manager to concentrate his activities as a director of the new Scottish Omnibuses.

As a leader of a business, Sword was ideal. He was able to delegate authority as with his airline while at the same time closely follow the course of the business. He was also able to develop influential contacts. Thus he became very friendly with the Air Minister, Lord Londonderry, during the period of his airline, sometimes flying him from London to his Northern Ireland home at the weekends. He also carried the Prime Minister, Ramsay MacDonald, on at least two occasions. Both the Air Minister and Prime Minister were present at the ceremony in Liverpool to launch the scheduled services between London and Belfast in April 1934. But as one of the obituaries recorded, he could 'walk with kings, nor lose the common touch'.

Sword's love of motoring led him to collecting veteran cars and at his farm near Irvine he assembled more than 250 vehicles. He also had a collection of over 200 clocks, model railway locomotives and was interested in pictorial art and fine furniture. In December 1951, he received the freedom of Airdrie. Towards the end of 1957 he opened an art exhibition of paintings from his own collection at Airdrie library. In the post-war period, he also took up sailing in the waters off south-west Scotland. In religion he was a Presbyterian, although he does not appear to have been active in the life of the church beyond the course of regular worship. He died on 27 March 1960, his funeral taking place at St Cuthbert's Parish Church, Prestwick.

JOHN KING

SOURCES

Unpublished

Correspondence and interview with William Sword
Department of Industry & Commerce and Railway records in PRO, Dublin
Railway and Air Ministry records in the PRO, London
Railway and Londonderry private records in the PRO of Northern Ireland, Belfast
Railway records in the Scottish Record Office, Edinburgh

Published

MacDonald, Neil, *The Western Way*, 1983
Motor Transport Year Book, 1937-8
The Scotsman, 28/3/1960

Sir James THOMPSON,

Railway manager; b. 1/3/1835, Kirtlebridge, Dumfriesshire, s. of Robert Thompson, contractor (goods carrier) and Jean Hope Burgess; m. 20/12/1865, Christina Robertson, d. of Captain James Adams, shipowner; 1 s., 3 d.; Ch, Caledonian Railway; d. 8/6/1906, Glasgow; g/v estate: £136,832 0s 3d.

James Thompson's 59 year working life was spent entirely in the service of the Caledonian Railway Company. Starting at the age of 12 in the lowest levels of the goods department, he rose to become the most distinguished Scottish railway manager of the late nineteenth century. Retiring at the age of 65, he was taken on to the board; within 18 months he was chairman of the company, a position he held until his death.

He was born in Kirtlebridge, Dumfriesshire, on 1 March 1835, the eldest child and only son of Robert and Jane Burgess Thompson. His father, variously described as a goods carrier or a coach operator, soon moved to Carlisle, where James was first educated at the Academy and then joined the Caledonian. In 1849, a year or so after the main line opened, he moved to Glasgow as a junior clerk in the goods department on an annual salary of £20. In 1856 he was selected by general goods manager William Mathieson as his chief clerk. Preferment continued to arrive at steady intervals. In 1865 he was made goods manager of the company's eastern district, with a salary of £250 plus a £50 bonus for every percentage point by which the ordinary dividend exceeded 5%. In the same year he married Christina Adams, ten years his junior and daughter of a Greenock shipowner.

At the start of 1867 he was moved to the goods managership of the southern and western division, a more important post rewarded by a salary of £350 and the same possibilities of bonus, and a mere seven months later by a rise of £150. In 1870, on Mathieson's retirement, he succeeded to the post of general goods manager on £700, still with the chance of bonuses. Clearly the board were well satisfied with his work, since his salary was increased by £100 in each of the next three years, and by £200 in 1877. The bonus provisions were not mentioned after 1873; if they were in fact dropped, it was unfortunate for Thompson that the years from 1875 to 1877 were the only period during his entire service with the company in which the dividend reached 6%.

Thompson's 12 years as general goods manager were in many ways a time of consolidation and steady prosperity for the Caledonian. The major acquisitions of the mid-1860s, when the Caledonian had taken over the Scottish Central, the Scottish North-Eastern, the Dundee & Perth, and the Forth & Clyde Canal, and had sponsored the technically independent Callander & Oban, were now integrated into the network. Continuing expansion was reflected in the capital account - the issued capital of £21,977,934 in 1870 became £37,158,115 by 1882. The major project of the period was the creation of Central Station in Glasgow with its associated bridge across the Clyde; since this was an attempt, even if not an adequate one, to solve the horrendous problem of Glasgow passenger traffic, it was not a scheme on which Thompson would have had much influence. But the goods department dealt with the greater part of Caledonian traffic. In Thompson's first three years as general goods manager, the department's receipts averaged £1,269,879 per year; they rose to a peak of £1,854,604 in 1877, and then fell back with the general recession to average £1,676,132 in 1879-81. From 1872 on, this represented each year between 62% and 64% of total Caledonian income on current account. To the company, the comprehensive pattern of lines with which it battled for the mineral and industrial traffic of Glasgow and Lanarkshire was as important as the more glamorous new routes to the north.

In 1882 James Smithells, the general manager since 1868, retired through ill-health, and Thompson was the obvious internal candidate to succeed him. The Caledonian tended to like internal candidates; Thompson himself was to remark with approval in 1897 that all the senior officers of the company had worked their way up through its ranks. He joined a group at the top of the company which included three men - the engineer George Graham, the secretary Archibald Gibson and the treasurer Alexander Ferguson - who had held their posts since 1852 or 1853. Even so, for the next 18 years Thompson was the principal, and often the controlling, influence on Caledonian affairs. Apart from his executive role in command of the management structure, he frequently initiated policies which in most companies would have come first from the directors. In particular, he was largely responsible for a policy of aggressive expansion of the network, often through theoretically independent subsidiary companies.

Aggression was nothing new in Scottish railway politics, where inter-company relations often resembled semi-controlled warfare, with occasional truces to allow both sides to recover from severe mutual damage. The Caledonian had been expansionist from the start; even before its original act of authorisation, it was planning (but failing to build) a subsidiary from Ayr to Berwick, straight across the territory of its two major rivals. The North British (which from 1865 included the Edinburgh & Glasgow) and the Glasgow & South-Western kept a wary eye on Caledonian ambitions, and occasionally made common cause against them. A few examples of the policies pursued by Thompson and the Caledonian board indicate their need to be watchful.

Ardrossan, the main port for the southern Firth of Clyde, was firmly in Glasgow & South-Western hands. However, much of the coal shipped through it from the 84 pits of the Hamilton area started its journey on Caledonian rails. In 1884 the Caledonian sponsored the Lanarkshire & Ayrshire project to run from the jointly owned Glasgow, Barrhead & Kilmarnock line through the South-Western heartland to a new pier at Ardrossan; it was also to send out branches to such South-Western strongholds as Irvine, the Nobel factory at Stevenston and the ironworks at Glengarnock. That the project passed parliament may have owed much to Thompson's noted skills as a witness before committees. Help came from numerous industrial interests in Ayrshire, who were not so much discontented with the South-Western as hopeful that they could only gain from railway competition; 560 traders and industrialists in Ayr unsuccessfully petitioned the company for a branch, promising to use it for at least half of their trade for ten years.

The Caledonian had long had access to Greenock, and from 1865 a subsidiary ran to Wemyss Bay, but it had shown little interest in Clyde shipping. The Glasgow and South-Western, with a better placed pier at Greenock and one at Ardrossan, had made arrangements with those steamer owners who were prepared to co-operate with the railways; the North British ran its own boats out of Helensburgh or Craigendoran. Access to Ardrossan, and the opening in 1890 of a branch to Gourock (where the company had bought the pier in 1869 in the hope of being allowed to create a terminal for ocean-going vessels) brought the Caledonian into the Clyde steamer business. Refused permission to run their own boats (which was embarrassing since they had already purchased a couple), and unable to find independent owners who would co-operate with them, they started the Caledonian Steam Packet Company under some of the railway directors in 1889. Six years of intense competition and ridiculous price cutting followed until an exhausted peace ensued.

On the north bank of the Clyde, Caledonian access was limited to running powers on the North British branch to Stobcross docks. In 1891 the company supported the Lanarkshire & Dunbartonshire project, whose board also included three prominent shipbuilders in John Denny, James Thomson and Sir Andrew McLean. The railway hugged the river, between the North British line to Helensburgh and the shipyards, with branches into such works as Yarrows and Beardmores (though the North British had managed to sign a monopoly agreement with the biggest prize, Singers). The Caledonian also managed to force the North British to accept joint management (though total lack of co-operation) on the line between Dumbarton and Loch Lomond. Having achieved what he wanted, Thompson announced in 1893 a peace agreement with the North British 'to take the bitter edge off the rivalry between the companies .... Surely, after all our strife it will be of most advantage to the public in the long run if each company is allowed to devote its energies to the cultivation and development of the traffic and resources of its own particular district'.

The schemes of expansion with which Thompson was most closely associated were in Glasgow. The Cathcart District railway, authorised in two sections by acts of 1880 and 1887 and finally opened throughout in 1894, supplied suburban services for the south side of the city. According to the chairman, Thompson had 'over and over again expressed his belief that there was a great future for this railway', and had given the crucial evidence before the House of Lords select committee on the bill. The Glasgow Central line, authorised in 1888, formally merged with the

Caledonian in 1890, and open in 1896, was according to Caledonian chairman James C. Bunten almost entirely Thompson's project. The line connected a Caledonian branch at Dalmarnock to the Lanarkshire & Dunbartonshire at Maryhill, passing through the city centre and Central Station (Low Level) in a 6.25 mile tunnel which was a major feat of cut-and-cover engineering. In 1893 Thompson noted that the work was providing up to 4,000 jobs and about £20,000 of wages per month, at a time of economic depression, and that Glasgow was also getting a new main sewer at Caledonian expense. When both lines were open, there were 89 trains per day on the Cathcart circle, and 260 passing through the Low Level station. Unfortunately, both found it difficult to compete with the municipally-owned horse trams, and faced stiffer competition when the trams were electrified from 1898.

'The Caledonian', according to the not unprejudiced *Bailie* in 1882, 'is new, eager and daring, the North British is old and safe'. At times perhaps the Caledonian was too daring; in 1900 the dividend, which in the mid-1890s seemed to have stabilised at 5%, dipped below 4%, and it only reached 5% again in one half-year during the remainder of Thompson's life. Part of the problem was the extra costs and inadequate returns of the Glasgow lines; part was the necessary rebuilding and expansion of Central Station which took place during Thompson's chairmanship from 1901 to 1905. Increased working expenditure, which rose above 50% of gross revenue for the first time since 1872, was largely due to the rising cost of coal. In 1901 the *Railway Times* reported that 'the Caledonian has been making strenuous efforts to introduce economy in working. The staff has been reduced where possible, and train mileage has been cut down'.

Caledonian enterprise was shown in improved customer facilities. Thompson pioneered third class bookings on all trains, and cheap return fares at 1.25 times the single rate. Cheap tours had been organised from the early 1870s on the initiative of Robert Currer, passenger superintendent of the company's southern division; by 1887 they went as far afield as Torquay, Scarborough and Ireland. The Caledonian introduced workmen's fares to Scotland; for first class passengers it started dining cars in 1892, later extending the facility to all passengers. Services were speeded up and rolling stock improved, particularly after the appointment of Dugald Drummond as locomotive superintendent in 1882. The abolition of the second class, following the example set by the Midland, was an acceptance of reality: as company chairman J C Bolton noted in 1882, 'the vexed question of whether it is desirable to supply second class accommodation seems likely to be soon solved by the public ceasing to use it'.

Appropriately for a man who had worked his way up through the goods department, Thompson was recognised as probably the finest exponent in Britain of the difficult art of adjusting rates. The legislation of 1888 and 1894 created enormous rating difficulties for railway managers; as Thompson noted in 1893, two-thirds of Scottish traffic was being carried at exceptional rates, and the Caledonian itself had 15,000,000 separate rates to calculate. His skills were recognised when he was called as a key witness to the select committee on railway rates and charges, and again in 1892 when the Conference of General Managers, meeting to consider the Clearing House rules, chose him as their president. By this time Thompson was a national figure who 'largely influenced railway policy throughout the three kingdoms'. In particular he was a first-class parliamentary witness, being reputedly the only man in Scotland who could stand up to John Walker of the North British; after Walker's death in 1891 he was himself without rival. 'Of railways and railway management', said *The Times*, 'Sir James Thompson's knowledge was perhaps unrivalled, and in the promotion before Parliamentary committees of successive schemes of extension his opinion carried great weight'.

His skills as a witness were required before the 1894 Royal Commission on Labour, which spent some time considering the Caledonian strike of 1890-91. As in an earlier strike in 1883, the main demand had been for recognition of the Amalgamated Society of Railway Servants, coupled on this occasion with a campaign for a ten hour day. Thompson was not sympathetic to either demand. Perhaps remembering the 16-hour day which he had worked at the start of his own career, 'the witness did not consider 11.5 hours an excessive day's work for six days a week' - besides which, he claimed, what the men really wanted was extra overtime. Neither union recognition nor any form of outside arbitration were acceptable: 'it is very necessary that the men who work on a railway should know that they are there to obey orders, and have no appeal from them to an outsider'. Within these criteria, however, Thompson was a benevolent disciplinarian, always willing to discuss difficulties with the employees (if not with their union) and generally given credit by them for attempting to look after their interests as well as those of the shareholders. The strikers of 1891 were almost all re-employed without penalty, and drivers of mineral trains even got their ten hour day. Caledonian employment remained popular; Thompson claimed that there were five applications for every vacancy, though the union did not believe him.

Thompson's leading role in railway management was recognised with a knighthood in the diamond jubilee honours of 1897 - the first Scottish railway manager to be thus honoured. The occasion produced the inevitable outpourings of unstinted praise; as a sample, William Patrick, his assistant general manager and eventual successor, stated on behalf of the staff that Thompson 'had enjoyed the confidence and respect of all the workers. He had gained for the company the reputation of being one of the best equipped and best managed railways in the world'. At least it was not obviously untrue, and tributes to Thompson's straightforwardness and probity came from quarters which had nothing to gain from flattery. Other honours followed. His knighthood was upgraded in 1904 to KCSI. In 1898 a 'large body of subscribers' presented him with his portrait by Sir John Watson, and a further presentation from the Clearing House and the Conference of General Managers came in 1900. In 1900 also, he was invited by Lord Roberts to serve on the South African Hospitals Committee, but declined for health reasons. He was a Justice of the Peace and Deputy Lieutenant for Glasgow and Lanarkshire.

In 1900 Thompson retired as general manager. His value to the company had been recognised by regular salary increases; the initial £2,000 of 1882 had been increased by £500 in each of the next two years and again in 1888 and 1890, to reach £4,000. During his term of office the issued capital of the company had risen from £37,158,115 to £47,750,512 and the annual gross revenue from £2,791,524 to £4,210,858; dividends throughout had almost always been 4% or 5%. On his retirement he was almost immediately elected to fill a casual vacancy of the board, while also being paid £1,500 per year, officially for consultancy services - an arrangement which lasted until his death. When Bunten died in 1901, Thompson became chairman of the company; he also occupied the chairs of two associated railways, the Callander & Oban and the Cathcart District. Outside railways, he was also a director of James Dunlop & Company. On 8 June 1906 he died at his Kelvingrove home from bladder cancer.

Apart from his work for the railway, Thompson's life centred on his family; his leisure time was spent as far as possible in family company at his country house, Inverardoch, Doune. His wife outlived him by 25 years. Of his five children, the only boy died six hours after his premature birth without being christened, and one daughter also died in childhood. The other three daughters married into the industrial and commercial world, to a London merchant, a Glasgow ironmaster and a Glasgow distiller. In private life Thompson was a sociable man, with 'a fund of pawky Scotch humour'. His devotion to the work of Robert Burns extended beyond massive and accurate quotation to arranging for the free carriage of the poet's statue to be set up in George Square, Glasgow. In politics he was Conservative, though he took no active role. His personal estate was valued at £136,832, mainly consisting of shares (£86,410) and debts due (£38,348); of the shares, £44,632 was in railways, led by a holding in the Caledonian of nominal value £30,389, though of actual value only £19,788. Other significant holdings included, not surprisingly, the Callander & Oban and the Lanarkshire & Dunbartonshire; more adventurously, the Grand Trunk

of Canada and the Chinese Imperial; and rather remarkably the North British. Apart from annuities for his sisters and a few other very small bequests, the estate was left to his wife and daughters.

Thompson became general manager of the Caledonian when, although strong, it was engaged in ferocious and apparently equal competition with its major rivals. He left it the clear leader in the Scottish railway world. And, as the *Scotsman* obituarist noted, he had been 'the architect of his own career, which was a brilliant example of what may be achieved by intelligence linked to integrity and perseverance, even with the handicap of no initial worldy advantages'.

C J ALAN ROBERTSON

SOURCES

Unpublished

Royal Commission on Labour, pp 1893-4, c6894-[XI] XXXII, evidence
SRO: BR/RAC(S)/1/4,1/93, Caledonian reports and accounts
BR/CAL/1/22, Caledonian minutes
BR/HRP(S)/51, Caledonian scrapbook
BR/SPC/6, Cuttings on Sir James Thompson
BR/GSW/4/7, Miscellaneous scrapbook
CEN 1861-91, Census records
SC 36/48/200, Inventory
SC 36/51/141, Will

Published

The Bailie, No 487, 15/2/1882; 20/7/1887; No 1289, 30/6/1897
Biographical Notices, Glasgow Men, Vol XVI
Glasgow Herald, 21/1/1893, 13/6/1897, 1/10/1897, 9/6/1906
Glasgow & Lanarkshire Illustrated, 1904
MacArthur, I C, *The Caledonian Steam Packet Co Ltd*, Glasgow, 1971
Nock, O S, *The Caledonian Railway*, London, 1961
Railway Times, 30/9/1882, 9/2/1907, 12/6/1906
The Scotsman, 9/6/1906, 9/6/1909
Thomas, J, *Regional History of the Railways of Great Britain, VII: Scotland, the Lowlands and Borders*, Newton Abbot, 1971
The Times, 9/6/1906
Who Was Who

William THOMSON,

Shipowner; b. 15/8/1839, Leith, Edinburgh; s. of William Thomson, shipowner and Sarah Wishart; m. 2/10/1883, Katherine, d. of Duncan Macnab, Free Church Minister; 6 s., 2 d.; Partner, William Thomson & Co; d. 27/11/1911, Edinburgh; g/v estate: £316,443 14s. 5d.

There is an unavoidable artificiality in selecting one member of the large Thomson family for such a biography as this. Important in business around the Forth from at least the later part of the eighteenth century, the family is still well known today as one of the leading contributors to the commercial life of Britain and the world.

The earliest record of a Thomson in business in Leith, identifies James Thomson, grandfather of William, as a builder. If he is the founder of the dynasty, it was his son William, father of the present subject, who founded the firm which bears his name, William Thomson and Company, the partnership which for almost 150 years controlled the merchant fleet of the Ben Line Steamers Ltd.

William Thomson II founded neither the dynasty nor the business. He was given one third of the business by his father in 1860 on attaining his 21st birthday, as was his brother James two years later. Until his father's retirement in 1875, he was a junior partner, and subsequently for many years shared the direction of the partnership with his brother.

He was not visibly responsible for any striking technological innovation. The company acquired its first steamship in 1870 whilst William I was the senior partner, but noticeably then purchased four more sailing vessels until the brothers assumed sole control.

During the period for which William and James were responsible, the fleet changed over entirely to steam, the Canadian timber trade was dropped, a new trade was opened to the Baltic, which lasted until the Russian revolution, and the main part of the company's business became concentrated where it remains today, in the provision of a high quality, fast cargo liner service beween Western Europe and the Far East.

Perhaps the most notable sign of development was the growth of the fleet during William Thomson's time in management from five wooden vessels totalling 4,359 grt to 12 triple expansion engined steel ships measuring 46,975 tons, as well as five steamers in the Baltic fleet of altogether some 10,000 tons.

As a measure of expansion of the enterprise, however, even this record is not especially dramatic when compared with the development of the great steam ship companies at the end of the nineteenth century, such as P & O and Blue Funnel.

Probably the most truly distinctive aspect of William's (and James's) achievements lie in the continuity of values, and of progress, inherited apparently from their father, and passed on, certainly, to their children and grandchildren, so that at all times were the highest standards observed of ship quality and maintenance, of care for their staffs and seamen, and of service to their customers, whilst at no time was the family's control of the business placed in any sort of jeopardy, in contrast to the records of many of their more dynamic rivals.

Examples of such prudence in business as well as in family life abound. On entering the partnership William 'willingly agreed' to his father's condition,

'That you give your entire and undivided attention to the business, strictly abstaining from all speculations on business foreign to the trade I have hitherto conducted unless my consent has previously been obtained to the same and particularly that to no person whatever you sign any accommodation Bill or grant security either in your own name or that of the firm, and your doing so shall be sufficient authority and warrant to me at once to close the Co-partnery without previous warning, the last condition I make most imperative upon you and not in any way to be evaded'.

There is no evidence that such a stringent condition was actually needed, but it covered the chances in a way symptomatic of the manner in which the family conducted its affairs. Similarly, William and his wife had a pre-nuptial contract of marriage.

The family never became over-extended, which is the obvious root of the business's sound, secure, but slow growth and development. It was a rule that of all income available, half was to be invested, and of that some 40% was to go into gilt edged securities, about 20% into non-shipping investments and a further 20% into the line. William Thomson's estate at death shows that he had punctiliously pursued these policies.

This conservatism was matched by equally punctilious integrity. In illustration, we may cite the fact that the expansion of the fleet was held back in order to enable William Snr to discharge all of his trusteeship obligations in full subsequent to the collapse of the City of Glasgow Bank.

Equally important were the less tangible aspects of quality through the ships and through people. The ships were invariably bought new from the builders, taking no advantage of possible second-hand bargains, but it became acknowledged that throughout the nineteenth century they were being bought about 1,000 tons too small, thus shortening their commercially viable life by some years. The reason for buying smaller ships than was desirable was lack of funds to buy larger.

The partners and associated investors put their own money into the ships, apparently with no recourse whatever to commercial borrowing. They could therefore only invest in new tonnage as they had been receiving regular dividends. Such was the timing of the profits cycle relative to the shipbuilding cycle that the phasing resulted, in all but one ship ordering decision, in the new vessel arriving just in time to catch the next upsurge in trade!

Merest reference to the vessels' voyage accounts also overwhelmingly vouches that the officers and seamen on Thomson ships were well provided for. The provisions were good and plentiful, many seamen returned for voyage after voyage, and William Thomson himself expressed a preference for the steady Shetlanders who would respond to good working conditions.

The man who played the leading role in developing and passing on these inherited policies was certainly exceptional. He was a scholar at Leith High School where he won the silver medals for 'English Classics' in July 1852 and 'Mathematics and Arithmetic' as well as for 'Lingua Latina' in July 1853. Clearly he showed early promise of being a good all-rounder. Following his entry to the shipping company's office it is clear that he served a comprehensive apprenticeship in all aspects of the business, and it can be inferred from references to travel that this included visits to agents and others throughout the world. He seems to have accepted literally his father's condition that he 'give his entire and undivided attention to the business', to the extent that he remained a bachelor until October 1883 when, at the age of 44, he married Katherine Macnab, a daughter of the Minister of Silvertonhill Free Church, Hamilton, who subsequently had six sons and two daughters, two of his sons succeeding him in the business.

He was widely connected. Both his Aunt Jemima and his sister, Sarah, married into the Henderson family of Glasgow shipowners, and he moved in a circle of business friends and relations including such names as John Jordan and the firm of Miller of Leith.

Following his father he held a directorship in the North British Rubber Company, and he had extensive non-business interests. He was a leading member of the Conservative Party, and of the Church of Scotland, first at St Mary's and later St George's, Edinburgh. He was a member of the Edinburgh Chamber of Commerce and of the Leith High Constables, as well as being a Justice of the Peace for the County of Linlithgow. He was also involved with local charities including, it appears, the Leith Hospital, the Edinburgh Royal Infirmary, and the Association for Improving the Conditions of the Poor in Leith.

Described as 'personally retiring', he had a modest lifestyle: his achievements are difficult to enumerate in any simple list. At root, however, there can be no doubt that he, with his brother James, took over a modest fleet of little wooden sailing ships and left behind a cargo line which was capable of becoming, by continuation of their policies, one of Britain's leading shipping fleets.

Perhaps most of all they epitomise the worth of the traditional Scottish business values of concentration, caution and attention to detail which, when adaptively applied to changing conditions, in this firm at least, ensured crisis-free survival, growth and development.

T E MILNE

SOURCES

Unpublished

Family & Company Contacts

Milne, T E, 'A British Shipping Company in the late Nineteenth and early Twentieth Cnturies', B Litt thesis, University of Glasgow, 1965

NRA(S): 281, 2214, The Ben Line Voyage Accounts, Wm Thomson & Co, Edinburgh

SRO: SC 70/1/522, Inventory
        SC 70/4/443, Will

Published

Blake, George, *The Ben Line. The History of a Merchant Fleet, 1825-1955,* Neilson, 1956

Men of the Period, London, n d

The Scotsman, 28/11/1911

Sir William Johnston THOMSON,

Engineer and bus operator; b. 2/2/1881, Muirend, Baillieston, s. of Thomas Thomson, blacksmith, and Esther McKay; m. 28/1/1908, Glasgow, Elizabeth Gilmour, d. of William Gilmour, telegraph clerk and Elizabeth Humphries; 1 s., 2 d.; Founder, Ch and MD of Scottish Motor Traction Co Ltd., Pres of Scottish Motor Trade Association, Pres of Scottish Amicable Building Society; d. 18/9/1949, Edinburgh; g/v UK estate: £286,766 13s 4d.

One of the pioneers of passenger transport was William Johnston Thomson who saw early on the wide range of opportunities that were being created by motorised transport. He was born on 2 February 1881 in Muirend, Glasgow. He was educated at Eastbank Academy, but left when he was 12 to get work and contribute to the family income. His first job was with D & J McDonald, a tobacco firm in the Gorbals. He earned 5/- a week and worked from 8.30 a.m.-6.00 p.m. However Thomson wanted to be an engineer. He asked his father if he could become an apprentice engineer, and although this meant a loss of 1/- a week in wages his father said yes. Thomson presented himself at Boyd's Engine Works, Shettleston, where he was taken on. After one year with Boyd's, Thomson was offered the chance to complete his apprenticeship with Pollok, McNab & Highgate, general engineers, Carntyne.

Thomson found ample scope for initiative in this firm which produced several types of engine. The motor car was coming into prominence while Thomson completed his apprenticeship, and when he left the Carntyne firm he became a mechanic at the Arrol Johnston Motor Works, Paisley. He was now earning 35/- a week. His skill and ability as an engineer was recognized and he became manager of a department of 200 men before he was 21. Only three years later he was chosen to build Arrol Johnston's first two racing cars, under the firm's managing director John S Napier. In 1905 at the First Tourist Trophy Race in the Isle of Man one of the cars came in first, the other fourth. This gained much recognition for Arrol Johnston as motor car manufacturers. Thomson could have stayed on at Arrol Johnston and taken further promotion, but he had ideas and ambitions of his own. He recognised the possibilities of motor bus operations and he decided to form a motor bus company. He was willing to put the few hundred pounds he had saved into a company, and interested some Edinburgh people, including his friend A J Paterson in his proposals. Paterson on agreeing with Thomson said he 'had a notion that motor buses in Edinburgh would prove profitable'. Thus, as a young engineer of 24, William J Thomson formed the Scottish Motor Traction Company on 14 June 1905, with a capital of £12,000 and no rolling stock. Thomson was the company's general manager, traffic superintendent and chief engineer.

Their first purchase was a 'Maudsley' chain-driven, solid tyre, two-decker motor bus which plied for passengers between the Mound, Edinburgh, and the outlying village of Corstorphine, from 1 June 1906. They soon had six buses and 20 employees. The venture initially proved a success and the buses were well patronised. Six more buses were bought. However after the company had been in existence only a few months it faced disaster. The solid tyres of the buses broke up in a short time and one by one the vehicles had to be laid up. The company did not have the money to replace the tyres, but Thomson averted the crisis by asking a firm to take him on trust and supply the company with new tyres. With the 12 buses back on the road Thomson's company went from strength to strength.

Even in these early days the Edinburgh magistrates approved timetables and routes and issued licences to operate. All vehicles were passed by a corporation omnibus and hackney carriage inspector, and the vehicles also had to come within the Edinburgh police regulations. Such statutory regulations were not the norm at this time, and outside Edinburgh most operations were unfettered by controls. Difficulties in obtaining suitable vehicles to meet with regulations most likely led to a new design of vehicle introduced by Thomson. Regulations limited the length of a passenger vehicle to 23 ft. Thus if the company wanted to carry more passengers Thomson realised that the driver must sit further forward at the side of his engine. The 'Lothian' was designed by Thomson and assembled by the company's works which had opened in 1910. It was an early forward control vehicle, giving the driver a position and a view of the road which at that time was unique. It could seat 32 passengers, accommodation which was not available with any vehicle type then marketed with a single-deck body. The 'Lothian' acquired its name in consideration of the three counties surrounding Edinburgh.

By the outbreak of the First World War Thomson's fleet numbered 35 vehicles, and had an annual mileage of 728,000. During the war the company was involved with munition transportation. At the end of the war Thomson had new problems to face. His fleet was worn out and buses had to be replaced. To deal with this the workshops were refurbished and new plant installed. However, more importantly the war had given impetus to the growth of motor transport, especially passenger transport. Many small operators set up and SMT found itself faced with stiff competition for passengers. However, many of these smaller operators often failed to survive the competition due to lack of experience or to commercial difficulties which made it hard to get a firm foothold in an area. SMT withstood the outbreak of competition as it had already established itself firmly, based upon Edinburgh and had a 'most cordial' relationship with the corporation of that city, which as Hibbs points out no doubt contributed to the company's virtual monopoly into the city from the country around.

By 1925 the SMT fleet consisted of 230 single-decker vehicles of which 85 were 'Lothians' and the rest mostly 'Maudsleys'. Services were established throughout the Borders and in 1926 a service to Glasgow was begun. This was important to SMT as most companies were trying to establish services to Glasgow. The middle twenties also saw the company's absorption of smaller independent companies. For example, a controlling interest was gained in the Peebles Motor Company in 1925, and with the purchase of various businesses in the south, including Brock and Amos in Galashsiels, in 1926, the company's control of the important south-eastern part of the Borders increased rapidly. In 1928 the first through route to England by SMT was established. This was to Newcastle, via Jedburgh. In this year the annual mileage had increased to 10,500,000 miles. A through route to London was inaugurated in 1930.

As the company increased its operations railway opposition to the competition for passengers began to develop. Under parliamentary legislation in 1928 the railways were allowed to develop an interest in road transport. An agreement was reached between SMT and the London, Midland and Scottish Railway and the London and North Eastern Railway. Under this regrouping both LMS and LNER acquired 25% of the company's shares each.

1930 witnessed the introduction of statutory restrictions which led to a greater degree of control over the passenger transport industry. The Road Traffic Act, 1930, also represented an amalgamation of the bigger operators in Scotland when SMT took over the interests of W Alexander & Sons Ltd, of J C Sword and R B Dick. The holding company for the combine became SMT itself. The new operating units were SMT covering most of Eastern Scotland south of the Forth, Central SMT Company Ltd in the Clyde Valley, the Western SMT Co Ltd based in Kilmarnock, and W Alexander and Sons Ltd, covering eastern Scotland from the Forth to Inverness. The Alexander, Sword and Dick families were all represented in the group. This move regulated competition and placed SMT at the forefront of bus operations in Scotland. By the end of 1930 the annual mileage of the group was nearly 40,000,000 miles, employees numbered 5,165, and the fleet had grown to 1,750 vehicles. Numerous operators were acquired at this time, and acquisitons continued during the 1930s. The company enjoyed continued success and by 1939 its employers numbered 16,620 and the fleet numbered 3,158 vehicles. By 1947 SMT was responsible for over three-quarters of Scotland's non-municipal passenger transport. In 1949 when the industry was nationalised the company's extensive road passenger transport undertaking was acquired by the British Transport Commission, along with the company's holdings in subsidiary concerns.

Although heavily involved in his business William Thomson still devoted much of his time to other interests and activities. He was greatly interested in local politics. In 1921 he entered Edinburgh Town Council as a representative of Haymarket Ward. He also served on many committees. In 1926 he was elected to the magistracy, heading a list of six new bailies. Thomson was a progressive in municipal politics, and he had taken a prominent part in the formation of the Progressive Party in the Town Council of which he was the first chairman. After serving for 11 years on the Town Council, Thomson was elected Lord Provost of Edinburgh in 1932. When his term of office expired in 1935 he was presented with his portrait, which had been painted by an Edinburgh artist, Captain Borthwich, in recognition of his services to the city.

During his term of office Thomson had been an ardent supporter of the Forth Road Bridge project, and under his leadership the public authorities concerned had been brought to a basis of agreement about the site of the Bridge and the general character of the scheme. He organised Edinburgh's celebration of the Silver Jubilee of King George V. He also placed great emphasis on the educational and cultural interests of the city.

It was during his term as Lord Provost that several honours were conferred on him. In October 1933 he received the honorary degree of LLD from Edinburgh University, when it was remarked of him that the same energy and foresight which characterised his business career had been brought to bear on the problems of civic administration. In 1934 he was knighted by King George V at Holyroodhouse. He was also Deputy Lieutenant for the city of Edinburgh and county of Peebleshire, as well as Justice of the Peace. Other distinctions conferred on Thomson included the Order of El Mohdad, class three, which Thomson received from King Abdulla of Transjordan, Knight of Grace, and the Order of St John of Jerusalem. He was also appointed to the extra-parliamentary panel of persons qualified to act as commissioners under the Private Legislation Procedure (Scotland) Act.

Thomson was associated with many groups and companies. He was vice-president of the Western Branch of the British Legion in Scotland, a director of the United Automobile Services, and of the Gilmerton Colliery Company, and president of the Scottish Amicable Building Society. He was a member of the Council of the Omnibus Owners' Association, and of the Council of the Institution of Automobile Engineers, chairman of the National Vehicle Builders' Association, and president of the Scottish Motor Trades Association, as well as chairman and managing director of the SMT Ltd. Thomson was also the founder of Scotland's SMT Magazine.

Thomson's recreational time was taken up by sports. He enjoyed golf and was a member of the Royal Burgess, Luffness, Gullane, Kilspindie and Dornoch golfing clubs. He liked to take part in curling matches at the Haymarket rink, and was fond of shooting and fishing. He became interested in farming later in his life with the acquisition of the farm of Blythbank, near Blyth Bridge, Peebleshire, in 1941. He devoted much of his spare time to its administration, and once said 'If you want good crops, you must take the scientist into consultation. If a farm is properly equipped, it must be more like an engineering shop', applying to his farm the same thoroughness and modern outlook characteristic of his commercial undertakings. Thomson was interested in the future of Scottish tourism, and his work as joint honorary treasurer of the Scottish Tourist Board occupied a great deal of his time and energy.

In 1908 Thomson married Elizabeth Gilmour, who had attended the same school as Thomson. They had one son and two daughters. Elizabeth had been involved in the company from the early days when she helped out at the Lauriston Street office. She was very supportive of all Thomson's work, and he was very appreciative of her support and had said 'that a great part of his success had been due to the lady whom he was fortunate enough to choose as his wife'.

Despite these many and varied outside activities William Thomson still devoted much of his time to the company. The company had continually grown and expanded under his leadership, until it was the largest concern in Scotland in its provision of non-municipal passenger transport. By 1947 SMT Co Ltd was carrying more than 561,550,000 passengers, travelling some 124,750,000 miles a year, and possessed a fleet of over 3,000 vehicles, an outstanding achievement for a man who had started with just six solid tyred vehicles in 1906. After the company was acquired by the British Transport Commission in 1949 Thomson still continued his involvement with SMT and attended various meetings. Indeed it was while he was attending an EGM of the SMT Company in Edinburgh in September 1949 that Thomson took ill. He died at his home on 18 September 1949. Thomson had had a prominent role in the formation of passenger transport in Scotland, and will best be remembered in conjunction with SMT which under his guidance and business acumen grew into a huge countrywide concern, and which was reputed to be in 1947 the second oldest surviving bus company in Britain. He was survived by his wife Elizabeth and his two daughters, and left a personal estate of £286,766 3s 4d.

THERESA BARTON

SOURCES

Unpublished

SRO: SC 70/1/1212, Inventory
       SC 70/4/944, Will

Published

Bruce, J Graeme, 'Bus Services of the Great North Road between Edinburgh and Darlington', in John Hibbs (ed), *The Omnibus,* Newton Abbot, 1971
Dyos, H J and Aldcroft, D H, *British Transport,* Surrey, 1971
Edinburgh Evening News, 23/1/1933
Evening Dispatch, 19/9/1949
Glasgow Herald, 19/9/1949, 22/9/1949
Hibbs, John, *The History of British Bus Services,* Newton Abbot, 1968
Motor Transport, 24/9/1949
The Scotsman, 5/9/1934, 17/3/1937, 19/9/1949
SMT Magazine, October 1949
Strong, L A G, *The Rolling Road,* London, 1956
The Sunday Post, 28/11/1937
The Times, 19/9/1949
Who Was Who, Vol IV

Andrew WEIR, Lord Inverforth, 1st Baron Inverforth of Southgate

Shipowner, b. 24/4/1865, Kirkcaldy, s. of William Weir, cork cutter, and Janet Laing; m. 1889, Tomania Anne, d. of Thomas K Dowie, coachsmith, Kirkcaldy; 1 s., 5 d.; Ch, Andrew Weir & Co, Bank Line Ltd, British Mexican Petroleum Co Ltd, etc, d. 17/9/1955, London; g/v estate: £548,214.

Andrew Weir was a Scot who had a long and varied business career, much of it outside Scotland, based in London. But the foundation of his wealth was his shipping business established in Glasgow in 1885, and this remained the core of the Weir enterprises throughout his long life.

Andrew Weir had no background in shipping, though his father and his maternal grandfather were in business as cork cutters in Kirkcaldy. His early life was focussed there and he took his elementary education at the Kirkcaldy High School. His first step into business was not with his father, but to train as a clerk and cashier in the office of the Commercial Bank of Scotland. It is clear that the routine of this job was not to Andrew Weir's liking and he quickly left for the more varied work of a shipping clerk in an office in Glasgow. In the 1880s Glasgow was on the upswing as a great mercantile and industrial city, and the River Clyde was expanding rapidly as a busy shipping centre. The ease of entry into shipping by buying into a secondhand sailing vessel, and the opportunity presented for making profits from the trade of the vessel, was not lost on the young Andrew Weir. In 1885, at barely 20 years of age, Andrew Weir purchased his first vessel, a sailing barque of 299 tons, the *Willow Bank*. From this small beginning there quickly grew the Bank Line of Andrew Weir & Co. It seems certain that such an early start in independent trade could only have been made possible by the young Andrew Weir drawing some financial support from his family.

Andrew Weir employed the *Willow Bank* initially in the coasting trade but he quickly added new sailing vessels engaging in trade to the Baltic. From there, like other shipping lines on the Clyde, he stretched farther afield to South America, with a particular interest in the Chilean nitrate trade.

All of Andrew Weir's business in his first decade in Glasgow, from 1885 to 1895, was conducted in sailing ships. Indeed the Clyde, somewhat against the United Kingdom trend, saw a huge increase in the registration of sailing vessels in these years. This is even more surprising since this was just at the time when the Clyde was making its name as the world leader in the construction of steel and steam vessels. However even as the steamship was being developed the economics of long haul and low value cargoes like grain and nitrates still favoured sailing vessels, where neither time nor regularity were critical issues in the voyage. Weir exploited this, benefiting from the lower capital cost of sailing barques, and the growing efficiency of this type of vessel as advances were made in the winches and in other equipment to reduce the manpower necessary to man and sail the larger vessels.

In establishing his business between 1885 and 1895 Andrew Weir specialised as a managing owner. He also took interest in a large number of single ship companies. It is reputed that his sailing fleet peaked in the mid 1890s at 52 vessels, making it the largest fleet of sailing vessels in single ownership in the United Kingdom at that time. By that time his brother William had joined him in partnership, and the firm of Andrew Weir & Co was poised to shift its headquarters from Hope Street in Glasgow to Lloyds Avenue in London. As ship managers, the lure of the metropolis with its commodity exchanges, its insurance houses and its network of brokers and access to clients, proved too powerful for Glasgow to retain Andrew Weir. In 1896, at the age of 30, Andrew Weir went to London and added the first steamship to his fleet. By then the days of sailing vessels were numbered, and Weir began the process of converting to steam. With him to London went his wife, Anne Dowie, whom he had married at Kirkcaldy in 1889. In 1897 his son Andrew Alexander Morton was born.

When Andrew Weir moved to London he had already diversified his shipping interests. Not only did he operate a large sailing fleet, the Bank Line, his interest had also extended into the newly emerging oil business. He was managing owner of Inver Tanker and Inver Transport & Trading. In the next decade he also opened offices at Middlesborough to expedite his business. His progress was rapid and by the beginning of the First World War Andrew Weir and his brother William were operating a fleet of 14 sailing ships and 23 steamers. The sailing vessels were still the core of the Bank Line, and represented a fleet of 28,000 grt. Seven of the 14 vessels had been built by Russell & Co at Port Glasgow, and only two vessels had been built outside the Clyde. The 23 steamers in the Weir's fleet were operated and managed as single ship companies such as the Comeric Steamship Co Ltd, the Elleric Steamship Co Ltd and so on. By this time the Weirs shipping interests had extended to the Far East and they had established a significant interest in the rice trade.

The First World War briefly interrupted this progress but at the end of it Andrew Weir was poised for expansion. Indeed, in spite of the difficult conditions between the wars, Andrew Weir pursued a vigorous building policy of new vessels. Between 1920 and 1928 he had constructed for him 88 new vessels for his various shipping interests, these totalling 342,329 grt. The major builder for Andrew Weir was Harland & Wolff who constructed 65 of the vessels. Another 12 ships came from Workman Clark & Co, 4 from Redhead & Sons, 3 from Doxford, 2 from Henry Scarr, and 1 each from Denny Brothers and John Brown. 37 of these new vessels bore Bank Line names; of these 18 were built on the Clyde at Harland & Wolff's Glasgow yard. Indeed Andrew Weir divided the 65 orders to Harland & Wolff at 35 vessels to Belfast, and 30 to Glasgow. However no Weir vessel was constructed on the Clyde after 1926, and the close association of Andrew Weir with shipbuilding and shipping on the Clyde was broken after a period of 40 years. Therefter building was mainly undertaken by Harland & Wolff at Belfast, or by Doxford and Redhead on the north east coast. Perhaps the most significant thrust of Andrew Weir & Co in these years was into the oil tanker business with his Inver Tanker Line, and other oil interests. Twenty-seven of the vessels built between 1920 and 1938 were new tankers for this growing trade.

By the First World War, Andrew Weir was metropolitan based in London. Through his strong support for the Liberal Party he was drawn by Lloyd George into public service. In 1917, following a report he drew up for Lloyd George on the commercial organisation of the supply branches of the army, he was appointed Surveyor General of Supply. He toured the trenches, and his plans for more efficient handling of supplies were reported to have saved millions of pounds for the government. So effective was he in administering this complex task, that in 1919 he was appointed Minister of Munitions with the responsibility of winding down wartime activities, contracts and commitments. He held this position until 1921. He then became chairman of the Disposals and Liquidation Commission, responsible for selling the vast stores of army surplus materials. His war efforts saw him created a member of the Privy Council in 1919, and in that year he was also created a Baron taking the title Lord Inverforth of Southgate. The government of the United States also recognised his services by awarding him the DSM.

After the war, while Andrew Weir still guided his shipping interests, it is clear that other members of the family had more day to day responsibility. Andrew Weir in contrast became more and more involved in a very wide range of other activities. During the war Weir had become a director of a lead manufacturing company, H J Enthoven & Sons Ltd; indeed he had tried to encourage all United Kingdom lead manufacturers to amalgamate to form one large company. To encourage a move in that direction he had also bought a controlling interest in the largest British lead company, Walkers, Parker & Co, but war diverted his attention from this ambition and some rationalisation of the lead industry was not realised till 1927 when Weir disposed of his holdings to the grouping formed as Associated Lead Manufacturers Ltd. By that time his main interest had turned to communications. He had become involved with the Marconi group of companies, becoming president of the Radio Communication Co, Marconi-International Marine Communication Co, and Cable & Wireless (Holding); he also became chairman of Marconi-EMI Television Co.

Even though Weir was busy in these directions his shipping interest still prospered. In 1919, encouraged by King George V, Andrew Weir was instrumental in establishing the British Baltic Trading Co, a joint partnership between British and Danish companies to compete with the Germans in the Baltic trade. Weir's involvement in this Baltic enterprise brought him a number of honours. In 1937 he received from Denmark the Grand Cross of Dannebrog; in 1938 he also received the Grand Cross of the Grand Duke Gedinimas of Lithuania. At the same time his interest in the oil trade also brought him new positions. He acquired numerous directorships of oil companies, including the chairmanship of the British Mexican Petroleum Co Ltd, the British Union Oil Co Ltd, the Aguri Petroleum Co Ltd and the Red Line Motor Spirit Co Ltd. Moreover his reputation as a shrewd investor was instrumental in his becoming chairman of the English, Scottish and Colonial Investment Co Ltd and the Forest Dale Trust Ltd. In addition he became a director of Lloyds Bank and also of the National Bank of Australasia Ltd. Finally his long connection with the Far East rice trade saw him take directorships in the Burma-Siam Rice Co, and the Anglo-Burma Rice Co Ltd.

Andrew Weir's business career clearly moved through a number of stages. The foundation of his business lay on the Clyde, a brief but critical period from 1885 to 1896, in which he established his shipping interests in sail with the Bank Line. The second phase lay in London from 1896 to 1914, in which he converted his sailing fleet to steam, though still retaining a significant sail tonnage in the Bank Line on the eve of the First World War. In that period he extended his interests into the rice trade and into the oil trade. Then during the First World War he became a public figure, demonstrating his first class administrative and business abilities. Next in the period between the wars he vigorously promoted his shipping interests especially in oil; at the same time he became a national figure in business spanning communications, shipping, investment, lead manufacture, and oil transport. Finally from the Second World War he clearly took a less involved role in his many business activities. His wife died in 1941 when he was then 76 years old. Thereafter Andrew Weir & Co grew more by momentum than directly at the urge of its founder. When he died in 1955 at the age of 90, he had still been attending his office in London regularly. His personal estate was valued at over £548,000, ample reflection of his long and successful business career.

ANTHONY SLAVEN

SOURCES

Unpublished

Birth Certificate, Kirkcaldy, No 167, 1865
Calendar of Confirmations, 1955
SRO: SC 70/7/869, Will

Published

Dictionary of National Biography, 1951-60
Directory of Shipowners, Shipbuilders and Marine Engineers
Glasgow Herald, 19/9/1955
Journal of Commerce, List of Shipowners
The Scotsman, 19/9/1955
The Times, 19/9/1955
Who Was Who, Vol 5

William WHITELAW,

Railway Company Chairman; b. 15/3/1868, Gartsherrie House, Coatbridge, Lanarkshire, s. of Alexander Whitelaw of Gartshore, MP, Ironmaster and Barbara Forbes Lockart; m. 1890, Gertrude, d. of T C Thompson of Milton Hall, Cumberland; 3 s., 3 d.; Ch, Highland Railway; Ch, North British Railway; Ch, London and North Eastern Railway; Deputy Governor, Bank of Scotland; d. 19/1/1946, Hatton House, Ratho, Midlothian; g/v estate: £731,735 17s 4d.

William Whitelaw was, in business terms, the most prominent of the four sons of Alexander Whitelaw. He was born in 1868 at Gartsherrie, overlooking the ironworks of the same name, which formed the heart of the great business empire of William Baird & Co. His father was the nephew, brother-in-law and close business confidante of James Baird, the longest lived and last active partner of the brothers who had created the large and extremely profitable iron and coal firm, reputed to earn £1,000,000 per annum profit at the beginning of the 1870s.

The Bairds had used their wealth to climb determinedly into the ranks of the landed gentry and their sons received an appropriate education - public school and Oxbridge or RMC - prior to life as a country gentleman/army officer and occasionally MP and railway company director. Alexander Whitelaw having, in his turn, earned a fortune from the firm provided

321

the same for his sons. All four attended Harrow and Trinity College, Cambridge.

The eldest, Alexander, who married Disraeli's niece, stood unsuccessfully for North East Lanarkshire in 1892 while the second son, Graeme, a captain in the 3rd Battalion Argyll and Sutherland Highlanders was MP for North West Lanarkshire 1892-5. William, who graduated BA at Trinity in 1890, seemed at first to have decided to aim at a serious political career. He was elected for Perth City as a Conservative in 1892, aged 24, but lost the seat in 1895 and contested it unsuccessfully in 1900. He failed again at Banffshire in 1907 and at the Stirling District by-election of 1908. He had very definite political views right from his first election campaign, in his early twenties, and, as with his opinions on railway matters he held to them consistently, in season and out. He supported tariff reform, and vigorously rejected Irish Home Rule, or any reform of the House of Lords. Had he secured a safe parliamentary seat it must be doubted that he would ever have achieved political prominence.

He had, between election campaigns, become involved in railway affairs and in December 1908 he decided to quit his position as prospective candidate for Stirling District and concentrate on 'that other work which somehow seems to have taken possession of me'. A third choice was available, namely to take a position in the family firm. His father's half-brother, William Weir, who until his death in 1913 was the senior partner, recognized his abilities and clearly hoped to draw him into the management. He made particular provision in his will for William, and his grand nephew David Euan Wallace, the grandson of a former partner, to receive 7,000 shares in the company. However, in June 1910 he gifted 2,500 of these shares to William, at the same time as Angus and McCosh, the other two key partners, gifted blocks of shares to their respective sons to smooth the succession within the company. The young Angus and McCosh joined the board but Whitelaw restricted his involvement to his existing position as trustee for the debenture stock holders, a post which he held till his death. His links with the firm remained strong. In the inter-war period he was the largest shareholder outside of the leading executive directors and at his death virtually half his estate, £361,000 out of £732,000 was in William Baird & Co stock.

Although he did not become active in the firm his family links were not without their relevance to his chosen career as a railway company executive. The family and the company - in so many respects the distinction between them was often hard to make - were intimately involved in the history of the Scottish railway network. From 1830 when Whitelaw's great-grandfather, Alexander Baird, joined the board of the Glasgow & Garnkirk Railway until 1900 the 'Bairds' provided 29 directors including five chairmen to railway companies. William's first step was a useful apprenticeship with the Highland Railway Co. He joined the board in 1898 when only 30 years old and while his long term future was still undecided. Although not one of the major railways in Scotland, let alone the UK, its very character as a fully fledged but modest system of some 438 miles proved an ideal training ground. Whitelaw was elected deputy chairman within two years and chairman two years later, retaining the post until 1912, the longest spell of any but the founding chairman. Although entirely lacking in any previous executive responsibility, and extremely young by the usual standards of railway boards he quickly made his presence felt. His election followed the financial scandal which had come to light when the previous, somewhat unsophisticated, board had been shocked to discover that a satisfactory share dividend had been maintained only by drawing on capital. He immersed himself in all the detail of railway working, travelling the length of the network, notebook at the ready, checking the entire operation. It was said that he practised the kind of personal involvement that was more typical of an American railroad president rather than a UK chairman, and that his familiarity and enthusiasm was such that he could have earned his living doing any of the jobs on a railway. This kind of intimate attention to detail seems to have been a family trait.

The new chairman immediately suspended dividend payments, and set about establishing the company on a secure financial footing. It was generally recognized that the Highland, serving a small scattered and predominantly agricultural community, owed more to local pride than to economics. Indeed some financial experts doubted whether it could ever be viable. It is all the more impressive therefore that under Whitelaw's direction it was paying 1% by 1903 rising to 2.5% in 1913. His other major concern was to end the wasteful rivalry between the Highland and the Great North of Scotland. A proposal for closer co-operation in 1904 came to nothing but Whitelaw returned with a more radical proposal for complete amalgamation in 1905. The press welcomed the scheme and it won majority support in votes among both bodies of shareholders. However, a much greater measure of support was shown among the Great North shareholders. The Inverness local interest, with the backing of the Duke of Richmond and Gordon, vigorously opposed the scheme, criticised Whitelaw's high handed tactics, disputed his evidence, and hinted obliquely at questionable motives in view of the 'Baird' holding of £237,544 of Great North stock. Whitelaw decided, given the size of the abstention, as well as the substantial no vote, not to continue with the scheme, although he was able to initiate a closer working agreement a few years later. Ironically it was suggested that the Highland remained independent thanks to shareholder satisfaction with the achievements of the Whitelaw regime.

It was about this time that he finally decided to give up all hope of a political career. A factor influencing his decision may have been his election to the board of the North British Railway in 1908. Although he contined as chairman of the Highland Railway until 1912 it no longer stretched him but the prospect of advancing to the chairmanship of the North British was a much more exciting challenge. Here, too, the Baird connection was significant. Whitelaw's cousin, J G A Baird, had been on the board since 1888 but the company's indirect influence came out into the open during the boardroom battle of 1899 when Lord Tweeddale resigned and attacked Sir William Laird - partner in William Baird & Co - only to have Laird elected in his place. On Laird's death in 1901 his place was taken by another Baird partner, A K McCosh. The family and firm controlled almost £500,000 of North British Railway stock and obviously exercised a powerful influence.

Whitelaw was elected vice-chairman in 1910, becoming chairman in 1912, a month after resigning from the chairmanship of the Highland Railway. He retained his connection with the smaller company, resuming the chair in 1915 at the height of the wartime emergency when the role of Scapa Flow placed an enormous strain on the Highland Railway's resources. But his main activity from 1912 to 1922 was to preside over the last decade in the life of one of Scotland's big two. Since the upheavals of 1899-1900 the company had settled down under the chairmanship of the Earl of Dalkeith but it was not as financially secure as its great rival, the Caledonian.

Whitelaw had little opportunity to initiate any major policy initiative before the outbreak of World War I placed the entire network under state control. This brought into sharp focus the whole question of the railways long term future about which the chairman of the North British had long held strong and rather idiosyncratic views. Soon after joining the Highland board in 1898 he became convinced that competitive rivalry between companies was a major source of loss both for the individual firms and for the economy as a whole. In 1902 he approached Sir Charles Bine Renshaw, a director and later chairman of the Caledonian, proposing a takeover. Although personally interested he suggested that Whitelaw speak to the legal adviser to the London and North Western, Mr Mason, who agreed to recommend the plan provided the Highland could be restored to the point where it paid 1% on its ordinary stock. Unfortunately, Mason died before this target was reached and a scheme which foreshadowed the 1921 grouping arrangement by almost 20 years never materialized. The proposal of 1905 for an amalgamation with the Great North of Scotland was therefore part of a long term Whitelaw vision.

He soon came to support some form of nationalization, insisting that there was nothing inherently socialist about the concept, and for a time during the war it looked as though leading politicians might take up the idea. There was at least widespread agreement that something had to be done. By 1917 Whitelaw was predicting that there would soon be a revolution in the railway world, expessing the certainty that the pre-war situation could never be restored, and hoping for the day when the state would have the wisdom to purchase the railways outright. By the time the Armistice was signed he was quick to realize that state enthusiasm for such radical solutions was cooling rapidly. The general question of what would replace state control soon became embroiled with the immediate question of compensation and in this the North British, with Whitelaw at its head, found itself thrust into centre-stage.

The North British had been in straitened circumstances in 1913 and by the time the war was over the situation was critical. The wages bill was up 297% and the condition of locomotive stock was such that as many as 22% were under repair at any given time. Whitelaw suspended dividend payments and applied for £616,000 on account of a compensation claim which eventually totalled £10,618,000. The government withheld payment and the matter dragged through the courts with Whitelaw protesting that the state had placed the company in a quagmire and was now leaving it to sink or swim. The dispute became a highly personal battle between Whitelaw and Sir Eric Geddes, formerly of the North Eastern Railway, and now Minister of Transport. The company eventually received £9,790,000 and Whitelaw 'the clever, canny Scot' emerged with his reputation enhanced while Geddes was tarnished by his behaviour in publishing private correspondence between them.

While this struggle was going on Whitelaw was simultaneously adopting a high public profile in the debate over the future of the railways, speaking at numerous gatherings mainly of Scottish business interests. Recognizing that outright state purchase was no longer a serious option his great fear was the creation of a unified system run by a London bureaucracy giving all the evils of nationalization with none of the benefits. His own proposal was for the existing 200 companies to be reduced to not more than six groups, and suggested that the government buy out the smaller companies and lease the working of them to a few of the bigger English ones. Thus the Scottish east coast traffic would go under the North Eastern Company, the west coast traffic under the North Western Company, and the Glasgow and South Western traffic under the Midland Company. He attacked the delaying tactics of the government in establishing a select committee as a policy of drift when the possible options were already obvious. When it then became clear that the government was considering the creation of a self-contained Scottish system, his opposition became unrestrained. He called on the leading industries, especially coal, steel, wool, and agriculture, to join with the railways to fight such a scheme. Referring to an almost unheard of degree of Scottish unanimity he urged everyone, 'to get rid of all their old political prejudices as he had done' and fight for Scotland. He pressed them all to support a grouping arrangement of parallel lines with the East and West of Scotland linked to their corresponding English networks, to ensure uniformity of rates on both sides of the border, and this is substantially what emerged in the Railways Act, 1921.

Whitelaw's entitlement to an important position within the new set-up was considerable but he had of course aroused deep hostility in certain govenment circles particularly at the Treasury and the Ministry of Transport, still headed by Sir Eric Geddes. For some, such as Lord Claud Hamilton, the idea of the chairman of a Scottish railway, for one of 'the big four' was asking for trouble. Geddes opposed his appointment on the grounds that 'he represents the bygone feudal system of railway management when railway directors regarded the general manager much as they would their bailiff or gamekeepers.' Despite such opposition he was offered the chairmanship of the LNER, although it was surely significant that he was virtually unique among senior Railway figures in that he never appeared in an honours list. He retained the chairmanship for 15 years, considerably longer than the heads of the other three networks. In some respects it was a repetition of his North British experience. He was again responsible for the smaller and weaker of two rival concerns, and it required all his skill in cutting costs and exploiting cheap but effective public relations innovations to avoid serious difficulties.

Three of the four groups settled for an organizational structure which was little more than existing practice. Only the LNER adopted a more fundamental review based on the premise that the scale of the new company required a fresh approach. Before the company came into existence in January 1923 the chairman-elect met with an organizing committee of future directors and agreed to establish a 'federal' system. Not only did this fit in with the chairman's long held views on decentralization but it avoided the costs of standardization and defused Anglo-Scottish rivalries.

The dominant issue throughout his chairmanship was economy. The LNER group included the poverty stricken Great Central, but the hope that the strength of the North Eastern would carry this burden was undermined by the inter-war depression. Of the four systems the LNER had the greatest dependence on freight and more especially on the type of freight which showed the greatest decline. Initially the company bowed to pressure and brought forward some grand investment schemes, notably for electrification of its suburban lines. Such proposals soon became quite unrealistic. Between 1927 and 1931 with revenues down 16.9% drastic economies were called for. In the half year, July to December 1930, Whitelaw cut expenditure by £1,606,000 and over the years 1927-31 the total reduction was 17.2% bringing about the lowest ratio (80.95%) of working expenses to receipts of any of the mainline companies. Nor was his response simply a negative one. The ancillary van and lorry service was expanded, shopper trains and discount fares established and the commencement in 1935 of the 'High Speed Train' introduced a term borrowed long afterwards by British Rail.

It was an impressive performance in difficult circumstances. Whitelaw, himself, felt that the system within which he was obliged to work was really a case of too little, too late. He believed that the railways were nationalized in all but name and by the 1930s he had come to the opinion that a practical 'non-socialist' solution would be for national ownership, but private management. His growing concern with what he considered unfair road competition also led him to advocate the need for an overall transport policy to co-ordinate road, rail, water and air services. In the short term he settled for closer pooling arrangements between the LNER and the LMS and he was never in any doubt that his ideas did not command much support among his colleagues. It is more than coincidence however that years after his retiral during the debate leading up to nationalization it was the LNER which was least opposed to the principle, and which proposed 'The Landlord and Tenant Scheme' embodying many of its former chairman's ideas. When nationalization did eventually come about the LNER bequeathed a particularly strong pool of young managers, the products of a special recruitment scheme under which a number of graduates and an equal number of promising but academically unqualified staff were given a specialist in-house training. This reflected Whitelaw's belief that although a university education might be useful a young man who had failed exams at 16 could, through practical experience, mature to the point where his real potential would show itself.

In 1938, shortly after the death of his elder brother placed him at the head of the family, he decided that, at the age of 70, it was time to retire having completed an unprecedented 36 years of unbroken railway company chairmanship. His other concerns were slight. He joined the board of the Bank of Scotland in 1914, becoming deputy governor in 1945, but apart from a few other minor railway posts he had no further business interests. He was elected president of the Institute of Transport in 1933 and served on its council until 1941. Throughout his life his other great interest was that abiding Baird devotion to the Church of Scotland. He was a regular and prominent attender and speaker at the General Assembly and other church gatherings and his enthusiasm for correspondence was reflected in his numerous letters to the press on church affairs. He was a trustee of the Baird Trust established in 1873 by his great uncle James with a gift of £500,000 to promote church interests and he served as convener of the Maintenance of the Ministry Committee.

His long career was not directed at building up his personal fortune. His earnings as a chairman, and indeed his personal shareholdings, were extremely modest. He seems to have been motivated by personal enthusiasm and a sense of public duty. All three of his sons were victims of the Great War and on his death his male heir was his grandson and namesake, William Whitelaw, created Viscount Whitelaw and leader of the House of Lords in 1983.

ROBERT CORRINS

SOURCES

Published

The Engineer, 25/1/1946
Glasgow Herald, 1892-1938, passim
The Railway Gazette, 25/1/1946
The Times, 21/1/1946
Transactions of the Royal Philosophical Society of Glasgow, 1932
Whitelaw, H V, *The House of Whitelaw*, Glasgow, 1928

William WORDIE,

Carrier and contractor; b. 23/3/1810, Stirling, s. of John W Wordie, carrier and contractor, and Janet Stewart; m. 20/12/1837, Janet Jeffrey, d. of Peter Jeffrey; 2 s., 2 d.; Founder and MD, William Wordie & Co; d. 9/10/1874, Kirkintilloch; g/v estate: £43,765 5s. 4d.

William's father, John Wordie, had carried on business as a general carrier between Stirling and Glasgow before the arrival of the railway. His business was on a small scale and not very successful, and by the time of his death in 1830 he had become bankrupt. Thus, at the age of 20, William faced the task of rebuilding or, more accurately, starting afresh in the same line of business, founding the firm which became the highly successful William Wordie & Co. The firm which he started in 1830 survived until the nationalisation of transport in the late 1940s, when it was purchased at full market value by the LMS Railway under the terms of a clause included in the first contract negotiated by the founder more than a century earlier.

The early years of the new firm are recorded as one of uphill struggle. Apart from the financial problems

of buying back the stock and equipment of its bankrupt predecessor, the prospects for a small firm, with less than half-a-dozen horses, engaged in the transport of goods by horse-drawn vehicles on the eve of the railway age must have been less than bright. It was William Wordie's response to the challenge of this new means of transport, however, that distinguished him from most other road carriers and ensured the survival and subsequent expansion of his firm. He had the foresight to see the advantage of seeking co-operation with the new railway companies. With the opening of the Edinburgh and Glasgow Railway in 1842 he started to build up a service of delivery and collection of goods between the terminal stations and the roadside stations. From this he developed a system of distribution of goods over a widening area of the country. When the Scottish Central Railway opened the Glasgow to Stirling line in 1848 he secured appointment as the recognised carrier. He signed his first contract with the Scottish Central Railway, a contract originally renewable on a six-monthly basis but which ran, with appropriate adaptations, right up to nationalisation. It was this original contract which included a clause giving the Railway Company the right to purchase Wordie's at full market value, the clause which was invoked at nationalisation.

In the following decades the firm experienced almost continuous expansion, reflecting the spread of the railway system itself. In the 1850s the main contracts were with the Edinburgh and Glasgow Railway and the Scottish Central Railway, and Glasgow became an increasingly important centre for the firm, although Stirling was still its main base. Premises were purchased in Glasgow in 1852 and in Stirling in 1854; further premises were constructed in Glasgow in 1857-60. At the same period Wordie's held the contract for the Scottish Northern Railway (subsequently taken over by the Caledonian Railway), which extended from Perth to Aberdeen, with a consequent spread of depots and stables. By the end of the decade the firm's records show a stock of some 200 horses, with stables and other property, located at ten main stations.

The rapid growth of the railway system was followed by growth in the size of the railway companies through amalgamation. In 1865 the Scottish Central amalgamated with the Caledonian Railway, and the Edinburgh and Glasgow amalgamated with the North British Railway. Again William Wordie made a wise choice in his decision to throw in his lot with the Caledonian which was to become the leading railway company in Scotland in the following period of railway growth. The subsequent expansion and prosperity of Wordie's closely reflected the similar development of the Caledonian. As the railway lines advanced throughout the country, so too did the depots and stables of William Wordie. In addition to the long-standing link with the Caledonian, Wordie's also acted as agents for the Highland and Great North of Scotland Railway with stations for their services as far north as Wick and Thurso. By 1869 the firm's stock of horses was appoximately 400.

William Wordie died suddenly of a heart attack in October 1874. In his 65th year, he had been active in the business up to the time of his death. At the start of his business career, 44 years previously, he had inherited a small bankrupt concern. From such a beginning he had built up over his lifetime a large and successful firm, chiefly as a result of his inspired decision to link his business with the new and revolutionary railway system emerging on the Scottish scene as he was struggling to restore his father's business. His timing was right and his business flourished on the coat-tails of the rapidly expanding Scottish railway system of the middle decades of the nineteenth century.

By the time of his death in 1874 the firm had become established in Glasgow where its largest depot and stables were located. Stations and stables on a smaller scale had been established at major ports and at towns throughout the length and breadth of the country. The stock of horses had expanded to 700, with an appropriate number of carts. A considerable property ownership had been built up, much of it in the form of stables and warehouses, but also including some shops and hotels.

William Wordie was succeeded by his two sons; John, already an active partner in the business, and Peter, a successful brewer. Under their management the firm continued to grow and prosper. Cartage for the railways continued to expand. In 1896 the firm became local agents for Caledonian at Newcastle-on-Tyne. They acquired agencies for various coastal steamship companies trading with Ireland, Campbeltown, Orkney and Shetland. Subsequently they extended their activities to Ireland, where they built up a considerable distribution network in conjunction with the various railway companies operating there. The scale of their operations was expanded further by the acquisition in 1903 of Robert Grierson and Co who operated a similar business, mainly in Glasgow and Paisley. The growth of the firm was accompanied by additions to property and equipment and by 1905 the stock of horses had increased to nearly 2,300.

John Wordie died in 1910 and the following year Peter Wordie took into partnership his two nephews, William Wordie, son of John, and Archibald Watson, son of Anne Wordie. Peter Wordie died in 1913 and the business was carried on by the two nephews.

The early 1920s brought a regrouping of the railway companies and Wordie's became the agents for LMS in 1923. There was some expansion of its traditional services for the two railway companies now operating in Northern Ireland, LMS and the Great Northern, with protracted negotiation over the rates to be paid. As the decade advanced, however, a number of factors unfavourable to the firm's traditional business became increasingly obvious and the scale of its operations

had to be severely cut back. The effects of the uncertainties facing the traditional heavy industries and of the increasing competition from road transport by motor vehicles, with implications for the fortunes of the railway companies, were magnified by the onset of world depression. The business recorded losses over the period 1925-1932. Its recovery to a position of profit in 1932 reflects a substantial reorganisation which was completed that year. The business was divided into two companies, Wordie Property Company and Wordie Carriers, with LMS acquiring a half share in the latter. In the same year most of Wordie's business in Ireland was taken over by the two railway companies, LMS and Great Northern, with suitable compensation. Wordie's retained part of its business in Londonderry, Belfast and Dublin, but agreed not to operate services there which would compete with the railways.

Archibald Watson died in 1934 and William Wordie became sole managing director. By the outbreak of World War II the company had established itself as one of the most successful haulage companies in Scotland. Although horse-drawn vehicles were still extensively used, the firm, in addition to a stud of over 800 horses, had built up a large fleet of motor vehicles and trailers, with garages and workshops at the main depots, and a staff of mechanics for maintenance work. While still acting as agents to the railway companies, the general road haulage services operated must have been increasingly in competition with the railways. Regular daily services were operated between Glasgow and Aberdeen, Dundee, Edinburgh, Inverness, Perth and Stirling, and between Glasgow and Newcastle-on-Tyne. In addition to the main company, Wordie & Co (Ulster) Ltd looked after business in Northern Ireland, Wordie & Co (Dublin) business in Eire and Wordies (North Eastern) Ltd the contract for the Great North of Scotland Section of the LNER. The company had also acquired a number of smaller transport companies in different parts of Scotland which were operated as subsidiaries.

William Wordie, the founder, entered into the first contracts with the railway companies when the development of rail transport was threatening the existence of his former business of road transport by horse-drawn vehicles. His grandson William lived to see the purchase of his railway cartage business prior to nationalisation, under the terms of a contract similar to that drawn up by the founder, and at a time when the rail transport system was yielding ground to the increasing competition of motorised road transport. William (the younger) died in 1952, but the Wordie Property Co continues under the management of the founder's great grandsons Sir John S Wordie, George T Wordie (chairman) and Peter J Wordie.

SARAH ORR

SOURCES

Unpublished

Death Certificate, Kirkintilloch, 1874, Entry No 193
Strathclyde Regional Archives:
  TD 190, TD 513, Records of William Wordie, 1853-1934
    T-MR/456, Sederunt Books, 1864-1937 (2 Volumes)

Published

Biographical Notices, Glasgow Men, Vol II
Glasgow Herald, 10/10/1874

Distributive Trades

The growth of the distributive network in the period 1860-1960 is seen in the great diversity of trades represented in this sector. Indeed, the distributive sector contains many of the trades found elsewhere in the *Dictionary of Scottish Business Biography*, such as the food and drink, clothing, footwear, iron and construction sectors. The rising opportunities for the distribution of goods and services was a notable feature of the economy. The complex nature of its structure is reflected in the growing number of categories contained in the trade guides which emerged in the period. The market opening for trade guides in the late Victorian period is, in itself, an indication of the plethora of general and specialist trades which sprang up to occupy the middle ground of supply and demand created by the mass market. This has created difficulties for the sector as many of the retail distributors were themselves large scale manufacturing companies producing most, if not all, of their stock in trade. As such they might have been equally well placed in the specialist sectors.

The arch-exponent of exploiting the mass market was (Sir) Thomas Lipton. He was neither the first nor the only grocer to progress from being a single shopkeeper to a multiple retail chain owner, he was however the most successful. The largest market for the retail sale of cheap staple foods lay in the West of Scotland. There, the crowded tenement streets of Glasgow housed a mass of industrial labour which Lipton mined with consummate skill. Tenements, with their ground floor shops, provided instant local custom in sufficient numbers to ensure profit maximisation. Lipton gave his customers more than a variety of cheap nourishing food for cash, he gave them audacious sales stunts and added colour and excitement to the business of shopping. When Lipton decided to centre his empire in London in 1894 he had branches in 243 cities in the United Kingdom and 12 plantations in Ceylon.

The size of the market for basic necessities allowed other substantial entrants to multiple retailing. Galbraith's, Massey's, Templeton's, Healey's and Cochrane's stores provided the West of Scotland with similar ventures at a less spectacular level than Lipton's. In the 1870s William Galbraith began in Paisley, and Alexander Massey in Crown Street, Glasgow. Both enterprises catered for the industrial market, selling hams, eggs, butter, cheese, tea and sugar to local customers. Massey, like Lipton, placed an emphasis on hams and entered into wholesale curing with massive investment in purpose built premises producing 130,000 hams a year by 1895. Galbraith too made the backward linkages with ham curing, tea blending and bakeries added to his empire of 159 grocery and 12 butchers shops by 1935.

The art of customer psychology pioneered by Lipton, brought standardised frontages and interiors by firms to facilitate customer recognition and loyalty. Customers expected to see Galbraith's uniform black and red fronted shops and Lipton's horse shoe counters and encouraged them to feel unsettled when shopping in rival stores. This in turn led to the retention of comfortably recognisable shop names when Home and Colonial Stores acquired Massey's in 1930 and Galbraith's in 1954.

Whilst Lipton, Galbraith and Massey concentrated mainly on locally based tenement custom, there was a great deal of wealth in Glasgow living side-by-side with working class areas. Thomas Bishop founded Coopers Stores Ltd, an institution based on middle class preference. Cooper sited his Glasgow stores on strategic thoroughfares: by city rail terminii or on the main treets bisecting affluent city areas. The Liverpool, Church Street branch, launched on similar lines, rose to providing his elite customers with birdsong and flunkeys. Underpinning this were the navvy camp shops he provided for construction camps of the highland railways built by his in-laws, the McAlpine's. Although the name Coopers Stores was synonymous with genteel shopping it too fell victim to the post war syndrome of mergers and takeovers, moving from Coopers to Presto to Gateway in the cannibalistic warfare of food retailing.

Scotland provides very few examples of resistance to the mergers and takeovers experienced by retail grocery chains in the post war periods. The Dundee based firm of William Low & Co, PLC, founded by William Low in the late 1870s, sold in a similar manner to the jute based Dundee industrial population. It grew to cover an extensive Scottish market and still retained its independent status. At a different level, the smaller independent single shopkeeper has weathered the continuous storm of competition from grocery multiples of whatever description through wholesale suppliers such as Watson and Philip. Also Dundee based, this firm was founded in 1873 by Thomas Watson and Joseph Philip as bakery supply commission agents. Watson and Philip continue to supply the small grocer with cut-price goods through the modern franchise system of the VG or Voluntary Group of grocers.

The combination of rising incomes and reliable, refrigerated shipping made Scotland a fruit eating nation through men like (Sir) Malcolm Campbell and Michael Simons. They represent the retail and wholesale aspects of the fruit trade respectively. Their backgrounds could scarcely produce a more marked contrast. Campbell, the product of a poverty stricken childhood, was working in the bleach fields of the Renfrewshire cotton industry at the age of nine. Simons, the eldest son of a Jewish wholesale fruit merchant, finished his education at the Glasgow High School. They entered the fruit trade in Glasgow in the early 1860s, Campbell as an errand boy, Simons as heir presumptive to his father's business.

Malcolm Campbell and Joseph Simons reached pre-eminent positions because they seized the opportunities offered by the nexus of incomes, availability and choice. Malcolm Campbell, rose through his ability to catch the mood of burgeoning city office and store life in the 1880s. He supplied passing trade with innovative window displays of exotic fruit, introducing the Scottish shopper to the banana with a fully grown fruiting tree. Basic local vegetables were sold on a seasonal basis mainly in his smaller shops in the working class areas and he contributed to the growth of the Scottish soft fruit industry. His name became known to millions through his chain of railway station kiosks selling everything that money could buy to the public travelling the length and breadth of Britain. The art of floral decoration reached its apogee in the late Victorian era and Glasgow's polite society owed much to Malcolm Campbell's flair for spectacular floral displays for social occasions.

Michael Simons introduced the wholesale distribution of exotic fruits through close co-operation with Spanish and Portuguese contacts. European fruit reached Glasgow within 40 hours and the market for grapes and oranges appeared unlimited. Glasgow became the first UK market for Almeria grapes. By the turn of the century Simons imported Spanish and Portuguese melons, nuts, olives, onions and pomegranates, Californian fruit and vegetables, Canadian eggs, and had extensive cold storage facilities for perishable goods. Both Simons and Campbell were instrumental in encouraging the Lanarkshire tomato growers in the 1880s and Simons financed some of Campbell's retail ventures. The improving dietaries of the middle and upper classes in this period is well charted. Perhaps the rise of men such as Campbell and Simons indicates a level of consumption of fresh fruit and vegetables by the poorer classes which may have escaped the view of dietary historians.

A great deal of the passing trade tapped by Campbell in his Glasgow branches came from customers who worked in nearby offices, warehouses, shops and department stores and forms part of the generally recognised shopping revolution of the late Victorian era. The great warehouses of Glasgow dominated, trading on a global scale through the Clyde based distribution network of imports and exports already noted in other sectors of the economy. The warehouses present the greatest problem of exposition in that many of them manufactured the clothing and soft goods sold to retail traders throughout the world. For this reason most entries have found their way into the clothing sector (Volume 1), but others such as Campbell's and Stewart & McDonald, and Arthur & Co Ltd, are represented here in the distribution sector.

The difficulties experienced by the warehouses after the dislocation of First World War, documented in Volume 1, are further illustrated by Matthew Pearce Campbell, when in 1922 he merged his long established firm of J & W Campbell & Co, with the equally long established Stewarts & McDonald Co Ltd. An indication of the business large warehouses still generated can be assessed by the new firm's authorised capital of £1 million of which £918,000, was issued. However, at his death two years later £1 preference shares in Campbells and Stewart & McDonalds were down to 18/9d and £1 ordinary shares down to 12/6d. The gradual demise of this great commercial concern was overseen by Edwin Ruthven Boyd, vice chairman and managing director to 1948.

The major warehousing firm of Arthur & Co, covers the life-span of the species. Mathew Arthur was born into a family already well grounded in the 'merchant prince' tradition. When he joined his father's firm in 1873 it employed 700 workers in 50 departments manufacturing and selling textiles of every description capitalised at £200,000 and exporting to America and the Colonies. In 1878, Arthur's became a private limited company with a capital of £1.2 million of which £1 million was paid up. Prior to the First World War Arthur's was known throughout the British Empire as 'the universal provider'. With his death in 1938, Mathew Arthur (Lord Glenarthur) escaped the commercial realism of the post 1946 era when the last vestiges of general warehousing were swept away by the multiple retail department stores.

The rise of the department store is again well charted by historians and Scottish cities present good examples of their popular adoption by the buying public. Like the warehouses, department stores were prodigious providers of employment and needed massive turnover to support their continued growth and to this end employed vigorous advertising campaigns. For a brief spell they occupied a junior position to the warehouses, but as their attraction grew shopping patterns changed from dependence on the small specialist retail outlets supplied by the warehouses to the department stores. Reasons for the change in shopping habits are easily recognised; the ability to 'look round'

Arthur & Co Ltd

without obligation to buy; the variety of choice; the spread of departments offering to the general public what wholesalers had previously offered to the retailers with the concomitant price savings.

Edinburgh and Glasgow provide the major locations for department store development and it is worth noting that all the entries were bred to the drapery trade in some degree or another. Perhaps the most glamorous, and independent, of stores is still *Jenners* of Princes Street in Edinburgh. Charles Jenner began to supply Parisian fashions and materials to Edinburgh ladies in 1838. He moved to Princes Street in 1858 and by 1890 the store was valued at £250,000. Two years later the store burned to the ground and was rebuilt as seen today. Jenner tapped the seam of affluence also identified by Patrick Thomson when, in 1900, he began business on Edinburgh's South Bridge. Five years later bustling business allowed him to expand into the Bon Marche and he renamed it Patrick Thomsons or 'PTs' as it was affectionately known by thousands of shoppers.

In Glasgow, John Anderson was the precursor of department stores when in the 1840s he introduced the concept of 'universal trading' into his Clyde Street warehouse and decided to sell retail at wholesale prices. By 1850 Anderson was making regular trips to France, Austria and Germany to stock his shop, buying some of the Emperor Napoleon's effects in 1848. In 1860 he moved into Argyle Street, trading as Anderson's Royal Polytechnic Warehouse. To this day its successor, Lewis's Ltd, is known to countless Glaswegians as 'The Poly'.

In the late 1880s, Walter Wilson changed course from wholesale millinery to retail selling of general goods at wholesale prices in his 'Colosseum' store in Jamaica Street. Cut priced goods were bought in from the continent, sales techniques were imported from America and wide advertising campaigns employed to keep his 500 employees engaged in selling. Branches were opened in the major Scottish cities. Further sallies into up-market venues in Sauchiehall Street were the ladies millinery establishment, Treron et Cie and Les Grand Magasins des Tuileries by 1904.

Sauchiehall Street replaced the Trongate as the fashion centre where James Daly had first opened as a warehouseman in 1846. Several moves and some years later his son took control of the business and moved it to Sauchiehall Street, changing the store's image in the process. Daly's became noted for its select clientele as did its neighbour, Copeland and Lye's. Pettigrew and Stephens joined their company in 1888 when (Sir) Andrew Hislop Pettigrew joined with William Stephens to open their first store selling heavy draperies. At Stephens death, Pettigrew acquired adjacent premises and rebuilt the store giving shoppers five sales floors and employed 600 workers. Andrew H Pettigrew's interests included the managing directorship of Stewarts & McDonald prior to its merger with J W Campbell's. Pettigrew and Stephens Ltd continued to expand under the chairmanship of John Campbell, a farmer's son who entered the drapery trade in 1892 and succeeded Andrew H Pettigrew in 1924. He was popular and treated 800 of his staff to dinner at the Ca'Doro Restaurant after they had presented him with his portrait in oils.

The master of the Scottish drapery trade must be Hugh Fraser, who was the third generation of drapers to bear that name. His grandfather set up as a warehouseman in Buchanan Street in 1849, like Anderson and Wilson selling at considerabe discounts. He was amongst the first warehousemen to insist on ready money and had ticketed prices. His sons then turned to department store retailing and in 1919, his grandson, Hugh Fraser, entered the firm and began his phenomenal rise. Hugh Fraser was the ultimate drapery tycoon. He assumed control of Fraser Sons in 1926 and by 1948 had acquired a further 15 Scottish drapery shops and had extended the Buchanan Street premises increasing profits five fold in the period. In 1949 he floated House of Fraser a public company with £1 million capital. Further incursions into England netted him Binn's, a Sunderland based group store, and John Barkers of London. In 1959 Hugh Fraser acquired Harrod's Limited after a fierce contest. Not content with Harrod's he built up the House of Fraser to contain 75 retail outlets with a turnover of £98.7 million at the time of his death in 1966.

One of the major facilities that these highly successful and profitable department stores offered their (mostly female) customers was leisure. In elegant surroundings shoppers took their time to choose. Shopping became a day's outing, often spent in the same store. All the stores offered restaurant or tea-room facilities and rest rooms. Out-of-town customers arrived by a transport network which took them within walking distance of their destination. But other restaurants and tea-rooms were available to them in all major towns and cities. Tea-rooms became the state-of-the-art of gracious shopping. Glasgow's tea-rooms have gained a degree of fame through Miss Cranston's use of the brilliant architect, Charles Rennie Mackintosh, to design the decor for her Buchanan Street and Sauchiehall Street establishments. The attribution is well placed but Miss Cranston is not represented in the sector because of the nature of selection of the entries. Mackintosh's design for the Willow Tea-rooms, however, which was later incorporated into Daly's department store has survived the break up of Daly's and has been refurbished as a commercial concern within the premises of Henderson's the Jewellers.

Less well known personally than Miss Cranston is John Urie, the founder of City Bakeries and the Ca'Doro restaurant. Urie was not a baker but an accountant who retained his professional life whilst building up the family baking business to become a recognisable feature of Glasgow and the West of Scotland. Once again customer emphasis lay with the office, shop, and warehouse workers and the shoppers. It was this market which Urie exploited with the products of his bakeries, culminating with his Ca'Doro venture. The Ca'Doro, opened in 1921, was a five storey palace

The City Bakeries Ltd

devoted to culinary delights ranging from formal banquets to quick cups of tea. But Urie's empire of shops and tea-rooms made him second only to J Lyons & Co by 1938 when he sold it to Garfield Weston.

A J Peacock was a baker to trade and R A Peacock's Ltd supplied what were commonly known as 'Purveys': all the necessary equipment and food for the venue of your choice, which could range from the ceremonial banquet with flowers provided by Malcolm Campbell, to the marriage festivities celebrated in a Glasgow 'single-end'. By 1928 Peacock's had 50 outlets including suburban branches, tea-rooms and restaurants. In addition to that, Peacock's specialised in wedding cakes, often exported to expatriate weddings.

The rise of confectionery and chocolate shops was quite marked in the period. The increasing availability of specialised ingredients, mechanised production methods, and low wholesale prices made retailing possible. John S Birrell founded one of the best known Scottish confectionery firms though he came from a farming background. He made an early living as a grocer but soon learned the reality that popular demand for sweets was the way to success. He began making sweets in 1900. By 1924 he formed a public limited company with a capital of almost half a million pounds. Birrell's major rival was Robert Smith McColl's chain of R S McColl shops.

McColl was the strangest entrant to the world of sweets and chocolate. He was a famous Scottish football internationalist who combined a flair for making sweets with that of goal scoring. McColl and his brother, Tom, set up business in a single windowed shop in a respectable Glasgow suburb in 1901 under the style of R S McColl to gain maximum publicity from his footballing fame. Quality in both aspects of 'Sweetie Bob's' life ensured success. R S McColl expanded rapidly with a factory and 30 branches throughout Scotland. However, their market was limited to domestic Scottish appeal. It did not survive the economics of the early 1930s and the McColl brothers sold the controlling interest to the Cadbury group in 1933. But the appeal of R S McColl's name has remained throughout a series of ownerships and at the present moment fronts a vast chain of tobacco and confectionery shops throughout the UK.

Though the majority of entries fall under the preceding sections there are other less well known aspects of the distribution network in the industrial, construction and livestock trades. William Connal began in 1845 in Glasgow as a commodity broker dealing in a variety of general goods. he caught the upsurge in the demand for Scottish pig-iron and commenced trading in his own right in 1864 as iron broker and warehouseman. He occupied the middle-ground between the manufacturers and the contractors constructing railways or shipbuilding, basing his business on storing the pig-iron until it was required by issuing warrants to the depositor. This brought about speculative trading in warrants as prices for pig-iron fluctuated according to demand.

William Jacks was a linguist of some distinction and put his expertise to work by trading in iron and steel on the continent before moving on to the world of politics and translating the classics and history, mainly in German. John Currie successfully built up a distribution chain of building materials before turning to the preparation and sale of Portland cement. John McLaren Fraser of Perth was responsible for instituting a major industry in the town, that of the Cattle Mart. The Perth cattle sales replaced the old droving and tryst system of selling cattle as it declined with the spread of railways. Fraser began auctioning cattle in 1864 in Mill Street with the firm of MacDonald and McCallum, who were originally land surveyors and civil engineers. Fraser eventually became a partner under the style of MacDonald and Fraser. The market opening for cattle auctioneering was pioneered by Fraser and led to wider application of pedigree cattle breeding. By 1876 Fraser was sole partner dealing with some £200,000 of stock a year and had placed Perth at the centre of the Scottish cattle trade with worldwide contacts and buyers.

The predominance of capitalistic enterprises in the distribution sector must be off-set by the successful Co-operative system of trading which provided an increasing variety of goods to members of local and Scottish co-operative societies. Early examples were the provision of cheap supplies of bread and other essential foodstuffs such as the United Co-operative Baking Society. Union

John Menzies Ltd Bookstall

activities often forced workers to band together and form co-operatives such as the Scottish Co-operative Ironworks Society. Local Co-operative Societies opened retail branches for general goods. However, the wholesale production and distribution of goods came in 1868 with the foundation of the Scottish Wholesale Co-operative Society, selling to many of the smaller co-operatives. James Borrowman was a founder member of the SCWS and an early advocate of insurance, but it was the Rochdale Pioneers who finally formed the Co-operative Insurance Society acknowledging Borrowman's ideas but leaving the SCWS as Scottish agents for the CIS from 1872.

(Sir) William Maxwell was a contemporary of Borrowman and he fostered the enormous build-up of wholesale activities at the SCWS factories at Shieldhall, Glasgow. Boot and shoe manufacture at Shieldhall presented a direct challenge to capitalistic enterprises, more especially in the production of labouring work boots. As chairman of the SCWS for 25 years, Maxwell oversaw the expansion of retail outlets for Shieldhall goods and was active in co-operative politics, bringing the co-operative movement to the support of the nascent Labour Party. He brought an international dimension to the movement with his work for the International Co-operative Alliance. His international contacts took him to USA and Europe where he instituted a direct buying policy for the SCWS factories and reduced costs to co-operative customers. At his retirement in 1908 the SCWS annual turnover had risen to £7.5 million.

The growth of the movement continued with Neil Beaton who planted SCWS retail outlets in the 'deserts' of the co-operative spirit: in rural and Highland Scotland. This was often much to the distress of landowners and idealists such as the writer Eric Linklater. Beaton became chairman of the SCWS from 1932 and he widened the product base still further. He was responsible for the Art Deco style light bulb factory, British Luma, at Shieldhall in 1938, having preceded this by, laundry, pharmacy and funeral undertaking. The spread of SCWS products often duplicated brand name goods and a form of commercial warfare broke out as firms such as James Marshall's, to protect his Farola sales, and Campbell Paterson his Camp coffee and pickle production lines. The SCWS refused to sell these, and other products in their stores and Marshall and Paterson refused to employ anyone with co-operative membership or sympathies. At his retirement in 1946 SCWS annual turnover stood at £44 million from sales which covered almost every product in general use. He was however mainly concerned with providing a wider selection of services to SCWS customers but the conservative nature of co-operative selling he generated failed to take account of changing consumer patterns in the post war period. The same can be said for many capitalist concerns as they too fell prey to the grocery supermarket chains and multiple fashion houses.

But whether they were capital or labour based, the entries in this distribution sector show a remarkably high incidence of community involvement either as public figures in municipal, national or union policies, or by contributing to the charitable and philanthropic concerns of their immediate locality.

BRENDA M WHITE

John ANDERSON,

Warehouseman; b. 1817, Aberfeldy, s. of Peter Anderson, goods carrier and Margaret Mac-Donald; m. 19/4/1838, Robina Deacon Graham; 5 s., 2 d.; Major Firm, Royal Polytechnic Warehouse, Glasgow; d. 7/6/1892, Glasgow; g/v estate: £21,191.

John Anderson, orphaned at an early age, served his apprenticeship in Perth. He moved to Glasgow in 1835 and in May 1837 opened a small drapery shop in Clyde Terrace on his own account. At that time most retailers depended upon the credit nexus but from the outset Anderson determined to buy and sell only for cash. Initially he worked single handed, living over the shop and re-ploughing most of the profits. In April 1838 he moved to larger premises at 4 Clyde Terrace and married Robina Deacon Graham who was to prove an invaluable business partner.

Customers thronged the store, despite its distance from fashionable Trongate, due to judicious and inventive advertisement of his low pricing policy. In 1845 Anderson introduced the concept of 'universal trading'. By selling a range of different goods under one roof his warehouse became one of the earliest precursors of the department store. Such tactics were opposed by other retailers whose own trade was undermined by Anderson's sale of cheap toys, perfumery, books, patent medicines and drapery. Attempts to boycott Anderson's suppliers met with little success.

In 1846 Anderson made his first job lot purchase and sold a massive consignment of a printed fabric at less than its wholesale price. The venture was a great success and the strategy was used repeatedly by Anderson in later years with bulk purchases of religious tracts in 1849 and of arrowroot in 1850. Such goods, purchased at 50% to 75% discounts, were heavily advertised and shown throughout the store until cleared. This kind of marketing which depended upon achieving massive turnover, was new to Glasgow retailers who had previously restricted themselves to small sales of bargain lots often acquired from the stock of bankrupts.

From 1850 Anderson made regular buying trips to France, Austria and Germany. He was always quick to take advantage of favourable purchasing conditions and in 1848, after the abdication of Louis Philippe, was able to buy on his own terms in the Paris market. He often bought at exhibitions and from special sales, such as that of Emperor Napoleon's effects, so that his stock was fashionable and novel as well as varied.

By 1859 the Clyde Terrace warehouse had become too small for the volume of trade being conducted and new premises, which included Polytechnic Hall, were rented in Jamaica Street. The store became known as the Royal Polytechnic Warehouse and the lofty showroom surrounded by tiers of galleries, in the French style, was the first of its kind in Scotland. Some years later rising rents prompted a further move to a similar building in Argyle Street.

Anderson was never active in public life but he was a committed Christian and as a generous philanthropist was particularly involved with religious charities. From 1866 the Royal Polytechnic Warehouse charged 2d admission during the New Year's holiday and donated the entire proceeds to charity.

Anderson retired from active involvement in the firm in October 1891 and his two sons, Alexander and Charles, who had assisted him for some years assumed control.

ALISON TURTON

SOURCES

Unpublished

Millar, A H, 'Glasgow Sketches', 1889

Published

The Bailie, 17 December 1873
Briggs, A, *Friends of the People*, London, 1956
Drapers Record, 11 June 1892
Evening Times, 8 June 1892
North British Daily Mail, 22 December 1891
The Royal Polytechnic Jubilee Banquet Proceedings, Glasgow, 5 May 1887

Sir Mathew ARTHUR, Lord Glenarthur,

Wholesaler; b. 9/3/1852, Paisley, s. of James Arthur, soft goods merchant and Jane Glen; m. 8/7/1879, Janet Stevenson Bennett McGrigor, d. of Alexander Bennett McGrigor, LL D; 1s., 1d.; Ch, Arthur & Co Ltd; d. 23/9/1928, Mauchline, Ayrshire; g/v estate: £50,181 5s. 8d.

At the forefront of a composite portrait painting of the elite of Paisley entitled *Paisley Cross, 1868*, stand Mathew Arthur's uncle Thomas Coats (qv), thread manufacturer, William Wotherspoon, starch manufacturer and his parents James and Jane Arthur of

Barshaw estate, Paisley. Portraits and paintings, like photographs, can be as valuable a primary source to the historian as any document, and much can be gleaned from *Paisley Cross, 1868*, about young Mathew's formative years. Born in Paisley in 1852, the first son and second child of a father who was to become one of Glasgow's 'merchant princes' and a mother (she is the only real woman in the painting, the other is an allegorical figure wearing a Paisley shawl) whose vigorous campaigning for the political and educational rights for women, and social and medical welfare of all children, earned her the respect and affection of her fellow citizens. Mathew Arthur grew up in the midst of Victorian affluence and influence. From his father he inherited one of the largest cloth manufacturing and wholesale concerns in Britain and from his mother a passion for political and social action.

The firm Arthur & Co, began life as Arthur & Fraser, when Mathew's father James, the owner of a successful drapery and silk mercery in Paisley, (which he had founded in 1837 at the age of 18 with borrowed capital), formed a partnership with Hugh Fraser, (qv) a lace buyer with a Glasgow draper, in 1849. Together they built up a successful retail and wholesale concern (though the emphasis was on the retail side) until about 1859, when the partnership was dissolved and both men formed separate businesses. It was from as early as 1856 however, that the wholesale side was run from separate premises in Miller Street, Glasgow,

under the name of Arthur & Co. From then until his death in 1885, James Arthur extended his firm to such a degree that the *Glasgow News* for 5 October that year was compelled to state that it had 'no knowledge of so extensive a business in conjoined warehousing manufacture. There is nothing like it in London or New York.' Certainly by then not only were the premises at Queen Street/Miller Street/Ingram Street colossal with nearly 50 departments and 700 salesmen, there were also 100 commercial travellers at home and abroad, branch warehouses in London, Edinburgh and Newcastle and factories in Glasgow, Londonderry and Leeds, producing shirts, collars and men and boys' clothing.

Mathew joined his father's 'empire' in 1873 at the age of 21, following a brief period of travel abroad. Before that he had been educated in a one-roomed, one-teacher school in Paisley (at which his cousin, George Coats, the future Lord Glentanner was also a pupil), and a private school in St Andrews and finally Glasgow University. Unfortunately none of his obituaries state what he studied but it may have been an arts course he attended. He was the first of his father's four sons to join the firm, beginning with an annual salary of £150. How much influence he had in the early days is difficult to gauge, for although he was the boss's son, James Arthur was known to be 'brusque' and had the 'look of one accustomed to giving orders and seeing they were carried into practice'. Furthermore, in 1870, the firm became a co-partnership, with capital stock of £200,000 with William Ogilvie (who had been with the firm since 1860), William Wingate and John Robert Kay, three men with considerable experience in wholesaling. Nevertheless, James Arthur was firmly in command, the co-partnership was divided into 100 shares, 88 of which were held by him and four each by the other three. Provisions were also made, if the need arose, for him (or two of his sons) to take over the whole concern and pay out the other three.

However, Mathew who became a partner in 1874, was at a senior level for 11 years until he took over the responbilities of chairman following his father's death in 1885. Broadly speaking the years circa 1860 to 1900 were very good ones for the wholesale clothing industry in general, and outstanding ones for Arthur & Co in particular. But as it is impossible to separate Mathew's career from his father's until 1885, it is important to examine the reasons for James Arthur's spectacular success (or at least what is known).

There were several, not the least of which were the introduction of the sewing machine, the growing acceptance and popularity for ready-to-wear clothes, the growth of the home and overseas markets, Glasgow's lead in shipping, labour availability, and the wholesalers commanding position in the clothing industry itself. All of these advantages and opportunities James Arthur exploited to the hilt. But he also had two outstanding personal qualities beneficial for an aspiring business man: the ability to remain calm in a crisis, and a belief in a strict adherence to detail.

As early as 1857 he found himself in financial difficulties owing to a panic in Glasgow caused by the Western Bank refusing payment to certain customers. By calling a meeting of his creditors and submitting a statement of his affairs (which were in effect good) he gained their confidence and more importantly their financial support. This was followed by a letter to his customers in January 1858, explaining in detail what was happening with a promise to pay off his liabilities as soon as possible. This too had the intended effect, James Arthur was seen as an honest and honourable man who could be trusted. From this crisis very early in his career in Glasgow, he not only recovered, but went 'ahead by leaps and bounds' (Barclay). His strict attention to detail led him to have exact knowledge of his stock and enabled him to monitor his stock control to an 'nth degree. It was his practice to have daily statements on the various departments prepared for examination. No bad stock was allowed to accumulate, and no parcels or pieces of goods were allowed to appear in two successive stocktakings without an enquiry taking place. This was no easy undertaking in a concern which carried (this is not an exhaustive list) items such as linens, flannels, merinos, shawls, carpets, ribbons, printed cottons, tweeds, umbrellas, stays, gent's shirting, boots and shoes, men's clothing, juvenile clothing, ladies underwear, blankets, sheeting and curtains.

But if James Arthur realised the importance of minutiae and gaining public confidence, he was not blind to the opportunities for growth and expansion nor was he afraid to take risks. When he began his career as a draper and silk mercer in Paisley about 1837, he probably sold piece goods to women who either made them up into clothes for their families, or had such work carried out by private dressmakers. He continued to do this of course, but on a greatly increased scale as a wholesale merchant in Glasgow, but the introduction of the sewing machine in the mid 1850s created new possibilities. From the early 1860s sewing machines 'poured into clothing factories' (Adburgham) giving an immense impetus to the clothing trade, and Arthur & Co, were among the pioneers in ready-made clothing. The making of men's shirts was probably the most important, with two factories being founded at Glasgow and Londonderry for their manufacture, but eventually ladies' mantles, jackets, corsets and stays were also produced. In 1880 a ready-made clothing factory specialising in men's and boy's suits, trousers and cape-coats opened in Leeds, one of the most important centres of British tailoring. Competition between rivals was keen, and for English customers at least, Arthur & Co were able to deliver direct from the factory, thus cutting the cost of carriage, and giving them an advantage over their competitors.

Paralleling this expansion of the firm in Britain was its establishment and growth overseas. The first markets abroad were in the British Colonies, but apart from the fact that the firm was represented by agents and on occasion travellers and that the demand was mainly for piece goods, very little is known about the firm's activities in the countries it exported to - Australia, New Zealand, South Africa and Canada.

All of this was forged by a small team, under the undoubted leadership of James Arthur. Although his partner, William Ogilvie, is credited with influencing him to have Arthur & Co converted into a private limited company in 1878 (capital £1,200,000 of which £1,000,000 was paid up) Arthur retained the right to choose the direction and confined the membership to his own family and former partners. The shares were not placed on the market, being held exclusively by the partners and their nominees.

On his death at the age of 66, he left a personal estate of just over £1,000,000. He was essentially a businessman giving little time to outside interests. Nevertheless, he gave his wife considerable moral support, especially in her campaign for votes for women, and he was very generous to educational establishments in Paisley - especially after Mrs Arthur became a member of the Paisley School Board in the early 1870s. She was the first woman in Scotland to stand for election to a school board.

However, although he was associated with a few other business concerns, most notably Young's Paraffin Oil Company (as a director), Lochline Shipping (a financier) and Clan Line Steamers, he refused all other invitations to become involved or give advice, in order to confine his obligations to Arthur & Co.

His son's biography is almost the exact opposite. At the time of his death in 1928 Mathew Arthur, although chairman of Arthur & Co (and by then elevated to the peerage) left an estate of only £50,181 5s 8d and was probably more noted for his contributions to political and public life in Glasgow and the West of Scotand than business accumen. Indeed, as its history for the early 1930s demonstrates, the fortunes of the firm over which he had presided, had been decidedly mixed since the early 1900s.

Yet it would be wrong to suggest that this was caused by Mathew's lack of entrepreneurial skills or concern for the business. For just as the economic and social conditions of the period, the market opportunities and the position of wholesalers vis-a-vis the retailer worked to his father's advantage, during Mathew's chairmanship, especially from the early years of the twentieth century, they worked against. Nevertheless, there was expansion and success during his chairmanship, especially in the overseas market.

Overseas trading was important in the firm's early years, but it was not until the twentieth century that it enjoyed continuous expansion and large profits. By then Arthur & Co could have boasted it had become 'the universal provider' in most countries in the British Empire and at least another ten or so throughout the world. One interesting result of this trade was that the warehouse (whose policy was to fulfil as many orders as possible) opened a furniture department about the end of the nineteenth century. In 1902, Arthur & Co (Export) Ltd was founded. Although it was created as a subsidiary with a capital of 50,000 £1 shares, fully paid, it was not run completely separately from the parent company. Arthur's exported to territories as far away from Glasgow and each other as the West Indies, Greece, South America, Iceland, India, New Zealand, Hong Kong, Denmark, China, Canada and Egypt. In most of these countries there was a representative or agent (not necessarily on the permanent pay-roll), and in South Africa and Australia there were branch warehouses. By 1904 the South African warehouse, which was situated in Port Elizabeth, employed 24 men. Probably the best years of the export trade were during the boom which followed the First World War. One account, in South America, was worth £50,000 per year, and in 1920 the value of the firm's export trade totalled over £1,000,000.

Nevertheless, this was a false dawn. The economic slump of 1920-21 cost Arthur & Co over £400,000 which had to be paid for cancellation of commitments, and by the mid 1920s the firm was heavily in debt to city bankers. But apart from the widespread economic situation (which affected practically everyone) whole-salers like Arthur & Co were having to cope with new adverse conditions. In particular there was the growth of the large retail department stores in large towns and cities, which either dealt directly with the manu-facturers or had their own workrooms especially for women's clothing. Freight and transport costs began to increase (especially as Glasgow's position as an entrepot began to decline and direct shipping abroad decreased) so too did rates, postal charges, and packing materials and after 1912 there was the employer's contribution to the National Insurance Scheme. Fin-ally, and probably the most important of all, were the changes in social habits and fashions which had been growing since about 1910, and accelerated after 1918.

High Victorian and Edwardian consumption was nowhere more conspicuous than in women's fashions - wide crinolines, bustle skirts, flowing trailing dresses, with trimmings, laces and ribbons, worn over layers of frilly underwear and corsets, were the hallmark of middle and upper class womanhood who had at least two changes of clothing a day.

But the growth of women's emancipation (which ironically Mrs Jane Arthur helped set in motion) and the increase in the number of women going out to work since the First World War, created a demand for simpler less constricting clothes. In the nineteenth century Arthur & Co listed separate departments for lace, trimmings, ribbons, ladies underwear and stays. There was also one dealing exclusively in black silks, which were probably used to make mourning outfits. The custom of dressing in black for months at a time after a bereavement, (which was strictly adhered to by nearly all sections of society) began to decline after the horrors of the First World War when 'the bitter

realism of this habit became too repulsive for most people's taste' (Cunnington). Significantly, when Arthur & Co embarked on a programme of reor-ganisation and rationalisation in the early 1930s it was departments carrying such stock which were either closed down altogether or merged. Further savings were made by selling off large parts of the warehouse which had previously housed the enormous stock of piece-goods, which had been such an important part of the company's sales since the mid 1850s, and which were now no longer in demand owing to the almost universal weaving of ready made cloths.

Preliminary discussions regarding reorganisation from which 'the firm emerged stronger than ever' (Barclay) had begun before Lord Glenarthur's death. However, despite the fact that he had been connected with Arthur & Co for 55 years, 43 of them as chairman, there is very little information about Mathew Arthur, businessman. His obituary notice in the *Glasgow Herald* lists his directorships (chairman of Lochgelly Iron and Coal Co; Glasgow and South Western Railway Co; Young's Paraffin Light and Mineral Oil Co) and then goes on to give a detailed picture of Mathew Arthur the public man and in reality that is what he was. perhaps maternal influence was stronger than paternal, for like his mother he dedicated himself to political and public life for most of his maturity. And it is perhaps not without significance that in less than two years following his father's death, although he inherited the chairmanship of Arthur & Co, he also entered the political and public life of Glasgow.

In 1886 he joined the Board of Management of the Western Infirmary, and the following year the West of Scotland Liberal Unionist Association. Both concerns occupied a great deal of his time, and both brought him satisfaction and fulfilment, in particular his work for the Western Infirmary. In 1904 he became chair-man of the board, a position he held until 1921. During that time, the Western Infirmary emerged as an exceptionally well-equipped and administered institution and one of the leading teaching hospitals in Britain. His status and influence on Scottish Con-servative circles were equally important.

Although the Liberal Unionist Association had been formed by Liberals opposed to Gladstone's home rule policy for Ireland, very soon it was working 'albeit rather secretly' (Ward) with the Conservative Party. From 1893 Mathew Arthur had been its chair-man and after it eventually merged with the Con-servative Party in 1912, he became president of the Scottish Unionist Association from 1914 to 1919. At the time of his death he was president of the Glasgow Unionist Association.

During the First World War he was joint chairman, with Sir William Robertson, of the Central Recruiting Committee for Scotland and along with his wife he was active in the Red Cross Society. He was Deputy Lieutenant for Ayrshire and Glasgow and a member of the King's Bodyguard for Scotland.

It seems most likely that the official honours he

received, a knighthood in 1902, elevation to the peerage in 1918, and finally an honorary degree of LL B from Glasgow University, were in recognition of his public and political work.

In his private life he was very much the 'country gentleman'. At his estate at Fullarton House, Troon, he bred horses, rode with the Eglinton Hunt, and supported several local organisations.

The inventory of his personal estate reveals that the £50,181 5s 8d he left, came mainly from the shares he held in the Lochgelly Oil Co, and that those he held in Arthur & Co were paying no dividend at the time of his death. He left £1,000 to the Western Infirmary, £800 to be divided amongst his principal domestic staff, and one year's salary to those who had five years service with him. The remainder was divided amongst his wife, son and daughter.

MAUREEN LOCHRIE

SOURCES

Published

Adburgham, Alison, *Shops and Shopping*, London, 1964

Barclay, John F, *The Story of Arthur and Company*

Cunnington, C Willet, *English Women's Clothing in the present century*, London, 1952

Glasgow Herald, Obituary

Slaven, Anthony and Checkland, Sydney, (eds), *The Dictionary of Scottish Business Biography*, Vol I, Aberdeen, 1986

Ward, John T, *The First Century, a history of Scottish Tory organisation 1882-1982*, Edinburgh, 1982

Neil Scobie BEATON,

Wholesale merchant; b. 18/8/1880, Assynt, Sutherland, s. of Neil Beaton, shepherd; m. Martha Miller Hay; 1 s., 2 d.; Dir, Ch, Pres, SCWS; d. 23/8/1960, Portobello, Edinburgh.

Neil Beaton was the third son of a shepherd in a family of seven sons and four daughters. Educated by the travelling schoolmaster, he walked five miles every other day to 'school', held in rotation in one of three shepherd's cottages. Schooling over, he became a grocer's apprentice in Dingwall, and then went to work for a multiple firm in Edinburgh in 1897. He subsequently secured employment with St Cuthbert's Co-operative Association Limited, thus beginning his lifelong work with the co-operative movement. Increasing involvement in trade union activities led him to resign from St Cuthbert's Association in 1912 to become secretary of the Edinburgh branch of the Shop Assistants Union, and within a few months he had secured the post of Scottish Organiser for the Union. His energy and commitment to trade unionism in a period of inter-union and employer/employee conflicts led to a number of national appointments, including chairman of the STUC Parliamentary Committee, treasurer of the STUC, president of the Shop Assistants Union and finally president of the STUC in 1918-19.

In 1919 he returned to the co-operative movement as a propaganda agent for the SCWS. Over the next five years he succeeded in establishing eight retail societies in co-operative 'deserts', and was also partly responsible for the foundation of the SCWS retail branch organisation which played an important part in further national expansion. In 1924, Beaton was elected to the Board of the SCWS and concentrated much of his effort in establishing co-operative branches throughout the Highlands, a process culminating in the achievement of his long-time ambition: the creation of a co-operative organisation in his native Sutherland. His vigour and drive were widely recognised within the co-operative movement, and in 1932 he was elected chairman of the SCWS above men of wider and longer experience.

Beaton's 14 year presidency falls conveniently into two equal parts: the thirties and the war years. In the pre-war years he pushed ahead steadily with the expansion of the SCWS retail branch network, shops being opened for example in Elgin in 1933, Nairn 1934, Stornoway 1936, Turriff 1936, Millport 1937, Forres 1937, Ellon 1937, Lossiemouth 1937, Kingussie 1938, Shetland 1938 and Arran 1938, sometimes against considerable opposition from local traders, landowners and notables (for example the writer Eric Linklater). Expansion was not merely geographical. Services were improved and some new services started: funeral undertaking in 1934, laundering in 1935 and pharmacy in 1936. New productive ventures were also launched: the Shieldhall cabinet factory in 1931, tomato growing in 1933 and the opening of British Luma (producing light bulbs) in 1938.

Thus, despite the depression, Beaton's presidency saw substantive expansion in several areas. However, with hindsight, his success was not unalloyed. He failed, for example, to give a sufficiently vigorous lead to the movement over the adoption of 'bazaar' trading, despite the absence of any considerable internal opposition. In 1935, and again in 1937, the question of starting Woolworth or Marks and Spencer-type retailing was canvassed. The replies from the retail societies were inconclusive and the leadership allowed the matter to drop, thus leaving a lucrative sector of the market to private enterprise. Beaton also failed to mobilise the movement in opposition to the imposition of a tax on reserve funds in 1933, something which had been resisted successfully for over half a century. Much of this tax could have been avoided by reducing prices (& thus reserves), but Beaton's financial conservatism precluded this response, his arguments against eliminating depreciation carrying the day.

In ideological terms, Beaton was a pragmatist. He was concerned with service to the people rather than initiating radical social and economic change. Significantly, it was during his presidency that Calderwood estate was sold to the government in 1935, at a loss of £66,000. This sale officially acknowledged the death of a co-operative ideal which had, at least in theory, informed the movement for almost a century: the establishment of Owenite self-supporting communities on the land. By the outbreak of war, the SCWS under Beaton was in reasonably good heart financially. Its 1939 sales were the third highest ever, although its combined share and loan capital had been dropping for three years. In a more general sense though, the picture is less clear. It may be argued that Beaton's conservatism inhibited any dynamic response to capitalist crises, and his pragmatism facilitated the movement's continuing incorporation within the capitalist system.

The Second World War distorted the development of the SCWS, as it did that of every other large Scottish enterprise, and Beaton's performance can therefore only be assessed contingently. His interest in physical expansion persisted in these later years; indeed between 1939 and his retirement in 1946 a further 60 or more SCWS retail branches were opened, an unprecedented growth rate which was never again approached. The most important venture was development in Dundee where five outlets opened in 1939-40. Beaton travelled extensively both nationally and internationally during his presidency, and was an effective ambassador for co-operation, being a courteous and affable man. His greatest success in this field was his 1942 visit to North America, when his talk on co-operative democracy was broadcast over 150 radio stations; in fact Beaton was christened by the Americans 'the white knight of co-operation', a reference to his white hair and his chivalrous defence of co-operation.

Under Beaton the SCWS made a significant contribution to the war effort, producing vast quantities of munitions, uniforms and other essential war materials. Beaton himself was constantly on the move, visiting SCWS factories across the nation, often accompanying government ministers like Lord Woolton, and doing everything he could to keep up morale and productivity. His most important personal initiative during these years was his impassioned advocacy of a merger between the SCWS and its much larger English counterpart, the CWS. However, despite English approval, the Scottish societies decisively rejected the merger in 1944, and it was to take almost 30 years before the rationalising step was taken, and then only to avert collapse.

Beaton retired from the presidency of the SCWS in 1946, and therafter his influence on affairs was slight, being confined to membership of a number of national commissions and committees in the later forties. During his chairmanship, SCWS annual sales almost trebled from £16m. to £44m. and combined capital increased from £9m to £24m. Financially then, his stewardship may be accounted successful. He was also responsible for an unprecedented expansion of SCWS retail branches in the highlands and islands of Scotland. Over 75% of all SCWS retail branches opened between 1914 and 1969 were opened during his 14 year presidency. These are solid achievements, but in a wider sense his performance is problematic. The long post-war stagnation of the movement, its failure to capture a significantly increased share of what was for long periods a buoyant market, must be attributed at least in some measure to the structures and policies created and evolved during Beaton's long presidency. But perhaps his failure to give sufficiently dynamic leadership to an essentially conservative movement should not be judged too harshly. It may be that the structural problems facing the co-operative movement in the 1930s were already too great for any one man, however, gifted, to resolve satisfactorily.

LEN CAMPBELL & JOHN BUTT

SOURCES

Published

Anon, *The SCWS at War 1939-1945*, n d, c 1946

Carr-Saunders, A M, et al, *Consumers: Co-operation in Great Britain*, London, 1938

Co-operative News

Glasgow Herald, 24/10/1960

Hall, F, and Watkins, W P, *Co-operation*, Manchester, 1934

Johnston, T, *Memories*, London, 1952

Kinloch, J & Butt, J, *History of the Scottish Co-operative Wholesale Society Ltd*, Manchester, 1981

Lawson, W E, *People and Places*, 1968

John Stewart BIRRELL,

Chocolate manufacturer; b. 1863, Rattray, Perthshire, s. of James Birrell, farmer and Janet Stewart; m. (1) Janet McKemmie Burns; (2) Mary Paterson Dougall; 2 s., 1 d.; Founder and Ch, Birrell Ltd; d. 9/12/1938, Glasgow; g/v UK estate: £113,597 2s 8d.

Born in Rattray, a Perthshire village near Blairgowrie, in 1863, John Stewart Birrell rose to become the head of one of the best known confectionery firms in Scotland. He came from a farming background. His father, James Birrell, was a farmer and though Birrell tried his hand at farming at the age of 12 it appears he did not find the rural life to his taste. After a while he moved into Crieff where he apprenticed himself to a grocer.

Little is known about the next few years of his life. When he was 22 he came to Glasgow and obtained a position in the grocery trade. From this he proceeded to become the owner of a number of grocery shops and laid the foundations of a successful business career. Until circa 1900 Birrell concentrated on the grocery trade. He then changed direction and began the manufacture of chocolate in one of his shops in Partick. He began in this rather modest way, but soon afterwards he built his first factory in Thornwood Avenue, Partick West.

A rapid expansion of business soon followed for Birrell, and around 1912 he found it necessary to move to a new site at Anniesland in order to accommodate this expansion. At the time of the move the Anniesland area was almost entirely underdeveloped - many of his neighbours were still farmers and there was no main road - and yet in the next 20 years one of the largest housing estates, Knightswood, was built. While the area around his factory developed so his business continued to expand. Birrells became a public limited company in 1924 with a capital of £485,000. Birrell was made chairman and managing director. The success of the company continued and another large extension of Birrell's premises became necessary.

The growth of the confectionery market can partly be explained by the greater spending power of the public leading to an increased demand for sweets; also the introduction of automatic machinery helped cheapen the price at which good quality sweets could be made. Birrell had seized this opportunity and took advantage of the growing demand for confectionery, hence the need for enlarged premises. The extension was a two-storey building with 28,780 sq ft of floor space. This much enlarged capacity was to house some of the existing departments and also for some 'new lines'. But in particular the extension was to house a new chocolate covering and cooling machine - a feature of which was a high chamber along which the trays of chocolates passed in tiers. This showed the increasing mechanisation of the confectionery industry, reflecting the changeover which was occurring from handiwork to mechanisation, which in turn would lead to a reduction in the prominence of women in the factory workforce.

Birrell Ltd built up a reputation for good quality sweets of a wide variety. These included chocolate, boilings, fondants, jellies and assortments of all kinds. They were particularly associated with fine chocolates made at their 'Milady' factory at Anniesland. This reputation for fine chocolates may have stemmed from the fact that Birrells was almost unique among Scottish confectionery firms in starting the chocolate making process from the cocoa bean itself (of which there were at least 30 different kinds, each having a distinctive flavour and character) instead of already prepared chocolate. The chocolates were made of roasted and ground cocoa beans, cocoa butter, sugar and various flavourings, and the refining of these ingredients was highly skilled work.

Birrell Ltd and their main Glasgow rivals R S McColls were two main outstanding examples of sweet making firms which combined confectionery manufacture with the ownership of a nationwide chain of retail shops. Glasgow was Birrell Ltd's main base, but there were shops around Scotland as well as in England, including London, Birmingham, Leicester, Carlisle and Newcastle, though the major outlets remained in Scotland. Glasgow was a suitable central point of distribution - which was shown to still be the case in the 1950s when Birrell Ltd was bought over by Mayfair Products, as the new owners still concentrated all its production in Glasgow. Having their own retail outlets had its advantages for Birrell. Customer tastes were reflected in branch sales and factory production could be changed to allow for the vagaries of customer demand. By Birrell's death there were over 180 branches of Birrell Ltd in Scotland and England with other new shops in various stages of construction.

Promotion of their confectionery was important to make the goods saleable and attractive. Thus Birrell Ltd made a feature of window displays. For window dressing purposes materials such as crêpe-de-chine, satin, silk and sateen were used to cover window bases, often in a rucked fashion. Trays of sweets were widely spaced and arranged in pyramid form. Displays included foliage, flower baskets and ribbon bows, and price tickets were fresh and well printed.

John Stewart Birrell was devoted to his work, and as such any other interests were secondary to his business. He was at his factory daily from 6 30 a m to 5 p m and had been at work until the Monday of the week before his death. He became ill and was moved to a nursing home in Claremont Terrace to undergo an operation. He died in the nursing home on 9 December 1938, aged 75. He left an estate of over £113,597 which was to be divided between his family.

Little is known about the personal life of Birrell. His strict working schedule left little time for his other interests of flowers and fishing, especially in the Tay, his favourite river. When he was young he took an active interest in the Foundry Boys Religious Society, and later he was, for a short period, on the Master Court of the Incorporation of Bonnetmakers and Dyers. He was also a member of the Incorporation of Barbers. He showed interest in Perthshire and helped his native village of Rattray in practical ways. He married twice; firstly to Janet McKemmie Burns, and then to Mary Paterson Dougall and had two sons, John and James, and one daughter, Janet. He was survived by his second wife and children. After his death his sons carried on the business. Birrell was a well liked man both privately and in the business community and at his death he left a business which he had founded and developed into one of the best known Scottish confectionery firms.

THERESA BARTON

SOURCES

Unpublished

SRO: SC 36/48/536, Inventory
SC 36/51/266, Will

Published

Confectionery News, 14/12/1938
Cunnison, J and Gilfillan, J B S, (eds), *Third Statistical Account of Scotland, Glasgow*, Glasgow, 1958
Oakley, C A, 'New Processes and Products' Article No 54, *Glasgow Chamber of Commerce Journal*, Glasgow, 1937
Oakley, C A, *Scottish Industry Today*, Edinburgh and London, 1937
Scottish Trader, 16/12/1938
Stock Exchange Official Intelligence, 1925

Thomas George BISHOP,

Wholesale grocer and tea merchant; b. 1846, Carlisle, s. of Thomas Bishop, saddler, and Margaret Donnison; m. 28/11/1871, Hamilton, Elizabeth Henderson; 1 s., 2 d.; Proprietor, Cooper & Co; d. 26/8/1922, Dalmore, Helensburgh; g/v estate: £467,422 9s 11d.

Thomas George Bishop's business career grew from fairly modest beginnings as Scottish agent for Tetley's Teas to become founder of the successful chain of high class general grocery and tea stores, Cooper & Co, based in Glasgow, with notable branches in Liverpool, Manchester and London. Bishop based his success on keen commodity pricing and a specially targeted clientele: the rising strata of middle and upper working class families found in the great port oriented bastions of late Victorian affluence. The importance of communications in supply, distribution and consumer networks played a key role in his marketing strategies. The great trading cities provided him with import and export facilities and a seemingly endless supply of custom. The site of each store was carefully chosen to maximise communications potential.

Bishop himself is a shadowy figure. He was born in Carlisle in 1846. Little is known of his early life other than his forebears were leather merchants, and burgesses of Hamilton, Lanarkshire. Bishop had more scientific leanings than the family trade allowed and he attended Glasgow's Andersonian University with the intention of studying medicine. Some unknown circumstance forced him to withdraw from his studies and around 1864 he left Scotland for London where he began an apprenticeship in the tea trade with Joseph Tetley & Co.

In the Tetley business he rose to become their Scottish agent based in Glasgow. His private relationships with the firm were close: when Bishop married Elizabeth Henderson in 1871, Joseph Tetley Jnr was Bishop's 'best man'. Marriage to Elizabeth Henderson brought Bishop a further business opportunity when her mother, Lilian Cooper, lent him enough capital to open his first store and in recognition of her generosity Bishop named his business venture Cooper & Co.

Thomas Bishop opened his first shop in Howard Court in 1871. Howard Street stood diagonally in the path of the busy thoroughfare between St Enoch railway station serving the Ayrshire and border rail network, and the Broomielaw, the Clyde dock area serving the Western Highlands and Islands. Proximity to the Clyde dock areas brought immediate access to imported goods. Such judicious location brought passing long distance custom and ensured low cost supply and distribution opportunities.

Bishop established a daring pricing precedent. He

sold retail for cash at wholesale prices. General groceries and tea were staple items but Bishop included luxury continental items in his stock. Many businessmen predicted Bishop's failure but the buying public ensured a resounding success. He dealt directly with continental houses, bypassing the Glasgow wholesaling merchants, passing the profit margin to his retail customers. Within two years he had built a sound basis for expansion. He took his brother-in-law, John Henderson into partnership in 1873 and together they embarked on a programme of expansion in Howard Street and in quick succession opened premises in Sauchiehall Street and Great Western Road. Sauchiehall Street traversed the prosperous Blythswood district of Glasgow. Great Western Road bordered Woodside and the Hillhead districts, new home of the University transplanted from its original High Street location to make room for railway development in 1871. These were pleasant living areas, with spacious terraced and tenement housing, inhabited by professional, merchant, trade and upper artisan classes. In an age preoccupied with the human cost of high industrialisation these favoured districts of Glasgow and its environs provided the city's Medical Officer of Health with the lowest mortality and morbidity statistics.

The expected lifestyles and dietaries of these prospective customers demanded quality and variety. Bishop supplied both. By 1880 he developed factories within the Howard Street and Sauchiehall Street premises to manufacture pure fruit essences, jellies, custards, sauces, crystalised fruits, calf's foot jelly, syrups and a full range of powdered culinary spices. This was in addition to Cooper's in-house blended teas and coffee. Later, in the 1890s, to uphold quality control, he added bakery and meat processing production to his empire and consolidated all manufacturing at purpose built premises. His window displays offered goods varying from delicately wrapped confectionery to 36 different cereals and 40 varieties of tea. Bishop did, in fact, supply much of the sustenance, artefacts and ephemera of Victorian middle class life carefully depicted by illustrations, artists and novelists of the day.

Seasonal press advertising promoted everything from cool summer fruit drinks and cooked meats to the indulgent fantasies of Halloween with dates, nuts, masks, musical instruments and novelty boxes of toys ranging from 4d to 4s 9d. Extravagant Christmas delicacies were extended from mere oriental and continental edible delights to embrace the more solid tokens of seasonal regard: perfume caskets, cigars, cosaques (crackers) and fancy leather goods. But there were always the economically priced staple foods: three qualities of boiled bacon from 10d to 1s 4d per lb, sliced brawn 7d, roast chickens at 2s 6d each, roast pork 1s 2d per lb.

Thomas Bishop's business success went further than offering variety and value for money. His promotional flair was allied to a willingness to invest heavily in the commercial application of scientific advances which his contemporaries often ignored. To finance this he engaged in complicated real estate transactions with his growing property assets. With such financial aid he offered his customers elegant surroundings for their basic shopping needs. The Sauchiehall Street branch, greatly extended and rebuilt in 1880, was not so much a cornucopia as a temple. Bishop commissioned the architects, Peat and Duncan to design the building. The grandiose polished granite exterior, the opulent plaster and mahogany interior decoration with wide use of mirrors and glass, was a fitting place to introduce electric lighting into the city's commercial life. It caused a sensation. Bishop used the system powered by the Brush Electric Light Machine Company. In the same year the Howard Street branch was connected to the main telephone exchange so that customers could order by telephone. Indulging his customers further, Bishop linked his three Glasgow stores by field telephone to facilitate stock availability, introduced overhead cash railways to cut down waiting time, speaking tubes to connect departments, and pioneered motorised deliveries in the Cooper livery.

Innovations like these spelt out success for Bishop and by the turn of the century he could count 43 branches throughout Scotland, the North of England and London. Though not all his branches attained the eminence of Sauchiehall Street, the Liverpool store was reputedly one of the largest in the world. Like many Cooper's stores it commanded a salient corner sight and was located at the junction of Church and Paradise Streets. As in Glasgow, Bishop began there in smaller premises in 1895 gradually extending his holding then rebuilding on a grand scale in 1914.

The Church Street store employed over 1,000 staff and essentially repeated the sumptuous prescription for success that Bishop had used in Sauchiehall Street. Liverpool gentility shopped at Cooper's to the tuneful trill of singing canaries. Pageboys were stationed at all doors to carry out parcels to waiting cars. Cultural barriers between clientele and local staff, engendered by this oasis of sophistication, could and did lead to misunderstandings as the lady who telephoned a drawled order for two lamb chops and received two alarm clocks found out.

The Liverpool store however was more important to Thomas Bishop and Cooper & Co through the person of (Sir) Bertram Chrimes. Chrimes, who joined Cooper's in 1896 as an apprentice worked his way through all the departments to become manager of the newly opened store in 1914. He was appointed general manager of the group in 1919. When Thomas Bishop died in 1922 the company, previously unincorporated, was publicly floated in 1923. Chrimes was appointed managing director and continued the successful policies employed by Thomas Bishop until new marketing trends appeared in post war Britain. In 1963 Cooper & Co was bought out by Associated British Foods through its subsidiary Fine Fare.

Chrimes retired and the long connection of personal service, leisurely shopping and Cooper & Co was gone. A decade later it was scarcely a memory.

Thomas Bishop retained control of Cooper & Co until his death. When his sole partner retired in 1910 Bishop appointed his son, Arthur Henderson Bishop and Robert Nicol (the Glasgow manager) as partners. In 1921, Thomas Bishop celebrated the double event of his golden wedding and the golden jubilee of Cooper & Co, at which the staff presented Mr and Mrs Bishop with their portraits painted by Harrison Mann. His wife died shortly afterwards and Bishop survived her by only a few weeks. Bishop's only son, A Henderson Bishop became chairman of the newly formed Cooper & Co Stores Ltd. The company's initial authorised and issued capital of £800,000 can almost be regarded as a monument to Bishop's enterprise and business skills.

In private life Thomas Bishop's abiding passion, other than the happy family life he enjoyed with his wife, son and two daughters, was the study and collection of Coleoptera. At 14 years of age he compiled a Journal of his interest in Entomology. He was befriended by the noted Scottish naturalist Dr David Sharp and together they wrote up their findings of new species of Coleoptera on Rannoch Moor. Bishop scoured the few wildernesses around Glasgow for new additions to the range of Scottish fauna. He continued his interest in the Lewisham area when apprenticed to Tetley's. In later life, Bishop returned to his youthful enthusiasm for natural science and with Dr Sharp made further valuable additions to the scientific knowledge of beetles. At various times in his life he also acquired the collections of well known coleopterists. His entire collection was finally given to the University of Glasgow by his grandson. Bishop's obituarist in the *Entomologists Monthly Magazine* regretted the fact that despite Bishop being a noted collector and discoverer of beetles he rarely wrote up his findings.

Thomas Bishop's children made interesting marriages. All married children of Robert McAlpine (qv), giant of the Scottish construction industry. When both families were younger they lived close together in Hamilton. The Bishop's moved to the fashionable Clyde coast town of Helensburgh in the late 1880s and eventually bought Dalmore. When the McAlpines moved to Helensburgh in 1893 old friendships were renewed and to their parents amazement three engagements followed. Bishop's eldest daughter Lilias married Robert in 1896, Mary Gibb McAlpine married Bishop's heir, Andrew in 1897, and in 1898 Margaret Bishop married William McAlpine. Marriage to the McAlpines brought the Bishops into the orbit of political life as one of McAlpine's daughters married Major Richard Lloyd George, son of the Prime Minister.

Marriage, and friendship, with the McAlpines also brought Thomas Bishop further business opportunities. In 1894 McAlpines were involved in the building of the Craigendoran to Fort William railway. Competition for labour was keen. McAlpine's largest navvy camp was at Kinlochailort and he built a bakery there to ensure fresh bread to keep his labour supplied. He invited Bishop to open a store there and 12 other stores along the route to supply the navvies with quality food, tea, tobacco and clothing at reasonable prices. The Kinlochailort branch of Cooper & Co appeared to be a convivial place, 'soirees' were held there by the employees. But conditions were hazardous too: in 1899 the store at Glenfinnan was swept away by melting snows which burst a nearby dam, killing the storekeeper. The railway had other sad memories. In 1898 Lilias Bishop McAlpine and Robert McAlpine Jnr lost their infant son while staying on site at Corpach, Fort William.

Thomas Bishop did not court public life, even the great firm he founded did not bear his name. He attended the St Columba Church, Helensburgh, and shortly before his death donated an undisclosed sum to clear its debt. His charitable gifts, like much of his life, were given anonymously. A man of taste he collected fine furniture and masters of the Dutch and British school of painting. The value of his household furnishings and contents of Dalmore and his Beattock estate was over £5,000. The total value of his movable estate was £455,053 9s 11d, heritable property after debts amounted to £12,369.

Bishop's Inventory reveals no complicated shipping or mining shares. Fully £350,000 was taken up with the combined goodwill and interest in Cooper & Co. The other major source of his estate came from extensive life insurance policies. These are interesting because of the accrued benefits involved. Nine policies varying from £3,000 to £30,000 paid out the assured sum of £80,000 with a further £25,000 in accrued benefits. This may indicate that some policies were taken out many years previous to Bishop's death. Bishop might have taken them to cover borrowed capital to fund his business extensions. Insurance companies found such Insurance and lending policies a lucrative source of income.

Thomas Bishop died at his house, Dalmore on 26 August 1922 surviving his partner of 51 years marriage by only seven weeks.

BRENDA M WHITE

WRITINGS

Entomologists Annual, 1865
Entomologists Monthly Magazine, 1868
Entomologists Monthly Magazine, 1907
Helensburgh and Gareloch Times, 23/12/1896, 28/7/1897, 13/4/1898, 17/8/1908, 28/7/1897, 20/7/1898
The Oban Times, 14/1/1899, 18/3/1899

SOURCES

Unpublished

SRO: SC 65/36/20, Trust Disposition and Settlement
SC 65/39/29, Inventory
Register of Sasines, Glasgow 1871-1900

Published

Messrs Cooper & Co, Grocers and Italian Ware-
housemen, *The Mercantile Age*, 1881
Entomologists Monthly Magazine, December 1922
Glasgow Herald, 29/8/1922
Glasgow Evening News, March, June, October and
December, 1899
Glasgow Scrapbooks, The Mitchell Library, Glasgow
The Grocer, 2/9/1922
Helensburgh and Gareloch Times, 30/8/1922
Liverpool Daily Post, 26/9/51, 17/8/65, 28/2/1972,
1/3/72, 15/12/72
Post Office Directory, Glasgow, 1870-1906
Russell, Iain, *Sir Robert McAlpine & Sons: The Early
years*, Carnforth, 1988
Stock Exchange Official Intelligence, 1924-63

James BORROWMAN,

Co-operative manager; b. 1826, Edinburgh, s. of
John Borrowman, joiner, and Jane McNab; m.
Agnes Campbell; 1 d.; Manager, Scottish Co-
operative Wholesale Society Ltd; d. 9/6/1892,
Glasgow; g/v estate: £84.00.

An ardent and outstanding propagandist for the co-
operative movement, James Borrowman was one of
the founders of the Scottish Co-operative Wholesale
Society. His great belief in co-operative production,
however, almost led to the bankruptcy of the SCWS.
This mistake was to overshadow Borrowman's entire
role in the co-operative movement. Although always
held in esteem by ordinary co-operative workers, it
was only in the final years of his life that Borrowman
was rehabilitated by the ruling bodies of the Scottish
co-operative movement. He is best known for his
position in the SCWS, but his activities extended
broadly from production to co-operative insurance.

Borrowman belonged to one of the early great
families of Scottish co-operation. His father, John,
had been elected in 1858 as the first president of the
St Cuthbert's Co-operative Association in Edinburgh.
A leading trade unionist, John had been dismissed by
his employer for union activities so he established his
own joinery business with William Low, the secretary
of the St Cuthbert's Society. In 1866 Borrowman Snr
was censured by his committee for establishing a new
society in northern Edinburgh after a dispute over
the closure of the branch at Stockbridge. He resigned
to become president of the new Northern District
Co-operative Society.

In these early days of co-operation, James, an
accountant, was a prolific writer in Scottish newspapers promoting the cause. He became directly
involved in the Anderston Society in the 1860s and
as secretary to the Crosshouse Society in Ayrshire.
He rose to prominence as champion of the movement
to inaugurate the Scottish Co-operative Wholesale
Society. The Crosshouse Society was already a shareholder in the English Co-operative Wholesale Society.
Borrowman chaired all the meetings to discuss the
issue and with J McInnes, visited Manchester to
study the business methods of English society. In
particular, Borrowman was anxious that the proposed
Scottish society should have a secure capital foundation through share issue and investment from
existing societies. It took four years for Borrowman
and McInnes to persuade Scottish co-operatives to
establish a wholesale society. The SCWS was finally
founded in April 1868 with Borrowman appointed as
manager and cashier in recognition of his role as
founder. In these roles he had considerable autonomy
in the day to day administration of the society. In the
first quarter sales amounted only to £9,697 and had
only 28 members but by the end of the first year sales
had risen to £81,094 with a profit of £1,504, from
which Borrowman established a reserve fund.

As a founder of the SCWS, Borrowman also rose
to prominence in the national co-operative movement.
He became the leading spokesman for the SCWS at
Co-operative Congresses. In the early 1870s he was
elected as the first chairman of the Scottish Co-
operative Union. He was also a member of the Central
Co-operative Board and, with McInnes, was the first
Scottish representative to the Co-operative Union of
Great Britain. This gave him a national platform for
one of his main beliefs - co-operative insurance. He
had raised the issue as early as April 1865 in an article
to the Co-operator. In a series of articles he warned
of the dangers to societies of a lack of fire insurance
and recommended the establishment of a national
insurance system based on a levy of so much per £100
insured by each store which would be administered
from Rochdale. During the early discussion on the
creation of the SCWS, Borrowman tried to raise the
issue of co-operative insurance but with little success.
Eventually when the Rochdale Pioneers published a
draft plan B, a Co-operative Insurance Society, they
relied heavily on Borrowman's ideas. By 1872 the
SCWS was acting as agent for the CIS in Scotland.

Having done so much to secure the prosperity of
the SCWS through the creation of a reserve fund and
insurance it was Borrowman's activities which almost

caused the collapse of the society in 1874. Wile acting as manager and cashier of the SCWS, Borrowman continued his activities in other co-operative spheres. In 1869, for instance, he became secretary of the United Co-operative Bakery Society. In 1871 he helped to fund the Kinning Park Retail Society while the following year he joined the United Co-operative Drapery Society. At the Congress of 1872, Borrowman declared his faith in co-operative production stating that 'the consumer who is a non-producer is a burden on labour'. The conflict of interest this raised with his role of manager of the SCWS passed unnoticed but it was to become evident with his controversial involvement in the Scottish Co-operative Ironworks Society.

The SCIS was founded in 1872 by shipworkers dismissed for union activities. From its inauguration the society suffered from financial difficulties. Borrowman was one of the principal advocates of the Ironworks Society and persuaded the SCWS to provide an overdraft of £9,800 for the SCIC. However, unknown to the Board of the SCWS, Borrowman authorised a further £9,000 of credit. When the true level of the overdraft was discovered at the March 1874 quarterly meeting, there was a major crisis of confidence in the SCWS, the total overdraft representing a quarter of the Wholesale Society's capital. Several private bondholders began to withdraw their investments and E V Neale suggested that the SCWS should freeze its assets. Borrowman was censured for endangering the society and asked to resign. It was then discovered that he had given credit to his father's failing retail society in Edinburgh and to the Hawick Hosiery Company which was not even a member of the SCWS. The Board, therefore, reduced the period of notice and an open argument between Borrowman and the Board ensued. James Borrowman was reluctant to resign at the earlier date and attempted to gain support from member societies for his stance. This involved a loss of credibility in the SCWS but, accepting that Borrowman's behaviour was questionable, the Board must also take its share of the blame for failing to act decisively at an earlier date. It was only late in 1873 that the Board voted to curtail Borrowman's external activities but never implemented the decision, and the Board even elected Borrowman to represent the SCWS at the Halifax Congress of 1874. In the long run, the crisis proved beneficial for the SCWS resulting in improvements of both financial structure and management. The losses sustained were recouped quickly through a scheme proposed by the Penicuik Society that one penny per £ of the dividend should be capitalised at 5% until the debt was cleared.

After the debate of the Ironworks affair, James Borrowman returned to work for the Kinning Park Co-operative Society which he had helped to establish in 1871. However, he still found it impossible to curtail his activities to one enterprise. He also still attended the quarterly board meetings of the SCWS as a representative, proving to be one of its fiercest critics. Borrowman continued to pursue his interest in co-operative production. In 1875 he became manager of the Glasgow Co-operative Cooperage Society which was to fail five years later through want of capital. This time, however, the sale of land owned by the society covered its losses. Meanwhile the Co-operative Drapery Society had failed for the same reason, as did one of Borrowman's later ventures, the Bo'ness Industrial Pottery Society. On the other hand, Borrowman's managerial skills helped to pull the United Co-operative Bakery Society through a financial crisis until by 1875 28 societies were members and the financial success secured. Although many of Borrowman's production schemes failed, they paved the way for the implementation of co-operative production under the auspices of the SCWS inaugurated by Sir William Maxwell (qv). Maxwell differed in concentrating on the production of goods for which there was a ready market, such as soaps, shirts, boots and shoes and flour. Borrowman's reputation was finally rehabilitated in 1884 when he was presented with £200 in recognition of his early services to the SCWS.

James Borrowman did not play as active a role in co-operative politics. In 1873 he had stood as a Labour Co-operative candidate for the local school board, polled 7,463 votes but still lost after incurring the opposition of local churches. His lack of involvement in co-operative politics is readily explained by the amount of his time devoted to other co-operative ventures. He continued to work for the co-operative movement despite failing health until his death in 1892 aged 66 years. In his last years he concentrated on the Kinning Park Co-operative Society, although was also the secretary of the Central District Co-operative Conference. His advocacy of effective communications continued with the publication of the Kinning Park Co-operator in June 1891. Borrowman remained in charge of the retail outlet of the Kinning Park Society and persuaded the committee to purchase land at the corner of Crookston Street and Ardgowan Street for the erection of new premises. In 1891, he laid the foundation stone for the new building at a ceremony attended by several co-operative dignitaries including Neale and Maxwell. Even here controversy followed for alcohol had been served during the ceremony. While the committee generally were censured an attempt to blame Borrowman personally failed. James was not to live to see the new building completed. His rehabilitation was completed at his deathbed, surrounded by the Kinning Park Committee and William Maxwell who heard the last oration urging the co-operative fight to continue.

In sum, James Borrowman was a complex personality. A brusque, dominating figure who could behave at times like a petulant schoolboy, as in the Ironworks episode, he was revered by co-operative workers as their representative. His relationship with the leaders of the co-operative movement ws uneasy. His fundamental belief in co-operative production clashed with his role in the retail societies and the SCWS. Yet while many of his production schemes failed, they were to lay the basis for the success which was to come. Where Borrowman failed was in allowing his zeal for co-operative production to overcome his business sense. At his best James Borrowman remained one of the great pioneers of the Scottish Co-operative Movement.

PATRICIA COLLINS

SOURCES

Published

Co-operative News, 18/6/1892

Dollan, P J, *Jubilee History of the Kinning Park Society Ltd*, Glasgow, 1927

Flanagan, J A, *Wholesale Co-operation in Scotland. The Fruits of Fifty Years' Efforts, 1868-1918*, Glasgow, 1920

Garnett, R G, *A Century of Co-operative Insurance*, London, 1968

Glasgow Herald, 10/6/1892

Kinloch, J and Butt, J, *History of the SCWS Ltd*, Glasgow, 1981

Maxwell, Sir W, *The First Fifty Years of the St Cuthbert's Co-operative Association Ltd 1859-1909*, Edinburgh, 1909

Maxwell, Sir W, *The History of Co-operation in Scotland. Its Inception and its Leaders*, Glasgow, 1910

Edwin Ruthven BOYD, MBE,

Chartered accountant, b. 14/10/1884, s. of James Boyd, writer, and Kathleen Morison; m. Gertrude Lyford; Vice-chairman and MD, Campbells and Stewart & McDonald Ltd; d. September, 1949, Ayr; g/v estate: £1,119.

Edwin Boyd was educated at Kelvinside Academy and Haileybury College and served his apprenticeship as an accountant with Messrs M-Clelland, Ker & Co, Glasgow. He became a member of the Institute of Accountants and Actuaries of Glasgow in 1908 and in the following year entered the employment of J & W Campbell & Co. Scarcely into the run of business Boyd served in the First World War in Palestine and France as Captain and Adjutant of the Battallion of the 8th Cameronians (Scottish Rifles). He was mentioned in Despatches for his courage when wounded. After the war he returned to business life with J & W Campbell and in 1922 was appointed secretary of the newly formed Campbells and Stewart & McDonald under the chairmanship of Matthew Pearce Campbell (qv). He became a director in 1926 and rose rapidly through the hierarchy and later became vice-chairman and joint managing director to

COURTESY OF THE MITCHELL LIBRARY

349

James Clark Campbell (see Matthew Pearce Campbell, qv).

Campbells and Stewart & McDonald were still one of the largest wholesaling concerns in Glasgow but theirs was a shrinking world. In 1936 the firm's authorised capital of £1 million (in 1922) was reduced to £523,797. This was done by writing off 4/- of the preference shares and 18/- off the ordinary shares, and dividend arrears from 1928 to 1935 were cancelled. The outlook for most warehousing concerns continued to decline and in 1938 another of the major concerns, Mann Byers (qv Cooper) was wound up. Campbells and Stewart & McDonald acquired the stock and goodwill of Mann Byers. As managing director and vice-chairman Boyd oversaw much of Campbells and Stewart & McDonald's activities during this gradual run down of the firm's influence. His own personal influence in the commercial life of Glasgow however deserves notice. Edwin Boyd had a long association with the Glasgow Chamber of Commerce. He became a director in 1933 and chairman in 1945. During his period of office he made notable contributions to the postwar re-assessment of industry. He was also a director of the Glasgow and West of Scotland Commercial College and promoted an interest in the study of business administration courses for ex-servicemen.

He was a director of the Royal Hospital for Sick Children and a director of the Merchants House of Glasgow. He was a member of the Royal Company of Archers (The Monarchs Bodyguard in Scotland) and a Justice of the Peace in Glasgow. During the Second World War Edwin Boyd was engaged on censorship duties and was awarded an MBE for this work. Failing health forced his retirement from business life in 1948, though he retained his seat on the board of Campbells and Stewart & McDonalds. He died at his home in Ayr in September 1949.

BRENDA M WHITE

SOURCES

Unpublished

SRO: SC 6/44/156, Inventory
SC 6/46/88, Trust, Disposition & Settlement

Published

The Accountant, 5/11/1949
Directory of Directors, 1949
The Drapers Record, 24/9/1949
The Glasgow Herald, 19/9/1949
The Stock Exchange Yearbook, 1920-49

George BOYD,

Ironmonger; b. Elie, Fife; m. 13/9/1849, Elizabeth Gibson Gillies; 3 s., 1 d.; Founder, George Boyd & Co Ltd, architectural ironmongers and engineers merchants, Glasgow; d. 10/6/1896, Gourock; g/v estate £2,944 18s 5d.

George Boyd was born in Elie, Fife where he lived with his parents until the 1840s when he moved to Glasgow. The Boyds had been in Fife since the early nineteenth century. In his early years George worked for tin-smiths and ironmongers, Barnet and Morton.

The reason for George's move to the west is unknown. Certainly there would have been few opportunities for him in Elie, a place more noted even then as a holiday resort than for its industry. Perhaps he met his wife there while she herself was on holiday from the west. In any event on 13 September 1849 he married Elizabeth Gibson Gillies at the Congregational Presbyterian Church in Parliamentary Road, Glasgow. They had four children, Jessie, George, Richard and James.

The year before his marriage George Boyd formed a partnership with a Mr Waddell to supply wholesale ironmongery. Their original premises were in Sauchiehall Street, Glasgow. This partnership cannot have lasted long for George Boyd appeared alone in the Glasgow Post Office Directory of 1855-1856. By this time the business is listed at 248 Buchanan Street. There seem also to have been works at Weaver Street, Townhead, and at some stage in North Hanover Street. The firm carried out smithwork and light engineering as well as manufacturing nuts and bolts.

The obvious success of the company was mirrored by George Boyd's changes of address. From North Hanover Street he moved to Garnett Hill then to 11 Windsor Terrace in the fashionable West End. By the 1880s George Boyd was living at Bloombury House, Gourock.

In the 1870s the need for more manpower and capital prompted George to take into partnership his son James and some new blood in the form of James McAlister Shepherd. The two families continued to be associated. George Boyd died on 10 June 1896, predeceased by his wife in 1860. He left an estate worth £2,944 most of which represented his partnership interests in George Boyd & Co.

George Boyd & Co was to make its name in distributive work, but they continued to manufacture mainly for contract work as around 1900 they produced a locking mechanism for Glasgow Corporation's street lighting. Contract work became very important in the Second World War, when day to day business was hard to find because of the shortage of metal.

After the Second World War the firm's great period of expansion began. In 1946 the worries about death

350

duties and government regulations plus the need to expand prompted the firm to become a limited company. The Boyd and Shepherd families continued to maintain an active and financial interest in the company. However new partners were acquired such as John W B Scott who was to become the firm's managing director and piloted the firm through the 1970s when it became part of the Graham Group under the holding company Thomas Tilling. Recently Thomas Tilling has itself become part of B T R. The firm is now based in the East End of Glasgow with offices in the other Scottish cities.

CHRISTOPHER LEE

Sources

Unpublished

Business Archives Council of Scotland: George Boyd & Co Ltd
SRO: SC 53/41/8 Inventory
  SC 53/47/5 Will

Published

Evening Times, 11/6/1896
Glasgow Herald, 12/6/1896
Groomes Gazatteer, Edinburgh, 1882
Post Office Directories, 1855-1856

John CAMPBELL,

Draper; b. 1874, Fife; bachelor; Ch and MD, Pettigrew and Stephens Ltd; d. 13/11/1940, Glasgow; g/v estate: £104,434.

An obituary to John Campbell described him as 'one of the most outstanding figures in the drapery trade in Scotland'. If anything that was something of an underestimate for his influence was enormous and his contacts myriad. If his career can be criticised it can only be on the grounds that he took little active interest in the drapery trades in England and probably neglected the possibility of extending his operations south of the border, an opportunity which was seized upon by his contemporary Hugh Fraser (qv).

Campbell was the elder son of a Fife farmer but nothing is known about his education. It was likely to have been in the local schools of his native Fife. He received his early business training in Markinch before moving to Glasgow, full of ambition, at the age of 18 in 1892. It was a buoyant time for the drapery trades as standards of living were increasing and the demand for all types of consumer goods was expanding at a rate never experienced before. Commensurate with this expansion was a growth in the number and types of retail outlets, especially in a large city like Glasgow. There were plenty of jobs and an abundance of opportunities for early promotion for young people with talent. The firm which Campbell joined when he arrived in Glasgow was Arnott and Company but within three years he had moved to Pettigrew and Stephens as a buyer.

It was with Pettigrew and Stephens that Campbell built his career. When the firm became a limited company in 1904 Campbell became a director. He was only 30. His talent had been spotted and encouraged by Sir Andrew Pettigrew whom he succeeded as managing director in 1924 and later as chairman.

From this position he consolidated and developed a series of connections with other firms. He was chairman of Cochrane's Stores Ltd, Daly and Sons Ltd, J & R Allan Ltd, and the Scottish Drapery Corporation Ltd amongst others. He was also on the board of several companies. His presence on these boards was especially valued for his clarity of thought and commercial sense. In particular he saw the possibilities for retailers to challenge for some of the business of the old wholesalers whose business was under pressure from a number of angles including the direct selling organisations of several manufacturers. He was also responsible for an extensive building and rehabilitation programme.

Campbell seems to have been a popular man with his staff for in 1925 they presented him with his portrait in oils and in response he treated 800 of them to dinner in the Ca'dora Restaurant. The speeches there made reference to Campbell's high sense of justice and humanity.

In addition to his extensive business connections Campbell also found time to devote to benevolent interests. He was a prominent member of the Trades House and of the Merchant's House and was Deacon of the Incorporation of Tailors in 1932 and a member of the Incorporation of Bonnet Makers and Dyers. He also represented the Trades as a director of the Royal Hospital for Sick Children. In 1924 when the Board of Trade appointed a standing committee of the Council of Art and Industry, to deal with matters affecting the relations between art and industry in Scotland, Campbell was appointed to the committee. For many years he served as an elder on the Kirk Session of Sherbrooke Church, Pollokshields.

CHARLES W MUNN

SOURCES

Unpublished

SRO: SC 36/48/566, Inventory
    SC 36/51/275, Trust Disposition and Settlement

Published

Directory of Directors, 1940
Drapers Record, 23/11/1940
Glasgow Herald, 14/11/1940

Sir Malcolm Brown CAMPBELL,

Wholesale and retail distributor; b. 1848, Kilwinning; s. of Duncan Campbell, colliery engineer and Agnes Brown; m. (1) 1868, Euphemia McKechnie, d. of Donald Mckechnie, blacksmith journeyman; 2s. 1d.; m. (2) Isabella Mellis; Ch, MD, Malcolm Campbell Ltd; d. 3/9/1935, Glasgow; g/v estate; £20,800 5s 7d.

Malcolm Campbell's name is synonymous with the fruit and greengrocery trade still carried on in his name by the family firm he founded. His business biography presents the classic example of the progress from rags to ermine, of hard endeavour surmounting early obstacles, of the triumph of entrepreneurial talent. He began his working life as a child labourer in the cotton factories of Renfrewshire and died a peer of the realm. Contemporaries knew him as the man who introduced the banana to the Scottish people, but he was also the founder of the Clan Campbell Society, a dedicated civic figure and a noted local philanthropist.

Malcolm Campbell's early life was nomadic. Born in Kilwinning, Ayrshire, his parents originally came from Argyll, home of the clan Campbell. The family moved to Kilmarnock when he was three years old where his father worked as a colliery engineman. Six years later his father died in a pit accident and his mother moved the family to Neilston in Renfrewshire where she could get work in the cotton factories. Malcolm Campbell, the eldest of the four children, began work at the tender age of nine in a bleachfield working from 6 am to 7 pm six days a week to keep the family from starvation. He stayed with his family until he was 16 and the other children were able to provide family support.

In 1864 he left Neilston for Glasgow on the strength of hearing that a greengrocer in Buchanan Street was looking for an errand boy. The shopkeeper was Mark Walker whose premises were on the site of the present Stock Exchange. Campbell got the job and stayed with his employer for the next 14 years, becoming Walker's assistant. The business premises were changed from Buchanan Street to the busier corner of Gordon Street and West Nile Street near the Central Railway Station. The years spent with Walker provided Campbell with a business training in a burgeoning trade. The population of Glasgow grew from around 417,000 in 1864 to 524,000 in 1878. Commerce flourished. The food and related industries began the metamorphosis from straggling back shops to the beginnings of chain stores serving either the artisan classes, such as Lipton's Stores (qv) or the carriage trade, such as Coopers Stores founded by TG Bishop (qv). There was every reason for the greengrocery trade to follow this pattern once refrigerated transport came on stream. The port of Glasgow brought fruit from many lands, Tasmanian apples and Spanish grapes and oranges. Those who could afford it became, to one observer, 'a fruit eating people who ate fruit simply because they had been made available for our comsumption'. The fruit market was housed, after the 1860s, in Glasgow at the Bazaar in the Candleriggs from 1817 but it saw rapid increases both in size and the gradual increase of fruit broking firms over the fruit retailing firms. Scarcely a desirable

COURTESY OF THE MITCHELL LIBRARY

fruit or vegetable was not cultivated or brought to Glasgow by the end of the nineteenth century. Foreign trade stimulated the home market. Fruit and vegetable growers proliferated and in the Clyde valley glass houses grew fruit and vegetables out of season to cater for an ever increasing market.

The professional and middle classes demanded a diet of variety and quality and were willing to pay for it, especially at the Christmas season. John Glaister, professor of forensic medicine at the University of Glasgow 1932-62 recalled his childhood christmases in the 1890s when his father, John Glaister Snr, also professor of forensic medicine, would order a variety of rare fruits ranging from custard apples to litchis and grapes for the festivities. The central position of Walker's shop provided the young Campbell with a vantage point from which to mark the changes and to see the possibilities of the fruit and vegetable trade in a rising market.

Campbell's opportunity came in 1878 when Mark Walker retired. Campbell, now aged 30, bought the business from Walker for an unknown sum. Campbell already had two shops of his own by this time, situated in the New City Road area. He had married Euphemia McKechnie in 1868 and, as she was a fruiterer's assistant before marriage, it is probable that she looked after these shops. By buying Walker's business, Campbell therefore had dual access to the market for fresh fruit and vegetables, the local housewife buying seasonal fresh vegetables in the working class districts and the growing force of commuting city workers and shoppers prepared to pay more for extravagant delicacies such as apples, oranges, melons and grapes imported from Europe, America and the Empire. Around 1878, Campbell changed his listing as fruiterer and greengrocer to that of fruit and vegetable merchant and achieved the Victorian Glaswegian's dream, a holiday house on the Clyde, at Gourock by 1880.

The Gordon Street shop became Campbell's showpiece with its spectacular window displays of new delights. The proprietor's zest for innovation matched only by his customers eagerness to buy the wares so temptingly arranged. The tomato, known only for its culinary flavouring use, leapt into popular demand once one of Malcolm Campbell's customers picked one from the display and ate it raw while still in the shop. Supplies of this fruit were made more freely available once cultivation under glass became a profitable business in England, Guernsey and the Clyde Valley. Malcolm Campbell's flair for the unusual did, in fact, lead him to introduce the banana to the Scottish public. In the late 1880s, Campbell learned that the head gardener at the Duke of Hamilton's estate had begun to cultivate this new fruit. He arranged for a full banana tree to be transported and displayed in the Gordon Street windows. The effect was, as he intended, dramatic. By 1911 he was a large scale importer of Canary Island bananas which made the long journey carefully swathed in cotton wool and newspaper wrappings in straw lined crates and which were then hung and ripened in Campbell's own fruit and vegetable storehouses. Added to this, Campbell also bought much of his seasonal and non seasonal fruit and vegetables direct from continental and American growers. He moved into wholesaling, selling to other retailers who needed smaller quantities.

It was not merely the exotic that Campbell dealt in. He took cognisance of the native fruits, often grown in hedgerows, such as the ubiquitous Scottish Bramble. By observing the demand for home-made preserves he arranged consignments of brambles for his Glasgow stores which sold at the rate of 800 lbs per day during the season. Of the soft fruits strawberries made the best impact. He brought them to Glasgow by express train from Southampton in specially fitted vans then arranged them all around Grodon Street piling punnet upon punnet in glorious abundance. Who could resist such temptation? Evidently very few for he sold a record three and a half tons in one day.

Malcolm Campbell was a consummate arbiter of public taste, and this was shown to perfection in the exquisite Rotunda he built for the great 1901 Glasgow International Exhibition held in Kelvingrove. In the flower garlanded building which flew the company's flag, Mrs Campbell presided over the sale of teas and confectionery to refresh the elegant, and the plainly dressed visitors. Part of Campbell's success was the accepted customary pattern of the lady of the house buying her own fresh fruit, vegetables and, quite often, cut flowers and potted plants. This allowed him to tap the ideals of the late Victorian society, part of which was the development of the visual arts for private and public functions in the form of ornate floral decoration.

Responding to this trend Campbell diversified into floral arrangements in the 1890s and took the telegraphic code 'Bouquet'. Campbell's displays decorated some of the most prestigious occasions of the day. The luncheon room and tables for guests at the *Lusitania* launch in 1907 were garlanded by Campbell's floral artists. So too were Tommy Lipton's 'Shamrock' occasions and this maritime tradition extended to decorated 'christening' bottles. Political dinners, society weddings, church functions, receptions, even the Stock Exchange's chairman's Christmas dinner all benefited from the sensory delights created in Campbell's St Vincent Street floral warehouse. Many of the blooms were grown under glass in Campbell's nurseries at Hughenden which were situated close to his Glasgow house, and at his Drumchapel and Scotstoun nurseries. Others were imported from England and the Continent.

In 1904 Campbell began a lucrative expansion of his business by opening a kiosk at St Enoch Railway Station selling in micorcosm all that his Gordon Street branch had to offer. In the decade following he opened similar kiosks at all the main Glasgow terminii and the coastal stations. In their heyday there were 60 such kiosks stretching from Stonehaven down to Crewe. At the end the kiosks, built to an easily recognisable pattern, made of mahogany and glass and surrounded by a large brass rail, the customers could barely see the assistants behind the goods on display. An appealing and colourful display of highly polished fruit, boxes of chocolates, nuts, dates, figs, tins of toffees, shortbread, Edinburgh rock, grapes, jars of honey, offered travellers all their fancied needs and emblazoned Malcolm Campbell's name on the mind of the travelling public. It was this amalgam of quality, colour variety and publicity, in all their branches, which helped Malcolm Campbell Ltd to weather the war years and the depressed 1920s and 1930s.

Malcolm Campbell formed his business into a public limited company in 1899 with his son, Donald and five others as subscribers taking one share each. The business was valued at £45,000 divided into equal amounts of £1 preference and ordinary shares. Campbell, as chairman and managing director, held all the initially issued shares: 14,525 ordinary and 10,000 preference. In 1901 he appointed his two sons, Donald and Malcolm as directors. Some indication of the volume of business generated at the turn of the century was given in the Scottish Trader when the 1905 dividend was paid at 10% ordinary and 5% preference. The reasons given for such generous dividends were the progress in the nursery and floral departments and the increased gross takings of £5,146 from the extended Gordon Street shop. In 1908, at an extraordinary general meeting, Campbell made the company into a private limited company, a position maintained to the present day.

As a person, Malcolm Campbell was tall, well built with great presence. He was a hard working, likeable, gregarious man who took his social responsibilities seriously. The course of his life from the early years of deprivation to the affluence made possible by business acumen made him a natural choice for membership of the City Parochial Board, which he served on for 18 years. Under Campbell's chairmanship the City and Barony Parochial Boards amalgamated into the consolidated City of Glasgow Parish. He was a director of the Glasgow Juvenile Delinquency Board for several years and was chairman of the Glasgow Burgh Distress Committee during a succession of hard winters in the late 1880s. He was elected to serve as councillor for the eleventh ward of Glasgow in 1880 under John Ure's Lord Provostship and was elected to serve as magistrate in the 1883 local elections, and sat on the bench regularly. These were busy years for Campbell coming as they did shortly after he began his own business in 1878. He quit active municipal work after 1886 to concentrate on the growing demands of his business.

A sincere interest in poor made him president of the Brown's Society, one of Glasgow's oldest benevolent societies, and chairman of the Fruit Trades Benevolent Society. His civic commitment brought him into the formation of the municipal museum known as the People's Palace, built in 1898 at a cost of £20,000. Campbell and some notable business men bought out a company called The People's Palace which operated a music hall off the Gallowgate. The company was then wound up and the title was then transferred to the new museum and the attached Winter Gardens.

He was an enthusiastic Free Mason and a Master of the Lodge Montefiore, 753. Campbell enjoyed a long association with the Montrose Congregational Church and was president of the Congregational Union in 1924. Other positions held by him were, Justice of the Peace for Glasgow, treasurer of the Glasgow Branch of the National Temperance Commercial Union, president of the Sandyford Burn's Club, president of the Scottish Poet's Club, president of the Grocer's Company of Glasgow, trustee of several insurance offices including the Scottish Legal and Industrial Life Insurance Society.

His generosity was legendary. In 1918 he gifted £2,000 to the Glasgow Royal Infirmary and several other Institutions. To celebrate his eightieth birthday Campbell gave all his 250 staff an extra weeks wages in recognition of their services. He remembered his harsh childhood and donated £300 each to the poor of Kilmarnock and Kilwinning and £200 to Kilwinning. Lenzie Convalescent Home received £100 and the Fruit Trades Benevolent Society £50.

In 1922 Malcolm Campbell was knighted for his services to the city and the fruit trade. In a proud moment he was the guest of honour at a dinner given by the Clan Campbell Society which had formed in the 1890s and of which he was the first president. In his speech of acknowledgement he said that 'although he had been so long in Glasgow he felt Argyllshire blood still in his veins'.

Sir Malcolm Campbell died in 1935 at the age of 87 at his home in Glasgow.

BRENDA M WHITE

SOURCES

Unpublished

SRO: SC 36/48/491, Inventory
     SC 36/51/252, Will
     SC 4399, Malcolm Campbell Ltd, Companies Registration Office

Published

The Baillie, No 897, 1889
Bell & Paton, *Glasgow, Its Municipal Organisation & Administration*, Glasgow, 1896

Centenary Booklet, Malcolm Campbell Ltd, 1978
Directory of Directors, 1935
Evening Times, 4/9/1935
Fruit & Flower & Vegetable Trades Journal, 7/9/1835
Glaister, J, *Final Diagnosis*, London, 1964
Glasgow Corporation, *Municipal Glasgow, Its Evolution and Enterprises*, Glasgow, 1914
Glasgow Herald, 2/1/1922, 31/1/1922, 30/11/1928, 4/9/1935
Post Office Directories
Scottish Trader, July, 1904 and November, 1905
Tweed J, *The Lord Provosts of Glasgow, 1833-1883*, Glasgow, 1883
Who Was Who, Vol III

Matthew Pearce CAMPBELL,

Wholesale warehouseman; b. May 1853, s. of William Campbell, merchant and Hannah Pearce; m. October 1881, Mary Helen Clark; 1 s.; Partner & Dir, J & W Campbell & Co, Ch & Dir, Campbells and Stewart & McDonald Ltd, Dir, British Linen Bank, Nobles Explosives, North British and Mercantile Insurance Co Ltd.; d. 2/8/1924, Glasgow; g/v estate: £93,160 15s 0d.

Matthew Pearce Campbell was born into a family of titans in the Scottish warehousing community whose owners were part of the British political system. The family firm of J & W Campbell was founded in 1817 by James and William Campbell. James Campbell was later to become Lord Provost of Glasgow 1840-43 and was knighted. His sons were James Campbell, MP for Glasgow and Aberdeen Universities, and Sir Henry Campbell Bannerman, one time Prime Minister. The second partner William Campbell, was Matthew Pearce Campbell's grandfather.

The original partners of J & W Campbell came from the Port of Menteith and began business in the Saltmarket area of Glasgow and gradually built up a magnificent empire in that particular part of town, moving, gradually, towards the imposing edifice in Ingram Street built in 1858 in the Scottish baronial style. This building is still a city landmark. Both brothers were involved in municipal politics and James bought Strachathro Estate and William bought Tullichewan Estate. When the original partners retired their places were taken by James A Campbell of Stracathro MP and Sir Henry Campbell Bannerman and their cousin James Campbell of Tullichewan. Matthew Pearce Campbell entered the firm in the counting house department and succeeded to the management of the department in 1884 when his cousin George Langlands retired. Campbell was at this time 31 and had recently married Mary Helen Clark. Under Campbell's partnership and directorship J & W Campbell's weathered the rigours of the First World War and the aftermath of broken lines of trade communications and lost markets. J & W Campbell's was originally a manufacturing and retail organisation but had turned wholly to being wholesalers in the 1850s and remained so. They sold all the staples of the warehousing trade in soft goods.

J & W Campbell's was something of an institution but in 1922 it merged with another old established Glasgow warehousing concern Stewart & McDonald's & Co Ltd. Matthew Pearce Campbell was chosen as chairman of the new company now named Campbells and Stewart & McDonald Co Ltd which was housed in the great Ingram Street warehouse of J & W Campbells. The new firm Campbells and Stewart & McDonald Ltd had an authorised capital of £1 million. £918,000 was issued, part in ordinary and part in preference shares of £1 fully paid; the preference shares were entitled to a cumulative 7% paid in March and September and to priority for capital without further participation. Of the two firms Stewart & MacDonalds appeared to be the partner most in need of the merger, their premises in Argyle,

COURTESY OF THE MITCHELL LIBRARY

Buchanan and Mitchell Streets carried mortgages of £233,000. The merger was part of a drastic shift in warehousing fortunes as the retail trade rose to take its place. It is interesting to note that the chairman of Stewart & McDonalds Ltd was Sir Andrew Pettigrew of Pettigrew & Stephens, a long established firm, which was floated as a public company under his aegis in 1904.

Matthew Pearce Campbell died shortly after the foundation of Campbells and Stewart & McDonald Ltd. He was succeeded by Andrew Pettigrew as chairman and joint managing director, and his own son James Clark Campbell as vice-chairman and joint managing director. As befitting the head of a large commercial concern with strong community lines M P Campell held a number of responsible positions. He was also a well propertied man with a small estate, Glenlora, at Lochwinnoch and a town house in Lynedoch Crescent in Glasgow's prestigious Park area.

As would be expected Matthew Pearce Campbell was connected with both the Trades and the Merchant House of Glasgow. In 1896 he became deacon of the Weavers Incorporation at the Trades House. In 1908 he was appointed Lord Dean of Guild and in the same year he became Deputy Lieutenant for the county of Glasgow for which he was also Justice of the Peace. His association with the Merchants House brought him to membership of the Clyde Navigation Trust from 1899 to 1904 and he was also, for a term, the patron of the Adam Smith Chair of political economy in the University of Glasgow. The Campbell family had a strong connection with the Glasgow Savings Bank; the original partners, James and William Campbell were two of the founders of the Glasgow Savings Bank in 1836. Following this family tradition Matthew Pearce Campbell was, for many years, the chairman of the committee of management and followed closely the business of the bank.

M P Campbell carried on much of the duties assumed by his grandfather, William Campbell, such as the chairmanship of the Maternity Hospital and the Glasgow Night Asylum. He was also a director of the Glasgow Chamber of Commerce and an honorary member of the Glasgow Merchants Club. Matthew Pearce Campbell represented the Campbell family on many other major concerns in the west of Scotland. He was a director of the British Linen Bank, of the North British and Mercantile Insurance Co and Nobles Explosive Co. He was a member of the departmental committee on the bankruptcy laws in Scotland and was also a representative on the juvenile delinquency board.

Campbell's life was not all business, he had literary and artistic pursuits and was for many years chairman of the choral and orchestral union in Glasgow and is said to have promoted much of the rising standards of musical appreciation within the city. Earlier in his life he was a member of the Volunteer Force and served for 27 years in the 1st Lanark Volunteers and held the honorary rank of major of 'the Greys'. During the war he was a member of the military appeal tribunal.

Matthew Pearce Campbell died at his Glasgow home on 2 August 1924. The gross value of his estate was £93,160 much of which was takn up by his holdings in Campbells and Stewart & McDonald Ltd and the various commercial concerns of which he was a director. It is interesting to note that of the 15,000 preference shares held in Campbells and Stewart & McDonald at a £1 were valued only at 18/9d. and the 81,985 ordinary £1 shares were valued at 12/6d, nevertheless, this accounted for a great deal of his wealth. A further indication of his taste and refinement were the comparatively large amounts attributed to the household furniture; £2,433 at Glenlora, Lochwinnoch and £1,568 at his town house, 9 Lynedoch Crescent.

BRENDA M WHITE

SOURCES

Unpublished

SRO: SC 36/48/357, Inventory
SC 36/51/204, Trust Disposition and Settlement

Published

The Bailie, 23/9/1896
Glasgow Herald, 4/8/1924, 6/8/1924
Post Office Directories, 1860, 1924 passim
Scottish Retail Drapery Journal, 1924
Stock Exchange Yearbooks, 1920-24
Stock Exchange Intelligence, 1972
Stratten's Commercial Glasgow, London, 1891
Who's Who in Glasgow, 1909

William CONNAL,

Commodity broker and warehouseman, b. 1819, Stirling, s. of Patrick Connal, banker, and M S Glass; m. Emilia Jessie Campbell, 5 s., 4 d.; Proprietor, Connal & Co, Ironbrokers & Warehousemen, Glasgow; d. 14/7/1898, Solsgirth, Dollar; g/v estate: £209,564.

William Connal and his cousin Michael Connal were taken into business by their uncle William Connal in 1845. William Connal Snr had come to Glasgow from Stirling around 1806, then being about 16 years of age. Six years later he joined the commodity brokers firm of Findlay, Duff & Co, which through a series of changes in partners and families, could trace its origins back to 1722 to the Virginia Merchants House of Cochrane Murdoch & Co. By 1822 the young William Connal had become a partner and the company had changed its name to Findlay, Connal & Co. In 1826 this company foundered in the cotton famine crisis of that year; the four partners then established themselves in four independent businesses. William Connal specialised in tea and sugar importing activities, and built a large bonded tea warehouse in York Street, Glasgow, to cope with the London buyers who came north to purchase their supplies in his sales. William and Michael Connal's uncle continued in business on his own account till 1845 when his two nephews joined him; William was then 26 and Michael 28. The business then became known as William Connal & Co.

The new company grew rapidly and quickly added a new commodity to its list - pig iron. The Connals' began in pig iron as brokers just as in their other commodities, but since the pressure quickly grew to establish an efficient distributive link between the many pig iron producers in the Monklands, and the large number of consumers in Scotland and elsewhere, the Connals also quickly became warehousemen. With their uncle's approval the young William Connal and his cousin Michael formed an independent company M & W Connal, to handle this branch of activity; William Connal managed this agency.

The elder William Connal, founder of the business, died suddenly in 1856. For the next eight years the two cousins worked the business between them. In 1864 however, they separated to form two independent companies. Michael Connal took over the tea, sugar and general commodity business. Somewhat confusingly, Michael Connal continued to trade with the established name William Connal & Co; William Connal then reverted to trading under the title Connal & Co.

Connal & Co, in which William was the sole proprietor, specialised in the pig iron business in which he was an iron broker and warehouseman. Commencing business on his own in 1864, he caught the Scottish pig iron industry in its upswing. Scotland at that time supplied a large part of Britain's needs of pig iron, and in Glasgow there developed the Glasgow pig iron market, an agency to act as an intermediary between suppliers and customers. Connal & Co introduced an unusual element into this commodity market business, by accepting physical deposits of pig iron normally in units of 500 tons. William Connal issued the depositor with a warrant proving ownership of the deposited iron. On presentation of the warrant to Connal & Co, and after payment of storage charges, the pig iron was released to the holder of the warrant. These warrants were in effect certificates or tickets which could be traded on the pig iron market as prices fluctuated. This device was initially intended to help contractors to even out fluctuations by purchasing warrants against future needs of pig iron in extended construction contracts, say in building railways or iron vessels. However, since price fluctuations in pig iron were substantial, the warrants also attracted speculators who gambled on the warrant prices and never had any intention of actually using the iron on deposit. William Connal effectively provided the foundation for this activity, but as pig iron production grew and new centres of production appeared, and as iron masters began to bypass warehouses in preference to directly supplying customers, the 'iron ring' in Glasgow Exchange began to diminish in importance. Nevertheless it dominated William Connal's business from the formation of his own company in 1864 to his death in 1898. By then Connal had established another warehouse complex at Middlesborough, but he could not dominate pig iron sales there as he had done in Glasgow. Connal's stores and warehouses were capable of handling immense quantities of iron, and the Glasgow stores peaked with deposits of 1,030,000 tons of pig iron in 1889. The system declined sharply with the run down in Scottish iron production, and the Pig Iron Ring was finally closed in 1916 by order of the Ministry of Munitions.

William Connal did not devote all his energies exclusively to business. He had an estate and farms at Solsgirth near Dollar, and spent much time there with his wife and large family of five sons and four daughters. He was not much interested in public office or affairs, but did have an interest and involvement in the Juvenile Delinquency Board, leaving its directors £200 for investment. His one indulgence was the collecting of works of art and he was a significant collector of paintings. On his death in 1898 in his eightieth year, his personal moveable estate was valued at £209,564. He had already transferred substantial shares in Connal & Co to his offspring, and at his death his own holdings in the company totalled only £6,150. Wealth and control in the business had already been passed on, particularly to his son William. Only £48,414 of his estate lay in Scotland, the balance of nearly £160,000 being invested in England, notably in railways. He had over £63,000 invested in the London & North Western Railway alone.

At the time of William Connal's death the mainstay of his company, pig iron, was in decline. In the hands of his sons and in-laws, Connal & Co reverted to more general commodity brokerage. In the First World War Connal & Co was especially involved in food storage and distribution. Later in the 1920s the company invested in road transport. In a hundred years Connal & Co had come full circle and had returned to being a more diversified brokerage, warehouse and investment enterprise.

ANTHONY SLAVEN

SOURCES

Unpublished

SRO: SC 36/48/163
    SC 36/51/119, Will

Published

Gibson, (ed), John C, *Diary of Sir Michael Connal 1835-1893*, Glasgow, 1895
Glasgow Post Office Directories
Mitchell, J O, *Two Old Glasgow Firms: W Connal and the Crums of Thornliebank*, Glasgow, 1894
Mitchell, J O, *The Old Hoose of William Connal & Co*, Glasgow, 1894
North British Daily Mail, 15 July 1898
Oakley, C A, *Connal & Co Ltd, 1722-1946*, Glasgow, 1946

John P CURRIE,

Cement merchant and building trades supplier; b. 1848, Glasgow, s. of Joseph Currie, classics teacher and author, and Margaret Robertson; m. Mary B Thomson; 1 d.; Founder, MD and Ch, Currie & Co, Glasgow, Edinburgh, etc.; d. 30/3/1919, Edinburgh; g/v estate: £33,723 2s 10d.

During the second half of the nineteenth century there evolved a significant group of companies which had been established primarily to service the demands of an increasingly sophisticated construction industry. These firms ranged from those involved in the extractive industries; quarriers such as Gibb and Fyfe of Aberdeen (qv), brick and fireclay goods producers such as Glenboig Union Fireclay, and timber merchants and saw-millers, such as Brownlees of Glasgow. Least glamorous of all these was the general builder's merchant, selling and distributing some of the items produced by those above, in addition to a variety of other products deemed essential to the public works contractor and house-builder. Typically firms involved in building supplies operated on limited capital within a small area. A significant part of the credit which fuelled much of the building industry originated with builders' merchants, who were consequently prone to failure as the fortunes of the industry fluctuated. One exception to these three features of builder's merchants was Currie & Co, who under the management of John P Currie became one of the largest firms in the trade in Victorian and Edwardian Scotland.

John Currie was born in Glasgow in 1848, where his father Joseph was classics master at Glasgow Academy. Currie was educated in the city, where he subsequently served an apprenticeship at the Greenhead mill of his relatives, the cotton spinners John Robertson & Co, where his training concentrated on the commercial rather than the manufacturing side of the business. In the late 1860s he moved to the office of John Orr Ewing & Co, the Turkey Red dyers, where he remained until 1873. In that year he began his own business as a commission agent and merchant, dealing principally (and somewhat curiously given his background) in Portland cement. At this time there were around 35 cement merchants in the city, dealing, in the case of Portland cement, with a material which was still regarded with some suspicion in some parts of the construction industry. However its use was increasing, largely due to its comparative cheapness and ease of preparation, and Currie's strategic decision to concentrate his business on cement was to be of immense importance to the firm. In order to secure a lead over his competitors Currie strove to gain agencies with some of the most prestigious firms in the business: Johnsons of London and Gateshead, Thomlinson & Salked of London, and the West of England Granite Company from Cornwall. His flagship product was Eagle Portland Cement, produced by one of the leading Kentish manufacturers, a material of high-quality that was in demand on many prestigious contracts. In 1880 the sustained growth in trade led him to move the firm's premises from Queen Street to Wellington Street in Glasgow. A store in Wallace Street, incorporating the frontage of a mock lime-kiln, was expanded in 1882 and again in 1889. With his younger brother, Joseph, who managed an identical business in Leith, Currie obtained 'some of the largest contracts then going' for cement, including cement for the Tay Bridge contracts. His customers soon included 'the principal contractors and builders, as well as public corporations' in Scotland, including firms such as James Young & Sons and John Best (qv).

Currie increased the range of goods the firm dealt with to include plasters, Scotch and Irish limestone, crushed granite, Arbroath and Caithness paving stones, slates and fireclay goods. In addition they acted as sole agents for a range of cement testing machines. Extensive advertising was undertaken in directories and trade-journals to boost sales; in 1881 the firm took a stand at the Glasgow Exhibition where they exhibited a number of models designed to illustrate the versatility of cement as a building material, including a model of the Bishop's Palace. In 1894 Curries' younger brother died, prompting him to take over the direct management of both the Glasgow and Leith businesses. A main office was set up in Edinburgh, and Currie moved his home from Uddingston on the outskirts of Glasgow to 4 Royal Terrace in Edinburgh. He also made preparations to merge the two firms through the floatation of a new company, which took place in 1898. John Currie was appointed managing director of the business which had a capital of £60,000; his fellow directors were Joseph Reid, G E Phillip and the timber merchant, Henry J Stewart.

The end of the nineteenth century was accompanied by a massive upturn in the fortunes of the construction industry, and it also witnessed a significant increase in the use of concrete by builders and contractors, leading to a massive rise in the use of cement. This can be illustrated simply by examining the experience of Glasgow, where the amount of London cement shipped into the Clyde increased from 82,000 tons in 1896-97 to 117,124 tons in 1906-7. Between 1900 and 1920, despite the disruptions to the industry and communications caused by the war (when imports of foreign cement virtually ceased, whilst those of English cement fell by over 60%) imports of foreign cement averaged some 22,000 tons per year, and those of English cement some 72,000 tons per year. In Glasgow increased business forced the firm to move to larger premises in Bothwell Street. Currie began to further expand the business during this period - branches were opened first in Greenock, then at Dundee and Perth. After the war additional depots were established at Kirkcaldy, Dunfermline, Stirling, Alloa, Grangemouth and Falkirk. All these branches, some of which were highly ornate, were named the Eagle Buildings, carrying somewhere on their exterior a figure of a large eagle made from cement, the firm's widely used logo.

John P Currie died in 1919 from pneumonia; he left a daughter, Roberta, his wife having predeceased him. His personal estate totalled £33,000 (this did not include the value of his bungalow at St Fillans where he was able to indulge in his hobby of gardening). The majority of his estate was tied up in shares in the company, worth over £18,000, a loan to the company for £4,000, and cash held on account with them to the value of £1,600. Some of these shares were distributed to his daughter, nephews and nieces, and a few trusted colleagues and employees, including

Joseph Reid who succeeded him as managing director of Currie & Co. However the bulk of his estate was intended to provide income for his daughter and her family; to this end Currie instructed his executors to retain any remaining shares in the company for as long as possible. Joseph Reid remained in charge of the business until 1938, and it continued to trade as an independent firm until the end of the 1950s. An unremarkable one perhaps, but in the context of building trades suppliers one of the few that, thanks to John P Currie, had developed (in terms of size and spread of operation) in the early twentieth century along the lines that were to dominate the industry in the 1970s and 1980s.

NICHOLAS J MORGAN

SOURCES

Unpublished

SRO: SC 70/1/637, Inventory
        SC 70/4/528, Trust Disposition and Settlement

Published

Building Industries, 16/4/1919
Clyde Bill of Entry, 1890-1920
Directory of Directors
Glasgow Post Office Directory
Hume, John R, *Industrial Archaeology of Glasgow,* Glasgow, 1974
Industries of Glasgow, Glasgow, 1886
Stock Exchange Official Yearbook

James DALY,

Warehouseman and importer; b. 16/8/1818, Rigside, Lanarkshire, s. of James Daly, warehouseman and Marion Brown; m. Janet Fairley; 2 s., 1 d.; Partner, Messrs James Daly & Co, Glasgow; d. 12/7/1907, Glasgow; g/v estate: £3,575 6s 7d.

James Daly was brought up in a mining village in Lanarkshire by his widowed mother and his educational background is obscure. As a young boy he gave elementary instruction to local children and later taught at a school in Muirkirk. In 1833 he was appointed assistant teacher at Canongate School, Edinburgh, but found the harsh disciplinary regime there unsupportable. In July 1833 he moved to Glasgow and, through the offices of a family acquaintance, he secured a position at John MacIntyre & Co, drapers, of Glasgow Cross. He remained with the firm for ten years and built up expertise in all aspects of the trade.

In November 1846 James Daly entered into partnership, with two other employees of John MacIntyre & Co, to open a new linen and woollen warehouse, Daly, Spence & Buchanan, at 98 Trongate. The firm proved successful and within five years had moved to larger premises at 97 & 99 Trongate. The store specialised in ladies' outfitting fabrics, trimmings and accessories.

In early 1855 Spence and Buchanan set up as warehousemen and importers in St Paul's Churchyard, London, and James Daly assumed a series of new partners. The store, known as Daly & Scott from 1855, Daly, Symington & Buchanan by 1860 and Daly Milwain, at 150 & 152 Trongate, by 1863, was eventually purchased by James Daly on his own account in March 1870. By 1881 the business employed around 60 hands and Daly had assumed his son, James, as partner.

In March 1882 the store moved to Tron House, 20,000 square feet of elegant showrooms at 60 & 62 Trongate. During the following years the premises were extended to accommodate the growing departments of men's outfitting, furnishing and shoes and a large mail order trade was established. The store advertised as 'a universal provider' but it was never a department store in the exuberant mould of such contemporary Glasgow retailers as Walter Wilson's Colosseum and John Anderson's Royal Polytechnic. James Daly retired from active management around 1890 and in 1894 his son, who had assumed control, moved the store to Sauchiehall Street, which had superceded Trongate as Glasgow's fashionable shopping promenade.

As sole enduring partner Daly Snr was probably responsible for the store's modern marketing policies between 1846 and 1890. The warehouse advertised copiously, sold a wide variety of goods at moderate cash prices, and served both retail and wholesale customers. Contemporary commentators make it clear that Daly was known in Glasgow for his probity and hard work rather than any innovative entrepreneurship. For the most part he adopted the practices made successful by other retailers and created a comprehensive drapery shop rather than a department store. He was however, a leading light in the city's early closing movement and his determination to provide good working conditions for his staff was an early initiative.

Such concern was typical of James Daly who was very active in church affairs. Founder and superintendent of the first Sabbath School at the Cameronian Church, Great Hamilton Street, he later became director of the South Eastern District Sabbath School Union. He served on the City's Parochial Board and was active in the management of the Glasgow Night Asylum for the Homeless and in the YMCA movement.

ALISON TURTON

COURTESY OF THE MITCHELL LIBRARY

SOURCES

Unpublished

SRO: SC 36/51/144, Inventory and Settlement

Published

The Bailie, 31 May 1899
Clydebank and Renfrew Press, 9/6/1899
Daily Record, 15/7/1907
Glasgow Herald, 13/7/1907
Glasgow Post Office Directory, 1847-1909
Lennox Herald, 17/2/1894

Stewart, R and Simpson, W, *Glasgow in Former Times*, Vol II, Edinburgh, 1848
Strattens' Glasgow and its Environs, London, 1891

Hugh FRASER,

Draper and Warehouseman; b. 19/5/1815, Cardross, Dunbartonshire, s. of John Fraser, ferryman and innkeeper; m. c.1848, Jane Bunting; 5 s., 3 d.; Partner, Arthur & Fraser, Glasgow; d. 12/2/1873, Glasgow; g/v estate: £55,660.

Hugh Fraser was the eldest son of John Fraser, a ferryman and innkeeper in Cardross, Dunbartonshire. He lived at his father's inn for many years employed as a local cloth salesman. During the mid-1840s he joined the wholesale and retail drapery warehouse of Stewart & McDonald in Buchanan Street, Glasgow. Promoted to lace buyer and warehouse manager, but disappointed in his expectation of a partnership, Fraser set up on his own account in October 1849 with James Arthur, an established retail draper and former customer from Paisley, Renfrewshire. Arthur was clearly the senior partner although it is not known precisely how the capital investment was divided. In 1856 Arthur's stake was £36,000, six times as large as that of Fraser.

The partners opened a retail drapery establishment, Arthur & Fraser, on the first floor of a mansion house opposite Stewart & McDonald in Buchanan Street, where they copied the most innovative Glasgow warehouseman in insisting on ready money and fixed ticketed prices - a policy which attracted custom, as goods were sold at considerable discounts. Later further showrooms were acquired on the second floor and a small display window was installed at street level.

In 1851 Arthur & Fraser opened a wholesale branch in adjacent premises in Argyle Street and built up a large trade by canvassing country shopkeepers. In 1856 premises were acquired in Miller Street to house the growing wholesale business which was to be operated by a separate partnership, Arthur & Co. Again Fraser was the junior partner, taking three-sixteenths of the firm's profits.

The wholesale business quickly began to demand the attention of both partners. As Fraser's absences became more frequent, Thomas Kirkpatrick, an experienced draper, was appointed to manage the retail branch. Turnover quickly increased and new showrooms were opened in Argyle Street and Buch-

anan Street. In late 1857, with the onset of a general commercial crisis heightened by the collapse of the Western Bank, the wholesale business began to experience severe cash flow problems and was only able to continue trading due to the forbearance of its major creditors. The retail side was little affected although Kirkpatrick resigned in January 1858 and was succeeded by Alexander McLaren, previously merino buyer at Arthur & Co.

During the early 1860s the wholesale business flourished, assuming new partners to fund continuing expansion. The retail operation was increasingly at odds with the firm's mainstream activities and relations between Arthur and Fraser became strained. In December 1865, by mutual consent, the firm of Arthur & Fraser was dissolved. Fraser retired from the partnership of Arthur & Co, which was controlled by the remaining proprietors as a separate concern, gaining total control of the retail branch. The retail business was worth £42,000 in 1866, modest in comparison with the wholesale firm which had an asset value of almost £1 million.

Fraser immediately entered into partnership with Alexander McLaren. As senior partner he was entitled to three-quarters of the profits and took all the major management decisions. During the late 1860s Fraser extended and consolidated the trade, introducing new

COURTESY OF HOUSE OF FRASER PLC

lines like furniture and such services as house and ship furnishing. In 1867 he purchased the recently modernised Argyle Street and Buchanan Street show-rooms with money borrowed on the security of the property. In 1872 the premises were devastated by fire and in process of reconstruction at the time of Fraser's death the following year.

Fraser was a cautious businessman, who lacked the bold, empirical approach of his former partner, and the character and scope of the store remained little changed. Although well-known in Glasgow he took no part in the city's public life. The terms of Fraser's will allowed his sons the opportunity to buy a share in the business. Three eventually did so although trustees continued to manage the firm until 1894.

ALISON TURTON

SOURCES

Unpublished

Millar, A H, 'Glasgow Sketches', 1889
SRO: SC 36/51/63, Will and Inventory

Published

Barclay, J F, *Arthur & Co Ltd, Glasgow*, Glasgow, 1953
Glasgow Post Office Directories, 1851-1871
Moss, Michael and Turton, Alison, *A Legend of Retailing ... House of Fraser*, London, 1989

Hugh FRASER, Lord Fraser of Allander,

Retailer; b. 15/1/1903, Glasgow, s. of Hugh Fraser and Emily Florence McGowan; m. 3/4/1931, Kathleen, d. of Sir Andrew Lewis, Aberdeen, shipbuilder; 1 s., 1 d.; Ch, House of Fraser Ltd; Scottish Universal Investments Ltd; d. 6/11/1966, Milngavie, Dunbartonshire.

Hugh Fraser, son of Hugh Fraser and Emily Florence McGowan, was educated at Warriston School and Glasgow Academy. After leaving school in 1919 he passed almost immediately into the family firm, Fraser

Sons, a Glasgow department store founded 70 years earlier by his grandfather. During the following years he made himself familiar with every detail of the store's operation and became an accomplished window dresser and buyer as well as opening several new departments. In 1924 he was appointed managing director of Fraser Sons and, in 1927, on the death of his father, he assumed sole control as chairman.

Fraser was more ambitious than his father and keen to take advantage of the economies to be made by expanding the firm in the aftermath of the depression. He extended the Buchanan Street premises adding a modern arcade frontage and, in 1936, purchased two other stores nearby. Between 1940 and 1948 the acquisition of a further 15 Scottish drapery shops brought a fivefold increase in profits before tax. In December 1947 the business was floated as a public company, House of Fraser Ltd, with a capital of £1 million.

A staunch defender of the department store and its capacity for merchandising in depth, Fraser also appreciated the need to refurbish stores and adjust stock to contemporary and local tastes. He understood the importance of monitoring sales and expenditure closely and gathered together a talented management team to advise on and implement his plans. Many of the company's acquisitions during the 1940s were motivated by Fraser's determination to keep English retail groups out of Scotland and he became spokes-man for the Scottish drapery trade, vociferously attacking the government's postwar policies on ration-ing, price-fixing and purchase tax.

COURTESY OF HOUSE OF FRASER PLC

Published

Glasgow Herald, 'A Cornerstone of Independence',
13/2/1985

Grierson, Mary G, *A Hundred Years in Princes Street,
1838-1938, Jenners Edinburgh on the occasion of
their centenary,* Edinburgh, 1938

Sunday Standard, 'Surprises in Store for the Gentry',
6/9/1981

Thomas Johnstone LIPTON,

General provisions merchant; b. 10/5/1850, Glasgow, s. of Thomas Lipton, grocer and Frances Johnstone; Bachelor; Sole Prop, Lipton Co, Ch, Lipton Co Ltd; d. 2/10/1931, Osidge Park, Southgate, Middlesex; g/v estate: £566,068 18s 6d.

Thomas Lipton opened his first 'Lipton Market' in Stobcross Street, Anderston, Glasgow in 1871, when he was 21. By the time he was 40 his stores were general over Britain. Eight years later, in 1898, he sold them together with his tea plantations to the public for two and a half million pounds, but remained in command. His name was now a household word, made so by the promotional devices that had popularised his shops. He lived for another 33 years. For most of this time he continued as head of the firm until ousted by shareholders' pressure. At the same time he sought to replace the image of grocer and tea seller with that of friend of royalty and the great, and as aristocratic sportsman, challenging for that most prestigious of yachting trophies, the America's Cup.

How could the son of poor Irish immigrants into Scotland create so triumphant a business, doing so between the 1870s and 1890s, when the British economy was showing its first signs of arrestation after the achievements of the high Victorian age? Part of the answer lay in opportunity. This arose from social changes in Britain and her food needs, together with improvements in transport. But another and essential part lay in Lipton's personality. His character had extraordinary strengths (as well as weaknesses), so that he was able to bring together a highly unusual blend of energy, market perception, organising ability and nerve. All of this was made to cohere and persist because of a driving determination to succeed. Lipton was, in a sense, as perhaps all great businessmen are, a man of the moment, able to perceive what the 'moment', embraced by his active years, could be made to yield.

With urbanisation accelerating by the 1870s it was only a question of time before a few innovative men discovered that the grocery business, catering to the working and lower middle classes, could be changed from an affair of selectively petty shopkeepers (the essence of Marx's petit bourgeoisie) into large-scale business and, indeed into a trading empire. This was not to be done by buying up existing shops, but rather building from the ground up, choosing one's own staff and sites. Thus Lipton gained his entry into the grocery trade by starting with a single shop, and then on the basis of the experience gained, together with retained profits, setting up others. The trade was such that entry was easy, beginning on a small scale, without great resources. As the number of Lipton's shops extended, further potential was discovered. Not only did Lipton strengthen his position as a purchaser because of the demand he wielded he could now build for himself distribution depots, gaining great economies and cutting out the middle man. Moreover, in the shops themselves he developed techniques of standardisation, so that a Lipton market was immediately recognisable. There was a wide horseshoe counter, piled with butter and cheese, with the ceiling hung with hams, the whole illuminated with gas jets in opal globes, with magic lantern pictures to attract

COURTESY OF THE MITCHELL LIBRARY

371

children. Customers were dealt with in a way to which they quite soon adjusted, and indeed began to expect.

The old concern of the grocer with individual preference gave way to a straight offer of known lines of goods, explicitly priced, and with no credit. The purposeful description of the stores as 'markets' made clear the intention to supply on these terms. Like other multiple shop firms including the Home and Colonial Stores, Sainsburys and the Maypole Dairy Company, Lipton learned to narrow the range of provisions and teas offered so that handling costs were minimised.

Lipton was a classic example of the incremental learner in business: at each level of scale he discovered what could lie beyond; he then acted energetically from this perception. In this way his own motivation was continuously reinforced. So it was that Lipton, once he had achieved a dozen shops or so, had raised himself above the mark of small scale grocers, so that, provided his energies did not flag, he had a vast open field of opportunity all financed by the ploughing back of profits.

By 1898, however, two new circumstances were present. The great day of the single owner-trader was passing. The Lipton business was now such, centred on its vast headquarters in the City Road, London, occupied in 1894, that it had to seek wider financing. There were branches in 243 cities and towns in the United Kingdom and 12 plantations in Ceylon. Competition among multiple stores was now formidable, making the business much more challenging than the period of hectic expansion and calling for new specialised skills. The plantations were a kind of empire in themselves. Moreover, Lipton, now approaching 50, though refusing to retire from the headship of the business, and still keeping his American business directly in his own hands, now wished a new role for himself.

How did Lipton acquire the character that powered such a career? His parents came from County Monaghan, Northern Ireland, fugitives from the great potato famine. They ran a tiny shop in Crown Street in the old core of Glasgow, selling mainly foodstuffs brought over from Ireland, from their home district, chiefly those staples of the Scottish urban working class diet, ham (bacon), butter and eggs. The Lipton parents were good Presbyterians. They gained a reputation for the strictest honesty, providing sound food at reasonable prices. Indeed they traded on the basis of years of acquaintance and friendship with their customers. They enjoyed a modest success, becoming well regarded members of the Church of Scotland Congregation of Hutchesontown. All his life Lipton idealised his mother. He was her only surviving child, born when she was 36. He consulted her constantly. His father seems to have been something of a cypher in his life. How far his implacable will to succeed involved proving himself to her or to her memory is hard to say. He never married. Instead he combined solitariness with self-reliance, sustained

by the exhilaration of cumulative success as his empire grew. His formal education was minimal, confined to some five years at St Andrew's Parish School facing Glasgow Green.

There was indeed some danger that he might have succumbed, as did so many young lads, to the casual employments that cast so many lives into blind alleys. He was successively an errand boy, worked for a shirtmaker and then as a cabin boy on the Burns Line steamers between the Broomielaw of Glasgow and Belfast. But the instinct of thrift and self-betterment from his parents gave him direction: he saved enough to pay his steerage passage to New York. There he spent four important years. Once more it seemed he might be caught in the trap of casual employment, working on tobacco plantations and in the rice fields as well as odd-jobbing. But a job in a prosperous and progressive grocery store in New York set him on course. He returned to Glasgow with savings of $500 and a rocking chair for his mother.

In his first shop in Stobcross he seems to have begun his trading as his parents had done, interesting himself in each customer's requirements, delivering goods himself where possible, exuding good cheer and optimism, working all day long and far into the night. In later life he liked to recall how that on many a night he slept under the counter so that he might be up bright and early for his customers in the morning. He knew also how to protect his interests: on the list of his beneficiaries in his early years in business was the police constable on the Stobcross beat. This was the very pattern, one of highly particular relationships, from which he had to learn to escape.

His obsessive drive, his ambition and his business acumen made it possible to discover the route to higher ground, made available by the possibility of a new form and scale of retail trade in foodstuffs. He pioneered another form of escape, namely that of the retailer from dependence upon the wholesaler. He made his first direct contact with primary suppliers through his purchases in Ireland, buying, for example, butter and cheese from 'the choicest dairies of Armagh, Clones or Enniskillen'. In this he followed the example of his parents. This kind of contact was extended to the pastoral economies of the Scandinavian countries, conveniently accessible to Scotland as was Ireland. His greatest coup in reaching back to the source of his foodstuffs was, however, in Ceylon. Visiting the island in 1890 he discovered that it was in a depression because of a fall in coffee prices. With estates going cheap he bought up tea plantations and processed and packed his teas in standard forms and quantities, fixing a price well below that of the small grocer, and launching a vigorous advertising campaign, using the slogan 'direct from the tea garden to the tea pot'. It was tea, with its pioneering of brand loyalty, its convenience of handling and its ease of storing, so different from the blending done to order in the more old fashioned shops, that made Lipton a neatly rich man whose name was known to every working class family. His plantations in Ceylon also produced coffee and cocoa. His American interests were developed on a considerable scale, including *Pork Packer*, Chicago and Lipton's Refrigerator Car Line.

All along, however, he had used promotional gimmicks, the spirit of which was inspired by his experience as a youth of the New York provision trade, his admiration for the showmanship of a man like Barnum, and his knowledge of his customers' psychology. 'If I could make people talk or, better still, laugh', said this solitary, work-obsessed man, 'I would, it seemed to my mind, be much nearer to solving the problem of effective advertising' and so it proved. His shop doors would be flanked with Lipton mirrors, the concave one of which produced a thin and haggard image of the pre-Lipton shopper and the convex one of which showed a stout party who had benefitted from Lipton's foods. He produced in the later 1870s a kind of pseudo currency of his own, a 'one pound note' on which was emblasoned the name *Lipton's Great Irish Ham, Butter and Egg Markets*, with 'the promise to give on demand at any of my Establishments Ham, Butter and Eggs as given elsewhere to the value of ONE POUND sterling for Fifteen Shillings'. This was a device that worked in Scotland because of that country's one pound currency notes; England had none smaller than £5. But it was perhaps the mountainous cheeses that conveyed the Lipton name far and wide: in 1881 two such, both weighing more than half a ton were brought from the United States to Scotland. The one for Glasgow was conveyed by traction engine from the Broomielaw to the Jamaica Street branch amid a fanfare of publicity. It contained golden sovereigns; it was sold within two hours, with the police in attendance to control the crowd. The monster cheese became part of the Lipton Christmas. At the time of the Golden Jubilee of Queen Victoria in 1887, Lipton offered to provide the monarch with a five-ton cheese; the unsolicited gift was declined. Lipton at once capitalised on this Royal rebuff by publishing the letter from the palace over the heading 'A Snub from Royalty'. He had greater success with royalty in 1895, being granted the Royal Warrant to supply the Queen with tea. Lipton's various stunts projected an image of his firm very different from the earnestness of the Co-operative movement; moreover he gave good value to those he drew into his shops so that they came again. He was never distracted by politics, having, in spite of his Irish loyalty, no interest in them. When asked about his politics his answer was 'my politics are to open a new shop every week'.

What was there Glaswegian about Lipton's success? An important element was the relatively high income of much of the artisan population, for Glasgow at this time was proudly the second city of the Empire with a population of skilled men unsurpassed anywhere. The families of such men, living in their tenements, spent a higher proportion of their income on food than did their English counterparts. The city was a closely-packed place, so that a shop could serve many people on a pedestrian basis. Lipton, born and raised in the city, knew needs, minds and tastes of its working people and was able to cater to these in such a way as to be able, in due course, to extend beyond Glasgow and Scotland. The early connections between Glasgow and Ireland that Lipton knew so well, and which were so convenient, were a great advantage in terms of sources of supply especially in the early phase.

In covering England with his shops, however, Lipton found that there was no real choice but to move his headquarters from Lancefield Street in Glasgow to London, for a national chain of shops and depots could not resist metropolitanisation. It had indeed been one of his dearest ambitions to conquer London. But while his parents, especially his mother, lived, he would not leave the home they shared at Cambuslang. There he had cherished his mother in every sense, providing her with a carriage and pair. When she died at the age of 90 in 1889, followed in a few months by his father, the vast magnet of London and the South East of England, already involving him in expending much of his time on the train, could exert its full force: he took 1,000 Scots to London with him.

In Southgate in Middlesex he bought Osidge Park (known by those who recalled its owner's business origins as 'Sausage Park') a large mansion in generous grounds. There he lived until his death, attended by his servants from Ceylon, with rice, cooked in the Singalese manner, a basic part of the diet for host and guests alike, cultivating orchids in his conservatory and wearing them in his buttonhole in the manner of Joseph Chamberlain. He blossomed from the loneliness and self-containment of his business years into a graceful host, entertaining fellow countrymen from business like Lord Dewar (qv) the whisky magnate (Lipton and Dewar were bracketed as 'The Two Scotch Toms'), William Blackwood who helped him with his autobiography, and Sir Harry Lauder the city-raised 'Highlander' of the music halls. Lipton performed, too, something of a seigneurial role, holding at Osidge staff parties and sports dominated by his presence.

There was to be no gentle eventide for Lipton after his firm became a limited liability company in 1898. At 48 he was by no means ready to give up his commanding position in the firm he had created; indeed his continued services were a selling point in promoting the new firm.

All seemed to go well for another 25 years. But between 1923/24 and 1925/26 the profit collapsed from £234,245 to £30,844. There was a strong movement among the shareholders to bring the top management under scrutiny. Sir Thomas as chairman now 75, was vulnerable. There is no doubt that he lacked the renovative urge which the firm by then needed. His two great business maxims had always been 'never take a partner' and 'never accept a loan'. These precepts, the key to the creation of the firm, were not appropriate in the new context of competition among a range of multiples, where a spreading of responsibility and initiative and a constant fight against the inertias of large scale, together with flexible loan finance, were necessary. At the centre things had become top-heavy, for Lipton's inability to delegate had had the paradoxical effect of allowing the staff to proliferate in an inefficient way. At the branches, a good many were now in the wrong place because of changes in the social morphology of the cities since the 1880s and 1890s. Perhaps most serious of all the branch managers were not as good as they had been, partly due to Lipton's defective choices. Moreover, Lipton's relations with his staff were autocratic; he fired at short notice, and when he had invited a pair of his managers to Osidge he was not above bugging the sofa on which they sat waiting to enter his presence.

Under pressure Sir Thomas stepped down in 1927 in favour of the banker Sir John Ferguson. He was deeply hurt at being ousted. A review was conducted of the company's future and an arrangement was arrived at with Meadow Dairies. Liptons Ltd had exhausted the potential of the retailing revolution of which it had been so dynamic a part, and now faced a future of holding its own in a world in which chain stores were a norm, competition with one another rather than with the petty trader.

Meanwhile Lipton had since his move to London in 1894 wished to move up the social scale. A national celebrity with the general public, he wanted recognition in more exclusive circles, and in more heroic terms. He had already discovered yachting, that sport of aristocrats, and now invaded it with his over-the-counter money, challenging five times for the America's Cup. Yachting was a Royal interest and the way up the social ladder for Lipton lay through Royalty, in the person of the Prince of Wales, soon, in 1901, to become Edward VII. Edward, with his selection of friends from orders of society that were unacceptable to the hostesses of the great aristocratic houses, gave Lipton his chance. There was a trade-off between the King and such men, for Edward, in return for admitting them to his circle, required a *quid pro quo*. Thus Sir Ernest Cassell, city financier, was very useful to the King in his financial affairs. Lipton first brought himself to Royal notice in 1897: Princess Alexandra, Edward's wife, set up a trust fund to provide a celebratory meal to 400,000 poor people all over Britain to mark the Diamond Jubilee of Queen Victoria. The public failed to respond. Lipton sent an anonymous contribution of £25,000 to the Lord Mayor of London, the custodian of the fund. The Poor Folks Royal Dinner, apart from the fact that charitable feeding on such a scale should be necessary at all, proved a splendid success. The identity of its rescuer reached the public and, of course, the Royal family. Lipton followed this up with a donation of £160,000 to set up a poor persons' and children's restaurant in City Road, London under the *Alexandria Trust*.

Edward was a yachting enthusiast, so that when Lipton proposed to challenge for the America's Cup in 1899, Edward gave enthusiastic moral support. Lipton began his regular visits to Balmoral and Sandringham, was knighted in 1898 and made a baronet in 1902. In return Edward expected hospitality for himself on Lipton's steam yacht *Erin*, causing elements of the press to criticise the King's cavalier treatment of Lipton. There was of course resentment at Lipton's social pretentions. Having become a member of most of Britain's ranking yacht clubs, he was excluded from the Royal Yacht Squadron not being elected until the very year of his death. All of his challenges for the America's Cup were issued through the Royal Ulster Yacht Club.

Lipton tried five times for the America's Cup with successively numbered *Shamrocks* (1889, 1901, 1904, 1920 and 1930) but with no success. He appeared in his old age in the yachting cap which, together with his blue polka-dot bow tie he had made his personal trademark, in newsreels and newspapers and so continued in the public eye. He was 80 at his final attempt in September 1930: his disappointment in failing in this last of his ambitions was profound, but was well hidden from the public. His autobiography appeared posthumously because he delayed it in the hope that he would win 'that blooming cup'. American admirers presented him with a gold loving cup inscribed 'To the world's most cheerful loser'.

At death at the age of 81 Sir Thomas Lipton, Baronet, returned to Glasgow. Great crowds gathered for his funeral, the service being held in St George's Church. He had been made a Freeman of the City in 1923, and Honorary Colonel of a Volunteer Batallion of the Highland Light Infantry, so largely recruited from Glasgow's working classes. Having no heir or family, he left his estate to various charities, many of his bequests being in memory of his mother, whose picture he had carried with him all his life. Glasgow and Cambuslang were among the major recipients, especially mothers with children in poor circumstances. Glasgow also gained the 84 volumes of press cuttings about himself. But Lipton's greatest gift to the British people was to lead the way to the provision of sound food sold efficiently and cheaply.

S G CHECKLAND

WRITINGS

(with William Blackwood), *Leaves from the Lipton Logs,* London, 1931

SOURCES

Unpublished

SRO: SC 58/45/34, Trust Disposition and Settlement
of A G Peacock, 4/1/1952
SC 58/42/116, Inventory, A G Peacock,
4/1/1932

Published

British Baker, 13/11/1931
Directory of Directors, 1910, 1930, 1931
Glasgow Herald, 28/11/1931
Industries of Glasgow, Glasgow, 1888
The Stock Exchange Yearbook, 1928-29
Stratten, *Glasgow and its Environs*, Glasgow, 1891
Third Statistical Account of Glasgow

Sir Andrew Hislop PETTIGREW,

Drapery Merchant; b. 14/4/1857, New Lanark,
Lanarkshire, s. of John Pettigrew, grocer and
Agnes Hislop; m. (1) 22/12/1880, Amelia Kirkwood, d. of Alexander McNaughton, druggist;
(2) 24/4/1919, Annie A MacLeod, d. of Angus
Thompson MacLeod, contractor; 2 s.; (3) 1938,
Joan Cottam, d. of H R Cottam; Founder, Pettigrew and Stephens Ltd; d. 15/7/1942, Glasgow;
g/v estate: £108,826 8s 10d.

Andrew Hislop Pettigrew was born and educated in
New Lanark, the model factory village created by
David Dale and Robert Owen during the Industrial
Revolution. His father, John Pettigrew, was in the
grocery trade but apprenticed his 12 year old son to a
draper in nearby Lanark.

In 1875 Pettigrew moved to Glasgow where he was
employed in several of the city's largest and most
innovative drapery and general warehouses - James
Daly & Co, Copland & Lye and Anderson's Polytechnic. As a linen buyer he was able to save sufficent
capital to set up on his own account. In 1888 he
purchased the stock and goodwill of an existing
business in Sauchiehall Street in partnership with
William Henry Stephens. The store, known as Manchester House, specialised in heavy drapery goods
and comprised a small corner shop and upper flat.
Pettigrew was responsible for both the buying and

selling of goods and the general supervision of the
business whilst Stephens managed only the counting
house.

The business prospered. Adjoining premises were
acquired and an extensive foreign and colonial connection added to the home retail trade. In 1893
Pettigrew negotiated a three-quarters share of the
profits and on the death of Stephens, four years later,
assumed sole control. Immediately he embarked upon
major rebuilding. The new store, completed in 1901,
comprised five sales floors and offered a huge range
of goods and services, including a restaurant.

In 1904 Pettigrew converted the business into a
limited company, Pettigrew & Stephens Ltd, with a
capital of £170,000. The store was then one of the
largest in Scotland, employing around 600 hands, and
continued to expand in subsequent years with the
aquisition of premises in adjoining Bath Street. In
1925 when Pettigrew retired from chairmanship of
the board, and sold the entire ordinary share capital
of the company to Clarence Hatry's Austin Friars
Investment Trust Ltd, the firm's annual profit
amounted to £43,000.

Pettigrew was also actively involved in other businesses. In 1908 he became managing director of
Stewart & McDonald Ltd, wholesale textile ware-

COURTESY OF THE MITCHELL LIBRARY

housemen. He was also a director of the Scottish Temperance & General Assurance Co Ltd. Pettigrew, a respected businessman, was often consulted on matters concerning the distributive industry. He was president of the Glasgow and West of Scotland Retail Drapers Association and gave evidence to a Parliamentary Committee investigating the living-in system for shop assistants. Pettigrew also served as Deacon of the Incorporation of Bonnetmakers and Dyers and as a member of the Master Court of the Tailor's Incorporation.

In addition to his business commitments Pettigrew performed many public services. Staunchly liberal in politics he was elected town councillor for Cow-caddens Ward in 1907/8 and later served as Justice of the Peace and Deputy Lieutenant of the County of the City of Glasgow. An ardent social reformer and generous philanthropist he chaired The Civic League dedicated to aiding the city's poor. He was also chairman of the West of Scotland College of Domestic Science, of the Scottish National Council of the YMCA and, in 1911, of the executive committee of the Scottish National Exhibition. Pettigrew was knighted in 1913 in recognition of his many public services and received an honorary degree of Doctor of Laws from Glasgow University in 1924.

Pettigrew was married three times and inherited a large estate from his second wife, Anne MacLeod, in 1937, by whom he had two children.

ALISON TURTON

SOURCES

Unpublished

Glasgow University Business Archives: House of Fraser PLC Company archive, Pettigrew & Stephens Ltd: HF 43/1/1, HF 43/4/1, HF 43/4/2
Naismith, Alexander & Gardener, solicitors, Glasgow: Lady Pettigrew's Trust 1937-46

Published

The Bailie, 19/8/1903, 23/9/1903
Drapers Record, 28/7/1942
The Eagle, 30/9/1909
Glasgow Herald, 16/7/1942
Glasgow Post Office Directory, 1888-1940
Parliamentary Papers, House of Commons, Report of the Departmental Committee on the Truck Acts, 1908, Cd 4444 lix533
Michael Moss & Alison Turton, *A Legend in Retailing ... House of Fraser* (Weidenfeld & Nicolson, 1989).

Scottish Biographies, Glasgow, 1938
Strothers Glasgow, Lanarkshire and Renfrewshire Christmas and New Year Annual, 1911-12
Who Was Who in Glasgow in 1909

Michael SIMONS,

Fruit broker; b. 1842, Covent Garden, London; s. of Benjamin Simons, wholesale fruiterer, and Hannah Crawcour; m. 1869, Alice Moses; 3 s., 4 d., Snr Partner, Simons Jacobs & Co, Ch, Simons & Co Ltd, Fruit Wholesalers and Brokers; d. 20/1/1925, Glasgow; g/v UK estate £24,496 0s 7d.

Michael Simons was born at Covent Garden, London, in 1842, the first son of Benjamin Simons, then a wholesale fruiterer. At the age of three Michael was transported with the rest of his family first to Newcastle, then to Edinburgh, and finally to Glasgow, where his father decided that business opportunities were brightest. In 1849 Benjamin Simons established the firm of Simons & Co, retail and wholesale fruiterers in the centre of Glasgow at Candleriggs, close by the city's main fruit market. Michael Simons at this time was being educated first at St James' School and then at Glasgow High School. At the age of 17 he joined the firm of Syme, Simons & Smith, seedsmen, nurserymen and fruiterers in the Argyle Arcade, the start of a business apprenticeship which was continued in his father's firm which he joined in 1861. Here he worked his way through all aspects of the business, learning the skills of the auctioneer in the Glasgow salerooms, and those of a buyer in journeys to Spain, the United States and Canada. His father conducted an increasingly extensive business through two partnerships, Benjamin Simons & Co, who dealt with merchanting, and Simons Jacobs & Co, fruit brokers, who received goods on consignment for sale at Glasgow. By the early 1870s Michael Simons was managing the Glasgow broking business in partnership with his father - a third partner, Samuel Jacobs, managed a branch of the business at Southampton. A fourth partner in the growing concern, which boasted other branches in London and Liverpool, was Michael Garcia.

During Michael Simons early years in the business the fruit trade in Glasgow witnessed a revolution, largely through a reduction in rail-freight charges (both in the United Kingdom and on the continent) and the introduction of steamers equipped with the technology to allow the carriage of perishable cargoes such as fruit. In addition to refrigeration reduced journey times cut the time for fruit to reach Glasgow from the continent to less than 40 hours. These advances placed Glasgow on an even footing with London as a market for the national distribution of fruit and vegetables, a situation which Michael Simons was quick to exploit. In particular he was influential in capturing for the firm a pre-eminent position in the marketing of Spanish and Portuguese oranges in the United Kingdom - the importance of his endeavours to the Spanish economy were recognised by the award of the Knighthood of the Order of Isabella la Catolica. The orange trade established Simons as a nationwide business and formed the basis of their later growth and success - the firm imported oranges both on their own account, and also dealt with consignments from Spanish and Portuguese agents, particularly towards the end of the season when the need to dispose of unsold stocks was at its greatest. Simon's involvement in this part of the business earned them only the grudging admiration of some, who claimed they were assisting 'the Iberians' in dumping produce at 'under the hammer' realisations. The size of the trade was prodigious, although subject to fluctuation through crop failure. In 1882 the Clyde Bill of Entry recorded consignments totalling 109,931 cases of oranges from ports such as Valencia, Seville, Oporto and Lisbon, destined for the Glasgow auction rooms of Simons Jacobs & Co. Similar quantities were also being shipped to the English branches.

Although oranges made up a substantial part of the fruit imported by Simons Jacobs & Co they dealt with an ever broadening range of imported and domestic produce. Lemons, melons, nuts, olives, onions and pomegranates were imported from Spain and Portugal, which also provided the firm's second most important product, the grape. Largely due once more to the efforts of Michael Simons, Glasgow became the first UK market for Almeria grapes, with a total sale of around 150,000 barrels per year. Apples (around 17,000 barrels in 1882 increasing to 28,000 in 1890) and pears were imported from New York (from whence came also consignments of coconuts), whilst links were established with Egypt, Jaffa, Malta and the West Indies. The Atlantic market also offered, by the turn of the century, the promise of Californian fruit and vegetables. Eggs also increased as an import item, coming largely from Canada in the winter months. Vegetables were brought to the Glasgow market, frequently from the continent via the Southampton or London subsidiaries with whom close communications were imperative. Although sometimes accused as working for the best interests of overseas agriculture the firm did not eschew domestic products, although the quantity of their output, combined with a price disadvantage caused by smaller units of production and less favourable overheads (particularly freight charges) made exploitation of the continental market an imperative. It was a harsh truth, as Michael Simons explained to a House of Lords committee in 1894, that 'it would be utterly impossible to satisfy the demands for fruit which exists all over the country, if we depended altogether on home growers'. Nonetheless they did seek to promote the best of Scottish produce, especially the tomato, virtually an unknown fruit in Glasgow before the 1880s. As increasingly large quantities came to be imported into Glasgow by Simons from Valencia so the firm also looked to local growers, such as T S Finlay at Baillieston in Lanarkshire, and D & W Buchan of Kippen, Stirlingshire, for the highest quality crop of this product which by 1898 possessed, in the words of Michael Simon's eldest son, Benjamin, 'every promise of a big future'.

The range and quantity of produce imported into Glasgow by Michael Simon's firm suggests a far higher proportion of fruit (sometimes exotic) in the Scottish diet than has normally been allowed by dietary historians. That fruit was of growing importance in the diet of all was certainly the view of contemporaries. Writing of Michael Simons' father, Benjamin, *The Bailie* magazine commented in 1880 that 'Fruit is no longer a luxury to our city - it is a daily article of food within reach of all, and it is to Mr Simons that we are indebted to this'. Increased availability stimulated demand, which was in turn met by a further expansion in the quantity and quality of produce available. The consequent vast increase in the importation of produce into Glasgow (and other southern ports) during the last two decades of the nineteenth century was largely due to the energies of Michael Simons and other lesser brokers in the city. As a Glasgow rival, Thomas Russell, explained in 1904, 'Scotland has been learning to eat fruit. The people have been educated for some years by the cheap fruit coming on the market. The fruit trade has grown considerably this last ten years, almost doubled'.

The availability of fruit was enhanced by improvement in the storage, distribution and retailing. Simons Jacobs & Co developed an extensive purpose-built warehouse and saleroom at Candleriggs (built in 1883 for some £22,000) on a property which Benjamin Simons had purchased shortly after arriving in Glasgow. The building, valued in 1926 at some £91,000, had a lane running through the centre to expedite loading and unloading, and steam lifts to distribute goods to the various specialist salerooms within the building; it offered, claimed one contemporary, 'exceptional modern facilities for the rapid and efficient handling of the business'. The firm also had warehouses at Montrose Street and at George Street, the latter being converted into a cold-store for the Scottish Cold Storage and Ice Co Ltd in 1896. With Michael Simons as its chairman the company had been established with a capital of £100,000 at a time when the demand for both ice-making plant and cold storage seemed inexhaustible. By 1900 this company was planning to increase the storage capacity of the George St building from 185,000 cubic feet to 255,000 cubic feet, whilst ice-making capacity was to be increased from 25 to 40 tons a day. The combination of depressed economy and a high-pressure climate led to a slump in business; in 1906 the directors of the company petitioned for voluntary liquidation and in 1907 the assets (including the George Street store) were sold to the Union Cold Storage Co Ltd, part of the Vestey empire. These adventures were matched by developments in the field of retailing with which Simons Jacobs & Co were closely involved, providing, for example, loans to entrepreneurs such as Malcolm Campbell (qv) for expanding retail outlets.

Benjamin Simons died in 1891, when the partnership comprised Benjamin and Michael Simons and Michael John Garcia. The style of the Glasgow business remained Simons Jacobs & Co although associated partnerships in London, Southampton, Liverpool and New York adopted differing titles as partnerships changed. Garcia died in 1894 leaving Michael Simons as sole partner in the business. Possibly as a result of a family disagreement, or due to their father's refusal to delegate business responsibilities, Michael Simons' three sons chose not to join the family business in which they had been trained but rather to form their own fruit-broking partnership of B & S H Simons, competing directly with their father in adjacent premises at Candleriggs. The success of this venture was marred by the bankruptcy of the eldest son, Benjamin Simons, a cause of considerable expense and embarrassment to Michael Simons. Simons' two younger sons, Samuel and Ernest, continued to work together in partnership as Simons & Co until 1919, when they joined their father as partners in Simons Jacobs & Co. In 1921, as Michael Simons began to withdraw from an active role in the business, the firm was formed into a limited liability company, Simons & Co Ltd, with Samuel and Ernest as the major shareholders, each holding shares to the value of £14,000, and Michael Simons with a shareholding of £7,500. In 1925 plans were laid for a rationalisation of the company's structure which were effected after Michael Simons' death in November of that year - a new limited company was formed which incorporated the branches at Southampton and Liverpool, and consolidated shareholdings in associated businesses in Liverpool, Boston and New York.

With the exception of his involvement in the Cold Storage Co Michael Simons kept his business interests outside of the family firm to a minimum. Only one other business concern substantially occupied his time, that of the theatre-owners and impressarios Howard and Wyndham Ltd. Here business was mixed with pleasure, as Michael Simons was able to indulge his love of the stage and music with the exercise of his prodigious administrative powers. He was one of the promoters of the company at its floatation in 1895, along with a Glasgow associate the wine-merchant David Heilbron, and acted as chairman from its inception until 1925. The company owned four theatres: the Royal and Royalty in Glasgow, and the Royal and Royal Lyceum in Edinburgh. In addition they leased the Tyne theatre in Newcastle. Simon's involvement in the company was largely restricted to the business side, with artistic management being undertaken by Fred Wyndham, director of many of the company's famous pantomimes. These were occasions that brought the greatest names in popular entertainment to the stages of Glasgow and Edinburgh, and success for participating artistes could secure future careers. One, Sir Harry Lauder, had great reason to thank Howard and Wyndham (no doubt the feeling was mutual) - he recalled that 'my work ... in Glasgow pantomime really put me on the map as a popular favourite in Britain'. In November 1905 he graced the Theatre Royal, Glasgow, with the first performance of 'I love a lassie' during the opening night of *Aladdin*, an occasion that was only bettered by the first performance of 'Roamin' in the gloamin' on the same stage five years later. Simons and Heilbron also became involved with the management of Robert Arthur Theatres Ltd, of which Simons was chairman from 1914 until his death.

In 1883 Michael Simons was elected as councillor for Glasgow's third ward, making an unusually strong impact on the running of the municipality. 'In everything of moment that has been done by the Corporation during the 12 months since his election', wrote one local commentator, 'Mr Simons has played a leading part'. Simons was responsible for a major investigation into the finances of the city and the running of the City Chamberlain's office, and also served on the City's Parliamentary Bills Committee. In 1887 he was elected a magistrate, retiring after only two years due to the increasing business pressures brought about by the failing health of his father. After the latter's death in 1891 Simons resigned as a councillor in order to take over the sole responsibility for the family business. His participation in municipal affairs was remarkable both for the vigour with which he approached the work, and also for his independence of spirit which marked him as a man apart from most of his contemporaries. Nonetheless his skills as an administrator had led during his brief career to an invitation to serve as Lord Provost which he declined. Despite his relatively short municipal career he was known throughout the city as 'the Baillie'. In 1888 Michael Simons was active in the promotion of Glasgow's first International Exhibition, acting as convener of the refreshments committee - 'to the management of these departments he brought to bear a business capacity, resourcefulness and originality in methods of working which contributed in material degree to the success of the exhibition'. He was equally active in the organisation of the 1901 exhibition, where he was convener for music, entertainments, sports and refreshments, a task that included the provision of cups of tea, of switchbacks and water-chutes, of orchestral performances, and of a charity cup tie between Third Lanark and Queen's Park. As part of his work for the exhibition Simons visited the Paris exhibition, and also President McKinlay in the United States. In 1906 he was appointed a deputy lieutenant for the city.

Michael Simons was the first member of Glasgow's small Jewish community, originally centred on the Candleriggs area near the fruit market, to hold a senior public office. His father had been prominent in the congregation since his arrival in Glasgow, serving as treasurer between 1857 and 1862. Benjamin Simons had been largely responsible for the moves of the congregation, first to a synagogue in George Street in 1858, and then to the Garnethill Synagogue in 1877. Michael Simons was also involved in this latter transfer, acting with his father and three others as trustee for the congregation. Michael Simons served as secretary to the Glasgow Hebrew Congregation for 24 years between 1872 and 1896.

When Michael Simons died in 1926 he left a modest estate of £24,496, not including the value of his house at Kensington Gate in Glasgow and a seaside villa at Port Bannatyne, Bute. He made no charitable bequests, 'having subscribed liberally to these' during his lifetime. He was survived by his three sons and four daughters, all of whom had been provided for before his death. His wife, Alice Moses, whom he had married in London in 1869, predeceased him some four years earlier. He was a man of great reputation, not only in the city, where his incisive business skills had been applied with vigour to the good of the municipality, but also in the world at large, where he was identified with the revolution in the distribution and consumption of fresh fruit and vegetables which his firm had done so much to bring about.

NICHOLAS J MORGAN

SOURCES

Unpublished

Companies Registration Office: SC 2858, Howard & Wyndhum PLC
SC 14381, Simons & Co Ltd
Register of Sasines, Glasgow
SRO: BT2/11877, Simons & Co Ltd
SC 36/51/104, Trust Disposition and Settlement, Benjamin Simons
SC 36/48/369, Inventory, Michael Simons
SC 36/51/209, Trust Disposition and Settlement, Michael Simons

Published

The Bailie, No 428, 29/12/1880; No 625, 8/10/1884; No 1490, 18/5/1901

Clyde Bill of Entry, 1880-1900
Directory of Directors
Fruit, Flower and Vegetable Trades Journal, 6/1/1945
Glasgow Herald, 21/11/1925, 29/12/1944
Hume, John R, *Industrial Archaeology of Glasgow*, Glasgow, 1974
Levy, A, *The Origin of Glasgow Jewry 1812-1895*, Glasgow, 1949
Moss, M S, *Iceman Glasgow*, Glasgow, 1984
Scottish Trader, 12/11/1898
Stratten & Stratten, Environs of Glasgow, London, 1891

Patrick THOMSON,

Draper; b. 12/12/1860, Edinburgh, s. of Thomas Thomson, draper and Elizabeth Clark; m. Catherine Alexandria Halliday; 2 d.; Founder, Patrick Thomson Ltd; d. 7/3/1907, Edinburgh; g/v estate: £9,364 5s 6d.

There is little information regarding Patrick Thomson whose name is so familiar in Scottish Drapery. His father was Thomas Thomson, who was a draper, and who at one time had his own business, known as Thomas Thomson. Later he added 'and Sons' to this, and later still it became Thomson and Allison. This business was in Princes Street and as a young man, one of six sons, Patrick went to work in his father's shop. He evidently found this less than satisfying so went off to London to make a career for himself.

When his father died, Patrick returned to Edinburgh and the family firm, but in 1900 the firm was dissolved and soon after that he set up in business on his own in a small shop on South Bridge.

Two years later, when the Coliseum Company gave up trading, Patrick Thomson leased the building, and renamed it the Iron Drapery as it happened to be opposite a building known as the Iron Church.

In the space of five years he had expanded the business to a considerable extent, and when the Bon Marche became available on the North Bridge, he decided to take it over as well. This was thought by many at the time to have been over-ambitious but it turned out to be the nucleus of the huge emporium which developed over the next 20 years or so. Initially, the Bon Marche was renamed the Cash Drapery Stores and it was 1906 before it was known as Patrick Thomson's, familiarly known by later generations of customers as 'Pat's' or 'P.T.s' Thomson died in 1907.

It was after the death of the founder of the business

that a limited company was formed, and developed by Mr A F Gardner as managing director.

Patrick Thomson was only 47 years old when he died, as a result of an operation for a duodenal ulcer with perforation. He was well respected by the business community in Edinburgh as the number of people attending his funeral testified. An obituary in the Drapers' Record notes that 'Representatives of the leading London houses were present. The route to the cemetery was lined by several thousand citizens ...'

Patrick Thomson died in his home in Hermitage Drive, Edinburgh, and was survived by his wife and two young children. He left £9,364 5s 6d, which included 100 fully paid up £1 shares in Parramon Company Limited worth only £5 in total when he died. The capital value of the firm was given as £8,000, but debts amounted to something over £5,000.

About 1927/28, the Scottish Retail Drapery Journal published an article about Patrick Thomson Ltd describing the progress made since the business began trading. The whole of the building, of which the Bon Marche had been only a small part, was gradually taken over by Patrick Thomson Ltd and extensions and additions were made from time to time.

At the time the article was written, the store consisted of five floors above street level and four below, with each floor a gallery so that the ceiling of the building could be seen from the centre of the ground floor.

The 40 departments included those of hairdressing, postal and telegraphic services, tobacco and cigarettes, and confectionery. There was also a hairdressing salon, a lounge and a restroom. Furniture removal was one of the services and also furniture storage, and cabinet making was done to order. A refrigeration and cold storage plant were recent additions and an arcade entrance had just been added to the building.

30 years after the originator's death, Patrick Thomson Ltd had a capital value of £300,000 and Mr A F Gardner who had been involved with the company from the beginning, was chairman and managing director. The business was taken over by the House of Fraser in 1952.

KATHLEEN DONALDSON

SOURCES

Unpublished

Inventory - Personal Estate

Published

Drapers' Record, March 1907
Scotsman, March 1907
Scottish Retail Drapery Journal, 1927/28

John URIE, OBE,

Chartered accountant, b. 17/1/1874, Paisley, s. of Robert Urie, flour merchant and Isabella Dunlop; m. (1) Jessie T Morgan, (2) Isabella Auchterlonie; 2 s. 1 d.; MD, City Bakeries Ltd; d. 5/11/1956, Glasgow; g/v estate: £70,000.

John Urie was born into the third generation of a family of Paisley bakers. He was not trained as a baker but as a chartered accountant, yet he took a small time enterprise and shaped it into a Glasgow institution, the City Bakeries. His father Robert Urie left Paisley and went to Glasgow in 1897 and bought the old established Friendly Baking Company in Clarendon Street. This was a workers co-operative bakery formed by industrial workers to ensure that they had cheap and wholesome bread. It was delivered by horse and cart round the doors. Bakeries, as such, seldom sold bread in Glasgow their products being teabreads, sweet breads, cakes, and biscuits. Grocery shops sold bread supplied by such progressive breadmakers as William Bilsland (qv) and William Beattie (qv) and it is still much the same today in Glasgow though some small home bakeries have survived. Robert Urie soon changed the name of the Friendly Bread Company to the City Bakeries Ltd in 1905 with 5,000 10/- shares all family owned. He, too, began to produce the sweet breads and fancy french cakes then being produced in Scotland by continental craftsmen.

Illness overtook Robert Urie early in the 1900s and John Urie turned from a promising career as a professional chartered accountant and put his expertise into the family business. For a time he continued to work in the office of (Sir) John Mann CA but in 1909 he gave his full-time attention to the family business, the City Bakeries. He was joined on the board by John Mann who acted as chairman and his own younger brother, William Urie. This was a relatively young and dynamic executive team and together they set about applying business efficiency methods to the polite world of the Glasgow tearooms. They did so at an admirable time (see A G Peacock qv). Glasgow's suburbs were expanding and baker's shops were popular in the new areas where vans delivered fresh goods three or four times daily. The city tearooms were the highlight of the day's shopping or a visit to the cinema or were the normal lunchtime venue for city office workers. Despite the wartime restrictions John Urie boosted the City Bakeries turnover from £58,993 in 1913 to £370,995 in 1919 with ten branches in the major suburbs and a highly efficient bakery still situated in Clarendon Street.

In 1919 John Urie bought the Ca'Doro Building which occupied the centre position on the corner of Union Street and Gordon Street. The Ca'Doro building built in the 1850s was designed by John Honeyman for F & J Smith's Furniture Warehouse. The building had always contained a restaurant of some description. In 1919 it was occupied by several small traders and a restaurant owner Mrs McColl, all of whom were dispossessed when Urie began to develop the site.

The Ca'Doro was a three-roomed renaissance Italianate building. Urie's plans necessitated the building of two extra storeys. He commissioned Gillespie and Kidd to design the two top floors on the top of the Ca'Doro building to be used as ballrooms, restaurants and banqueting halls. This task fell to a young architect, Jack Coia who had just begun work in the Gillespie & Kidd office. The Ca'Doro was financed by a further issue of shares although the firm of City Bakeries still remained a private limited company with £1,500,00 in £1 preference shares, 980 £1 shares for employees and 18,000 ordinary shares. With the Ca'Doro, Urie entered into direct competition with the Cranston tearooms, long associated with the Glasgow architect Charles Rennie Mackintosh, and the tearoom chain of James Craig who, together with R A Peacocks (qv G A Peacock) set the tone of Glasgow's café society.

In the Ca'Doro the bakery shop was on the ground floor, the tearoom on the second floor, the third floor held the restaurant and the fourth and fifth floors banqueting halls. The new additions were popular function suites for balls and banquets although, because of strict licensing laws, Urie was refused a licence for the two suites and customers had to apply for a special licence to the Glasgow magistrates. Despite this inconvenience the Ca'Doro was an extremely popular venue.

But there was a hard side to John Urie and shortly after the Ca'Doro complex was opened an unsavoury and unpopular incident occurred. In 1922, 31 members of the restaurant staff were arrested by the police as they left the premises late one evening in February. The 6 men and 25 women were kept in police cells for two nights without bail. The charge was theft, pressed by the Ca'Doro board, and considerable amounts of foodstuffs, confectionery, cutlery and napery were confiscated at the time. Fines ranged from 10/6 to 5 guineas or 15 days in prison. The incident is worth recalling because it reveals the current state of wages in the trade at that time. Young waitresses earned 16/- a week and could later expect a 2/- bonus, however, in the initial period of their employment they had 5/- a week deducted from their salary to pay for their uniforms. With the 11d for national insurance this left young waitresses with 10/1 take home pay. Questions about the propriety or necessity of keeping people imprisoned for two nights for pilfering were raised in the city magistrate's meeting and there was considerable ill-feeling against the City Bakeries board at this time.

The incident contrasts sharply with John Urie's policy towards employees at the time. Employee shares had been instituted in 1914 when £135 at 10/- a share was allocated to the employees mainly for shop assistants and inspectors which could be paid for on the instalment plan and that rose to £980 in 1921 and £1,800 in 1926. The incident obviously made an impact on Urie and to redress the situation he began a detailed extension of worker's benefits such as a canteen, a holiday camp for apprentices in the summer, dances, concerts, cinema shows, dramatic class; sewing and physical exercise were all pursued in the winter months by the employees. The City Bakeries were also pioneers in staff training. Every girl who entered the selling staff underwent a methods course of salesmanship before obtaining a post in a branch shop.

In 1928 Urie bought over the long established tearoom and bakery business of Walter Hubbard & Co and also Colquhouns of Glasgow. The new companies retained their names but were supplied by the City Bakeries from the Clarendon Street bakery. By 1937, next to J Lyons & Co, the City Bakeries were the largest private firm of retail bakers in Great Britain. This brought them to the attention of Garfield Weston. In 1938 Garfield Weston successfully bid for the City Bakeries when he founded Weston Foods Ltd with his biscuit concerns. It had an issue capital of £2 million. The City Bakeries retained their name and John Urie remained as chairman of the company until 1944 when he retired.

Apart from his interests in the City Bakeries John Urie was a former deacon of the incorporation of bakers and devoted much time to the benevolent work of the Glasgow Trades House. There was a strong element of patriotism in John Urie. During the First World War he worked with John Mann on the financial side of the Ministry of Munitions and was afterwards awarded the OBE for this work. During the Second World War he made a gift of £5,000 to the Ministry of aircraft production, more or less as a thanks offering for the safety of his son, John Urie, who, when he was in the RAF was involved in an aerial dog-fight and his machine was destroyed during the battle. As a further indication of his patriotic spirit out of more than a half of his £70,000 estate was accounted for by victory bonds, national savings bonds and national savings certificates. The value of these holdings had fallen considerably since they were bought. For instance the £1,000 savings bonds at 3% yielded only £757 and the £34,000 invested in 4% victory bonds yielded only £30,604.

John Urie died at his home in Winton Gardens, Glasgow, in November 1956. In his obituary notice in the *Accountant's Magazine* it was noted that John Urie was admitted to the Glasgow Institute in 1896 and that there were still only 11 members of the Institute surviving who were admitted earlier at the time of John Urie's death.

BRENDA M WHITE

SOURCES

Unpublished

SRO: SC 36/51/012, Testamentary Disposition for John Urie, 30/11/1956
SC 36/48/848, Inventory, 30/11/1956
SC 3672, Company Registration File, City Bakeries

Published

The Accountant's Magazine, November, 1956
The Bailie, Vol 2543, 13/7/1921
British Baker, 9/11/1956
Country Life, 19/6/1969
The Directory of Directors, 1952
Glasgow Chamber of Commerce Journal, Vol 18, No 6, 6/6/1932 and No 52, 1967
The Glasgow Herald, passim, February/March 1922, 1923, 1924, 1938, 1956
Jeffries, J B, *Retail Trading in Britain 1850-1950*, Cambridge, 1954
Oakley, C A, *Scottish Industry Today*, Edinburgh, 1937
The Post Office Directories
The Stock Exchange Yearbook
Third Statistical Account of Scotland

Thomas WATSON,

Produce broker and merchant; b. 1850; m.; 2 s., 2 d.; Partner, Watson & Philip Ltd; d. 7/7/1934, Dundee; g/v estate: £70,424 4s 5d.

Joseph PHILIP,

Food importer; b. 1850, Dundee, son of William Philip, master joiner and Charlotte Lonie; m. 4/8/1875, Annie, d. of James McGlashan, manager to Alex Henderson & Sons; 2 s., 3 d.; Partner and Dir, Watson & Philip Ltd; d. 19/7/1930, Eildonhurst, Dundee; g/v estate: £75,154 8s 6d.

The foundations of the firm of Watson and Philip, PLC, whose turnover in 1985 amounted to a record £114,825,000, were laid in 1873 when Thomas Watson and Joseph Philip set up in business with a small loan from the Commercial Bank.

Watson and Philip had both been employees of William and James Miller, commission agents, Dundee. Watson remained with them until the death of William Miller, the surviving partner and then arranged to continue the firm in partnership with Philip, who had for some years prior to 1873 been gaining experience of the provision trade in Manchester.

The new firm's main activity was the supply of commodities to the bakery trade. They imported flour, lard, butter, sugar, fruit and sold them to bakers from a small warehouse in the dock area of Dundee. A chain of agents was formed in Liverpool, Canada, Russia and the West Indies to keep them in touch with the best quality goods at the best prices around the world. They were equally careful to be made aware of the respectability and financial standing of their customers and kept detailed notes about the credit worthiness of every baker and shopkeeper with whom they dealt.

It is interesting that this firm, based on the importing of white flour, was established only two years after the opening of the first steam powered flour mill in Dundee. The partners were apparently unafraid of competition from home grown, home milled flour. The demand was growing for white bread and bakery products. A population with a high proportion of wives and mothers employed for long hours in the jute trade and housed in tenement flats without ovens was becoming more and more dependent upon shop bought food.

By 1896 the firm was in a position to build new offices and a warehouse on the Esplanade, close to both docks and railway stations. The following year William, Joseph's son, joined the firm. Profits were invested in the Samnugger Jute Company, the Titaghur Jute Company, New York Central Railroad, the British Investment Trust, the National Investment Company, the Dundee and District Tramway Company, Willmar and Sioux Falls Railway, North America Trust, the Balaena Whale Fishing Company, Bovril Ltd, the Imperial Ceylon Tea Company and in house property for renting. The income from investments in 1898 was £1,507 15s.

In 1900, Watson's two sons, Preston and James, joined the firm and a branch was opened in Aberdeen. Preston Watson was later renowned for flying an aircraft of his own design perhaps earlier than the Wright brothers. In 1919 a private limited company was then formed whose directors were William and James Philip and James Watson, Preston having been killed in the First World War. A Glasgow branch opened in 1920. In 1927 the nominal capital was £120,000, 50,000 preference shares ad 60,300 ordinary shares taken up. The shareholders were then Thomas Watson and Joseph Philip, listed as flour importers, and James Philip, senior and junior, and James Watson, shown as importers of foodstuffs. From its beginnings as suppliers to the bakery trade the firm had expanded into supplying the retail grocery trade.

Joseph Philip took a prominent part in public life. He became president of Dundee Grocers Benevolent Society in 1884. He was elected to the Harbour Board in 1899 and sat as a member for 21 years, acting as deputy chairman from 1911 to 1913 and as finance convener from 1913 to 1920. He became a governor of University College, Dundee in 1902. During the First World War he was appointed by the Ministry of Food to supervise flour distribution in Scotland. He was president of Dundee Liberal Association in 1921 and became honorary president in 1924. Dundee Chamber of Commerce elected him president in 1921 and in 1920 he was president of the UK Association of Flour Importers. Other interests included the Sick Poor Nursing Association, of which he was a director, Dundee Floorcloth and Linoleum Company, of which he was one of the founders, and Dalhousie Golf Club of which he was captain in 1914. He was a member of St John's Church Kirk Session and a Justice of the Peace. He died in July 1930 and was succeeded on the Board of Watson and Philip by his grandson, Herbert.

Thomas Watson died four years later in July 1934, aged 84, at his home, Balgowan, a large villa close to his partner's home, Eildonhurst, in Perth Road. Less involved in committee work than Philip, he was a very keen sportsman throughout his long life and a faithful church goer. His only public appointmet was as chairman of Dundee Industrial Schools. On his death he left only small bequests outside te family, to local hospitals and to the Society for the Prevention of Cruelty to Children. The cash payable on shares in Watson and Philip at the time of the first partners deaths was in each case £25,000.

After the First World War expansion was rapid and association with the catering trade developed and extended. From the 1950s the firm adopted its own trade name and supplied imported groceries packaged under the name 'Pinnacle'. The first cash and carry depot, now the oldest cash and carry depot in Scotland, was opened in 1959 and moved in the following year to premises within the old Blackness Foundry. In 1964 Watson and Philip were successful in gaining the VG service franchise, becoming the first and only operator under the Voluntary Group sign in Scotland. By this means, providing independent retail grocers with a comprehensive marketing service, Watson and Philip were able to counter the supermarket chains' attempt to dominate the grocery trade and became responsible for the survival of many small grocers' shops.

The policy paid handsomely. Sales increased from £2,033,151 in 1960 to £14,080,000 in 1969. In that year the firm went public, with a market capitalisation of £1,500,000 at 12/6d (62.5p) per share. It was over-subscribed 14 times. The growth in sales continued, from £14,080,000 of 1969 to £18,979,000 in 1972 and to the £114,825,000 of 1985. The share price doubled in the four years from 1969 to 1972, from 62.5p to 128p.

On Herbert Philip's retirement the company appointed its first chairman from outside the families of the original partners, James Hadden, hitherto the firm's accountant, and now retired, under whose care it continued to expand and succeed. There is still one member of the original family on the Board of Directors, maintaining a connection of more than a century. From modest beginnings and very small capital investment in a flour importers' warehouse, Watson and Philip has spread its interests to anticipate public demand first for white flour, shop bought bread, then for goods pre-packed in small quantities, then for convenience shopping in self service stores.

ENID GAULDIE & KATHLEEN DONALDSON

SOURCES

Unpublished

Calendar of Confirmation, 1934, Thomas Watson

Register of Governors, University College, in University of Dundee Archive

SRO: SC 45/31/107, Inventory of Joseph Philip
SC 45/34/60, Trust Disposition and Settlement of Joseph Philip

Watson & Philip Archive, Blackness Buildings, Dundee

Published

Dundee Advertiser, 21/7/1930, 7/7/1934
Dundee Chamber of Commerce Centenary Publication
Dundee Directories, 1873-1969

Walter WILSON,

Hosiery agent; b. 21/8/1849, Glasgow, s. of Arthur Wilson, grocer; m. Jane Williams Binnie; 1 s., 3 d.; Founder, Walter Wilson & Co (Glasgow) Ltd, Millinery Business; d. 17/10/1917, Harrogate; g/v estate: £14,902.

Walter Wilson's father, Arthur Wilson, owned two grocery and general stores on the south side of Glasgow and his grandfather and uncle had both been tea merchants in the city centre. He was educated locally at Mrs Alexander's School and the Gorbals Youths' School.

In 1863, he was employed by a Glasgow hosiery agent and during the next six years took up three futher positions with wholesale provision merchants in the city. In August 1869, with a capital of £100, he entered into partnership with Hugh Kean to carry on the business of hat cleaning and blocking. The partnership of Wilson, Kean & Co. was, however, short-lived and Walter Wilson soon became the sole proprietor of a new concern.

COURTESY OF THE MITCHELL LIBRARY

For ten years Walter Wilson & Co. traded in hats alone, and by 1879 employed 150 assistants and carried a regular stock of 25,000 hats. Thereafter Wilson added a variety of new lines and acquired adjoining premises in Jamaica Street. By 1889 the warehouse, known as 'The Colosseum', employed 500 staff and sold drapery, millinery, shoes, upholstery, gloves, books and tea in 23 departments. Wilson had also opened a tea room and reading rooms for the convenience of shoppers who thronged the store daily.

The Colosseum's phenomenal success was entirely attributable to the inventive buying and marketing policies of Walter Wilson. From the outset he insisted on ready money and sold quality goods at low prices in order to profit from large turnover rather than the customary high mark ups. The sale of single, high fashion hats at wholesale prices caused a sensation. Such practices had already been adopted by a few like-minded Glasgow retailers, but were still very progressive. During the late 1870s Wilson decided to purchase, rather than manufacture, his stock and, by buying in bulk for ready money, persuaded manufacturers to supply him direct despite boycott threats by wholesalers. Wilson personally undertook many buying trips to London and the continent and visited the United States on two occasions to see different kinds of retail enterprise.

On the marketing side, Wilson's success was founded upon promotion of a kind unprecedented in Scotland. He advertised regularly in the local press, using such devices as coded text and unusual layouts to catch the attention of readers, on circulars, posted from the top of the Eiffel Tower in 1889 and over-printed with campaign maps during the Egyptian War in 1882, and on sandwich boards carried by Glasgow's unemployed in 1886. He also introduced sky signs to the city. His resourcefulness was endless and numerous competitions, processions and Christmas toy fairs were organised to boost sales.

Wilson was well aware that the growth of the suburbs in the south had made Jamaica Street a major thoroughfare and he was determined to attact casual custom. Visitors were invited to browse without buying, and the showrooms, replete with goods and magnificently decorated, were designed to seduce shoppers. In 1882 he introduced electric light as a further novelty, some ten years before it was adopted by Glasgow Corporation.

The expansion of the business prompted Wilson to make a partner of Robert Binnie, his brother-in-law and general manager of 12 years standing, in 1887. In 1874 Wilson had experimented unsuccessfully with opening other shops in Glasgow. In late 1890, possibly on the suggestion of Wilson's friend, Thomas Lipton, the idea was revived and branches were opened in Sauchiehall Street, Greenock, Dumfries, Inverness, Kirkcaldy and Arbroath. In 1891 and 1892 a further 20 stores were established in Scotland as well as seven in England and Ireland including a London branch selling drapery of Scottish manufacture. All were managed by Wilson, from Glasgow, using a team of inspectors. The profitability of the whole enterprise was, however, undermined by the tendency of branch managers to set up on their own account and poach trade. The last branch store was closed in 1902.

In April 1894 the firm adopted the title of 'The Grand Colosseum Warehouse' and Wilson's hectic and innovative marketing continued. In 1896, for example, he introduced the motor car for the delivery of parcels and, in 1901 published the 'The British Almanac' which included special offer coupons.

In 1901 The Caledonia Railway Co was authorised to purchase property in Jamaica Street for siting a new station and Wilson, believing that the Colosseum was threatened, opened Les Grand Magasins des Tuileries, in Sauchiehall Street, in March 1904. The new store, an elaboration of a high class millinery establishment which Wilson had earlier opened under the style of Tréron et Cie, was handsomely fitted out with luncheon and retiring rooms. It was agreed that Binnie would manage the Colosseum whilst Wilson concentrated in the new store with his son, Arthur, as a department manager. At Les Magasins, Wilson allowed credit purchases for the first time through a system of deposit accounts. He encouraged forenoon shopping by offering morning discounts, and in 1913 opened Glasgow's first bargain basement. The store incorporated many concepts he had seen in operation in America in contrast to previous warehouses in the city which had imitated Parisian models. The store flourished although government taxes on imported hats proved onerous during the First World War.

The assumption of a partner allowed Wilson to become involved in civic affairs. In 1887 he was elected to the Town Council for Gorbals Ward determined to ensure the more economic use of city funds. He was an active member of many committees and served on the Council for nine years. Wilson was appointed a magistrate in 1893, and served as convener of the Printing and Advertising Committees for the Glasgow Exhibitions of 1888 and 1901. He was a member of the Merchants' House and Grocers' Company.

Wilson was also an extravagant philanthropist and personally financed numerous schemes to help the city's poor and aged. In 1886, for example, he arranged a series of day trips to Rothesay for 1500 children and, in 1887, a fête for 37,000 children on Glasgow Green to celebrate the Queen's Jubilee. Wilson's staff were also well treated. Their working conditions were relatively good and dining and recreation rooms were provided in 1887.

Wilson died in Harrogate in 1917 whilst visiting for the benefit of his health. In 1919 his trustees registered Walter Wilson & Co. (Glasgow) Ltd and Tréron Ltd as private limited companies.

ALISON TURTON

SOURCES

Unpublished

Millar, A H, 'Glasgow Sketches', 1889
SRO: SC 36/48/288, Inventory
      SC 36/51/180, Settlement

Published

The Bailie, 10/2/1875, 3/1/1883, 9/11/1887
Glasgow Herald, 18/10/1917
North British Daily Mail, 22/12/1891
Who's Who in Glasgow, 1909
Wilson, Arthur, *Walter Wilson, Merchant, 1849-1917*, Glasgow 1920

Sir Alexander ANDERSON,

Financier and company promoter; b. 10/6/1802, Strichen, Aberdeenshire, s. of William Anderson, Minister of Religion, and Helen Findlay; m. Rachel Johnston; 1 s., 2 d.; Partner, Adam and Anderson, solicitors; d. 11/4/1887, Aberdeen; g/v estate: £22,094.

Joint-Stock Companies formed by Sir Arthur Anderson, 1836-1874

	Number	Capital*
Total	19	£3.77m
Railways	7	3.0
Banks	1	0.25
Insurance	3	0.08
Investment	3	0.19
Gas	1	0.05
Property	2	0.17
Commercial	2	0.03

* Initial paid-up capital

Sir Alexander Anderson was born in Strichen, Aberdeenshire, where his father was the minister, on 10 June 1802 and died at Blelack, Aberdeenshire, on 11 April 1887. He was educated at Aberdeen Grammar School and then at Marischal College, Aberdeen, while his early training was with David Hutcheon, of Marischal Street, Aberdeen. A partner in the legal firm of Adam and Anderson, from 1827 until 1866, he was responsible for promoting, among others, such companies as the North of Scotland Bank, the North of Scotland Assurance Company, the Aberdeen Railway, the Great North of Scotland Railway, the Northern Agricultural Company, and the City of Aberdeen Land Association. He was knighted by Queen Victoria in 1863 and was Lord Provost of Aberdeen from 1859 to 1866.

Alexander Anderson's upbringing and early career was conventional for as a son of the manse, school, university and the law were all a natural progression. However, when Anderson entered the legal profession, the business of a lawyer was not merely confined to the narrow practice of law, but extended into every sphere in which an educated, knowledgeable, and respected man of affairs could be expected to give advice and render practical assistance. The lawyer was an agent for business, financial, estate and legal matters and it was upon the former, rather than the latter, that Adam and Anderson concentrated. In particular, they cultivated the Aberdeenshire landed gentry, acting as general estate factors for many of them, as in the case of Lord Saltoun.

As a consequence of this, Anderson numbered many of the region's wealthy among his clients, and his firm was often entrusted with the safe-keeping or investment of substantial sums of money. This made him very aware of the needs and interests of investors, and it was here that his strength and success as a company promoter lay. He could easily assess the capacity and willingness of investors to finance a particular project, while he was also in the position of knowing, either personally or professionally, many of the potential investors, who could be approached and interested in a scheme at its inception. At the time when Anderson was in business there were no indviduals or institutions specialising in the promotion of joint-stock enterprise, and the task fell naturally to the local lawyer, with his knowledge and contacts.

The first company Anderson prmoted was the North of Scotland Fire and Life Assurance, which appeared in 1836, and the last was the City of Aberdeen Land Association, which was formed in 1874. Between these two Anderson was involved in a further 23 projects. Twenty-five companies were promoted by Anderson, of which a total of 19, with a paid-up capital of £3.8m, actually came into existence. Only six companies were not taken up by the public and, of these, four were railway concerns promoted in 1844-5, temporarily abandoned, only to re-appear at a later date in much the same form. Consequently, Anderson had a 90% success rate in the companies he promoted, although some had to renew their appeal to the investor before they were firmly supported. His only real failures were with two local property ventures, namely the Aberdeen Building Association (1843) and the Aberdeenshire Land Company (1872).

There was little novelty about the companies formed by Anderson for, with few exceptions, they either duplicated existing enterprises operating in the region, or imitated concerns promoted elsewhere. For example, the first two ventures he promoted were an insurance company and a bank in 1836 and they were modelled on flourishing Aberdeen firms established the previous decade by John Ewing, another Aberdeen lawyer. Similarly, the Aberdeen New Gas Light Company (1843) and the Northern Agricultural Company (1854) both competed with established local joint-stock concerns, while the marine insurance company (1839), the railways (1844-5 and 1852-5), the investment/exchange company (1845), the property companies (1838 and 1874), and the steam traction company (1872), comprised the Aberdeen component of a national mania for such concerns.

The only really novel enterprise promoted by Anderson was the Illinois Investment Company, which appeared in 1837. This had as its objective the raising of money in the Aberdeen area, where interest rates were low, and lending it on property in Illinois, where they were high. This had been done before but the

Illinois Company was the first venture that intended to operate on the joint-stock principle and offer the opportunity to small ivestors. It was to be another 30 years before the concept gained widespread acceptance, though there was a flurry of such ventures in Aberdeen between 1837 and 1840, following the early success of the Illinois. These included an Australian investment company and a Wisconsin insurance company promoted by Anderson.

Despite the lack of originality about most of the enterprises founded by Anderson, their creation was a major achievement for him. Anderson was not unique in recognising the opportunities for new joint-stock ventures in the north-east of Scotland. In railways, for instance, Anderson's Great North of Scotland railway faced competition both from a rival Aberdeen group and from an Inverness consortium that wanted the line under its control. In the end the Anderson project was the preferred route, but control of the last section was lost to the Inverness interests. Similar battles were fought over Anderson's other railway promotions but, almost invariably, it was his company that gained the support of the investing public.

Anderson's strength as a company promoter lay not in what he promoted but in his ability to mobilise financial support for his creations. Although the local press was used to advertise prospectuses and obtain favourable comment, it was through a network of influential legal contacts and legal investors that Anderson filled the subscription lists for one venture after another. In the promotion of the North of Scotland Bank in 1836, for instance, Anderson marshalled assistance from substantial lawyers in the other main towns of the region, and this gave him a favourable reception from their clients. As a result the North of Scotland Bank attracted the most numerous shareholding of any bank in Scotland. When Anderson promoted the City of Aberdeen Land Association in 1874, he was still using the same methods. They again proved successful, despite the feeling among some of his legal colleagues that the task was impossible. Moreover, success bred success not only in widening contacts and instilling confidence in potential investors, but also through Anderson's ability to use his own and the resources of established companies to promote other ventures. Anderson, for example, borrowed extensively from the North of Scotland Bank in the mid 1840s to finance his railway projects so that, by 1852, his firm, Adam and Anderson, owed the bank over £200,000.

Essentially, contacts, confidence and capital were the keys to Andersons' success as a company promoter. Yet all three were weakened in 1866 when he suffered financial embarrassment due to unwise investments on borrowed capital.

Since 1846 he had been carrying 3,000 shares of the North Staffordshire railway, as well as a considerable holding of Great North of Scotland stock, while he had also purchased land on the outskirts of Aberdeen for £75,000 in 1863. In the longer run these were to prove remunerative investments, especially the land, but, when he was asked to repay his debts of £127,000 during the 1866 crisis, he was unable to do so, and it was only when he sold the land for £134,000 to the City of Aberdeen Land Association in 1874, that he regained solvency. By then, however, the firm of Adam and Anderson had been dissolved, and though Anderson formed a new partnership with Lachland Mackinnon Jnr, his time was largely occupied with the affairs of the City of Aberdeen Land Association - especially during the aftermath of the City of Glasgow Bank collapse. At that time the Association had outstanding loans of £158,000 in Glasgow financed by Aberdeen deposits of £125,000, which could be withdrawn on one month's notice. It required careful husbanding of the company's resources to avoid a panic and Anderson, a director of the Association until his death, was largely responsible for their survival.

However, even before the financial difficulties of 1866 Anderson had been withdrawing from active company promotion. In 1859, he began on a new career as Lord Provost of Aberdeen which lasted until 1866. During that period he placed his considerable skills at the disposal of the council, and became involved in the re-organisation of the city's water supply and sewage system; the building of new streets and schools; and he initiated the construction of a new Town Hall. Clearly, Anderson regarded his civic duty as an extension of his business practice and applied the same principles and methods to that as he did to the formation of new companies and, as a result, the city gained excellent public facilities.

What evaluation can one place on Sir Alexander Anderson? As a company promoter and mobiliser of local capital he was without a peer in the north-east of Scotland, being responsible for the region's largest bank, insurance company, property company and agricultural supply company, as well as most of the railways. Of the companies he formed, only two of the overseas ventures turned out to be failures, though some of the others came close to disaster, even with Anderson's guidance, such as the North of Scotland Bank in the late 1840s and the City of Aberdeen Land Association in the late 1870s. Despite his success in pulling the Land Association through its difficulties, Anderson was not a careful manager. He thought too much of newer and more ambitious projects and too little of making the companies that he established operate successfully. That task he largely left to others. Alexander Anderson was a promotional genius who saw opportunities and knew the possibilities of success, but did not have the talent to run a successful company - luckily there were others who did.

RANALD MICHIE

SOURCES

Unpublished
SRO: SC 1/36/101, Inventory
    SC 1/37/98, Will

Published
Keith, A, *The North of Scotland Bank Ltd, 1836-1936*, Aberdeen, 1936
Mackinnon, L, *Recollections of an Old Lawyer*, Aberdeen, 1935
Macmillan, D S, *Scotland and Australia, 1788-1850: Emigration, Commerce and Investment*, London, 1967
Michie, R C, *Money, Mania and Markets: Investment, Company Formation and the Stock Exchange in Nineteenth Century Scotland*, Edinburgh, 1981
Smith, A E, *George Smith's Money: A Scottish Investor in America*, Maddison, 1966

Robert FLEMING,

Financier and investment trust founder; b. 1845, Dundee, s. of John Fleming, jute mill overseer, tea merchant and Ann McIntosh; m. 14/2/1881, Sarah Kate Hindmarsh; 2 s., 2 d.; Founder and Secretary, Scottish American Investment Trust and Founder and Ch, Robert Fleming & Co; d. 31/7/1933, Bridge of Orchy; g/v estate: £2.2 million.

Robert Fleming's businesses as a financier straddled three cities - Dundee, Edinburgh and London, yet his field of operations covered the world for, as an investor, he needed an accurate and detailed knowledge of opportunities overseas as well as in Britain. He is often given credit for being the founder of the investment trust movement but there were organisations, similar to his own, in existence before he began his investment activities and there were others, such as William J Menzies (qv), who developed institutions in tandem with Fleming's activities. There is no doubt, however, that he was an entrepreneur and a pioneer and that his ideas on how to run an investment trust were widely copied.

Fleming received his early education in Free Church of St David's School in Brown Street, Dundee, where he won a scholarship to go to Dundee High School. At the time of Robert's birth his father, John Fleming, was an overseer in a jute mill who later became a tea merchant and he placed great store on the value of a traditional education followed by a commercial apprenticeship.

Fleming's business training began about 1859 in the office of the merchant James Ramsay Jnr and by 1866 he was a book-keeper and private clerk to the senior partner, Edward Baxter, in the offices of Messrs Edward Baxter and Son, textile manufacturers. There was therefore little about his early life to suggest that he was destined for greater things but Baxter tutored him in the management of his investments and eventually put him in charge of his own portfolio. He made his first visit to the United States in 1870. The training which Fleming received and the knowledge which he was able to accumulate of commercial affairs in many parts of the world were soon to be put to more positive use.

In July 1873, when he was only 28 years old Fleming issued a prospectus for the Scottish American Investment Trust, the intention being to raise £150,000 for investment in North America. The only mistake which he made was to underestimate the demand for the Trust's services and the prospectus had to be withdrawn, to be replaced with another asking the public to subscribe £300,000, even this was over-subscribed. The launch was an enormous success. The idea of Dundee people investing in overseas securities was not new as at least one of the local banks, the Dundee Banking Company, had been placing some of its reserve funds in various types of investment since the 1830s. What was new was that the Scottish American Investment Trust gave potential investors the opportunity to take direct advantage of the specialist knowledge of local people like Fleming. That this chance was taken up with such enthusiasm must, in part at least, be due to the fact that the rate of interest being paid on bank deposits was very low. Savers and investors were clearly prepared to accept the higher risk of overseas investment, via the medium of an investment trust, for the sake of a higher rate of return. The coupon rate was six per cent.

Fleming became the secretary of the new organisation, in effect its chief executive. Four well known local businessmen became the trustees with John Guild as chairman. Such was the success of the Trust that before 1876 he had formed two more trusts in Dundee. All three trusts continued to pay their dividends even when market conditions were difficult. Reserve funds were built up. He kept in close touch with other people in Dundee who were active in overseas investments. For example in 1881 he became a director of William Mackenzie's Dundee Mortgage Company. The Dundee investors were a close knit community. It was not long before others tried to emulate their success. Fleming also became involved in setting up the British Investment Trust in Edinburgh (1889), the Investment Trust Corporation in London (1886) and the Scottish Western Investment Trust in Glasgow whose first chairman was Andrew Bonar Law. It is difficult to determine the exact nature and extent of Fleming's involvement in these other trusts. At very least he was involved because of his experience and success in Dundee and because he had firm ideas about how the business of this type of financial institution should be conducted. He became a director of all of these trusts.

His move to London was a gradual process in the sense that it was not a sudden decision, but the market for American investments was more easily operated from London than from any Scottish city and London was rapidly emerging as the world's major financial sector. Most of the Scottish banks opened offices there in the 1860s and 1870s. Fleming finally opened an office there in 1900. When settled in London Fleming became increasingly aware of the opportunities open to him for financial innovation. He continued to pursue his interests in investment trusts but began to take a wider view of the financial markets. The firm which he set up, Robert Fleming and Co, was in effect, a merchant bank. It is often said that a merchant banker lives by his wits while a commercial banker lives by his deposits. In Fleming's case that was not true for he could draw on, or at least influence, the direction of investments by several large trusts. By the late 1920s he could influence 56 trusts which controlled over £100 million. This gave him a clear advantage over some other merchant bankers. His activities in this area included raising money for American railroads. Fleming was justifiably proud of his achievements and maintained that American farmers and railroad promoters got a better deal from British financiers than they did from their own countrymen in New York. In pursuing these interests Fleming made 64 visits to North America where he became acquainted with many leading bankers and investors including J P Morgan. Other involvements included the setting up of the Anglo-Persian Oil Company (later British Petroleum).

Although Fleming made his home in Grosvenor Square, London, and at Nettlebed in Oxfordshire, he never neglected his Scottish interests and he served for a time as a director of the Royal Bank of Scotland. Moreover he made several charitable donations in his native city, in particular to the city itself and to University College, Dundee. In 1928 he gifted £155,000 to the city for slum clearance and redevelopment. Within five years more than 500 families had been rehoused. Also in 1928 he was made a freeman of the city and St Andrews University conferred on him the honorary degree of LLD.

Apart from business Fleming took a great interest in farming and forestry. His hobbies included deer stalking and he was a first class rifle shot. In 1881 Fleming married Sarah Kate Hindmarsh of St Andrews. They had two sons and two daughters but their elder son, Major Valentine Fleming, MP for Oxford, was killed during the First World War. Robert Fleming died in 1933 at Bridge of Orchy, at the age of 89. His estate was valued at £2.2 million.

CHARLES W MUNN

SOURCES

Published

Glasgow Herald, 2/8/1933
Jackson, W Turrentine, *The Enterprising Scott*, Edinburgh, 1968
Kerr, W G, *Scottish Capital on the American Credit Frontier*, Austin, Texas, 1976
Scott, J and Hughes, M, *The Anatomy of Scottish Capita*, London, 1980
Stewart, D, 'Robert Fleming of Dundee, Father of the Investment Trust Movement', *Scottish Bankers Magazine*, August 1979
The Times, 2/8/1933
Weir, R B, *A History of the Scottish American Investment Company Ltd 1873-1973*, Edinburgh, 1973.

William Henry FRASER,

Writer to the Signet; b. 2/3/1876, Edinburgh, s. of William S Fraser, Writer to the Signet, and Annabella Nelson; m. Katherine M Cowan, d. of Alexander Cowan, papermaker; 2 d.; Ch, National Bank of Scotland; d. 26/6/1966, Edinburgh.

William Henry Fraser was educated at Edinburgh Academy, where he was dux of the school, and at Edinburgh University where he studied law. As was the tradition he also spent some time at Bonn University. His apprenticeship was served with Cowan and Dalmahoy, WS, in Edinburgh and he himself became a Writer to the Signet in 1900 in the family firm of Fraser, Stoddart and Ballingall, WS. This was the firm from which he retired in 1964.

Fraser's working life, therefore, was spent as a lawyer but he is better remembered as a member of the Edinburgh financial community. His entré to that community probably came via his wife's family. In 1903 he married Katherine Cowan, daughter of Alexander Cowan, papermaker. Various members of the Cowan family were active members of the Edinburgh financial community and this gave Fraser his start. By 1925 he was a director of 11 companies, the most important of which were the Caledonian Insurance Company, the Edinburgh Investment Trusts and the National Guarantee and Suretyship Association (of which he was chairman). By 1939 his list of directorships numbered 18 and now included the National Bank of Scotland and Alex Cowan and Company Ltd -

his father-in-law's firm. The Cowan papermaking business had got into difficulties in the inter-war years and Fraser was called in to sort out the problems.

Fraser's primary motive in joining all of these boards was to try and bring in business for his legal firm and in this he was highly successful. But it was not long before the experience which he gained in investment, insurance and banking made him one of the most experienced men in the community. This experience, combined with his personal qualities of integrity, sagacity and good humour placed him in great demand.

Probably the largest organisation to which he contributed his skills was the National Bank of Scotland. He joined the board in 1925 and became chairman in 1942, a position which he retained unil 1956. He remained on the board after his spell as chairman and later served on the board of the merged bank the National Commercial Bank of Scotland. He also served as a director of Lloyds Bank in London which was the parent company of the National Bank. These were very frustrating times for bankers as government controls on lending prevented them from developing their business in the way that they would have wished. After the Second World War the British banks co-operated in the setting up of the Industrial and Commercial Finance Corporation Ltd. William Fraser represented the Scottish banks on the board of this new organisation and made sure that Scottish interests were not forgotten.

William Fraser does not seem to have had much interest in politics but he was an active churchman. As a child he, his brother and father attended Free St George's Church, while his mother and sister went to St John's Episcopal Church. Following his marriage to Katherine Cowan in 1903 he too attended the Episcopal Church. Fraser had a number of charitable interests including the Sick Children's Hospital and Trades Maiden Hospital.

Fraser's main recreation was shooting and he was a well known after dinner speaker noted for his sense of humour. He was a member of New Club and of Edinburgh University Club.

CHARLES W MUNN

SOURCES

Unpublished

Interview with daughter, Mrs M Peters
SRO: SC 70/1/1646, Will

Published

Checkland, S G, *Scottish Banking: A History, 1695-1973*, Glasgow, 1975
Directory of Directors
Glasgow Herald, 21/12/1956, 28/6/1966
Kinross, J, *Fifty Years in the City*, 1982
Who Was Who

Charles GAIRDNER,

Banker, b. 6/1/1824, Ayr, s. of Charles Dalrymple Gairdner, bank manager and Agnes Cowan; m. Hannah McNairn, d. of James McNair, merchant; 2 s., 6 d.; General Manager, Union Bank of Scotland; d. 18/2/1899, Broom, Newton Mearns; g/v estate: £72,601 11s 6d.

Charles Gairdner's business career began in 1839 in the office of James McClelland, accountant in Glasgow. McClelland was an Ayrshire man and was well known to Gairdner's father who had banking and estate management interests in that county. Gairdner's father had secured the apprenticeship for his son but when the four year indenture was concluded the terms offered for a clerkship were not to the liking of either father or son and a clerkship was acquired for Charles with Peter White, accountant and stockbroker in Glasgow, with the intermediation of Andrew Mitchell, writer in Glasgow. Mitchell, together with James Finlay of James Finlay and Co, was also able to secure the Glasgow agency of the Globe Insurance Co for the young Gairdner who was then only 19 years old. Gairdner's early career therefore gained experience for him in the developing areas of accountancy, stockbroking and insurance.

White, who was also an Ayrshire man, was keen to develop the stockbroking side of his business and when the Glasgow Stock Exchange Association was formed in 1844 he became one of the founding members. He offered Gairdner a partnership the following year and the firm then traded as White and Gairdner. Charles became a member of the Glasgow Stock Exchange Association in 1845, and a member of its managing committee in 1855-6.

If anything, Gairdner's main interest was in accounting rather than in stockbroking and in 1853 he was one of the young accountants who petitioned their seniors to found a professional association for accountants. Accordingly, the *Institute of Accountants and Actuaries in Glasgow* was set up and received its Royal Charter in 1855. (It is now part of the *Institute of Chartered Accountants of Scotland*). James McClelland was the first president and Peter White the first treasurer and second president. Gairdner was therefore associated with the exclusivity of membership and professionalisation of standards to two professions.

Gairdner's reputation as an accountant was sufficiently well established for him to be appointed as assistant liquidator of the Western Bank of Scotland following its failure in the crisis of 1857. He was subsequently principal liquidator until 1865 when he handed over this task to the firm of McClelland and MacKinnon. James McClelland had retired from the firm by that time and had been replaced by his son. Gairdner's own son later became a partner in the firm.

As a result of his experience as liquidator of the Western Bank and possibly also through his father's influence, (Gairdner Snr's bank, Hunter and Co of Ayr had been taken over by the Union Bank in 1843), Charles Gairdner was invited by the directors of the Glasgow based Union Bank of Scotland to carry out a general investigation of their bank's affairs in 1861. What he discovered disturbed him greatly and as the directors were far from satisfied with the performance of their general manager, James Robertson, they appointed Gairdner to be the joint general manager in 1862 and when Robertson retired in 1865 Gairdner then became sole general manager. He joined the

board in 1868 where he remained until his retiral in 1895. Following his appointment to the bank he resigned from the Glasgow Stock Exchange Association and allowed his membership of the Institute of Accountants and Actuaries to lapse.

Gairdner proved himself to be a cautious lender and a good manager. Several new systems were introduced which were designed to enhance the flow of management information, eg a systematic 'opinion book' was initiated which recorded both outgoing and incoming correspondence regarding the credit worthiness of customers. By the time that Gairdner had entered fully into his general managership, however, the Scottish banks had agreed to standardise rates and charges and so a large part of the competitive element was removed from the Scottish banking scene. Glasgow banks had often offered higher deposit rates than their Edinburgh counterparts in the past but this option was now denied to them. When Gairdner became general manager in 1865 the Union Bank had the largest deposits of any Scottish bank but by 1870 it had slipped to fourth place and when he retired in 1895 it had gone done still further to sixth place. It is, of course, impossible to unravel all the causal strands to this decline but there can be no doubt that at best some of the blame must be attributed to Gairdner's general managership.

These were difficult years for the Scottish economy, particularly in the west, witnessing as they did the decline of the cotton industry and the somewhat painful birth of the steelmaking and shipbuilding industries. The bank was involved in all of these industries, financing expansion or contraction as required. On occasion Gairdner was not beyond involving himself directly in the internal affairs of his customers, eg the shipbuilding firm of J & G Thomson was a major debtor of the bank, indeed the bank had financed the transfer of their operation from Finnieston to a more extensive site at Dalmuir, Clydebank in 1874. By 1881 the bank had advanced £124,000 to Thomsons but a bad fire in that year, and commissioning trouble in 1883, put the firm's future in jeopardy. Gairdner was then in the difficult position of not knowing whether to finance reconstruction or to write the debt off as bad. To help him make up his mind he commissioned an investigation by Chartered Accountants, including McClelland, MacKinnon and Blyth. As a result of this enquiry the firm's debts were restructured, a new manager was appointed and the firm was eventually launched as a public company in 1889. This episode in the bank's history was fraught with difficulty and hazard for both bank and shipbuilder alike but the end product was a great success. Debts were repaid, Thomsons became the most modern yard on the Clyde, and Clydebank emerged as a new industrial town. The Thomson case is perhaps the most extreme example of Gairdner's involvement with the internal affairs of his customers but it does indicate the lengths to which he was prepared to go in order to defend his bank's position. What is also significant in this is the very intimate relationship between Gairdner, representing the bank, and the accountancy firm of McClelland, MacKinnon and Blyth.

Following the failure of the City of Glasgow Bank in 1878, but before the passage of the Banking and Joint Stock Companies Act in August 1879, Gairdner had moved to re-assure public opinion about the safety of his bank by asking the deputy chairman as 'the official representative of the proprietors, as distinguished from the board of directors' to appoint independent auditors. Those appointed were William MacKinnon of McClelland, MacKinnon and Blyth in Glasgow and James Haldane of Lindsay, Jameson and Haldane in Edinburgh. The latter was a liquidator of the City of Glasgow Bank. The auditors were of course the leading members of their profession but given the close relationship between MacKinnon's firm and Gairdner and the fact that the appointment was not made by the shareholders but at Gairdner's suggestion, it seems that the 'independent' nature of the audit must be called into question. The London Times, however, believed that the audit 'appears to have been of a very thorough character and completely independent'.

Too much might not be made of this one case but Gairdner's only other directorship was in the North British and Mercantile Insurance Co which was then Britain's second largest composite insurance company. In 1883 Gairdner was responsible for having the appointment of auditors made a duty of the Board of Directors rather than the shareholders. In this case, Haldane was appointed. What is clear in all this is that as far as Gairdner was concerned the rise of independent auditing, which is so often associated with this period, was a sham.

Clearly, Gairdner believed in keeping matters closely under his own control and indeed his management style could be said to have been autocratic. This characteristic is also reflected in his dealings with his peer group. It is said of him that at some of the bank managers meetings which he attended in Edinburgh, instead of giving free expression to his ideas, he would take out of his pocket and read a paper on the main topic for discussion, then hurry away to catch the return train to Glasgow.

This aloofness is not, however, reflected in his other activities for he was otherwise a clubable man who was a member of the Royal Northern Yacht Club. He also founded the Adam Smith Club in Glasgow which he moulded on the Political Economy Club of London which he had attended on occasion. He was a member of the economics section of the Glasgow Philosophical Society and president of the Society in 1887. He eschewed all overt political activity, as all good bankers must, but he corresponded with a wide range of businessmen, economists and politicians, including Campbell-Bannerman, although he personally contributed to the Conservative party.

Gairdner wrote extensively on banking matters and several pamphlets were published. From these it is clear that he was hostile to the Banking Acts of 1844 and 1845 and believed that they were damaging to the economic system. Nor did he believe in fixed reserve ratios but instead advocated that these should be allowed to vary according to circumstances.

He advocated that banks should possess large capitals and that they should have unlimited liability, but if they adopted limited liability then there should be a reserve liability of callable capital to cover note issues and so protect note holders. These ideas were published in 1872 several years before the failure of the City of Glasgow Bank when they came into the arena of public debate before being incorporated into legislation. It is not certain, however, that Gairdner originated the principle of reserve liability.

He was a noted public speaker and lectured widely in Scotland and England. When in 1866 the Counsel Superieure du Commerce de France approached the Glasgow Chamber of Commerce on the subject of banking and currency, Gairdner was chosen to reply. His answer attracted the attention of M. Chevalier, a leading authority who was very complimentary and said that he thought the French ought to copy the system followed by the Scots banks. He also gave evidence to the Parliamentary Committee on Banks of Issue (1875). He was awarded the degree of LLD by the University of Glasgow in 1889.

Gairdner was fond of foreign travel and was noted for his charitable donations. He retired due to ill health in 1895 and was succeeded in the Bank by Robert Blyth a partner in McClelland, MacKinnon and Blyth. He died in 1899 at Broom, Newton Mearns.

CHARLES W MUNN AND NORIO TAMAKI

WRITINGS

Paper money, 1866
The Rate of Discount and the Bank Acts, 1873
Fluctuations in Trade, 1977
Economy on the Use of Gold as Practised in Scotland, 1886
Constitution and Course of the Money Market, 1888
The Royal Commission on Gold and Silver, 1889
National Gold Reserves, 1890
The Making of the Gold Reserves, 1891
Mr Goschen's Scheme for Reform of the Bank Acts 1892

SOURCES

Unpublished

Gairdner Correspondence, Bank of Scotland (Glasgow) Archives

Information provided by Charles G D Tennant, Blairgowrie, from Family archives

Calendar of Confirmations, 1899

Published

Anon, *Scottish Banks and Bankers*, 1900

The Bailie, 'Men You Know Series', No 330, No 344 and No 825

Checkland, S G, *Scottish Banking: A History 1695-1973*, 1975

Gairdner, C D, *Autobiography of C D Gairdner of Auchans*, 1902

Glasgow Herald, 20/2/1899

Kennedy, Ian M, 'Some Scottish Banking Families', *Scottish Genealogist*, Vol 6, No 1, 1959 and Vol 7, No 2, 1960

Tamaki, N, *The Life Cycle of the Union Bank of Scotland 1830-1954*, 1983

Tennant, C G D, 'The Gairdner Correspondence', *Scottish Industrial History*, Vol 2, No 2 and 3, 1979

Thomas Johnstone Carlyle GIFFORD,

Writer to the Signet; b. 14/1/1881, Ingleston, s. of Patrick Gifford, farmer, and Barbara Sloan Grierson; m. (1) 11/6/1907, Maud Oriel Riata Pearson, d. of Hon Charles Henry Pearson, LLD, Fellow of Oriel College, Oxford; (2) 4/5/1960, Sophia Mary Wharton Miller, d. John Hepburn Millar, Advocate; 1 s.; Snr Partner, Baillie, Gifford & Co, Investment Trust Managers; d. 24/1/1975.

Baillie and Gifford, WS was founded by Augustus Baillie NP whose partner in law had died in 1901. Baillie's limited qualification forced him to seek a partner who could practice law. He consulted Lyon Mackenzie, a member of the Bar, who then consulted William Purves of Messrs W and F Haldane, WS. This network of private contacts came up with the name of Thomas Johnstone Carlyle Gifford, a 25 year old Writer to the Signet who had served his apprenticeship with Ward J Cook, WS and was then private clerk to Sir Henry Cook.

T J Carlyle Gifford became Baillie's partner at a salary of £300 per annum with a one-third share of profits (increased to half share the following year). Gifford's own recollection was that the firm was quite small relying very largely on a network of family contacts for the bulk of its business. Nevertheless they found employment for five clerks. The firm had some early contacts in the rubber industry, being secretaries to the Third Mile Rubber Company and it was from this connection that the expansion was to come.

At the suggestion of a friend, Alistair McGregor, who was a rubber planter in Malaya, the Straits Mortgage and Trust Company was set up in 1909 to lend money to rubber planters to help develop their estates. The Trust was only modestly successful at first and although Gifford did not become a director, he was intimately connected with its management as Baillie, Gifford and Co were its managers and secretaries. The Trust's name was changed in 1913 to Scottish Mortgage and Trust Co Ltd.

Within the firm, Gifford came to play a leading role for Baillie spent a lot of his time hunting. In fact the two men complimented one another very well for while Gifford applied himself to the business, Baillie applied himself to finding new clients - a task for which his wide ranging social contacts and his membership of New Club, of which Gifford also became a member, helped enormously.

In the years before the First World War, Gifford took an interest in various aspects of the law which, although seemingly unrelated, were to have an important effect upon the future development of the firm. His particular interests were in the law as it affected Stock Exchange Transactions and land law, especially as it concerned the rent on pastoral farms. His involvement with these issues prompted him to write several articles on these subjects which were published in the Scots Law Times. His interests in these and related matters led him to be invited onto the boards of several Edinburgh investment trusts, eg Investors' Mortgage Security Co Ltd, which was managed by Shepperd and Wedderburn, WS; Scottish and Canadian General Investment Co Ltd, which was managed by Maxtone, Graham and Sime, CA; and the United States Trust Company of Scotland Ltd which was managed by R G Simpson, CA. In short, by 1925, Gifford was on the boards of companies in all the Edinburgh Fund management Houses where he met and became better acquainted with such names as A W Robertson Durham and W H Fraser (qv). As was the general practice, he was just as likely to be a member of a fund managed by another house, as of one managed by Baillie, Gifford, WS By 1925 he was a director of 13 companies, most of which were investment companies and trusts but which included the Scottish Widows Fund Life Assurance Society and by 1939 his directorships numbered 22, including 8 chairmanships. After the Second World War he became a director of Alliance Trust. Gifford was also a founder director of several companies.

By 1957 Baillie, Gifford and Co of which Gifford was by then the senior partner had become the largest of the Scottish investment trust managers - a position which they retained at the time of his death in 1975 by which time he had been semi-retired for a number of years.

In building up the investment side of the business of Baillie, Gifford, WS, Gifford became conscious during the explosive growth of the 1920s of the need to employ non-lawyers. His solution to this problem was simple. It was to have two firms - one to be lawyers and one to be fund managers. In 1927 two investment managers were employed and this began the separation which reached its climax in the early 1970s by which time there were no common partners in the firms. The legal side of the business had become Biggart, Baillie and Gifford, WS, while the fund management side remained Baillie, Gifford & Co. Both, however, continued to share the offices at 3 Glenfinlas Street which were purchased in 1914.

Gifford was in the forefront of the growth in investment trusts in the inter-war years and this led him to set up trusts in London as well as in Edinburgh. In 1929 he set up the Abbots, Friars and Monks Trusts and the Winterbottom Trust. His great interest in trusts and his obvious entrepreneurial zeal led him to be a member of the steering committee which set up the Association of Investment Trust Companies in 1931. He became the first deputy chairman, responsible for Scottish trusts - a position which he held from 1932-34 and from 1936-51. He was the second chairman of the Association from 1934-36.

During the Second World War his great experience of investment led him to be called into Government service. In the closing months of 1939 he was invited by the Governor of the Bank of England to join a committee formed to advise the Treasury on the requisition and realisation of British and foreign securities and by February 1940 he was described in *The Times* as the 'special British Treasury agent in charge of the sale of British holdings of American securities'. He spent almost two years in the United States and was also involved in the disposal of other assets. It is a tribute to his ability that only one dispersal caused any great controversy and that was the sale in March 1941 of the American Viscose Company which was owned by Courtaulds and which Churchill later claimed had been sold at too low a price. In this, however, Sir Edward Peacock and not Gifford was the principal negotiator. Nevertheless, both men objected strongly to Churchill's claim.

Aside from gaining a number of lasting friendships in the American banking community, Gifford's sojourn in the United States did two things for him. Firstly, it reinforced an already strong belief in the free enterprise system. When British Government plans for the Civil Aviation Industry were published in 1945, Gifford wrote to *The Times* advocating a free enterprise system based on the American model.

Secondly, it confirmed his commercial judgment on the growth potential of the American economy so that after the cessation of hostilities when he had returned to Glenfinlas Street, he advocated investment in the United States even although this meant paying the dollar premium for overseas investment funds which was necessitated by the Exchange Control regulations. This began the return to overseas investment which had been such a notable feature of the British (especially the Edinburgh) financial scene for over 80 years. Gifford's judgment in this was well rewarded by the rise to premier position of Baillie, Gifford and Co amongst the Edinburgh fund managers.

His interest in fund management, however, was only one of a substantial list of activities with which he was concerned. As a lawyer he is remembered as being good at pleading - especially in tax cases. He was a name at Lloyds. He was a member of the Court of Edinburgh University. He had a small farm at Humbie in East Lothian where he bred Herefords, not terribly successfully.

He was a noted sportsman and played tennis well into middle age when he took up golf and became a member of the Honourable Company of Edinburgh Golfers at Muirfield. He was also an enthusiastic bridge player.

He was an atheist and was given to occasional acts of charity. Gifford is remembered by his colleagues as a man who set very high standards and who was good at delegating work. He had a gift for spotting errors and for getting to the heart of problems. One acquaintance remembers him as 'an outstandingly wise man who so often got his timing of investment decisions spot on'.

CHARLES W MUNN

SOURCES

Unpublished

White, J G Charles, 'A Personal and Anecdotal Memoir of T J Carlyle Gifford', 12/2/1979

Published

Directory of Directors, 1925, 1939
The Scotsman, 7/3/1959
The Scots Law Times, 1914
The Times, 27/2/1975

James IVORY,

Chartered accountant and fund manager; b. 3/12/1862, Edinburgh, s. of William Ivory, advocate, and Janet H Rankin; m. 1877, Florence T Wyckoff of New York; 2 s., 2 d.; Founding partner of Ivory and Sime, CA and manager of the British Assets Trust; d. 11/1939, Edinburgh; g/v estate: £103,466.

James Ivory belonged to that relatively small band of Edinburgh businessmen, whose interests in managing his own and other people's money, made Scotland's capital city into a major financial centre. The interlocks between these men and their families crossed the generations. Despite commercial rivalries they often sat on the boards of directors of each other's investment firms and many of them served as directors of one or more of the large life assurance offices and banks. In short the Edinburgh financial community, despite a relatively large and growing number of firms, was led by a relatively small number of men all of whom knew one another.

The family into which James Ivory was born in 1861 was intimately connected with the law. His father William was Sheriff of Inverness, Elgin and Nairn while his grandfather was Lord Ivory. The young James was sent for his education to Harrow and from there he went to Germany where he spent some time in Hanover. He then returned to Edinburgh, to an apprenticeship with Moncrieff and Horsburgh, CA, but his independent spirit rebelled against the slow career path which was stretching out before him and, as soon as he had qualified in 1886, he set up business on his own as a chartered accountant.

In 1895 Ivory took as his partner Thomas Watson Sime, CA and the two men worked together until 1907 when Sime emigrated to Canada. From then until 1925, when he admitted his elder son, Ivory had no partner. His younger son was also later admitted as a partner.

In late nineteenth century Edinburgh many lawyers and accountants were becoming interested in the management and investment of other people's money. The investment trust movement had got underway in 1873 when William Menzies (qv) set up the Scottish American Investment Company Ltd and there were a number of others, such as Robert Fleming (qv) who followed and refined his example. James Ivory was one of the most conspicuously successful of these innovators. In 1898 he started the British Assets Trust with a capital of £15,000. By the time of his death in 1939 it had funds under management of over £7m. Ivory was the fund's manager and did not become a director until 1928. What he created was one of the most successful of the Edinburgh fund managers.

Although the Trust's records have been deposited with Glasgow Univeristy Archives these have not yet been examined. The inventory of James Ivory's estate, however, is revealing about his investment policy which was doubtless reflected in the investment strategies which he followed in business. What is particularly interesting is its modernity and its scope. There were many investments in up and coming organisations such as Tube Investments, Marks and Spencer and Lever Brothers as well as in several electrical supply companies. The bulk of the portfolio was in trusts, life assurance companies and even a building society and the foreign investments were in such organisations as United States Steel and Sears Roebuck. Doubtless Ivory had once been fond of railway stocks but by the time of his death he had sold every single one of them. He clearly believed that railways had had their day. Cars were the transportation of the future and Ivory had a few hundred pounds invested in the Chrysler Corporation.

In 1920, not content with one Trust, the British Assets Trust acquired the share capital of the Edinburgh American Land Mortgage Company which was renamed as the Second British Assets Trust in 1925.

The influence of men such as Ivory was much wider than their trusts, for the expertise which they acquired as fund managers was in demand by other businesses. In 1906 James Ivory became a director of the Standard Life Assurance Company and for many years was influential in formulating its investment policy. His presence in Charlotte Square helped enhance the reputation of that part of the city as a place where those with money to be managed would go in search of advice.

Although his chief interest was in business James Ivory developed many other interests and talents. As a young man he was a keen athlete but a sports injury left him slightly lame and put an end to his sports career. He became an enthusiastic fisherman, using rods which he made, and flies which he tied, himself.

Following his marriage in 1887 Ivory became interested in antique furniture and later in silver and needlework. Yet his was not the behaviour of the selfish aesthete, for he enjoyed showing his collections and frequently made pieces available for exhibitions. He was also an enthusiastic gardener with special interests in herbaceous and wild gardens. He lived at Laverockdale House, Colinton in Edinburgh and at Brewlands in Angus. Both houses and their gardens were widely known and appreciated by horticulturalists.

His wide interests were developed with an enquiring mind which was always ready to try something new. He was a man of independent mind. A pioneer motorist he was also an early exponent of personalised number plates. His number, S3, graced several vehicles.

James Ivory was also an active philanthropist, although he endeavoured to keep his charitable acts private. Among his many interests was the Pleasance

Trust which ran one of the best equipped welfare centres in Scotland and to which he and his wife made a number of donations over several years. Mrs Ivory survived her husband by almost 20 years and in that time she continued the family's interest in the work of the Trust.

CHARLES W MUNN

SOURCES

Unpublished

Calendar of confirmations
SRO: SC 70/1/1015, Inventory

Published

Scott, J and Hughes, M, *The Anatomy of Scottish Capital*, London, 1980
The Accountants' Magazine, 1939
The Evening Dispatch, 21/1/1939
Glasgow Herald, 21/1/1939
The Scotsman, 21/1/1939, 24/1/1939, 29/9/1958

commitment to the profession is underlined by the fact that, together with Esson and Donald Lindsay, he was amongst the founder members of the Society of Accountants in Edinburgh, established in 1854. For a while the three men practised as Lindsay, Esson & Jamieson, but in 1856 George Esson left to take a public appointment and the firm was re-styled Lindsay & Jamieson. Two years later they were joined by James Haldane and the firm became known as Lindsay, Jamieson & Haldane, a title it was to hold for over a century, with its offices at 24 St Andrew Square, Edinburgh.

The firm had already been guided to a prominent position by Donald Lindsay, who had been in practice since 1823 and in partnership with Esson since 1838. From 1837 until his retirement in 1871, Lindsay acted as auditor of the Scottish Widows Fund and, like both Jamieson and Haldane, was a director of the Royal Bank of Scotland. Through the 1850s, 60s and 70s, the partnership's activities widened to take in auditing work for a large number of Scottish companies and landed estates, as well as receiving frequent remits from Courts of Session and minor judicatories. By 1865, when testifying to the Royal Commission on Hypothec, Jamieson claimed, 'We have the charge, more or less directly, of several estates in various parts of Scotland ... the aggregate rental of (which) ... is about £100,000 a year'. As the reputation of the firm, and of Jamieson in particular, grew, the remits

George Auldjo JAMIESON,

Chartered accountant; b. 1/5/1828, Castle Hill, Aberdeen; s. of James Jamieson, Doctor of Medicine, Royal Navy and Anna Maria Esson; m. (1) Mary Souter Robertson; (2) Susan Helena Oliphant; 5 s., 2 d.; Senior Partner, Lindsay, Jamieson & Haldane, CA, Edinburgh; d. 18/7/1900, Edinburgh; g/v estate: £188,023 19s 0d.

George Auldjo Jamieson was born at Castle Hill, Aberdeen, on 1 May 1828, the son of a medical doctor, formerly of the naval service. Little is known of his early life or education prior to his graduation from Aberdeen University in 1846. Together with his younger brother, James Auldjo, he then entered the offices of Messrs Chalmers, advocates, in Aberdeen, before moving to Edinburgh, around 1849-50, to follow a career in accountancy. This move appears to have been suggested by George Auldjo Esson, a relative and fellow Aberdeen graduate, who arranged a position in his firm of Lindsay & Esson, accountants. Jamieson was soon made a partner and his early from the judicial system increased in importance and in 1879 he was appointed judicial factor in the Orr-Ewing case, in which the Glasgow firm of Archibald Orr-Ewing & Co successfully brought an action to restrain the London firm, R Johnston & Co, from infringing their trade-mark for Turkey red dye. The case was a notable one, particularly in its resolution of conflicts between Scots and English law. Jamieson's adept handling of the complex financial issues involved enhanced his growing reputation amongst businessmen and accountants in both Scotland and England. Jamieson's position as one of Scotland's leading chartered accountants was further underlined when, together with Haldane, he was appointed one of the four liquidators of the City of Glasgow Bank, which failed in 1878. This difficult task was only completed in October 1882.

A significant development in Jamieson's business career occurred after 1880, with his increasing involvement in the overseas capital market. During the 1880s and 1890s Edinburgh rapidly matured as an international financial centre, with Jamieson and many of his fellow chartered accountants leading the way in mobilising investment capital, and directing it towards ranching, mining and trust companies operating in the United States, Australia and elsewhere. By the early 1880s his firm was already gaining experience of overseas conditions in acting as auditors for a number of expatriate Scottish companies, such as the Cloncurry Copper & Smelting Co Ltd, which between 1883 and 1888 unsuccessfully attempted to work some mines in Queensland. At this time Jamieson's personal interest in mining was growing, although some of his early experiences were not happy ones. In 1881 he joined a group of prominent Scottish investors, such as Sir George Warrender, in taking up the shares of the Scottish Pacific Coast Mining Co Ltd. This company attempted to exploit some Californian mining leases, but had gone into voluntary liquidation by 1885. On this occasion, Jamieson's loss was limited to £300. Subsequent investments in mining were more successful and by the time of his death Jamieson held shares valued at £20,639 in 55 individual overseas mining companies. Of this, £10,582 was invested in the United States and £4,444 in Australia. His total stake in overseas issues amounted to £51,505 of the £146,333 probate valuation of his shareholdings (including £4,010 in foreign railway stocks).

Almost certainly the most important area of Jamieson's business career was his involvement in the Arizona Copper Co Ltd. This was first registered, in Edinburgh, in August 1882 with a nominal capitalization of £875,000, to purchase mines and smelters in a desolate part of south-eastern Arizona, near the towns of Clifton and Morenci. Promoted by directors of the influential Scottish American Mortgage Co, with copper prices at a high £67 a ton, and glowing reports of massive ore-bodies, Scotland's investors eagerly bought the company's £5 shares. However,

it soon became clear that the mines were poorly developed, with large-scale investment needed. The area was also 70 miles from the nearest rail-head and still subject to occasional Apache attacks. To compound the company's problems, copper prices began to fall throughout 1883 and 1884, ending at just £47 a ton. Amidst rumours of share-rigging by members of the original board, Jamieson was appointed chairman in November 1883, despite only being a minor shareholder (he had taken up 200 shares early in the year). A large number of shareholders had pressed for his appointment, calling for a man of proven integrity to steer the firm out of its difficulties. Through the following five years Jamieson led the company through a major reconstruction (August 1884), the floating of the Arizona Trust & Mortgage Co, to lend the Copper Co £350,000 (December 1883), and a major modernisation programme at the mines. A temporary rise in copper prices, to around £80 a ton in 1888, brought about by French speculation, helped the company to make substantial profits and clear its accumulated debt. By 1895 the loans were repaid, the Trust & Mortgage Co absorbed, and the Arizona Copper Co was finally set on a course of expanding output and rising profits. In the period 1884-90, average annual production of smelted copper had been just 2.63 thousand tons; by 1895-1900 this rose to 7.1 thousand tons (and, after Jamieson's death, in 1912-19, was to peak at an average 16.9 thousand tons per annum). The first dividend declared, in 1898, amounted to £83,000 and the accumulated dividends, by 1918, amounted to around £6.0 million. Once it had surmounted its birth pangs, the Arizona Copper Co became, by a long margin, the most profitable British mining investment in North America before 1920, and one of the best British overseas investments altogether. Jamieson's role in this success was significant; from being the architect of the company's survival in 1883-87, he steered it to a position of technological leadership in the south-western United States, pioneering both copper leaching and low-grade ore-extraction techniques. Jamieson made an extensive tour of the United States in 1892, during which he visited the Company's operations. After his death his obituary could claim that the Arizona Copper Co was '... a concern which his business ability has raised from what looked a hopeless state of depression to one of flourishing prosperity'.

Jamieson was undoubtedly one of the most successful and influential chartered accountants in Scotland during the last two decades of the nineteenth century. He was a director of seven companies by the late 1890s, including the Royal Bank of Scotland and the North British & Mercantile Insurance Co, both at the heart of Scotland's close-knit financial community. He moved in high circles, being involved with members of investment trusts and banking concerns, such as the Fleming family, Sir George Warrender, Holmes Ivory, W J Menzies (qv), J Duncan Smith and J Guthrie Smith. He was also a leading light in his profession. According to a recent historian of accountancy, he '... became almost a legendary figure among the early Edinburgh chartered accountants'. He was an examinator of the Society of Accountants in Edinburgh, 1872-82, and its President, 1882- 88, at that time an unprecedentedly long term of office. Together with Donald Lindsay and George Esson, he was also a member of the Faculty of Actuaries in Scotland, and a signatory to its Royal Charter of Incorporation, October 1868. He was clearly a man who was conservative in many ways, and deliberated long over complex issues. His obituary stated that '... his business training made him a believer in the importance of figures...' but '... his speeches were of great length... he was more earnest than tactful'. However, it continued, 'he had great confidence in himself...' and 'the labours of his private business were gigantic'. Like a number of his contemporaries, the apparent conservatism and business caution of his profession and Episcopalian beliefs were belied by the great energy and acumen displayed in recognising investment opportunities overseas.

His wide knowledge of financial affairs brought him onto a number of Royal Commissions. In 1865 he gave evidence to the Commission on Landlords' rights of Hypothec in Scotland, at which he professed '... a pretty extensive knowledge of the tenantry of Scotland' and argued against a change in the law. In 1889 he sat as a member of the Commission on Mining Royalties, and in 1895 on the Commission on Company Law. As early as 1860, he was elected a Fellow of the Royal Society of Edinburgh, and in 1887 he attended the Manchester meeting of the British Association, contributed two papers on finance, and was elected a member.

Jamieson was a Conservative in politics and in 1885 stood unsuccessfully as parliamentary candidate for Edinburgh West. He was for a long period chairman of Edinburgh West Conservative Association. In 1889 he entered Edinburgh City Council as member for St Luke's Ward, a seat he held until his death. He was an active council member and at various times was chairman of its Law Committee and also sat on the Lord Provost's, Treasurer's, Electric Light and Water Trust Committees. He was also for a time a Commissioner of Supply for the City and County of Edinburgh. He was an ardent opponent of the municipal takeover of gas, tramway and electric lighting operations, but was outvoted on all these issues. According to his obituary, '... considering he was otherwise so busy a man, (he) was a fairly regular attender at the meetings of the Council and its committees'.

Religion played a strong part in his life and he was a member and office-bearer of St John's Episcopal Church, Edinburgh, as well as Chancellor of the Episcopal Diocese of his home city, Aberdeen. He also supported a number of charitable organisations such as the Edinburgh Association for Incurables.

Jamieson died suddenly at the New Club, Edinburgh, on the evening of 18 July 1900, following an influenza attack. He was survived by his second wife, four sons and a daughter. His eldest son, Lindsay Auldjo had died in 1895; his second son Claude Auldjo was also a chartered accountant, but died in 1902 of wounds received in the Boer War. Another son, Harry Auldjo was active during the 1920s in numerous investment trusts and three grandsons, W H, G L A, and J A J Jamieson were active in investment trusts, the Fleming Bank and the Scottish Mortgage & Trust Co into the 1970s. George Auldjo Jamieson left a gross estate valued at £188,817. He was buried at Dean Cemetery, Edinburgh, in a ceremony attended by the Earls of Aberdeen and Haddington, the Municipal Coporation of Edinburgh, Alexander Fleming, Quintin Hogg and numerous business and personal friends.

CHRISTOPHER SCHMITZ

SOURCES

Unpublished

SRO: BT2/1018, Scottish Pacific Coast Mining Co Ltd
BT2/1144, 1375 Arizona Copper Co Ltd
BT2/1304, Arizona Trust & Mortgage Co Ltd
SC 70/1/396, SC 70/1/397, SC 70/1/424, SC 70/1/476, Additional Inventory
SC 70/4/325, Will
SC 70/1/395, Additional Inventory

Published

Brown, Richard, *A History of Accounting and Accountants*, Edinburgh, 1905

Colquhoun, James, *The History of the Clifton-Morenci Mining District*, London, 1924

Davidson, Andrew R, *The History of the Faculty of Actuaries in Scotland, 1856-1956*, Edinburgh, 1956

Edinburgh and Leith PO Directory, 1860-1900

Jackson, W Turrentine, *The Enterprising Scot: Investors in the American West after 1873*, Edinburgh, 1968

Lindgren, Waldemar, *The Copper Deposits of the Clifton Morenci District Arizona*, Washington DC, 1905

Marwick, W H, *Economic Developments in Victorian Scotland*, London, 1936

The Mining Journal, 16/12/1882, 9 & 16/6/1883, 3 & 24/11/1883, 2/2/1884, 26/4/1884, 6/12/1884, 14/3/1885, 15/1/1887, 11/6/1887, 18/2/1888, 26/5/1888, 15/2/1890, 28/3/1891, 19/3/1892, 1/4/1893, 17/2/1894, 13/2/1897, 19/2/1898, 11/2/1899

The Mining Manual, 1887-1900

Parsons, Arthur B, *The Porphyry Coppers*, New York, 1933

'Recent illustrations of the theory of rent, and their effect on the value of land' and 'Limited liability' (synopsis of paper), in *Report of the 57th Meeting of the British Association for the Advancement of Science (Manchester 1887)*, London, 1888

'Report of the Commissioners Appointed to Consider the Landlord's Rights of Hypothec in Scotland', *Sessional Papers, House of Commons*, 1865 [3546, 3546 - I], XVII, 413, 441

'Report of the Departmental Committee relating to Joint Stock Companies Incorporated with Limited Liability under the Company Acts, 1862 to 1890', *Sessional Papers, House of Commons*, 1895 [c 7779], LXXVIII, 151

'Report of the Royal Commission appointed to Inquire into the Subject of Mining Royalties', *Sessional Papers, House of Commons*, 1890 [c 6195], XXXVI, 1

Scotsman, 20, 23, 25/7/1900

Scott, J & Hughes, M, *The Anatomy of Scottish Capital*, London, 1980

'Scottish Capital Abroad', *Blackwood's Edinburgh Magazine*, CXXXVI, 828, October 1884

Spence, Clark, C, *British Investments and the American Mining Frontier 1860-1901*, Ithaca, New York, 1958

Stewart, J A, *Pioneers of a Profession: Chartered Accountants to 1879*, Edinburgh, 1977

The Stock Exchange Official Intelligence, 1885-1900

Wendt, Arthur, F, 'The Copper Ores of the South-west', *Transactions of the American Institute of Mining & Metallurgical Engineers*, XV, 1886-87

Ian Wilson MacDONALD,

Chartered accountant; b. 1907, s. of Alexander Buchanan Macdonald, minister, and Mary Bowman Wilson; m. 7/10/1933, Helen Nicolson, d. of James Nicolson, rubber manufacturer; Ch, Royal Bank of Scotland; d. 11/1/1989.

Following his education in Perth Academy and Edinburgh Academy, Ian Wilson Macdonald sought and obtained an apprenticeship as a chartered accountant with the Glasgow firm of Kerr, MacLeod and Macfarlan in 1924. An active apprenticeship as a committee member of the CA Students Society followed and culminated in him being admitted as a qualified member of the Institute of Accountants and Actuaries

in Glasgow in 1930. He was assumed as a partner in Kerr MacLeod and Macfarlan in 1933.

A busy career in professional practice followed and as auditor or consultant he was in close contact with a wide range of industrial and commercial companies. In 1938 he was invited to become the Johnstone Smith Professor of Accountancy in the University of Glasgow. This was a part-time appointment which enabled the holder to continue in private practice. He held the chair until the period of appointment terminated in 1950.

His association with Scottish banking commenced with his appointment in 1945 as a joint auditor of the Commercial Bank of Scotland. He retired from that office in 1947 to allow him to join the Board of the Bank as a part-time director. At that time he anticipated that his professional career in accountancy would continue to be his main activity. However, an unforeseen event completely changed his course. In 1953 the retiral of Sir John Erskine, the General Manager of the Commercial Bank was imminent, and his likely successor became a casualty through ill health and other possibles were not in the right age group. So the Board asked Ian Macdonald to retire from professional practice and be appointed as John Erskine's successor. His acceptance of this invitation created some furore in Scottish banking circles as it followed hard on the heels of the appointment of William Watson, also a CA, to be Treasurer (ie General Manager) of the Bank of Scotland. The fact that men who had not been part of the Scottish banking scene since leaving school could be appointed to such elevated positions upset the traditionalists who believed that only time served bankers should fill these posts. Nothing was to be served by such ill-feeling, however, and within a short time the matter ceased to be a topic for comment.

When he became its general manager, the Commercial Bank ranked third of the seven Scottish banks of note issue but by 1955 it had slipped to fourth position because the amalgamation of the Bank of Scotland and Union Bank of Scotland (both of which had been smaller than the Commercial), in 1954 created an organisation which ranked first amongst the Scottish banks. This event doubtless confirmed in Macdonald's mind that his intention to seek a partner for the Commercial was essential. When he became general manager, Macdonald had drawn up a three point strategy for the future of his bank. His ideas were first of all to seek growth through amalgamation, secondly to diversify the Bank's interests and thirdly to set up a merchant banking arm of the bank. The attempt to diversify the bank's interests was the first of these aims to meet with success. In 1954 the Commercial Bank bought the entire share capital of a hire purchase company - the Scottish Midland Guarantee Trust which was a wholly owned subsidiary of the Scottish Motor Traction Company. In doing so the Commercial Bank had not thought it necessary to consult in advance the Bank of England

Norie-Miller was fortunate in acquiring experience of accident insurance on the eve of the explosion in growth in this form of insurance which took place between 1900 and 1914. Similarly, he found himself at the head of a concern whose affairs he could control with freedom at an early age. He attributed these chances to the fact that he preferred to be a big fish in a small pool. Yet he built on these advantages with imaginative underwriting and an energetic capacity for organisation.

He underwrote with competitive panache, leading the market and taking dramatic risks. In the early days, in 1887, he achieved a coup by providing free insurance cover against injury from a railway accident for anyone carrying a particular publisher's diary, thus inaugurating coupon insurance. In 1890 he started to underwrite burglary insurance and in 1896 motor vehicle insurance. In both cases, though the precise details of the first policy to be issued are unclear, General Accident can undoubtedly be the principal pioneering company of both types of insurance. General Accident remained outside the tariff arrangements established to regulate premium rates in both fire and accident insurance markets almost throughout its history. This enabled it to adopt an independent and aggressive rating stance in the market. From 1906 the company offered bonus payments for householders' policies that were free of claims for a number of years. In the motor insurance market it led the market in the use of 'no-claim bonuses' as a form of competitive discrimination. In the 1920s it turned the motor insurance market upside down by arranging a scheme whereby every new Morris sold was provided with a year's free insurance. Within the two years the scheme operated 90,000 policies were issued and General Accident's market position was transformed as it gained new agents and policy-holders. In 1923 a subsidiary was established to finance car hire purchase which brought with it tied insurance business.

These underwriting successes were backed up by remarkable organisational and marketing powers. Contemporaries described Norie-Miller as being formidably active and industrious. Throughout his career he travelled extensively in Great Britain and abroad. By 1935 he had made 39 business trips to the United States alone. As early as 1906 General Accident controlled 27 home and foreign branches with 12,000 agents. This organisation was held together on a tight rein, providing the necessary service at modest cost, relative to many of the London based companies and enabling competitive premium rates to be sustained. Organisational costs were also contained by the pioneering of the diversification across insurance markets so that the modest revenues available from accident underwriting could be augmented by business from other markets to beat down overheads. The move into fire insurance in 1895 was one of the first steps taken in the move towards the composite insurance company which characterised

the insurance market in the Edwardian years. This strategy was rounded off after the war when in 1923 General Accident purchased the Road Transport and General, a leading non-tariff motor insurer, and in 1924 when the long established General Life Assurance Company was taken over to provide a substantially larger life department. By the mid-1930s the company's British branch organisation of 137 offices was larger than all its competitors except the large industrial life offices and the service this offered motor policy holders, along with an extensive network of local directors, was an important feature in its domestic growth.

The growth in General Accident and the concentration of its headquarters in Perth meant that Norie-Miller inevitably became a figure of civic importance: a magistrate for 47 years. He was prominent in the administration of education in the city and county of Perth as chairman of the education committee for 18 years and in 1907 was made a Fellow of the Educational Institute of Scotland. He was chairman of Perth Royal Infirmary for 15 years, treasurer of the diocese of St Andrews and he was a regular attender at the Scottish Episcopal Cathedral of St Ninian's. He was awarded a medal by the King of the Belgians for refugee work carried out in the First World War. At a by-election in 1935 he was elected Member of Parliament for Perth as a result of a joint approach by the local Conservative and Liberal Associations, but did not stand again in the general election which immediately followed. In the following year he was created a baronet.

Norie-Miller married Grace Harvey Day, the daughter of the vicar of Cheshunt, in 1884. They had two sons and a daughter. The elder son, Claud, who had been employed by General Accident in Canada, was killed on active service in the Mediterranean in 1917. The younger son, Stanley, succeeded his father as general manager of General Accident in 1933 and later as chairman and managing director. Francis Norie-Miller's first wife died in 1931 and in 1934 he married his secretary, Florence Jean Belfrage McKim. He enjoyed fishing, shooting, golf, poetry and the countryside. He retired from an active involvement in business in 1944 and died at Cleeve, his home near Perth, in 1947.

OLIVER M WESTALL

SOURCES

Unpublished

Information supplied by General Accident, Fire and Life Assurance Corporation PLC
SRO: SC 49/31/391, Inventory
SC 49/32/93, Will

Published

Dinsdale, W A, *History of Accident Insurance in Great Britain*, London, 1954

Glasgow Herald, 5/7/1947

The Insurance Shareholder's Guide 1920-21, Manchester

Post Magazine & Insurance Monitor, 12/7/1947

Scottish Biographies, Glasgow, 1938

Supple, Barry, *The Royal Exchange Assurance, A History of British Insurance 1720-1970*, Cambridge, 1970

The Times, 5/7/1947

Who's Who, 1946

Alexander Rennie STENHOUSE,

Insurance broker; b. 6/3/1876, Lenzie, s. of John Stenhouse, builder and Sarah Janet Goodwin; m. 31/3/1908, Hughina, d. of John Cowan, wine merchant; 4 s., 2 d.; Ch, A R Stenhouse & Partners Ltd; d. 3/11/1952, Chryston; g/v estate: £170,346 16s 5d.

A R Stenhouse left the village school at Millerston at the early age of 12. His mother had been widowed when her three children were infants and this left the family in straitened circumstances. Stenhouse became an errand boy in a newsagents, but became connected with the insurance business in Glasgow while still quite young. At the age of 21 he migrated to the United States, where he was fortunate to find employment with the Hartford Insurance Company. This progressive concern had taken an early lead in the encouragement of automatic sprinkler fire protection through the offer of large discounts for protected risks and the provision of sprinkler leakage insurance.

In 1903 he returned to Scotland, eager to exploit his experience with this growing class of insurance. He was briefly employed by the National of Great Britain, an early specialist sprinkler office based in Glasgow. However, in December 1904 he set up as an insurance broker at 154 St Vincent Street, Glasgow, sharing an office with Adam Ker, an accountant who was to remain an associate throughout his business career.

In the following years he became an agent of change in the Scottish fire insurance market, attracting any business he could, but particularly exploiting the competitive opportunities created by the possibility of large sprinkler discounts offered for hazardous industrial and commercial risks. He was able to capitalise on this idea successfully, through his easy personal manner, which was marked by great charm and a powerful memory for attaching names to faces. He always left his office door open so that clients visiting the business could be engaged in conversation, thus strengthening his wide range of associations and facilitating the formidable flow of information he received from throughout the Scottish commercial and industrial community. Behind this clubbable exterior however, there was a fertile and determined business brain which generated more than sales talk. When, for example, he met resistance to the cost of installing sprinklers, he arranged finance which could be serviced out of the large discounts that became available for protected risks. He also demonstrated his capacity for organised thought in the production of several carefully argued pamphlets circulated to the insurance world on such themes as the organisation of marketing in insurance and investment in insurance shares.

The growth in business was such that in 1911 he persuaded James M Hope and William P Blyth to join him as partners, though he retained a controlling financial stake in a business initially capitalised at £8,000. Hope became a peripatetic business winner, travelling all over Scotland and the north of England. Blyth, an expert on the new credit insurance, became the 'office' man, always available in case of need and whose forte was the settlement of delicate negotiations within the business and with clients. This increase in capacity made it possible to open an office in Edinburgh by purchasing an existing broker's firm and retaining its female manager.

The First World War restricted all insurance marketing. At its end, the firm instituted an important departure by recruiting G A Edmunds, a company trained technical expert of great authority, who revolutionised the service the firm offered its clients. He supervised the preparation of detailed reports which appraised their insurance requirements in the broadest possible way, suggesting adjustments in the type and scale of cover and providing a free valuation of their premises. The firm dealt on equal terms with the companies. Indeed, in subsequent years Edmunds submitted memoranda to the Fire Offices' Committee that were instrumental in securing major revisions in the terms of some of its tariffs, including that covering the jute trade and the paper industry. As a result, in the 1920s and 1930s, the firm was able to attract substantial business from these two sources.

This created a reputation for the Stenhouse firm that clearly differentiated it from most brokers. Competing on the quality of the service it offered, as much as the rates it could obtain, it became the leading insurance broking concern in Scotland. Stenhouse himself had been an early member of the Association of Insurance Brokers and Agents formed in 1906 (to become the Corporation of Insurance Brokers in 1910) and in 1911 he led the formation of a separate committee for Scotland which he chaired for many years.

Office expansion continued - in Dundee and Perth

in 1920; in Newcastle upon Tyne in 1922. These developments were facilitated by the addition of the buoyant loss of profits, liability, accident and motor insurance business to the more stable fire income in this period - though this change itself required the addition of new types of technical expertise at the Glasgow head office. In the mid-1920s fire insurance still accounted for some 60% of the firm's business. Attempts were made to start life assurance but it required a quite different type of staff and was not seriously essayed until after the Second World War.

Business was strengthened by the increasing diversification of Stenhouse's own activities. From the start of his business career, Stenhouse had always taken the broadest possible view of the scope of his activities. He became deeply involved in investment, and insurance broking eventually became conveniently complementary to these wider interests. By the early 1920s, it was said that these had made him a millionaire. Though he always knew exactly what was happening in the insurance business, from the 1920s the technical aspects of the business were almost entirely delegated to his partners and staff.

His approach to investment was dominated by two features. He was convinced of the value of investment in insurance company equities, partly, no doubt, because his involvement in the business enabled him to make informed judgements about the quality of their managements and prospects. It is likely that he made money from the sharp fluctuations in insurance equity values during the First World War, and from the restructuring of the industry as many smaller insurers were taken over in that period. He also watched carefully the growth of the General Accident of Perth under Sir Francis Norie Miller (qv) and this would undoubtedly have given enormous scope for capital appreciation. Between 1916 and 1919 this company's ordinary shares rose nearly twelvefold.

He also placed a great emphasis on a personal acquaintance with the managements of companies. When considering a move he would invite them to lunch at the Malmaison Restaurant near his office in Glasgow, and only proceed if he was thoroughly convinced of their capacity.

Stenhouse founded the Scottish Western Trust (to be distinguished from Scottish Western Investment, established by Robert Fleming and Bonar Law in 1906) in 1922 to manage his private family interests. Such was his success that in the 1920s he became involved in the formation of a number of trusts with a group of Scottish business associates who had made money which they wished to invest. He was a director of the privately owned Glasgow Financial Trust; the publicly quoted Great Northern Investment Trust (1924); the Home and Foreign Investment Trust (1926); sometime chairman of the Midland-Caledonian Investment Trust (1928) and the Clyde and Mersey Investment Trust (1929). He managed these trusts with a panache and individuality that sometimes disconcerted his fellow directors, yet, for the most

part, produced successful results. Their approach was naturally much in line with his own outlined above. At one time, for example, some 80-90% of the Great Northern Investment Trust's assets were devoted to insurance equities. In addition, the Glasgow Financial Trust at least, undertook the underwriting of new issues for industrial concerns.

At the same time, he began to devote himself to advising in the most general way on company affairs. His wide range of contacts throughout Scotland and his imaginative approach to business were supplemented by a firm grasp of the technical aspects of financial organisation. He assisted companies in obtaining finance, facilitated mergers and joined the boards of a number of private companies in the Glasgow area. Much of this work derived from initial connections made through his insurance business. When, for example, a large Sheffield engineering concern ran into financial difficulties, the managing director turned to Stenhouse, its insurance broker, for help, and he found the substantial funds necessary. This work thus cemented existing insurance connections, and in some cases provided an excellent introduction to new firms. Stenhouse did not charge for his services, but it was assumed that his firm would be given an opportunity to discuss insurance business, in addition to any financial interest he might take himself.

These wider concerns involved him in the chief crisis in his business career. The 1929 crash created a temporary disaster for Stenhouse's private affairs. His investments were put in trust and severe economies instituted in his private life. His domestic staff were cut from 16 to two and his family moved temporarily into a factor's house on an estate he owned. On top of this, Stenhouse became implicated in allegations that the underwriting of the flotation of Scottish Amalgamated Silks by the Glasgow Financial Trust had taken place on a fraudulent basis. In February 1931 he, along with 16 other businessmen, was arrested and detained for three weeks until bail was granted. This caused a sensation in Glasgow's financial and commercial circles and even led to a sharp reaction on its Stock Exchange. Only after a year, and two days before the trial was due to open, were the charges against Stenhouse dropped. He and his partners had to use the full weight of their considerable reputations in the insurance market to reassure clients and companies, backing this by a commitment to pay all insurance funds into a trust account. There is little doubt that this episode temporarily halted business development.

Nonetheless, in the 1930s progress was resumed. Within three years of the crash it is believed that Stenhouse's personal fortune had been restored to at least two million pounds. The wider range of his activities and the marketing work carried out by Hope expanded English business and in 1929 the firm had opened an office in the city of London. The Glasgow office was expanded and progress in the south was

419

such that quite soon larger premises were taken in London. New Scottish industries such as paper making, electrical and metal manufacturing were particularly important sources of premium income. As the partnership grew in capacity with an increasing number of qualified staff, it became difficult to retain them as purely salaried employees. Thus, in 1938 it was converted into a private limited liability company - A R Stenhouse and Partners Ltd - with a nominal capital of £10,000. A R Stenhouse became chairman holding £2,000 of this, but his family stake was increased by his sons, J G Stenhouse, A R Stenhouse Jnr, and H C Stenhouse who had now joined the business and were allocated £500 each. Despite his senior position in the firm, Stenhouse continued to attend business regularly, making himself available to staff and continuing his long standing routine of touring the office twice each day, checking the cash books, insurance company ledgers and new order books to form an estimate of the firm's day by day progress. The cessation of investment activity during the Second World War enabled him to give more time to insurance broking, when so many staff were undertaking military service. He remained closely involved in all his affairs within and outside the firm until his death, which was unexpected.

Stenhouse devoted most of his time to business and its inevitable social concomitants. He was a member of the Incorporations of Bonnetmakers and Dyers, Hammermen, and Wrights, and the Society of Deacons. When he enjoyed free time he spent it walking in the country district around the home he built himself at Garnkirk, near Stepps, in 1937. While insisting on formal dress in business hours and the importance of a hat, even if only carried, he was a sober dresser, allowing himself only the luxury of a bright tie, but usually exhibiting a trail of ash from an inevitable cigarette. He was a passionate aficionado of Burns and could recite long stretches of his verse off the cuff. He died in 1952 survived by his wife, four sons, three of whom were directors of his business, and two daughters. A large proportion of his wealth had already been distributed to his family and his estate therefore bears little relationship to the fortune he accumulated. By his wish, this was consolidated in the Scottish Western Trust which became the vehicle for his family's financial interests.

In the post-war years the most dynamic source of growth for A R Stenhouse and Partners had been the English market, where Hugh Cowan Stenhouse, A R Stenhouse's third son, had in 1949 established the London branch as a separate company under his own management. Such was his success that, after a brief interlude following his father's death, he became the natural successor as chairman of the main company. He consolidated this position by buying out the original partners, thus restoring the close family control which his father had always been loth to lose.

OLIVER M WESTALL

SOURCES

Unpublished

Information supplied by Stenhouse Holdings PLC
SRO: SC 36/48/776, Inventory
      SC 36/51/376, Will

Published

Directory of Directors, 1925, 1930, 1935, 1945, 1950
Glasgow Herald, 1931-1932 passim: see references to Scottish Amalgamated Silks and Scottish Artificial Silks; see also obit 4/11/1952
The Policy Holder, 13/11/1952
Westall, Oliver M, 'David and Goliath: the Fire Offices Committee and non-tariff competition, 1898-1907' in *The Historian and the Business of Insurance*, Manchester, 1984

Hugh Cowan STENHOUSE,

Insurance broker; b. 29/6/1915, Kilsyth, s. of Alexander Rennie Stenhouse, insurance broker and Hughina Cowan; m. Rosamund; 3 s., 1 d.; Ch, A R Stenhouse & Partners, Glasgow; d. 25/11/1971, Leicester.

Hugh Cowan Stenhouse, youngest son of Alexander Rennie Stenhouse of Craig-en-Goin, Kilsyth, was born in 1915. He attended Warriston Preparatory School, Moffat, and completed his formal education at Sedbergh, near Kendal.

Possibly inspired by his father's flourishing business as an insurance broker, founded about 1904, and other industrial interests, the young Hugh, when he left school, got a place on the staff of the Caledonian Insurance Company in 1932. The company's name seems significant, for he became a dedicated Scotsman who could tolerate no suggestion that Scotland had 'had it' nor that the Scots were dependent on English goodwill or charity, and it was his ambition to encourage industrial success in Scotland. Having had all round insurance experience during his six years with the Caledonian he transferred his experience to the family firm in 1938.

The Second World War caught up with him in 1939; he served in France with the RASC, survived Dunkirk to take part in the Eighth Army Campaigns in Africa and Italy, and attained the rank of Lieutenant-Colonel.

On returning to the family business after the war he set about diversifying and extending the business beyond Scotland, and not only to England and the European Continent but also to Australia, New Zealand and Southern Africa, founding the Stenhouse Group of which he became chairman in 1957, striving to make A R Stenhouse and Partners the biggest firm of insurance brokers in the world. He became chairman of John Wallace & Sons, the holding company of the John Wallace Group of industrial companies, by 1963. In 1970, Stenhouse Holdings showed a profit of £2,486,000 before tax, an increase of £1,113,000 over the 1969 figure.

By 1965 the premises at 117 St Vincent Street, Glasgow, could no longer contain the Stenhouse Group business and it was essential to move. The Stenhouse Group bought the Commercial Union Assurance building at 145 St Vincent Street which is now named Alexander Stenhouse. In 1971 Hugh Stenhouse's interests covered over some 40 'takeovers' with a vast range of industries. As an employer his motto was 'A good day's work for a good day's pay'.

He held many important appointments including chairmanship of the Great Northern Investment Trust, chairmanship of Govan Shipbuilders (this, at the request of the Government), which brought him international recognition,. He was a member of Fairfield's board and had invested £50,000 in this concern in 1966, indeed he had hopes of a covered shipyard on the Clyde and he deeply regretted that time ran out before his hopes could be achieved. Within a few days of the Upper Clyde Shipbuilders' shop stewards defying the Government he won their confidence, which earned him great credit. Another of his hopes was to see a deep water port at Hunterston - he was chairman of the Hunterston Development Company.

Reticent about his private benevolence he did admit to helping children and the church. He was a member of the Strathclyde University Court and being interested in the training of the coming generation he donated £150,000 to that university towards setting up a building for teaching management studies; the building to be a memorial to his father. He donated a sum to the McAlpine Nursing Home (as it was at the time) to name a room in memory of his mother.

He was a Governor of Drumly School, Ayr, and a staunch supporter of his old school, Sedbergh, conscientiously wearing his old school tie. In 1971 the University of Strathclyde conferred on him the honourary degree of Doctor of Laws. Politically he was a true blue Tory, succeeding the late Lord Fraser of Allander as national treasurer of the Conservative Party in Scotland in 1967. Applying his dynamic personality and business methods for the benefit of the party he set up a large capital reserve and working fund which enabled the political battle for votes at the general election to be carried through without using any of the capital reserve.

He relaxed in his dear Scotland spending time in the management of his farms in Renfrewshire and Dumfriesshire, shooting over his Maxwelton Estate, Moniaive, occasionally restoring his home there at Maxwelton House and in visiting his place on the shores of Loch Fyne.

It was with deep regret that the city learned that while on a business trip to visit a textile factory in the Stenhouse Group, Mr Stenhouse had been instantaneously killed when his chauffer-driven car crashed going towards Leicester about 6.30 pm on 25 November 1971. A private funeral took place at Maxwelton House and a public memorial service was held in St Columba's Church of Scotland, Pont Street, London, which many notable mourners attended. Mr Stenhouse was survived by his widow, Rosamund, three sons and a daughter.

DORIS BLACK

SOURCES

Unpublished
Calendar of Confirmations, 1972

Published
Glasgow Herald, 26/11/1971, 27/11/1971
Glasgow Herald Review, 1972
London Times, 27/11/1971
Scotland, July 1965, April 1968
Scottish Field, September 1971

William Thomas THOMSON,

Actuary; b. 1813; m. Christian Anne Seaman; 2 s.; Manager, Standard Life Assurance Co; d. 16/9/1883, Edinburgh; g/v UK estate: £23,936 11s 11d.

William Thomas Thomson was a key figure in the development of the life assurance industry within the United Kingdom during the middle decades of the nineteenth century. Appointed to the post of Secretary of the Edinburgh-based Standard Life Assurance Company at the early age of 21, he was selected to succeed James Cheyne as that office's manager in November 1837. It was a position that he was to hold until ill health compelled him to retire in 1874.

Thomson's lengthy tenure of the managerial chair coincided with a major transformation in the Standard's fortunes. In the late 1830s the company still operated within a strictly limited geographical framework. Apart from a token number of policies issued in England and Ireland, its life underwriting activities were exclusively confined to Scotland. Indeed, even within a Scottish context it operated on a regional rather than national stage since it derived relatively little business from the industrialising towns of the West Central belt. By the mid-1870s on the other hand its agency network had been extended to cover all the principal centres of population in the United Kingdom and it had also acquired a firm foothold in most of the areas of white settlement in the British Empire. What these changes actually represented can best be expressed in statistical terms. Whereas in 1838-9 the amount of new business that was secured marginally exceeded £200,000, the comparable figure for every year during the 1865-75 decade never fell below £1,000,000. Viewed from another perspective, if the Standard still fell some way short of being the most dynamic Scottish life company in 1838-9, it decisively outstripped all its competitors during the 1865-75 period when it generated an aggregate total of new business greater than that of any other office in the United Kingdom.

The dimensions of this advance did not, of course, mean that the Standard's progress in the intervening years followed an unbroken upward path. Business had usually been checked both by periodic crises in the financial markets and by the downswing phase of the trade cycle. Furthermore, for much of the 1850s and during the early 1860s the company's annual returns were more distinguished by stability rather than rapid growth, while between 1865 and 1870 there was an actual decline in the volume of new assurance obtained within the United Kingdom compared with the preceding quinquennium. Finally the colonies proved to be a less fruitful source of new contracts in 1870-75 than during the second half of the 1860s. Nevertheless, when all these qualifications have been entered, they do not obscure the impressive nature of the company's overall achievements. For there was ample justification for the claim, made around the time of Thomson's retirement, that the Standard had become an "A one" office in the Estimation of the Press and the World'.

Thomson's contribution to this transformation has to be kept in perspective. In the first place some of the main initiatives that were taken to extend the Standard's horizons were the direct sequel to the deliberations of the board of directors. This was above all true of the campaign that was launched in the late 1830s and early 1940s to broaden the office's slender base of operations in Ireland and of the later decision, taken in the aftermath of the Irish Famine, to entertain favourably applications for loans based upon the security of Irish land. Again, the major restructuring of the rates of commission paid to the company's

agents which took place in 1854-5 and which was of vital importance in the struggle for new business in the English market, owed everything to the prompting of H Jones Williams, the Standard's resident secretary in London. Similarly the slow progress that was made in Canada in the late 1860s and early 1870s towards the adoption of a more liberal assurance contract flowed primarily from the advice tendered by W Ramsay, the office's principal full-time official in Montreal.

Secondly it is clear that some of Thomson's business judgements exercised a decelerating effect upon growth. Thus, although he was one of the first life assurance managers to make use of an inspectorate system to improve the efficiency of agents in England, he was reluctant to apply the same approach in a Scottish context. Instead he was content to rely upon the revising work, north of the Border, of the Edinburgh-based Agency committee, supplemented by his own sporadic tours of his company's widely scattered Scottish representatives. In addition, as more than one critical observer noted, he made little attempt in Scotland to recruit members of the shopocracy to the Standard's service to tout for custom amongst the rapidly expanding ranks of the lower middle class. The net result of this neglect was that from the mid-1850s to the early 1870s the volume of new business that was secured in Scotland consistently disappointed the expectations of the board. Furthermore it must be emphasised that Thomson's defence of an organisationl infrastructure that had been inherited from an earlier period was not confined to the Standard's home territory. Thus, in the competitive climate in England in the late 1860s and early 1870s he displayed little enthusiasm for branch offices, manned by a salaried secretariat, as a more systematic means of tapping the whole life market than part-time representatives remunerated upon a commission basis. This kind of institutional conservatism was also to manifest itself in the same period in his dealings with the Standard's officials in Canada where, despite the challenge of new and more flexible forms of organisation pioneered by American offices, he was unwilling to depart too far from the traditional methods that had served the Colonial Life Assurance Company well in the 1850s.

Nevertheless while these negative aspects of his career must be acknowledged, they do not obscure the central role that Thomson played in carrying through a largely successful strategy of orderly and organic development of the company over time. The salient characteristics of that strategy can in their turn best be defined when they are discussed within a chronological framework. During the first 13 years of Thomson's management (1837-50) he sought to achieve two distinct, and yet inter-related objectives. In the first place he paid particular attention to investment policy since it was only through the careful investing of the company's funds that it could be possible to attract new clients by producing substantial reversionary bonuses to participating policy holders at the periodic declarations of profits. When a bonus of 1.25% per annum was announced at the conclusion of the 1840 and 1845 investigations into the office's finances, this was accepted by the assuring public as ample vindication of the fact that this first goal had been realised. But, as Thomson had long accepted, the growth of new premium income did not exclusively hinge upon the company's ability to generate profits. It was also crucially dependent upon the realisation of his other objective, the decisive penetration of the lucrative English whole life market by the Standard. Initially the most formidable barrier that Thomson had to surmount in this sphere was the limited vision of his own board which had shown little inclination to mount a vigorous campaign for English business during Cheyne's occupancy of the managerial chair.

By the early 1840s, however, Thomson had persuaded them both to move in that direction and to circumvent some of the difficulties that the Standard expected to encounter by taking over, and using the agents of, an existing English office, the York and London Insurance Company. Nonetheless, even when the takeover negotiations, largely conducted by Thomson, had been concluded in 1844 and the York and London's directors had been retained to form a London-based board with wide powers over the Standard's English operations, progress was still far from smooth. For fresh problems arose when the newly constituted London directorate, having unsuccessfully challenged the overriding authority of Edinburgh, resigned *en masse*. During the lengthy interregnum (1846-8) which ensued between the departure of the York and London officials and the creation of a new London board, Thomson assumed much of the responsibility of sustaining the Standard's campaign for 'first class' lives in England. By the late 1840s, however, the fruits of his persistence had already started to surface when England for the first time became a major contributor to the company's premium income.

For the next decade and a half (1850-64) Thomson's prime aim was to consolidate the Standard's position by operating largely within the administrative and technical infrastructure that had been assembled during the previous 25 years. Such a policy was in part a response to external pressures, for the spectacular growth of 'bubble' companies in the late 1840s and early 1850s gave rise to fears, freely expressed in the insurance press, about the financial probity and future stability of the industry. Although most of these fears proved to be groundless, established offices had to devote time and energy to impressing upon the insuring classes that the rubrics of prudent management that they had hitherto pursued, provided the best guarantee that all whole life contracts would be honoured. But this strategy also owed something to Thomson's belief, shared by the Edinburgh board, that it would be unwise to interfere drastically with an organisational structure that had yielded good returns in the immediate past. Nonetheless the adoption of such a stance did not exclude the adoption of a cluster of changes that were designed to enhance the Standard's position in an increasingly competitive market. Thus Thomson was able to persuade his directorate to press ahead with a more rigorous pruning of the company's English agents and, between 1851 and 1861, to ease progressively many of the constraints that had been placed upon policy holders who wished to travel or reside abroad. On the other hand when in 1855 and 1860 he drew attention to basic weaknesses in the Standard's current 'with profits' schemes, he obtained little support for his advocacy of a new form of participating contract.

Yet even in the short term this last reform was essential for the company's economic health since by the late 1850s its original 'with profits' plan, adopted in 1825, possessed two fundamental weaknesses. At one level the premium rates which it levied upon younger age groups were higher than those of several of the Standard's rivals. Equally important, the bonuses which had been declared in 1855 and 1860 were below those which had accrued to relatively recent insurers with such major offices as the Scottish Widows' Fund. In other words, failure to initiate change in this area was bound to inhibit future growth prospects. Scarcely surprisingly, therefore, Thomson during his last decade (1864-74) as manager sought to defend the Standard's market position by persuading his directors to sanction signficant discontinuities in policy. Firstly, a decade after he had raised the issue, he at last secured in 1865 their endorsement of a new participating scheme which possessed none of the drawbacks of the existing plan. Secondly, with his board's approval, he launched the most ambitious takeover strategy in the company's history. In 1864-5 the Minerva Life Assurance company was taken over with the explicit aim of strengthening the Standard's English base. Less than 12 months later the Victoria Life Assurance Company of London and the Colonial Life Assurance Company of Edinburgh were also absorbed. The immediate cause of these last two mergers was Thomson's desire to prevent the severance of those strong but informal ties which had subsisted between the Colonial and the Standard, for he had also served as manager and actuary of the first named office since its inception in 1846. But he was probably more strongly motivated by a desire to extend the Standard's influence abroad by making use of the Colonial's extensive connections in the empire. Notwithstanding, therefore, those organisational weaknesses which have already been mentioned, these major shifts in direction enabled Thomson to maintain the company's dominant position among life offices within the United Kingdom and to hand over to his son Spencer a managerial chair whose influence in the assurance world had in large measure been shaped by its third incumbent.

Thomson's influence, however, was not exclusively

determined by the manner in which he exercised entrepreneurial skills in the service of the Standard. It also owed something to the catholicity of his work and interests in the broad realm of the life assurance industry from the early 1850s onwards. He was, for instance, a leading figure in the moves to formalise and institutionalise the training of actuaries in Britain, thereby ensuring that life offices would be provided with a growing number of practitioners skilled in the actuarial arts. In a very real sense the Institute of Actuaries, formed in 1851, and the Faculty of Actuaries, the separate Scottish organisation which was established in 1856, were indebted for their existence to his enthusiasm and vision. In addition he played a prominent role in the formation of the Edinburgh Actuarial Society, whose main aim was to bring together young actuaries and others interested in the technical and statistical aspects of life assurance, to discuss questions of mutual interest. Finally, he was an enthusiastic supporter in its formative years of the Association of Managers of Life Offices in Scotland, a body which was concerned with securing, where possible, a common approach to specific practical problems that beset the industry. Later, drawing on this experience, he was instrumental in trying to persuade English companies to emulate this example of fruitful consultation and co-operation.

JAMES H TREBLE

SOURCES

Unpublished

Standard Life Assurance Co archives, preserved in Edinburgh and Peebles
SRO: SC 70/1/228, Inventory
SC 70/4/204, Will

Published

Post Magazine and Insurance Monitor, September 1883
The Scotsman, 18/9/1883

Sir James WATSON,

Stockbroker; b. 10/3/1801, Paisley, s. of James Watson, merchant and Jane Armour; m. Rachel Rattray; 5 d.; James Watson (later James Watson and Smith), stockbroker; d. 14/8/1889, Row, Dunbartonshire; g/v UK estate: £125,152 16s 0d.

James Watson, the son of a merchant, was born in Paisley on 10 March 1801 and died at Row, Dunbartonshire, on 14 August 1889. He married Rachel Rattray early in life and had five daughters. His education included attendance for five years at Paisley Grammar School and, later, Young's Greek classes at Glasgow University in 1813. However, like many of his contemporaries he did not obtain a degree. He was chairman of the Glasgow Stock Exchange from its inception in 1844 until 1865 and again from 1875 to 1878. Between times he was Lord Provost of Glasgow, from 1871 to 1874, and was knighted in 1874. His business connections included the Ayrshire Iron Company, the Edinburgh and Glasgow Railway, the Glasgow, Paisley, Kilmarnock and Ayr Railway, and the Clydesdale Bank.

Although his father had been a merchant, James Watson inherited neither a business nor wealth and until 1830 his career appeared to be heading nowhere. After sampling University life he tried a variety of occupations. At first he spent two years with a mercantile house, but abandoned that for a position with the Thistle Bank, where he spent seven years. There he gained a training in accountancy. However, he left the bank to become head clerk with McCall & Co, which was the largest firm of grain merchants in Glasgow at the time. He stayed with that firm for two years and managed their large provision department, then went on to become a partner with Robert Stewart, a Glasgow wine and spirit merchant, in an accountancy firm. Stewart, however, became heavily involved in the formation and management of the Union Bank of Scotland and so the partnership was discontinued, leaving Watson to practice on his own as an accountant. It was from that foundation that his career as a stockbroker emanated.

When Watson entered accountancy around 1830 it was an emerging profession in Scotland, though it did not yet challenge the central position in financial affairs occupied by the lawyer. The role of the accountant was a general one which ranged from the advising of individual and institutional clients on all financial matters, to the undertaking of such tasks as bookkeeping, arranging insurance, handling investments, actuarial work, and the management of bankrupt estates. Watson's varied career had equipped him well for such a profession.

Outwith Edinburgh in the early 1830s, there did not exist any recognised stockbrokers in Scotland. It was only in the mid- 1820s that they had made their first appearance in the country. The stockbroker's functions of buying and selling stocks and shares and advising on investments in securities was shared by a variety of other groups, which included lawyers, agents, retail merchants, and accountants. As early as 1831, Watson was conducting a stockbroking business in association with his accountancy, and it was that activity upon which he concentrated increasingly during the 1830s. This transition made by Watson, from accountant to stockbroker, was a normal one for the period, when the parameters of professions were very blurred. It was also a common one, with many of Glasgow's stockbrokers beginning their careers as accountants, and continuing that business as an ancillary activity. Watson classified himself as an accountant and insurance agent until 1835/36, when he listed stockbroker as the second of his occupations. It was not until 1845/46 that stockbroking became his principal activity, and 1856/57 before accountancy was dropped altogether.

Although Watson himself claimed to be the first stockbroker in Glasgow, this was not strictly true. During the mid-1820s a number of Glasgow accountants and booksellers had added stockbroking to their occupations and publicly declared themselves as such. However, when the speculative mania collapsed in 1825 these individuals reverted to their main businesses, so that when Watson set up as an accountant a few years later there were no recognised stockbrokers in the city. Nevertheless, there were many other than the banks who did buy and sell securities for clients, and so Watson did not have the field to himself. The difference between Watson and the others was that he saw the possibility of making stockbroking a permanent, full-time occupation rather than an occasional part-time activity. In this he deliberately followed the example set by John Robertson in Edinburgh, who had established himself as Scotland's first stockbroker in 1824. Consequently, during the 1830s, Watson set himself the task of becoming an acknowledged expert on Scottish joint-stock enterprise and the state of the share market in Scotland. The circular that he produced for his clients became much more than the normal list of stocks and shares for sale and wanted. For in it he expressed his opinion on the contemporary situation and future prospects, as well as producing an annual survey of Scottish share prices. These opinions and statistics were then regularly quoted not only by the local press but also by publications elsewhere in Scotland and England. For the next 40 years Watson's financial opinion was to carry considerable weight, especially in Glasgow.

During these early years, Watson developed an extensive business and important contacts. He was painstaking in the care of his largely local clientele, for example, regularly travelling out to Paisley in the 1840s, to advise Peter Brough, a substantial investor. Along with a few other accountants, he represented the Glasgow market in shares, which was growing rapidly throughout the 1830s with the growing number of local banks, insurance companies, utilities and railways, as well as wealthy shareholders. In addition, Watson developed a strong working relationship with John Robertson in Edinburgh and, between them, they formed the most substantial component in the developing Scottish securities' market, by regularly exchanging information and completing orders on behalf of each others' clients. For example, on 17 February 1834 Watson wrote to Robertson, as part of a continuing correspondence:

'If you can procure £160 a share for ten shares Bank of Scotland Stock dividing expenses please dispose of them. The nearness to the dividend and the scarcity of the stock in the market may enable you to procure this price.

I wish you could sell the National Bank Shares at £14. If you cannot sell at this price dividing expenses you can perhaps procure an offer at this price the seller paying expenses to wait a reply from Newcastle.

Please give me your quotations.'

Similarly, on 3 March of that year, he indicated to Robertson that:

'I have several orders for Scottish Union Insurance Co's Stock at 17/- dividing expenses. If you can get 100 shares at this price or 300 shares at 17/- seller paying expenses, please take them.

If you could get up the price of Bank of Scotland Stock I could send you a good deal.'

Despite his influential position in stockbroking, Watson did not initiate the establishment in June 1844, of the Glasgow Stock Exchange, the first to be formed in Scotland. This role fell to Peter Dixon, another Glasgow accountant and stockbroker. Watson, with his much longer experience, had much less faith in the permanency of the vastly increased business generated by the railway mania. However, he was one of the 28 founding members and was elected the first chairman, a position he occupied continuously for the next 21 years. In the early years, this was not an easy task. The Glasgow Stock Exchange had to meet competition from rival exchanges in Glasgow and it was only slowly that the members of these were either absorbed or driven from the field. Additionally, though a set of rules governing the conduct of business on the exchange had been established from the outset, it was not an easy matter to ensure that these rules were both obeyed and that their interpretation was understood. Consequently, there were numerous disputes between members, which had to be adjudicated by the chairman and his committee, while the rules themselves had to be continuously amended to make their intention clearer or to fit changing practice. This all meant considerable work for the chairman as the Exchange operated with minimal administrative assistance. Accordingly, much of Watson's time was occupied by these unpaid duties rather than by stockbroking. Eventually, in the mid-

1850s, he was joined in the firm by James Smith, who had been his clerk for a number of years and the partnership was changed to James Watson and Smith. James Smith, and later his successor F J Smith, undertook an increasing burden of the work of the partnership, but Watson did not retire from active involvement until 1881, when he was 80, and even then retained a financial stake in the firm until his death. Even in his later years he was still astute enough to invest his fortune in US railroads bonds rather than more familiar securities.

Watson proved himself well suited to administration and, under his control, membership of the Stock Exchange rose from 45 in 1845 to 55 in 1865, after a considerable drop in the intervening years. Membership then rose to 102 in 1878, which was his last year as chairman, during his second spell of duty. By then the Glasgow Stock Exchange was established as the most important British exchange outside London, and had occupied its own imposing new building in the heart of Glasgow.

However, Watson's business activities were not confined to stockbroking and the stock exchange. In the mid-1830s he was actively involved in the promotion of both the Edinburgh and Glasgow Railway and the Glasgow, Paisley, Kilmarnock and Ayr Railway. Andrew and Dugdale Bannatyne, Glasgow lawyers, were the principal characters behind the schemes but Watson acted as secretary to both companies in their formative years, and was instrumental in obtaining the necessary financial support, with the aid of John Robertson in Edinburgh. Watson was also called upon to assist in the liquidation of the ill-fated Ayrshire Malleable Iron Company, which collapsed in 1847/48 with debts of £250,000. It took him five to six years to wind-up the tangled affairs of that concern. However, by the mid-1850s, Watson had few outside business connections, and those that he did undertake, such as a directorship in the Clydesdale Bank, between 1886 and 1888, were largely honorary posts.

Increasingly Watson was devoting himself more and more to his philanthropic and civic interests and less and less to business, in all its forms. As early as the 1820s he had been conducting a Sunday School in the Trongate while, in 1823, under the leadership of Dr Barclay he was involved in the formation of the Glasgow Mechanics' Institution, and became its first chairman. This was the first such institution established in Britain, and was copied by other towns throughout the kingdom.

This flurry of activity was followed by a period of quiescence during the 1830s and early 1840s, when he established his business and participated in local railway developments. However, famine in the Highlands in the mid-1840s revived his outside interests, and he became chairman of a committee which sought to provide employment in the lowlands for destitute highlanders in 1845/46. Though this scheme was not a success, his next, in 1847, was. Under the leadership

of Provost Blackie, a Glasgow publisher, Watson was a major force behind the establishment of model lodging houses. By 1857 three houses had been set up and they gave temporary accommodation to up to 500 people at any one time. Eventually, the city took over this role and the private committee which managed the lodging houses handed their considerable assets to the Royal Infirmary.

Watson's next involvement was in a major scheme for urban renewal, namely the City of Glasgow Improvement Trust, which came into being in the mid-1860s. This was again under the instigation of Provost Blackie with Watson becoming deputy chairman and later chairman until 1871. The aim of the Trust was to rebuild and re-house an area of Glasgow covering over 50 acres inhabited by nearly 60,000 people and with property valued at £1.2 m. By 1872, £900,000 had already been spent on re-development though the programme had only been inaugurated in 1866.

With this history of civic activity, it was only natural that Watson would become a member of Glasgow Town Council, which he did in 1863. From that it was a steady progression to the position of Lord Provost, which he occupied from 1871 until 1874. When Watson became Provost his administrative skills were taxed to their utmost for the previous Provost had resigned because he had been unable to work with the town clerk, Angus Turner, who had become something of an autocrat. Eventually Turner resigned and Watson chose the safe course of appointing James Marwick, the town clerk of Edinburgh, in his place. As Provost, Watson was noted most for his administrative ability rather than any particular development, although during his tenure considerable improvements continued to be made in Glasgow, such as the beginning of the tramway system and the opening of a new fish market. To crown his achievements Watson was knighted on 2 March 1874. Even after Watson ceased to be Provost, or even a councillor, he continued to take strong interest in various civic and charitable activities.

What assessment can one make of James Watson as a businessman and a person? Certainly, he was not an innovator since all the pursuits in which he had indulged had been pioneered by others, such as Robertson in stockbroking, Dixon in the Stock Exchange, the Bannatynes in the railways, Barclay in the Mechanics' Institution, or Blackie in the model lodging houses and the slum clearance programme. Nevertheless, Watson was an ideal partner to these men for he was a most capable and conscientious administrator, who could bring other people's ideas to fruition through careful and cautious management. He gave willingly of his time to the institutions and city of which he was a part. As the *Bailie* commented on 23 October 1872:

'..., there has been no scheme for the benefit of the poor, or, for the good of the town, in which he has not been found able and willing to bear his part.'

However, after his early pioneering work in stock-broking, he left the further development of that business to others. Rival firms eclipsed his in size, success and prestige since he neglected his own interests for wider concerns. Thus, on his death, he left only a modest fortune of £125,000.

Consequently, though Watson failed to create a substantial business bearing his stamp, he did leave behind such institutions as the Glasgow Stock Exchange and the Improvement Trust, which ran the more smoothly and efficiently through his guiding hand in their formative years.

RANALD MICHIE

Improvements in Glasgow and the City Improvement Acts, London, 1879

On Improving the Sanitary Condition of Large Towns, Glasgow, 1877

A Paper on the Present Railway Crisis, Glasgow, 1846

SOURCES

Unpublished

Glasgow Stock Exchange Association Minutes, 1844-1914

Glasgow University Ms Gen 531/13, Watson/Robertson Correspondence

SRO: SC 36/48/126, Inventory
SC 36/51/99, Will

Published

The Bailie, 23/12/1872

Glasgow Directory, 1824-1900

Glasgow Herald, 30/3/1877, 15/8/1889

Jeans, J S, *Western Worthies,* Glasgow, 1872

Local and Municipal Souvenir of Glasgow, 1837-1897, Glasgow, 1897

The Lord Provosts of Glasgow, Glasgow, 1883

McIlwraith, *The Glasgow and South-Western Railway: Its Origin, Progress and Present Position,* Glasgow, 1880

Memoirs and Portraits of One Hundred Glasgow Men, Glasgow, 1886

Michie, R C, *Money, Mania and Markers: Investment, Company Formation and the Stock Exchange in Nineteenth Century Scotland,* Edinburgh, 1981

Rait, R S, *The History of the Union Bank of Scotland,* Glasgow, 1930

Records of the Glasgow Stock Exchange Association, 1844-1898, Glasgow 1898

Records of the Glasgow Stock Exchange Association, 1844-1926, Glasgow 1927

Reid, J M, *The History of the Clydesdale Bank, 1838-1938,* Glasgow, 1938

Report of Proceedings at the Presentation of his (Sir James Watson) Portrait to the Corporation of Glasgow, Glasgow, 1882

Conclusions: Some characteristics of Scottish entrepreneurs

At the outset of the research which we have conducted into the Scottish businessmen represented in this two volume study, three broad conditions quickly became clear to us. First, apart from a clutch of prominent names which could be identified in any industry, the general population of Scottish businessmen was largely anonymous. Second, although there was much anecdotal observation on particular men, we had little hard information on the origins, training, and public roles of our entrepreneurs; and third, while it was relatively easy to identify a number of famous firms in most industries, we had little real knowledge of the number, scale, and significance of the participating firms at any point in time.

In preparing these volumes a great deal of information has been collected which helps bring these three issues into focus. The data are far from complete, and no systematic analysis has yet been conducted, but some observations are now possible. It is clear, for example, that in each industrial sector there were a number of 'core' firms headed by men who played a leading role in their industry, and around whom there clustered an extensive penumbra of smaller enterprises. The 'core' firms, and the 'leading' businessmen have been clearly identified in these volumes, and taken together they represent a number of coalitions of interest in different sectors, each capable of exerting considerable influence on the general conduct of their industry. In the Dundee textile trades, for example, the Cox's and the Baxters clearly represented such influential groupings. In coalmining the dynasties of the Bairds, the Wilsons, and others, held similar positions for a time. Similar dominant groups can be identified in every sector reviewed in these studies.

However, while such broad observations have some utility they do not tell us very much on more detailed issues. In spite of the fact that systematic analysis remains to be done, we are at this stage able to offer some general comment on a range of features such as lifespan, origins, patterns of ownership and control, education and training, wealth holding, public service, patronage, philanthropy and religion in the Scottish business community during the last hundred years.

A preliminary analysis of our biographic subjects indicates that Scottish businessmen as a group were a long-lived lot. The average age of death of our men was 74 years. Considering the high infant mortality rates current in Scotland in the early part of our study, and the correspondingly low expectation of life, the long life-span suggests that hard work and daily involvement in business affairs was certainly not generally detrimental to health. Indeed it is clear that most of our men of business died in harness, very few giving up active control of their firms, or influence in the business, before death claimed them. A legitimate question must be whether the general unwillingness to withdraw from business leadership with advancing years had a detrimental effect on the long term development, and success or failure, of Scottish business.

The origins of these long-lived men of business also present some interesting features. In the start-up phase as an industry is expanding rapidly it is clear that men entered textiles, or coalmining, or shipbuilding, or any other trade from very diverse backgrounds stretching all the way from farming, through virtually every traditional craft to the professions. However, as the industries consolidated, entry was much more dictated by experience of the business, by existing patterns of ownership, and occasionally by the ability to supply scarce skills. In shipbuilding, for example, of the group of 18 men studied here, many had no direct experience of the industry in their family background: Charles Randolph's father was a printer and stationer, David Rowan's father a slater; John Kincaid and William B Thompson both had fathers who were ship's captains. In the same vein Joseph Russell hailed from a Minister's family and William T Lithgow emerged from a yarn merchants household. In the second phase of development, however, virtually all the more important Scottish shipbuilders emerged from the founding families and rose to the positions of leadership in their firms by dint of being sons, nephews or relatives of the founding and established concerns. Family networks rapidly became more important than individuals, and this is a common pattern in all the main sectors of Scottish business reviewed in these volumes. It is clear that family control was a dominant influence in Scottish business for much of the period, and family influence and involvement continued to be prominent even when firms took the form of limited companies.

Family patterns of ownership also had another implication for the recruitment of talent into senior positions in Scottish business. It is generally the case that access to senior and controlling positions in the boardrooms of Scottish business was strongly linked to family ownership, and family preferment, thus accelerating promotion and involvement for sons, nephews, and relations by marriage. It would not be true, however, to say that such family structures entirely excluded the entry and rise of professional managers to senior and influential positions. Many such men can be found in every sector studied here, but it was rare for such men to acquire any significant holding in the capital of these firms. By and large they remained salaried managers.

These patterns of family ownership and control were also linked to some characteristic features of the education and training of Scottish men of business. By far the largest number of these men had little more than elementary schooling; their recruitment and training in business owed less to formal education than to traditional apprenticeship training. In effect gaining experience of the business through training on the job remained the norm for most proprietors of Scottish business. Many indeed graduated through apprenticeship to journeyman and foreman moving among a number of firms before setting up in business on their own account. However, once families were in control, sons, nephews and relations pursued a general training by shifting quickly around departments to get a feel for the business before being admitted to partnership, or to the board of directors.

While this 'in-house' training remained the norm, more formal technical and academic qualifications became more common among the owners of Scottish business after 1900; even then it was combined with shop floor experience, however brief. The qualification threshold for Scottish entrepreneurs clearly varies among the sectors. In some like textiles, construction, and timber and furniture, few men had any formal technical qualification. In steel, engineering, shipbuilding and mining, technical qualifications became more common as time progressed. However it is probably true to say that in general terms, Scottish entrepreneurs were rarely men of great technical expertise or profound learning.

It is a maxim of economics that in operating their companies the principal objective of businessmen is to maximise profits. The evidence of the men and companies presented here would not support such a bold conclusion, but it is nevertheless clear that many men of business in Scotland amassed considerable family and personal wealth. A systematic analysis of wealth holding has not as yet been conducted, but some illustrative evidence can be presented. A preliminary analysis of the textile men indicates that the average value of personal moveable estates of the textile entrepreneurs at death was £400,193, ranging to £1.4m of James Caird to £16,732 of Thomas Fairgrieve. Indeed among the textile men reviewed there were seven millionaires. Among these men, a large part of the wealth was held in their own businesses; 38% of the total wealth was tied up in shares in their own concerns, ranging from over 92% for Sir John Muir of James Finlay & Co, to the other extreme like John Colville who held no shares in any cotton concern at death, having earlier sold out his holdings in the Glasgow Cotton Spinning Co to English speculators. Similarly, among the 18 shipbuilders studied in these volumes the average value of estate was £226,712 ranging from a high of £1,069,669 to a low of £23,615. The same type of pattern emerges also in the Mining and Quarrying sector where the average estate of the 29 men was £297,111.

In general it would seem that the textile men were on average much wealthier than those in mining, metals, or engineering: indeed they appear to have been the wealthiest on average of all the men of business; but insufficient analyses of our data has been undertaken to make that conclusion secure. It is clear that every sector generated great wealth for some of its families, and generally the earlier the establishment of the firm, the greater the wealth accumulated. However changes in death duties and taxation from the turn of the century encouraged buinessmen to protect their estates, to transfer holdings to sons or trusts long before their demise, and the records of personal estates in the twentieth century give little clear guide to the true wealth of our later businessmen or their families. It is not possible to say at this stage whether wealth making diminished, or became harder and less common as the twentieth century progressed.

While it is not clear what the achievement in wealth making has been for all our businessmen, we have a much clearer idea of how these men used their wealth, both in their lifetimes, and after their death. In almost every sector successful men used part of their wealth to buy country houses, and often landed estates. While some enjoyed country pursuits, few abandoned their businesses in pursuit of gentrification, and for most of our entrepreneurs the acquisition of the landed estates was an adjunct to their business success, not an escape from business, or an alternative to it. In some sense however it was a diversification of the family portfolio, for while most of our men and their families kept large portions of their personal wealth in their businesses, they did so only as long as the business remained profitable over the longer term; they did not however see the continuance of the business as a duty beyond the protection of their personal wealth.

They did however take a general view that they had a responsibility for their local community. Certainly before the First World War our men of business took an active role in local affairs, and used their position as employers and wealth holders to shape, and in some measure direct, the development of their own communities. There can be few Scottish towns of any size that do not boast a library, a school, a civic centre, a hall, a park, a hospital, or some other public facility that does not bear the name of local business families as patrons and benefactors. In Dundee the Caird Hall; in Edinburgh the Usher Hall; in Glasgow the Mitchell Library; in Kilmarnock the Dick Institute and so on. This patronage was a characteristic feature of business success and public leadership, and virtually every university, college, hospital and museum owes something to business patronage as part of the community leadership exercised by Scottish entrepreneurs.

One particular area of business philanthropy was the Church; the Lithgows were generous endowers of the Church of Scotland and the Iona Community. In similar vein the Templeton family supported the home and foreign missions of the United Free Church. Most of our businessmen at least professed some religious observance, and many were active in their churches. The evidence is unclear and not fully analysed on church allegiance, but it is clear that the Church of Scotland was the dominant affiliation, with perhaps up to two-thirds of our recorded religious observance falling in that sect, while the various branches of the United Presbyterians, the United Free Church, and the Free Church of Scotland held an extraordinary allegiance among the business community, probably claiming in excess of 20% of our businessmen as members. More analysis and research is however required before the pattern of religious observance can be confidently articulated.

These tentative observations give some indication of the range of analysis which this biographic investigation of our men of business can support. The interested reader will be able to explore most of the points developed here by a careful scrutiny of the information contained in the biographies collected in each sector, but much more work remains to be undertaken before these initial propositions can be confidently advanced as generalisations on the origins and characteristics of Scottish businessmen. It is nevertheless clear that even such preliminary observations are capable of illuminating our understanding of the origins and role of businessmen in Scotland, and that our understanding of the springs of economic growth, of business motivation, success and failure, can be greatly advanced by a focus on business biography. It is, as these studies make plain, a powerful tool of analysis that is only just beginning to illuminate and redress the long anonymity of our men of business and their achievement.

ANTHONY SLAVEN

Index of Personal Names

Subject Index